Cupid and Psyche

Trends in Classics – Pathways of Reception

General Editors
Franco Montanari and Antonios Rengakos

Editorial Board
Lorna Hardwick, Craig Kallendorf, Fiona Macintosh, Miltos Pechlivanos

Associate Editors
Anastasia Bakoianni and Rosanna Lauriola

Volume 1

Cupid and Psyche

The Reception of Apuleius' Love Story since 1600

Edited by
Regine May and Stephen Harrison

DE GRUYTER

ISBN 978-3-11-077748-2
e-ISBN (PDF) 978-3-11-064158-5
e-ISBN (EPUB) 978-3-11-064200-1

Library of Congress Control Number: 2019956357

Bibliographic information published by the Deutsche Nationalbibliothek
The Deutsche Nationalbibliothek lists this publication in the Deutsche Nationalbibliografie; detailed bibliographic data are available on the Internet at http://dnb.dnb.de.

© 2021 Walter de Gruyter GmbH, Berlin/Boston
This volume is text- and page-identical with the hardback published in 2020.
Typesetting: 3W+P GmbH, Rimpar
Printing and binding: CPI books GmbH, Leck
Cover image: Paul Klee, Hauptweg und Nebenwege

www.degruyter.com

Preface

This book presents a selection of papers delivered at a conference on the *Reception of Cupid and Psyche from 1600* at Leeds in July 2016, organised by Regine May and Stephen Harrison, which had twenty-nine speakers of national and international acclaim.[1] It is part of an ongoing research collaboration by the editors to explore the reception of Apuleius' story from 1600 to today.

This project's focus on images as well as books has allowed us to display some of the resulting research in various physical and online exhibitions. An online exhibition 'Facets of Apuleius' *Golden Ass* in the Brotherton Collection at Leeds' at https://library.leeds.ac.uk/special-collections/view/1594 showcases several of the items discussed in this volume as well as others not included here. Our thanks go to Leonardo Costantini for taking the images, and the colleagues at the University of Leeds Brotherton Special Collections for all their support in making this possible. Two exhibitions associated with the project went ahead for February 2019: 'Treasures at the Brotherton: *Cupid and Psyche*. The story of Love and the Soul in Leeds' in the Brotherton Library, Leeds, and 'Love and the Soul: Apuleius' tale of *Cupid and Psyche* in European Culture since 1600' as a Proscholium Display at the Bodleian Library in Oxford. Again the editors would like to thank library colleagues in both Leeds and Oxford for helping to bring *Cupid and Psyche* to a wide audience inside and outside academia, especially Sallyanne Gilchrist and Dot Little from the Bodleian exhibitions team at Oxford.

This research project would not have been possible without generous financial support from the British Academy / Leverhulme Small Research Grant, the Hugh Last Fund, the Audrey Barrie Brown Memorial Fund and the Donald Atkinson Fund, as well as from Corpus Christi College Oxford.

Our helpers during the conference and afterwards, Eleanor OKell, Anthi Chrysanthou and Maria Haley, deserve our thanks for their excellent work, including on the online exhibition. Eleanor OKell organised several Leeds Light Night outreach events around our research on Apuleius, ancient novels and *Cupid and Psyche*, encouraging each time more or less the whole Leeds Classics Department to get involved in this endeavour. Maria Haley, furthermore, helped with the editing of the manuscript and created the index. Further thanks go to our colleagues at Leeds and Oxford for their encouragement and support.

---

[1] http://cupidandpsyche.leeds.ac.uk/

At de Gruyter, we would like to thank the *Trends in Classics* team for taking on the volume, especially the general editor Antonios Rengakos for his kindness and enthusiasm for the project.

Finally, Regine May would like to thank her family, especially Amrita May-Singh, for never tiring of hearing new stories about Psyche. Stephen Harrison would like to thank the Leverhulme Trust for a Major Research Fellowship for 2017–20 with which this book is associated.

While this book was in production, in July 2019, we were shocked and saddened to hear of the early death of Christoph Leidl, our friend and contributor. We dedicate this volume to his memory.

Regine May
Stephen Harrison
September 2019

List of contributors

Zacharias Andreadakis is a Research Assistant in the Department of Education, University of Oslo, Norway.

Geoffrey Benson is Assistant Professor of the Classics, Colgate University, USA.

Robert Carver is Associate Professor in the Department of English Studies at the University of Durham, UK.

Friedemann Drews is DFG-Heisenberg-Stipendiat at the Institut für Klassische Philologie at the University of Münster, Germany.

Julia Haig Gaisser is Eugenia Chase Guild Professor Emeritus of the Humanities and Professor of Latin at Bryn Mawr College, USA.

Stephen Harrison is Professor of Latin Literature at the University of Oxford, UK.

Paula James is Honorary Associate, Faculty of Arts & Social Sciences, Open University, UK.

† Christoph Leidl was Akademischer Oberrat, Seminar für Klassische Philologie, University of Heidelberg, Germany.

Lisa Maurice is Senior Lecturer in the Department of Classics, Bar-Ilan University, Israel.

Regine May is Associate Professor of Latin Literature at the University of Leeds, UK.

Hendrik Müller is an independent scholar and founder of the Hamburg-based business consultancy *"Beratung &Denkanstöße"*. He teaches Business Ethics at the University of Applied Science Hochschule Fresenius.

Maeve O'Brien is Lecturer in the Department of Ancient Classics, Maynooth University, Ireland.

Michael Paschalis is Professor of Classics Emeritus at the University of Crete, Greece.

Lucia Pasetti is Associate Professor in the Department of Classical Philology and Italian Studies, University of Bologna.

Vernon Provencal is Professor of Classics at Acadia University, Canada.

Tiziana Ragno is Ricercatore in the Dipartimento di Studi Umanistici, University of Foggia, Italy.

Holly Ranger is a Research Associate at the Institute of Classical Studies, University of London.

Christiane Reitz held the Chair of Classics at the University of Rostock 2000–2019.

Luca Ruggeri is completing his PhD at the Scuola Normale Superiore at Pisa, Italy.

Clemence Schultze was formerly a Lecturer in the Department of Classics and Ancient History at the University of Durham, UK.

Janice Siegel is Associate Professor of Classics, Hampden-Sydney College, USA.

Jared A. Simard is Postdoctoral Faculty Fellow in Liberal Studies at New York University, USA.

Table of Contents

List of contributors —— 7

Regine May and Stephen Harrison
Introduction —— 1

I Baroque and the Influence of La Fontaine

Tiziana Ragno
'Del soffrir degli affanni è dolce il fine'. Ancient myth and comic drama in G.F. Fusconi's libretto (with G.F. Loredano and P. Michiel) for F. Cavalli, *Amore innamorato* (1642) —— 31

Stephen Harrison
Apuleius at the court of Louis XIV. *Psyché* (1671, 1678) and its English version (1675) —— 47

Christiane Reitz
How to use a wallpaper. *Psyché et Cupidon—notice explicative* —— 61

Jared A. Simard
Psyche in the salon. French interior decoration in the eighteenth century —— 79

II Romanticism and Philosophy

Maeve O'Brien
'Pensive pleasures' in prose and poetry. Apuleius, Mary Tighe and eighteenth-century Ireland —— 101

Robert H. F. Carver
The Platonic Ass: Thomas Taylor's *Cupid and Psyche* in Context (1795–1822) —— 119

Regine May
Keats's 'Ode to Psyche'. Psyche as poetry and inspiration —— 147

Michael Paschalis
Sir Walter Scott's *Kenilworth* and Apuleius' tale of *Cupid and Psyche* —— 167

Zacharias Andreadakis
Kierkegaard as a reader of Apuleius' *Metamorphoses* —— 181

Luca Ruggeri
Robert Bridges' *Eros and Psyche* and its models —— 203

III *Fin de Siècle* and Psychology

Lucia Pasetti
From Psyche to psyche. The interiorisation of Apuleius' *fabella* in D'Annunzio, Pascoli, and Savinio —— 225

† Christoph Leidl
Between Symbolism and Popular Culture.
***Cupid and Psyche* in *Fin de siècle* Book Illustration** —— 247

Geoffrey C. Benson
Psyche the psychotic. *Cupid and Psyche* in Dr. Franz Riklin's *Wishfulfilment and Symbolism in Fairy Tales* —— 273

Clemence Schultze
Psyche and Cupid in the Novels of Charlotte M. Yonge and Sylvia Townsend Warner —— 289

IV Twentieth Century and Modernism

Julia Haig Gaisser
**Eudora Welty's *The Robber Bridegroom*.
Cupid and Psyche on the Natchez Trace** —— 307

Friedemann Drews
***Cupid & Psyche* and C.S. Lewis' *Till We Have Faces*.
A Christian-Platonic metamorphosis** —— 323

Vernon L. Provencal
Faulkner's reception(s) of Apuleius' *Cupid and Psyche* in *The Reivers* —— 339

Holly Ranger
'I have tried to be blind in love'. Psyche and the quest for feminine poetic autonomy in Sylvia Plath's *House of Eros* —— 357

V New Audiences

Lisa Maurice
***Cupid and Psyche* for children** —— 381

Hendrik Müller
***Cupid and Psyche* on stage in the 21st century** —— 397

Janice Siegel
**Undertones of Apuleius' *Cupid and Psyche*
in Guillermo del Toro's *Pan's Labyrinth*** —— 415

Paula James
***Beauty and the Beast* as a myth and metaphor in the contemporary world.
Looking forward with Apuleius' fable of *Cupid and Psyche*** —— 433

List of Figures —— 451

Index —— 455

Regine May and Stephen Harrison
Introduction

Few love stories from the Graeco-Roman world have been more popular in European culture than the tale of *Cupid and Psyche*, written in the second century CE as the centrepiece embedded narrative of Apuleius' Latin novel *Metamorphoses or the Golden Ass*.[1] It describes the love between Psyche (or 'Soul'), the most beautiful woman on earth, and Cupid, the god of Love, who meet each other, are separated, experience adventures, and finally achieve reunion in heaven through Psyche's happy apotheosis. Over the last two millennia, authors, painters, composers, film-makers and psychologists have engaged with this story in many different creative ways, and inspired further readings of *Cupid and Psyche* through every kind of medium.

There are excellent recent scholarly surveys of the reception of the whole of the *Metamorphoses* up to the seventeenth century.[2] The date of 1600 is therefore a good starting point for the present volume; it is also, in matters of reception, an important watershed, as the Renaissance and its love for ancient (and especially Latin) literature had by this point firmly gripped the imaginations of all Europe. This volume's specific focus on *Cupid and Psyche* since 1600 thus covers new ground in two different ways, chronologically and thematically, and the material is rich, since during these last four centuries, the reception of *Cupid and Psyche* has blossomed in multiple and ever varied responses throughout the Western world.

This volume contains a selection of the papers delivered at an international conference, organised by Regine May (Leeds) and Stephen Harrison (Corpus Christi College, Oxford) at Leeds, UK in July 2016.[3] Its detailed case studies cover the reception of *Cupid and Psyche* in European and North American literature, visual art, music, theatrical production, and film; they showcase the story's versatility, as it lends itself to classicising and radically modern, comic

---

[1] For the life and career of Apuleius (125-after 170 CE), a Latin-speaking public intellectual, Platonising philosopher and prolific writer in many genres, based in Roman North Africa, especially Carthage, see Harrison 2000, 1–39.
[2] Carver 2007; Gaisser 2008.
[3] See May 2017 and http://cupidandpsyche.leeds.ac.uk/ (accessed October 20th, 2017). The editors thank Maria Haley and Eleanor OKell for their work on this during the conference and afterwards. An online exhibition 'Facets of Apuleius' *Golden Ass* in the Brotherton Collection at Leeds' at https://library.leeds.ac.uk/special-collections/view/1594 (accessed February 28th, 2018) showcases several of the books discussed in this volume.

and serious, myth-affirming and myth-busting interpretations, and it can be made the carrier of serious philosophical and psychological messages, or the source for pictures of beautiful bodies whose nakedness is sanctioned by antiquity.

1 *Cupid and Psyche's* reception in this volume

Reception studies have gained much attention in Classics in recent years, with a rapidly developing bibliography[4] and spectrum of methodologies.[5] These latter range from an emphasis on the lasting power of the 'great tradition' with the classical original 'pushing' its way through later receptions to a stress on the freedom of classical reception to 'pull', modify and appropriate its originals,[6] and a focus on the generation of meaning at the point of reception.[7] Most recently, we have seen the 'intellectual archaeology' model of reception in 'Deep Classics', concerned to investigate 'the very pose by which the human present turns its attention to the distant human past',[8] and a restatement of the lasting aesthetic value of the 'classical tradition' via the linguistically-rooted idea of classical 'reflexes' which argues that much of Western culture is classicising in some sense.[9] In general, advocates of the classical tradition have tended to emphasise the high aesthetic value of canonical works and their long-lasting cultural diffusions, while advocates of classical reception have tended to emphasise the impact of the historical and intellectual conditions of a particular receiving culture.

Against this background, the authors in this volume engage with reception as two-way traffic; not only does the discussion of reception throw light on the receiving text, but it also helps us to understand *Cupid and Psyche* better

---

4 It is notable that the three major UK classical publishers now have lively reception monograph series: Classical Presences at OUP (80 titles since 2005), Classics After Antiquity at CUP (two titles since 2013), and at Bloomsbury Studies in Classical Reception (12 since 2013). OUP is also engaged in a major survey of classical reception in English literature, the *Oxford History of Classical Reception in English Literature* (*OCHREL*)—for relevant volumes so far see Cheney and Hardie 2015, Hopkins and Martindale 2012, Vance and Wallis 2015.
5 For an interesting range of debate see Martindale and Thomas 2006.
6 For the 'push/pull' formulation see usefully Goff 2005: 12–14, and note the counterpart Blackwell Companions to the classical tradition (Kallendorf 2007) and to classical receptions (Hardwick and Stray 2011)
7 See famously Martindale 1993, 3.
8 Butler 2016, 14.
9 Silk, Gildenhard and Barrow 2014.

in itself.[10] Meaning is created by the receiving text engaging with the ancient text, but the discussion always throws light on both, even if that happens in varying proportions. As a result, the volume offers a fresh and challenging study, incorporating different though related methodologies, applied to widely varying genres, texts and artefacts, all held together by a uniform desire to explain both Apuleius' story and the last four centuries of its reception, illuminating both the ancient story of love and the soul and the reactions to a classical myth within the vernacular cultures in which the receiving texts and artefacts were composed. The volume sets out why and how people a millennium and a half after Apuleius wrote his story are still interested in it, and how this interest might express itself in ever varying forms, in high literature and popular entertainment, in art and in music, in philosophy and psychoanalysis up to the present day. The receiving texts are creations of their own time, and we as modern scholars of historical receptions of classical texts are engaged in not a two-way, but a three-way reading of Apuleius, encompassing the original context of the Roman empire, the particular detailed context of reception in a time before our own, and our own context of a particular modernity which can be different for each individual.

In this volume, we set out to showcase the breadth and depth of the story's influence, and by doing so to cover new territory in the understanding of *Cupid and Psyche*; this agenda speaks both to the idea of the classical tradition, the deserved afterlife of a rich and attractive story, and to that of classical reception, the specific and culturally determined appropriations of a narrative in many different later contexts and forms. The earlier reception of the *Metamorphoses* as a whole up to the seventeenth century, including the works of Shakespeare, has been treated in depth by two scholars who also appear in this volume, Robert Carver and Julia Haig Gaisser.[11] This book focuses on the inset tale of *Cupid and Psyche* by itself since 1600, and looks at literary and non-literary genres up to our own contemporary period. We are not here presenting an encompassing history of the reception of *Cupid and Psyche* for the period; we hope to trace some of its main European lines in a separate co-authored monograph on the literary reception of the story. Instead, this edited volume offers representative snapshots of in-depth studies of specific authors or genres from 1600 to today, and moves beyond literary reception into other genres such as art or theatre history, music, film, philosophy or psychology.

---

10 Here we follow Hardwick 2000.
11 Carver 2007; Gaisser 2008; Carver and Schaaf 2010.

This wide scope of the volume is intended to encourage further discussion of the reception of the *Metamorphoses* in general and *Cupid and Psyche* in particular throughout Classics and neighbouring disciplines. Interdisciplinarity has been shown to be an important aspect for the study of classical reception,[12] and this wide range of disciplines is impossible for a single author to cover; a group of international scholars was brought together in order to provide this uniquely wide range of reception and approaches. For this reason, the authors in this volume were free to decide whether they wanted to study direct reception, i.e. of a receiver interacting carefully and innovatively with *Cupid and Psyche* read either in Latin or in translation, or whether they would define the idea of reception in a wider sense, as a type of 'cultural' or 'secondary' reception, where the received text or artefact engages with *Cupid and Psyche* without direct and detailed knowledge of the original.[13] Often a conscious intertextual reference to the work of Apuleius is a given for the authors in this volume; others are more circumspect about claiming a direct 'influence' of Apuleius on the receiver.

2 The novel and its centre. *Cupid and Psyche* in the *Metamorphoses*

Cupid and Psyche is the centrepiece of Apuleius' best-known work, the only completely extant Latin novel *Metamorphoses or The Golden Ass* in eleven books, which displays Apuleius' idiosyncratic style and interest in archaic and classical Greek and Latin philosophy and literature in its rich literary texture.[14] Its date within Apuleius' career is sometimes disputed.[15]

The plot of the *Metamorphoses* has something of a picaresque colour. The novel's protagonist, a young Corinthian nobleman called Lucius, describes in a first-person narrative how he travelled through Greece and, driven by insatiable curiosity, was accidentally transformed into a donkey by magic. As a donkey, un-

---

[12] For emphasis on this aspect see e.g. the work of the collaborative research centre 644 'Transformations of Antiquity' at the Humboldt Universität in Berlin (https://www.sfb-antike.de/en/644) and Brockliss et al. 2012.
[13] This is an important way in which this volume distinguishes itself from the idea behind OCHREL (see n.4 above), where the focus is on 'the close and sophisticated critical engagement with the complex interaction between classical and English literary texts from the early Middle Ages to the present.' (Hopkins and Martindale 2012, xi).
[14] For guides to this rich literary texture see e.g. Finkelpearl 1998. May 2006 and Harrison 2013.
[15] Dowden 1994, 419–34 argues for an early date in the 160s AD, whereas Harrison 2000 and 2013 argues for a later date in the 180s.

able to speak but still with human rationality, he is sold from owner to owner until he finds salvation at the hands of the benevolent Egyptian goddess Isis, who instigates his retransformation into human form. In eternal gratitude, Lucius becomes a priest in Rome of the cult of Isis and her brother-god Osiris in the closing words of the novel.

The seriousness and meaning of the Isiac ending is a much discussed issue in scholarship; some see it as a satiric take on contemporary salvation narratives,[16] others as a deliberate riddle,[17] or as a serious retelling of a religious conversion.[18] The accurately observed religious detail of the Graeco-Roman Isis cult betrays Apuleius' detailed knowledge of this mystery religion,[19] but its playful tone, in parallel with the rest of the novel's style and continued allusions to previous literature,[20] suggest that literary entertainment is at least part of the work's intentions.

In his time as a donkey, Lucius overhears many stories that his owners tell each other, and he narrates them in the novel to his readers. They form by themselves a large part of the novel's text and engage with the themes and narratives of the main story, by echoing, anticipating or illustrating them. By far the longest and most important inset tale is the story of *Cupid and Psyche*. An old woman tells it to a girl captured by robbers in order to calm her down. Lucius-ass stands nearby and overhears it, too. At the end of the tale, Lucius understands neither the story's complexities nor its reflection of his own experiences, and simply regrets not having the means to write down the *bella fabella*, the 'pretty story' (*Met.* 6.25) he has just heard. This elaborate tale covers the space of two of the eleven books of the novel, and straddles three of them by running from *Met.* 4.28 to 6.24.[21]

3 The tale of Cupid and Psyche

We summarise Apuleius' tale. Psyche is the youngest daughter of a king and queen, and the most beautiful of three sisters. So beautiful is she, in fact, that

---

16 Harrison 2000.
17 Winkler 1985.
18 Shumate 1996.
19 Egelhaaf-Gaiser 2000, Keulen et al. 2015.
20 For recent reconciliatory positions see e.g. Graverini 2007, Tilg 2014.
21 For modern commentaries on the Latin text of *Cupid and Psyche* see Kenney 1990, Moreschini 1994 and (especially detailed) Zimmerman et al. 2004 in the Groningen Commentaries on Apuleius series, plus the accompanying volume of essays, Zimmerman et al. 1998.

she is worshipped by everyone as an image of the goddess of love, Venus, whose temples as a consequence are empty and uncared for. Whereas Psyche's sisters are married, Psyche is uncourted and left to mourn her solitude. Her father asks the oracle of Apollo for advice, and is told to expose Psyche on a lonely rock, so that she can be married to a monster. Psyche agrees to her terrible fate, and soon thereafter she is left alone in the wilderness, to be married (all expect) to death. Instead of dying, however, she is carried off by the wind Zephyrus and taken to a beautiful palace, where invisible servants take care of all her needs and prepare her for her wedding night. In the dark, Psyche's invisible husband arrives, and he leaves again before sunrise.

This state continues for some time, and Psyche is soon pregnant. Her still unknown husband makes her promise never to try to discover his identity. If she were to break this taboo, he would leave her immediately, and their unborn child would be born a mortal rather than immortal, but an immortal child would be her reward were she to keep her promise. Psyche agrees to this condition, but her loneliness during the day takes its toll. She asks her invisible husband repeatedly to be permitted to let her two sisters come and visit her. After several requests, her husband reluctantly agrees, but warns her against their treachery. With Zephyrus' assistance for their transport, Psyche welcomes her two sisters to her splendid palace. The sisters become jealous of Psyche's good fortune and guess the divine nature of her husband, especially after they realise that she does not know what he looks like. They persuade her that she is married, as the oracle had predicted, to a monster, who will eat her in due course, once she is heavily pregnant with her unborn baby.

Psyche, terrified, follows their instructions to stab her husband to death in his sleep. When she lifts her lamp and her dagger to kill him, she immediately realises that he is not a monster at all, but Cupid, the god of love, in the shape of a beautiful young man with feathery wings. His iconic bow and love-inducing arrows are leaning against their bed. In wonderment, Psyche handles the weapons and pricks her finger, which makes her fall deeply in love with the god of Love. Just then, a drop of oil from her lamp burns him; he wakes up and flies away from her with a rebuke, leaving her behind, heartbroken and alone.

It has become clear by now that Venus, his mother, jealous that Psyche was worshipped instead of her, had sent Cupid to make Psyche fall in love with a man of low social status. Cupid however had himself fallen in love at first sight with the girl and had deliberately wounded himself with his own arrow, disobeying his mother's command and therefore having to hide Psyche away from the other gods, in his beautiful palace.

Now, angered by her breach of trust, Cupid has left her, apparently forever. Psyche, distraught and planning revenge on her sisters, travels to their palaces and persuades them that Cupid had expelled her and had asked for each sister's company instead. Greedy for Cupid's love, the sisters throw themselves off the rock where Psyche had been exposed, but instead of being carried to Psyche's palace by Zephyrus as before, they fall to their deaths.

Meanwhile, Psyche searches for Cupid far and wide. She asks the goddesses Ceres and Juno for help, but they are too much in awe of Venus' powers to aid her. Finally, driven by despair and loneliness, Psyche gives herself over to Venus. Gloating, Venus has Psyche beaten by her servants, and then sets her four impossible tasks to perform: to sort a pile of grains, retrieve golden fleece from flesh-eating sheep, collect water from the river of the Underworld, and lastly to fetch a box of beauty from the goddess of the Underworld, Proserpina. Psyche despairs at her tasks and needs to be prevented several times from committing suicide. She receives help throughout her ordeal from magical creatures like helpful ants, speaking reeds and towers, or Jupiter's talking eagle. Just as she ascends from the Underworld with Proserpina's box, her customary curiosity overwhelms her again, and she opens the box. She falls into a death-like sleep, but Cupid reappears, his wound having healed, and reawakens her. He has made a deal with Jupiter, the highest of the gods, who has agreed to make Psyche immortal and marry her to Cupid, in exchange for Cupid promising Jupiter even more success in his extra-marital affairs. Psyche is raised to Olympus, where she is immortalised and married to Cupid in everlasting bliss. In due course, a daughter called Voluptas, 'Pleasure', is born to the couple.

This inset tale of *Cupid and Psyche* sits at the centre of the *Metamorphoses* as a whole and in many ways reflects and echoes the story of Lucius as the novel's miniaturising mirror, or *mise en abyme*.[22] It is important and central for the novel's interpretation. To careful readers, Psyche's lonely travels echo Lucius' journeys through Greece as a donkey, and both share an insatiable curiosity which leads to their peril; in book 11 we are told that it was not merely a magical accident but Lucius' own curiosity which had caused his transformation into a donkey (11.15). Both Lucius and Psyche fail at their tasks and need to be rescued from their terrible fates by the intervention of benevolent deities. Psyche is rescued by Cupid, and Lucius by Isis, although he never acknowledges these parallels to his own life in the telling of the tale, which he, naively, only ever sees as a 'pretty story'. Just as Lucius' Isiac conversion contains some elements of ambiguity, which may worry Apuleius' readers but never Lucius himself, *Cupid and Psyche*, too, has its own ambiguous ending: the birth of a daughter rather than of

---

[22] For this technique by which one part of a literary work reflects its whole see Dällenbach 1989.

the promised son, whose morally ambiguous name 'Pleasure' denies a straightforward interpretation of the ending to its more sceptical readers.

Despite this close interconnectedness between the two stories, *Cupid and Psyche* can easily stand alone, as a tale by itself without Lucius' story as its frame. Reading the tale in isolation from Lucius' fate allows for some of its inherent features to shine through more clearly. For example, the focus of the tale becomes less an anticipation and echo of Lucius' fate and his ultimate salvation, but instead concentrates the readers' minds on the love story between Cupid and Psyche, the god of love and the mortal princess, whose name means both 'butterfly' and 'soul' in Greek. It should be noted, though, that even though contemporary and later images of Psyche portray her with butterfly wings,[23] she never has any wings in Apuleius' tale, where, despite her name, she is an ordinary mortal until her apotheosis at the end.

4 The originality of *Cupid and Psyche*

Cupid and Psyche is very likely Apuleius' own creation.[24] The frame narrative, the tale of the young man turned into a donkey, is found in a now lost Greek novel by a now unknown author whom some believe to be the Greek satirist, and exact contemporary of Apuleius, Lucian of Samosata. The author of this lost novel (named *Metamorphoseis*, the Greek equivalent of Apuleius' title) is erroneously named by Byzantine readers after the novel's protagonist: 'Loukios of Patrae'. Apuleius adapted and expanded it, and changed the ending significantly from a farcical retransformation of Loukios from donkey to man in public view in a theatre and subsequent rejection by a woman who had been in love with the donkey, to a salvation narrative of divine intervention. An epitome of the *Metamorphoseis*, called *Loukios or the Ass* or *Onos*, survives in the corpus of the works of Lucian, which allows us to compare Apuleius' version with what his Greek source would have been like.[25] Other fragmentary versions of prose texts involving donkeys have come to light, too.[26] Despite the availability of many versions of the frame narrative, it is generally accepted that the story of *Cupid and Psyche* is

---

23 See Schlam 1976.
24 Fulgentius *Mythologiae* 3.6 mentions a parallel but otherwise unknown Greek text by Aristophontes of Athens, which might have been either a Greek model or a later adaptation of the Latin: see Dowden 2007, 145; Stramaglia 2010, 166–176 discusses possible evidence from material culture for pre-Apuleian versions of *Cupid and Psyche*.
25 Mason 1978; Van Thiel 1971 and 1972.
26 See further May 2009.

not found in the Greek versions and is entirely designed by Apuleius as the centrepiece of his novel to deliberately echo and anticipate the fate of his hero Lucius.

It is itself a very literary tale, told as a deliberately invented story by an old woman within an elaborate work of fiction; this enables *Cupid and Psyche* to offer a wide scope for later receptions by allowing them to revive various strands already present in the text. It alludes to and often parodies high classical literature.²⁷ Echoes include Plato's philosophical dialogues, especially *Phaedrus* 248c, where Plato describes a soul weighed down by forgetfulness, which is comically echoed in *Met.* 5.24, when Psyche tries in vain to hang on to the fleeing Cupid's feet but falls down to the ground, heavy with the forgotten taboo and her own pregnancy, or on the nature of love (the *Symposium*). In some sense, Apuleius offers a comic version of a serious philosophical text.²⁸

The *Metamorphoses* has clear affinities with elevated epic literature such as Homer or Vergil, which Apuleius engagingly uses and parodies. Whereas Homer's Odysseus is pursued by the god Poseidon for blinding his son Polyphemus, and Vergil's hero Aeneas is pursued by the angry goddess Juno for being a Trojan and causing the future destruction of her favourite city Carthage by the Rome that his descendants will found, Apuleius' Psyche is pursued by the angry goddess of love Venus, who is jealous of Psyche's beauty and the homage paid to her by admiring humans. Psyche's *katabasis* to the Underworld in *Met.* 6 to retrieve Proserpina's beauty treatment echoes Aeneas' descent in *Aen.* 6 to gather knowledge for his future mission to found the Roman race.²⁹ But at least in some respects, the timid maiden Psyche's 'epic' tasks, involving 'feminine' items such as wool, fetching water and cosmetics, are less dangerous than an epic hero's, and more domestic and comic.³⁰

There are also dramatic intertexts, for example clear literary allusions to Greek tragedies: the sacrificial death of a maiden on the eve of her wedding, the apparent prospect for Psyche at the start of the story, recalls Sophocles' *Antigone* or Euripides' *Andromeda*, while Apuleius explicitly echoes Ennius' *Medea* in Psyche's distress when no suitor for her hand appears (*Met.* 4.32). Again, Apuleius toys with the tragic nature of his intertexts and finds the comic side. Indeed, Roman comedies, such as Plautus' or Terence's works, are used by Apuleius in the plot as well as the language of *Cupid and Psyche*. For example,

---

27 See especially the material collected in Zimmerman et al. 1998 and Zimmerman at al. 2004.
28 For a similar analysis of the references to Plato's *Symposium* as comic see Harrison 2013, 166; 2016, 85.
29 Harrison 2016, 78–80.
30 See especially Harrison 1998.

the portrayal of Cupid's illicit love for an unsuitable girl to whom his parents object and who is belatedly raised to his own social status for a lawful marriage echoes several New Comedy plots.[31] This versatility of Apuleius' plot in its adaptation of tragic and comic patterns of action allows his later readers to create both tragic and comic versions themselves with some fidelity to Apuleius' own story.

The Platonic subtext of a story involving the 'Soul' (Psyche) and 'Love' (Cupid) is easily recognised (see above on echoes of the *Phaedrus* and *Symposium*), and has led to an important strand of literary reception of the story from the earliest point, but other seeds of literary textures bear fruit in the story's reception in drama, epics or other poetic kinds. This self-conscious playing with canonical ancient texts was obvious to Apuleius' contemporaries and later readers alike. This playfulness led to reactions in reception of a similar playful nature, although a serious Platonist interpretation of the story was one of the most important continuous strands of reception throughout. The story helped in shaping Renaissance and later understanding of the Classics and Platonism, but also informed the early writers of fairy tales, and influenced composers keen on recreating ancient theatre in operas and ballets, as well as authors of modern novels looking back to their ancient counterparts.

5 The early reception of *Cupid and Psyche*

A story this rich in its reception of previous high and low literature is a natural candidate to inspire by itself many different lines of reception, some of which revisit Apuleius' own literary tapestry by highlighting some of the motifs he integrated into his own work. Apuleius' story, in itself extremely intertextual, holds continued fascination for later readers as an accessible link to further classical works. For the first millennium and a half of its reception, only a few examples can be given here.[32]

Cupid and Psyche's Platonist subtext allowed for early reception as an allegorical text which was easily Christianised (e.g. in Fulgentius' *Mythologiae* 3.6, early sixth century AD), as the story of Love and the Soul who are united in heaven despite earthly temptations and tribulations. This allegorisation was facilitated by the story's early separation from the rest of the novel, first evidenced in

---

31 May 2006 studies the influence of Greek and Latin drama on Apuleius, Pasetti 2007 focuses on Plautine language, and Hindermann 2009 studies the use of love elegy in the novel.
32 For the rich early reception of *Cupid and Psyche* see in more detail Carver 2007 and Gaisser 2008.

Fulgentius; it was followed for example by Giovanni Boccaccio (1313–1375), who made his own copy of the main manuscript of Apuleius after its rediscovery in Florence. In *On the Genealogy of the Gods of the Pagans* (*Genealogia deorum gentilium*, 1360–1374), Boccaccio tries to bring order into the genealogy of the pagan gods of Greece and Rome, and it quickly became a reference work for many generations. Book 5, chapter 22 retells the story of Psyche, and gives two contradictory genealogies for her: at first Boccaccio identifies her, following some late antique sources, as the daughter of Apollo, the god of the Sun, but then diligently and in detail summarises Apuleius' story where she is a princess born of mortal parents, up to the point where Cupid deserts her because she broke the taboo and looked at her sleeping husband. The rest of the tale is told very briefly. Boccaccio then explains its interpretation allegorically: Psyche is the soul, and Apollo the god of true light, who therefore has to be her father; this Platonist philosophical explanation is in some tension with Apuleius' tale, but Boccaccio allows the two to stand next to each other. Boccaccio's double reception is yet again evidence for the story's versatility for its later readers.

The novel as a whole was printed early on, by Arnold Pannartz and Konrad Sweynheim for Giovanni Andrea Bussi in 1469,[33] which boosted the reception of Apuleius in Europe, turned the novel into an important text of the Renaissance, and resulted in several translations into vernacular languages, e. g. by M.M. Boiardo into Italian (*Apulegio volgare*; Venice 1518) or by Johann Siedler into German (printed 1538).[34] William Adlington's 1566 translation into English inspired Shakespeare to include, for example, the transformation of Bottom into a donkey in *A Midsummer Night's Dream*.[35]

6 *Cupid and Psyche* after 1600

In this section we try to plot the location of the papers in this volume on the extensive map of Apuleian reception after 1600, a period in which *Cupid and Psyche* became widely influential in European culture. The papers are organised in roughly chronological order, but also grouped into five (sometimes overlapping) influential areas of reception, to demonstrate the changing focus of readers of *Cupid and Psyche* over the centuries.

---

[33] The only non-defaced copy of this incunabulum is kept in Manchester's John Rylands Library, Deansgate.
[34] See Moreschini 1994, 12–26; Plank 2004; Küenzlen 2005.
[35] See Moore 2015.

The story's dramatic dimension, already recognised in Renaissance Italy,[36] is explored in plays such as Thomas Heywood's masque *Love's Mistress* (1636), which received an elaborate staging with expensive costumes and sets involving singing and dancing performed for the London royal court.[37] Some further early modern theatrical adaptations of *Cupid and Psyche* are however lost, despite their obvious popularity: 'the anti-theatricalist Stephen Gosson referred/contemptuously in 1582 to works such as *The Golden Ass* and *Amadis* being "ransacked" for the stage, and a play of *'The golden Ass & Cupid & Psiches'* by Dekker, Day, and Chettle was written around 1600.'[38]

Cupid and Psyche's potential as a narrative of epic or romance was picked up throughout the centuries, too. Roger Boyle (*Parthenissa*, 1651–69) modelled his English romance on French heroic romances based on Heliodorus, but already includes a painting of Psyche, which then 'triggers a mini-retelling of her story', making it an inset tale in yet another romance.[39] There is a cameo-like adaptation in Edmund Spenser's *Faerie Queene* (1590), where 3.6.50 summarises the story briefly (motifs from Apuleius' novel as a whole are used recurrently throughout this poem).[40] Sir Philip Sidney's *Arcadia*, too (unfinished and in two versions, late 1570s to his death in 1586), incorporates motifs from *Cupid and Psyche*).[41] Shackerley Marmion's *Cupid and Psyche* (1638), on the other hand, devotes two books of heroic couplets to the story, turning it from an allusive intermezzo into an independent plot. Other philosophical, tragic, comic, philosophical, epic, lyric and multiform literary responses followed and continue to follow until today.

A key event in the reception history of *Cupid and Psyche* was the publication in 1669 of Jean de La Fontaine's *Les Amours de Psyché et de Cupidon*, the influence of which is the focus of section I ('Baroque and the influence of La Fontaine') of this book. It is an extensive prose adaptation of the tale (with some intercalated poems) which is double the length of the Latin original. It begins *Decameron*-style with a brief frame narrative, concerning four friends in contemporary Paris: Acante, Poliphile, Ariste and Gelaste, who go to the palace-park of Versailles to hear Poliphile's version of the story of *Cupid and Psyche*. The opening sequence of the work is dedicated to an elaborate description of some of the

---

36 See Moreschini 1994, 16 on the 1499 five-act *Nozze de Psiche e Cupidine* of Galeotto del Carretto.
37 See Harrison forthcoming.
38 Moore 2015, 295–96.
39 Moore 2015, 292.
40 Carver 2007, 384–428.
41 Carver 2007, 365–83; Moore 2015, 295.

wonders of the gardens of Versailles, then being laid out by Le Nôtre, which find their echo later in the descriptions of the palace of Cupid in the main story, but otherwise the text is a fairly faithful adaptation of the original, with a supplement in the form of a dialogue between the four friends of the frame-narrative about the relative merits of tragedy and comedy, and the addition to Psyche's story of an episode where she takes refuge with a fisherman's family in the forest, taken in general outline from Canto VII of Tasso's Italian romance *Gerusalemme Liberata*. This addition itself became popular in the story's reception, especially in the visual arts in France. For instance, it is clear that the Parisian wallpaper on display in Bad Doberan and its descriptive booklet find its inspiration in La Fontaine's version, as Reitz shows.[42] It comprises a set of twelve classicistic panels designed by Merry-Joseph Blondel and Louis Lafitte, produced after 1815, and one panel portrays Psyche meeting a fisherman, which corresponds to one of the scenes added by La Fontaine's version. The same can be said about the cycle of paintings in the Salon de la Princesse in the Hôtel de Soubise in Paris, discussed in this volume by Simard, who shows that the identification of the room's female occupant with the beautiful Psyche is a desired outcome of the representations. La Fontaine's version was adapted into English for an aristocratic wedding in 1764 by John Lockman (1698–1771), and proves to be one of the most important landmarks in the tale's reception, with its impact felt long into the nineteenth century.

La Fontaine's version marks the key connection between the reception of *Cupid and Psyche* and the history of the modern European fairy tale, since it provided a point of dispute for Charles Perrault in the preface to his *Contes en Vers* of 1697, a fundamental fairy-tale text which contained early versions of such classics as *Cinderella* and *Bluebeard*. Perrault praises the story of Psyche, specifically as mediated by La Fontaine's adaptation, for its attractiveness and ingenuity, but criticises it for its lack of an obvious moral allegory: Psyche clearly signifies the Soul, he says, but the fact that she comes to grief when she recognises Cupid/Love is hard to interpret. His conclusion is that *Cupid and Psyche*, like all ancient tales, was written to charm and entertain rather than edify. This is thoroughly in tune with modern interpretations, but for Perrault the lack of moral content was a major fault, and was one more proof that the Moderns were superior to the Ancients in the so-called 'Quarrel of the Ancients and Moderns' in which both Perrault and La Fontaine had been involved on opposite sides for a decade (see Fumaroli 2001). For Perrault, his traditional moralising fairy tales represented

---

[42] See further Winkler-Horaček and Reitz 2008.

a better and more edifying body of literature than classical narratives such as that of Apuleius.

La Fontaine's version rapidly became the source text for dramatic adaptations with Jean-Baptiste Lully's music: 1671 saw the ballet and tragicomedy *Psyché* based on a text by Molière at the French royal court, and 1678 a *tragédie lyrique* or opera of the same name based on a libretto by Thomas Corneille; on Lully's operatic adaptations see the chapter by Harrison in this volume. Lully's ballet became popular in England in an adaptation by Thomas Shadwell (ca. 1642–1692), a poet and comic playwright, again discussed in Harrison's chapter. Shadwell succeeded Dryden as the English poet laureate in 1689 after aligning himself with the successful Protestant faction in the Glorious Revolution. He provided the libretto for the semi-opera *Psyche* (1675), one of the earliest English operatic works, for which Matthew Locke (1621–1677) wrote the music.[43] The opera was first performed in 1675 in London's recently opened Duke's Theatre with lavish staging, typical for Restoration theatre, and was soon loosely parodied on the London stage in a 'mock-opera' comedy *Psyche Debauch'd* by Thomas Duffett (1675).[44]

Cupid and Psyche thus formed an important influence on the development of Baroque music and opera; even before Lully, Pier Francesco Cavalli (music) and G.B. Fusconi (formally designated as the author of the libretto, in fact by several hands) produced *Amore inamorato* in Venice in 1642 (for this opera and its influences see Ragno in this volume). In subsequent centuries a wide range of comic, tragic and tragicomic versions of the story were brought to the musical stage,[45] a tradition which continues today, where *Cupid and Psyche* is still reinvented and performed as stage plays with or without music (on 21st century operas and plays see Müller in this volume).[46]

Simultaneously with Perrault, and similarly using La Fontaine, the earliest versions of the 'Beauty and the Beast' story emerge in this same French context: 'The Green Serpent' (*Serpentin Vert*) of Marie-Catherine D'Aulnoy (published in 1697) plainly presents a re-working of *Cupid and Psyche* in which a dreadful snake turns out in the end to be a handsome prince, while a generation later we find the first tale actually entitled 'Beauty and the Beast' (*La Belle et la*

---

43 See Degott 2008.
44 See DiLorenzo 1972.
45 See Müller-Reineke 2009.
46 The theatre practitioner Emily Snyder, who herself had adapted *Cupid and Psyche* in blank verse for the stage, gave a paper at the Leeds conference via You Tube on her methods of adaptation, which is still available (accessed 12/06/2017): https://www.youtube.com/watch?v=fME6UcNksVI&feature=youtu.be

Bête) by Gabrielle-Suzanne de Villeneuve (1740), establishing a tradition which would underlie such modern phenomena as the Disney cartoon film *Beauty and the Beast* of 1991,[47] and its semi-animated remake of 2017. This genetic link with the Apuleian original is important for the interpretation of *Cupid and Psyche* in its Latin version, since it shows that the fairy-tale elements of the story are in fact generated from the ancient source itself rather than being parallel and separately transmitted versions of some archetypal folk-tale.[48] Thus the later interpretations and adaptations (see e. g. James' chapter in this volume) of *Cupid and Psyche* as a fairy tale actually reflect its key role in the origins of the European fairy tale itself. Amongst these are versions which consciously mix fairy tales with more literary ambitions, as Gaisser shows for the 1942 American novella *The Robber Bridegroom* by Eudora Welty (see below). The story's perceived fairy-tale-like character continues to be an important aspect in its modern reception, even with wide ranging consequences for modern psychology, since *Cupid and Psyche* became the focus of early psychoanalysis, where the analysis of fairy tales as primal narrative patterns is a common theme, as Benson discusses in his chapter.

During European Romanticism, the story became popular as a love story, as a contemplation of the human condition, and for its Platonic themes as well as as a fairy tale, as set out in Section II: 'Romanticism and Philosophy'. Translations into modern languages proliferated[49] and helped to spread interest in the tale. In Germany, August von Rode's translations of *Cupid and Psyche* on its own and then of the *Metamorphoses* as a whole (1780 and 1783) became classics in their own right and are still in print. In Britain, the neo-Platonist Thomas Taylor similarly translated *Cupid and Psyche* together with selected sections of Plato's *Symposium* (1795), followed (1822) by all of Apuleius' works. Apuleius had made Plato accessible, at least for Taylor (others show less deference to the philosophical background); Taylor's contribution is discussed in this volume by Carver, who also covers English translations between Adlington (1566) and Gildon (1708).

Although Platonist readings dominated in this period, other philosophical schools could find Apuleius' eclecticism inspiring, and the Danish philosopher Søren Kierkegaard (1813–1855) found Lucius' and Psyche's anxieties useful in developing his own proto-existentialist ideas, as Andreadakis demonstrates in his chapter.

---

[47] See Warner 1994, 273–97.
[48] Here we follow the important but sometimes neglected argument of Fehling 1977.
[49] For German translations since 1780 see Stephan 2015.

Platonism, however, was the dominant channel through which Romantic poets engaged with Psyche.[50] In Germany, for example, the dramatist and novelist Christoph Martin Wieland (1733–1813) composed 'Bruckstücke von Psyche, einem unvollendet gebliebenen allegorischen Gedichte' ('Fragments of Psyche, an allegorical poem which remains incomplete') in 1767. During the same period in which he wrote this incomplete poem, he also wrote the *Bildungsroman* ('novel of development') *Geschichte des Agathon* (*The Story of Agathon*), in which he describes his own personal development, but disguises this thinly by setting the novel in the historical context of the 5th and 4th century BC. At the same time, Wieland systematically translated Shakespeare into German prose. His poetic fragment has a Boccaccio-style frame set in the same time period: the story of Psyche is told to Aspasia, a romantic high priestess, by her Platonic lover Alkahest, a handsome young Zoroastrian magician, on a number of summer evenings. The story itself is coloured by its Platonist and philosophical context, and very freely adapted from Apuleius. For example, the goddess Isis, who plays a major role in the last book of Apuleius' *Golden Ass*, is here Psyche's creator.

In England, too, poetic reactions to the story were found. In 1799, Hudson Gurney (1775–1864), a politician and antiquary, published his *Cupid and Psyche: a Mythological Tale from The Golden Ass of Apuleius*. This poem in quatrain stanzas includes the frame from the original, the old woman telling Charite the story to distract her, but the frame is never closed; the poem ends with the birth of Pleasure. For Gurney, too, Apuleius is a Platonist and a mystic, who wishes to 'typify, after various trials and probations, the final union of the soul of man to Divine Love in a state of immortality'. Gurney's justification for his adaptation of *Cupid and Psyche* is specifically his genteel female readership:

A FEMALE relation of the AUTHOR'S, having seen a manuscript version of the Story of CUPID AND PSYCHE, mentioned it to him as a subject peculiarly susceptible of poetical embellishment, and recommended him to attempt it.—He at one time thought of giving an analysis of the fable, but finding that each commentator explained almost every subordinate circumstance in a different manner, he resolved to decline the task. …'[51]

The concerns with the story's suitability for female readers is a recurring phenomenon; this reflects both the fact that it is one of the few classical narratives in which the protagonist is female, as well as the need to render it in the vernacular owing to fewer opportunities for women to learn the classical lan-

---

50 See Holm 2006.
51 Both quotes are from Gurney [1801] on the page after the title page (no pagination).

guages. It is also found in Mary Blachford Tighe (1772–1810), who wrote a Spenserian adaptation of *Cupid and Psyche* in six cantos: *Psyche or The Legend of Love*, which was at first privately published in 1805.[52] The first two cantos are closely based on Apuleius' story, whereas cantos III-VI are a much freer response to the tale. After Psyche's and Cupid's separation, Psyche, Cupid in disguise as a knight errant, a lion (symbolising passion), and their page-boy Constance go on a quest to find the urn of beauty, and encounter on their journeys many personifications, who either help or hinder their quest. In the end, Cupid and Psyche are reunited. The poem brought Tighe fame and the nickname 'Psyche', identifying the author with her subject, a conflation ironically frequent for her source text, too—already St. Augustine of Hippo (354–430) had mistaken the author Apuleius for his fictional first person narrator Lucius, and claimed that the author had experienced the novel's story of adventure and witchcraft himself (*CD* 18.8). Tighe's *Psyche* is analysed in this volume by O'Brien. Tighe's third edition from 1811 was read by John Keats, who at first admired Mary Tighe enthusiastically, but afterwards became disenchanted with her poetry. His 'Ode to Psyche' depicts Cupid and Psyche in a close embrace; Keats's reading of Apuleius' story and its continued influence on how Keats defines his poetry is studied in this volume by May.

Long poetic and prose texts from earlier periods developed into the modern novel, and Apuleius' story formed a natural source for interested authors in search of a classical model to emulate ostentatiously. These novels, too, could themselves interpret *Cupid and Psyche* in many different ways. An early example, the neo-Latin novel *Psyche Cretica* (1685) by Johann Ludwig Prasch, once again uses the symbolism of Psyche as the human soul, but places the tale in a thinly veiled discussion of contemporary German Protestantism.[53]

With the increasing domination of the novel as the literary form of choice in the 19th and 20th centuries, Apuleius' novel, too, became an inspiration for many authors. It is therefore not surprising that *Cupid and Psyche*'s reception in novels is amply represented in this volume, and developments of this most versatile form of prose fiction can be traced in the different ways allusions to Apuleius are treated. Walter Scott, the last Romantic and first great historical novelist, as is shown in this volume by Paschalis, knew *Cupid and Psyche* well and integrated the story into the plot of at least one of his novels (*Kenilworth*) to characterise his lonely heroine, while both Edward Bulwer-Lytton's *The Last Days of*

---

52 On Tighe and Apuleius see May (forthcoming).
53 On Prasch see Gärtner 2013.

Pompeii (1834) and William Makepeace Thackeray's *Pendennis* (1848 – 50) shape their loving couples after the relationship of Cupid and Psyche.[54]

Walter Pater (1839 – 1894) [55] was a writer and critic of English romantic poets and Renaissance art, as well as a friend of William Morris (see below), whom he admired greatly. His novel *Marius the Epicurean* (1885) is set in the lifetime of Apuleius. It describes the life of Marius, a young Roman, who follows various philosophical schools after being disenchanted with traditional religion, including Epicureanism and Stoicism, which he experiences as the emperor Marcus Aurelius' secretary. Early on in the novel, the hero Marius and his friend Marianus read Apuleius' *Metamorphoses*, which includes the story of *Cupid and Psyche*, at a dinner party. The story of the *Metamorphoses* in general is only summarised and discussed by the two boys, who admire Apuleius' learned style:

> ... in an age when people, from the emperor Aurelius downwards, prided themselves, unwisely, on writing in Greek, he had written for Latin people in their own tongue; though still, in truth, with all the care of one writing a learned language.[56]

But the story of *Cupid and Psyche* in particular is extensively included in translation, in Chapter V: 'The golden book' (an allusion to Apuleius' title *Metamorphoses or The Golden Ass*). Pater describes *Cupid and Psyche* admiringly: 'With a concentration of all his finer literary gifts, Apuleius had gathered into it the floating star-matter of many a delightful old story.' As Pater charts his hero's development through various philosophical schools, Apuleius, who appears as a character in Pater's novel, and the story of *Cupid and Psyche* which he narrates in person represent and speak for Platonism, in the tradition of Fulgentius and Taylor.[57]

During the same period, poetic adaptations of the story abound, and are especially fruitful in the Victorian age, when long poetic narratives were fashionable.[58] Elizabeth Barrett Browning's *Paraphrases on Apuleius* (1845) is a cycle of ten poems which closely follows Apuleius' story, as does William Morris' *The Earthly Paradise* (1868 – 70). Morris (1834 – 1896) was a founder of the Arts and Crafts Movement, designer and author, as well as a social reformer. His (very) long epic *The Earthly Paradise* combines Morris' two favourite periods in history in a retelling of twenty-four tales, two for each month of the year; twelve

---

54 See Harrison 2018.
55 On Pater as classicist see Martindale, Evangelista and Prettejohn 2017.
56 Pater 1885, 61.
57 See further Brzenk 1978; Harrison 2004.
58 See the recent OUP volume on Victorian epic by Tucker 2012.

from classical sources; the other twelve from medieval Latin, French and Icelandic originals. Like Boccaccio (*Decameron*) and Chaucer (*Canterbury Tales*), Morris uses a frame story of a group of narrators, here mediaeval Norse Wanderers fleeing the plague who after many years of travels encounter some city Elders who still live according to ancient Greek customs. The Wanderers settle and the two groups exchange stories twice a month. *Cupid and Psyche* is the classical story for May. It follows Apuleius' plot quite closely, but differences are obvious, too. Morris' version is more sentimental, for instance, especially in the portrait of Psyche, who is less vengeful and more gentle than her Apuleian ancestor, who, for example, successfully plots revenge on her sisters for inducing her to reveal her unknown husband's identity.[59]

Robert Seymour Bridges (1844–1930) was poet laureate from 1913 to his death. Originally a physician, he had to retire from his profession in 1882 because of ill health. He dedicated the rest of his life to poetry. Interested in the Classics, his work included masques on themes like Prometheus and Demeter, but also sonnets and religious hymns. His 1885 work *Eros and Psyche: A Poem in Twelve Measures* is a narrative poem, divided into twelve cantos, each representing a month of the year.[60] Each canto has the same number of stanzas as the month has days. Bridges adds a note to the end of the poem in which he claims that 'the beautiful story is well known, and the version of Apuleius has been simply followed', even though he admits to some learned additions: 'the addition made to Homer's description of Hera's dress is an orientalism of the present writer'. He never, he says, read an English version of the story (i.e. not even Adlington's widely available translation), but this can be doubted.[61] Many allusions to other ancient and more modern authors make this a learned, intertextual poem, e.g. the citation from Dante, *Purgatorio* canto XVI. Bridges' adaptations of the novel and use of previous poetry are studied in this volume by Ruggeri.

The time around the turn of the twentieth century (the era of the birth of the discipline of modern psychology) saw a focus on the internal mentalities of the characters of the novel, especially of Psyche (Section III: 'Fin de Siècle and Psychology'). In Italy, Giovanni Pascoli (1855–1912), a classicist and poet, picks up the themes of mortality of the soul in his contemplative diptych of poems on Psyche, which he juxtaposes with Platonism to explore symbolist ideas, as Pasetti explores in this volume.

---

59 For a treatment of Morris' version of our story see Harrison 2015.
60 For a brief account see Harrison 2018.
61 His structure plainly echoes that of Morris, see Ruggeri below.

There is no space to do enough justice to the rich reception of *Cupid and Psyche* in art, often inspired by Apuleius' text, and often by one of the many adaptations discussed here.[62] In this volume, the focus is on artistic reactions to specific texts which themselves prove to be literary receptions. La Fontaine again proves influential here, as the papers by Reitz and Simard (see above) show. But in parallel with the wide-spread interest in the story by Victorian readers, there is also a notable rise in paintings and prints of the story.[63] Although already the earliest translations illustrated this colourful story (the early German and Italian versions by Siedler and Boiardo contained remarkably fine woodcuts),[64] the nineteenth century with artists like Morris and Burne-Jones (1833– 1898) showed an almost unprecedented fascination with the story. Burne-Jones' oeuvre includes over two hundred images of the story.[65] Various versions of his 'Cupid finding Psyche', themselves become important influences, for example on the Italian Decadent poet Gabriele D'Annunzio (1863–1938) in his 1892 poem *Psiche giacente*, discussed in this volume by Pasetti. Illustrations by Morris and Burne-Jones, including 'Psyche carried by Zephyrus' (Figure 1), were designed for the Kelmscott Press version of *The Earthly Paradise*: forty-four were engraved on wood in line, consciously imitating the methodology of German Renaissance book printing. About thirty-five were executed by William Morris, the rest by others, but they were not used after all for *The Earthly Paradise*.[66]

In Germany, too, especially fine book illustrations were produced at the end of the nineteenth century and in the first half of the twentieth. Leidl's richly illustrated paper in this volume shows how contemporary illustrations reflect popular interpretations of the story through symbolist, psychological, and erotic lenses.

This focus on the psychology of the characters led Jungian critics to discuss Psyche like a patient on their psychologist's couch. One example of this treat-

---

[62] See for these the full listings in Davidson Reid 1993, and most recently Scippacercola and Scippacercola 2016, an expanded published version of their well-illustrated paper at the Leeds conference, as well as Cavicchioli 2002.
[63] Charles Martindale and Liz Prettejohn gave a fascinating paper on *Cupid and Psyche* in Victorian art and its refraction in contemporary literature at the conference.
[64] For Siedler see Gaisser 2008, 254. For the woodcuts in Boiardo see the appendix in Zimmerman 2009 and the cover of May 2013.
[65] See Christian and Sidey 2007; Harrison 2016, 112–113. On Victorian illustrations see Maxwell 2002.
[66] See Harrison 2016, 112–113. Some are now published in Dufty 1974.

Figure 1: William Morris, 'Zephyrus and Psyche'. Source: William Morris and Sir Sydney Carlyle Cockerell: *A note by William Morris on his aims in founding the Kelmscott Press. Together with a short description of the Press by S.C. Cockerell, & an annotated list of the books printed thereat.* Kelmscott Press 1898. Reproduced with the permission of Special Collections, Leeds University Library (Brotherton Collection)

ment of the story is discussed by Benson, who focuses on Franz Riklin's analysis of the story as Psyche's wish-fulfilment fantasy.

As Schultze shows in this volume, both Charlotte M. Yonge (*Love and Life* 1880) and Sylvia Townsend Warner (*The True Heart* 1929) adapted the ancient love story to describe quite different ways in which modern women fall into love and develop their identities. This theme is also pursued by Eudora Welty's 1942 novella *The Robber Bridegroom*, which explores the love of lonely Rosamund and the dashing Lockhart, who keeps his identity hidden from her, as explored by Gaisser in this volume, the first paper in Section IV: 'Twentieth Century and Modernism'. As a counterweight to this more romanticised rewriting of the myth, Pasetti looks at two novels by Alberto Savinio (1891–1952), whose versions combine postmodern deconstructions of the myth with revisionist and ironic tendencies (*Angelica o la notte di maggio* 1927, and *La nostra anima* 1944).

An important milestone in modern reception is C.S. Lewis' 1956 novel *Till We Have Faces*, in which Psyche's sister whom he names Orual tells the story of Psyche/Istra's love for the God of the Mountain (Cupid). The first part of the novel follows Apuleius' plot fairly closely, although the narrator's perspective is shifted from that of the quasi-omniscient old woman in Apuleius to Orual's fallible human perspective (she misunderstands some plot-events). Lewis deepens Apuleius' narrative psychologically and tries to find explanations for some often incomprehensible actions in the original story. In the second part, an old Orual revises her first version after having received some divine visions, not unlike Lucius. In these visions, Orual finds herself completing some of the tasks that Apuleius' Psyche had to undertake, and in the end finds Psyche again, and gains her and the God of the Mountain's forgiveness and mercy before she dies. Drews' chapter focuses on the philosophical learning and development of the novel's characters, especially Orual.

William Faulkner's *The Reivers* (1962), a novel as a whole richly inspired by Apuleius' *Metamorphoses*, doubles up the story of *Cupid and Psyche* into two interwoven narrative strands, one comic, one idealistic, in yet another echo of Apuleius' Platonic philosophy, as shown by Provencal in this volume.

As a representative of modern, feminist receptions of *Cupid and Psyche*, Sylvia Plath's poetry is a reaction, as Ranger demonstrates, to both the novels by the Brontë sisters—themselves readers and receivers of *Cupid and Psyche*; Charlotte Brontë used Apuleius in *Jane Eyre*—and by Apuleius. It is especially the female perspective of Psyche that fascinated Plath, who herself explored female life experiences throughout her work.

The twenty-first century now sees the expansion of Cupid and Psyche reception to 'New Audiences' (Section V). Not only Pulitzer-Prize-winning novels like *The Reivers*, but also simple children's stories could be inspired by *Cupid and*

Psyche. In her chapter, Maurice traces the development of readings of the old story related to child psychology and modern feminism in children's books from the 19th to the 21st century, which reflect contemporary attitudes to love, sex and children's behaviour. Other new media, such as YouTube or experimental film, allow even more young audiences to experience the story and reinterpret it in their own way for our contemporary society, as Müller shows in his overview discussion of recent adaptations of the tale. The volume concludes with the most modern of reception genres: film. Siegel shows in her discussion of Guillermo del Toro's film *Pan's Labyrinth* (2006) how our knowledge of Psyche's tale enables us both to understand the film's heroine Ofelia better and to find added meaning in the story's terrifying setting. James, as already noted, shows how the story of *Cupid and Psyche*, to modern audiences often channelled through popular adaptations of the *Beauty and the Beast* fairy tale, illustrates modern anxieties about the human condition and our encounter with the uncanny and the divine.

7 Conclusion

Because of the strategy of reading the text as a Platonic allegory, present in reception since the very early Middle Ages, *Cupid and Psyche* could be seen as a respectable work of instructive fiction by Renaissance scholars. Because of its adaptability, the story could be used both to showcase something ancient and also be rewritten into something recognisably contemporary. The tension between the alien and the contemporary is one of the key themes that comes to the fore in the studies in this book. Apuleius' fiction has had something of a mixed reputation across the centuries, due both to the often risqué nature of the novel itself and its florid, 'late' language which has often been contrasted with the 'classical' prose style of Cicero.[67] Focusing on the chaste and elevated episode of *Cupid and Psyche* has, however, enabled readers and artists throughout the centuries to avoid the problems of the frank eroticism and low-life elements of the rest of the *Metamorphoses*, and concentrate on the higher form of the ancient 'fairy tale' and edifying love story of Soul and Love. It is not entirely surprising that a remarkably large group of women writers engaged with *Cupid and Psyche* and wrote reactions of their own—a phenomenon that is much less in evidence for more classical authors such as Horace or Vergil. Female authors and readers specifically took to the story's female protagonist Psy-

---

[67] See Harrison 2013,17–24; May 2013, 41–43; 46 discusses the Renaissance controversy between Ciceronians and Apuleians.

che, a feature rare indeed in classical literature, whose experiences became rationalised, inverted, eroticised or allegorised. Children and young adults could see their own experiences of growing up reflected in versions adapted to focus on Cupid's, and especially Psyche's, feelings as teenagers in love. Studying *Cupid and Psyche* and its reception therefore also gives voice to the hitherto voiceless. As many of the papers in this volume demonstrate, this desire to make Psyche more comprehensible to their contemporary readers results in a considerable rewriting of her character: gone most often are her pregnancy and her involvement in the death of her sisters; furthermore, the love story between Cupid and Psyche becomes more often one between equals, where Psyche is less passive than her Apuleian ancestor, and Cupid, absent in large parts of Apuleius' tale, becomes more active and visible throughout. Time and again the papers demonstrate that the love of Apuleius' characters can be adapted to demonstrate contemporary yet changing ideals of love, resulting in each receiving author's demonstration of their own originality in a crowded field.

At times, the erotic elements in the novel of Lucius turned into a donkey are 'smuggled' back into the more 'harmless' reception of *Cupid and Psyche*, offering a 'guerilla' approach which allows the receiving author to surreptitiously engage with the dangerously erotic *Metamorphoses* while at the same time ostentatiously preserving their decency by also overtly engaging with the philosophically and sexually 'safe' *Cupid and Psyche* story. In some sense, this inverts Apuleius' own methodology, who condensed the story of the *Metamorphoses* and its protagonist Lucius into the inset tale of Psyche, which reflects the novel's main plot and character, often in unexpected yet recognisable ways (see above). Surprisingly often, Apuleius' tale was seen as an essentially 'Greek' text in Latin clothing, which yet again added to its respectability to some more modern recipients. Apuleius' relative lateness in the canon of classical authors also becomes exploitable by more modern readers who saw themselves as latecomers to literature; using Apuleius became an attractive statement about their own reception of antiquity and desired position in the literary canon. Especially during the literarily self-conscious periods at the end of the eighteenth and throughout the nineteenth century, the engagement with ancient texts is very deliberate, the comparison of two authors and styles is positively invited, and *Cupid and Psyche*, with its equally conscious play on previous literatures, becomes a valid and useful modern story. The more modern reactions to Apuleius are, too, ironic, undermining, and reflective. All these different versions and adaptations invite us to look back at Apuleius' original tale and rediscover the seeds of so many different receptions within it: the love story between god and human, the allegorical tale, vivid visualisations and human conflict, but also its psychological depth, The story has been, and continues to be, an important inspiration for authors, artists and film-makers, and its study is not only a history of the literary reception of an ancient tale, but also an exploration of human tastes and preoccupations over many centuries.

8 Bibliography

Bastianini, G./Casanova A. (eds.) (2009), *I papiri del romanzo antico*. Atti del convegno internazionale di studi Firenze, 11–12 Giugno 2009, Florence.

Brockliss, W./Chaudhuri, P. /Lushkov, A.H. /Wasdin, K. (eds.) (2012), *Reception and The Classics*, Cambridge.

Brzenk, E.J. (1978), 'Apuleius, Pater and the Bildungsroman' in: Hijmans/van der Paardt, 231–38.

Butler, S. (ed.) (2016), *Deep Classics: Rethinking Classical Reception*, London.

Carver, R.H.F. (2007), *The Protean Ass. The Metamorphoses of Apuleius from Antiquity to the Renaissance*, Oxford.

Carver, R.H.F./Schaaf, I. (2010), 'Apuleius von Madaura' in: Walde, C., (ed.) *Die Rezeption der antiken Literatur. Kulturhistorisches Werklexikon* (= Der Neue Pauly, Supplemente, Band 7), Stuttgart and Weimar, 45–68.

Cavicchioli, S. (2002), *Le metamorfosi di Psiche. L'iconografia della favola di Apuleio*, Venezia.

Cheney, P./Hardie P. (eds.) (2015), *The Oxford History of Classical Reception in English Literature. Vol. 2. 1558–1660*, Oxford.

Christian, J. and Sidey, T. (2007), *Hidden Burne-Jones. Works on Paper by Edward Burne-Jones from Birmingham Museums and Art Gallery*, London.

Dällenbach, L. (1989), *The Mirror in the Text*. Translated by J. Whiteley and E. Hughes, Cambridge.

Davidson Reid, J. (1993), *The Oxford Guide to Classical Mythology in the Arts, 1300–1900s*, Oxford, II: 939–66.

Degott, P. (2008), '"Amongst the Gods I Psyche will translate": la réécriture par Thomas Shadwell de la tragédie-ballet Psyché (1671) de Molière, Corneille et Quinault', *Revue LISA* 6: 20–35 https://www.lisa.revues.org/1128

DiLorenzo, R.E. (1972), *Three burlesque plays of Thomas Duffett. The Empress of Morocco, the mock-tempest, Psyche debauch'd*, Iowa City.

Dowden, K. (1994), 'Apuleius' Roman Audience', in: Tatum, 419–34.

Dufty, A.R. (ed.) (1974), *The Story of Cupid and Psyche, with illustrations designed by Edward Burne-Jones, mostly engraved on the wood by William Morris; the Introduction by A.R. Dufty*, London, Cambridge.

Egelhaaf-Gaiser, U. (2000), *Kulträume im römischen Alltag. Das Isisbuch des Apuleius und der Ort der Religion im kaiserzeitlichen Rom*, Stuttgart.

Fehling, D. (1977), *Amor und Psyche*, Wiesbaden.

Finkelpearl, E. (1998), *Metamorphosis of Language in Apuleius. A Study of Allusion in the Novel*, Ann Arbor.

Fumaroli, M. (2001), *La Querelle des Anciens et des Modernes*, Paris.

Gaisser, J.H. (2008), *The Fortunes of Apuleius and the Golden Ass*, Princeton.

Gärtner, T. (2013), 'Die *Psyche Cretica* des Regensburgers Johannes Ludwig Prasch (1685). Eine christliche Apuleius-Adaptation' in: Tilg/Walser, 135–41.
Goff, B. (ed.) (2005), *Classics and Colonialism*, London.
Graverini, L. (2007), *Literature and Identity in the Golden Ass of Apuleius*, Columbus.
[Gurney, H.] (1801), *Cupid and Psyche: a Mythological Tale from the Golden Ass of Apuleius*, London (3rd ed., published anonymously).
Hardwick, L. (2000), *Reception Studies*, Cambridge.
Hardwick, L./Stray, C. (eds.) (2011), *A Companion to Classical Receptions*, Oxford.
Harrison, S.J. (1998), 'Some Epic Structures in *Cupid and Psyche*', in: Zimmerman et al., 51–68.
Harrison, S.J. (2000), *Apuleius. A Latin Sophist*, Oxford.
Harrison, S.J. (2004), 'Two Victorian Versions of the Roman Novel', in: Zimmerman/van der Paardt, Leuven and Paris, 265–78.
Harrison, S.J. (2007), 'The Reception of Horace in the Nineteenth and Twentieth Centuries', in: Harrison (2007a), 334–46.
Harrison, S.J. (ed.) (2007a), *The Cambridge Companion to Horace*, Cambridge.
Harrison, S.J. (2013), *Framing The Ass. Literary Texture in Apuleius' Metamorphoses*, Oxford.
Harrison, S.J. (2015), 'William Morris', in: Vance/Wallace, 559–78.
Harrison, S.J. (2016), 'Nachwort', in: Norden, E. (ed.), *Apuleius Amor und Psyche. Übertragen von Eduard Norden. Mit Buchschmuck von Walter Tiemann*, Leipzig. 66–126.
Harrison, S.J. (2018), 'Psyche amongst the Victorians. An Aspect of Apuleian Reception', in: Harrison and Thorsen, 177–94.
Harrison, S.J. (forthcoming), 'An Apuleian Masque? Thomas Heywood's *Love's Mistress* (1634)' in: Boidin, C. / Mouren, R. / Pedeflous, O. (eds.) (2020), *The Afterlife of Apuleius*. London (forthcoming).
Harrison, S.J./Thorsen, T., (eds.) (2018), *Dynamics of Latin Prose. Biographic, Novelistic, Apologetic*, Berlin.
Hijmans, B.L. Jr./van der Paardt, R.Th. (eds.) (1978) *Aspects of Apuleius' Golden Ass*, Groningen.
Hindermann, J. (2009), *Der elegische Esel. Apuleius' Metamorphosen und Ovids Ars amatoria*, Frankfurt am Main.
Holm, C. (2006), *Amor und Psyche. Die Erfindung eines Mythos in Kunst, Wissenschaft und Alltagskultur (1765–1840)*, Berlin.
Hopkins, D./Martindale, C., (eds.) (2012), *Oxford History of Classical Reception in English Literature. Vol. 3. 1660–1790*, Oxford.
Kallendorf, C. (ed.) (2007), *A Companion to the Classical Tradition*, Oxford.
Kenney, E.J. (1990), *Apuleius Cupid and Psyche*, Cambridge.
Keulen, W. / Tilg, S. / Nicolini, L. / Graverini L. / Harrison S.J. / Panayotakis, S. / van Mal-Maeder D. (eds.) (2015), *Apuleius Madaurensis. Metamorphoses Book XI: Groningen Commentaries on Apuleius*, Leiden.
Kitzbichler, J. / Stephan, U. (eds.) (2015), *Studien zur Praxis der Übersetzung antiker Literatur. Geschichte—Analysen—Kritik*. Berlin and New York.
Küenzlen, F. (2005), *Verwandlungen eines Esels. Apuleius' Metamorphosen im frühen 16. Jahrhundert*, Heidelberg.
Martindale, C. (1993), *Redeeming the Text*, Cambridge.
Martindale, C. (ed.) (1997), *The Cambridge Companion to Vergil*, Cambridge.

Martindale, C. / Evangelista, S. / Prettejohn, E. (eds.) (2017), *Pater the Classicist*, Oxford.
Martindale, C. / Thomas, R. (eds.) (2006), *Classics and the Uses of Reception*, Oxford.
Mason, H.J. (1978), 'Fabula Graecanica. Apuleius and His Greek Sources.' in: Hijmans Jr/van der Paardt, 1–15.
Maxwell, R. (2002), *The Victorian Illustrated Book*, Charlottesville.
May, R. (2006), *Apuleius and Drama. The Ass on Stage*, Oxford.
May, R. (2009), 'An Ass from Oxyrhynchus. P.Oxy. LXX.4762, Loukios of Patrae and the Milesian Tales', *Ancient Narrative* 8, 59–83.
May, R. (2013), *Apuleius* Metamorphoses *or The Golden Ass. Book 1. With an Introduction, Translation and Notes*, Oxford.
May, R. (2017), 'The Reception of Apuleius' *Cupid and Psyche* from 1600 to Today. Leeds, University of Leeds, 13th – 15th July 2016', *Bolletino di Studi Latini* 57, 276–78.
May, R. (forthcoming), 'Echoes of Apuleius' Novel in Mary Tighe's *Psyche*. Romantic Imagination and Self-Fashioning', in: Boidin, C. / Mouren, R. / Pedeflous, O. (eds.) (2020), *The Afterlife of Apuleius*. London (forthcoming).
Moore, H. (2015) 'Prose Romance' in Cheney / Hardie, 291–310.
Moreschini, C. (1994), *Il mito di Amore e Psiche in Apuleio*, Naples.
Morris, W. / Sir S. Carlyle Cockerell (1898), *A note by William Morris on his aims in founding the Kelmscott Press. Together with a short description of the Press by S.C. Cockerell, & an annotated list of the books printed thereat*, Kelmscott.
Müller-Reineke, H. (2009), 'Recent theatrical and musical adaptations of Apuleius' *Metamorphoses*', *New Voices in Classical Reception Studies* 4, 1–26.
Norden, E. (2016 and 1902), *Apuleius Amor und Psyche. Übertragen von Eduard Norden. Mit Buchschmuck von Walter Tiemann*, Leipzig.
Paschalis, M. / Panayotakis, S. / Schmeling, G. (eds.) (2009), *Readers and Writers in the Ancient Novel*, Groningen.
Pasetti, L. (2007), *Plauto in Apuleio*, Bologna.
Pater, W. (1885), *Marius the Epicurean. His sensations and ideas*, London.
Plank, B. (2004), *Johann Sieders Übersetzung des 'Goldenen Esels' und die frühe deutschsprachige 'Metamorphosen'-Rezeption*, Tübingen.
Plantade, E. and N. 'Libyca Psyche. Apuleius' Narrative and Berber Folktales' in: Todd Lee/Finkelpearl/ Graverini, 174–202.
Schlam, C.C. (1976), *Apuleius and the Monuments*, Pennsylvania.
Scippacercola, N. /Scippacercola, R. (2016), 'La bellezza di Psiche tra testo e immagine', *Classico Contemporaneo* 2, 23–64.
Scobie, A. (1983), *Apuleius and Folklore. Toward a History of ML3045, AaTh567, 449 A*, London.
Shumate, N.C. (1996), *Crisis and Conversion in Apuleius' Metamorphoses*, Ann Arbor.
Silk, M., Gildenhard, I./Barrow, R. (2014), *The Classical Tradition. Art, Literature, Thought*, Oxford.
Stephan, U. (2015), 'Deutsche Übersetzungen der *Metamorphosen* des Apuleius seit 1780' in Kitzbichler Stephan, 277–360.
Stramaglia, A. (2010), 'Le *Metamorfosi* di Apuleio tra iconografia e papri', in: Bastianini /Casanova, 165–192.
Tatum, J., (ed.) (1994), *The Search for the Ancient Novel*, Baltimore and London.
Tilg, S. (2014), *Apuleius' Metamorphoses. A Study in Roman Fiction*, Oxford.

Tilg, S. /Walser, I. (eds.) (2013), *Der neulateinische Roman als Medium seiner Zeit*, Tübingen.
Todd Lee, B. /Finkelpearl E. /Graverini, L. (eds.) (2014), *Apuleius and Africa*, Abingdon and New York.
Tucker, H., (ed.) (2012), *Epic. Britain's Heroic Muse 1790–1910*, Oxford.
van Thiel, H. (1971–72), *Der Eselsroman. Vol. I. Untersuchungen*, München 1971. *Vol. II. Synoptische Ausgabe*, München.
Vance, N. /Wallace, J. (eds.) (2015), *The Oxford History of Classical Reception in English Literature Volume 4: 1790–1880*, Oxford.
Walde, C. (ed.) (2010), *Die Rezeption der antiken Literatur. Kulturhistorisches Werklexikon* (= *Der Neue Pauly*, Supplemente, Band 7), Stuttgart and Weimar.
Warner, M. (1995), *From the Beast to the Blonde. On Fairy Tales and their Tellers*, London.
Winkler-Horaček, L. and Reitz, C. (2008), *Amor und Psyche. Eine Erzählung in zwölf Bildern*, Rahden.
Winkler, J. J. (1985), *Auctor & Actor. A Narratological Reading of Apuleius's* Golden Ass, Berkeley.
Zimmerman, M. (2009), 'Food for Thought for Readers of Apuleius' *The Golden Ass*' in: Paschalis /Panayotakis /Schmeling, 218–240.
Zimmerman, M. /van der Paardt, R.Th. (eds.) (2004), *Metamorphic Reflections. Essays presented to Ben Hijmans at his 75th Birthday*, Leuven and Paris.
Zimmerman, M. et al. (eds.) (1998) *Aspects of Apuleius' Golden Ass II: Cupid and Psyche*, Groningen.
Zimmerman, M. et al. (eds.) (2004), *Apuleius Madaurensis Metamorphoses Books IV 28–35, V and VI 1–24. The Tale of Cupid and Psyche*, Groningen. (Groningen Commentaries on Apuleius).

I **Baroque and the Influence of La Fontaine**

Tiziana Ragno
'Del soffrir degli affanni è dolce il fine'. Ancient myth and comic drama in G.F. Fusconi's libretto (with G.F. Loredano and P. Michiel) for F. Cavalli, *Amore innamorato* (1642)

"Cette fable eût pu faire inventer l'opéra, tant elle y est propre":[1] Antoine Houdar de La Motte's 1757 remark on *Cupid and Psyche* is indeed confirmed in general not only by the many operatic versions of this story,[2] but also by the fact that at the beginnings of this musical genre of melodrama[3] *Cupid and Psyche* inspired the storyline of some key examples.[4]

The first instance, whose author is assured (at least for the music), is Francesco Cavalli's lost opera, *Amore innamorato*, performed at the Teatro San Moisè in Venice in 1642.[5] While the music has disappeared, the libretto has survived: it was ascribed to Giovan Battista Fusconi,[6] although scholars lean more towards a

---

[1] Houdar De La Motte, 'Examen de l'opéra de Psyché' *Mercure de France*, Avril 1757, 2: 48.
[2] For the reception of this myth in Italy, see De Maria 1899. For Italy and other countries: Puleio 1992; Moreschini 1994, 7–48; Moreschini 2000; Acocella 2001; Candiani 2001; Ussia 2001; Cavicchioli 2002; Carver 2007, especially 384–428; Sozzi 2007; Gaisser 2008, especially 110–121 and 184–196; Iacovelli 2008, 11–48.
[3] For the main features of seventeenth-century Venetian opera, cf. recently Heller 2003.
[4] For seventeenth-century Italian operas inspired by the tale of *Cupid and Psyche* cf. e. g. D. Gabrielli for A. Leardini, *Psiche* (Mantova, 1649), F. Di Poggio for T. Breni, *La Psiche* (Lucca, 1654), G.F. Savaro for M. Cazzati, *La Psiche deificata* (Bologna, 1668), G.D. De Totis for A. Scarlatti, *La Psiche, ovvero Amore innamorato* (Napoli, 1683), M. Noris for [C. Pallavicino], *Amore innamorato* (Venezia, 1686), N. Minato for A. Draghi, *Psiche cercando Amore* (Vienna, 1688).
[5] The Venetian opera *Amore innamorato* has to be considered the first melodrama focusing on the myth of *Cupid and Psyche*, as G.B. Cini for A. Striggio and F. Corteccia, *Psiche e Amore* (Firenze, 1565), although staged earlier, merely consists of 'intermedi' for the comedy *La Cofanaria* written by F. D'Ambra. For *Amore innamorato* see Rizza 1984, 482–484; Candiani 2001, 149–52 and 156–158; Ussia 2001, 42–3; Sozzi 2007, 52–53, n. 9; Iacovelli 2008, 40–2. The quotations in this paper from the libretto are from [Fusconi] 1642 and cited as *Amore innamorato*. The English translation of individual excerpts is mine. In general, for the main features of seventeenth-century Venetian opera, cf. at the very least Rosand 1991 and Heller 2003.
[6] The signature following the dedication to Carlo Cervetti is that of Fusconi, who refers to the libretto as his own work ([Fusconi] 1642, 3).

threefold authorship, given that Pietro Michiel and Giovan Francesco Loredano[7] seem likely to have also contributed to the text.[8]

These three authors are sufficient to ascribe this libretto to the renowned Venetian Accademia degli Incogniti, of which Loredano and Michiel themselves were co-founders and of which Fusconi was secretary (the last wrote, among other things, the dedication of the volume *Le glorie de gli Incogniti overo gli huomini illustri dell'Accademia de' Signori Incogniti*, 1647).[9] The text indeed reveals a full conformity to the principles being theorized and practiced by the Incogniti either in general terms (e. g. the need to alter or even mock the classics) or in connection with specific aspects (e. g. the reliance on certain stock characters typical of the seventeenth-century Venetian context, such as the vile procuress).

1 The *Accademia degli Incogniti* and the classics

At the heart of the literary theorization established within the *Accademia degli Incogniti* was the notion that the distortion of the ancient tradition through imitation is appropriate and necessary. 'The stories are merely stories and the pagan gods are foolish entities, so we can joke merrily about them': so declares Giulio Strozzi in the preface to *Delia* (1639). To disrupt the classics by flouting their authority was the purpose of the *Incogniti*, whose extensive creation of parodies, burlesque travesties, and mocking rewritings revealed, however, a strong mastery of the literary tradition.

Well-known stories were rearranged so that they were provided with unprecedented meanings and narrative potentials, and also retained specific elements that could be recognized by the learned audience–an audience which, with regard to seventeenth-century Venetian opera (a genre in which the contribution of the *Incogniti* was noticeable), was multifaceted: aristocratic patronage aside, opera in Venice appealed to a heterogeneous public, made up of not only middle-class ticket-buying Venetians, but also foreigners of different classes (noble

---

[7] On Michiel and Loredano respectively cf. Giachino 2001 (preceded by Cicogna 1886) and Miato 1998, 15–55.
[8] On the roles played by Michiel, Loredano and Fusconi (a drama, initially entitled *La Psiche*, may well have been written by the former and conceived as a "favoletta per musica", on the basis of an outline of the plot provided by Loredano, and Fusconi would then have supplemented it with a few sections for the purposes of the performance), cf. Cicogna 1886, 392–3 and 394–5, who, however, erroneously refers to Agostino–instead of Giovan Battista–Fusconi, and Rosand 1991, 37–40.
[9] On the Accademia degli Incogniti cf. e. g. Miato 1998, 57–120.

men, ambassadors) who attend carnival entertainment such as operas. Such circumstances necessitated, for the purposes of seventeenth-century Venetian melodrama, a happy ending.

With the myth of *Cupid and Psyche*, a special turn of events *in extremis* to ensure a happy ending was not needed: it had actually already been provided by its source, Apuleius' text.[10] The three librettists instead focus on the deliberately distorted imitation (in a paratragic or elegiac sense) of elements of the plot and on the creation of humorous scenes which mainly ridicule the gods as characters in the piece, following the heroic-comic genre modeled after Francesco Bracciolini's *Lo scherno degli dèi*, 1618.

Rich in thought and abstruse in style, the libretto reflects baroque images and devices: adapted to the demands of the audience, the myth recreated by Fusconi, Michiel and Loredan follows contemporary laws of taste and inspiration and displays both aspects of novelty (the altered imitation of original traits, the comic side, the witticism in thought and style) and references to intermediate models. This story is less elevated than the drama of the French court a generation later, described by Harrison in this volume, but still full of baroque playfulness with its focus on all aspects of love.[11]

2 *Amore innamorato*, the imitation and parody of myth

2.1 The paradox of 'Love in love'

This title (albeit not unprecedented)[12] suggests a theme recurring throughout the drama: the paradoxical position of Love who is a victim (and not the origin) of falling in love.[13] It is the protagonist himself who admits that 'the beauty of Psy-

---

10 See Penwill 1998.
11 See below, especially n. 76 on Marino.
12 Compare Antonio Minturno's *Amore innamorato* (1559) and Lucrezia Marinella's *Amore innamorato et impazzato* (1618).
13 Cf. Marino, *Adone* 3.174.6–8; earlier, Nicolò da Correggio, *Rime* 241 for similar phrases. In general, Marino's *L'Adone* seems to be imitated by the librettists (on the influence of Marino's version of *Cupid and Psyche*, cf. Candiani 2001, 151). Further evidence for echoes of *L'Adone*: *Amore innamorato* I.4: 'If they [Cupid's eyes] were open..., they would act as a double sun ["doppio Sole"]' (on the face of Cupid) with *Adone* 4.38.1–3: "Veggio doppio oriente e veggio dui/cieli, che doppio Sol volge e disserra,/dico que' lumi..." (on the face of Psyche). See also nn. 78, 98 and 111. Furthermore, the motif of Venus' quest for Cupid, which exists in *Amore innamorato*

che's face has enveloped Love with strands of love' (*Amore innamorato*, I.1). The proximity between the two homonyms (Love as a character; love as a passion) highlights the unusual circumstance of the god who is not promoting love, but is gripped by it, a paradox that continued to fascinate later readers of *Cupid and Psyche*, such as Mary Tighe.[14]

Yet, the paradox of 'Love in love' reveals itself to be apparent enough to be in fact subverted in accordance with the inherent nature of the god. This is a stance embraced, albeit indirectly, by Aeolus, a new character in the myth who does not appear in Apuleius: in a short tirade against love (I.5), he refers to the case of Cupid as a basis for comparison *a fortiori* in order to demonstrate that every lover who idolizes his own partner is insane, given that even the god of love is forced to flee from his adored Psyche (and this he does, despite generally being accustomed to the consequences of love). In this instance, a sort of principle of identity (Love as an expert in love) undoes the paradox and, rather, lets the case of Love in love slip into an obvious pleonasm.

The debate between the two opposing viewpoints embodied by Venus and Cupid, in a scene which imitates (albeit with many variations) Apuleius' corresponding passage (5.29–30), is paradigmatic. Venus accuses Cupid of using false pretences in order to justify a position which is clearly unnatural: indeed, now 'Love lets his tears flow and sighs because of love' (II.3), whereas by his very nature 'Love was born with the aim of inspiring other people with the delights of love and not of falling in love' (*ibidem*).[15] Conversely, the connection between Cupid and love appears not at all peculiar from the viewpoint of Cupid himself, assuming that 'it should be surprising if Indignation or Hate aims to love: however, why would it be surprising if Love loves?' (*ibidem*).

The use of homonyms, polyptoton and affected word order highlights Cupid's bizarre (or tautological) being in love and reveals a fitting aptitude for wordplay which agrees well with *Amore innamorato*'s Baroque-style virtuosity. *Mutatis mutandis*, the seventeenth-century authors perhaps recognised this skill in Apuleius,[16] where e.g. in addition to the repeated wordplay on the soul of Psyche (*Met.* 5.6.9; 5.7.6; 5.13.4; 6.2.5), a subtle pun is connected with the observation that love-passions (*amores*) also exist within the family of Venus, the goddess of love: involved in upholding Cupid's right to fall in love, Ceres and Juno, in dialogue with Venus, come to the conclusion that, since

---

and not in Apuleius, had already been developed by Marino: it features also in Ercole Udine's *La Psiche* (first edition: 1599), which was in fact one of Marino's sources (Ussia 2004, 11–12).
14 See O'Brien in this volume, chapter 6.2 for a more serious use of this pun.
15 Cf. Marino, *Adone* 4.201.6–202.4.
16 Cf. Nicolini 2011.

she is used to imposing passion on whole peoples, Venus herself should not suppress harshly (*amare*) those same affections (*amores*) which are now felt in her own family (*Met.* 5.31.6 'But who... will tolerate your disseminating passions everywhere among the people, when you bitterly—*amare*—punish the love-affairs—*amores*—of your own house?').[17]

Thus, in Apuleius, too, the case of Love in love both raises potential objections of substance (objections denied here) and plays on words which, at least in this instance, look to a long-standing literary tradition (the motif of 'bitter love').[18] Moreover, in the translation of Agnolo Firenzuola (*L'Asino d'oro*, 1550 with many further editions), the same passage of Apuleius, misunderstood in terms of meaning, maintains an effortless witticism inspired by the fact that it is Loves (Cupids) who love ('Hence, who would tolerate you nowadays? You, who have always journeyed far and wide lustfully sowing your seeds, now do not want Loves to love at your door'—'in casa tua amino gli Amori']).[19] Furthermore, the hidden source can be found in the ancient model itself, where, albeit with regard to Psyche's—and not Cupid's—falling in love, the expression artfully employed by Apuleius (*Met.* 5.23.3 *in Amoris incidit amorem*, '[Psyche] fell in love with Love') seems in fact to draw attention to the unusual circumstance of a sentiment involving a deity who is generally the cause, rather than the victim, of this emotion.[20]

2.2 The tragedy of Psyche

The ability of the librettists to change the ancient source, while adopting at the same time some of its individual elements, is prominent in the main scene of the play, the feverish moments which precede the 'crime' driven by the curiosity of Psyche. This is a situation which, already in Apuleius, shows tragic traits.[21]

At dusk (*Met.* 5.21.4), the heroine prepares to carry out the deed, setting up the equipment and also embodying the emotional mindset which usually char-

---

17 Apuleius' text follows the edition by Zimmerman 2012; the translation, Zimmerman 2004.
18 Cf. e.g. Plaut. *Cist.* 68, *Trin.* 260. For the same image without the pun, see Apul. *Met.* 4.31.1 (*dulcia vulnera... mellitas uredines*).
19 Firenzuola 1863, 125.
20 For this play on words and the one that follows in *Met.* 5.23.3 *cupidine flagrans Cupidinis*, Harrison 2000, 225, n. 82 and 252, n. 197.
21 See e.g. Kenney 1990, 166–167; Moreschini 1994, 208; Zimmerman 2004, 265 and 267; May 2006, 211. Schiesaro 1988, 145–150 and, again, May 2006, 209–212 focus on further tragic elements in the tale.

acterizes every circumstance of malice aforethought. Left alone, Psyche is beset by doubts, worries and contradictory feelings which cause her to fluctuate between resolution and fear (5.21.3–4 *adhuc incerta consilii titubat multisque calamitatis suae distrahitur affectibus. Festinat differt, audet trepidat, diffidit irascitur*, 'she still wavers, unsure of her decision and she is torn apart by the many emotions provoked by her distress. She is impatient, she procrastinates, she is courageous, she panics, she has no confidence, she becomes angry').

In terms of emotions (as a soul tortured by divergent sentiments) and in terms of performance (as a character on the verge of committing a crime), her position is obviously similar to that of tragic heroes and heroines (the case of Medea,[22] both in Euripides' and Seneca's versions, is paradigmatic albeit not unique). Moreover, despite the allusion to a female character who is more elegiac than tragic (such as Catullus' Ariadne),[23] Apuleius highlights an explicit tragic connotation by mentioning the 'fiendish' Furies who agitate the mind of Psyche (*Met.* 5.21.3 *infestis Furiis agitata*).

The Italian librettists appear to pick up on Apuleius' idea and force it to undergo, as expected, a significant theatrical rearrangement by both condensing and enriching it with elements which do not exist in the source but are consistent with the tragic approach outlined there. In the libretto, the female protagonist recognizes the emotions which disturb her; hence, she addresses her own heart (a pattern already set out by ancient female tragic characters: see, again, Medea and her address to her own θυμός or *animus*[24]):

> Qual moto inusitato in seno
> fa sentirsi il mio core...
> Ma par che indietro mi respinga i passi, insolito timore
> Ardisci, ardisci o core,
> e col levar queste coltrine, leva
> il sospetto, e 'l timore anco a te stesso.
>
> How unusual this sensation within my heart feels to me... It seems to be stopping me in my tracks, this is an unfamiliar fear.—I dare you, oh my heart, and, by removing these small curtains, move the suspicion and the fear away as well. (*Amore inamorato*. I.4)

---

22 For the link between Psyche and Medea, cf. also Apul. *Met.* 4.32.4 *aegra corporis, animi saucia* ~ Enn. *Medea* 216 Jocelyn *Medea animo aegro amore saevo saucia*: e.g. Mattiacci 1998, 136 and n. 30.

23 Compare Apul. *Met.* 5.21.3 and 5.23.4 (*saucia mente fluctuat*) with Catull. 64.6 (Ariadne); Verg. *Aen.* 4.532: Harrison 2013, 144–145 and 226–227. For the same metaphor, cf. also Sen. *Med.* 939–943 (below, n. 87). Moreover, Catull. 64.127.

24 Cf. Eu. *Med.* 1056–1057 (in addition to 1242–1250) and Sen. *Med.* 937–944 (in addition to 895–896 and 976–977) respectively—see also, below, p. 96. See further Paduano 2006.

Although echoing Apuleius' own approach, here the adoption of this tragic motif reveals itself as to some extent gratuitous: this is not only because the scenario is situated *in medias res* without any reference to the background situation (which will be reported in flashback much later), but also because there is no explicit mention of the prohibition against discovering the identity of Cupid which leads to Psyche's infringement and offence.

Further confirmation of the pretentious use of this *cliché* occurs later when Psyche is preparing to commit her second offence (the discovery of the 'rouge' delivered to her by Proserpina in order to be offered to Venus). In Apuleius this action is again attributed to the maiden's mind 'seized with a rash curiosity'—*temeraria curiositate* (*Met.* 6.20.5); the same motive had been ascribed, of course, to Psyche's first offence, namely seeing Cupid (e.g. 5.6.6 *sacrilega curiositate*, 5.19.3 *de vultus curiositate*, 5.23.1 *Psyche... curiosa*, 6.19.7 *curiosius*). So, possibly on the strength of this analogy, the librettists equate the second crime with the first and, again albeit without mention of any restriction violated by Psyche (differently from the text of Apuleius: 6.19.7), they replay the motif of the alternation between daring and anxiety, combining it with the commonplace apostrophe to Psyche's heart and her 'murderous' hand.

This brings to light the (direct or indirect) influence of the tragic models and, in particular, of the scenarios which, in the myth of Medea, are a prelude to the infanticide.

> ἀλλ' εἶ' ὁπλίζου, καρδία·τί μέλλομεν
> τὰ δεινὰ κἀναγκαῖα μὴ πράσσειν κακά;
> ἄγ', ὦ τάλαινα χεὶρ ἐμή, λαβὲ ξίφος
> Come, put on your armour, my heart. Why do I put off doing the terrible deed that must be done? Come, wretched hand, take the sword. (Eur. *Med.* 1242–1244)[25]

> Ah no, non fia la mano
> a par del core ardita...
> Ma nulla fa chi non ardisce...
> Su cor, su mano ardita
> apri il chiuso vasello.
>
> Oh, no! Do not let the hand be as audacious as the heart... But who does not dare does not gain anything... Come now heart, come now audacious hand, open the closed small jar. (*Amore inamorato.* V.1)

---

[25] For the motif, cf. also Eur. *Med.* 1055–1057; Sen. *Med.* 951–953 and 976–977. Among the modern adaptations, cf. e.g. F. Romani for V. Bellini, *Norma*, II.1: cf. recently Ragno 2016, 252–258.

The corresponding speech patterns highlight their dependence on grand (and so quite different) tragic precedents. As a result, this distancing effect (similar to a parody) matches, to some extent, the most unprecedented elements of this text, namely, the comic side of the drama.

2.3 Psyche *alias* Ariadne

In Apuleius the character of Psyche reveals elegiac traits,[26] starting with allusions to the above-mentioned myth of Ariadne. This element perhaps plots a course for this rewriting: and indeed, Fusconi's libretto seems to be influenced by an operatic pattern (Claudio Monteverdi's *Lamento d'Arianna*, 1608) which was certainly considered essential at the time for seventeenth-century Venetian opera.[27]

Hackneyed questions[28] modeled on the device of the *addubitatio*[29] and inspired by the overall 'rhetoric of desperation',[30] and furthermore the repeated use of the adjective *misera* ('wretched')[31] portray Psyche's efforts to restore the lost contact with her beloved.[32] Hence, Psyche appears to take on the role of the ancient (Catullus' and Ovid's)[33] or modern Ariadne, especially in the scenario of her own inconsolable lament (I.6).[34]

---

[26] Cf. the survey in Mattiacci 1998.
[27] For the possible influence of Monteverdi's *L'Arianna* on contemporary versions of *Cupid and Psyche*, cf. Cavicchioli 2002, 143.
[28] E.g. *Amore innamorato*, I.4: 'What do I do? What do I say?'; III.4: 'Wretched me! ... Which ground do I tread?'.
[29] Cf. e.g. Macr. *Sat.* 4.6.11 and Quint. *Inst.* 9.2.19.
[30] Fowler 1987. In Apuleius *Met.* 5.30.3 and 6.5.3, a similar pattern is attributed to Venus and Psyche respectively, albeit in very different contexts (Keulen 2000: 57–59).
[31] E.g. *Amore innamorato*, I.6 and II.4 for "misera" referring to Psyche (Cupid is described as "misero", mourning his lost beloved: II.1). The corresponding epithet, mostly in a derivative form, had already featured in Apuleius (*misella*: *Met.* 4.34.1; 5.5.4; 5.18.4; 5.26.3; 6.9.3; 6.17.3; 6.21.4; *misera*: 5.7.2; *miseranda*: 5.24.1; 6.2.1; 6.2.5).
[32] E.g. *Amore innamorato*, I.6: '... An exhausting walk and an intense gaze... I would like to make my footsteps and my eyes go onwards following the tracks of my heart in order to find my fugitive love'.
[33] For rhetorical questions, cf. e.g. Catull. 64.177; Ov. *Her.* 10.59; 64. For Ariadne's demeanour (e.g. her tumultuous flight to the sea) also in the form of a *teichoscopia*, cf. Catull. 64.52–53; 61–62; 126–128; Ov. *Her.* 10.19–20; 25–28.
[34] Probably prompted also by a brief reference in Apuleius: *Met.* 5.25.1 *Psyche [...] extremis affligebat lamentationibus animum*.

For his part, her partner (who, though not an adulterer, is nevertheless a 'fugitive' lover[35]) is described by Psyche as a harsh man, hardhearted and unresponsive (like an oak, a piece of marble, a heart covered in enamel). This is the reason why Psyche addresses, albeit pointlessly, the forces of nature (the wind, the echoes from the caves), so they can make her complaints, which have fallen on deaf ears, resonate. The combination of our myth with that of Ariadne (and Theseus as a *perfidus hospes*[36]), particularly in Monteverdi's *Lamento*, is noticeable also at the point where, after hysterical ravings, she returns to reality, which is marked by a sudden change in her agitated speech.[37]

Here, too, the connection with the models seems to be based on a higher principle of literary conventionality. Intended to present a love interrupted then finally restored, the myth of *Cupid and Psyche* has quite a different conclusion to the story of Ariadne and others who were permanently abandoned by their 'runaway' true love. Hence, recalling elegiac patterns appears to illustrate above all the deliberate intention to show off, through imitation, the mastery of a long-established literary (and musical) tradition that without doubt appealed to the spectators of the day.

2.4 The comic side

Thus, the strategies of rewriting applied to *Amore innamorato* reflect for the main part the expectations of the audience. This is a predictable principle in itself in relation to every case of adaptation and even more so in a popular genre like the opera.

This applies, too, to the additions which represent the comic side of the piece, as set out in the preface of the text ('With a view to the piece's absurd aspect, a few *canzonette* have been inserted'). The occurrence of '*canzonette*' as 'in-

---

35 "Fuggitivo" is already in Marino's *L'Adone* (4.173.2), uttered, again, by the abandoned Psyche. For possible operatic echoes, cf. Moreschini 1994: 22; Moreschini 2000: 30. An analogous elegiac demeanour features, furthermore, in E. Udine, *La Psiche*, 4.55–65.
36 Theseus: Catull. 64.136–138; 164–166; Ov. *Her.* 10.22–24; 107–110; 131–132; *Ars am.* I.531. Again O. Rinuccini for C. Monteverdi, *Lamento d'Arianna*: "Ahi, che non pur risponde;/ahi, che più d'aspe è sordo a' miei lamenti". Compare, too, Dido, Verg. *Aen.* 4.365–371. For similarities between Psyche and in particular Dido see Lazzarini 1985, 145–146 and Schiesaro 1988, 143ff.; cf. also n. 86 above.
37 *Amore innamorato*, I.6: "Ah, che vaneggio" ('How I rave!') ~ O. Rinuccini for C. Monteverdi, *Lamento d'Arianna*: "Che parlo, ahi, che vaneggio?". Moreover, E. Udine, *La Psiche*, 4.56: "Ch'errore/or fo? Vaneggio?".

termedi' aside, the insertions consist of certain characters or whole scenes embedded in the main action.

The characters of Vulcan and Aeolus are unprecedented in Apuleius; the former is involved first in a 'work song' along with his colleagues, the Cyclopes, intent on forging Jupiter's thunderbolts and, then, in dialogue with Venus in a hilarious skirmish between a 'troublesome' wife and a 'cuckolded' husband (I.2 and I.3 respectively); the latter is introduced, after a brief comment about the misfortune of Cupid (I.5), in order to play the part of a 'consoling god' (I.6), a part which in Apuleius had been played by the god Pan.[38] Furthermore, having succeeded in consoling the heroine, Aeolus, as the ruler of winds, incites their 'graceful dance' (I.6). Here, a kind of exhortation, which usually indicates the start of terrible storms,[39] is transformed into a kind of 'stage direction', which prepares the audience for a happy interlude. So, promoted (or downgraded) to a light-hearted pause, Pan's action of consoling Psyche in Apuleius[40] becomes a performance in itself.

The insertion of the procuress as a character reflects a very familiar feature of the Venetian society of the day, which was linked to the interests of the *Incogniti*, since, in 1642, the year of the premiere of *Amore innamorato*, the Academician Ferrante Pallavicino defended the type of rhetoric to be used by prostitutes in his *La retorica delle puttane*.[41] As procuresses are able to subvert the moral code, their technique is praised as a sort of 'magic art' able to accomplish *adynata*, which are of course impossible in themselves (II.6: 'I could act so that Diana becomes a courtesan…').

This new character interacts with Psyche immediately before the maiden ventures into the Underworld (III.3): the procuress' 'tempting speech' is aimed not so much at discouraging Psyche from fulfilling this endeavour as at dissuading her from being '*univira*' (tied to Cupid as a sole lover) and to turn her towards

---

[38] E.g. *Amore innamorato*, I.6: 'Oh, maiden, put a stop to the laments emanating from your lips… Dry your tears… because I am aware of your situation' ~ *Met.* 5.25.4–6 *utcumque casus eius non inscius… ad se vocatam sic permulcet*: '*Puella scitula… Verum si recte coniecto… Luctum desine et pone maerorem*'.

[39] *Amore innamorato*, I.6: 'Having been freed from your chains, move away from this enclosure ruled by Aeolus'. For this *cliché* see Verg. *Aen.* 1.124–156.

[40] For Pan as a *senex sapiens*, cf. Panayotakis 1997, 32.

[41] The work contains fifteen lessons given by an elderly procuress to a young maiden: for a modern edition, cf. Coci 1992. On prostitutes or procuresses (and courtesan-like women) within seventeenth-century Venetian opera, cf. Heller 2003, 266–268. One of Michiel's poems focuses on the character of a procuress (Giachino 2001, 80).

'love in common'.[42] The novelty of this addition, possibly also inspired by Roman elegy such as Propertius 4.5 or Ovid *Amores* 1.8, does not exclude the possibility that it originates from an informal reading of the text of Apuleius where Venus slanders the maiden with her analogy between Psyche and a courtesan,[43] along with the consequent, self-mocking (and genuinely comic[44]) definition of Venus as a procuress, who encouraged Cupid and Psyche to meet.[45] Again, an element already sketched by Apuleius seems to be developed into a theatrical mode and altered in order to modernize certain aspects of the plot.

An equally essential role is that taken by Charon: this figure, albeit mentioned fleetingly in Apuleius, appears unprecedented here not only because of his conversion into a fully theatrical figure (from a mute character to a *persona loquens*), but also because of the comic treatment applied here. Introduced in the prophetic report attributed to a tower in Apuleius, Charon confirms, in the libretto, his own identity as an avaricious ferryman (IV.2), just as in *Met.* 6.18.5, but from the viewpoint of Charon himself: a change of perspective which creates a certain ridiculous effect. As constant witness to a vile and ragtag humankind, Charon introduces an amusing series of characters, where, by means of a brief outline in a few verses for each, he pronounces judgements on several representatives of professions (the ignorant philosopher, the arrogant soldier, the idiot astrologer, the foolish and sly pedagogue, the failed poet, the insolent musician who cannot memorize his part, and the inevitable procuress).

Yet, the presence of Charon is also significant in terms of the structural aspects of the drama: in his long scene with Psyche (IV.3), the maiden reports on the background situation which, offstage, had preceded her love-idyll and then the separation from Cupid.[46] So, the account of the previous events in the latter part of the piece returns the audience to the starting point of the play: in the interests of the spectators, every narrative gap is filled, thereby pushing the melodrama forward towards its bright and embellished finale.

---

42 The arguments of the procuress—the advantage (*utile*), related to the enjoyment of youth, and the morally worthy, *honestum* (compliance with the imperative 'follow nature', *sequi naturam*)—reproduce patterns dating back to Plautine comedies (e.g. Plaut. *Most.* 157 ff.: Minarini 2006).
43 Apul. *Met.* 5.28.4.
44 May 2006, 237–239 and n. 153.
45 Apul. *Met.* 5.28.9.
46 For the removal of the first part of the myth and all trials bar the sole *katabasis*, cf. Rizza 1984, 483.

2.5 The 'rouged' Hades

In Apuleius the *katabasis* to the Underworld is undertaken to obtain a part of Proserpina's beauty for Venus. The Latin passage uses the abstract word *formonsitas* for both the object of the request of Venus and a characteristic of Proserpina partially asked for by Venus herself (*Met.* 6.16.4 *petit de te Venus... modicum de tua mittas ei formonsitate*, 'Venus asks you to send her a little bit of your beauty').[47] Transferred, however, to the genteel atmosphere of the Venetian seventeenth century, the objective pursued by Psyche becomes more concrete, namely the 'rouge' which displays a notion of overly elaborate make-up (*Amore innamorato* III.2: 'Make sure you bring me Proserpina's most admired rouge [*belletti*], with which she artfully presents a rosy face'). Dictated perhaps by reasons of performance but not unprecedented,[48] this change illustrates a more general intention of prettifying a rather terrifying experience.

Acting as 'courteous and trusted security guards' of Psyche (IV.4), the Spirits, too, comply with the agreeable setting, thereby rendering their role very unlike the authoritative guide embodied by the tower in Apuleius (*Met.* 6.17.2–19.6).[49] Indeed, whereas in Apuleius the trial of initiation involves the fulfilment of specific instructions (namely, those related by the tower), in the libretto the actions of Psyche seem to be inspired by languishing inertia or chance which operates beyond the individual character as if driven by a mysterious will.

Hence, mostly described as a 'prodigy' (IV.4), the miraculous descent of Psyche seems appropriate to the Baroque 'maraviglia' required by contemporary melodrama: Psyche, too, highlights, through a clever wordplay, how her position as a living woman (among the dead) is marvellous, albeit not at all certain, because she has actually now 'died of love' (IV.3: 'It is true: I am still living, assuming that those of us who would far prefer to die of love continue to live'). Thus, like Orpheus reborn not only because of the privilege of crossing unscathed the boundaries between life and death, but also because of being prohibited from seeing or discovering who or what emerges from Hades (Eurydice, in the case of Orpheus; Proserpina's beauty, in the case of Psyche—at least in Apuleius),[50] the maiden, far from being naïve and unsophisticated, exploits even this thorny situation in order to show off the urbane virtues of a witty 'lover's discourse',

---

[47] For *formonsitas* in *Met.* 6.16.4, cf. Panayotakis 1997, 35–36; Zimmerman 2004, 489–490.
[48] Marino, *Adone*, 4.278.1–2: "E taccio come poi le venne audace/di quel belletto d'Ecate desio".
[49] Lamarque 1989.
[50] Harrison 2013, 152–153 and 210.

which is similar—as are many other elements in this bizarre Underworld—to the charming worldly pleasures of the Baroque era.

2.6 The moral of the story

Finally, hedonism could be considered the distinctive trait of this rewriting, especially in the scenario of the *katabasis* when Proserpina[51] introduces Psyche to the affected atmosphere of her own court (IV.5). From this perspective, the distance from the corresponding passages of Apuleius (*Met.* 6.19.4–5; 6.20.2–4) could not be more striking. In the Latin text, the ritual which takes place in the Underworld[52] demands that everything happens rapidly (6.20.4 *statim*) without interval or luxurious interlude (6.19.4 *molliter*); conversely, in the libretto, Psyche welcomes the opportunity of enjoying the amenities of Proserpina's comfortable house.[53]

Yet, the final interlude, which the maiden attends after accomplishing her endeavour, also seems to exemplify a 'moral'. Created certainly because of the requirements of the performance (the necessity to insert, between one act and another, amusements and marvellous settings, like the dance of the winds, the lullaby sung for Cupid, the comforting words uttered by little cupids),[54] this scene appears to evoke a message valid for hell and the entire existential experience of humankind. If 'even in Hell, we often delight in joy and pleasure' because niceties have a place 'even amongst tears' (IV.5), it is not difficult to imagine how well the Venetian audience of the time received this kind of radical hedonistic message. More profoundly, this dominant voluptuous idea matches the principle of the reversibility of pain: it seems possible to escape (or, at least, to be freed temporarily) from suffering which, albeit unavoidable, is never-ending.

Thus the last part of *Amore innamorato* suggests that human relationships are ruled by 'inconstancy':[55] inconstancy of affections like love and hate, which are considered to be more fickle than the wind by the expert Aeolus

---

51 Again, a minor character in Apuleius, *Met.* 6.19.4 and 6.20.2–3, is made speaker here.
52 For Psyche's *katabasis* e.g. Finkelpearl 1999; Harrison 2013, 150 ff. and 170.
53 In Apuleius, too, the Underworld is the sumptuous house of Proserpina (*Met.* 6.20.2–3) and Proserpina herself appears as a courteous hostess (cf. Zimmerman 2004, 517).
54 See *Amore innamorato*, at the end of the first, second and third act respectively.
55 The constancy (or inconstancy) of lovers or destiny is one of the most popular motifs developed within seventeenth- and eighteenth-century Venetian opera: e.g. F. Piccoli for P.A. Ziani, *L'incostanza trionfante overo il Theseo* (1658), V. Cassani for T. Albinoni, *L'incostanza schernita* (1727).

(IV.1); and inconstancy of destiny which 'often changes', thereby subverting for the better 'the adverse fate' by the wise exhortation 'not to despair' (IV.3).

Far from appearing as a genuine expression of the 'conciliatory and edifying solution'[56] found in numerous Renaissance and even Baroque adaptations,[57] the 'morality' ultimately set out by Mercury seems to refer to a fatal conclusion to the misfortunes of Psyche, since the dynamics of a superior law of existence lie beyond the control of humans:

> Ecco qual frutto coglie,
> chi ne' suoi lunghi mali
> di sofferenza humil veste le spoglie
> apprendete, o mortali.
> *Del soffrir degli affanni è dolce il fine.*
> E principio al salir son le rovine.
>
> It is this which is reaped, as the fruits of reward, by the person who throughout his long troubles humbly puts on the vestiges of pain. Learn, mortals. *The ending of sorrow is sweet.* And ruin is the start of ascension. (*Amore inamorato.* V.9)

Embracing fully the purpose of pleasure always and everywhere, the librettists seem to reject the idea of sublimation and evolutionary development underlying the experience of Psyche not only in Apuleius, but also in the most recent adaptations. Indeed, in Marino (who is, nevertheless, dear to the *Incogniti*) this myth continued to be interpreted as a struggle between the Fate and the soul strengthened by its own 'constancy':

> Non desperi mai sì che si sommerga
> chi per quest' oceano spiega le vele,
> ma de' flutti e de' venti al fiero orgoglio
> faccia un'alta costanza ancora e scoglio.
>
> He who unfurls sails over the sea should not allow despair to submerge him; he should however counter the intrepid pride of the waves and the wind with profound rock- and anchor-like constancy. (*Adone.* 4.2.5 – 8)

In *Amore innamorato*, however, the happy ending seems to be safeguarded by the possibility, beyond the will of humans, to enjoy pleasure at the end of (but not because of) tribulation. This playful adaptation invites us to look again at the joyful wordplay in the Apuleian original as a characterization tool

---

[56] Thus Sozzi 2007, 46.
[57] See e. g. G. Del Carretto, *Noze de Psiche e Cupidine* (1499?) and, much later, V. Cassani for B. Marcello, *Psiche, intreccio scenico musicale* (ca. 1711).

which adds emotional depth, and at the plot's tragic and comic possibilities, and appreciate the changing moralities of the Apuleian and the baroque periods in their respective attitude to love and erotic fulfilment.

Finally, the paternalistic incitement of Mercury 'to learn' aside,[58] the delight in reality appears to be not so much the 'fruits of reward' derived from choice or the goal of a path inspired by individual responsibility, but rather the final destination of the inconstancy embodied by the souls of human beings (or of the gods), by their variable affections and ultimately by the caprice of destiny. It is this context which allows Psyche, and by extension all humankind, to continue to have hope, after all, in the 'sweet ending' of their own misery.

3 Bibliography

Acocella, M. (2001), *L'Asino d'oro nel Rinascimento. Dai volgarizzamenti alle raffigurazioni pittoriche*, Ravenna.
Candiani, R. (2001), 'Metamorfosi e riletture di una fonte classica: la favola di "Amore e Psiche" di Apuleio', in: Sala Di Felice, 136-158.
Carver, R.H.F. (2007), *The Protean Ass. The* Metamorphoses *of Apuleius from Antiquity to the Renaissance*, Oxford and New York.
Cavicchioli, S. (2002), *Le metamorfosi di Psiche. L'iconografia della favola di Apuleio*, Venezia.
Cicogna, E. (1886), 'Cenni intorno la vita e le opere di Pietro Michiel, poeta del secolo XVII', *Memorie dell'I.R. Istituto veneto di lettere, scienze ed arti* 13, 387-400.
Cipriani, G. and Ragno, T. (eds.) (2016), *Tra Passato & Presente*, Campobasso—Foggia 2016.
Coci, L. (1992), *F. Pallavicino. La retorica delle puttane*, Parma.
De Maria, U. (1899), *La favola di Amore e Psiche nella letteratura e nell'arte italiana*, Bologna.
De Martino, F. (ed.) (2006), *Medea: teatro e comunicazione*, Bari.
Finkelpearl, E. (1999) 'Psyche, Aeneas, and an ass: Apuleius' *Metamophoses* 6.10-6.21', in: Harrison, 290-306.
Firenzuola, A. (1863), *L'asino d'oro di Apuleio*, Milano.
Fowler, R.L. (1987), 'The rhetoric of desperation', *HSPh* 91, 5-38.
[Fusconi], G.F. (1642), *Amore innamorato. Favola da rappresentarsi in musica nel Teatro San Moisè l'anno 1642*, Venezia.
Gaisser, J.H. (2008), *The Fortunes of Apuleius and the* Golden Ass. *A Study in Transmission and Reception*, Princeton—Oxford.
Giachino, L. (2001), 'La sensualità in Barocco. L'esperienza lirica di Pietro Michiel tra erotismo e concettismo', *Quaderni veneti* 33, 67-107.
Harrison, S.J. (2000), *Apuleius: a Latin sophist*, Oxford.
Harrison, S.J. (2013), *Framing the Ass. Literary Texture in Apuleius*, Oxford.

---

58 Rizza 1984, 484 refers to a "ton vaguement moral".

Harrison, S.J. (ed.) (1999), *Oxford Readings in the Roman Novel*, Oxford.
Heller, W. (2003), *Emblems of Eloquence. Opera and Women's Voices in Seventeenth-Century Venice*, Berkeley, Los Angeles and London.
Hofmann, H./Zimmerman, M. (eds.) (1997), *Groningen colloquia on the novel 8*, Groningen.
Iacovelli, E. (2008), *Diamante Gabrielli. Psiche*, Bari.
Kenney, E.J. (1990), *Apuleius. Cupid & Psyche*, Cambridge.
Keulen, W. (2000), 'L'immagine evocata dal testo: la rappresentazione drammatica della Venere apuleiana', *Fontes* 5-6, 55-72.
Lamarque, H. (1989), 'Une tour douée de parole dans le Conte d'Amour et de Psyché d'Apulée', *Pallas* 35, 65-68.
Lazzarini, C. (1985), 'Il modello virgiliano nel lessico delle *Metamorfosi* di Apuleio', *SCO* 35, 131-60.
Mattiacci, S. (1998), 'Neoteric and elegiac echoes in the tale of *Cupid and Psyche* by Apuleius', in: Zimmerman, 127-49.
May, R. (2006), *Apuleius and drama: the ass on stage*, Oxford.
Miato, M. (1998), *L'Accademia degli Incogniti di Giovan Francesco Loredan, Venezia (1630-1661)*, Firenze.
Minarini, A. (2006), 'Dialoghi delle cortigiane in Plauto e Terenzio', *BStudLat* 36, 3-24.
Moreschini, C. (1994), *Il mito di Amore e Psiche in Apuleio: saggio, testo di Apuleio, traduzione e commento*, Napoli.
Moreschini, C. (2000), 'Amore e Psiche. Novella, filosofia, allegoria', *Fontes* 5-6, 21-44.
Nicolini, L. (2011), *Ad (l)usum lectoris: etimologia e giochi di parole in Apuleio*, Bologna.
Paduano, G. (2006), 'Variazioni sul grande monologo di Medea' in: De Martino, 497-522.
Panayotakis, S. (1997), '*Insidiae Veneris*: Lameness, Old Age and Deception in the Underworld (Apul. Met. 6.18-19)', in: Hofmann/Zimmerman, 23-39.
Penwill, J.L. (1998), 'Reflections on a "happy ending": the case of Cupid and Psyche', *Ramus* 27, 160-82.
Puleio, M.T. (1992), 'La favola di Amore e Psiche nel Cinquecento tra Italia e Francia', *Studi di Letteratura francese* 19, 157-72.
Ragno, T. (2016), 'Medea (o Norma) senza infanticidio. Mito e melodramma fra riscrittura e redenzione', in: Cipriani/Ragno 205-86.
Rizza, C. (1984), 'Autour de Psyché' in *Papers on French Seventeenth Century Literature* 11, 475-95.
Rosand, E. (1991), *Opera in Seventeenth-Century Venice. The Creation of a Genre*, Berkeley.
Sala Di Felice, E. et al. (eds.) (2001), *Intersezioni di forme letterarie e artistiche*, Roma.
Schiesaro, A. (1988), 'La "tragedia" di Psiche: note ad Apuleio, met. IV 28-35', *MD* 40, 141-50.
Sozzi, L. (2007), *Amore e Psiche: un mito dall'allegoria alla parodia*, Bologna.
Ussia, S. (2001), *Amore innamorato. Riscritture poetiche della novella di Amore e Psiche. Secoli XV-XVII*, Vercelli.
Ussia, S. (2004), *E. Udine. La Psiche*, Vercelli.
Zimmerman, M. et al. (eds.) (1998), *Aspects of Apuleius' Golden Ass. Vol. II, Cupid and Psyche. A collection of original papers*, Groningen.
Zimmerman, M. et al. (2004), *Apuleius Madaurensis. Metamorphoses. Books IV 28-35, V and VI 1-24. The tale of Cupid and Psyche. Text, Introduction and Commentary*, Groningen.
Zimmerman, M. (2012), *Apulei Metamorphoseon Libri XI*, Oxford.

Stephen Harrison
Apuleius at the court of Louis XIV. *Psyché* (1671, 1678) and its English version (1675)

1 Introduction

This paper forms part of the ongoing project on the reception of Apuleius' narrative of *Cupid and Psyche* from the *Metamorphoses* in Western European literary culture since 1600, mentioned in the introduction to this volume.[1] One key early episode of this reception history occurs at the court of the young Louis XIV in the 1660s and 1670s, involving some of the greatest names of French Golden Age literature. In 1669 Jean de La Fontaine published *Les Amours de Psyché et de Cupidon*, his extended prose retelling of the episode, with a frame narrative set in the palace-park of Versailles, then under construction.[2] His version became highly influential in the Francophone reception of *Cupid and Psyche*, turning Apuleius' story into a talking point for fashionable society at court.[3] This soon stimulated two further versions of the tale, both with music by Jean-Baptiste Lully (1632–87): the tragicomedy and ballet *Psyché* of 1671, based on a text co-authored by Molière (Jean-Baptiste Poquelin, 1622–73), the tragedian Pierre Corneille, and Lully's regular librettist Philippe Quinault, and the opera (*tragédie lyrique*) *Psyché* of 1678, with a libretto adapted by the dramatist Thomas Corneille (Pierre Corneille's brother) and the future philosopher and essayist Bernard Le Bovier de Fontenelle from the 1671 version.[4] This paper sets out in a preliminary study to compare and contrast these two versions of the story from the 1670s, paying due attention to their different dramatic genres, and adds as a coda some analysis of Thomas Shadwell's 1675 English adaptation of the first of them.

---

[1] I here reiterate my warm gratitude to the Leverhulme Trustees for their generous and enlightened support of this research project.
[2] For my analysis of this work and its reception of the Apuleian original (with further bibliography) see Harrison (2018), and for a convenient English translation see Powell http://www.personal.utulsa.edu/~john-powell/Psyche.
[3] See the papers by Reitz and Simard in this volume.
[4] For much useful information on both see the rich resources gathered by John Powell at http://www.personal.utulsa.edu/~john-powell/Psyche.

2 The two French versions[5]

2.1 *Psyché. Tragicomédie et ballet* 1671[6]

Prologue: Flora and her followers summon Venus to participate in their games (in celebration of the peace that Louis XIV has brought to the world). Venus arrives in a fury, however, and breaks the hitherto musical atmosphere of the prologue. She sends her son to punish Psyche, despite his reticence.

Act one: Psyche's jealous sisters attempt to attract the attention of her two most recent suitors, without success. Psyche refuses both suitors before being called away by a messenger. The messenger then informs Psyche's sisters that she must be sacrificed on the mountain top and devoured by a monster. The sisters confess their delight before a group of mourners arrive on stage and sing the first *intermède* (song between acts), a *plainte italienne* (mode of lament).

Act two: The King informs Psyche of her fate. She accepts it unflinchingly, though her father prefers to defy the gods. After bidding him farewell, her sisters arrive and seem unwilling to leave her alone. Psyche pushes them to save themselves, but they reply that oracles are always mysterious and perhaps her fate will not be so hard after all. They finally leave, and Psyche believes herself to be alone at last to face her doom when her suitors appear to defend her. She chastises their impiety. Their attempt to defend her is in any case vain, as she is carried away by zephyrs. The set changes for the third act, representing a magnificent palace. This time, Vulcan sings the second *intermède*, encouraging his crew of Cyclopes to finish building the palace.

Act three: Zephyr informs Cupid that he has successfully brought Psyche to her new palace and expresses his surprise at Cupid's new, adult appearance. Psyche wakes up and is confused by her splendid surroundings. Rather than being attacked by a monster, Psyche is greeted by the dashing figure of Cupid who declares his love for her. After a love scene, Psyche impresses upon Cupid (whose identity she still does not know) that she must share her happy fate with her sisters and father. Cupid resists, but finally concedes and sends Zephyr

---

5 These summaries draw on various materials from Powell and elsewhere.
6 For the full libretto, published in that year, see http://gallica.bnf.fr/ark:/12148/bpt6k70160j (accessed 30th June 2017).

to fetch Psyche's sisters. For the third *intermède*, Cupid invites a putto Cupid and a Zephyr to sing a *divertissement* in honour of Love.

Act four: Psyche's sisters, having seen Psyche's new home, are envious and keen to spoil her happiness. They feed her curiosity regarding the identity of her lover and make her fear his unfaithfulness, suggesting that all the palace may be no more than a lie, an enchantment. Zephyr takes them away. Psyche demands to know the identity of her lover. Cupid resists, saying that to know his identity is to lose him forever, but swears that he will tell her if she wishes it absolutely. She insists, and Cupid confesses his identity, then disappears, taking the palace with him. Alone in a lugubrious setting, Psyche bemoans her fate, and resolves to drown herself in the river. The River God stops her, saying the heavens forbid it and that an easier fate may be in store. Venus arrives to chastise and to punish Psyche. In the fourth *intermède* Psyche descends to Hell, where eight furies dance a ballet to celebrate the rage they have inspired in so sweet a goddess as Venus. Psyche crosses in Charon's boat with the box Venus had ordered her to obtain from Proserpine.

Act five: Psyche is in Hell and meets her two suitors. They recount how they threw themselves from the rock on which Psyche was sacrificed, having been unable to prevent her death. They also recount the death of her sisters, who voluntarily threw themselves off a cliff, proudly believing that Zephyr would carry them back to Cupid's palace. Psyche, determined to regain the love of Cupid, opens Proserpina's box, hoping to enhance her beauty. But a poisonous vapour comes out of the box, rendering her unconscious. Cupid descends to lament her apparent death and forgives her. Venus appears and chastises Cupid for his rebellion. He confronts his mother for her cruelty towards the object of his love. He calls on Jupiter for aid, who takes his side and grants Psyche immortality (she is revived by Venus). The scene changes from Hell to Heaven and a great ballet is danced by the followers of Apollo, Bacchus, Momus and Mars to celebrate the union of Cupid and Psyche.

2.2 *Psyché: Tragédie en musique* 1678[7]

Prologue: practically identical with Molière's.

Act one: Psyche's sisters learn with the spectators that Psyche must be sacrificed to a serpent that has been ravaging the kingdom. The *plainte italienne* from Molière's play is sung to represent the mourning of the people. The sisters flee at Psyche's arrival, and it is her father who informs her of the oracle that has pronounced her doom. Psyche unhesitatingly climbs the rock to offer herself in sacrifice, much to her father's consternation, and is carried away by Zephyrs to Cupid's domain.

Act two: Vulcan and his Cyclopes are building a palace for Psyche at Cupid's bidding. Vulcan is surprised by his wife Venus who discovers that her son has betrayed her. She quarrels with her husband and vows revenge against her son. Psyche awakes and is courted by Cupid. The act ends in a happy love scene, but Cupid must hide his identity and begins a *divertissement* sung by three Nymphs to divert Psyche's attention.

Act three: Venus disguises herself as a Nymph and gives Psyche a lamp with which to discover the identity of her lover. Psyche is overjoyed to learn that her lover is Cupid himself, but the light of the lamp awakes the god, who flees. At the same time, the palace disappears, and Psyche is left in a desolate wilderness. Venus exposes her treachery to Psyche and further accuses her of trying to marry her way into immortality. She forces her to descend to Hell and recover a box in which Proserpina keeps her beauty. Psyche, in despair, attempts to drown herself, but is saved by the River God who peacefully accompanies her to the underworld.

Act four: Psyche resists the torture of the three Furies in order to meet the Nymphs of the Acheron. These Nymphs banish the Furies, give Psyche the box she is looking for and conduct her to Venus's garden where act five is set.

Act five: Psyche opens the box, hoping to restore any beauty she might have lost during her recent hardships. But instead of beauty, the box exudes a poisonous

---

[7] For the complete libretto see the edition by Luke Arnason at ftp://ftp.cs.umanitoba.ca/pub/arnason/ala/Psyche.pdf, (accessed 4th July 2017), and for a modern recording see that by Paul O'Dette and Stephen Stubbs with the Boston Early Music Festival Orchestra and Chorus (2008) on the CPO label, catalogue number 777 367–2.

vapour that renders Psyche unconscious. Venus appears to rejoice and brings Psyche back to life in order to gloat and torture her further. She is amazed to see that Psyche is still in love with her son despite so many hardships, but she is resolved to continue punishing her. Mercury descends and begs her to stop, recounting the chaos and suffering in the universe that has been produced by Cupid's displeasure. Venus takes no heed and Jupiter descends himself to calm the goddess and pronounce Psyche immortal. The lovers are united and the opera ends with a magnificent ballet, identical to the one closing the 1671 version.

2.3 Comparison of the two versions

La Fontaine's 1669 retelling of the Apuleian story is naturally the prime source for the libretti of both stage versions. Here I should like to focus on three points: some elements shared by the two performance texts which are not present in La Fontaine or Apuleius which have contemporary cultural significance, some differences between the two which reflect their generic differences, and two aspects of the 1671 version, of which the 1678 version is in effect a rapid adaptation:[8] its modifications of certain elements in the original, and its introduction of non-Apuleian classical models.

Both the 1671 and 1678 versions open with references to the peace Louis XIV has brought to the world. This focus on the monarch is natural, given the royal contexts of the first performance both of the 1671 version, first presented in part at the royal palace of the Tuileries in January of that year, and of the 1678 version, first given at the Académie Royale de Musique in April of that year.[9] In both contexts the praise of Louis as peacebringer is appropriate: in 1671 the War of Devolution with Spain (1667–8) was several years over, following the Treaty of Aix-la-Chapelle of 1668, while in spring 1678 France was moving towards the end of a six-year war with Holland and the Treaties of Nijmegen of 1678–9 (peace was declared in August).

Three modifications of the Apuleian plot in both versions look to its seventeenth-century cultural context and are shared with La Fontaine. First, in both Psyche accepts her fate unflinchingly and as a matter of willing self-sacrifice; this plays up an element present but less prominent in Apuleius, no doubt under the influence of the figure of the similarly self-sacrificing princess Iphige-

---

8 Accomplished in only three weeks, according to a contemporary source—see Powell (no year).
9 See Powell (no year) for this and other performance details.

nia, who was particularly popular in seventeenth-century French drama, e. g. in the 1674 *Iphigénie* of Racine.[10] Second, the courtship of Cupid and Psyche takes place not in darkness and ignorance with little verbal interchange, but in extensive open conversation, much more in tune with contemporary ideas about romance as found in early novels such as Honoré d'Urfé's *Astrée* (1607–28), which indeed had an influence on La Fontaine's version.[11] Third, the original's references to Psyche's pregnancy during her wanderings are cut out; such premarital sexual contact is clearly indecorous for this cultural level at this period, even though the happy ending of lovers marrying when the girl is pregnant is a standard topic of Roman New Comedy (e. g. in Terence's *Adelphoe*).

The different genres of the two stage versions are reflected to some extent in their different treatments of the original story. The 1671 *tragicomédie-ballet*, a new hybrid genre, innovated in harnessing the previous experience of Molière and Lully in *comédie-ballets* such as *Le Bourgeois gentilhomme* (1670), integrating ballet and comic drama, with a more serious mythological plot (but still with a happy ending), and showed a particular concern with exploiting newly available stage machinery and spectacular effects. In the 1678 version we find Lully's emerging style of musical *tragédie lyrique*, first seen in *Cadmus et Hermione* (1673), the first of many collaborations in the genre with Philippe Quinault, co-librettist with Molière of the 1671 *Psyché*. This also sought integration of music and dance into the whole, but was more ambitious and serious in its text, using the elevated tragic tone of Corneille and Racine with declamatory recitative and high spectacle.[12]

Some of the key differences between the two stage plots seem to reflect this generic contrast. For example, the 1671 sub-plot of Psyche's sisters who maliciously tempt her to seek her husband's identity against his instructions and are duly punished by being deceived into suicide, a key element in both Apuleius and La Fontaine, is excised in 1678, to be replaced by Venus herself as the enemy who suggests the fatal move: this is one of a number of simplifications in this hastily-executed adaptation, but may suggest that the low and ignoble jealousies of Psyche's sisters are not suitable for the more elevated world of tragic opera. In 1678 the sisters appear only in the opening act, where they are dignified and sympathetic towards their sister in her sufferings. Another omission in 1678 is that of the sub-plot of Psyche's suitors, itself an addition to Apuleius and La Fontaine; in Act 5 Scene 1 of 1671 they appear to Psyche in the Underworld, recount-

---

10 cf. Philippo 2013.
11 cf. Gély 1996.
12 For the various genres in this period see Powell 2000; Bartlet 2007; Sadler 2007.

ing their own deaths and those of the sisters; this is not especially low in tone (indeed, characters narrating their own modes of death are typical of the Underworld scenes of classical epic, e.g. in the *Odyssey* or the *Aeneid*), but creates a little more erotic interest. In 1671 Psyche insists on Cupid revealing his identity to her personally, another element of more romantic treatment in stressing interplay and converse between the lovers; in 1678 we revert to the Apuleian revelation by lamplight. In 1678 the royal father, rather than a messenger (as in 1671 and elsewhere), pronounces the fatal oracle about Psyche's husband, introducing more dignity and drama, and there is more emphasis on divisions in the divine family of Olympus, again a Homeric and Vergilian trait.

Examination of the 1671 version also shows that it used a wide range of classical sources outside Apuleius, perhaps in the realization that Apuleius' own tale itself uses a spectrum of models from different classical genres, but differently from Apuleius, who includes low genres like mime, the focus here is on more acceptable and respectable 'high' classical genres.[13] Ovid is an obvious source: in the Prologue we find several divinities who have extensive back-stories in Ovid's major works—Flora, goddess of flowers, with Nymphs (cf. Ov. *Fast.* 5.183–378), Vertumnus, god of trees and fruit (cf. Ov. *Met.* 14.623–771), and Palaemon, a god of the sea (cf. Ov. *Met.* 4.464–542, *Fast.* 6.504–48).[14] Proper names can also be drawn from Ovid: Psyché's sister Aglaure (Act 1 Scene 1) appropriately bears the name of the princess Aglauros, daughter of Pandion, king of Athens, who like her counterpart felt envy of her sister's union with a god (Ov. *Met.* 2.555–61), while her sister Cydippe is a homonym of the beloved of Acontius in the *Heroides* (Ov. *Her.* 20–21); these names are needed in the stage-play as Apuleius does not name the sisters, and nor does La Fontaine. Likewise, the two suitors introduced to the plot (see above) need names, too (Act 1 Scene 2): Agenor is named after the king of Tyre, the father of Europa (Ov. *Met.* 2.858), while Cleomenes recalls not an Ovidian hero but a historical king of Sparta (Livy 34.28.1), both appropriately royal for these two princes. Another Ovidian name is that of Lychas, the unwelcome messenger who brings Apollo's oracle (Act 1 Scene 4), evidently drawn from the unfortunate Lichas, killed by Heracles for bringing the deadly gift of the poisoned robe (Ov. *Met.* 9.211–18, originally from Sophocles' *Trachiniae*).

Epic and tragedy also have their place. The building of Cupid's palace by Vulcan and the Cyclopes in Act 2 Scene 1 (already found in Thomas Heywood's

---

13 For the details see Zimmerman et al. 1998 and Zimmerman et al. 2004.
14 Palaemon also makes a brief appearance at the start of Apuleius' *Cupid and Psyche* (*Met.* 4.31.6).

Love's Mistress of 1636)[15] is plainly drawn from the glimpse of Vulcan's workshop with the Cyclopes making Aeneas' new arms at *Aeneid* 8.416–53, while the helpful River God of Act 4 Scene 4 clearly owes something to Vergil's Tiberinus in the same book of the *Aeneid* who likewise prophesies a happy outcome for the protagonist at a time of doubt (8.36–65), confirming the Roman future for Aeneas. As we have already seen, the Iphigenia story was prominent in France in the period, and the dilemma of Psyche's father between his role as parent and his role as monarch in the matter of sacrificing his daughter clearly looks back to the famous dilemma of Agamemnon as expressed in the *Agamemnon* of Aeschylus (205–217) or the *Iphigeneia at Aulis* of Euripides (1255–75).

3 The English version. Thomas Shadwell, *Psyche* (1675)

Molière's 1671 version was adapted within a few years (1675) into English by Thomas Shadwell,[16] later (1688) successor to Dryden as Poet Laureate and soon to be attacked by the latter for dullness in *MackFlecknoe* (1676, published 1682), who had already adapted several of Molière's comedies for the English stage.[17] Shadwell's *Psyche* was done for the London actor-manager Thomas Betterton of the Duke of York's Theatre, who had visited Paris and was keen to imitate French theatrical successes in a court and society that looked to France for cultural prestige and fashion.[18] The text was set by the composer Matthew Locke[19] as what is known as 'semi-opera', a mixture of speech and song, in some ways the beginnings of opera in English, though William Davenant also has some claim to this with the earlier *The Siege of Rhodes* (1656, revised and expanded version 1661).[20] In 1674 Betterton had produced a version of *The Tempest*, with music by Locke and others, but the classicizing plot of *Psyche* clearly looks to French influence

---

15 For this adaptation of the *Cupid and Psyche* story see Carver 2007, 349–54; Harrison (forthcoming). Heywood's work may have been known in France.
16 For the 1675 edition see http://quod.lib.umich.edu/e/eebo/A59443.0001.001/1:2?rgn=div1; view=fulltext (accessed 3rd July 2017), the text cited here, and for resources on Shadwell see Slagle 1996. Shadwell claims in his preface to have adapted the French work in five weeks.
17 See Bennett 2004.
18 See e.g. Hayward 2015.
19 For a recording see that by Philip Pickett and the New London Consort (1995) on the L'Oiseau-Lyre label, catalogue number 444 336–2OH.
20 For this piece and even earlier candidates see Pinnock and Wood 2008.

and to Molière in particular[21] rather than the already rich tradition of performing Shakespeare with song and dance accompaniment.[22]

It has been plausibly suggested that Locke's designation of the piece as 'the English opera' on the title page of his score (1675)[23] is an explicit challenge to the more openly French operas being produced by the rival opera company the King's Men such as Louis Drabu's *Ariane* (1674), but again the key reception context for *Cupid and Psyche* is that of the fashionable royal court. Shadwell's libretto is dedicated to Charles II's illegitimate son James Scott, Duke of Monmouth, seen as the Protestant rival for the succession to the king's brother James, Duke of York, who had emerged as a Roman Catholic in 1673. Once again I summarise the plot:

Act one: In a pleasant landscape, Psyche discusses possible marriage and is entertained by Pan and nymphs: Ambition, Power, Plenty and Peace appear, as do the Furies and Envy. Psyche's rival lovers Nicander and Polynices arrive and are reconciled by Psyche; Psyche's envious sisters Cidippe and Aglaure call upon Venus to attack Psyche—she agrees.

Act two: Psyche's family gather at Apollo's temple to receive the dark oracle—her sisters rejoice, her father despairs, while the two lovers are sceptical about priests and religion. Two minor pairs of unhappy lovers commit suicide. Psyche is exposed but rescued by Cupid.

Act three: Vulcan and the Cyclopes build Cupid's palace; Cupid and Zephyr prepare for Psyche's arrival; she is courted by Cupid who does not reveal his name. On earth the rival lovers appear with priests and followers of Mars and scorn the love of the sisters in their devotion to rescuing Psyche. Psyche asks for her sisters to visit.

Act four: The envious sisters visit Psyche's palace and meet Cupid; they sow doubt in her mind. Psyche asks Cupid's name; he confesses and leaves. Psyche's father dies, the lovers still seek her. The sisters plot with soldiers to kill the lovers, and abuse the abandoned Psyche, who attempts suicide; she is prevented by the River God who foretells a happy ending. Psyche confronts an angry Venus

---

21 For more on the adaptation (not focussing on the classical elements) see Lefkowitz 1979–80 and Degott 2008.
22 For the latter see e. g. Brissenden 1981.
23 For an illustration see https://library.leeds.ac.uk/special-collections/view/1603 (accessed 4th July 2017).

who sends her to the Underworld; the lovers follow her in suicide, and Cupid sends the sisters there, too.

Act five: Psyche is in the Underworld with Furies and devils. Her sisters abuse Psyche, but Pluto and Proserpina release her to the world above and condemn the sisters to Hell. The dead lovers remain in the fortunate parts of the Underworld. Psyche takes Proserpina's box and opens it—and faints, apparently in death. Venus initially refuses to revive her, then agrees if there is no contact with Cupid; but Jupiter intervenes and makes Psyche a goddess out of fear of Cupid. The gods celebrate the marriage of Cupid and Psyche.

Once again, modifications of the original (Molière, with little sign of return to Apuleius)[24] are instructive. This version introduces groups of soldiers, both as Psyche's rejected lovers and warlike defenders, and as the supporters of her two evil sisters: we might compare the rival armies of Cordelia and her sisters in *King Lear*, a play similarly including three sisters, one good, two bad, already deployed in Heywood's *Love's Mistress*.[25] This military presence also perhaps reflects the fact that England was still in war mode; the Third Anglo-Dutch War (1672–4), in which England had supported Louis XIV against the Netherlands, had not long finished, and Shadwell's preface makes it clear that most of his libretto was written during that period.[26] Shadwell's version also gives a much increased role to priests, who are shown in a negative light, no doubt reflecting the author's desire to stress his anti-Catholicism (he had earlier been suspected of Catholic sympathies),[27] consistent with the work's dedication to the Protestant champion Monmouth (see above).

Unusually, in Shadwell's text Cupid gets to meet Psyche's wicked sisters, who never encounter him in any of the previous versions; this gives a firmer basis for their jealousy, the kind of change Shadwell alludes to in his preface when he claims that he had made the plot more like a proper play. The sisters themselves are worse than usual, perhaps (as already noted) under the influence of Goneril and Regan in *King Lear*, and are consequently sent to the Underworld by Cupid for eternal punishment rather than being deceived into suicide. An interesting touch is the introduction of a desert scene in Act 1 with two pairs of despairing lovers who kill themselves, presumably a contrast with Psyche who

---

[24] Shadwell's preface alludes to Apuleius as model for the French work, but does not suggest any direct use.
[25] See n.2 above.
[26] It claims that most of it was finished 16 months before, i.e. some time in 1674.
[27] But later wrote anti-Catholic satire; for both see Bennett 2004.

shows resolution in her desperate situation of prospective marriage with a serpent. We also find a particularly positive presentation of Proserpina and Pluto, monarchs of the Underworld, who behave graciously to Psyche, no doubt a compliment to the English king and queen.

Shadwell also follows the lead of Molière (and as we have already noted, of Apuleius himself) in bringing in elements from other classical genres. In Act 2, one of Psyche's rival lovers (Polynices, borrowing a name from the son of Oedipus)[28] comments on her father's acquiescence in the prophecy of Apollo that Psyche must marry a monster:

> Thus the great Agamemnon was betray'd,
> And Iphigenia thus a Victim made:
> Such horrid ills Religion can persuade.

The last line plainly translates a famous verse of Lucretius, also referring to Agamemnon's sacrifice of Iphigenia (1.101) *tantum religio potuit suadere malorum*; here the contemporary English popularity of Lucretius[29] is added to the French interest in the sacrifice of Iphigenia (see above).

Similarly, the presentation of the Underworld in Act 5 owes much to Vergil *Aeneid* 6, also a source for Apuleius (but here recalled in different ways). When Psyche reaches there, she asks information from her now deceased former lovers whom she encounters, just as Aeneas repeatedly questions the Sibyl about the world below:

> *Psyche:*
> Stay, Princes! and declare where, and what it is,
> This everlasting place of Bliss?
>
> *Nicander:*
> In cool sweet Shades, and in immortal Groves,
> By Chrystal Rivulets, and eternal Springs;
> Where the most beauteous Queens and greatest Kings,
> Do celebrate their everlasting Loves.
>
> *Polynices:*
> In ever peaceful, fresh, and fragrant Bowers,
> Adorn'd with never fading Fruits and Flowers;
> Where perfum'd Winds refresh their heat,
> And where immortal Quires their Loves repeat.

---

28 His rival, Nicander, seems to be named after the general of the Seleucid Antiochus III (Livy 35.12, 29).
29 See e.g. Norbrook et al. 2015.

> There your great Father we have seen,
> Where he afresh enjoys his beauteous Queen.

The shades and groves of Bliss look to Vergil's Elysium with its *locos laetos et amoena virecta / fortunatorum nemorum sedesque beatas* ('the joyous places and pleasing green spaces of the fortunate groves, and the happy homes', *Aeneid* 6.638–9). The reuniting of Psyche's dead royal parents recalls Vergil's reunion of Dido and Sychaeus (*Aeneid* 6.474–4), but might also evoke the fairly recent reunion in death of Henrietta Maria (d.1669) with her long-dead husband Charles I, a potential compliment to their son Charles II.[30]

Shadwell's rapidly-confected piece seems not to have been a great success,[31] but it is certainly of interest for historians both of English theatre and of Apuleian reception and for its reflection of English royal court politics.

4 Conclusion

The three works outlined here represent an intense phase in the theatrical reception of the tale of *Cupid and Psyche* in France and England in the 1670s; three adaptations within seven years is a remarkable hit-rate, even if all are closely textually related to each other. All three versions reflect a key feature of Apuleius' original, its capacity to use characters and scenes from various literary genres. These three texts confirm the key importance in the story's reception history of La Fontaine's 1669 retelling as a stimulus for further versions in the Paris of Louis XIV and its imitators in London, and offer interesting perspectives on the different influences of literary/musical forms and socio-political circumstances on the resulting versions, as well as playing a significant role in the development of early opera on either side of the English Channel.

5 Bibliography

Bakogianni, A. (ed.) (2013), *Dialogues with the past. Classical reception theory & practice.* London. (*BICS Suppl.* 126, 2 vols.)

Bartlet, M.E.C. (2007), '*Comédie-ballet*', in: *The New Grove Dictionary of Opera.* Oxford. http://www.oxfordmusiconline.com [Accessed 4th July 2017].

---

[30] For the increased interest in *Cupid and Psyche* leading up and during the rule of Charles I see Carver in this volume.

[31] See Lefkowitz 1979–80.

Bennett, K. (2004), 'Shadwell, Thomas (c.1640–1692)', in: Cannadine, D. et.al (eds.) *Oxford Dictionary of National Biography*. Oxford. http://www.oxforddnb.com/view/article/25195 [Accessed 4th July 2017].

Brissenden, A. (1981), 'Jacobean Tragedy and the Dance', *Huntington Library Quarterly* 44, 249-62.

Carver, R.H.F. (2007), *The Protean Ass. The Metamorphoses of Apuleius from Antiquity to the Renaissance*, Oxford.

Degott, P. (2008), '"Amongst the Gods I Psyche will translate": la réécriture par Thomas Shadwell de la tragédie-ballet Psyché (1671) de Molière, Corneille et Quinault', *Revue LISA* 6: 20-35 https://www.lisa.revues.org/1128 [Accessed 4th July 2017].

Finkmann, S./Behrendt, A./Walter, A.(eds.) (2018), *Antike Erzähl- und Deutungsmuster. Zwischen Exemplarität und Transformation*, Berlin-Boston.

Gély, V. (1996), 'La Fontaine entre Ovide et Puget de la Serre. Des Amours des dieux aux Amours de Psyché, un art d'aimer lire', *L'Information littéraire* 48, 10-19.

Harrison, S.J. (2018a), 'Psyche amongst the Victorians. An Aspect of Apuleian Reception', in: Harrison/Thorsen, 2018, 177-94.

Harrison, S.J. (2018b), 'Apuleius in France: La Fontaine's *Psyché* and its Apuleian Model' in Finkmann et al, 2018, 385-99.

Harrison, S.J. (forthcoming), 'An Apuleian Masque? Thomas Heywood's *Love's Mistress* (1634)', in: Boidin, C. / Mouren, R. / Pedeflous, O. (eds.) (2020), *The Afterlife of Apuleius*. London.

Harrison, S.J./Thorsen, T., (eds.) (2018), *Dynamics of Latin Prose. Biographic, Novelistic, Apologetic*, Berlin.

Hayward, M. (2015), 'Dressing Charles II. The King's Clothing Choices (1660–85), *Apparences* 6. https://apparences.revues.org/1320_[Accessed 4th July 2017].

Lefkowitz, M. (1979-80), 'Shadwell and Locke's 'Psyche'. The French Connection', *Proceedings of the Royal Musical Association* 106, 42-55.

Norbrook, D./Hardie, P./Harrison, S (eds.) (2015), *Lucretius and the Early Modern*, Oxford.

Philippo, S. (2013), 'Accidental Creativity'. Scribes, Scholars, Translators and the Iphigenia Dramas of Seventeenth-Century France', in: Bakogianni, 381-99.

Pinnock, A. and Wood, B. (2008), 'A Mangled Chime. The Accidental Death of the opera libretto in Civil War England', *Early Music* 36, 265-84.

Powell, J., http://www.personal.utulsa.edu/~john-powell/Psyche [Accessed 30th June 2017].

Sadler, G. (2007), '*Tragédie en musique*', in: Sadie, S. et. al. (eds.) *The New Grove Dictionary of Opera*, Oxford. http://www.oxfordmusiconline.com [Accessed 4th July 2017].

Slagle, J.B., ed. (1996), *Thomas Shadwell Reconsider'd. Essays in Criticism*, special number of *Restoration: Studies in English Literary Culture, 1660-1700*: 20.

Zimmerman, M. et al. (eds.) (1998), *Aspects of Apuleius' Golden Ass II. Cupid and Psyche*, Groningen.

Zimmerman, M. et al. (2004), *Apuleius Madaurensis Metamorphoses Books IV 28-35, V and VI 1-24. The Tale of Cupid and Psyche*, Groningen.

Christiane Reitz
How to use a wallpaper.
Psyché et Cupidon—notice explicative

Some years ago Lorenz Winkler-Horaček and I became interested in a scenic wallpaper which depicts the story of *Cupid and Psyche*.[1] The French wallpaper consists of a sequence of 12 images. Several copies are preserved, among them one complete set in Rostock and one in the Ducal Palace in Bad Doberan on the Baltic, nearby.[2] The wallpapers in grisaille, using eight different shades of grey and sepia, were designed by the French painters Merry-Joseph Blondel (1781–1853) and Louis Lafitte (1770–1828). These artists were themselves inspired by various sources, most importantly the engravings after the pictures by François Gérard which accompanied an edition of the *Contes de La Fontaine* by Didot, Paris 1797, and which were exhibited in the Salon of 1808. A painting by Pierre-Paul Prud'hon, entitled 'Vénus et l'Amour endormi, caressés et réveillés par les Zéphirs' was also exhibited on this occasion.[3] The adjustment of the designs to the format of the wallpaper (with a height of 183 cm each, and a width varying from 61 to 215 cm) was executed by Xavier Mader who was a member of the atelier Dufour. 26 'lés', lengths or panels, form 12 'tableaux', pictures. The *Cupid and Psyche* wallpapers were designed and first printed by the atelier Dufour in Paris from 1815 onward, and were sold after 1865 in a simpler reprint by the manufacturer Desfossé and Karth, until 1931. They were a huge commercial success.[4]

---

[1] See Reitz and Winkler 2008a for a brief discussion, Winkler and Reitz 2008b, and Thümmler 2008 for a more detailed treatment in connection with an exhibition (Berlin and Rostock 2009, Hannover 2010), and Reitz and Winkler 2011.
[2] The Rostock exemplar was shown in the Schifffahrtsmuseum in Rostock, formerly Kunst- und Altertumsmuseum. For its history see Reißmann 2003 and 1996. It has unfortunately now been put in storage and is at the moment no longer viewable by the public. The wallpaper in Bad Doberan was acquired in Paris for the newly erected Grand Ducal Palace of Frederick Francis I of Mecklenburg-Schwerin in the 1820s; documents concerning the negotiations for its acquisition have been preserved. See also Woods and Jacqué 1995 for a British exemplar.
[3] The Salon of 1808 took place in the Musée Napoléon, as the Louvre was then called, and exhibited 834 works of art.
[4] See e.g. the exemplar in the Tapetenmuseum Kassel, a reprint by the manufacturers Desfossé and Karth. For the wallpaper's commercial success see Haase 1978, 8–9; Nouvel-Kammerer 1990, and Lang 1994, 144–9. On the influence of ancient art on 19th cent. interior design see e.g. Brunner 2003.

In our research, it proved rewarding to focus both on the relationship of both text and image with the literary version (or versions) and the pictorial design, and on the reception of ancient iconography, art, artefacts and architecture in the pictures. We have to keep in mind that under the reign of Napoleon I, Paris and the Musée Napoléon housed temporarily what was then probably the world's largest collection of ancient sculpture. The same public that would have visited the 'originals' which had served as models for the wallpaper's design would shortly afterwards attend the 'Exposition des Produits de l'Industrie Nationale' where the wallpapers were put on display and awarded a silver medal.[5] The wallpapers were sold together with a booklet which served as a thematic introduction, and provided instructions on how to arrange and glue the single panels in the correct order onto the walls—the 'avis pour le colleur'.[6]

This little booklet[7] forms the focus of my paper. It testifies to the cultural role this expensive luxury product played for the customers; it gives an idea of the impact such a product had for the self-fashioning of a social and economic elite. When we talk about luxury items, such as porcelain centrepieces or the like, we presume that they served, and still serve, as conversation pieces for their owners and their guests. In our booklet, we have the instruction manual to hand and may gain from it an insight into the tastes and the literary background of a group of consumers. Just as an industrial product can offer broader and more telling insights into the fashions, tastes, and conventions current among their buyers than a unique artefact,[8] so the manual can guide us to their motives and give us an idea of the polite conversations of a Parisian-- and later international—salon. Beyond being a mere instruction leaflet, the guide allows us a glimpse into contemporary society's pretensions, and with its literary quotations to illustrate images realigns the visual and literary reception of both Apuleius' and La Fontaine's texts.

---

5 Apparently, Dufour was disappointed and saw himself as the subject of an intrigue which downgraded the industrial product in favour of the 'true' work of art. See the analysis in Pastiaux-Thiriat and Pastiaux 2000, 25 f.
6 I am very grateful to the Musée du Papier Peint in Rixheim, and to its director M. Philippe de Fabry, for providing me with a copy of this almost inaccessible document.
7 The full title is: *Psyché et Cupidon; Tableaux-tentures en papier peint, de la manufacture de Joseph Dufour et C.ie, de l'imprimerie d'Abel Lanoe*, 1815. The booklet is mentioned by Clouzot 1931, 174. As far as I can see, it was more common, for merchandising purposes, to accompany wallpapers by lithographic reproductions. Booklets were produced by Dufour and by Zuber et Cie. (founded in 1797), but not for all their panoramic wallpapers. I am thankful to Sabine Thümmler (Berlin) for this information.
8 For a fuller discussion of the influence of Napoleonic ideological imagery, see Winkler and Reitz 2008b, and Nouvel-Kammerer 2008.

That the myth of Cupid and Psyche is one of the most fruitful topics in art does not need to be discussed here. The evidence has been collected by Christel Steinmetz, Christiane Holm and others,[9] and some striking examples are presented in this volume.[10] Yet, while considering what previous knowledge possible owners of the wallpapers would have had, we have to keep in mind that whole pictorial cycles as well as works choosing single episodes and motives from the myth had formed the aesthetic perception of the story. The literary reception of the tale in France would have been much more influenced by La Fontaine's rendering of the story than by the Latin novel of Apuleius, an influence, as Harrison shows in this volume, which moves beyond French borders. Though new contextualisations like Raphael's fresco cycle in the Villa Farnesina in Rome (1515) and allegorical interpretations like Giulio Romano's cycle for the Palazzo del Te in Mantua (1535) were known, symbolic meaning and the ancient concepts of death and immortality do not play the main roles. Jean de La Fontaine's *Les amours de Psyché et de Cupidon* of 1669[11] is more focused on retelling the story itself and on its framework. Its overall structure introduces a group of learned friends who tell the story, with inserted verse passages, in the surroundings of the park of Versailles. Multiple editions of La Fontaine's work, some of which were illustrated, were to follow. As mentioned above, the 1797 illustrations based on François Gérard especially influenced Dufour's wallpapers. There are, however, substantial differences between the pictures of the printed version and the wallpapers, according to the express wish of Dufour himself. In the book version the protagonists are nude, while they appear fully clothed on the wallpapers. Several attributes and architectural vistas present in the wallpapers do not appear in the print version. The narrative on the wallpapers includes one episode which appears only in La Fontaine, not in Apuleius: Psyche is given shelter by a fisherman. The emphasis placed on individual episodes varies. Thus Psyche's bath is one of the central pictures, after the motive of the 'Toilette de Vénus'.[12] In Apuleius, the bath is only briefly mentioned, as a normal part of daily life (*Met*.5.2–3).

---

9 Steinmetz 1998, 4; Holm 2006; cf. Leidl 2008; de Jong 1998; Cavicchioli 2002; Weiland-Pollerberg 2002.
10 See e. g. the chapters by Simard and Leidl in this volume. But it is important to acknowledge the difference between a unique work of art, like the decoration in the Hôtel de Soubise, and a reproducible product like Dufour's wallpapers, however expensive they might be.
11 Vol. 8, 21–234 of the ed. by Regnies (1892). I quote from the 1990 edition by Charpentier. For a recent treatment of its adaptation of Apuleius see edition by Harrison (2018b).
12 The complicated relationship between Venus and Psyche is underlined by the fact that Psyche is depicted in the position of many statues who show Venus, unfastening her sandals. See

It should be noted that the wallpapers featured subtitles for the individual scenes, but these were sometimes cut off for reasons of space. The twelve panels show the following scenes: the enquiry from the oracle; Psyche transported by Zephyrus; Psyche's bath in the palace (Figure 2); the visit of her sisters; Psyche trying to stab Cupid; Psyche sitting on the rock; Psyche encountering the fisherman (Figure 3); the delivery of the vase with Stygian water (Figure 4); Proserpina's box and Psyche in the underworld; Psyche opening the box; Psyche reconciled with Venus; the marriage of Cupid and Psyche.

On the whole, the pictorial narrative follows the course of events and the choice of elements of the story as told by Apuleius and by La Fontaine. We have to take into account that there was another recent, maybe even more popular, version of the story. Charles-Albert Demoustier[13] in his adaptation of the story includes other elements of ancient mythology, and at times mixes items of information freely with the original plot. His *Lettres à Èmilie sur la mythologie* of 1786 had been a publishing success, and had also been translated into many languages. A German edition illustrated with engravings appeared in 1803,[14] and was reprinted several times, and Mary Tighe (discussed by O'Brien in this volume) admits to having read it alongside La Fontaine, though she claims to have not used them. La Fontaine and Demoustier are both mentioned in the booklet's foreword, and serve as its main sources.

1 The *Notice*

The small booklet of 30 pages contains an 'Introduction' (pp. I-VI), a 'Notice Explicative' in 12 numbers in accordance with the individual panels of the wallpapers (pp. 1–28), and an 'Avis pour le colleur' (pp. 29–30).

First of all, the term 'tableaux-tentures en papier peint' ('pictorial hangings in painted paper') makes quite clear the aims Dufour was pursuing. The product is promoted as an artefact, and as such invites comparison with the traditional visual arts. This is evident from the general introduction where the first artists mentioned as predecessors in the history of illustrating 'la fable de Psyché' are 'Raphael ... et Jules-Romain (i.e. Giulio Romano), son élève.' (p. I). At the same time, the educational aspect is foregrounded: the *fable* offers a selection

---

Winkler-Horaček 2008, 20. Venus' bath is a well-known motive in painting, cf. e.g. the famous painting by Peter Paul Rubens, now in Vienna.
13 In the *Notice*, he is called Dumoustier. I adopt the more familiar spelling of the printed editions.
14 Demoustier 1786; German edition Dresden 1803 and many others.

of some of the most interesting personalities in the works of Hesiod and Homer. The pictorial attraction of the *fable* lies in its presentation of a heroine in changing situations, laughing and crying, and always attracting the viewer's interest. The two literary sources are mentioned on p. 2, first Apuleius, who gave a 'paraphrase assez compliquée' ('a relatively complicated paraphrase'), then La Fontaine, whose is praised for his 'imitation fort agréable' ('very pleasant imitation'). Dufour states that the main reason for preferring La Fontaine's version to Apuleius' lies in its popularity: 'qui est entre les mains de tout le monde' ('which is in the hands of the whole world'). The foremost features of La Fontaine's 'petit Roman' ('short novel') are, so Dufour, its 'finesse' and a certain 'malice' (p. III). On the other hand, the author of our notice accuses the famous 'vainqueur d'Ésope' ('conqueror of Aesop') of a lack of 'style'. He proudly states that in contrast to the simple plot as unfolded by La Fontaine, where he claims that adequate characterisation and suitable description of both characters and the scenery of the plot were missing, his *tentures* ('hangings') stick to the conventions of time and place. The most important point in his product lies in the scrupulous observation of detail in architecture and accessories, thereby achieving 'l'élégante et belle simplicité des Grecs, qui savaient si bien allier la grâce à la magnificence' ('the elegant and beautiful simplicity of the Greeks, who knew so well how to ally grace and splendour'). Two errors must be avoided: 'l'affectation et la pesanteur' ('affectation and ponderousness').

This said, the reader is left in no doubt about the main target group of the wallpapers, and of the accompanying little book. It is a female spectatorship and audience whom the author wishes to attract and to entertain. First of all, women, the 'sexe aimable' ('lovable sex'), are responsible for interior decoration, being naturally talented for the task, as the author implies, and also staying more at home. Secondly, the subject matter of the decorative wallpapers should be neither too trivial, nor too far-fetched. It is only here that the author mentions models for his design who are much closer than Raphael and Giulio Romano: Gérard, Prudhon (sic) and Meynier (p. IV), and furthermore Fragonard and the marble group by F-J. Bosio.[15] A ballet with choreography by 'one of the best artists of the time' is also mentioned; possibly this refers to the version after Molière with music by Jean-Baptiste Lully (*Psyché: tragicomédie et ballet*, 1671).[16]

In the following passage of the introduction, the educational aspect of the *notice* and its length are discussed. Its purpose is not only to make the *Tableaux*

---

[15] Interestingly, the group by A. Canova, sculpted between 1787 and 1793 and henceforth in the Louvre, is not mentioned.
[16] See Harrison's chapter in this volume.

easier to understand, but also to refresh the owners' memory of the whole story, or even to serve as a replacement of the original source text. In order to analyse the literary function of our little text it is appropriate to quote this statement in full:

> Notre intention, en lui donnant quelqu'étendue, a été, non-seulement, de faciliter l'intelligence de nos Tableaux, mais encore de le faire avec une certaine liaison, qui rappelât complétement et avec exactitude, l'histoire de Psyché à la mémoire de ceux qui n'en auraient qu'un souvenir confus ou imparfait, et même de remplacer, au besoin, l'ouvrage entier auquel, néanmoins, nous renvoyons toujours nos lecteurs, persuadé qu'ils éprouveront un nouveau plaisir à le lire avec tous ses développemens.
>
> Our intention, in giving it some space, has been not only to ease the understanding of our Pictures, but also to do so with a certain kind of connection recalling the story of Psyche completely and accurately to the memory of those who have only a confused or imperfect recollection, and even to replace, when needed, the complete work, to which we nevertheless continually refer our readers, convinced that they will feel a new pleasure in reading it in all its developments. (p. V)

This statement resembles in content and intention the well-known technique of the (late)antique *epitomai*.[17] The author of the *notice* is aware of the danger that such a product could be too dry and therefore quotes literary passages in verse. And finally, he points to the timeless value of his product, quoting the last sentence of both Apuleius' and La Fontaine's version of the story, about the birth of *Voluptas*, and proudly states that his product induces the viewer to engage with the poetic genius of the Greeks, and their allegorical treatment of metaphysical ideas. This is indeed no mean claim.

The following explications first give the number and title of the *tableau* in question,[18] pointing (the workman) to its size, i.e. the number of single panels. Then the story is re-narrated in brief, sometimes making use of (unidentified) quotes from the original source, and inserting into most chapters one or more passages in verse. These passages vary in length, from 4 to 10 verses, with the exception of one longer piece of 20 verses in panel 4. Furthermore, the length of the narrative parts varies, from the brief concluding panel which is less than a page long, to the extensive narrative for panel 8. For each panel, the pas-

---

17 See the fundamental overview by Opelt 1962, Horster and Reitz 2010, 3–14, and Horster and Reitz, 2018. A handy definition is given by Gärtner and Eigler 1997: 'Epitomḗ (from ἐπιτέμνειν; epitémnein, "abbreviate", "cut to size", Aristot. *Soph. el.* 174b 29; Theophr. *Hist. pl.* 6,6,6): as an ideal type, it is a form of reduced written text somewhere between an excerpt and a paraphrase, generally of prose works.'

18 The titles of the narrative explications are identical with the subtitles of the wallpapers.

sage which points to the illustrated part of the story on the corresponding wallpaper is marked by an asterisk in the text and on the margin. In the following, I give an overview of the data, and quote the passage with the asterisk in full:

> 1: Les parens[19] de Psyché consultant l'oracle d'Apollon (p. 1–4, 4 verse passages, two by La Fontaine, two by Demoustier). ('The parents of Psyche consulting Apollo's oracle')
>
> Sujet du tableau: A ces terribles paroles, Psyché s'évanouit sur le sein de sa mère, qui semble accuser la rigeur des Dieux; le roi contemple, dans un morne silence, cette scène d'affliction; et Cupidon, témoin invisible de l'effroi qu'il cause, sourit en se reconnaissant dans le portrait du monstre qui doit être l'époux de Psyché.
>
> Subject of the picture: at these terrible words, Psyche faints on the breast of her mother, who appears to blame the cruelty of the gods; the king, in a miserable silence, contemplates this scene of suffering; and Cupid, an invisible witness of the terror he is causing, smiles as he recognizes himself in the portrait of the monster who is to be the husband of Psyche

The long story about the situation in the kingdom of Psyche's father, and the consultation of the oracle, closes with the description of the scene in question. Just before that, the oracle in verses by La Fontaine had been quoted. Adjectives like 'morne' and the expression 'scene d'affliction' hint at the emotional aspect, whereas the mention of the hidden Cupid focuses on the invention and innovation of the image, which in this form appears in none of the literary sources.

> 2: Psyché enlevée par les Zéphyrs (pp. 4–5, 2 verse passages, one by Demoustier, one by La Fontaine) ('Psyche after being taken away by the Zephyrs')
>
> Sujet du tableau: Zéphyr, par l'ordre de Cupidon, profite de ce moment, et la transporte à travers les airs, dans le magnifique palais où l'attend son époux.
>
> Subject of the picture: Zephyr, on the orders of Cupid, takes advantage of this moment, and carries her through the air to the magnificent palace where her husband awaits her.

The narrative emphasizes Psyche's horror at being exposed on the rock; Zephyr's role is not explained. This is astonishing, as in Demoustier, Zephyr and his enlistment by Cupid is described at length, even inserting a long passage on the god of Sleep, his entourage and his house.[20] The image of the wallpaper focuses on the sleeping Psyche, whose relaxed position recalls the famous sculpture of the reclining Ariadne.[21]

---

19 The original orthography of the *notice* is maintained.
20 Lettre LIV; German edition of 1803, 64. Brief.
21 For archaeological commentary, see Winkler and Reitz, 2008b.

Figure 2: Atelier Dufour, Wallpaper no. 3 = Psyche's bath in the palace. Copyright: Tapetenbilder aus dem Ovalen Saal des Großherzoglichen Palais in Bad Doberan. Edeltraud Altrichter, ITMZ Universität Rostock

3: Psyché au bain (p. 6–7, 3 verse passages by Demoustier) ('Psyche in the bath')

Sujet du tableau: [On la mène dans une salle préparée pour le bain;] *les Nymphes s'empressent de la servir: l'une la débarrasse de ses vêtements et détache le voile léger qui flotte sur son front; une autre verse dans l'onde rafraîchissante des essences parfumées; toutes admirent les charmes de Psyché, et Cupidon, caché entre les colonnes d'un peristile, voit avec orgueil et délice la beauté de celle qui sera bientôt son épouse, surpasser celle de ses divines compagnes, comme un beau lys éfface, par son éclat et sa majesté, toutes les fleurs d'un parterre.[22]

Subject of the picture: she is taken into a room prepared for bathing; the Nymphs hasten to serve her; one of them removes her clothes and takes away the light veil which floats over

---

22 This poetical comparison appears neither in La Fontaine, nor in Demoustier, where the bath is not even mentioned. The asterisks in the text are present in the original and inform the reader where the description of the picture begins.

her forehead; another pours perfumed essences into the refreshing water; all of them admire Psyche's charms, and Cupid, hidden between the columns of a peristyle, sees with pride and pleasure that the beauty of her who will soon be his wife surpasses that of her divine companions, just as a beautiful lily outshines, by its impact and splendour, all the flowers in a border.

The bath is mentioned in some detail by La Fontaine, and does not feature in Demoustier. The female attendants are important for both narratives, La Fontaine's and Demoustier's. Demoustier follows Apuleius here more closely; his servants are invisible, whereas La Fontaine and, of course, the wallpapers, let them appear 'in flesh and blood'. Again, the text of the notice points the viewer to the detail of Cupid as an observer, hidden on the margin of the scene.

> 4: Psyché montrant ses bijoux à ses soeurs (pp.7–9, 4 verse passages, all by Demoustier) ('Psyche showing her jewels to her sisters').
>
> Sujet du tableau: Psyché revoit ses sœurs, les accable de caresses, leur fait admirer la magnificence de ce beau séjour, leur montre les bijoux que son époux lui avait donnés, et leur en fait des cadeaux.
>
> 'Subject of the picture: Psyche sees her sisters again, covers them with caresses, invites them to admire the magnificence of this fine residence, shows them the jewels which her husband has given her, and makes them presents from these'.

Here the commentary at the end of the short narrative points to the future disaster which Psyche's decision to trust her sisters will cause. It evokes an emotional response from its readers, but the image itself purveys no such foreshadowing; it delights in antiquarian and architectural detail.

> 5: Psyché voulant poignarder Cupidon endormi (pp. 10–12, 2 verse passages by Demoustier) ('Psyche planning to stab Cupid in his sleep')
>
> Sujet du tableau: [Et jugez de ce qu'elle éprouve à la vue du monstre qui s'offre à ses yeux!] * Tout entière à l'étonnement, à l'admiration, le poignard est échappé de ses mains, et son projet meurtrier s'est évanoui!
>
> Subject of the picture: imagine what she thinks at the sight of the monster before her eyes! Wholly overcome by astonishment and admiration, the dagger fell from her hands, and her murderous enterprise has vanished!

This is the closing sentence of the brief chapter. In the sequence of the wallpapers, this is certainly a centrepiece. The antiquarian allusions are manifold. The drama of the scene is established by strong contrasts of light and shadow and by the dynamic movement of both Psyche and the escaping pigeons in the upper part of the image.

6: Psyché abandonnée (pp. 12–13, 2 verse passages, one by La Fontaine, one by Demoustier) ('Psyche abandoned').

Sujet du tableau: [Il voit Psyché; interdite et confuse, un poignard à ses pieds; il] * devine tout, et s'envole, lançant sur la coupable un regard courroucé, qu'il accompagne de ces paroles menaçantes: 'Vous m'avez vu, Psyché! vengez-moi de vos sœurs.'

Elle reste abandonnée sur le rocher rendu à son aridité première; la mer gronde sous ses pieds, les vagues écumantes engloutissent le palais où naguère elle fut adorée; et parmi ses débris flottans, surnage encore le glaive fatal qui devait percer le sein du plus aimable des Dieux.

Subject of the picture: he sees Psyche, taken aback and disturbed, a dagger at her feet; he guesses everything, and flies away, with a furious glance at the guilty girl, accompanied with these threatening words: 'You have seen me, Psyche! Take revenge for me on your sisters!'. She stays abandoned on the rock, restored to its original bare nature; the sea groans beneath her feet, the foaming waves engulf the palace where just now she was an object of adoration; and amongst its floating remains, there bobs the fatal blade which was to pierce the breast of the most lovable of the gods.

The rather long passage captures the movement of both the characters and their emotions and the narrative very well—the wallpaper shows exactly the instant where Cupid has already nearly vanished from Psyche's eyes, and the palace has fallen into ruins.[23]

7: Psyché recueillie par un pêcheur (p. 13–15, no verses) ('Psyche received by a fisherman')

Sujet du tableau: Ils gravissent avec peine un escalier taillé dans le roc; déjà ils sont arrivés à la vue de la cabane, d'où les deux petites-filles du viellard considèrent, avec une curiosité mêlée de surprise, la belle inconnue que guide leur aïeul.

Subject of the picture: they clamber with difficulty up a staircase cut in the rock; soon they arrive in sight of a hut, from which the two granddaughters of the old man scrutinise, with a mixture of curiosity and surprise, the beautiful stranger being led by their grandfather.

The narrative stresses Psyche's physical and emotional despair and vividly describes the appearance of the fisherman. The absence of verses may have its cause in the fact that the episode does not feature in Demoustier at all, and that in La Fontaine, verses are put in Psyche's mouth only after her arrival and short stay at the fisherman's hut.

---

23 It is perhaps telling that when I first saw the wallpapers, the exemplar in question was cut down and in frames, so that the palace ruins were not visible. I mistook the scene for Psyche exposed on the rock.

How to use a wallpaper. *Psyché et Cupidon—notice explicative* —— 71

Figure 3: Atelier Dufour, Wallpaper no 7 = Psyche encountering the fisherman. Copyright: Tapetenbilder aus dem Ovalen Saal des Großherzoglichen Palais in Bad Doberan. Edeltraud Altrichter, ITMZ Universität Rostock

Figure 4: Atelier Dufour, Wallpaper no. 8 = The delivery of the vase with Stygian water. Copyright: Tapetenbilder aus dem Ovalen Saal des Großherzoglichen Palais in Bad Doberan. Edeltraud Altrichter, ITMZ Universität Rostock

8: Psyché apportant à Vénus un vase d'eau de la fontaine de Jouvence (p. 15–21, one verse passage by La Fontaine). ('Psyche bringing Venus a vessel of water from the fountain of Youth').

Sujet du tableau: Psyché, de retour au palais de Vénus, se jette à ses pieds, lui présente, à genoux, le vase rempli de l'eau de jeunesse, et les Grâces sont bien aises de voir celle, que, de concert avec la Nature, elles on si généreusement dotée, revenue triomphante de cette périlleuse expédition.

Subject of the picture: Psyche, returned to the palace of Venus, throws herself at her feet, presents on her knees the vessel filled with the water of youth, and the Graces are well pleased to see the girl that they, together with Nature, have so richly endowed, returning in triumph from such a dangerous expedition.

The long narrative describes the different tasks assigned to Psyche by Venus; Psyche's delivery of the water of Youth appears at the end of the passage. The wallpaper plays with the imagery of triumph and submission, known e.g. from Roman coins and deliberately re-integrated into Napoleonic propaganda. The author of the notice identifies the three female figures with the Graces, but the iconography really does not fit; they might rather be the cruel servants mentioned in the story.

9: Psyché allant aux enfers (pp. 21–23, no verses)

Sujet du tableau: Arrivée à la porte des enfers, elle approche du chien à trois têtes, qui garde l'entrée de l'immense habitation des mânes: elle met un de ses gâteaux dans chacune des gueules du monstre, qui ressent aussitôt les premières atteintes du sommeil, et voit déjà devant elle, la barque de l'impitoyable Nocher, et les ondes sinistres du fleuve infernal.

Subject of the picture: once arrived at the gates of the underworld, she approaches the three-headed dog who guards the immense quarters of the spirits; she puts one of her cakes into each mouth of the monster, who immediately feels the first onset of sleep, and sees already before her the boat of the pitiless ferryman, and the sinister waves of the infernal river.

The absence of verses is noticeable, as, e.g., in La Fontaine Psyche enchants the infernal dragon with a song which would have lent itself well to the purpose of entertaining the reader. Demoustier's version would have offered the following verses:

Les Ombres à l'envi planèrent autour d'elle,
Cerbere, en murmurant, lécha ses jolis pieds,
Et l'avare Caron, deux fois dans sa nacelle,
Lui fit passer le Styx sans lui dire : Payez.

('The Shades in envy wandered about her,
Cerberus, murmuring, licked her pretty feet,
And the miser Charon, twice in his basket-boat,
Let her cross the Styx without saying to her: Pay').

La Fontaine even lets his narrator use alexandrines, the metre used by tragic authors like Corneille and Racine, to mark the sublime register of the underworld adventure.

10: Psyché revenant des enfers (pp.23–24, one verse passage by Demoustier) ('Psyche returning from the underworld').

Sujet du tableau: A peine a-t-elle atteint la sortie des enfers dont elle aperçoit encore les flammes vengeresses, que, ne pouvant plus résister, elle ouvre doucement la boîte: elle ne contenait rien qu'une fumée épaisse et noire, qui lui monte au visage. Hélas! cette fois Vénus a réussi!

Subject of the picture: hardly had she succeeded in leaving the underworld, whose vengeful flames she could still see, when, unable to resist further, she gently opened the box: it contained nothing more than a thick black smoke, which rose to cover her face. Alas! This time Venus has succeeded!

The author inserts a verse passage by Demoustier, illustrating Psyche's curiosity at the moment of opening the box, and then describes the act itself as a climax at the end of the chapter. The inconsistency between the story as told by Apuleius and by the French authors is not mentioned. In Apuleius' version, Psyche falls into a death-like sleep, whereas La Fontaine describes the fumes which come from the box and cover Psyche's face and bosom in black. Demoustier, again, follows Apuleius in that in his version Psyche falls into a trance. But his Psyche opens the box not out of curiosity, but by sheer misfortune. Perhaps the unfortunate Psyche in the letters to Emilie is more a subject for identification for the young addressee than the over-curious and incautious Psyche of the other two authors.

11: Réconciliation de Vénus et de Psyché (p. 25–27, one verse passage by Demoustier) ('Reconciliation of Venus and Psyche').

Sujet du tableau: [elle croyait qu'elle avait péri; de sorte que,] *quand elle parut, les yeux baissés, avouant sa faute, et tenant encore cette boîte qui avait trop bien servi une haine injuste, son cœur s'ouvrit à la plus tendre pitié, et passant d'un extrême à l'autre, elle la reçoit dans ses bras.

Subject of the picture: she believed that she had perished, so that when she appeared with lowered eyes, confessing her fault and still holding that box which had served an unjust hatred only too well, Venus' heart was opened to the most tender pity, and passing from one extreme to the other she received her in her arms.

The description captures the emotional moment of reconciliation; before that, the consequences of opening the box, and the reunion of the two lovers are told in emotional style. The reconciliation scene (not in the Apuleian original) is of high iconographic interest: the towering figure of Venus and the downcast, modest and girlish Psyche form a striking contrast. The scene takes place against a splendid architectural setting, and recalls an Italian landscape, with the well-known outline of Mount Vesuvius in the background.

12: Hymen de Psyché et de Cupidon (p. 27–28, no verses) ('Marriage of Psyche and Cupid').

Sujet du tableau: Cupidon emmena son épouse dans son palais de nuages, et délia, prés du lit nuptial, la ceinture d'Hymenée; le Plaisir, sous la figure d'un jeune enfant ailé, pose, en voltigeant, sa couronne de roses sur leurs têtes, et va leur présenter sa coupe divine, remplie du plus charmant délire.

Subject of the picture: Cupid took his bride away to a palace of clouds, and unbound, next to the bridal bed, the girdle of Hymenaeus; Pleasure, in the guise of a young winged child, hovers and places his garland of roses on their heads, and is about to present them with his divine cup, filled with the most charming delirium.

The well-known image of the banquet of the Gods which features so prominently on the ceiling of the Villa Farnesina (Raphael) and in the Palazzo del Te (Giulio Romano)[24] does not form part of the series of wallpapers. Instead, the final image depicts a very intimate scene between bridegroom and bride. La Fontaine alludes to the erotic context of the story by a decent *praeteritio:* 'Je décrirai encore moins les plaisirs de nos époux...' ('I will describe even less the pleasures of our nuptial couple'); Demoustier is even more chaste and does not even mention anything between Jupiter's consent and the birth of little Voluptas.

2 Conclusion

Without the commentary in the *notice*, which stresses French literary intertexts, the viewer of the wallpapers would identify mainly ancient models and famous iconography.[25] The models are adapted and transformed in varying intensity; sometimes, the allusion is marked clearly, sometimes hardly at all. The notice adds emotional depth for the benefit of the wallpaper's spectators, tapping into fashionable literature which adds baroque detail to Apuleius' story which is not always explicit about the motivations of the characters. The different types of reception range from quotation and allusion to topical use of omnipresent antiquarian details and decorations. In a subtle way, the viewers are led to generate their own version of the story, and to question, interpret and reinterpret the visual narrative. On the other hand, the *notice* recalls and epitomises the story, inserts verse which is suitable for quotation and delectation, and subtly points the observant reader to the innovative aspects and inventions of the decorative wall coverings.

---

24 See e.g. Leidl 2008.
25 See in more detail Reitz and Winkler 2011.

3 Bibliography

Brunner, A. (2003), *Renaissancen. Antikenrezeption in der Angewandten Kunst des 15. bis 19. Jahrhunderts*. Ausstellungskatalog. Hannover.

Cavicchioli, S. (2002), *Amore e Psiche*, Milano.

Clouzot, H. (1931), *Psyché et Cupidon, tableaux-tentures en papier peint de la manufacture J. Dufour et Cie.*, Paris.

Danke-Carstensen, P. (ed.) (2003), *Bürgerstolz. 1841–1903–2003 Museum in Rostock*, (Kleine Schriften des Schifffahrtsmuseums Rostock, Heft 3), Rostock.

de Jong, J.L. (1998), "Il Pittore a le volte è puro poeta'. Cupid and Psyche in Italian Renaissance Painting', in: Zimmerman, 189–215.

Demoustier, C.A. (1786), *Lettres à Èmilie sur la mythologie*, Paris.

Futre Pinheiro, M.P./Harrison, S.J. (eds.) (2011), *Fictional Traces. Receptions of the Ancient Novel. Vol. II*, Groningen (*Ancient Narrative Suppl.* 14).

Gaisser, J.H. (2003), 'Allegorizing Apuleius. Fulgentius, Boccaccio, Beroaldo, and the Chain of Receptions', *Acta Conventus Neo-Latini Cantabrigiensis*, Tempe, Arizona, 23-41 (Arizona Center for Medieval and Renaissance Studies).

Gärtner, H.A./Eigler, U. (1997), 'Epitome', in: H. Canick / H. Schneider (eds.) *Brill's New Pauly, Antiquity*, Leiden. http://0-dx.doi.org.wam.leeds.ac.uk/10.1163/1574-9347_bnp_e333570 [English version accessed 20 May 2017].

Haase, G. (1978), *Bildtapeten*, Leipzig.

Holm, C. (2006), *Die Erfindung eines Mythos in Kunst, Wissenschaft und Alltagskultur (1765–1840)*, München.

Horster, M./Reitz, C. (2018), 'Handbooks, Epitomes, Florilegia. Late Antique Variations on the Short Form', in: McGill and Watts, 431–50.

Horster, M. /Reitz, C. (eds.) (2010), *Condensing Texts—Condensed Texts*, Stuttgart (Palingenesia 98).

Icard-Gianolio, N. (1994), 'Psyche', in: *Lexicon Iconographicum Mythologiae Classicae (LIMC)* 7, 569–85.

Lang, P. (1994), *Ein Blick auf Amor und Psyche um 1800. Katalog zur Ausstellung Kunsthaus Zürich 20. Mai–17. Juli*, Zürich.

Leidl, C. (2008),'Räume und Feste der Liebe. Darstellungen von Amor und Psyche bis 1700' in Winkler and Reitz 2008b, 100–12.

McGill, S./Watts, E. (eds.) (2018), *Blackwell Companion to Late Antique Literature*, Chichester.

Nouvel-Kammerer, O. (1990), *Papiers peints panoramiques*, Paris.

Nouvel-Kammerer, O. (2008), Les ailes du papillon sous l'Empire napoléonien', in: Winkler/Reitz 2008b, 94–9.

Opelt, I. (1962), 'Epitome' in: *RAC* 5, 944–73.

Pastiaux-Thiriat, G./Pastiaux, J. (eds.) (2000), *Un créateur de papiers peints. Joseph Dufour (1754–1927)*, Catalogue de l'exposition Tramayes.

Reißmann, S. (1996), Die Psyche-Tapete, eine Kostbarkeit in den Sammlungen des Schiffahrtsmuseums', in: Schriften des Schiffahrtsmuseums, 75-81.

Reißmann, S. (2003), 'Vom Kunst- und Altertumsmuseum zum Schifffahrtsmuseum', in: Danke-Carstensen, 21–27 and 48–53.

Reitz, C./Winkler-Horaček, L. (2011), 'Love on a wallpaper. Apuleius in the boudoir', in: Futre Pineiro/Harrison, 95–107.

Schriften des Schiffahrtsmuseums der Hansestadt Rostock (1996), *Unter Wasser—über Wasser. Beiträge zur maritimen Technik- und Kulturgeschichte Mecklenburgs und Vorpommerns.*

Steinmetz, Ch. (1989), *Amor und Psyche. Studien zur Auffassung des Mythos in der bildenden Kunst um 1800.* Diss. Köln 1989.

Thümmler, S. (2008), 'Psyché et Cupidon. Ein Liebestraum unter den französischen Panoramatapeten', in: Winkler/ Reitz 2008b, 61–8.

Weiland-Pollerberg, F. (2002), *Amor und Psyche in der Renaissance. Medienspezifisches Erzählen im Bild.* Petersberg.

Winkler-Horaček, L. /Reitz, C. (2008a), 'Liebe auf Tapeten. Bericht über ein Projekt zur Antikenrezeption', *Gymnasium* 115, 481–3.

Winkler-Horaček, L./Reitz, C. (eds.) (2008b), *Amor und Psyche. Eine Erzählung in zwölf Bildern.* Rahden/Westfalen.

Woods, C. /Jacqué, B. (1995), *The Story of Cupid and Psyche*, Manchester, The Whitworth Art Gallery.

Zimmermann, M. et al. (eds.) (1998), *Aspects of Apuleius' Golden Ass. Vol. II. Cupid and Psyche*, Groningen.

Jared A. Simard
Psyche in the salon. French interior decoration in the eighteenth century

1 Introduction

The Hôtel de Soubise, an aristocratic mansion located in the third *arrondissement* of Paris, dates to the fourteenth century, but it is most widely known today for its eighteenth-century exterior and restored rococo interiors.[1] In particular, the Salon de la Princesse, an oval room on the first floor, is one of the finest examples of rococo interiors for eighteenth century France. Painted by Charles-Joseph Natoire, eight panels decorate the room, each one depicting a scene from the story of *Cupid and Psyche* found in Apuleius' *Metamorphoses*. Natoire's *Story* [*Histoire* in French] *of Psyche* is intriguing for its narrative qualities and the sheer number of panels. In addition, the context of the panels in the larger decorative program of the Hôtel de Soubise points to a gendered and intellectual playfulness characteristic of the rococo and trends in interior decoration for the nobility in the eighteenth century. After examining Natoire's cycle in detail, this chapter utilizes comparisons with both contemporary and earlier cycles of the myth in art to understand Natoire's own narrative sequence and themes. Finally, placed in the context of the overall decorative program of the Hôtel de Soubise and the occasion for its remodeling, Natoire's cycle suggests that an association with love and marriage remains a popular form of appropriation for the myth, and is evidence for La Fontaine's influence on the French reception of Apuleius reaching well into the eighteenth century.

2 Charles-Joseph Natoire's *Story of Psyche*

Natoire's eight panels date from between 1737 and 1739.[2] Natoire's first panel in the sequence, 'Psyche Carried Away by Zephyrus' (1739), dramatically begins his version of the tale with Psyche simultaneously abandoned and rescued (Figure 5). Her family descends the mountain at the lower right. Two figures, a woman

---
[1] For a brief history of the Hôtel de Soubise and information on restoration efforts in the modern period see Castagnet 2012, 121–7. For an overview of the rococo see Kimball 1943.
[2] For a table with the titles and dates of each panel see Lavezzi 2001, 307. The dates for panels six and eight are unknown.

Figure 5: Charles-Joseph Natoire, 'Psyche Carried Away by Zephyrus', Salon de la Princesse, Hôtel de Soubise. Paris. Copyright: Jared A. Simard

and a man, presumably her parents, turn their faces back to Psyche as the procession whisks them along. Psyche herself is momentarily alone, distraught, and weeping. She raises a handkerchief to her left eye as her gaze meets that of Zephyrus, seen swooping in to rescue her with arms wide open. She wears white clothing like that of a sacrificial virgin, and her right breast is exposed. Natoire's opening panel establishes Psyche firmly in the human realm. Psyche is abandoned, yet is simultaneously about to embark on a journey. Thus, there is a chronological compression in the very first panel.[3] Zephyrus' presence and that of the many putti fluttering about Psyche signal that her fortunes are going to change for the better. Indeed, as Élisabeth Lavezzi has pointed out, Psyche's family and Zephyrus are moving in opposite directions, which emphasizes that Psyche is about to be transported to the divine dimension.[4] The reason for Psyche's presence on the mountain crag is elided by beginning the visual narrative at this point in the myth. By removing Venus from the very beginning, Natoire focuses his version on Psyche and her perspective, turning her into a protagonist with whom the viewers can identify. Throughout all panels, the focus is always on her emotional journey, while, as we see in the second panel, Natoire

---

[3] Lavezzi 2001, 305.
[4] Lavezzi 2001, 309. Psyche is quite literally transported to the divine dimension since her movement is towards the eighth panel where she is raised to Olympus in Cupid's embrace.

also adds Cupid into the story in a more obvious manner than Apuleius, and thus places the couple at the centre of the suite of paintings.

Natoire's second panel, 'The Nymphs Greet Psyche with Flowers on Cupid's Palace Threshold,' again elides and changes parts of the myth.[5] Psyche here seems to step up to the palace from Zephyrus' cloud and is immediately greeted by nymphs. She does not fall asleep in a garden. In fact, it seems there is no garden at all; instead, the palace appears to be located up in the clouds. The nymphs offer baskets of flowers to Psyche, who reaches delicately to pick one up. Here, Natoire has necessarily made the nymphs visible because of the medium, while the flowers are a possible reference to the aforementioned garden episode. More importantly, Psyche's mood has shifted. She is not entirely free from the fear and sensation of impending death when Zephyrus first came to her. Nonetheless, she asserts her own agency by approaching the nymphs and seems at the very least to regard them as friends, not foes. Cupid is shown hiding in the clouds just behind Psyche, while Zephyrus points to Cupid's new bride. In this way, Natoire affords the viewer a sense of dramatic irony just as Apuleius includes hints as to her husband's identity for the reader.[6] We know her husband is Cupid, but Psyche is still ignorant of this. Furthermore, the gaggle of nymphs on the balustrade is not unlike a receiving line in the court. The white façade of the palace and its gilded accents directly mirrors the white base of the walls in the salon and its heavy use of gilding.[7] In this way, Natoire and his narrative of the myth connect the Salon de la Princesse and the Princess de Soubise with Psyche, by focusing entirely on Psyche's female experience.

Natoire's narrative continues with his third panel, 'Psyche Shows Her Treasures to Her Sisters.'[8] In this panel, Psyche is seated to the left of centre, while her sisters hold up treasures on the right. Attendants are seen bringing additional treasures in the background. Psyche is fully clothed in a pale-yellow dress and watches her sisters. She is the most secure in this panel, having come far from the abandoned woman left for dead. She is living a life of relative comfort and luxury. In this way, Psyche here mirrors the host in the salon. She holds court over those who come to visit her; Psyche dazzles with her treasures while the *salonière* does so with her sophistication and wit.

The next panel depicts the well-known consequence of the sisters' visit with Psyche. The fourth panel, 'Psyche Contemplates Her Sleeping Husband', reveals

---

5 For an image of Natoire's "The Nymphs Greet Psyche with Flowers on Cupid's Palace Threshold," see Béchu 2004, 367.
6 For a discussion of the mystery novel aspects of the myth see Winkler 1985, 89–93.
7 For images of the room and panels *in situ*, see Béchu 2004, 358 and 364.
8 For an image of Natoire's 'Psyche Shows Her Treasures to Her Sisters,' see Béchu 2004, 368.

Figure 6: Charles-Joseph Natoire, 'Psyche Contemplates Her Sleeping Husband', Salon de la Princesse, Hôtel de Soubise. Paris. Copyright: Jared A. Simard

a slumbering, youthful Cupid (Figure 6). In a departure from Apuleius' version, Natoire has Psyche hold just the lamp. The absence of the weapon marks a more innocent Psyche than in the original tale. This panel is the first climax in the series. The first three panels have taken Psyche from destitution on the mountainside to wife in a luxurious palace with attendants. Thus, panels one through four take Psyche from her lowest position through to the discovery that she was sleeping with the god of love himself. If we ignore the elusive image of Cupid in the second panel, the fourth panel also marks the resolution of the mystery of who sent Zephyrus to rescue Psyche in the first panel. If Cupid had not been jolted awake by dripping oil from the lamp, the story could easily have ended here.

Natoire, like Apuleius, does not end his tale with the recognition scene. This half-way point proceeds into the fifth panel, 'The Nymphs Pull Psyche's Still Body Out of the Water.'[9] Psyche is shown lifeless and limp as four nymphs hoist her body onto a riverbank. A river god is shown in the upper left corner of the panel. While it can be assumed that this scene was preceded by one of Psyche's many suicide attempts, here, nonetheless, Psyche is rescued again just as she was in the first panel. In this way, the first and the fifth panel each begin a

---

[9] For an image of Natoire's 'The Nymphs Pull Psyche's Still Body Out of the Water,' see Béchu 2004, 369.

Figure 7: Charles-Joseph Natoire, 'Psyche with the Shepherds', Salon de la Princesse, Hôtel de Soubise. Paris. Copyright: Jared A. Simard

sequence of four panels; each one begins with Psyche at her lowest point in imminent need of rescuing and simultaneously in the process of being rescued. Panels one through four also consistently depict Psyche just left of centre, while panels five through eight will depict her just right of centre, furthering the division and symmetry between them.[10] Finally, just as with the putti in the first panel, the nymphs in the fifth panel herald a happy ending for Psyche.

Natoire changes the narrative in his sixth panel, 'Psyche with the Shepherds,' (Figure 7), a clear indication of La Fontaine's influence, as this scene is not found in Apuleius. Psyche is downcast, doing her best to gather her clothing as a shepherd leads her to a shaded grotto where his daughters are at work. Sheep are seen in the distance. A billy-goat is in the foreground along with a basket of fruits. Psyche's breasts are once again exposed, further signaling her change of fortune. In this way, this panel directly reverses the narrative of the third panel where Psyche was fully clothed and surrounded by her treasures and her sisters in a luxurious environment. She is now in the countryside with an unknown family. Nonetheless, panels two and six remain coordinated with each other: each follows a scene where Psyche is rescued and each depicts Psyche safe and being introduced to a new group, albeit of different status, the

---

10 For a discussion of the symmetry of the salon and how this related to the panels see Lavezzi 2001, 306–7.

Figure 8: Charles-Joseph Natoire, 'Psyche Faints From Fright Before Venus', Salon de la Princesse, Hôtel de Soubise. Paris. Copyright: Jared A. Simard

nymphs and palace in panel two and the shepherd's family and countryside in panel six. Thus, there is a complex play between the series of panels as they reveal Natoire's narrative of the myth.

The story nears its completion in the seventh panel, 'Psyche Faints from Fright before Venus' (Figure 8). In this panel, Psyche is shown asleep in the arms of Cupid, who gestures towards Venus, who looms over the scene in the clouds. The title of the panel is perhaps an error because the iconography seems to suggest this is the moment when Psyche has opened the jar from Persephone and subsequently succumbed to sleep. The torch at her side and opened jar lid in her hand seem to confirm this interpretation. Cupid then comes to her rescue and appeals directly to Venus. Thus, as Lavezzi has noted, this panel has a significant amount of chronological compression.[11] Most importantly, this panel depicts a Psyche reconnecting with Cupid for the first time since the fourth panel when she discovered her lover's true identity. The return of Cupid signals a happy ending to come in the eighth and final panel.

In 'Psyche Taken to Heaven by Cupid,' Psyche embraces Cupid who points the way towards Olympus (Figure 9). Venus is off to the left discussing the matter with other divinities as she points to the council of the assembled gods behind her. A few doves appear just behind her right shoulder on the far left of the panel

---

11 Lavezzi 2001, 305.

Figure 9: Charles-Joseph Natoire, 'Psyche Taken to Heaven by Cupid', Salon de la Princesse, Hôtel de Soubise. Paris. Copyright: Jared A. Simard

identifying the goddess. Zeus and Hera are clearly shown in the clouds in the far left background of the panel. Natoire ends Psyche's journey at the same place Apuleius does, with her apotheosis, her happily ever after. Natoire also preserves the overall character of Psyche as she is depicted in Apuleius' novel. In the last four panels, Psyche is completely helpless and dependent on others for her safety and well-being. In particular, the final three panels each depict Psyche at the mercy of multiple figures who all gesture with their right hand in the same manner. She is either being led to greet new characters or her saviour appeals to others on her behalf. Thus, the focus remains on Psyche as each panel subtly shifts the viewer's interpretation of her fortunes, ultimately ascending from the rustic countryside to Olympus.

3 François Boucher: A contemporary tapestry Psyche

François Boucher was a more well-known and successful French artist than his contemporary Natoire.[12] He was commissioned in the 1730s for both paintings

---

[12] For an updated take on Boucher see Hedley 2004 and Hyde 2006. Older but still good is

and tapestries. Boucher also worked on panels for the remodeling of the Hôtel de Soubise which began in 1737.[13] That same year Boucher received a commission from King Louis XV for a series of six tapestries to be woven at the royal Beauvais tapestry manufactory. Boucher ultimately produced five tapestries depicting scenes from the Psyche myth.[14] Boucher's set covers a similar narrative scheme to Natoire's, namely: 'The Arrival of Psyche at Cupid's Palace', 'The Toilet of Psyche', 'The Treasures of Psyche', 'The Abandonment of Psyche', and 'Psyche and the Basket-maker.'[15] Of these five, only the toilet scene has no parallel in Natoire's cycle. In addition, Cupid appears only in Boucher's abandonment tapestry. The remarkable absence of Cupid in Boucher's short cycle focuses the story on Psyche alone in a way that removes the myth further from Apuleius' version. Boucher's Psyche seems far less mythical and could just as easily be the depiction of a woman who experiences court life and then becomes destitute. As Kathryn Heisinger puts it, Boucher's tapestries tell a story of 'riches-to-rags.'[16] By comparison, Natoire's extended cycle is much more grounded in the love story, as Cupid is featured multiple times, and more of Psyche's journey is shown, as is her interaction with Venus and ultimately her apotheosis at the Olympian court. Boucher's focus stems from his royal commission. His cycle is meant to entertain and demonstrates how prevailing tastes could shape the story of Psyche.[17]

What Natoire and Boucher choose to include and exclude shows the ease with which the Psyche myth can be manipulated according to the patron's demands. Both artists have similar audiences, the nobility in Natoire's case and royalty in Boucher's. The luxury of Cupid's palace and the treasures and easy life found within facilitate comparisons to the physical surroundings of each series. Boucher's depiction of the sudden abandonment of Psyche constitutes a fall from grace, and warns the court nobility of the impermanence of favour. The display of luxury in Natoire's second and third panels corresponds to the fashionable remodeling of the Hôtel de Soubise. Both artists also elide the most myth-

---

Block 1933. For an understanding of the prejudices against Natoire dating to the 1750s and his directorship of the *Académie de France à Rome* see Benhamou 2015.

13 Langlois 1922, 171–2. It is known that Boucher did at least one overdoor for the princess's ceremonial room titled 'The Graces Presiding Over the Education of Cupid'. The panel is dated 1738.
14 The definitive study of these tapestries is Heisinger 1976.
15 For a detailed accounting of each of the six sets, their commissions, and their present locations see Heisinger 1976, 7.
16 Heisinger 1976, 21.
17 Heisinger 1976, 21.

ical elements of Psyche's story, her many labours. The river setting and nymphs in Boucher's abandonment tapestry represent an even more allusive reference to Psyche's labours and many suicide attempts than is found in Natoire's fifth panel, which more closely references one of them. In addition, Boucher's more obviously radical reinterpretation of the myth foregrounds Natoire's standard narrative. Just as with the tapestries, patronage, audience, and context are equally important factors in understanding Natoire's Psyche.

Finally, the dating and potential sources for both series are important factors to consider. Natoire and Boucher both worked on commissions for the Hôtel de Soubise, and thus it is highly likely that Boucher was already familiar with Natoire's Psyche panels in 1737 when he received the royal commission for the tapestries. Heisinger has argued that the allusivity of Boucher's tapestry cycle likely stems from a letter to the artist sent from Louis Petit de Bachaumont, a contemporary critic and connoisseur. Bachaumont suggested a much more involved set of ten paintings (not tapestries) to Boucher. Of critical importance is Bachaumont's encouragement to take a look at earlier French source material, namely La Fontaine and Molière.[18] Heisinger goes on to argue convincingly that Boucher seems to have also worked with source materials independently from the advice he received in Bachaumont's letter and whatever he may have learned from Natoire while working at the Hôtel de Soubise.[19] Heisinger suggests that Boucher shared Bachaumont's letter with Natoire, but Bachaumont's letter is undated.[20] Furthermore, Natoire had previously been commissioned in 1735 for a series of four canvas paintings on Psyche for Louis-Denis de La Live de Bellegarde's salon in his Château de la Chevrette at Saint-Denis.[21] Three of the four works have been identified: 'Venus showing Psyche to Cupid,' 'Psyche Obtaining the Elixir of Beauty from Proserpine,' and 'The Toilet of Psyche.'[22] What is most striking in similarity between Boucher's and Natoire's series is the inclusion of the scene with Psyche and the shepherd. This scene would seem to be a direct reworking of La Fontaine's retired fisherman episode, as it appears nowhere in

---

18 Heisinger 1976, 11. For La Fontaine, Molière and Quinault's versions of the story see Harrison's chapter in this volume.
19 Heisinger 1976, 12–15 argues that Boucher's first three tapestry scenes garner evidence he worked independently from Bachaumont's advice.
20 Heisinger 1976, 10.
21 For a discussion of this commission and the subjects of the panels see Bailey 2002, 36–8; 176, and Bailey 1992, 348–51.
22 The three panels are now separated. The first is in a private collection, the second is located at the Los Angeles County Museum of Art, and the third is located at the New Orleans Museum of Art.

Apuleius.²³ Natoire's panel is undated and therefore it is impossible to determine when it was conceived. Thus, while it remains inconclusive whether Natoire worked directly with Apuleius, considering his previous commissions and the popularity of the works of La Fontaine, Molière and Quinault well into the early 1700s, it is safe to claim that Natoire likely worked with the French material and was undoubtedly well aware of the entire Psyche myth.

Another point of contact between the two series is their respective first scenes. Boucher begins with Psyche's arrival at the palace, which corresponds to Natoire's second panel, the only panel to date from 1737. Natoire's first panel also seems to be the last panel completed, dated to 1739.²⁴ Thus, it is possible that Natoire and Boucher each began their narratives at the same point, and that Natoire came back and added a new beginning at a later date in order to develop the symmetry between panels one through four and five through eight which I have discussed already. It is also now more likely that Natoire originally began with panel two independently, and went back and added panel one at the end after Boucher shared Bachaumont's letter, because Natoire and Bachaumont both begin with a Zephyrus scene followed by Psyche's arrival at Cupid's palace.²⁵ It should be noted, however, that like Boucher later, Natoire worked independently of Bachaumont's sequence since he diverges greatly from Bachaumont's suggestions. Furthermore, Natoire's previous commission for the Château de la Chevrette demonstrates that he was aware of a wider narrative of the *Cupid and Psyche* myth than is depicted in the Hôtel de Soubise. Thus, the comparison with Boucher's tapestries is an important context for the deliberate choices Natoire made in his overall narrative.

4 Historical parallels

4.1 Loggia of Psyche, Villa Farnesina

In addition to the contemporary Psyche cycle executed by Boucher, there were several important historical parallels to Natoire's cycle in the Hôtel de Soubise. In 1505, Agostino Chigi bought land on the banks of the Tiber River near Porta Settimiana in Rome. Construction began soon thereafter and likely ended by

---

23 Heisinger 1976, 20; Cavicchioli 2002, 190–7. For an alternative reading of Boucher's shepherd tapestry see Hussman 1977.
24 Lavezzi 2001, 307. The sequence of completion for the four panels that date to 1738 is unknown.
25 For the titles of Bachaumont's suggested panels see Heisinger 1976, 21, n9.

1510, although finishing touches possibly continued until Chigi's death in 1520.[26] The building, now known as the Villa Farnesina, was designed by architect Baldassare Peruzzi.[27] Many of the great artists of the day received commissions to decorate the interior rooms, including Raphael. The Hall of Galatea and the Loggia of Psyche are two of the most impressive rooms in the villa. Raphael supervised the decoration of the Loggia of Psyche, but the execution was likely that of his pupils, including Giulio Romano.[28] Letters definitively date the completion of the painting in this room to 1517.[29] The decoration is one of Raphael's finest and depicts the adventures of Psyche in the pendentives or spandrels, while the sovereignty of love is shown in the curvilinear triangles with cupids holding the iconographical attributes of other gods. Finally, the vault was covered by two large *trompe l'oeil* 'tapestries' (really paintings) which depict a Council and Banquet of the Gods respectively.[30]

For the purposes of this chapter, two features stand out in any analysis of the Loggia of Psyche. While the room is called the Loggia of Psyche, the actual decoration has more to do with Cupid, Venus, and the gods than it does with the Psyche story as told by Apuleius, in direct contrast to the focus on Psyche's human experience as depicted in Natoire and Boucher. Of the ten spandrels, Psyche appears in just three of them. She is in both of the ceiling depictions. The overwhelming force of the room has more to do with Venus enacting her jealousy and Cupid either showing dominion over all of the gods or pleading for Psyche than it does with depictions of Psyche and her adventures.[31] The first time we see Psyche in the sequence of the spandrels is in the seventh spandrel where she holds the vessel from her final labour, followed by the eighth spandrel where she presents the vessel to Venus, and then again in the tenth spandrel where Mercury lifts her up to Olympus. In the ceiling depictions, Psyche is passive while Cupid pleads to Zeus for her hand in marriage, and then in the Banquet panel she reclines next to Cupid. This sequence hardly tells the tale of Psyche in any complete form.

---

26 Gerlini 2006, 10. Over the years, various restoration efforts have done both good and harm to the original structure and decorations. The most recent and definitive restorations were conducted by Dr. R. Varoli Piazza and were completed in 2001. For a discussion see Gerlini 2006, 3–9.
27 Gerlini 2006, 10.
28 Gerlini 2006, 49. Other pupils were Francesco Penni, Raffaellin Del Colle, and Giovanni da Udine who likely painted the festoons and maybe the animals as well.
29 For a discussion see Gerlini 2006, 50.
30 For a discussion see Rak 2011, 87–90 and Gerlini 2006, 54–6.
31 For a discussion of the dominance of love in this room see Dempsey 1995, 23–4.

The second aspect of importance of the Loggia of Psyche is its location in the villa and its relationship to other parts of the villa. The room housed the original entrance to the building.[32] Guests would have entered through the garden. Thus, the garlands of fruit and nuts that border the entire vault and outline each of the individual spandrels, triangles and ceiling were meant to be a reflection of the garden.[33] The garlands in the Loggia therefore blurred the lines between inside and outside, and marked the Loggia of Psyche as an extension of the exterior garden space. And while it is possible the room is a testament to Chigi's love for his wife Imperia, its location as the entrance hardly seems to convey that message.[34]

4.2 The Chamber of Psyche, Palazzo del Te

Like the Villa Farnesina, the Palazzo del Te was the masterpiece of its time. Federico II Gonzaga held his ducal court in Mantua and commissioned Giulio Romano, the disciple of Raphael, to design the Palazzo del Te; we have already seen that Romano was very likely involved in the decoration of the Villa Farnesina. Construction likely took place between 1525 and 1534.[35] The Chamber of Psyche is located in the northeast corner of the compound overlooking an expansive forecourt. The tale of *Cupid and Psyche* is told at length across the ceiling and lunettes in over twenty-two panels.[36] The gilding of the architectural elements paired with the darkened chiaroscuro effect used by Romano lends a sense of drama to the room while allowing the individual characters to emerge strikingly from the darker background. Romano's depiction leaves out very few episodes from the myth. Unlike Raphael's Loggia of Psyche, the walls of Romano's Chamber of Psyche also portray mythic love scenes.[37] In the curvilinear triangles directly above the lunettes, cupids are shown holding various implements and iconographical attributes. Thus, similar to Raphael's composition, the room's

---

[32] Gerlini 2006, 7.
[33] Gerlini 2006, 49.
[34] For a discussion see Gerlini 2006, 53. It has been speculated that Imperia was perhaps the model for the image of Psyche, but it is also possible that Fornarina, Raphael's obsession at the time, served as the model.
[35] For a discussion see Bazzotti 2013, 16–18.
[36] For a detailed discussion of this room see Bazzotti 2013, 161–9. For a different perspective see Rak 2011, 90–2.
[37] Bazzotti 2013, 167–8.

decorative program displays the triumph of Love/Cupid over all of the gods.[38] The Psyche myth is then just one example of love depicted in the room, albeit the most detailed and important one, and again the focus is on the divine experience and not on Psyche's human emotions.

The location of the Chamber of Psyche adds weight to its decorative program. It opens onto two other rooms which were used as bedrooms by Federico Gonzaga.[39] In this way, the decorative program signals the movement of the guest into the Duke's private sphere. The triumph of Cupid legitimized his own life-long affair with Contessa Isabella Boschetti.[40] Coupled with the fact that this room also contains the dedicatory inscription for the villa, it becomes clear that this was its most important room.[41] The myth of Psyche perfectly complements Gonzaga's sentiments and celebrates his love for Boschetti.

Both the Villa Farnesina and the Palazzo del Te were constructed at times when their owners exerted their greatest influence. Both patrons commissioned some of the greatest artists of their day to depict the myth of *Cupid and Psyche* in important locations in their buildings. Finally, both may have appropriated the story as a representation of their affection for their own lovers. Of the two depictions, while Raphael's Loggia of Psyche is perhaps more well-known, Romano's Chamber of Psyche in the Palazzo del Te more closely follows Psyche's journey and utilizes other myths of desire to create a miniature programmatic theme for that portion of the Palazzo Te. These two interior representations of Psyche are important precursors to Natoire's series of panels in the Hôtel de Soubise.[42]

5 L'Hôtel de Soubise. The context

The Hôtel de Soubise had been acquired in 1700 by François de Rohan, Prince de Soubise. His wife was Anne Julie de Rohan, the one-time mistress of Louis XIV. Of his eleven children, Hercule Mériadec de Rohan, Prince of Maubuisson, Duke of Rohan-Rohan, would inherit the property in 1712 upon his father's death. At

---

38 For a discussion of the eye's movement across the room and how the room extolls the 'sacredness of marriage' see Bazzotti 2013, 168–169.
39 Bazzotti 2013, 35.
40 Bazzotti 2013, 161.
41 Bazzotti 2013, 161.
42 Natoire won the Prix de Rome in 1721 and spent 1723–1728 in Italy so it is likely that he was aware of the depictions of the Cupid and Psyche myth at the Villa Farnesina and the Palazzo Te.

the royal court, the House of Rohan was allowed the rank of Foreign Prince.[43] Thus, that of the Rohan-Soubise was one of the most noble of families. Hercule married his second wife, Marie-Sophie de Courcillon, in 1732. Marie-Sophie was the granddaughter of the Marquis de Dangeau, the famous memoir writer for the court of Louis XIV. This was the second marriage for both. Marie-Sophie was now Princess de Soubise by marriage. This marriage occasioned the remodeling of the Hôtel de Soubise, for which noted architect and designer Germain Boffrand was commissioned.[44] Boffrand positioned the prince's chambers on the ground floor, while the princess was allocated the first floor for her suite. For the interior decoration, only the great painters of the day were commissioned.[45] In addition, Boffrand was in touch with the trends of the time. After the death of Louis XIV, the nobility retreated from Versailles to Paris and built fashionable mansions for themselves.[46] Away from the court, rank and status still reigned: the more rooms a guest traversed, the greater the status of the owner. Also, rococo decorative schemes grew in elaborateness as one approached the final room along the *enfilade*, a series of rooms with aligned doorways. In this way, interiors both architecturally and decoratively reproduced social hierarchy.[47]

Arriving at the Hôtel de Soubise, a guest first experienced the vast colonnaded forecourt and the impressive exterior of the mansion which deliberately echoes Versailles. Upon entering the mansion, the guest could proceed forward on the ground floor toward the prince's suite, or could take the grand staircase to the right and ascend to the first floor toward the princess's suite. Doing so brought the guest to the grand antechamber. Next, following the path along the *enfilade*, the guest entered the assembly hall. The princess's ceremonial room followed next. The *enfilade* terminated in the princess's salon. Following the logic of the *enfilade*, the ceremonial room was often the most prestigious,

---

[43] For a detailed discussion of *les princes étrangers* at the French court see Antonetti 2000, 33–7. For a discussion of the fortunes of the House of Rohan see Antonetti 2000, 49–51.

[44] A previous remodeling of the exterior was commissioned by François de Rohan in the early years of the eighteenth century. At that time, Pierre-Alexis Delamair designed the exterior to mirror Versailles. The statues of the four seasons were done by Robert Le Lorrain. For more information on this period see Castagnet 2012, 123–6 and Ayers 2004, 68–70. For information on Boffrand and his style see Kalnein 1972, 207–20 and Hellman 1997, 151–5.

[45] Castagnet 2012, 125. Jean Restout, Pierre Charles Trémolières, Charles-André van Loo, François Boucher, and Charles-Joseph Natoire all received commissions. For a brief introduction to each and some of their works for the Hôtel de Soubise see Levey 1972.

[46] For information on some of these mansions see Gallet 1972. For a discussion of the nobility in Paris after the death of Louis XIV see Beik 2009, 336, 342–3.

[47] For a discussion see McKay 1994, 72–4 and Scott 1995, 104–16. The rococo was also criticized at the time. For a discussion see Gutwirth 1992, 3–22.

and in rococo interiors, the most elaborate room.⁴⁸ Boffrand's design alters the traditional sequence by placing the ceremonial room, where the princess would receive guests according to rank, as the penultimate room in the sequence. The salon, which in eighteenth century France was not a ceremonial room, is placed last, affording it the most prestige and the most elaborate decoration. By means of a secret door, one could also gain access from the salon to the princess's private sleeping chamber and an accompanying antechamber. Thus, as Sherry McKay has noted, the salon of the princess became an important interstitial space that connected the ceremonial rooms, which hearkened back to traditional representations of rank at the court of Versailles, and the newly-constructed private chambers of the princess, which embodied the emerging values of privacy and family life in the eighteenth century.⁴⁹

The remodeling of the Hôtel de Soubise follows the remodeling of the Hôtel du Maine in 1720. Here, the ambitious Duchesse du Maine sought to challenge via architecture the boundaries of gender, status, and power in the *ancien régime*.⁵⁰ Boffrand was undoubtedly aware of this remodel since the duchess had commissioned him for some of her other projects.⁵¹ The layout of rooms in the Hôtel de Soubise is similar to the Hôtel du Maine in that the suites for the great ladies were located on the first floor, thus raising their perceived status because guests would be forced to use the grand staircase and traverse more rooms to reach their ceremonial room.⁵² Boffrand innovates in his design for the Hôtel de Soubise in the location of the princess's salon and its connection to the private quarters.⁵³ In addition, the liminal space of the salon and its accompanying Psyche panels reminds one of the location of the Chamber of Psyche at the Palazzo del Te. Both chambers are located near private sleeping quarters, directly making a connection with the theme of love, the marriage of the owners, and the architecture of the space. Unlike the Loggia of Psyche at the Villa Farnesina and the Chamber of Psyche at Palazzo del Te, however, Natoire's *Story of Psyche* focuses acutely on Psyche and her journey.⁵⁴ This draws a closer

---

48 Scott 1995, 108.
49 For a discussion see McKay 1994, 74–75. For privacy in eighteenth century Paris see DeJean 2011, 33–51.
50 For an in-depth analysis of the remodeling of the Hôtel du Maine see Lewallen 2009.
51 Lewallen 2009, 2.
52 Lewallen 2009, 16. As due their status, both made use of a balustrade. Both rooms were of crimson colour.
53 Boffrand's design thus afforded Hercule an oval salon directly below the princess's.
54 It should be noted that the salon in the Hôtel de Soubise also features a series of putti just as in the Psyche rooms at the Villa Farnesina and Palazzo Te. Instead of demonstrating the dominance of love as a programmatic theme, here the putti add to the rococo decoration of the room.

connection then between the marriage of Marie-Sophie to Hercule Mériadec, which occasioned the remodeling, and the figure of Psyche depicted in Natoire's panels.

What further distinguishes the representation of Psyche in the princess's salon at the Hôtel de Soubise from its predecessors is the decorative scheme of the entire *enfilade*. The Loggia of Psyche in the Villa Farnesina was but one room on the theme of love. The same can be said of the Chamber of Psyche at the Palazzo Te. Boffrand's decorative scheme established one theme for the whole suite of rooms. From what can be pieced together, the ceremonial room and the salon both featured the theme of love in their decorative commissions. As the two most important rooms in the *enfilade* and from their shared thematic program, the two rooms were clearly in conversation. In this way, while the salon was undoubtedly interstitial and could be closed to the *enfilade*, becoming a private extension of the princess's sleeping chamber, decoratively it had a much closer affinity to the ceremonial presentation room.

The decoration of the princess's ceremonial room established the theme of love and increased the amount of gilding and elaborateness associated with the rococo than was found in the assembly hall. For example, the overdoors in the ceremonial room featured Minerva teaching a young girl the art of weaving and the Graces educating Cupid.[55] Furthermore, the four gilded wall medallions as well as the four gilded medallions in the cornice corner angles all depict various loves of Zeus. Even many of the stucco reliefs depict love stories such as Venus and Adonis, Bacchus and Ariadne, and Diana and Endymion. The relief of Diana and Endymion is located directly above the ceremonial bed and thus draws a close connection to notions of sleep, love, and the marriage of Marie-Sophie to Hercule Mériadec. As the relief is also on the theme of love, it further strengthens the connection between the ceremonial room and the salon, where Natoire's fourth, fifth and seventh panels all feature a slumbering lover. In particular, panel seven and the relief bear a resemblance in terms of the devotion of the god for their mortal lover.

The difference between the decoration of the ceremonial room and the private chambers just on the other side of the salon could not be more striking by comparison. Both the salon and the ceremonial room display the theme of mythic love, which was appropriate considering their public audience. For the princess's private sleeping chamber, however, located through the concealed door from the salon, the overdoor panels depict scenes appropriately private, though

---

[55] Langlois 1922, 171–172. Charles Trémolières, *Minerva teaching a young girl the art of tapestry*, 1737. François Boucher, *The Graces presiding over the education of Cupid*, 1738.

not necessarily solitary for the nobility: Boucher's *Venus Bathing* and Carle Van Loo's *The Toilet of Venus*. Beyond the overdoor panels, not much else is known about the decoration of the princess's private sleeping chamber or the accompanying antechamber. However, there was enough of a stark contrast to the theme of love based on the overdoors to indicate a very different use for the newly remodeled private chambers and more closely align them with the emerging notion of privacy in the eighteenth century. Nonetheless, the location of the salon joined to both the public ceremonial room and the private sleeping chamber reflect the fact that love could have a public and private aspect to it.

The programmatic theme of love was not limited to the suite of the princess. The important ceremonial chamber for the prince, located on the ground floor, mirrored that of the princess, but with modifications. The entire suite of the prince had a more restrained rococo interior, with much less gilding used throughout. For the prince's ceremonial room, four overdoors were commissioned. Each depicted a pair of gods: Charles Trémolières' *The Wedding of Hercules and Hebe*, François Boucher's *Aurora and Cephalus*, Jean Restout's *Neptune and Amphitrite*, and Carle van Loo's *Mars and Venus*.[56] Thus, the theme of love was carried through the entire remodeling of the Hôtel de Soubise. The occasion of the second marriage for both Hercule Mériadec and Marie-Sophie was represented in the rococo love theme depicted in the paintings of both suites. Hercule Mériadec, as head of the noble house of Rohan, had legitimate divine couples portrayed in his ceremonial chamber. While the myths of Cephalus and Mars are not entirely positive in their conception of love, their depictions in the prince's room sanitize the myths, rendering them appropriate for the space and occasion. Indeed, there was a very large portrait of Marie-Sophie done by Jean-Marc Nattier which hung near the ceremonial bed of the prince to make the connection clear between the marriages of the gods and that of Hercule Mériadec and Marie-Sophie.[57] Thus, everlasting married couples grace the prince's chamber, while the passionate loves of Zeus, as well as other mythic couples, decorate the princess's ceremonial chamber. The *Story of Psyche* in the princess's salon is thus not out of place and not isolated. Within the context of the programmatic decorative scheme of the remodeled Hôtel de Soubise, the Psyche myth is one of many examples on the theme of love meant to illustrate and celebrate the recent marriage of Hercule Mériadec and Marie-Sophie. Nonetheless, Natoire's *Story of Psyche* stands out in this overall theme by virtue of its location in the salon, its elaborate rococo decoration, and its extended narrative of the myth.

---

56 For a discussion see Hedley 2004, 58.
57 Garnier 1879, 99.

6 Conclusions

The eight panels that comprise the *Story of Psyche* in the Hôtel de Soubise have a multitude of contexts. They are unquestionably part of the rococo and firmly situated in the decorative tastes of early eighteenth-century France. Nonetheless, Natoire's narrative of the myth is simultaneously in conversation with previous receptions of the Psyche myth in French culture. The story as told by La Fontaine at the court of Louis XIV brought the Psyche myth into the culture of the royal court and responded to the nobility's taste for Arcadia and the countryside as well as entertainment. François Boucher's series of tapestries on the myth followed in this line of development. Natoire's cycle also borrowed some of the taste for the bucolic from La Fontaine, but was more heavily indebted to the long history of the myth's use to commemorate marriages of the nobility.[58] In the Hôtel de Soubise, a comprehensive decorative program connected the myth more closely to other myths of divine marriage and love in both the prince's own remodeled suite, and that for his new bride. Architecture and decoration underscored the centrality of this theme to the remodeling and closely connected the myth of Psyche to Marie-Sophie because of the location of the salon in the suite of rooms and its elaborate decorative program. Much like the myth itself, the Psyche panels in the Hôtel de Soubise continue to survive as a testament to an undying belief in marriage and love. Despite this focus on Psyche's human emotions and her story's happy ending, these paintings are a far cry from Apuleius' much less genteel depiction of Psyche's adventures, which involve her torture at the hands of a cruel goddess. Natoire's, and to a lesser extent Boucher's, versions ask us therefore to revisit Apuleius' text and find evidence for ardent mutual love, especially in Apuleius' portrait of Cupid.

7 Bibliography

Antonetti, G. (2000), 'Les Princes Étrangers' in: Durand 2000, 33–62.
Auraix-Jonchière, P./Volpilhac-Auger, C. (eds.) (2001), *Isis, Narcisse, Psyché entre Lumières et Romantisme*. Clermont-Ferrand.
Ayers, A. (2004), *The Architecture of Paris. An Architectural Guide*, Stuttgart.
Bailey, C.B. (2002), *Patriotic Taste. Collecting Modern Art in Pre-Revolutionary Paris*, New Haven.

---

[58] It should be noted here that the characteristic butterfly representing the soul is absent from Natoire's panels, which further distances this series from the philosophical interpretation. For a previous example of the myth used in connection with marriage, see Gaisser 2008, 119–120.

Bailey, C.B./Hamilton, C.A. (1992), *The Loves of the Gods. Mythological Painting from Watteau to David*, New York.
Banham, J. (ed.) (1997), *Encyclopedia of Interior Design*, London.
Bardet, J.-P. (ed.) (2000), *État et société en France aux XVIIe et XVIIIe siècles, Mélanges offerts à Yves Durand*, Paris.
Bazzotti, U. (2013), *Palazzo Te. Giulio Romano's Masterwork in Mantua*, transl. G. Crerar-Bromelow, London.
Béchu, Philippe and Christian Taillard. (2004), *Les Hôtels de Soubise et de Rohan-Strasbourg*, Somogy éditions d'art.
Beik, W. (2009), *A Social and Cultural History of Early Modern France*, Cambridge.
Benhamou, R. (2015), *Charles-Joseph Natoire and the Académie de France in Rome. A Re-Evaluation*, Oxford.
Block, M. (1933), *François Boucher and the Beauvais Tapestries*, New York.
Bremer-David, C. (ed.) (2011), *Paris Life & Luxury in the Eighteenth Century*. Los Angeles
Castagnet, V./Barret, C./Pegeon, A. (2012), *Le Service éducatif des Archives nationales Par Chemins de traverse*, Villeneuve-d'Ascq.
Cavicchioli, S. (2002), *The Tale of Cupid and Psyche, An Illustrated History*, New York.
DeJean, J. (2011), 'A New Interiority. The Architecture of Privacy in Eighteenth-Century Paris', in: Bremer-David, 33–51.
Dempsey, C. (1995), *Annibale Carracci. The Farnese Gallery, Rome*, New York.
Futre Pinheiro, M.P./S.J. Harrison. (eds.) (2011), *Fictional Traces. Receptions of the Ancient Novel*, Groningen.
Gaisser, J.H. (2008), *The Fortunes of Apuleius and the Golden Ass. A Study in Transmission and Reception*, Princeton.
Gallet, M. (1972), *Paris Domestic Architecture of the 18th Century*, transl. J.C. Palmes, London.
Garnier, E. (1879), 'L'Hôtel de Soubise', *Revue Archéologique* 38: 87–108.
Gerlini, E. (2006), *The Villa Farnesina Alla Lungara*, Rome.
Goodman, D. (1989), 'Enlightenment Salons. The Convergence of Female and Philosophic Ambitions', *Eighteenth-Century Studies* 22, 329–50.
Gutwirth, M. (1992), *The Twilight of the Goddesses. Women and Representation in the French Revolutionary Era*, New Brunswick, N.J.
Hanser, D.A. (2006), *Architecture of France*, Westport, Ct.
Hedley, J. (2004), *François Boucher. Seductive Visions*, London.
Hellman, M. (1997), 'Boffrand, Germain 1667–1754', in: Banham,151–5.
Hellman, M. (2011), 'Enchanted Night. Decoration, Sociability, and Visuality after Dark', in: Bremer-David, 91–113.
Hiesinger, K.B. (1976), 'The Sources of François Boucher's 'Psyche' Tapestries,' *Philadelphia Museum of Art Bulletin* 72, 7–23.
Hussman, G.C. (1977), 'Boucher's 'Psyche at the Basketmakers': A Closer Look,' *The J. Paul Getty Museum Journal* 4, 45–50.
Hyde, M. (2006), *Making Up the Rococo. François Boucher and His Critics*, Los Angeles.
Joulie, F. (2004), 'Natoire and Boucher. Two Studies for a Don Quixote Tapestry', *Metropolitan Museum Journal* 39, 153–159.
Kalnein, W.G. and Levey, M. (1972), *Art and Architecture of the Eighteenth Century in France*, transl. J.R. Foster, Harmondsworth.
Kenney, E.J. (2004), *Apuleius: The Golden Ass or Metamorphoses*, Harmondsworth.

Kimball, F. (1943), *The Creation of the Rococo*, New York.
Lacroix, P. (1963), *France in the Eighteenth Century. Its Institutions, Customs and Costumes*, New York.
Langlois, C.-V. (1922), *Les Hôtels de Clisson, de Guise & de Rohan-Soubise au Marais*, Paris.
Lavezzi, É. (2000), 'Du regard interdit au regard exalté. Le cycle de Psyché peint par Natoire à l'Hôtel de Soubise (1737–1739)', in: Auraix-Jonchière/Volpilhac-Auger, 301–12.
Levey, M. (1972), *Painting and Sculpture in France 1700–1789*, New Haven.
Lewallen, N. (2009), 'Architecture and Performance at the Hôtel du Maine in Eighteenth-Century Paris', *Studies in the Decorative Arts* 17, 2–32.
Mason, H.J. (2011), 'Charikleia at the Mauritshuis' in Futre Pinheiro/Harrison, 3–18.
McKay, S. (1994), 'The 'Salon de la Princesse'. 'Rococo' Design, Ornamented Bodies and the Public Sphere,' *RACAR: reveu d'art canadienne/Canadian Art Review* 21, 71–84.
Praz, M. (1982), *An Illustrated History of Interior Decoration from Pompeii to Art Nouveau*, London.
Rak, M. (2011), 'From word to image. Notes on the Renaissance reception of Apuleius's *Metamorphoses*', in: Futre Pinheiro/Harrison, 83–93.
Reitz, C. and Winker-Horacek, L. (2011), 'Love on a wallpaper. Apuleius in the boudoir', in: Futre Pinheiro/Harrison, 95–107.
Scott, K. (1995), *The Rococo Interior Decoration and Social Spaces in Early Eighteenth-Century Paris*, New Haven.
Whitehead, J. (1992), *The French Interior in the Eighteenth Century*, London.
Winkler, J.J. (1985), *Auctor & Actor. A Narratological Reading of Apuleius' Golden Ass*, Berkeley.
Zimmerman, M. et al. (2004), *Apuleius Madaurensis, Metamorphoses, Text, Introduction, Commentary, Books IV 28–35, V, and VI 1–24*, Groningen.

II Romanticism and Philosophy

Maeve O'Brien
'Pensive pleasures' in prose and poetry. Apuleius, Mary Tighe and eighteenth-century Ireland[1]

Psyche or The Legend of Love by Mary Tighe (1772–1810), based on Apuleius' story of *Cupid and Psyche*, was famous in its day and published in 1795 (privately), 1805, and again in 1811 after her death in 1810.[2] The eighteenth century saw the beginnings of political debate, still live, about the nature of Irish national identity.[3] This paper aims to read Tighe as an Irish author who, adopting elements from the Irish stylised *aisling* poetical form, found her own voice in re-working Apuleius' Latin prose into English verse.[4] The following remarks seek to locate 'the Irish', until lately unseen in any of Tighe's poetry.[5]

1 Historical contexts and literary traditions

This Irish poet has suffered the neglect meted out to writers writing in English in Ireland between 1780 and 1820 by literary historians reluctant to grant 'Irishness'

---

[1] 'Pensive pleasures', *Psyche or the Legend of Love*, Canto 3.341; p.94. My grateful thanks to the editors for their many helpful suggestions.
[2] The text of Tighe I am using is Wordsworth 1992. All page numbers in quotations from the poem are from this text. I add the line numbers in Kramer Linkin 2005.
[3] For example, Morley 2017 explores vernacular song and verse by the Irish speaking populace between the late seventeenth-century and the early nineteenth century. Each chapter presents a text, translation and a commentary. On the turbulence of eighteenth-century Irish politics, historian Jacqueline Hill writes: 'The last decades of the seventeenth and eighteenth centuries were watersheds in Irish history. The 1690s ushered in a new era of penal laws for Catholics and witnessed the start of regular meetings of a more assertive Irish parliament; the 1790s saw the virtual dismantling of those laws and the abolition of that parliament,' (2001, 222).
[4] Ó Buachalla 1992, 43, on the ornate and stylised genre of the *aisling*. The dictionary definition is a dream, vision, a poetical description of an apparition, a scene or picture called up by the imagination in waking hours, Dineen 1927, under *aisling*.
[5] Kramer Linkin 2015, 190, on poems in the archive which pay 'close attention to contemporary aesthetics ... and engagement with national politics.' Behrendt 2007: 'the finest poem of the period by an Irish woman ... paradoxically, contains absolutely nothing that identifies it as unmistakably Irish.' Bourke *et al* 2002 (Vol. IV), esp. Raughter 2002: M. Tighe is mentioned, 509–510.

to writing in English, because to be Irish one had to write in the Irish language.[6] Declan Kiberd's essay 'English and Irish in the Eighteenth Century' in *Idir Dhá Chultúr* ('Between two cultures'), though not mentioning Tighe, does state that literary traditions both Irish and English then enjoyed more cross-pollination and inter-communication than has previously been acknowledged.[7] Recently, Siobhán McElduff's examination of an eighteenth-century Irish language parody of the *Aeneid* shows the links between 'a classical text, a lower class poet's usage of that text to find his own voice, and Ireland's own historical situation.'[8] The question for me is how Tighe remakes what she has found in her study of classical Latin, into a contribution to the creation of her own Irish identity.

Instead of neglect, faint praise at best characterises assessment of Tighe's poetic achievement from the 'second culture', to use Kiberd's term. For example, Keats's own remarks and his high value as a poet have obscured any debt he has to Tighe, and have resulted in a devaluation of her poetry due to Keats' low estimate of it. He says in one of his letters, noting the 'weakness' of her poetry, that Tighe's poetry has 'nothing', and this after he made full use of the work of this Irish poet, as Weller has shown and as May discusses in this volume.[9] The influential Irish classical scholar W.B. Stanford described *Psyche: Or the Legend of Love* as 'pallid' in the nineteen-seventies, and this has been the accepted assessment of her poetry until recently.[10] Her most influential legacy may perhaps be the inclusion of her two fountains of Sorrow and Joy in Canto I, where Cupid 'tempers his unerring darts' in Bulfinch's (1855) summary of *Cupid and Psyche*, which still has avid readers today, as Maurice shows in this volume.[11]

---

6 Vance 1980, 216: 'Life and Literature came to an end in 1690, leaving only an alien Anglo-Irish tradition of writing, inseparable from the culture of the British mainland and undeserving of the name or dignity of Irishness.' Vances's view is that this is wrongheaded, and he sees in the end of the eighteenth century a neglected first Celtic 'revival', 238.
7 Kiberd 1993, 1–25 (chapter I): 'An Béarla agus an Ghaeilge san Octú hAois Déag', 4; and 1: he notes Dean Swift's translations from Gaelic into English, that English with Latin and Greek was taught in hedge schools, that Carolan, the harper, was employed in both Catholic and Protestant houses.
8 McElduff 2011, 243.
9 In December 1818 Keats writes at length to his brother George 'Mrs Tighe and Beattie once delighted me—now I see through them and can find nothing in them—or weakness—yet how many they still delight! Letter 98 in Forman 1935, 259; Kramer Linkin 2005, xviii. Also: Weller 1928; even Weller cannot resist blaming Tighe for 'sentimentalism' in Keats' poetry, xvi.
10 Stanford 1976, 92; Kramer Linkin 2005, xviii-xix 'Introduction', on her popularity in the nineteenth century and her re-evaluation as a Romantic poet in the twentieth.
11 See Tighe 1811, 18–20 (quotation from p. 20).

The Cavan poet Charlotte Brooke (1740–1793) advocated the unity of the Irish (elder) and English (younger) muses of poetry to bridge the two cultures (*Reliques of Irish Poetry* p.vi, 1786). Her 'cultural unionism,' Cathal Ó Háinle's phrase, is clear-eyed about the difficulties of such a consummation: it cannot happen because of the difficulties of rendering the nuances of poetry in the Irish language into English.[12] Brooke fitted into the development of safe 'patriotic antiquarianism' aimed at promoting Irish culture and heritage, though not the Irish language, to first place in Europe.[13] The safe study of romantic antiquarianism which produced looser idealised translations or interpretations of early Irish poems such as those of Brooke dominated the last quarter of the 18th century.[14]

Tighe's version of this political engagement is the 'eloquence of tenderness' to soothe all ills (*Sonnet Addressed to my Mother*). Tighe negotiates between the two cultures by engaging with Latin instead of the Irish language. Though there is no actual Irish or Latin in *Psyche*, the poem engages in a variation of the antiquarianism popular in contemporary Irish culture because it reaches back to the second-century Apuleius. This antiquarianism resulted in the 1793 publication of James Hely's English translation of Roderic O'Flaherty's *Ogygia*, over a century after the Latin original—an indication of how influential O'Flaherty's work was throughout the eighteenth century.[15] In bestowing common 'Milesian' ancestry on both James II and on early Irish kings, *Ogygia* had worked the common links between Ireland and Britain in its own way. Tighe's 'patriotic antiquarianism' appealed to one culture by writing in English, but at the same time sought common links rather than divisions by using Latin, between Irish and English poetic cultures for her era.

Because acknowledging classical debt was then a marker of class, gender and learning, it is easy to understand why Tighe resorted to the classics, even though the classics were for men.[16] Yet, Latin in particular was valued and taught in Irish schools, including hedge schools, and was available to even

---

12 Ó Háinle 1982, 43.
13 Vance 1980, 235. As O' Halloran 2004, 2 says, the practice of antiquarianism in Ireland followed the Renaissance in its interest in Classical antiquity but included also an interest in pre-Christian pre-classical Irish history.
14 Vance 1980, 221.
15 James Hely, *Ogygia, or a chronological Account of Irish Events, collected from ancient documents written originally in Latin by Roderick O'Flaherty Esq*, Translated into English by Rev. James Hely, 2 vols. W. M'Kenzie, Dublin (1793). O'Flaherty's Latin *Ogygia* was published in 1685.
16 Whalley 1972, 195 on the as yet unformed distinction between 'classical' and 'romantic'; Homans 1990, 348 on gendered Classics. The 'romance of antiquity' led to Irish enthusiasm for the Tale of Troy, *Pharsalia*, and the Theban cycle of myths, see Flower 1947, 137.

'lower-class' parties, as noted by McElduff.[17] Spenser's Errour in *The Faerie Queene*, which Tighe admired, has classical antecedents.[18] Thomas Moore, a friend of the Tighes', published translations of Anacreon in 1800.[19] Sidney Owenson's Glorvina in her *The Wild Irish Girl* (1806) also acknowledges such learning, but with humorous references to classical culture and to those who professed expertise in the Greek and Latin classics. Despite her 'unpolished ignorance', Lady Glorvina 'spouts Latin' (p. 42–3) faster than her priestly tutor; the anti-hero Horatio is an expert in Horace, but only in one of his more well-known odes (p.22); and arguably, in a parody of the *aisling* vision in Tighe, Glorvina appears to the ill Horatio by his bed as a cherub in a dream (p.60).[20] Humorous parodies were common in Irish literature, notably in Brian Merriman's (1740–1808) poem, *The Midnight Court* (*Cúirt an Mheán Oíche*), the awful woman who appears to the poet is a parody of the godlike woman (*spéirbhean*) or young beauty (*ógbhean*) of the *aisling*. Tighe thought *The Wild Irish Girl* affected because of all its Latin borrowings, which were often misread or mistranslated.[21] Tighe may have been taking the novel too seriously, but an example of 'Latin' from the novel that may have annoyed Tighe is the *ignus* [sic] *fatuus* of Horatio's love for Glorvina (p.165). Tighe knew her Latin, learned at home, and she makes no mistakes in, for example, rendering Apollo's oracle into English verse (*Met.* 4.33 & *Psyche or the Legend of Love*, Canto 1.298–306; p.26).[22] In the *Metamorphoses*, the narrator of the entire novel steps in and says that although the oracle of Apollo at Miletus normally speaks Greek, really the prophecy must be delivered in Latin because the author of the *Metamorphoses* understands Latin better. Tighe recognises Apuleius' joke and trumps it by translating the oracle almost word for word into English, showing she, too, has command of anoth-

---

17 McElduff 2011, 243; on the classical education offered in hedge schools, O'Higgins 2007, 421–450 and 2017; also McManus 2002, 107–34.
18 See Pheifer 1984, 127–174. *Psyche: The Legend of Love* is composed in six cantos of Spenserian stanzas: rhyme scheme: abab bcbc cdcc; Kramer Linkin 2005, 295 n.6.
19 Stanford 1976, 90–112 (Chapter 5 'Anglo-Irish Literature'), for these and more examples.
20 Kirkpatrick 1999. The Tighes and Lady Morgan were acquainted, Kramer Linkin 2005, 324 n. 57.
21 Buchanan 2011, 99. Ó Crualaoich 1983, 69: Tighe picked up her knowledge of Latin where she could as did Keats and the Irish poet, Brian Merriman. On the latter, see Welch 1996, 363 and 127.
22 Her mother Theodosia in her journals maintains that Mr Henry Tighe, Mary's husband, taught her: 'he (i.e. Henry) saw that his wife did not love him though he loved her. She always spent her mornings in study and it was from him that she acquired her knowledge of Latin. To her industry in this respect may be attributed the fact that she was afterwards able to undertake the difficult task of composing "Psyche"' (*Wicklow papers NLI MS* 4810).

er language, Latin, though her poem is written in English. Her joke is learned and alive to the nuances of translation and interactions between cultures.

2 The poem: *Psyche or The Legend of Love*

Tighe addresses her ideal reader directly:

> Oh you for whom I write! Whose hearts can melt
> At the soft thrilling voice whose power you prove,
> You know what charm unutterably felt,
> Attends the unexpected voice of Love.
> (Canto 1.451–454; p.34).

Her ideal reader knows the power and charm of the 'unexpected voice of love.' She can best tell the 'rapture Psyche feels/when Love's ambrosial lip the vows of Hymen seals.' (Canto 1.458–9; p.34). Tighe explores Psyche's psychological state, her sadness, her soul 'dismayed', she is the 'mournful bride' alone and tended only by female voices, yet Psyche also feels 'rapture' and joy (Canto, 1.470; p. 35). The reason emphasised for Psyche's desolation in Apuleius is that all have forsaken Venus' shrines to 'worship' Psyche. Psyche is removed from her family in an offering to assuage Venus. Although Psyche's physical beauty causes her loneliness and dislocation, the effect of her beauty on others is the focus in the *Metamorphoses* and sets the plot in motion.[23] In contrast, Psyche's own state of mind when she is faced with this situation is what Tighe chooses to explore in six cantos in *Psyche, or The Legend of Love*. In the Latin version, Apuleius continues to exploit the fairy-tale-style narrative for the inner thoughts of his heroine. Psyche, a recently married princess bride (*novam nuptam*, *Met.* 5.4), is afraid because she thinks she is married to the 'wild and snake-like' monster foretold in the words of the oracle (*Met.* 4.33).[24]

Throughout Psyche's wanderings, before she is restored to her husband and her knight, Tighe matches the fairy-tale atmosphere of Apuleius where Psyche meets and speaks to Pan (Hircuosus), a Green Reed, an Eagle, and a tower in

---

23 Panayotakis and Panayotakis 2015, 136–7. On how Tighe's syntax, used for example in 'men her wondrous beauty deified' (Canto 1.57), underscores the reflexivity of male admiration, revealing how their admiration of her objectifies them, while they admire Psyche as an object of beauty, Kramer Linkin 2005, xxvi ('Introduction').
24 And the reader who is attentive is informed by the narrator (who is not Psyche) that her wedding was not an ordinary wedding, it was celebrated with the solemnities of a funeral (*feralis thalami*, *Met.* 4.34).

her quest to regain Amor/Cupid, though Tighe extends the length of the quest. She admits in the poem's preface that she has followed the outline of Apuleius' story in the first two cantos only.²⁵ Cantos 4–6 express the longing of one individual for another, or, allegorically, of the soul's longing for love. Apuleius' *Cupid and Psyche* has been interpreted allegorically as a fable about divine Love and the Soul almost from the time it was composed.²⁶ In the Preface (x) to *Psyche* Tighe maintains that 'innocent love' obviously approximating to the emotion denoted by *diligere* is her theme.²⁷ She feels the need to reinforce this point, especially stressing the 'innocent' idea in the sonnet to her mother that precedes *Psyche or the Legend of Love*. This suggests that she was aware that the passion of love as a literary topic by a woman involving a female character at this time in the late eighteenth century/early nineteenth century would cause some censure, which she is anxious to avoid.²⁸ Tighe counters any arguments from her readership about 'veiled forms of allegory' hiding an immoral or even a treasonous story in poetry. She avers, with some humour, that 'perplexed allegory' is always a poetic device, and not a cover or a dissimulation: 'I have however remembered that my verse cannot be worth much consideration, and have therefore endeavoured to let my meaning be perfectly obvious.' ('Preface', p. xii). She takes the opportunity her Latin source offers to describe a woman's strong emotion, meaning the female voice is 'perfectly obvious' in her poem to those who would hear it.²⁹ For this, her poetry has been criticised as sentimental

---

25 Tighe acknowledges her debt to Apuleius in her preface to *Psyche:* 'The loves of Cupid and Psyche have long been a favourite subject for poetical allusion, and are well known as related by Apuleius: to him I am indebted for the outline of my tale in the two first cantos; but even there the model is not closely copied.'
26 Purser 1910: xliv-lxv ('Introduction') and 128–31 ('Excursus II'); Kenney 1990, 27–28. Arkins 2002, 222: what makes Apuleius count for W.B. Yeats is 'a reading of *The Golden Ass* as an allegory of soul searching for truth.'
27 Tighe must surely have noticed the difference in terminology in *Met.* 5.6 when Psyche pleads with her husband: 'I love you (*diligo*) as much as I love my own soul', and that Apuleius uses *diligere*, spoken by the woman before she actually sees Cupid. This Latin verb denotes family love that is between children and their parents or between siblings. Yet, after she looks upon the sleeping Cupid the power of Psyche's passion, her changed love is reflected in the Latin words *inhians* 'avidly gazing' and *efflictim* 'passionately' (*Met.* 5.23).
28 Schellenberg 2005, 2 ('Introduction: "building on public approbation"').
29 On her 'coterie of readers' who might just so do, and recognise the parallels between Psyche and Tighe as beautiful women not permitted to marry the men of their choice, see Kramer Linkin 2010, 304.

and excessively wearying.³⁰ Yet, sentimentalism can be seen as a strategy to validate the power of personal and private feeling in the eighteenth century.³¹

Tighe's reading also included many works of Irish antiquarianism.³² It may be apposite to seek out an obvious female voice in poetry composed in Ireland, specifically in the *aisling* or dream-vision allegorical poem written in Irish. The learning, poetic talent and eloquence of the male poets who composed *aisling* poetry was greatly esteemed. Aodhan Ó Rathaile (1670–1726), the author of the first political *aisling, Mac an Cheannai* ('The Redeemer's Son'), or Eoghan Rua Ó Súilleabháin (1748–1784), author of 'Ceo Draíochta' ('The Magic Mist'), are more known in Ireland today than Mary Tighe or her poem. 'The Mower' (*An Spealadóir*) by Ó Súilleabháin illustrates the basic elements of the *aisling*: the poet addresses the reader 'in my dream I wandered far' and met 'a star,/ more fair than earthly maidens are'; the beauty of the woman is formulaic, her hair is luxuriant and flowing and her ornate headdress is decorated with: 'blithe Cupid ... his quiver full of darts, as poets tell'. Her 'skin the lily put to shame,/Her posture that of swan on stream,/Her chiselled brows a classic frame/For roses in cheek'; they converse: 'her gentle voice was soft and low... I ventured on the tranquil scene,/and modestly approached my queen/her lineage to seek.... She answered me between her sighs, ... "Behold in me the rightful queen,/the spouse of Charles"; she is sad and lonely 'with my hero o'er sea'; she yearns for a time 'when at last the Gaels arise,/the music of the Saxon sighs/will bring more gladness to mine eyes than the mower's sweet lay.'³³

Tighe may have had knowledge of these poems from wandering ballad sellers with their chapbooks, from Thomas Moore, or from her charity work with the young women in her mother's and uncle's hospital.³⁴ This may have inspired her to create

---

30 Hogan 1979, 1189: Psyche is 'utterly conventional and excessively wearying'. Motion 1997, 95: Leigh Hunt's poem *The Story of Rimini* (1816) is 'closely akin to the sentimental work of Mary Tighe.'
31 This is not my topic here, for further on the value of sentimentalism as a strategy to validate the power of personal and private feeling as opposed to public and legal codes, see Rodgers 1982, 143 'The Liberating effect of Sentimentalism'. White Beck 1996, 2 on the 'denigration of passion' in eighteenth-century philosophy and, p.5, how this attitude was challenged by Rousseau and Burke for example.
32 NLI papers, MS 4804 'Reading Journal' of 1806–1809, existence of journal noted in Kramer Linkin 2005, 258–9.
33 Translation by O'Sullivan 1960, in Caerwyn Williams and Ford 1992, 231–4. For twenty-one other poems by Ó Súilleabháin, see Muldowney 2002. Also, Ó Tuama and Kinsella 1981, 186–91.
34 Edward Tighe (b. 1740-?), Member of Parliament for Wicklow, was her mother's brother, and Henry, the poet's husband, was his son. Theodosia and her brother co-operated as devout Meth-

a longer poem than the *aisling*, but inspired by the latter's use of the device of the dream-vision.³⁵ Despite characterizing her poetic activity as courting repose in 'slumbery lay' in her introductory stanza and bidding farewell to any more 'visionary scenes' in the final stanza, Tighe is not the dreamer within the English poem. It may be the case that there is a doubling of the *aisling* form in the sense that Tighe sees a vision of Psyche, who then sees a vision of Cupid. 'Solitary' (Canto 1.46; p.12) similar to the *aisling* male dreamer, Psyche lies down to rest in the shade of woodland, a 'quiet spot' (Canto 1.31; p.11). Yet, in pointed contrast to the *aisling* dream, the scene shifts and Psyche's vision appears when she sleeps indoors (Canto 1.217–225; p.21), and her dream 'of mingled terror and delight' (Canto 1.262; p.24) exhausts her at the start of the poem, not at its end, as is the case in the Irish *aisling*.³⁶ The poet of the Irish *aisling* inserts himself into the dream where he tells how a beautiful godlike woman appears to him in a lonely place outdoors; this woman and the poet converse and she identifies herself as the bereaved wife of the rightful Irish King, usually the exiled Stuart king, who has been usurped; she prophesies his return and restoration to her.³⁷ The woman represents 'Ireland' in the *aisling* of the eighteenth century, making this type of poetry part of a political discourse in which 'Eire' bereft and lonely is ever yearning for her husband's return to her and to his country.³⁸ As with Psyche in Tighe's poem, the female figure is depicted as dignified, 'centre stage', making a political message 'accessible' in the eighteenth-century *aisling*. This is achieved, as the eminent scholar Máirín Nic Eoin says, simply by giving her a familiar name, like Cathleen or Síle, so 'that the female figure comes centre stage, and it is the depiction of a symbolic female figure in familiar guise which makes the political message in these poems accessible to a popular audience.'³⁹ Psyche makes a different political message 'accessible'. Tighe's Psyche reflects a yearning for a freedom of sorts, from 'the politics of beauty and the compulsion to marry well' felt by women especially in eighteenth century culture.⁴⁰ Just as the sleeping poet in the *aisling* longs for change in Irish society, for the roles of those in authority and those who had no power to be reversed, 'unhappy Psyche' seeks freedom from 'the pining sorrows which her soul oppress' (Canto 1.253 and 259; p.23).⁴¹

---

odists in founding a home for abandoned girls in Dublin in 1791, Bourke *et al* 2002 (Vol. V), esp. Roughter 2002, 687–8.
35 Ó Tuama and Kinsella 1981, xxvi-xxix ('Introduction'). Welch 1996, 9–10 on the *aisling*.
36 Leerssen 1986, 271.
37 McQuillan 2011, 21 outlines the *aisling* 'archetypal form.'
38 See Murphy 1939, 40–50.
39 Nic Eoin 1996, 7 and 20.
40 Kramer Linkin 2005, xxxi ('Introduction').
41 Ó Buachalla 1992, 45.

Recently, Ní Úrdail has pointed to 'the female voice markedly audible' in Irish language poetry about expectations men and women had of love and marriage in 'uninhibited, and often robust' language.[42] At the close of *The Legend of Love*, Psyche becomes immortal and enjoys a 'bliss too vast for thought' (Canto 6.277; p.205), presented in the most robust language in the poem. Cupid and Psyche are united: 'in one rapturous glance their mingling souls they tell' and the knight, who is of course Cupid/Love/Amor, is revealed on marriage ('unveiled his charms appear': Canto 6.465–68; p.205), and the poet urges Psyche to turn and see him at last. In *Metamorphoses* 5.4, Psyche is described as *nuptam* denoting her marriage to Cupid; *nuptam* also means 'covered' according to Young's Latin-English dictionary popular in the late eighteenth-century—an edition also published in Dublin in 1793 was possibly used by Tighe.[43] Tighe's knight 'beaming delight and love unspeakable' (Canto 6.467; p.205), enters Psyche's world of emotion. Cupid is married, and Cupid's new status is denoted when, his helmet fallen from his face, his charms are unveiled. Now the Latin verb *nubere* is used of women in Latin to denote marriage, as it is for Psyche in Apuleius. Tighe thus appropriates *nubere* for the male participant in the marriage ceremony, creating a kind of syntactical equality, because this verb is rarely used in Latin to denote a man who is marrying. He has made the psychological journey, and both lovers have achieved equal status like two tapers joined in one flame: 'Two tapers thus, with pure converging rays,/In momentary flash their beams unite' (Canto 6.469–470; p.205).[44] The poem ends with an address to Fond Youth. This personification, unlucky in love, is urged never to give in to despair, and to always seek the final 'one dear embrace' (Canto 6.495; p.206) and to identify with Psyche: 'And catch that softly pleasurable sigh,/That tells unutterable ecstasy!' (Canto 6.508–9; p.207). Observe that while Tighe emphasises the power of love here, the motif of the loneliness of the human love in this figure of Fond Youth and the possibility of betrayal in love are also emphasised. Loneliness and betrayal, the opposites of the unmingled bliss of trust and unity, are equal elements in the power of passion. The eighteenth-century *aisling* in the

---

42 Ní Úrdail 2007, 150.
43 I have not been able to check whether Tighe did use this dictionary. William Young (d.1757), *A New Latin-English Dictionary* (1792). The title states: 'Designed for the General Use of Schools and Private Gentlemen. By the Rev. Mr. William Young, Editor of Ainsworth's Dictionary'. One of the later editions published in London in 1792 was published in Dublin, printed by William Porter, in 1793. The entries are not detailed, so that under *nubo*, meanings are listed as '1. to cover, 2. to cover or be married *de feminis*' and so on. See Eighteenth Century Collections Online (*ECCO*): image 743, *nubere*.
44 Wordsworth 1992, 5 ('Introduction').

Irish language also deals in dreams where betrayal and loneliness are common motifs.

The dream device in the opening scenes of *The Legend of Love* (Canto 1.217–222; p.21). 'sets the scene': Cupid 'wrapt in a cloud unseen by mortal eye' (Canto 1.217; p.21) appears to Psyche 'her radiant eyes a downy slumber sealed' as she sleeps (Canto 1.222; p.21):

> Nor was it quite a dream, for as she woke,
> Ere heavenly mists concealed him from her eye,
> One sudden transitory view she took
> Of Love's most radiant bright divinity;
> From the fair image never can she fly,
> As still consumed with vain desire she pines;
> (Canto 1.280–285; p.25).

Psyche sees Cupid in her mind's eye, 'not quite a dream', in a type of vision or *aisling*. Tighe makes a couple of changes to the use of this device in the *aisling* poem: the male figure appears to the female here; and the male is the godlike figure, whereas the female is the goddess in the *aisling*. After the wedding night, when Psyche in her mind's eye sees her husband as 'some Being nigh' (Canto 1.450; p.39), her reference to him points to his divine status. Because Psyche had '*seen*' the beauty of her husband in her dream, she is conditioned by this dream to identify his beauty with the ringletted beauty of Cupid: 'Oh, by those beauties I must ne'er behold!/the spicy-scented ringlets of thine hair' (Canto 1.532–33; p 39).[45] In Apuleius, Psyche does not know who her husband is, so when she actually looks upon him as *he* sleeps, punning humour takes precedence over psychological motivation, as she says:

> te, quicumque es, diligo aeque ut meum spiritum, nec ipsi Cupidini comparo.
>
> You, whoever you are, I love you as much as I love my own soul and I do not compare you to even Cupid himself. (Apuleius, *Met.* 5.6).

Cupid and Psyche do not speak in Tighe's dream scene, and she departs from that convention in the *aisling*, concentrating on its vision imagery instead. The dream scene in *The Legend of Love* is lavished with attention; literary play around notions of sight and vision is relished by Tighe just as it is by Apuleius

---

45 This description in Tighe mirrors the one in Apuleius when she actually does look on Cupid 'she looks upon her lover's golden-haired ringlets wafting with heavenly scent: *videt capitis aurei genialem caesariem ambrosia temulentam* (*Met.* 5.22).

and by the composers of the Gaelic *aislingí*. Placing Psyche centre-stage even though she has lost her beauty means that her mind, her soul, her thoughts, not her looks, are pointed to as the main concern. In Apuleius, Psyche is the very image of Venus, so much so that she is characterised as a vision, a statue 'they all wonder at her as at a statue (*simulacrum*) consummately finished by a sculptor': *ut simulacrum fabre politum, mirantur omnes* (*Met.* 4.32).[46] In *The Legend of Love* when Cupid appears to Psyche in the dream his 'smooth neck's unblemished ivory' (Canto 1.246; p.23), make of him a sort of *simulacrum*, and his smooth ivory form becomes the admired one:

> Of wond'rous beauty did the vision seem ...
> His form she oft invokes her waking eyes to bless.
> (Canto 1.271, & 279; p.24).

Keats, *Ode to a Nightingale:* 'was it a vision or a waking dream? Fled is that music: do I wake or sleep?' attests to the power of these lines.[47] Psyche, who views Cupid's *fair image* on her own (Canto 1.284; p.25), sees a sight to inspire 'grateful transport.' His image is so 'wondrous' it invokes her to prayer, in a reading of Apuleius' *mirantur omnes* (*Met.* 4.32), where Apuleius' phrase describes the 'image' of, not Cupid but Psyche, whose beauty is worshipped by all, causing Venus' shrines to be neglected in her favour. In Tighe's poem, Psyche's inner mental state causes her to lose her outward beauty: 'Unhappy Psyche! Soon the latent wound/The fading roses of her cheek confess' (Canto 1.253–4; p.23), not a symptom the woman possessed of 'roses in cheek' in the *aisling* suffers, because despite all her difficulties that woman is a goddess. The reason Psyche feels as she does is because in the dream she has had, Love has wounded her; the symptom of her deep psychological passion is illustrated by her subsequent illness. Cupid is now the object gazed at and praised, mirroring the way the Apuleian Psyche, *specimen gloriosum* (*Met.* 4.29), was looked upon and praised (*spectatur... laudatur, Met.* 4.32). Cupid, 'Love's most radiant bright divinity' (Canto 1.280; p.25), renders *divinam speciem* as Psyche was (*Met.* 4.32). Cupid's 'fair image' (Canto 1.284; p.25) unseen by mortal eye rereads Venus's *imaginem meam*, 'my double Psyche' who is looked at by all (*Met.* 4.30). Aware, too, of the Latin where Cupid's proper name is nearly always rendered Amor and where *amor* denotes the emotion love, the keen eighteenth-century language student

---

[46] She is the image of me, says Venus, *imaginem meum circumferet puella moritura, Met.* 4.30. Also on Cnidos Venus' altars and statues are not tended: *Met.* 4.29, *incoronata simulacra et arae viduae frigido cinere foedatae.*
[47] As Weller 1928 notes, lines 79–80.

foregrounds the emotion *amor* or love in her poem whose alternative title is *The Legend of Love*.

Punning in Apuleius is turned to serve a serious purpose by Tighe in her treatment of the pun on the wounded soul in *Metamorphoses*. The reason emphasised for Psyche's desolation in Apuleius is that all have forsaken Venus' shrines to 'worship' Psyche. The people's worship of Psyche means that she has no friends, no lover, just devotees. She has no lover—who wants to embrace an image, a statue? Wounded to the core, sick in spirit (*animi saucia*, *Met*. 4.32); here we find the conventional metaphor of sickness reserved for one who has a lover in Latin poetry, as noted in Kenney's commentary; she hates her beauty.[48] The pun on her name here is repeated when 'Psyche in her innate curiosity' (*Met*. 5.23.1) injures herself with one of Cupid's darts while he sleeps (*Met*. 5.23.2), and wounds him with hot oil from her lamp (*Met*. 5.23.4). And so Psyche falls unawares in love with Love:[49]

> Sic ignara Psyche sponte in Amoris incidit amorem...Tunc magis magisque cupidine flagrans Cupidinis, prona in eum efflictim inhians...
>
> Then ever more on fire with desire for Desire she hung over him gazing (*inhians*) in her distraction (*efflictim*) and devoured him with quick wanton kisses... (Apuleius, *Met*. 5.23.1–3).

This famous description of the sleeping Cupid, where the Apuleian Psyche burns Cupid with oil from her lamp and wounds herself with one of his arrows in a breaking of the taboo he enjoined on her, is reprised in Tighe's version in two different places. The wounding is set in the dream description in Canto I when Cupid wounds Psyche and his own 'smooth neck's unblemished ivory' with one of his own darts as he gazes at her while she sleeps (Canto 1.244–6; p.23). It is only later in *The Legend of Love* that Psyche looks at Cupid by the flickering light of a lamp (Canto 2.177–8; p.55). There is no taboo in *The Legend of Love*, because Cupid abandoned Psyche first and wounded her and himself in the dream in Canto 1, making the rest of the poem about her quest to find love, a cure for love's 'latent wound.' Cupid becomes the unseen cause of Psy-

---

48 Kenney 1990, 29–130; Zimmerman *et al*. 2004, 81–2.
49 References abound: *Met*. 5.22.1: *Tunc Psyche et corporis et animi alioquin infirma*: 'then Psyche though naturally weak in body and mind'; *Met*. 5.22.3: *Psyche tanto aspectu deterrita et impos animi*: 'Psyche was unnerved at the sight as was no longer mistress of herself'; *Met*. 5.22.5 ...as she [i.e. Psyche] gazed and gazed on the beauty of the god's face, her spirits returned (*recreatur animi*); *Met*. 5.23.1: *insatiabili animo Psyche*; *Met*. 5. 23.4. *tanto bono percita saucia mente fluctuat* 'carried away by this enjoyment, the prey of her conflicting passions.' Translations are from Kenney 1990. For a comic version of this pun and its frequency in the reception of Cupid and Psyche see Ragno in this volume.

che's physical decline noticed by all, a decline that mirrors the strong effect seeing him in her dream had on her 'soul' or *psyche*. Tighe delivers Psyche from her Apuleian epithet *ignara* ('unknowing') and breaks a different taboo by allowing herself space to reveal Psyche's desires and passions. In her use of the motif of dream vision of the *aisling*, and in her rereading of Apuleius, she reveals the power of the emotion of love in the story when it is told by a woman about a woman.

The dream in Canto 1 foregrounds the love between Cupid and Psyche. Love is privileged as the driver of the action rather than (as in Apuleius) the hatred of Venus for her false *imago* Psyche. The dream vision (not in Apuleius) is an Irish dream vision, an *aisling*, with one important variation, as Cupid (male) appears to the sleeping Psyche who is lying asleep, whereas in the *aisling* the 'fairy woman' appears to the poet (always a man) sleeping. Otherwise, the similarities are striking: the *aisling* mourns the loss of some happy time in the past; Psyche mourns the loss of her love because Tighe's poem begins after she has lost him; the *aisling* hopes for a return to happiness in the future victorious time; Psyche does this also.[50] Tighe's (unhappy) Psyche has already 'lost' love and she knows it:

> Forgetful of the dangers of her way
> imagination oft would Psyche bear
> to her long travel's end, and that blest day
> when Love unveiled should to her eyes appear.
> (Canto 3.361–4; p.95).

Psyche does not see love 'for real' until Canto 6 only after she has heroically avoided the Bower of loose Delight (Canto 3), Disfida's Castle (Canto 4), Castabella's palace of Chastity and the coast of Spleen (Canto 5), and finally Glacella's cold land of Indifference (Canto 6). The land she finds love in is as a place imagined in a dream 'her soul intent' might survey (Canto 6.424–5; p.203) The description in Canto 6 of 'each well known scene' of 'sloping green' speaks to Psyche's soul and recalls the land of her dream in Canto 1 where over the 'varied scene' Eternal Spring spread her 'mantle green' (Canto 1.140; p.17). The notion of the 'cup of amorous delight' (Canto 1.192; p.20) becomes the urn Psyche now places on the altar of Venus (Canto 6.460; p.205). It is at this point that Psyche and her knight see one another. In the earlier dream Psyche cannot join with Desire because of 'Fortune's envious spite' (Canto 1.193; p.20), and because mortals cannot 'drink unmingled of that current bright' where Desire stands. In Canto 6, Cupid and Psyche unite and, at last, Psyche is a goddess. The apotheo-

---

50 Ní Úrdail 2007, 133.

sis of Psyche completes the poem: her charms become immortal and she enjoys heavenly bliss (Canto 6.531; p.208).

3 Conclusion

'Dreams of Delight farewell!' Psyche has left the page and 'the visionary scenes no more I see' says the poet in the final stanza of the poem (Canto 6.532 and 539; p.209). Tighe achieves her objective of emphasising how a woman should deal with 'power of mighty Love' (Canto 1.11), by re-reading Apuleius' tale about Psyche and her lost love. Yet, longing to return to a lost love whom the unhappy lover cannot see is a characteristic element not only in Apuleius but also in the *aisling*. The taboo on looking at Cupid prevents Psyche looking in Apuleius, the exigencies of history prevent the union of the *spéirbhean* (god-like woman) and her lover, and her scheming sisters and her own 'mortal chillness' separate Psyche from her beloved in Canto 2 (2.245; p. 59). Tighe exploits the vision imagery in the Latin story and appropriates the dream device from the *aisling* poem to assert 'her own right to look as a visionary woman poet.'[51] Pensive pleasures are her delight:

> They do not love, who can to these prefer
> The tumult of the gay, or folly's roar;
> The Muse they know not.
> (Canto 3.43–345; p.94).

She uses an acceptable form, a classical tale, and reforms it to negotiate erotic affect in *Psyche or the Legend of Love*. Similarly, Seamus Heaney has revealed how Brian Merriman's Gaelic poem *The Midnight Court*, contemporary with Tighe, is backlit by the myth of Orpheus as it appears in Ovid's *Metamorphoses*.[52] The myth of Cupid and Psyche as it appears in Apuleius, *Metamorphoses*, and the female presence found centre stage in the *aisling*, allows Tighe to illumine Psyche in 'vivid colours' (Canto 6.540; p.209). Mary Tighe's source is Apuleius, and 'the words or images which floated upon my mind' as she says in her Preface (xiv) from the Latin prose of Apuleius and from the Gaelic lyric *aisling*, make her reception of her classical source at once international and Irish.

---

[51] Kramer Linkin 2005, xxv.
[52] Heaney 1995: 57 ('Orpheus in Ireland'), on Merriman (1748–1805) *The Midnight Court*.

4 Bibliography

Arkins, B. (2002), 'The Roman world in Irish writers', *Irish University Review* 32, 215–24.
Behrendt, S.C. (2007), *Ireland and Romanticism*, Alexandria, VA. 42pp., in: *Irish Women poets of the Romantic period,* http://lit.alexanderstreet.com/iwrp [accessed 30th May 2017].
Bourke, A. et al. (eds.) (2002), *Field day anthology IV. Irish women's writing and traditions*, New York.
Boyce, D., Eccleshall, R./Geoghegan, V. (eds.) (2001), *Political discourse in seventeenth- and eighteenth-century Ireland*, Basingstoke.
Buchanan, A. (2011), *Mary Blachford Tighe. The Irish Psyche*, Newcastle upon Tyne.
Bulfinch, T. (1855), *The Age of Fable: Stories of Gods and Heroes*, Boston.
Connolly, P.G. (ed.) (1982), *Literature and the changing Ireland*, Totowa NJ.
de Brún, P./Ó Coileáin, S./Ó Riain, P. (eds.) (1983), *Folia Gadelica*, Cork.
Dineen, P. (1927, repr. 1970), *Foclóir Gaedhilge agus Béarla/An Irish-English Dictionary, being a thesaurus of the words, phrases and idioms of the modern Irish language, with explanations in English.* Irish Texts Society, Dublin.
Eichner, H. (ed.) (1972), *'Romantic' and its cognates. The European history of the word*, Toronto.
Flower, R. (1947), *The Irish Tradition*, Oxford.
Forman, M.B. (ed.) (1935), *The Letters of John Keats*, Oxford.
Harrison, S.J. (ed.) (2015), *Characterisation in Apuleius' Metamorphoses. Nine studies*, Newcastle upon Tyne.
Heaney, S. (1995), *The Redress of Poetry*, New York.
Hill, J. (2001), 'Politics and the writing of history. The impact of the 1690s and 1790s on Irish historiography', in: Boyce/Eccleshall/Geoghegan, 222–39.
Hogan, R. (ed.) (1979 and 1996), *Dictionary of Irish literature. Revised and expanded edition* (M-Z), London.
Homans, M. (1990), 'Keats reading women, women reading Keats', *Studies in Romanticism* 29, 341–70.
Kenney, E.J. (1990), *Apuleius: Cupid and Psyche*, Cambridge.
Kiberd, D. (1993, reprint 2002), *Idir Dhá Chultúr*, Dublin.
Kirkpatrick, K. (1999), *Sidney Owenson, Lady Morgan, The Wild Irish Girl. A National Tale*, Oxford.
Kramer Linkin, H. (2005), *The collected poems and journals of Mary Tighe*, Lexington.
Kramer Linkin, H. (2010), 'Mary Tighe. A portrait of the artist for the twenty-first century' in: Wright, 291–309.
Kramer Linkin, H. (2015), 'Reassessing Mary Tighe as a lyrical and political poet. The archival discovery of Tighe's *Verses Transcribed for H.T.* (1805)', *Women's Writing* 22, 189–208.
Leerssen, J. (1996), *Mere Irish & Fíor-Ghael. Studies in the idea of Irish nationality, its development and literary expression prior to the nineteenth century*, Amsterdam.
McElduff, S. (2011), 'Not as Virgil has it. Rewriting the *Aeneid* in 18th century Ireland', *International Journal of the Classical Tradition* 18, 226–45.
McManus, A. (2002), *The Irish hedge school and its books, 1695–1831*, Dublin.
McQuillan, P. (2011), Loneliness versus delight in the eighteenth-century aisling,' *Eighteenth-Century Ireland/Iris an dá chultúr* 25, 11–32.

Morley, V. (1997), *The popular mind in eighteenth-century Ireland*, Cork.
Motion, A. (1997), *Keats*, London.
Muldowney, P. (2002), *Eoghan Rua Ó Súilleabháin: Nah Aislingí/Vision Poems*, Cork.
Murphy, G. (1939), 'Notes on aisling poetry', *Éigse* 1, 40–50.
Ní Úrdail, M. (2007), 'The representation of the feminine. Some evidence from Irish-language sources', *Eighteenth-Century Ireland/Iris an dá chultúr* 22, 133–50.
Nic Eoin, M. (1996), 'Secrets and disguises? Caitlin Ní Uallacháin and other female personages in eighteenth-century Irish political poetry', *Eighteenth-Century Ireland: Iris an dá chultúr* 11, 7–45.
Ó Buachalla, B. (1992), 'Irish Jacobite poetry', *The Irish Review* 12, 40–9.
Ó Crualaoich, G. (1983), 'The vision of liberation in *Cúirt an Mheán Oíche*', in: de Brún/ Ó Coileáin/ Ó Riain, 95–104.
Ó Háinle, C.G. (1982), 'Towards the revival. Some translations of Irish poetry 1789–1897', in: Connolly, 37–57.
Ó Tuama, S. and Kinsella, T. (1981), *An Duanaire: An Irish anthology 1600–1900. Poems of the dispossessed*, Philadelphia.
O'Halloran, C. (2004), *Golden ages and barbarous nations. Antiquarian debate and politics in Ireland c. 1750–1800*, Cork.
O'Higgins, L. (2007), '(In)felix Paupertas. Scholarship of the eighteenth-century Irish poor', *Arethusa* 40, 421–50.
O'Higgins, L. (2017), *The Irish Classical Self. Poets and Poor Scholars in the Eighteenth and Nineteenth Centuries*, Oxford.
O'Sullivan, D.J. (1960), *Songs of the Irish. An anthology of Irish folk music and poetry with English verse translations*, Dublin.
Panayotakis, C./Panayotakis, S. (2015), 'The human characters in the tale of Cupid and Psyche (Metamorphoses 4.28–6.24)', in: Harrison, 125–45.
Pheifer, J.D. (1984), 'Errour and Echnidna in *The Faerie Queene*. A study in literary tradition', in: Scattergood, 127–74.
Purser, L.C. (1910), *The story of Cupid and Psyche as related by Apuleius*, London.
Raughter, R. (ed.) (2002), 'Eighteenth century Protestant and Catholic women', in: Bourke, 490–516.
Raughter, R. (ed.) (2002), 'Philanthropic institutions of eighteenth-century Ireland', in: Bourke 2002, 681–90.
Rodgers, K.M. (1982), *Feminism in eighteenth-century England*, Brighton Urbana.
Scattergood, J. (ed.) (1984), *Literature and learning in Medieval and Renaissance England*, Blackrock.
Schellenberg, B.A. (2005), *The professionalization of women writers in eighteenth-century Britain*, Cambridge.
Stanford, W.B. (1976), *Ireland and the classical tradition*, Dublin.
Vance, N. (1980), 'Celts, Carthaginians and constitutions. Anglo-Irish literary relations 1780–1820', *Irish Historical Studies* 22, 216–38.
Welch, R. (ed.) (1996), *The Oxford companion to Irish literature*, Oxford.
Weller, E.V. (ed.) (1928), *Keats and Mary Tighe. The poems of Mary Tighe with parallel passages from the works of John Keats*, New York.
Whalley, G. (1972), 'England/Romantic-Romanticism', in: Eichner, 157–262.
White Beck, L. (1996), *Eighteenth-century philosophy*, New York.

Williams, J.E.C./Ford, P.K. (1992), *The Irish literary tradition*, Cardiff.
Wordsworth, J. (1992), Mary *Tighe. Psyche, with Other Poems 1811.* Oxford.
Wright, J.M. (ed.) (2010), *A companion to Irish literature. Volume I and II*, Oxford.
Young, W. (1792), A *new Latin-English dictionary; containing all the words proper for reading the classic writers; with the Authorities subjoined to each Word and* ..., London.
Zimmerman, M./Panayotakis, S./Hunink, V./Keulen, W./Harrison, S.J./McCreight, T./Wesseling, B./van Mal-Maeder, D. (eds.) (2004), *Apuleius Madaurensis, Metamorphoses. Books IV 28–35, V, and VI 1–24. Text, introduction and commentary*, Groningen.

Robert H. F. Carver
The Platonic Ass: Thomas Taylor's *Cupid and Psyche* in Context (1795–1822)

1 Introduction

The great French encylopaedist Pierre Bayle (1647–1706) opens his long (and still surprisingly relevant) entry on Apuleius with what appears to be a truism:

> APULEIUS (LUCIUS) a Platonist known to all the world by the famous work of the *Golden Ass*.[1]

But what are the options available to an English reader in the 1790s who actually wants to put his (or her) hands on this eminent Platonist's 'famous' *Ass*? As late as 1821, Thomas Jefferson Hogg can observe:

> there are many editions of the Metamorphoses; old and new, but principally old; large and small, but chiefly large; with and without notes, but commonly choked up with piles of animadversions. We sometimes see one, or two lines of text at the top of a full quarto page, like the chimneys and roofs and battlements of a town rising above a flood; sometimes only a dreary waste of waters, when the Ruhnken and the Wower, the Oudendorp and the Elmenhorst have broken their banks, and laid the smiling face of the [166] text under commentary;[2] then the blank of paper above and the blank of annotation below meet in one uniform line; and the weary eye seeks in vain along the dull Dutch horizon an object to repose upon.[3]

As we know, the contributions of Dutch and German scholars, printers and publishers to the dissemination of all things Apuleian constitute a long, distinguished, and still-vibrant tradition. But Hogg had a point: Apuleius' 'famous' *Ass* was

---

1 *A general dictionary, historical and critical: in which a new and accurate translation of that of the Celebrated Mr. Bayle, with the corrections* ... (London, 1734), vol. 2, p. 116. = M. Pierre Bayle (1647–1706), *Dictionnaire historique et critique*.
2 For a contemporary account of these editions, see Dibdin 1808: I, 166–71. The 'Preface' notes (p. 2) that Apuleius is one of thirteen authors who have been added to the work since the second edition (1804). Dibdin observes (I, 171) of Oudendorp's edition: 'The curious sometimes illustrate this edition of Apuleius's most entertaining work, with plates, and other appropriate graphic ornaments. It is daily becoming scarcer and dearer'.
3 [Hogg] 1823, 165–66. For the attribution to Hogg, see Markley 2003, 122–3.

https://doi.org/10.1515/9783110641585-009

quite difficult to access, especially in English.⁴ There were several French versions in circulation; and the fortunate (or persistent) book-hunter might be able to procure a copy of the earliest English translation, that by William Adlington, first published in 1566, with new editions in 1571, 1582, 1596, and 1639 (this last re-printing coinciding, on the eve of the English Civil War, with the resurgence of interest in Apuleius within the court of Charles I which produced adaptations of the tale of 'Cupid & Psyche' by Thomas Heywood and Shakerley Marmion).⁵

Copies of Adlington's *Golden Asse* feature occasionally in eighteenth-century book-sellers' catalogues, and examples of the 1639 edition, at least, are not especially expensive – the fact that they were printed in a heavy gothic typeface (the damning note, 'black letter', often appears in the description) seems to have kept their value relatively low (sometimes as little as one or two shillings). In 1798, a London auction catalogue for the books of the late Robert Masters includes a copy of the 1566 edition of 'Apuleius's Golden Ass, by Adlington, interleaved, bound in Morocco', together with the comment: 'N. B. For the Rareness of this Translation, see a Note at the End of the Epistle'.⁶

The reality seems to be that Adlington's translation loses its currency during (or soon after) the English Commonwealth – the *Golden Asse* remains pretty much dead or dormant until it is revived by Charles Whibley in the 'Tudor Translations' reprint of 1893,⁷ and then adopted by Stephen Gaselee as the basis for his modified English version in the original Loeb Library edition of 1915.⁸

In 1792, demand was evidently sufficient for a translation of *The Golden Ass* to be published in England, but it was in Italian, not English: *Apuleio, dell'asino d'oro, traslato da Messer Agnolo Firenzuola, di latino in lingua toscana*.⁹ Firenzuola's *L'asino d'oro* had first appeared in Italy in 1550, a full sixteen years before William Adlington's version; and it represents a recasting of Apuleius' text, rather than a 'faithful' translation (if such a thing can ever be said to exist): the first-person singular space established by Apuleius in his opening line (*At ego ...*) has been usurped by the translator himself, who becomes the subject

---

4 Cf. 'The Mirror of Fashion', *Morning Chronicle*, Friday, 24 April 1818, p. 3: 'will it not be deemed singular, in the opinion of foreign scholars, that in England APULEIUS should be called an author of extreme rarity?'
5 For possible later connections to Charles II see Harrison in this volume.
6 Arrowsmith and Bowley s.n., 1798, 27, item 884.
7 Note that Taylor's 1822 complete translation is reprinted (in 600 copies) at about the same time (Birmingham: W. J. Cosby, September 1893).
8 For evidence of post-Commonwealth circulation of Adlington, see May in this volume.
9 (London: Richard Edward, 1792).

of the erotic and asinine adventures, not in ancient Greece but in early-modern Italy.[10]

While searching eighteenth-century sources for traces of Adlington's translation, one may be puzzled by references (such as the following, from 1713) to an illustrated edition of Apuleius published 'in English' in 1708:

> (Miscellanies in English, Octavo.)
> Apuleius's Golden Ass, with Cuts, 2 Vol. 1708[11]

Another catalogue (from 1795) provides details of the contents of the two volumes, as well as valuable indicators of perceived genre. *The Golden Ass* is classed with the *Arabian Nights* under the running head 'Romances, Novels, Tales, &c.':

> 2027 Apuleius's Golden Ass, 2 vol. 7s
>   Vol. I. The Lady's Taste, Mercenary Gallant, Gamester, &c.
> 2028 Vol. II. Fair Extravagant, Julio and Sempronia.
> 2029 Arabian Nights Entertainments, 4 vol. 12s[12]

It only becomes apparent on closer inspection that the items described as 'Apuleius's Golden Ass' are actually copies of Charles Gildon's *The new metamorphosis: or, the pleasant transformation: being The golden ass of Lucius Apuleius of Medaura* [sic]. *Alter'd and improv'd to the modern times*, 2 vols (London, 1708; reprinted 1709 and 1724), with fashionable engravings ('cuts') by William Hogarth.

Gildon's *The new metamorphosis* is an engaging work in itself, but, as his own title suggests, it is a long way from Apuleius' *Ass* (even further removed than Firenzuola's adaptation which may have given Gildon the impetus to 'transform' the original, 'altering' and 'improving' it to meet the tastes and demands of

---

10 Carver 2007, 254–6; Gaisser 2008, 275; Carver 2018, 223–4.
11 *The student's library: or, a choice collection of books, in all faculties and parts of learning; in Hebrew, Greek, Latin, &c. with their best editions, by these celebrated Printers, viz. Wechelius, Aldus, Junta, Plantin, the two Stephens, and the Sen. Elzivir, &c. recommended to all Students in Divinity, Law, Physick, &c.*, London: printed by John Humfreys, in Bartholomew-Lane, and sold by E. Curll, at the Dial and Bible, over-against St. Dunstan's Church in Fleet-Street, T. Harrison, at the West Corner of the Royal Exchange in Cornhill [London], and Steph. Fletcher, Bookseller in Oxford, [1713], p. 87.
12 *A catalogue of the Minerva General Library, Leadenhall-Street, London. Containing upwards of five hundred thousand volumes, in all classes* ... ([London], [1795?]), p. 67. Cf. Warburton 1742: Vol. II, Book IV, Sect. IV, p. 123: 'The foundation of this *allegorical* Tale [sc. Apuleius' *Metamorphoses*] was a *Milesian Fable*, a Species of polite trifling then much in Fashion; and not very unlike our modern *Arabian Tales*.'

'modern times'). For more than 110 years, however, Gildon's version was the closest that monolingual English readers were likely to get to Apuleius' novel. As Hogg puts it in 1821:

> It is no wonder, therefore, that the Golden Ass is but little known: it is a vain attempt, with a few hands, to tow a heavy vessel against a strong wind and a strong tide; but it is as well to take hold of the rope; winds and tides have changed; and we owe all that is precious to vain attempts.
>
> If the curiosity of one person only shall be excited to read the work by these remarks, the pleasure which he will derive from it will repay whatever labour the composition of them has demanded.[13]

Ten years earlier, Hogg had chosen to join Shelley in being sent down from Oxford for their joint parts in the publication of *The Necessity of Atheism* (1811 and 1813). Hogg's essay on Apuleius was completed early in 1821 for the *London Magazine*, but never published there. When Shelley and Leigh Hunt accepted it for the second volume of their new journal, *The Liberal*, they may have felt that the 'winds and tides' had indeed 'changed', and that it was a good moment to launch a second Apuleian vessel, albeit a light one, following the publication of Thomas Taylor's version of the *Golden Ass* the year before (1822) – the first new English translation of the complete work in two and a half centuries.

Before this date (1822), of course, there is no shortage of editions, translations, explanations, and adaptations of 'Cupid and Psyche', but there is a tendency to deal with the tale in isolation from the context of the novel, a habit initiated by Fulgentius in the sixth century AD. As late as 1884, we hear John Evelyn Barlas claiming in his 'Cupid and Psyche':

> I found a fallen rose-bud
> Where the mire lay gross and crass,
> One sweet Milesian story
> In the filthy Golden Ass ...[14]

The 'filthy Golden Ass' at least gets a mention here. More often than not with adaptations of 'Cupid and Psyche' during this period, the novel as a whole is ignored, in keeping with 'the common View' decried by Bishop Warburton (1698–

---

13 [Hogg] 1823, 167.
14 Douglas 1884, 230.

1779) that the inset tale (being 'visibly allegorical throughout') was 'entirely foreign to all the rest of the Work'.[15]

2 Taylor's Programme

Cupid & Psyche (1795) forms part of Thomas Taylor's campaign to make the ancient Platonic tradition accessible to English readers in its entirety. Plato's stock in the 1790s was low. Rejecting any stark dichotomy between 'rational' and 'metaphysical', Taylor embodies a neo-Platonic belief in the essential unity of Plato and Aristotle: Aristotle's *Metaphysics* appears in 1801; the first English translation of the complete works of Plato in 1804, 'revising and completing the work begun by Floyer Sydenham' who had died in destitution in 1787.[16] But Taylor's insistence on viewing Middle- and neo-Platonic writings not as degenerate derivatives but as the fullest expression of Platonic truths invited the disdain of an Establishment still shaped by Enlightenment values; and his lack of academic credentials (and alleged philological deficiencies) made him vulnerable to attack. In November 1789, the 'half-witted' Taylor's 'blundered translation' of Proclus provides satirical *pabulum* for Horace Walpole as he contemplates the founding of 'the world's future religion' by the neo-Platonists' 'new apostle'.[17] Richard Porson derides him as someone who, 'without staying to learn even the inflexions of Greek words, has plunged into the very bottom of Pagan philosophy'.[18] T. J. Mathias mocks 'The Hymns, that Taylor, England's gentile priest, / Sung spousal at fair Psyche's marriage feast', describing Taylor (in an appended note) as 'the would-be restorer of unintelligible mysticism and superstitious pagan nonsense'.[19] As late as 1825, the Irish critic William Maginn can declare

---

15 Warburton 1742, Vol. II, Book IV, Sect. IV, p. 131. For Warburton, the fable of 'Cupid and Psyche' was 'the finest and most artful preparation for the Subject of the *eleventh*' book (*ibid.*), the 'true Design' of the *Golden Ass* being 'to recommend *Initiation into the Mysteries*, in opposition to the *New Religion*' [*sc.* Christianity] (p. 130). Taylor (1822: xvi) rejects, as 'singularly ridiculous and absurd', Warburton's claims for a hidden anti-Christian agenda: 'it is wholly incredible, that [...] Apuleius should have written a work one part of the intention of which was to ridicule *latently* that which, *without any concealment*, and with the sanction of the existing government, was generally despised.'
16 Louth 2004.
17 Letter to Lady Ossory, in: Walpole 1965 vol. 34, 82–3.
18 Porson 1798, 262.
19 Mathias 1796, 5.

that 'the man is an ass' and 'knows nothing of the religion of which he is so great a fool as to profess himself a votary'.[20]

Taylor was sensitive to such barbs, but he learned, over the course of a long life (1758–1835), to commodify his own notoriety as a pagan and polytheist, and to respond to market forces. Taylor devotes an appendix in *Cupid & Psyche* to the defence of another work of obvious appeal to art historians – his translation of Pausanias, which he completed, in ten months, for the paltry fee of £60.[21] Taylor chooses to publish *Cupid & Psyche* himself, using the book auctioneers Leigh and Sotherby to distribute copies – he is willing to assume the financial risks in the expectation of higher profits. *Cupid & Psyche* is reasonably short (compared to Pausanias), relatively simple in style (compared with *The Golden Ass* as a whole), and (in contrast to much of his Platonica and neo-Platonica) is aimed at a wider audience. An advertisement from December 1797 presents Taylor's translation as a new publication,[22] quotes tendentiously from reviews, and seeks to capitalize on the popularity of highly spectacular 'dramatic entertainments' such as the London revivals of Jean-Georges Noverre's *Psyché et l'Amour* (Stuttgart, 1762)[23] and Pierre-Gabriel Gardel's *Psyché* (Paris, 14 December 1790):[24]

---

20 [Maginn] 1825, 737–38. For the attribution to Maginn, see Latané 2013, 324.
21 Taylor 1795, 148.
22 This may be evidence of a re-printing, or merely an attempt to shift un-sold stock.
23 Advertisements appear in *True Briton* (p. 1) and the *Morning Post and Gazetteer* (p. 1) on the same day as Taylor's puff (26 October 1797) for a performance at the Theatre Royal, Covent Garden, of the 'Grand Ballet of Cupid & Psyche composed by Mr. Noverre'. A reviewer of the first performance (13 December 1796) notes: 'The story of Cupid's Amour with Psyche is represented with the most exquisite charm of spectacle and fancy. [...] the spectacle approaches to the sublime terror and passion of an opera. [...] The torches and swords of fire in the hands of the Furies produced so tremendous an effect, that part of the audience seemed petrified at the agonies of Psyche. A higher compliment to a scene of acting we never witnessed. Much of this effect was produced by the strong reflection from the glass panels of the new boxes; and after this first night, the spectators will learn, that though terrible in appearance, it is perfectly safe.' See 'New Opera', *The Sporting Magazine, or Monthly Calendar*, 9. 51 (December 1796), 143. Nares (1788, 23) describes Noverre's ballet as the 'wonder of the present year'. He admits the inherent potential of the fable for 'the strongest effect and contrast of scenery' and, 'what is more important, the most striking contrasts of passions and situation' (26), though he laments that 'After the tremendous leap of Psyche into the flaming gulph, [...] the work of the carpenter is perfectly conspicuous; and the bursting flames, which ought to fill the soul with horror, are seen to issue through a regularly square opening of planed wood' (34). For confirmation of Nares' authorship, see the reprint of this pamphlet in Nares 1810, I, 69–108. The pamphlet is followed (109–21) by 'a part of the argument [*sc.* to the ballet] which was sold at the time [1788] in the theatre' (108).
24 *The Times* (Tuesday, 26 September 1797, p. 1) advertises five performances (in the 'Amphitheatre of Arts, Astley's, Westminster Bridge') of a work ('now performing at Paris with universal applause') which is probably Gardel's (or based thereon): 'a Grand, Serious, and Comic Panto-

> This day was published, price 4s. in boards, THE Fable of Cupid and Psyche, By THOMAS TAYLOR
> Author of a Dissertation on the Eleusinian and Bacchic Mysteries; and Translator of the Hymns of Orpheus; of the Works of Plato, Pausanias, Plotinus, Proclus, &c. &c.
>
> ...
>
> This Fable at the present moment has excited a very lively interest in the public mind, by being made the ground of several favourite dramatic entertainments.
> The Authors of the British Critic speak of the present translation, as very accurate;[25] and the Critical Reviewers assert, that the Poetical parts of the Volume possess considerable harmony and spirit.[26]

Noting that the Fable 'has been a favorite subject of the most eminent artists, ancient and modern', Taylor dedicates his 'Translation and Explanation' of *Cupid & Psyche* to 'the President, Council, and Members of the Royal Academy'.[27] In the 1780s, Taylor had given a course of twelve lectures on Platonic philosophy at the London house of the sculptor, John Flaxman, who (in 1776) had supplied the jasperware maker, Josiah Wedgwood, with a relief plaque model ('The Marriage of Cupid and Psyche') based on the famous 'Marlborough Gem'.[28]

Flaxman's circle also included William Blake, who seems to have embarked on an abortive course of tutorials from Taylor on Euclidean geometry.[29] In about 1794, Blake made some engravings which appeared in George Cumberland's *Thoughts on Outline* (1796),[30] including one depicting the moment in 5.24

---

mime Spectacle, in Four Parts, called CUPID and PSYCHE: Interspersed with a most splendid Variety of Scenery, Machinery, Transformations, &c. &c. with new Dresses, Decorations, Music, &c.' On Gardel's original Paris production, see Chazin-Bennahum 2004, 64: 'Psyché endures classic suffering for her sins while the stage is filled with dazzling scenic spectacles. What contributed to the fortune of this ballet was her costume. The *robe à la Psyché* became one of the most touted fashions of the time. *Le Journal de la Mode et du Goût* of December 25, 1790, mentioned that this costume was tastefully designed to suggest one breast exposed.'

25 i.e. Robert Nares and William Beloe, eds, *The British Critic* (Jan. 1796), 571–72 (Art. 68). Beloe's translation of *The Attic Nights of Aulus Gellius* also appeared in 1795 (the notes contain several references to Apuleius).

26 *Star* (London), Thursday, 26 October 1797. See *The Critical Review, or, Annals of Literature* (Sep. 1795), 33–7.

27 Taylor 1795: preliminaries. Cf. Louth 2004: 'In 1797 Taylor obtained the post of assistant secretary to the Society of Arts, which he resigned in 1806 to devote himself more completely to translation.'

28 The Marlborough Gem, now in the Boston Museum of Fine Arts, is catalogued there as a 'Cameo with the Wedding of Cupid and Psyche, or an initiation rite'. For the Platonism lectures, see Louth 2004.

29 King 1972, 153–7. Cf. Pierce 1928, 1121–41.

30 Cumberland 1796: Figure 13 [= Image 69 of 80 on ECCO]. The plate is entitled 'Psyche repents'.

Figure 10: William Blake, 'Psyche repents' (1794/1796). Copyright Chetham's Library, Manchester

when Cupid flies off, and Psyche clings to his right leg with both hands (figure 10). The coincidence of dates and subjects suggests the possibility that, in the late 1780s and the 1790s, Taylor and Blake are working in concert, playing off one another as they engage with Platonic and Apuleian themes.[31]

In 1810, Blake observes, in his Notes on *A Vision of the Last Judgement*: 'Apuleius's Golden Ass & Ovid's Metamorphosis & others of the like kind are Fable yet they contain Vision in a sublime degree, being derived from real Vision in

---

31 Cf. Louth 2004: 'Taylor was also lampooned as "the modern Platonist" in Isaac Disraeli's novel *Vaurien* (1797), and is perhaps the model for Sipsop the Pythagorean in Blake's *An Island in the Moon*; in both cases fun is made of his fondness for animals, especially cats.' Taylor may be a better fit for Blake's 'Obtuse Angle'. See Erdman 1977, 98–102 and 507: 'The text taken literally implies that Obtuse Angle had a "study" located in Blake's house; that could conceivably be true of Thomas Taylor – not requiring Blake to go out of his way to be shown Euclid's angles.'

More Ancient Writings'.[32] In early works like the *Book of Thel* (1789) and the *Visions of the Daughters of Albion* (1793), Blake gives new poetic and narrative form to Platonic myths about the fall of the Soul. In his unfinished *Four Zoas*, he is more specifically Apuleian, drawing, for example, on the description of Cupid's palace for the details of the divinely made house.[33]

But it is Blake's painting, *The Night of Enitharmon's Joy* (completed in 1795, the same year as Taylor's *Cupid & Psyche*, and now housed in London's Tate Britain), that is most suggestive of a joint Apuleian programme. The painting (figure 11) is also known as *The Triple Hecate* because of the ambiguity of the tri-form central figure. Hecate, in Classical mythology, mediates between the heavens (Selene), earth (Artemis), and the underworld (Persephone), but, in Book Eleven of the *Golden Ass*, Isis identifies 'Hecate' as one of the names by which she is known (11.5).[34] So, in the cave-like world of the painting (a setting appropriate to Apuleius as well as to Plato), the central female figure may be both a goddess and a magician (witness the book). The two figures behind her, forming her second and third sides, could be read as wingless versions of Psyche and the curly-locked Cupid: close, but not touching; hands awkwardly positioned, almost as though bound. The reptilian figure to the left will then be the imagined serpentine nature of Cupid, gazing intently on the half-concealed female we have posited as representing Psyche. The owl and the donkey suggest the emblem of wisdom into which Lucius hoped to be turned, and the embodiment of stupidity and lust that he actually becomes. The donkey is so distinctive – and so out of keeping with Blake's usual iconography – that it must surely be Apuleian: an ass forced to eat thistles, instead of the roses that would return it to human form.

A potential mediator here is an image that Blake may have encountered through his association with Cumberland: the engraving (attributed to the 'Master of the Die' and dating to the 1530s/1540s) of Charite listening to the tale of *Cupid and Psyche* [figure 12].[35] We may note similarities in the position of the ass relative to Charite; the orientation of the female face; the heaviness of the limbs; the draping of her garb to display her naked feet. Blake seems (almost

---

32 Blake 1982, 556; Raine 1969b, I, 182.
33 Haigney 1987, 119–120: 'During the "O Enion" plaint, Tharmas is a bearded adult; for the "O Vala" song, he has become a child again, a "little Boy" to whom Vala exclaims: "How are ye thus renewd" (130, 510–11; E 398).'
34 Cf. *Met*. 11.2, where Lucius suggests 'dreaded Proserpina, with tri-form aspect' (*horrenda Proserpina, triformi facie*) as a possible identification of the goddess who has appeared to him.
35 On the indebtedness of the engravings to Raphael, and their influence, in turn, on such works as Perin del Vaga's frescoes for Pope Paul III's apartment in the Castel Sant'Angelo, see Cavicchioli 2002, 154–7, 166–7.

Figure 11: William Blake, *The Night of Enitharmon's Joy* (1795). Reprinted with permission of The Tate Gallery London

teasingly) to represent everything at once: re-embedding the tale of *Cupid and Psyche* in the wider context of the novel, while embodying, in the central female figure, not merely Hecate-Isis, but Photis, Psyche, and Charite as well.[36]

3 Allegoresis: Taylor's 'Explanation' of *Cupid and Psyche*

In 1822, Taylor quotes Apuleius' *Apologia* (64.3) on the title page of his translation of *The Golden Ass:*

> "Platonicâ familiâ nihil novimus nisi festum, et lætum, et solemne, et superum, et cæleste. Quin altitudinis studio, secta ista etiam cælo ipso sublimiora quæpiam vestigavit, et in extimo mundi tergo degit."— APUL. *Apol.*

---

[36] On the inter-relatedness of these figures, see Carver 2013, 243–74.

The Platonic Ass: Thomas Taylor's *Cupid and Psyche* in Context (1795–1822) —— **129**

Figure 12: 'Master of the Die', Engraving 1 (1530s/1540s). Copyright Stephen Harrison

> In this Platonic family, we know nothing except the festive, and the happy, and the solemn, and the lofty, and the celestial. Indeed, in its zeal to elevate itself, this sect has investigated things more sublime than the sky / heaven, and has endured on the outermost surface of the cosmos

In 1795, by contrast, Taylor is at pains to emphasize the pecking order within that 'Platonic family'. He observes of Apuleius that, 'though he was a man of extraordinary abilities, and held a distinguished place among the Platonic philosophers' of his own time (i.e. what we would now call the 'Middle Platonists' of the second century AD), 'yet he was inferior to any one of that golden race of philosophers, of which the great Plotinus stands at the head' (Taylor 1795: ii).

Warburton's image of the hierarchy had been the inverse of this: Apuleius 'had imbibed his platonism, not at the muddy streams of those late Enthusiasts [viz. 'the fanatic *Platonists* and *Pythagoreans* of the latter ages'], but at the pure fountain-head of the Academy itself'.[37] In *A Dissertation on the Eleusinian and Bacchic Mysteries* (1791) – designed 'to vindicate the wisdom of antiquity from [Warburton's] malevolent and ignorant aspersions' – Taylor declares that while 'a representation of the descent of the soul' was 'occultly insinuated by Virgil' (*Aen.* 6.748–51), it was given 'openly by Apuleius' in the 'prayer addressed by

---

37 Warburton 1755, Vol. I, Book II, Sect. IV, 324.

Psyche to Ceres' (*Met.* 6.2).³⁸ For Warburton, 'the Fable of *Cupid* and *Psyche*' is 'a *Philosophical Allegory of the Progress of the human Soul to Perfection, in the Possession of Divine Love and the Reward of Immortality.*'³⁹ According to Taylor, it shows 'the lapse of the human soul from the intelligible world to the earth' (1795: iii).⁴⁰ Since Psyche equals the Soul, she is 'transcendently beautiful', as, indeed, is every human soul before that soul 'merges itself in the defiling folds of dark matter' (p. vi). The account of Psyche 'descending from the summit of a lofty mountain into a beautiful valley' signifies the descent of the soul from the intelligible world into a mundane condition of being, but yet without abandoning its establishment in the Heavens.' Her husband's palace is therefore said to be 'not raised by human, but by divine, hands and art.' The gems on which she walks are 'symbolical of the stars', while the disembodied voices 'which attend upon Psyche' are symbolical of 'this mundane, yet celestial condition of being', since 'outward discourse is the last image of intellectual energy according to which the soul alone operates in the intelligible world.' Thus the voices are subordinate to the 'intelligible', but 'superior' to the earthly ('a terrene allotment').

So long as Psyche's husband is invisible, all is well: Psyche is 'established in the Heavens' (Cupid's palace) and 'united with pure desire', 'in other words, is not fascinated with [viii] outward form'. 'But in this beautiful palace she is attacked by the machinations of her two sisters, who endeavour to persuade her to explore the form of her unknown husband' (p. viii). Taylor's allegoresis of the principal characters can be schematized as follows:

Jealous Sister 1 = Imagination ('phantasy')
Jealous Sister 2 = Nature ('vegetable power')
Psyche (Sister 3) = Reason (the 'rational part' of the soul)

Love 1 (the invisible Cupid before Psyche's fall and his flight) = 'pure desire'
Love 2 (the visible Love with whom Psyche falls in love by the light of the torch) = 'impure or terrene desire'.

Psyche's quest for Cupid represents the Soul 'in search of Love, or pure desire' (p. ix). The sleep caused by Psyche opening Proserpina's box of infernal Beauty

---

38 Taylor 1791, 1 and 83–84. Taylor quotes and translates *Met.* 11.5 (*En adsum tuis commota, Luci, precibus* ...) at 74–76, and *Met.* 11.25 (*Te Superi colunt*) at 77.
39 Warburton 1742, Vol. II, Book IV, Sect. IV, 131 (original emphasis).
40 Cf. Taylor 1822, xv: 'the very ancient dogma of the pre-existence of the human soul, its lapse from the intelligible world to the earth, and its return from thence to its pristine state of felicity, are most accurately and beautifully adumbrated.'

symbolizes how 'the soul, by considering a corporeal life as truly beautiful, passes into a profoundly dormant state, and it ap-[xiv]pears to me that both Plato and Plotinus allude to this part of our fable in the following passages':

> 'He who is not able, by the exercise of his reason, to define the idea of *the good* [...] *will descend to Hades, and be overhwelmed with a sleep perfectly profound*'
> (Taylor 1795: xiii-xiv, quoting Plato, *Republic* VII [original emphasis]).

> 'The death of the soul is, while merged, or baptized, as it were, in the present body, to descend into matter, and be filled with its impurity, and after departing from this body, to lie absorbed in its filth till it returns to a superior condition, and elevates its eye from the overwhelming mire. *For to be plunged into matter is to descend to Hades, and fall asleep*'
> (Taylor 1795: xv, quoting Plotinus, 'in *Ennead* I, lib. 8, p. 80' [original emphasis]).

The birth of *Voluptas* at the end of the tale (6.24) is explained thus: 'Cupid, however, or pure desire, at length recovering his pristine vigor, rouses Psyche or soul, from her deadly lethargy. [...] the natural result of this union with pure desire is plea-[xv]sure or delight' (Taylor 1795, xiv-xv).

Robert Nares and William Beloe's response to Taylor's 'Explanation' is politely dismissive:

> The story of Cupid has been again and again translated, and is probably familiar to every description of our readers. Mr. Taylor, whose diligence we should be glad to see exercised more beneficially to himself, as well as to the public, tells us, that this fable was designed to represent the lapse of the human soul from the intelligible world to the earth. At his mode of making out this position, some will smile, and others will stare.[41]

For 'Tay, jr.' in *The Monthly Review*, Taylor's *Cupid & Psyche* represents the attempted 'fulfilment' of Gemisthus Pletho's prophecy at 'the synod of Florence' that 'mankind would at length unanimously renounce the gospel and the koran for a religion similar to that of the pagans'.[42] The 'fine arts', 'the composition of theatric pageants', and 'the occasional sportive play of fancy and learning' pose no risk of 'serious impiety' or 'the revival of classical superstition' (51); but the 'various movements of the pupils of philosophy throughout Europe', especially in revolutionary France ('their Pantheon of Paris'), 'aim in concert at the

---

41 *The British Critic* (Jan. 1796), Art. 68, 571–2. Nares (1788, 50) rejects Fulgentius for 'allegorizing too minutely', but concedes: 'The really extraordinary circumstance is, that that there does actually appear to be concealed under this seeming fairy tale, some allegory of very high importance' (52). Nares reluctantly adumbrates a 'general outline' (55) of this allegory, designed to emphasize the congruences between Psyche's 'curiosity and disobedience' (56) and the Edenic Fall and its sequelae in the Judaeo-Christian tradition (55–8).
42 *The Monthly Review, or Literary Journal*, 18 (Sep. 1795), 51–5, at 51.

restoration of idolatry', and 'the crowd, ever prone to change, seems but too willing to forsake the cold abstractions of a metaphysical devotion, for the fascinating allurements of a ceremonious and sensual religion' (52):

> Among the most zealous and industrious, although not among the most able, priests of a dangerous sectarism, is the modern Gentile—Thomas Taylor [...] and certainly he has chosen, on the present occasion, one of the most beautiful fables of the heathen system, and one that is arrayed in all the luxurious embellishments of the gorgeous style of Apuleius, in order to display his talents at spiritualizing an amusive legend, and at engrafting abstrusely mystical interpretations on a highly romantic narrative. Still we think that a more rational plan of exposition were as yet better calculated to attract an avowed adherence to his fanaticism, than the recondite unintelligible allegory which he so devoutly patronizes, and which is much fitter to satisfy the initiated than the aspirant.

John Robison, Professor of Natural Philosophy and Secretary to the Royal Society of Edinburgh, may have had Taylor in mind when he provided his own 'rational' reading of 'Cupid and Psyche' in 1797:

> Search Apuleius, where you will find many female characters *in abstracto* – You will find that his little Photis was nearest to his heart, after all his philosophy. Nay, in his pretty story of Cupid and Psyche, which the very wise will tell you is a fine lesson of moral philosophy, and a representation of the operations of the intellectual and moral faculties of the human soul, a story which gave him the finest opportunity, nay, almost made it necessary for him, to insert whatever can ornament the female character; what is his Psyche but a beautiful, fond, and silly girl; and what are the whole fruits of any acquaintance with the sex? –Pleasure.[43]

A good deal of Taylor's allegoresis (e.g. the allocation of parts to the two elder sisters) does not appear to be a huge advance on the exegeses provided by Fulgentius, or the medieval commentators on Martianus Capella, or the vulgate version of Boccaccio's *Genealogy of the Gods*.[44] It makes no convincing attempt to engage with the implications of narrative, character, tone, and so on; and it requires some awkward accommodations of details that do not quite fit the philosophical *muthos* (Taylor makes no mention, for instance, of the fact that the sisters also persuade Psyche to cut off her husband's head).

The Plotinus passage does furnish, however, some very suggestive parallels to Psyche's soporific katabasis. The most compelling part of Taylor's exegesis may be his discussion of Book 5.5 of the *De insomniis* by Synesius of Cyrene (c. AD 373-c. 414):

---

[43] Robison 1797, 264.
[44] See Carver 2007, 36–47, 102–3, 133–41.

When the soul descends spontaneously to its former life, with mercenary views, it receives <u>servitude as the reward of its mercenary labours</u>. But this is the design of descent, that the soul may accomplish <u>a certain servitude</u> to the nature of the universe, prescribed by the laws of Adrastia, or inevitable fate. Hence when the soul is <u>fascinated with material endowments</u>, she is similarly affected to those who, though <u>free born</u>, are, for [xi] a certain time, hired by wages to employments, and in this condition <u>captivated with the beauty of some female servant, determine to act in a menial capacity under the master of their beloved object</u>. Thus, in a similar manner, when we are profoundly <u>delighted with external and corporeal goods</u>, we confess that the <u>nature of matter</u> is beautiful, who marks our assent in her secret book; *and if, considering ourselves as free, we at any time determine to depart,* <u>*she proclaims us deserters*</u>, *endeavours to bring us back, and openly presenting her mystic volume to the view, apprehends us as* <u>*fugitives from our mistress*</u>. Then, indeed, the soul particularly requires fortitude and divine assistance, as it is no trifling contest to abrogate the confession and compact which she made. Besides, in this case force will be employed; for the material inflic-[xii]tion of punishments will then be roused to revenge by the decrees of fate against the rebels to her laws.'[45]

We can extract, from Synesius, a useful gloss on Venus' odd insistence ('odd' because it has no basis in the foregoing narrative) that Psyche is the goddess's 'runaway' slave and, as such, needs to be arrested and punished (6.7–8). But the further attraction of this passage is that it seems as equally applicable to Lucius as to Psyche, especially in terms of his affair with Photis, and his voluntary subjection to erotic and necromantic servitude.[46]

4 Taylor as Translator

Despite his attacks on 'verbal critics' such as Beloe and Porson, and his hierophantic insistence that 'grammatical skill avails but little where intellect must be principally employed',[47] Taylor shows an astonishing commitment to the *verba ipsissima* of 'Cupid and Psyche':

> Taylor 1795, 32: 'But the two sisters ... direct their course with *precipitate velocity* [5.14: *praecipiti cum velocitate*] ... and ... leap on high with *licentious temerity* [*licentiosa cum temeritate*]

---

[45] Taylor 1795, x-xii (Taylor's italics; underlined emphasis added). Fitzgerald (Synesius 1926 & 1930, vol. II, 337) makes easier sense of the opening sentence: 'For, descending into the first life *voluntarily as a maid of service*, this *soul, instead of serving, becomes enslaved.*'
[46] On the philosophical implications of the *servitium amoris* trope in Apuleius, see Carver 2013, 255–71.
[47] Taylor 1795, 147–52 and 150.

> Taylor 1795, 33: 'turning their discourse to the *destined fraud*ulent snares' [5.15: *ad destinatam fraudium*]
>
> Taylor 1795, 37: 'But if you are wedded to the *vocal solitude* [5.18: *uocalis solitudo*] of this country retreat, or to the filthy and dangerous enjoyment of *clandestine venery* [*clandestinae ueneris*], and the embraces of a *poisoned serpent* [*uenenati serpentis*], we have at least acted like pious sisters'.

In many places, Taylor simply fails to convert the Latin into communicative English. Thus, Taylor's sisters describe Psyche's invisible husband as 'a vast serpent who glides along the plain *in various volumes* [5.17: *multinodis uolumnibus serpentem*]' (Taylor 1795, 36), while Hanson's enable us to visualize: 'It is a monstrous snake gliding with many-knotted coils' (Hanson 1989). When the theophany of Cupid finally comes, Taylor's literalism once again frustrates sense: 'On the shoulders of the *volatile* god' [5.22: *Per umeros volatilis dei*] (Taylor 1795, 43).

Is Taylor being ignorant, indolent, or inept; or could this be intentional, even intelligent? It may well be a bit of both. As one reviewer notes, 'his translation ... is faithful, but exceptionally tumid in point of style, though perhaps Mr. T. studied to make it so.'[48]

At times, Taylor's technique almost seems to anticipate Louis Zukofsky's magnificently perverse homophonic 'translation' of Catullus (1969):

> Miser Catulle, desinas ineptire,
> Et quod vides perisse perditum ducas.
> Fulsere quondam candidi tibi soles ...
> Miss her, Catullus? don't be so inept to rail
> at what you see perish when perished is the case.
> Full, sure once, candid the sunny days glowed, solace ...[49]

The two techniques are not equivalent, obviously, but there is *some* overlap. Zukofsky's versions can be wonderful, especially for readers with a precise (and active) knowledge of the Latin.[50] Taylor's willingness to employ the closest equivalent in form and sound is an attempt, one suspects, to conserve as much of the philosophical content and nuance of the original as possible.

---

[48] Anon., *The British Critic* (Jan. 1796), Art. 68, 571–72. The review continues: 'The author must not be offended with us if we honestly confess that we can by no means praise his poetry. We will not give extracts which would degrade Mr. T. in the public opinion, but we must in justice observe, that his lines are generally heavy and prosaic.'
[49] Catullus 8; Zukofsky 1969.
[50] On the significance of Zukofsky's *Catullus* in terms of translation theory and practice, see Horáček 2014, 106–31.

That is clearly his intention in 1822:

> In translating these treatises, I have endeavoured to be as faithful as possible, and to give the manner as well as the matter of the author; since a translation in which both these are not [xxii] generally united, must necessarily, as I have already observed, be essentially defective. I have also availed myself of the best editions of the works of Apuleius, and among these, of the Delphin edition, which I think is excellent on the whole, though the editor frequently in his interpretation substitutes other words for those of the original when this is not necessary. There is an ancient translation into English of the Metamorphosis by one Adlington, the first editions of which were printed in 1566 and 1571, and the last edition in 1639; and there are other intermediate editions; but as he every where omits the most difficult, and the most elegant passages, his work is rather a rude outline or compendium than an accurate translation. (Taylor 1822, xxi-xxii)

In a footnote, Taylor mentions some French translations, but claims (astonishingly) that 'I have not consulted any of these translations, because I have no knowledge of the French tongue.'

For his 1795 production, he might have taken advantage of Lockman's translation of La Fontaine (*The Loves of Cupid and Psyche*, 1744; on La Fontaine see Harrison 2018b). What is more surprising is the extent of Taylor's indebtedness to Charles Gildon's *The New Metamorphosis*. Gildon and Taylor could scarcely be further apart as exegetes. For the former, 'The story of Psyche, and Cupid, so valu'd of Old, and so admir'd in various Authors, is both a Lesson against the Curiosity of the Sex, and a pregnant Proof of a certain if not speedy Deliverance of Providence from the cruelest of Misfortunes' (Gildon 1709: II, 141). But while he radically updates and transforms the vast majority of Apuleius, Gildon preserves the tale of 'Cupid and Psyche' intact, as a story set in a faraway place, in distant times: 'THERE was a King and a Queen of a certain City in Greece, and in the Ancient Days of Paganism, who had three Beautiful Daughters' (Gildon 1709, II, 142).

Taylor appears to be translating Apuleius with both the Latin text and Gildon in front of him. The consummation scene (5.4) reveals Taylor's close, but not servile, engagement with Gildon:

> her unknown Husband approaches, ascends her Bed, makes her his Wife, and retires before the Dawn of comfortable Morning. And the Voices attending in the Chamber took care of all things Necessary on that Occasion. This Course was continued for a long time, and the Novelty Naturally, by its constant Repetition, confirm'd her Pleasure; and the Solitude lost its Terror in the Attendance of those vocal Companions. (Gildon 1709, II, 154)

> ... And now the unknown Husband approached, ascended the bed, made her his wife, and hastily left her before the rising of the morning light. Immediately the attendant voices, who were ministers of the bedchamber, took care of every thing Necessary on the Occasion. This Course was continued for a long time; the novelty, by its constant repetition, (as it was nat-

ural it should) became at last delightful; and the sound of the uncertain voices was the solace of her solitude.⁵¹ (Taylor 1795, 16)

If it is simply quotidian detail (what we might call mere 'realism'), Taylor seems content to take his cue from Gildon. But where he detects even the possibility of a Platonic inflection, he pays close attention to the particularities of the Latin (*Met.* 5.10):

'But I am the most miserable of my Sex, being curs'd with a Husband more aged, than my Father, bald as a Gourd, and shorter than a Pigmy [...] BUT I, assum'd the other Sister, am condemned to support a Fellow grown almost double with the Gout; And tho' he very seldom takes Care to reward my Pains with conjugal Comfort, yet I am forced to spend all my Time in rubbing his distorted Fingers almost turn'd into a Stone; acting the Surgeon [medicae] more, than Wife, I defile my fine Hands with stinking Fomentations, nasty Rags, and stenchy Plaisters. You, my Sister, seem to bear this Partiality of Fortune with a Temper too Patient, and serene' (Gildon 1709: II, 161)

'"But I, miserable creature, am, in the first place, tied to a husband more aged than my father; and, in the next place, to one who is balder than a gourd, and shorter than a pigmy [...] "But I," replied the other sister, "am destined to endure a husband whose body is distorted with an articular disease [articulari ... morbo]; and though on this account he seldom rewards my pains with conjugal embraces, yet I am forced to spend a great part of my time in rubbing his distorted fingers, which are almost hardened into stone, with fetid fomentations, defiling these delicate hands with nasty rags and stinking Poultices; acting, by these means, the part of a surgeon more than that of a wife. You, indeed, my sister, seem to bear all this with patient or rather servile soul [patienti uel potius seruili [...] animo]"' (Taylor 1795, 25 = 1822, 104)

Here, for example, the distinctions between 'heart', 'mind', 'fancy', and 'soul' clearly matter to Taylor:

Age iam nunc ut voles et animo tuo damnosa poscenti pareto: tantum memineris meae seriae monitionis cum coeperis sero paenitere. (Apuleius, *Met.* 5.6).

'Do then as you wish and obey the ruinous demands of your heart. Only be mindful of my stern warning when – too late – you begin to be sorry.' (Apuleius, *Met.* 5.6, transl. Kenney 1990, 55).

---

51 Cf. Kenney 1990, 53: 'while the sound of the unseen voice solaced her solitude.' Despite her revolutionary credentials, Mary Shelley's (unpublished) version from 1817 is prim by comparison: 'Now when kindly night approached a sound struck her ears which filled her with fear and horror; not knowing what the evil was that she expected her dread augmented. Her unknown bridegroom approached and after having passed the night with her quitted before break of day. The voices hastened to approach & aided her to dress' (Shelley 2002, 289). See Markley 2003, 126–27.

'Dismiss your Tears, do now what you please, <u>submit to the obstinate Dictates of your Fancy</u> which prompts you to things of the last [157] Prejudice to your Happiness and Peace. But when you too late repent of your Folly remember my timely and serious Admonitions.' (Apuleius, *Met.* 5.6, transl. Gildon 1709, II, 156).

'But come, act now as you please, and <u>comply with the pernicious desires of your soul</u>; however, when you begin too late to repent of your folly, call to mind my serious admonitions.' (Apuleius, *Met.* 5.6 transl. Taylor 1795, 19).

Sic affectione simulata paulatim sororis invadunt animum. (Apuleius, *Met.* 5.15).

'THUS by degres [sic] with a dissembled Affection and false Love they invade the unguarded <u>Mind</u> of their innocent Sister'. (Apuleius, *Met.* 5.15, transl. Gildon 1709, II, 167).

'Thus by a dissembled affection they gradually invade the <u>soul</u> of their sister' [animum; Kenney 1990: 67: 'heart']. (Apuleius, *Met.* 5.15, transl. Taylor 1795, 33).

Despite 2000 years or more of Aesopic beast fables, Gildon is uncomfortable with the notion of speaking animals, so his chief ant communicates with his neighbours 'in sounds mistically signifying these Words':

'the Leader execrating the Step-Mothers Cruelty summons together all the busie Legions of the Neighbouring Emets <u>in sounds mistically signifying these Words,</u> — Take pity ye active Nurselings of the <u>Omniparent</u> Earth! Take Pity, and with speed make Haste to my Assistance of the Wife of Love, a beautiful young Woman and in danger of Ruin.' (Gildon 1709, II, 199).

Taylor has no such anxieties. He shares, with William Blake, the neo-Pythagorean view that 'every thing that lives is holy' (*The Marriage of Heaven and Hell* [1790–1793], 27):

'execrating the step-mother's Cruelty <u>towards the wife of the mighty god Cupid, rapidly</u> summoned together all the busie Legions of neighbouring ants, and thus addressed them: "Take pity, ye active Nurselings of the <u>all-parent</u> Earth! Take Pity, and with prompt celerity, assist the wife of Love, a beautiful young Woman who is now in a dangerous situation."' (Taylor 1795, 72).

Sometimes Taylor's deviation from Gildon is subtle, as in Met. 6.12–13:

'But when she came to the Brink, the River God inspir'd the Reeds with harmonious Murmurs, which breath forth these Words in soft Music.—Psyche exercised in great Sorrows, Polute not my holy Streams … [201] THUS the compassionate River God by the Murmuring Reed gave Psyche instructions how to return in safety' (Apuleius, *Met.* 6.12–13, transl. Gildon 1709: II, 200–1)

'But when she came to the brink, a reed, the sweet nurse of music, being divinely inspired, thus <u>prophetically</u> spoke in soft and harmonious murmurs: "Psyche, exercised in mighty sorrows, neither pollute my sacred waters … [75] Thus the simple and humane reed taught the wretched Psyche how to accomplish this dangerous enterprise with safety.' (Apuleius, *Met.* 6.12–13, transl. Taylor 1795, 74–5)

It is important to Taylor (as it seems to be to Apuleius, though not to Gildon) that the reed is singular: Taylor's 'simple' may remind us that Psyche herself is often called *simplex* (or *simplicissima*). And humane/*humana* – with its etymological link both to *homo* and to *humus* – emphasizes the fact that Psyche and the reed are–like the helpful ants–'Nurselings of the all-parent Earth'.

And in *Met.* 5.19, Taylor (unlike Gildon) is sufficiently accurate to have his wording adopted by E. J. Kenney:

'THE poor hapless Psyche full of Simplicity and Fear, is strook with a pannick Terror with the terrible Story; and being thus quite out of her Wits, she reveals to them all the Admonitions her Husband had given her against Enquiries into his Person, and Form; and her Promises to curb so natural a Curiosity in the Sex. By this Folly precipitating herself from the highest Point of Happiness into the Abyss of Calamities.' (Apuleius. *Met.* 5.19, transl. Gildon 1709: II, 171)/

'being thus quite beside herself, loses the remembrance of all her husband's admonitions and her own promises, and hurls herself headlong into a profound abyss of calamity' (Apuleius. *Met.* 5.19, transl. Taylor 1795, 37).

'Beside herself, she totally forgot all her husband's warnings and her own promises, and plunged herself headlong into an abyss of calamity'. (Apuleius. *Met.* 5.19, transl. Kenney 1990, 71).

Taylor is often accused of lacking a poetic ear. The proto-Byronic anapestic rhythms in the description of the sea-gull 'who swims with his wings on the waves of the sea' (Apuleius, *Met.* 5.28) might suggest otherwise:

'Then that extremely white Bird, the sea-gull, who swims with his wings on the waves of the sea, hastily merged himself in the profound bosom of the ocean' (Taylor 1795, 52).

It may seem disappointing, therefore, that the best parts of the sentence belong to Gildon:

'then that white Bird call'd Gavia, or the Sea-Gull, who Swims with his Wings on the Waves of the Sea, div'd down to the profound Bosom of the Ocean' (Gildon 1709, II, 182).

But at least Taylor had the good sense not to mutilate Gildon's line.

It is also worth noticing what Taylor omits. In Book Five, Psyche's jealous sisters advise her (in Hanson's translation) to 'Take a very sharp razor, whet it with the application of your soft stroking palm, and secretly conceal it that side of the bed where you usually lie' (5.20: *Novaculam praeacutam adpulsu etiam palmulae lenientis exasperatam tori qua parte cubare consuesti latenter absconde*). Harvard University really ought to attach a health warning to this passage: if you attempt to apply your palm to the blade, you will cut your hand to ribbons. As traditional barbers know, the correct procedure is to apply the blade to the palm.

Taylor's translation is not inaccurate (or hazardous), but it makes no attempt to reproduce the intense mimetic localization of the original Latin: 'Secretly conceal a very sharp razor, which has been perfectly well set', 'set' here being used in the *OED*'s 75th sense of 'To put an edge on (a cutting instrument, esp. a razor).'[52]

The *nouacula* is an implement accustomed to having an intimate relationship – both with the person who wields it (usually a *tonsor*) and the person upon whom it is wielded. Apuleius – transformative as always – is putting the 'novelty' back into *nouacula*. It is a small blade which makes the shav-ee 'feel like new'; but the blade is itself metamorphic: blunted by bristles, but periodically honed (the edge made new) by contact with the palm.

The *lector scrupulosus* might wonder what need anyone has of a razor in Cupid's palace; or why the sisters would consider it a suitable instrument for decapitating a man-sized serpent; or how royal princesses have acquired such detailed technical knowledge of the *tonsor's* craft. Some of these concerns seem to drive the lexical choices of certain translators:

> 'Carefully hide [...] a Sword, whose edge may be as sharp as the Whetstone can make it.'[53] (Lockman 1744, 29).
>
> 'Get hold of a very sharp carving knife, make it sharper still by stropping it on your palm'; (Graves 1950, 132).
>
> 'Take a very sharp blade and give it an additional edge by caressing it on your palm'. (Kenney 1990, 73).

Both for practical and thematic reasons, however, Psyche's *nouacula* needs to be a razor, with a blade no longer than the width of a palm if injury is to be avoided during hand-stropping. One might also think back to that earlier passage in *The Golden Ass* (2.17), describing the titillating contact between Photis' 'rosy' palm and her *glabellum feminal*: 'Diligently, also, through bashfulness, rather shading than covering her depilous private parts with her rosy expanded hand [...]' (Tay-

---

52 Taylor 1795, 39 = Taylor 1822, 111. Cf. Adlington 1566, repr. 1639, 98: 'Take a sharpe razor and put it under the pillow of your bed'; and Gildon 1709, 172: 'Take care to hide a Razor perfectly well set'.
53 See his note on *novaculam*.

lor 1822, [405]: 'Passages Suppressed': p. 33, line 27).⁵⁴ Or forwards to the headshaving that Lucius will undergo in the eleventh book to mark his initiation, after he has taken Isiac roses from the hands of the priest, Mithras. Or sideways, to the destructively metamorphic threat made by Venus to Cupid (5.30):

> 'Then I shall think my Injury attoned when I have shaved off those Locks [...] and crop'd off those Wings' (Gildon 1709: II, 185).

> 'Then I shall believe atonement has been made for the injury I have received when I [sic] have shaved off those locks [...] and cut off those pinions'. (Taylor 1795, 56).

The instrument chosen for Psyche has also featured significantly in the medieval reception of the tale. In a twelfth-century commentary on Martianus Capella attributed to Bernard Silvester, we find an exegesis of Psyche's *nouacula* which anticipates William of Ockham's notorious 'Razor':

> Novacula est ratio quia utile ab inutile, honestum ab inhonesto, iustum ab iniusto, verum a falso secernit. Hac Cupido expellitur quia ratio et temporalium appetitus in eodem simul non morantur.

> The razor is Reason because it separates the useful from the useless, the honest from the dishonest, the just from the unjust, the true from the false. Cupid is driven away by it because Reason and the appetite for temporal things do not tarry at the same time in the one being.⁵⁵

5 Legacy

When the most celebrated of the American Transcendentalists, Ralph Waldo Emerson (1803–82), met Wordsworth for the second time in 1848, he expressed his incredulity that 'no one' in England 'knew anything of Thomas Taylor, the Platonist, whilst in every American library his books are found'.⁵⁶ Emerson's own library included a copy of Taylor's 1822 translation of Apuleius' *Metamorphoses*.⁵⁷ Indeed, 'Apuleius' appears in Emerson's 'List of Books' (seven lines

---

54 Taylor excluded some of the more explicit passages from the text and published them separately as 'passages suppressed'. Some copies of the 1822 edition have these bound in at the end.
55 *The Commentary on Martianus Capella's 'De nuptiis Philologiae et Mercurii' Attributed to Bernardus Silvestris*, ed. H. J. Westra (Toronto: PIMS, 1986), 171–72. On the role of Fulgentius in bridging the Apuleian and Capellan traditions of Psyche in this passage, see Carver 2007, 102–3.
56 Emerson (1960–82), Vol. X (1847–1848), 559.
57 Emerson (1960–82), Vol. XIII (1852–1855), 370.

below the word 'Favourites') in one of his Topical Notebooks.⁵⁸ Emerson also observed:

> Tis curious that Thomas Taylor, the Platonist, is really a better man of imagination, a better poet, or perhaps I should say, a better feeder to a poet, [282] than any other writer between Milton and Wordsworth. He is a poet with a poet's life and aims.⁵⁹

'Feeder' might mean a 'channel or conduit', supplying the information, imagination, and inspiration needed to make a poet; but it can also suggest a 'nurse' or 'Pastor' – a 'shepherd' in the biblical sense, as in Jesus' words of commission to Peter just before His Ascension: 'Feed my sheep' (*John* 21:17, KJV).

English Romanticism drew much of its inspiration from an expansion and reinvigoration of the Platonic tradition – a process to which Taylor devoted the whole of his working life.⁶⁰ As early as 1796, the young Coleridge had declared: 'Metaphysics, & Poetry, & "Facts of mind" – (i.e. Accounts of all the strange phantasms that ever possessed your philosophy-dreamers from Tauth, the Egyptian to Taylor, the English Pagan,) are my darling Studies'.⁶¹ Taylor's advocacy of the *Platonica familia* in its totality, and his insistence upon a profound philosophical truth underlying the surface of 'Cupid and Psyche' (so often the occasion of purely 'decorative' treatments in the visual arts, and 'spectacular' ones in the dramatic) helped to fuel the remarkably rich reception of Apuleius by poets of the Romantic period, encapsulated in Keats's vow, in the 'Ode to Psyche', to 'be thy priest, and build a fane / In some untrodden region of my mind' (1819, quoted and discussed in this volume by May). In a letter to Hogg dated 8 May 1817, Percy Bysshe Shelley wrote: 'I am in the midst of Apuleius – I never read a fictitious composition of such miraculous interest & beauty. – I think generally, it even surpasses Lucian, & the story of Cupid and Psyche any imagination ever clothed in the lan[g]uage of men. Peacock is equally enchanted with it.'⁶²

It is not always easy to separate specific debts to Taylor's translations of 'Cupid and Psyche' (1795) and the *Metamorphoses* (1822) from the broader stream of Taylor's influence as a platonizer, but W. B. Yeats's 'Leda and the Swan' (September 1923) may be a late and brilliant example. Taylor's contribution to Yeats's mystical-philosophical outlook (articulated most infamously in *A Vision*) was sig-

---

58 Emerson 1993, II, 236–37, 385.
59 Emerson 1993, II, 281–82. Cf. Emerson, (1960–82), Vol. XIII (1852–1855), 138 (1853).
60 Notopoulos 1936 and 1949 (Shelley); Vigus 2009 (Coleridge).
61 Coleridge, Letter to John Thelwall, 19 November 1796, 13.
62 Quoted by Markley 2003, 125.

nificant.⁶³ Yeats was also interested in Apuleius' treatment of zoophilia (*Met.* 10.19–23): 'Our words must seem to be inevitable. Apuleius describes a woman & donkey having connection in a crowded circus.'⁶⁴ Could a scintilla of his reading of Taylor have penetrated a sonnet initially titled (in Yeats's early drafts), 'A Pagan Annunication'?:

> A sudden blow: the *great wings beating* still
> Above the *staggering girl*, her thighs caressed
> By the dark webs, her nape caught in his bill,
> He holds her helpless breast upon his breast.
>
> How can those *terrified vague fingers* push
> The *feathered glory* from her loosening thighs?
> And how can body, laid in that white rush,
> But feel the strange heart beating where it lies?
>
> A shudder in the loins engenders there
> The broken wall, the burning roof and tower
> And Agamemnon dead.
>   Being *so caught up*,
> So mastered by the brute blood of the *air*,
> *Did she put on his knowledge with his power*
> Before the indifferent beak could let her *drop*?

The description of Leda, post-impact, as 'the staggering girl' may involve, from the poet's conscious point of view, the 'inevitable' words for the occasion. But the phrase is certainly distinctive, and arguably disruptive. Taylor observes in his preface: 'It is remarkable that Psyche, after falling to the ground, is represented as having "*a stumbling and often reeling gait*";" for Plato, in the [ix] Phædo, says, that the soul is drawn into body with a *staggering* motion'.⁶⁵ Taylor is recalling Pan's inference, *ab isto titubante et saepius uacillante uestigio* (5.25), that Psyche 'labor[s] under an excess of love' (*amore nimio laboras*; transl. Taylor 1795: 48). Apuleius' *titubante* echoes *titubat* in the slightly earlier description (5.21) of Psyche's irresolution as she prepares to decapitate Cupid: 'yet now she was beginning to *apply her hands* [*manus admovens*] to the impious work, *she staggers* with uncertain determination [*adhuc incerta consilii titubat*], and is distract-

---

63 In the 1890s, Yeats was a member of Madame Blavatsky's Theosophical Society which had championed Taylor's work in England as well as America since the 1870s.
64 Letter to Dorothy Wellesley, 3 May [1936]. ALS Meisei. Wade, 854–5.
65 Taylor 1795, viii-ix; original emphasis. Cf. *Phaedo* 79c: καὶ αὐτὴ πλανᾶται καὶ ταράττεται καὶ εἰλιγγιᾷ ὥσπερ μεθύουσα ('it wanders about and is confused and dizzy like a drunken man'; transl. Harold North Fowler).

ed with the apprehension of her approaching calamities [...] in the same body she loves the husband and hates the beast [*in eodem corpore odit bestiam, diligit maritum*]' (Taylor 1795: 41; emphasis added).

The coincidence (or concurrence) of 'staggering' in Taylor and Yeats may not constitute a clear 'allusion'.[66] But it creates, at the very least, an echo-effect; and it invites us (as Apuleianists, Platonists, or Yeatsians) to collocate, to co-read these two mythological narratives, both of which involve highly transgressive, but ultimately productive encounters between powerful, 'feathered' deities and ambivalently resistant (or reactive) young women who are subsequently 'dropped' by the fathers of their offspring.[67]

Such resonances should remind us that, when it comes to the wider manifestations of mythological fable and Plato's 'dear gorgeous nonsense',[68] 'All' is, indeed, 'One'.[69]

6 Bibliography

Adlington, William, transl. (1566; repr. 1639), *The XI. Bookes of The Golden Asse containing the Metamorphosie of Lucius Apuleius, interlaced with Sundry Pleasant and Delectable Tales: with an Excellent Narration of the Marriage of Cupid and Psyches, set out in the Fourth, Fifth and the Sixth Bookes*, London: Printed by Thomas Harper, for Thomas Alchorn, and are to be sold at his shop at the signe of the Greene Dragon in Pauls Church-yard.

Arrowsmith and Bowley (1798), *Bibliotheca Mastersiana. A Catalogue of the Genuine and Singulary* [sic] *Valuable Library of Books, of the late Robert Masters, B. D. & F. R. S. Author ...*, London: s.n.

Bayle, P. (1734), *A General Dictionary, Historical and Critical: in which a New and Accurate Translation of that of the Celebrated Mr. Bayle, with the Corrections ...* London.

Blake, W. (1982), *The Complete Poetry and Prose of William Blake*, ed. David V. Erdman, commentary by Harold Bloom, Newly revised edn, Berkeley and Los Angeles.

Carter, A. (ed.) (2004), *Rethinking Dance History. A Reader*. London.

Carver, R. H. F. (2007), *The Protean Ass: The 'Metamorphoses' of Apuleius from Antiquity to the Renaissance*, Oxford.

---

[66] In the third section of 'Nineteen Hundred and Nineteen' (1921), however, Yeats invokes 'Some moralist or mythological poet' who 'Compares the solitary soul to a swan' (1–2), and 'Some Platonist' who 'affirms that in the station / Where we should cast off body and trade / The ancient habit sticks' (14–16). O'Neill 2004: 159 offers possible identifications: Shelley as 'poet', Thomas Taylor as 'Platonist'.

[67] Ranger in this volume makes a case for Sylvia Plath's use of the same myth in a poem alluding to *Cupid and Psyche*.

[68] Coleridge, Letter to John Thelwall, 31 December 1796.

[69] Plato, *Parmenides*, 128a-b; cf. Heraclitus, Fr. 50.

Carver, R. H. F. (2013), 'Between Photis and Isis: Fiction, Reality, and the Ideal in *The Golden Ass* of Apuleius', in: Paschalis/Panayotakis, 243–74.

Carver, R. H. F. (2018), 'Bologna as Hypata: Annotation, Transformation, and Transl(oc)ation in the Circles of Filippo Beroaldo and Francesco Colonna', in: Futre Pinheiro/Konstan/MacQueen, 221–38.

Cavicchioli, S. (2002), *The Tale of Cupid and Psyche: An Illustrated History*, New York.

Chazin-Bennahum, J. (2004), 'A Longing for Perfection: Neoclassic Fashion and Ballet', in: Carter, 59–68.

Cumberland, G. (1796), *Thoughts on Outline, Sculpture, and the System that Guided the Ancient Artists in Composing Their Figures and Groupes: Accompanied with Free Remarks on the Practice of the Moderns, and Liberal Hints Cordially Intended for Their Advantage. To which are Annexed Twenty-four Designs of Classical Subjects Invented on the Principle Recommended in the Essay by George Cumberland*, London: printed by W. Wilson, St. Peter's-Hill, Doctors'-Commons; and sold by Messrs. Robinson, Paternoster-Row; and T. Egerton, Whitehall.

Dibdin, T.F. (1808), *An Introduction to the Knowledge of Rare and Valuable Editions of the Greek and Latin Classics*, 3rd edn., London.

Douglas, E. (pseudonym of John Evelyn Barlas) (1884), *Poems, Lyrical and Dramatic*, London.

Emerson, R.W. (1960–82), *The Journals and Miscellaneous Notebooks of Ralph Waldo Emerson*, ed. William H. Gilman, 16 vols, Cambridge, MA.

Emerson, R.W. (1993), *The Topical Notebooks of Ralph Waldo Emerson: Volume 2*, ed. Ronald A. Bosco, Columbia, MI.

Erdman, David V. (1977), *Blake: Prophet Against Empire*, 3rd edn., Princeton.

Firenzuola, A. (1792), *Apuleio, dell'asino d'oro, traslato da Messer Agnolo Firenzuola, di latino in lingua toscana*, London.

Futre Pinheiro, M./Konstan, D./MacQueen, B.D. (eds.) (2018), *Cultural Crossroads in the Ancient Novel*, Berlin.

Gildon, C. (1708; repr. 1709 and 1724), *The New Metamorphosis: or, the Pleasant Transformation: Being The Golden Ass of Lucius Apuleius of Medaura. Alter'd and Improv'd to the Modern Times*, 2 vols, London.

Graves, R. (1950), *The Transformations of Lucius, otherwise Known as The Golden Ass by Lucius Apuleius*, Harmondsworth.

Hagstrum, Jean H. (1977), 'Eros and Psyche: Some Versions of Romantic Love and Delicacy', *Critical Inquiry*, 3.3, 521–42.

Haigney, C. (1987), 'Vala's Garden in Night the Ninth: Paradise Regained or Woman Bound?', *Blake: An Illustrated Quarterley*, 20.4: 116–24.

Hanson, J. A. (ed. and transl.) (1990), *Apuleius: Metamorphoses*, 2 vols, Loeb Classical Library, Cambridge, MA.

[Hogg, Thomas Jefferson] (1823), 'Apuleius', *The Liberal*, 2. 3 (Jan. 1823), 151–76.

Horáček, J. (2014), 'Pedantry and Play: The Zukofsky *Catullus*', *Comparative Literature Studies* 51. 1, 106–31.

Kenney, E. J. (ed. and transl.) (1990), *Apuleius: Cupid & Psyche*, Cambridge.

King, James (1972), 'The Meredith Family, Thomas Taylor, and William Blake', *Studies in Romanticism* 11: 153–57.

Latané, D. E. (2013), *William Maginn and the British Press: A Critical Biography*, Farnham.

Lockman, J. (1744), *Loves of Cupid and Psyche; in Verse and Prose from the French of La Fontaine, Author of the Celebrated Tales and Fables. To which are Prefix'd, a Version of the Same Story, from the Latin of Apuleius. With a New Life of La Fontaine, Extracted from a Great Variety of Authors. The Whole Illustrated with Notes by Mr. Lockman*, London.
Louth, A. (2004), 'Taylor, Thomas (1758–1835)', *ODNB*.
[Maginn, W.] (1825), 'Note-Book of a Literary Idler. No. I', *Blackwood's Magazine*: 736–44.
Markley, A. A. (2003), 'Curious Transformations: Cupid, Psyche, and Apuleius in the Shelleys' Works', *The Keats-Shelley Review*, 17.1, 120–35.
Mathias, T. J. (1796), *The Pursuits of Literature, or What You Will. A Satirical Poem in Dialogue. With Notes. Part the Third*, London: printed for J. Owen, No. 168, Piccadilly.
[Nares, R.] 1788, *Remarks on the Favourite Ballet of Cupid and Psyche; with Some Account of the Pantomime of the Ancients, and other Observations*, London: printed for John Stockdale, opposite Burlington House, Piccadilly.
Nares, R. (1810), *Essays and other Occasional Compositions, Chiefly Reprinted, Volume 1*,
Notopoulos, J. A. (June 1936), 'Shelley and Thomas Taylor', *PMLA*, 51.2: 502–17.
Notopoulos, J. A. (1949), *The Platonism of Shelley: A Study of Platonism and the Platonic Mind*, Durham, NC.
O'Neill, M. (2004), *A Routledge Literary Sourcebook on the Poems of W. B. Yeats*, London.
Paschalis, M./Stelios, P. (eds.) (2013), *The Construction of the Real and the Ideal in the Ancient Novel*, Groningen: Barkhuis Publishing & The University Library Groningen.
Pierce, F. E. (1928), 'Blake and Thomas Taylor', *PMLA* 43.4, 1121–41.
Porson, R. [pseudonym 'Mythologus'] (1798), 'Orgies of Bacchus. Part I', in *The Spirit of the Public Journals for 1797. Being an Impartial Selection of the most Exquisite Essays and jeux d'esprits, Principally Prose, That Appear in the Newspapers and Other Publications*, London: printed for R. Phillips. Published by Mess. Richardsons, Royal Exchange; Mr. Symonds, Paternoster-Row; Mr. Clarke, New Bond-Street; Mr. Harding, St. James's Street; and Sold by all other Booksellers, 262–67.
Priestman, M. (2000), *Romantic Atheism: Poetry and Freethought, 1780–1830*, Cambridge.
Raine, K. (1969a), *Blake and Tradition*, 2 vols, London.
Raine, K./ Mills Harper, G. (eds.) (1969b), *Thomas Taylor the Platonist: Selected Writings*, Princeton.
Robison, J. (1797), *Proofs of a Conspiracy against all the Religions and Governments of Europe, Carried on in the Secret Meetings of Free Masons, Illuminati, and Reading Societies*, Edinburgh.
Sanford, O. M. (1885), 'Works of Thomas Taylor the Platonist', *Book-lore* (Nov 1885), 169–76.
Shelley, M. (transl.) (2002), 'Cupid and Psyche', in: P. Clemit/A. A. Markley (eds.) *Mary Shelley's 'Literary Lives' and Other Writings: Volume 4*, London, 282–95.
Synesius (1926 & 1930), *De insomniis*, in: *The Essays and Hymns of Synesius of Cyrene, Including the Address to the Emperor Arcadius and the Political Speeches*, transl. A. Fitzgerald, 2 vols, London.
Taylor, T. (transl.) (1788–89), *The Philosophical and Mathematical Commentaries of Proclus; Surnamed, Plato's Successor, on the First Book of Euclid's Elements. And His Life of Marinus. Translated from the Greek. With a Preliminary Dissertation on the Platonic Doctrine of Ideas, &c. By Thomas Taylor*, 2 vols, London.

Taylor, T. (transl.) (1795), *The Fable of Cupid and Psyche, Translated from the Latin of Apuleius: To which Are Added, A Poetical Paraphrase on The Speech of Diotima, In The Banquet of Plato; Four Hymns, &c. &c. With an Introduction, in which the Meaning of the Fable Is Unfolded*, London.

Taylor, T. (transl.) (1822), *The Metamorphosis or Golden Ass, and Philosophical Works, of Apuleius. Translated from the Original Latin*, London.

Taylor, T. (transl.) (1893), *The Metamorphosis or Golden Ass of Apuleius, Translated from the Original Latin*, Birmingham.

Vigus, J. (2009), *Platonic Coleridge*, London.

Walde, C./ Egger, B. (eds.) (2012), *The Reception of Classical Literature*, transl. D. Smart/M. H. Wibier, Brill's New Pauly Supplements, Leiden and Boston.

Walpole, H. (1965), *Horace Walpole's Correspondence*, vol. 34, New Haven.

Warburton, W. (1738–41), *The Divine Legation of Moses demonstrated, on the Principles of a Religious Deist, from the Omission of the Doctrine of a Future State of Reward and Punishment in the Jewish Dispensation*, 2nd edn, London: Executors of Fletcher Gyles.

Warburton, W. (1755), *The Divine Legation of Moses*, 4th edn, corrected and enlarged, 2 vols, London: J. and P. Knapton.

Webb, T. (1982), *English Romantic Hellenism, 1700–1824*, Manchester.

Zukofsky, L. (1969), *Catullus*, New York-London.

Regine May
Keats's 'Ode to Psyche'. Psyche as poetry and inspiration

John Keats (1795–1821) frequently showcases the reception of antiquity in his poems, and uses Apuleius' story for widely different, contrasting reasons—classicism and innovation.[1] In this paper I will show that Keats engaged more deeply and creatively with Apuleius' novel, and particular *Cupid and Psyche*, than generally assumed. Keats first knew *Cupid and Psyche* from reading Mary Tighe's *Psyche* and the translation of the whole of the *Metamorphoses* by William Adlington (1566).[2] Although at first Keats highly admired Tighe's work, its sentimental nature eventually clashed with his own romantic ideas. Still, his love for *Cupid and Psyche* survived his disillusionment with Tighe, and Keats makes recourse to Apuleius' story at important stages of his own personal and poetic development, especially focusing on the character of Psyche as a metaphor for poetic inspiration. I believe that for Keats the way he characterises himself against the narrator and author of the original *Metamorphoses* is also important for his definition of what he wants to achieve poetically, which has an effect on how we see his self-fashioning as a poet and what he sets out as his inspiration. I will map Keats's poetic development as he defines poetry as Psyche, and eventually sees himself, like Apuleius or Lucius, as a priest,[3] and reassess our understanding of Keats's continued engagement with Apuleius.

Keats's knowledge of Latin is often underestimated, but he read Latin literature in the original as well as in easily available translations.[4] At school Keats studied and translated classical authors such as Vergil and Horace. Just like other Cockney poets from the mid 18th century onwards,[5] Keats was drawn to more marginalised, less canonical Latin authors such as Catullus and supplemented his school knowledge of the Augustan poets Vergil and Horace with dictionaries and handbooks on his subject, but he was also especially attracted to pre- (Catullus) and post-Augustan (Apuleius) writers.

---

1 Stead 2016, 19. On Keats's knowledge of the Classics see also Aske 1985, especially 101–109 on Psyche.
2 For Tighe see O'Brien in this volume.
3 Apuleius' priesthood(s): Harrison 2000, 8.
4 Stead 2016, 278.
5 On the resurgence of study of Catullus and other 'marginal' Roman authors during Keats's lifetime: Stead 2016, 8 and 274–8.

https://doi.org/10.1515/9783110641585-010

But Keats found inspiration closer to home, too: Tighe's third edition of *Psyche* from 1811[6] was read enthusiastically by the young poet,[7] and in 1815 he refers to the 'blessings of Tighe' in 'To Some Ladies'; In 1818, however, he claims to see through Mrs. Tighe and can find 'nothing in [her] but weakness' (letter to his brother and sister in law).[8] Nevertheless, his 'Ode to Psyche', 'Lamia' and 'Eve of St Agnes' all show many verbal allusions to Tighe.[9] Tighe is quite possibly his first encounter with the story of Psyche, and he still relies on her somewhat sentimental portrait in his first engagement with the tale.

1 'I Stood Tip-Toe'

While still enthusiastic about Tighe, Keats wrote 'I Stood Tip-Toe upon a Little Hill'. Completed December 1816 and the first poem in the 1817 volume (*Poems 1817*), it programmatically defines the nature of poetry,[10] and in it the poet seeks solace for erotic anxiety in the freshness of nature. He describes a perfect poetic experience as when a tale is 'moving on luxurious wings/The soul is lost in pleasant smotherings' (l. 131–2). He already associates the soul with wings, and claims that this exactly is the emotion that the author of Psyche must have felt, in lines 141–150:

> So felt he, who first told, how Psyche went
> On the smooth wind to realms of wonderment;
> What Psyche felt, and Love, when their full lips
> First touch'd; what amorous and fondling nips
> They gave each other's cheeks; with all their sighs,
> And how they kist each other's tremulous eyes:

---

[6] He probably read the poems in Tighe's 3rd edition from 1811.
[7] Weller 1928, xxiii collected Keats's allusions to Tighe, sometimes overenthusiastically; see also White 2010, 161. See Bush 1935, 794; 1969, 102 n.30 and Finney 1936, 614–15 for similarities between Adlington and Keats.
[8] On Keats's disillusionment with Tighe see Chandler 1998, 395–408; Finney 1936, 66–67 (who plays down Tighe's influence on Keats); Hartman 2011 argues that Apuleius' status as a later author in the Latin canon is reflected by Keats's Romanticism placing a challenge to the 18th century's 'Augustan' age.
[9] Gross 1990 argues that *Cupid and Psyche*, too, is influential on Keats's 'Lamia', a poem only a few months later than 'Ode to Psyche'. Similarities include the union of a mortal and immortal (p. 152), but he is sceptical about Keats' continued interest in Tighe at the time of his writing 'Ode to Psyche' (p. 154).
[10] Bush 1969, 84 describes it as 'Keats's first full affirmation of the identity of nature, myth, and poetry'. Schulz 1960, 56, oddly, does not identify Apuleius as the source.

> The silver lamp,—the ravishment,—the wonder—
> The darkness,—loneliness,—the fearful thunder;
> Their woes gone by, and both to heaven upflown,
> To bow for gratitude before Jove's throne.

The mutuality of love here is very much described as in Tighe: the couple appear equal and experience emotions together, albeit there is much left to the imagination. Compare for example the moment of mutual gazing and love that is not found in Apuleius, but described in Tighe, and where Psyche has a celebrated dream vision of Cupid, allowing the couple to fall in mutual love at the same time (p. 25):

> Nor was it quite a dream, for as she woke,
> Ere heavenly mists concealed him from her eye,
> One sudden transitory view she took
> Of Love's most radiant bright divinity;

The importance of this passage in Tighe has been shown by O'Brien in this volume. Keats's 'fearful thunder', too, may be taken from Tighe (p.58), when Cupid's palace disappears around her; there is nothing comparable in Adlington's version.

> Tremendous thunders echo through the halls,
> While ruin's hideous crash bursts o'er the affrighted walls.

Keats's plot outline is vague; although some imagery is taken from Tighe, Keats here importantly identifies the male author, Apuleius, as the tale's inspired first narrator ('he, who first told', l. 141). The mutuality of the couple's love continues in the story summarised in ll. 147–150. The cameo includes the story from the moment Zephyrus places Psyche in Cupid's palace, to her apotheosis—compare 'Psyche went/on the smooth wind' (l. 141f.), which echoes Adlington's (p.93) 'meek winde' (cf. *Met*.4.35 *mitis aura*). A mere two lines allude to the couple's separation and Psyche's trials. In these the focus is mostly on the couple's shared experience, and just slightly more on Psyche and her emotions than on Cupid's, as it is she (rather than he) who lifts the lamp or feels loneliness and fear of thunder; the allusiveness of the two lines, though, allows Cupid to remain included despite his actual absence from most of Apuleius' story, until at the end it is both of them again who fly to Heaven, as a happy and equal couple.

It is Keats's Psyche, not Cupid, who experiences darkness, loneliness and fear during their separation in a much more Apuleian set of emotions. Tighe's Psyche is not really apart from her Cupid, who travels with her as a knight in disguise, and both have quite an entourage –a page, a tame lion and a dove are constantly with them. Tighe's Psyche has offers of partnership of some sorts beyond Cupid's, while Apuleius' and Keats's Psyche experience loneliness and desolation while Cupid is away.

The last two lines of Keats's segment unite the two lovers and their actions again. In a few lines, Keats allusively summarises the story to its very end. Assuming that the tale is widely known, he uses it to define the nature of his poetry and describe the perfect poetic experience, but based on a prose author's joy when he first told the story of mutual love. This author is unequivocally male, anticipating Keats' valediction to Tighe and subsequent identification with a different kind of poetry before he openly denounces her in 1818.

Consequently, though Keats mostly focuses on the couple's emotions and love, he sees the story through the eyes of the author who wrote about it first, and who is an inspired creator: Apuleius. Despite his echoes of a text written by a female with a female focus (Tighe), his poet-narrator is male, and although the couple's emotions appear in the foreground of the story, it is essentially Apuleius' feelings that Keats ultimately identifies with. The repetition of 'first' disenfranchises Tighe, even more so since in her *Psyche* she, too, claims inspiration from the muse of poetry for herself, making her an inspired poetess in her own right (e.g. p. 56). Psyche's erotic story becomes the object which defines poetic inspiration, Psyche becomes poetry. Although much in the couple's portrait is from Tighe, Apuleius' influence is keenly felt.

So, 'I Stood Tip-Toe' already imperceptibly begins to move on from Tighe's sentimental femininity and refocuses on Apuleius the male author. It also uses motifs from the novel which move beyond Tighe's adaptation. The story becomes eroticised, but Psyche is not yet singled out as a character, specifically as the poem afterwards focuses on Cynthia and Endymion, and 'Endymion' is the original title by which Keats refers to it in his letters.[11] Psyche and Apuleius have yet to gain the grip on Keats's imagination that can be seen in 'Ode to Psyche'. Here it is only the first myth in a group of stories from mythology, which also include Pan and Syrinx, Narcissus and Echo. Still, the important identification of Keats with the male author Apuleius shows that this programmatic poem is important for Keats's poetic development.

---

11 See Cook on Keats 1996, 223n. 27.

2 'Ode to Psyche'

Keats returns to Psyche in 1819, and announces an important change in poetic direction, again by making Psyche the first in a set; the set of his carefully composed major odes.[12] In addition to using Tighe and Adlington in his poem, he also consulted several handbooks:[13] For example, he used Joseph Spence's (1699–1768) *Polymetis*,[14] an attempt to show how closely ancient poetry and art were dependent on each other, a book that Keats's friend Leigh Hunt held in scant regard.[15] Spence discusses Raphael's portrait of the marriage of Cupid and Psyche in the Villa Farnesina (see Simard's chapter), Roman statues of Cupid,[16] and the famous Roman statue group that Spence describes and depicts, and which resembles Keats's portrait (Figure 13).[17]

Keats could hope his readership would recognise the image he draws in his poem, and he announces its intertextual nature in l. 2 with 'remembrance'. He transcribes 'Ode to Psyche' in a letter to his brother George and his sister-in-law at the end of April 1819, and discusses his inspiration, research and manner of composition:[18]

> 'You must recollect that Psyche was not embodied as a goddess before the time of Apulieus the Platonist who lived after the Augustan age, and consequently the Goddess was never worshipped or sacrificed to with any of the ancient fervour – and perhaps never thought of in the old religion—I am more orthodox tha[n] to let a hethen Goddess be so neglected—
>
> ...

---

[12] The other major odes are 'Ode on a Grecian Urn', 'Ode on Indolence', 'Ode on Melancholy', 'Ode to a Nightingale', and 'To Autumn'.
[13] Jack 1967, 202 suggests *The Faerie Queene's* Garden of Adonis, *Comus*, and Erasmus Darwin's *The Botanic Garden* as further available literary inspirations for 'Ode to Psyche'. Further inspirations are Milton's 'On the Morning of Christ's Nativity' for some phrases, and Claude Lorrain's paintings *The Enchanted Castle* and *The Father of Psyche Sacrificing at the Milesian Temple of Apollo*, which he would have seen at least as engravings; see e.g. Brown 1976, 53; White 2010, 102f.; Roe 2012, 221; 317. Bush 1935, note 36 is sceptical about the use of Adlington in 'Ode to Psyche'.
[14] Stead 2016, 274–5; Buxton-Forman on Keats 1900 vol. II, 106.
[15] Hunt was scathing about the uses of Spence's *Polymetis*: Leigh Hunt's Journal 1 90, 66 (Wednesday 28th May 1834); cited in Stead 2016, 20.
[16] On pp. 69–71 ('Dialogue the Seventh'), especially p. 70 and plate VI.
[17] Spence, *Polymetis* plate VI (between p. 82 and 83), reproduced with the permission of Special Collections, Leeds University Library (Brotherton Collection Ltq SPE).
[18] Cited from White 2010, 160, with Keats's spelling retained.

Figure 13: Spence, Joseph (1747), *Polymetis. Or, An Enquiry Concerning the Agreement Between the Works of the Roman Poets, And the Remains of the Antient Artists. Being an Attempt to Illustrate them Mutually from One Another.* In Ten Books, London, plate VI (between p. 82 and 83). Reproduced with the permission of Special Collections, Leeds University Library (Brotherton Collection Ltq SPE)

'The word signifies *the soul* ... Psyche is generally represented with the wings of a butterfly, and on that account, among the ancients, when a man had just expired, a butterfly appeared fluttering above, as if rising from the mouth of the deceased.'

Keats gives us a glimpse into his thought processes when writing this first of his great odes. Although he does not say so explicitly, he here paraphrases, as is often noted, Lemprière's *Classical Dictionary* s.v. 'Psyche':

'PSYCHE, a nymph whom Cupid married and carried into a place of bliss, where he long enjoyed her company. Venus put her to death because she had robbed the world of her son; but Jupiter at the request of Cupid, granted immortality to Psyche. The word signified the soul, and this personification of Psyche first mentioned by Apuleius, is posterior to the Augustan age, though still it is connected with ancient mythology. Psyche is generally represented with the wings of a butterfly to imitate the lightness of the soul, of which the butterfly is the symbol, and on that account, among the ancients, when a man has just expired, a butterfly appeared fluttering above, as if rising from the mouth of the deceased.'

Still, differences here are important. The dictionary entry gives a somewhat garbled summary of the novel, and crucially does not mention Apuleius' *Platonist* leanings, which is how Keats introduces the author to his readers. Keats could have picked this up from Adlington's work, who identifies Apuleius as a famous Platonist throughout *The Golden Asse*. A Platonist reading of the tale leads on naturally to the identification of Psyche as the soul, an approach to the soul's immortality which was an important concept underlying e.g. Wordsworth's 'Immortality Ode' or Shelley's 'Epipsychidion',[19] although this is not the space to study the poem's implications for Keats' attitude to the 'vale of soul-making' since Keats sees the soul not as god-given and permanent, but as something that develops, especially through its exposure to pain in the world.[20]

There is no direct evidence that Keats read the works of the contemporary Neoplatonist Thomas Taylor (1758–1835), although Taylor's Platonic and polytheistic approach would have been received favourably by Keats and his friends,[21] who had engaged with Taylor's Orphic and Platonic interpretations

---

19 For the concept see Haekel 2014.
20 See e.g. Jack 1967, 205–7 for both, and Haekel 2014, 117–20 for the nature of Psyche's 'soul'.
21 Raine 1968, 256 thinks it likely that Keats had read Taylor; Jack 1967, 205 considers it a possibility, since Keats and his friends were attracted to widely available Platonist readings of the story. Jack 1967, 203 cites a passage from Hazlitt's *Table-Talk* (*Complete Works*, viii.200–1), illustrating conversations about Greek and Latin novels.

and would have found Apuleius' Middle Platonism attractive.[22] Taylor's engagement with *Cupid and Psyche* is discussed in detail by Carver in this volume.

It is clear, though, that Keats had read Apuleius' novel itself, not merely the dictionary article; Lemprière's summary of the story sounds oddly un-Apuleian, and Keats tacitly omits Lemprière's errors, which indicates that he knows the story independently. In Apuleius, Venus tortures Psyche but does not kill her (as Lemprière claims), and it is Psyche's own curiosity which puts her into a death-like sleep, not Venus. Venus does not pursue her because Psyche had robbed the world of Love—instead, Venus is driven by jealousy of Psyche's beauty and worship. Where Lemprière is successful, though, and this is important for Keats, is in his stress on the visual image of Psyche, usually portrayed with the wings of the butterfly, which in itself encourages Keats to focus on the visual aspects of the scene in front of him beyond Apuleius, whose Psyche does not have any butterfly wings.

Spence, too, identifies Psyche with the soul and the butterfly (p. 71). Reading this same information in both Spence and Lemprière will have reinforced the association for Keats, an association which is not emphasized in Apuleius or Tighe. In all other details he tacitly uses the Apuleian version of the story he had found in Adlington's text.

In terms of its plot, 'Ode to Psyche' picks up the story where Apuleius, 'I Stood Tip-Toe' and even Tighe left off, namely with the life of the divine couple after Psyche's apotheosis. No longer does Keats talk about another author's feelings, but addresses Psyche directly, as a poet to the goddess.[23] This reflects Keats's frequent engagement with myth beyond transmitted stories, as he creates a version very much his own and without 'false archaism.'[24]

The situation is however at first comparable to 'I Stood Tip-Toe'; again the poet wanders through an idealised landscape, and in a forest he sees a couple embracing in a pose reminiscent of Spence's description of the Roman pair of statues, again near a brook among the flowers. They either have kissed or are about to kiss. The poet is not sure whether it is a dream, a vision or something real that he sees (ll. 5–7):

---

[22] See Haekel 2014, who also argues for aestheticism's importance for the Romantic concept of the soul.
[23] I disagree therefore with Chandler's 1998, 409–10 assessment that in Keats the story of Cupid and Psyche never takes off.
[24] Vendler 1983, 51.

> Surely I dreamt to-day, or did I see
> The winged Psyche with awaken'd eyes?
> I wander'd in a forest thoughtlessly,

Again the description of the couple stresses mutuality, they both do the same things at the same time, and again the focus is on their embrace (ll. 9–10; 15–17):

> Saw two fair creatures, couched side by side
> In deepest grass, beneath the whisp'ring roof
> ...
> They lay calm-breathing, on the bedded grass;
> Their arms embraced, and their pinions too;
> Their lips touch'd not, but had not bade adieu,

Whereas in 'I Stood Tip-Toe' the couple's 'full lips/First touch'd' (l. 143 f.), this couple's 'lips touch'd not' (l. 17); their passionate embrace has already happened. The events of the novel are over, *Cupid and Psyche* becomes Keats's own story. Though Keats recognises the 'winged boy',[25] he needs to stop for a moment to work out the female's identity (ll. 21–2):

> But who wast thou, O happy, happy dove?[26]
> His Psyche true!

Cupid then fades into the background and Keats focuses entirely on Psyche and displays his research in Lemprière: her late addition to the pantheon,[27] her beauty which surpasses other goddesses, and the lack of normal worship for her. As such, she is particularly meaningful for Keats, who often felt himself to be an outsider and latecomer to antiquity.[28] For Keats, of course, the 'Augustan age' also had the connotation of the classicising literature of the 18th century, against which his work reacted, thus allowing him to display both a literary and a personal statement by the mere inclusion of Psyche in his network of classical references. *Ode to Psyche* shows that Keats is not merely an insecure Cockney poetaster, but an imaginative reader of Apuleius' text.

---

[25] Cupid is not name-checked until the very last line ('warm Love'); 'Love' is also used instead of 'Cupid' in 'I Stood Tip-Toe'.
[26] Tighe once addresses Psyche as 'Pure spotless dove!' (p. 46); either comparison is apt, since doves mate for life (I am grateful to Roger Brock for the bird lore).
[27] Ll. 36–7: 'though too late for antique vows,/Too, too late for the fond believing lyre'.
[28] Aske 1985, 102: 'As a human 'goddess' too late for the glory of mythology, Psyche is a perfect figure for Keats's own belated age.'

A list of negatives shows this lack of conventional worship (ll. 28–35):

> Fairer than these, though temple thou hast none,
> Nor altar heap'd with flowers;
> Nor virgin-choir to make delicious moan
> Upon the midnight hours;
> No voice, no lute, no pipe, no incense sweet
> From chain-swung censer teeming;
> No shrine, no grove, no oracle, no heat
> Of pale-mouth'd prophet dreaming.

Unmentioned by Keats, though, this lack of worship is a new experience for this Psyche, who actually had many worshippers when she was still a human girl. The admirers' adoration is much underplayed for Tighe's timid Psyche, who shrinks from such worship and hides from her suitors. In Apuleius' version, when Psyche was falsely worshipped as a goddess though a mere mortal, she enjoyed all these things she no longer has now, as Psyche's beauty deprived Venus of her sacrifices which are now offered to her younger, virginal, replacement Psyche. As Keats's goddess, paradoxically, Psyche does not receive this kind of worship any more.[29] Keats transfers Venus' loss of her own ancient and traditional worship to her rival Psyche, whose veneration in Apuleius is replaced by a complete absence of worshippers in Keats:

> 'the Citisens [...], came daily by thousands, hundreths, and scores, to her fathers palace, who was astonied with admiration of her incomparable beauty, did no less worship and reverence her with crosses, signes, and tokens, and other divine adorations, according to the custome of the old used rites and ceremonies, than if she were the Lady Venus indeed, [...]
>
> ... a contempt grew towards the goddesse Venus, that no person travelled unto the Towne Paphos, nor to the Isle Gyndos, nor to Cythera to worship her. Her ornaments were throwne out, her temples defaced, her pillowes and cushions torne, her ceremonies neglected, her images and Statues uncrowned, and her bare altars unswept, and fowl with the ashes of old burnt sacrifice.'
>
> (Adlington p. 89–90).

Keats knows that Psyche's apotheosis was too late for ancient pagan worship and for inspired poetry to be written about her at the time, and it seems that, paradoxically, his description of Psyche's lack of veneration as a goddess is based on Apuleius' description of Psyche's worship as Venus' substitute, when Psyche did receive the adulation of the masses instead of the goddess.

---

29 Also noted by Chandler 1998, 411.

Yet, Apuleius, the author of the novel summarised in 'I Stood Tip-Toe', as the narrator of the human Psyche's fate, does not qualify as the poet of the lyre that immortalised Psyche requires and deserves now—he is not mentioned. 'Ode to Psyche' is a new story, and Psyche needs a new, inspired poet—Keats himself. Consequently, Keats, who has just seen Psyche in his vision himself, replaces the Apuleius from 'I Stood Tip-Toe' (ll. 43–51) to tell of Psyche's life after Apuleius' story has ended:

> I see, and sing, by my own eyes inspir'd.
> So let me be thy choir, and make a moan
> Upon the midnight hours;
> Thy voice, thy lute, thy pipe, thy incense sweet
> From swinged censer teeming;
> Thy shrine, thy grove, thy oracle, thy heat
> Of pale-mouth'd prophet dreaming.
> Yes, I will be thy priest, and build a fane
> In some untrodden region of my mind,

One by one he goes through the items of worship that Psyche currently lacks, and promises to supply them himself. He will be her poet and her priest, and he will build her the temple she deserves, but inside his own mind and imagination. This idea might echo Vergil *Georgics* 3.12–18, where Vergil promises to build a temple for Augustus through his own poetry.[30] Keats's temple sits in the landscape of his own 'working brain', but resembles the green bower in which he had found Cupid and Psyche embracing.[31]

This complex poem is the first of the great odes, which all deal with poetic inspiration, and sees Keats become Psyche's priest. Previously he had acknowledged Apuleius' role in propagating her story, but now denies him any agency in ensuring that Psyche receives her worship. Instead, Keats offers to be the person who tells her story himself, facilitated by picking up the story where Apuleius himself had left it (and also leaving behind Tighe, another inspired poetess who addresses Psyche, and praises her at epic length). Apuleius, as it were, told the story of the mortal girl, and Keats picks up from there and tells her story as the goddess from the perspective of her newly-appointed priest/poet or *vates*.[32]

---

30 I owe this suggestion to Stephen Harrison. See Stead 2016, 272; 275–8 for Keats's knowledge of Vergil.
31 See also Vendler 1983, 60.
32 On the theme of mutability and immortality in 'Ode to Psyche' see Waldoff 1977.

3 Keats's Apuleius beyond *Cupid and Psyche*

As Psyche's poet, Keats usurps Apuleius' identity and inverts and reshapes Apuleian allusions not only in the portrayal of Psyche's lack of worship. Allusions to the rest of the *Metamorphoses* beyond *Cupid and Psyche* and the 'Ode to Psyche' show that this stolen imagery is functionally connected to Keats's self-identification as an inspired poet.

Psyche's name appears one more time in Keats's work, in his 'Ode on Melancholy' (ll. 6–8; composed during 1819):

> Nor let the beetle, nor the death-moth be
> Your mournful Psyche, nor the downy owl
> A partner in your sorrow's mysteries;

Psyche is neither a moth nor a beetle, as Keats knows well, but a butterfly and an image for the soul;[33] both associations are prominent here. Interesting in an Apuleian context, and hitherto unnoticed by Keats scholars, is that the name 'Psyche' is only the first in a set of potential Apuleian elements, sourced from *Cupid and Psyche* and, surprisingly, the *Metamorphoses* as a whole: the second is the owl, into which the witch Pamphile transforms, as part of what Apuleius calls the 'mysteries' or 'secrets' of magical metamorphosis, which here forms the third allusion within two lines.[34] Carver in this volume, too, argues that the owl is a powerful Apuleian symbol.

At the beginning of 'Ode to Psyche', Keats offers to be the mystagogue for Psyche's own cult, too: 'thy secrets should be sung' (l. 3). Apuleius' preoccupation with mystery initiations both false (*Met.* 1.3, into magic) and real (*Met.* 11, into the Isis cult) are adapted by Keats into poetic initiations. This magical initiation of Lucius by Photis results in Lucius' transformation into a donkey, and Photis' jealous warning against observing the mystery of transformation becomes Keats's advice on how to develop one's soul through poetry.

Furthermore, the Ode's 'sorrow' picks up on the relationship between Lucius and his 'mystagogue' Photis, as she repeatedly causes Lucius 'sorrow', for example when she unwittingly harmed him by botching Pamphile's magical ingredients:

---

[33] Keats uses the image of the soul as a fleeting butterfly in *Endymion*, e.g. 2.60–93.
[34] Adlington p. 64 translates Pamphile's owl metamorphosis as a mystery: 'now shal you know the hidden secrets of my mistres, unto whome the powers of hel do obey'.

'And thinke you not that I did willingly procure this anguish and *sorrow* unto you' (Adlington p. 63).

The word recurs p. 68, after Lucius had requested to be metamorphosed into an owl:'Then said Fotis, Wil you go about to deceive me now, and inforce me to work my own *sorrow?*'

Photis causing Lucius 'sorrow' is a running theme in their relationship, which is picked up by Keats, who adapts the erotic relationship of Lucius and Photis into a portrait of his own inspiration. Consequently, these few lines of 'Ode on Melancholy' contain a complicated web of allusions to both Lucius and Psyche which explain inspired poetry as a mystical initiation.

When we return to 'Ode to Psyche' to look for further Apuleian allusions, a few important images crystallise specifically around the portrait of the author-poet. In Apuleius, Psyche only falls in love with Cupid at the moment she sees him, months into their marriage, when she breaks the taboo, holds the lamp over him and accidentally handles his arrows. Tighe's couple fall in mutual love at the same time that they first ever see each other, but in 'Ode to Psyche' we have a *ménage à trois*, as the speaker joins Cupid and Psyche as her worshipper after he happens to come across them embracing in the woodland grove where he sees the couple, unmoving, as in a dream vision.

Keats poses at the beginning of the poem as an accidental observer chancing upon a goddess. This scenario, I would argue, recalls the statue of Actaeon that Apuleius' Lucius finds in his aunt Byrrhaena's atrium—an obviously attractive passage for Keats who loved and found inspiration in artwork and statues in particular.[35]

> On the contrary part, the image of the Goddesse Diana was wrought in white marble, which was a marvellous sight to see, for shee seemed as though the winde did blow up her garments, and that she did encounter with them that came into the house. [...] and while I beheld the running water, which seemed to spring and leap under the feet of the goddesse, I marked the grapes which hanged in the water, which were like in every point to the grapes of the vine, and seemed to move and stir by the violence of the streame. (Adlington p. 37–8)

In general, the Actaeon myth may well have inspired the observational aspect of Keats's poem, but there are also specifically Apuleian features. Keats's statue-like couple have a river at their feet (l. 12 'A brooklet, scarce espied'), and are framed by a canopy of greenery, just as Apuleius' Diana statue is reflected in

---

[35] See Scott 1994 for Keats's interest in ekphrasis.

a stream framed by grapes and flowers. Actaeon watches Diana, and Lucius observes the two of them (a pair of statues), just as Keats observes the kissing couple Cupid and Psyche (another pair of statues).

The clearest evidence that Keats is thinking of this statue group is however found in in 'I Stood Tip-Toe' l. 135–7, where again grapes and a babbling brook surround him, which indicates that already when composing this early poem Keats knew this scene from the novel itself:

> O'erhead we see the jasmine and sweet briar,
> And bloomy grapes laughing from green attire;
> While at our feet, the voice of crystal bubbles
> and grapes above their heads like the lovers

As an observer of a couple surrounded by grapes and water, Keats writes himself into the same situation as Apuleius' narrator Lucius. This identification is especially pertinent if we remember that Adlington followed a tradition found ever since at least Augustine of Hippo (354–430 AD), who identified Lucius with Apuleius, e.g. in Adlington's short 'biography' of the author, which merges elements of Apuleius' life, such as his birthplace and marriage to Pudentilla, with Lucius' fictional parents Theseus and Salvia (p. 9):

> LUCIUS APULEIUS African, an excellent follower of Plato his sect, born in Madaura [...] his father called Theseus had passed all offices of dignity in his countrey with much honour. His mother named Salvia was of such excellent vertue, that she passed all the Dames of her time, borne of an ancient house, and descended from the philosopher Plutarch, and Sextus his nephew.

This identification of author and his protagonist is facilitated by a famous passage in the novel, *Met.* 11.27, where a prophecy about Lucius suddenly identifies him as 'a poore man of Madaura'. Madaura/us is the birthplace of the author Apuleius, whereas Lucius is from Patras in Greece.[36] Already Apuleius himself toyed with conflating his own identity with that of his literary creation Lucius,[37] and Keats follows this through by adding his own identity.

Apuleius-Lucius is in a similar situation to Keats in Byrrhaena's atrium, and the two observers experience similar characterisations. The 'he' from 'I Stood Tip-Toe' completes his transformation into the 'I' from 'Ode to Psyche', a meta-

---

[36] For a discussion of the passage see Sandy 1978. Gildon 1709 (whose adaptation is discussed in this volume by Carver) repeats this biographical fiction about Apuleius, but focuses much less on Apuleius' Platonic pedigree than Adlington.

[37] See the discussion and bibliography in Keulen et al. 2015, 451 and 465–7.

morphosis already anticipated by the poet's earlier musings on how 'he' must have felt. This identification of Keats with Apuleius-Lucius is a logical step forward from a thought already planted in the earlier poem, and as Keats's conscious poetic choice and important step in his poetic self-expression.[38]

Furthermore, when Keats declares himself Psyche's priest performing her mysteries, he uses, though in an impressionistic manner, further Apuleian imagery (ll. 58–60):

> And in the midst of this wide quietness
> A rosy sanctuary will I dress
> With the wreath'd trellis of a working brain,

Although at the end of *Cupid and Psyche*, the couple are indeed showered with 'roses and other sweet smells' (Adlington p. 121), the involvement of a priest in a temple is not found in that text, which ends in a wedding feast on Mount Olympus.

Roses and priesthood, however, point to yet another link with Lucius' own metamorphic experiences towards the end of his own story: in *Met.* 11, Lucius is rescued from his donkeyhood by a priest carrying roses (Adlington p. 223):[39]

> For the great Priest which bare the restoration of my human shape, by the commandement of the goddes, Approached more and more, bearing in his left hand the timbrill, and in the other a garland of Roses to give me, to the end I might be delivered from cruel fortune. (Adington p. 223).

Lucius regains his identity with the help of this priest, just like Psyche gains her worship through Keats's assumption of her priesthood. Even this promise to become Psyche's priest and create a sanctuary for his goddess echoes *Met.* 11, where Lucius in the end becomes the priest of the goddess Isis, in whose sanctuary in Rome he comes to live. Like Psyche, Isis is herself another (relatively) late addition to the Roman pantheon.[40] Given that Keats's temple to Psyche is

---

[38] See Haekel 2014, 186 for the fluid nature of Keats's poetic identity.
[39] Interestingly, he does so in imagery that may also be associated with Tighe, where Psyche approaches a temple decorated with 'immortal roses' and encounters a priest of the Egyptian god Ammon (64); Keats, likewise, will become a priest, decorating Psyche's temple with roses. The declaration to become her priest may also be inspired by Spenser, *Amoretti* xxii: Bush 1935, 802.
[40] Even after its establishment in Rome in the early first century BCE, the Isis cult continued to be seen as foreign and suffered sporadic persecution. See Orlin 2010, 204–11.

inside his own inspired mind, the last few lines of the poem, which return to Cupid,[41] become significant, too:

> And there shall be for thee all soft delight
> That shadowy thought can win,
> A bright torch, and a casement ope at night,
> To let the warm Love in!
> (ll. 64–67)

Keats's mind-temple has excluded Cupid, who needs to come back into the scene and the poem. These last few lines seem to allude to Cupid's palace in Apuleius, where Psyche at night was not allowed to see her unknown lover who left before the sun rose (see e. g. *Met.* 5.4). Now there will be a bright torch to ensure that they can take visual delight in each other: brightness and warmth indicate that the union is now acknowledged, sanctified (by the wedding torch) and public.[42] So, although Cupid is neglected throughout the poem, he comes back into the inspired poet's mind, i.e. into the temple of the soul. Just as Keats has already inverted the terms of Psyche's worship, he now inverts her previous loneliness and dark nights with Cupid. As her priest he has promised her his 'heat' (l. 48; see 34), and now fulfils his promise with 'warm Love'. Identifying with the author who sings about Psyche as poetic inspiration is no longer enough; in order to be the poet he wants to be and master his poetic inspiration, Keats needs to become the author Apuleius (as in 'I Stood Tip-Toe'), Lucius the observer of lovers, and Love himself (as in 'Ode to Psyche'). Although he addresses Psyche, the poem is ultimately about his own experience as an inspired poet, whose own soul is both immanent in the body of a statuesque girl and transcendent.[43] Talking about the soul allows the poet to speak about himself.[44] Psyche is of course both a beautiful maiden and heroine of a romanticised tale, but her name, Greek for soul, recalls for both the Middle Platonist Apuleius and the Romantic poets the Platonic idea of the immaterial immortal soul.

---

41 Here I agree with Yost 1957. Ferris 2005, 404 argues that Cupid reappears in the poem as the gardener Fancy.
42 On the imagery see Sheats 2001, 89. Several images of Cupid in *Polymetis* show him holding torches. On Keats's knowledge of ancient wedding ritual including torches see Bush 1935, 786. Compare Adlington, 213: 'Cupidoes, either to have flowne from heaven or else from the river of the sea, for they had wings, arrowes, and the residue of their habit according in each point, and they bare in their hands torches lighted, as though it had beene a day of marriage.'
43 Haekel 2014, 117–20.
44 See Haekel 2014, 14 f., who traces the diversification and development of the concept of the soul in Romanticism.

4 Conclusion

Keats used the Psyche story in three important poems, which demarcate important turning points in his poetic development. 'Ode on Melancholy's' Psyche displays some complex allusions to the *Met.* with Psyche embodying the butterfly soul that should push against the sorrows of melancholy, and a focus on the importance and mysteries of poetic inspiration.

In 'I Stood Tip-Toe' Keats emulates Apuleius while searching for his own inspiration, and in 'Ode to Psyche' he claims new inspiration and treatment of the subject of Psyche for himself, identifying with Apuleius' creation, the rose-carrying priest of Isis who happily lives in a goddess' sanctuary, a goddess herself newly added to the Roman pantheon. If 'Ode to Psyche' is a continuation of the thoughts of 'I Stood Tip-Toe' as it is a continuation of its story, then Keats associates himself here not only with Apuleius, the first person who told the story of the girl, but also with the protagonist of Apuleius' novel beyond *Cupid and Psyche*, its hero Lucius, in a form of identification of the two that is already suggested by the novel itself and especially Adlington's, the translator's, introduction. As her poet, Keats partakes in the immortality that he helps to provide for Psyche,[45] as her worshipper, her 'heat', he ultimately becomes her Cupid, her 'warm Love'. Apuleius himself becomes subsumed into and surpassed by Keats, who not merely catalogues the feats of a mere mortal girl, but becomes the inspired priest and divine admirer of his poetic goddess and inspiration, Psyche, who is at the same time a beautiful girl, a goddess, and the transcendent human soul. Keats engages with the *Metamorphoses* as a whole, and not *Cupid and Psyche* alone, and does so more intensely and creatively than has been hitherto noticed. As a latecomer, Keats seeks association with Apuleius as an ancient yet similarly 'late' teller of stories in his own post-Augustan age, and his development as an individualistic, inspired poet can be traced in the changing ways he treats the story of *Cupid and Psyche*.

5 Bibliography

Adlington, W. (1566; transl.), *The Golden Asse of Lucius Apuleius*, without year; first printed 1566; reprinted from an edition from 1639, London (The Abbey Classics VI).
Allott, K. (1968), 'The Ode to Psyche', in: Stillinger, 17–31.
Aske, M. (1985), *Keats and Hellenism. An Essay*, Cambridge.

---

[45] See Allott 1968: 21.

Brown, H. (1976), 'Creations and Destroyings. Keats's Protestant Hymn, the "Ode to Psyche"', *Diacritics* 6: 49–56.
Bush, D. (1935), 'Notes on Keats's Reading', *PMLA* 50, 785–806.
Bush, D. (1969), *Mythology and the Romantic Tradition in English Poetry*, Cambridge Mass.
Chandler, J. (1998), *England in 1819. The Politics of Literary Culture and the Case of Romantic Historicism*, Chicago.
Ferris, E. (2005), 'Owing to Psyche', *European Romantic Review* 16, 399–415.
Finney, C.L. (1963), *The Evolution of Keats's Poetry*, New York.
Gildon, C. (1708; repr. 1709 and 1724), *The New Metamorphosis: or, the Pleasant Transformation: Being The Golden Ass of Lucius Apuleius of Medaura. Alter'd and Improv'd to the Modern Times*, 2 vols, London.
Gross, G. (1990), '*Lamia* and the Cupid-Psyche-Myth', *Keats-Shelley Journal* 39, 151–165.
Haekel, R. (2014), *The Soul in British Romanticism: Negotiating Human Nature in Philosophy, Science and Poetry*, Trier.
Harrison, S. (2000), *Apuleius. A Latin Sophist.* Oxford.
Hartman, G. (2011), 'Listen Up! Keats's "Ode to Psyche"', *The Yale Review* 99, 86–93.
Hijmans, B.L./van der Paardt, R. T. (eds.) (1978), *Aspects of Apuleius' Golden Ass*, Groningen.
Jack, I. (1967), *Keats and the Mirror of Art*, Oxford.
Keats, J. (1900), *The Complete Works of John Keats*, ed. H. Buxton-Forman, New York, 2 vols.
Keats, J. (1966= 1996), *Selected Poetry*, ed. With Introduction and Notes by Elizabeth Cook, Oxford.
Keulen, W.H./Tilg, S./Nicolini, L./Graverini, L./Harrison, S.J./Panayotakis, S./van Mal-Maeder, D. (eds.) (2015), *Apuleius Madaurensis Metamorphoses. Book XI. The Isis Book. Text, Introduction and Commentary*, Leiden.
Lemprière, J. (1788), *Classical Dictionary containing a full Account of all the Proper Names mentioned in Ancient Authors*, Reading.
Motion, A. (1997), *Keats*, London.
Orlin, E.M. (2010), *Foreign Cults in Rome: Creating a Roman Empire*, Oxford.
Raine, K. (1968), 'Thomas Taylor, Plato, and the English Romantic Movement', *The Sewanee Review* 76, 230–257.
Roe, N. (2012), *John Keats. A New Life*, London.
Sandy, G. (1978), 'Book 11. Ballast or Anchor?', in: Hijmans/van der Paardt, 123–40.
Scott, G.F. (1994), *The Sculpted Word. Keats, Ekphasis, and the Visual Arts*, Hanover N.H.
Schulz, M.F. (1960), 'Keats' Timeless Order of Things. A Modern Reading of "Ode to Psyche"', *Criticism* 2, 55–65.
Sheats, P.D. (2001), 'Keats and the Ode', in: Wolfson, 86–101.
Spence, J. (1747), *Polymetis. Or, An Enquiry Concerning the Agreement Between the Works of the Roman Poets, And the Remains of the Antient Artists. Being an Attempt to Illustrate them Mutually from One Another. In Ten Books*, London.
Stead, H. (2016), *A Cockney Catullus. The Reception of Catullus in Romantic Britain, 1795–1821*, Oxford.
Stillinger, J. (ed.) (1968), *Twentieth Century Interpretations of Keats's Odes. A Collection of Critical Essays*, Englewood Cliffs, NJ.
Tighe, M. (1811), *Psyche. With Other Poems. By the Late Mrs. Henry Tighe*, London.
Vendler, H.H. (1983), *The Odes of John Keats*, Cambridge Mass.
Waldoff, L. (1977), 'The Theme of Mutability in the "Ode to Psyche"', *PMLA* 92, 410–19.

Weller, E.V. (1928), *Keats and Mary Tighe. The Poems of Mary Tighe with Parallel Passages from the Work of John Keats*, New York.
White, R.S. (2010), *John Keats. A Literary Life*, Basingstoke.
Wolfson, S.J. (ed.) (2001), *Cambridge Companion to Keats*, Cambridge.
Yost, G.J. (1957), 'An Identification in Keats's "Ode to Psyche"', *Philological Quarterly* 36, 496–500.

Michael Paschalis
Sir Walter Scott's *Kenilworth* and Apuleius' tale of *Cupid and Psyche*

> A CERTAIN degree of success, real or supposed, in the delineation of Queen Mary, naturally induced the Author to attempt something similar respecting 'her sister and her foe,' the celebrated Elizabeth. He will not, however, pretend to have approached the task with the same feelings; for the candid Robertson himself confesses having felt the prejudices with which a Scotsman is tempted to regard the subject; and what so liberal an historian avows, a poor romance-writer dares not disown. But he hopes the influence of a prejudice, almost as natural to him as his native air, will not be found to have greatly affected the sketch he has attempted of England's Elizabeth. I have endeavoured to describe her as at once a high-minded sovereign, and a female of passionate feelings, hesitating betwixt the sense of her rank and the duty she owed her subjects on the one hand, and, on the other, her attachment to a nobleman who, in external qualifications at least, amply merited her favour. The interest of the story is thrown upon that period when the sudden death of the first Countess of Leicester seemed to open to the ambition of her husband the opportunity of sharing the crown of his sovereign.[1]

Sir Walter Scott's novel *Kenilworth*, published in three volumes in 1821, narrates the unhappy relationship of Amy Robsart with Robert Dudley, Earl of Leicester, the favourite courtier and intimate friend of Queen Elizabeth I to whom the novelist assigns a central role in the plot. In the opening lines of the Introduction to the Magnum Opus edition quoted above, Scott explains that he was in a sense obliged to write about Elizabeth after his successful treatment of Mary, Queen of Scots in *The Abbot* (1820) and emphasizes the highly sensitive nature of such a topic for a Scotsman like himself. According to the account given by Scott's son-in-law John Gibson Lockhart in his *Memoirs of the Life of Sir Walter Scott* (1837) it was Scott's publisher Archibald Constable who requested him to write about Elizabeth 'as a companion to the Mary Stuart of *The Abbot*' and suggested the title *Kenilworth*. Constable's original idea was to write a novel bearing the telling title *The Armada*, but Scott made instead the exciting as well as risky choice of involving Elizabeth, both as a queen and as a woman, in Dudley's relationship with Amy Robsart and the story of her alleged murder:

> Scott would not indeed indulge him with the choice of the particular period of Elizabeth's reign, indicated in the proposed title of *The Armada*; but expressed his willingness to take up his own old favourite, the legend of Meikle's [i.e. Mickle's] ballad. He wished to call the

---

[1] Scott 1831, 5.

https://doi.org/10.1515/9783110641585-011

novel, like the ballad, *Cumnor-hall*, but in further deference to Constable's wishes, substituted 'Kenilworth.'[2]

Regardless of other reasons, it might have sounded tactless if Scott had treated Elizabeth's greatest triumph, the defeat of the Spanish Armada in 1588, after telling in *The Abbot* the story of Mary's imprisonment, abdication, defeat at the Battle of Langside and flight to England, where she put herself at the mercy of her cousin (1568). Elizabeth threw her into prison and much later (1587) had her executed; in 1575, when the story of *Kenilworth* takes place,[3] Mary has been Elizabeth's prisoner for seven years.

Let me first give a synopsis of the plot of *Kenilworth:*

> The heroine Amy Robsart enters into a secret marriage with the Earl of Leicester, spurning her fiancé, Edmund Tressilian, a Cornish gentleman. A favourite of Queen Elizabeth, Leicester feels obliged to conceal his marriage in order to maintain his position at court. Having fled her father's house, Amy is therefore kept a virtual prisoner in Cumnor Hall, an old country house. Tressilian believes that Amy has been abducted by Leicester's Master of the Horse, Varney, whom Leicester has used as a covering for his own amorous intrigues. With the backing of Amy's distraught father, Sir Hugh, Tressilian accuses Varney before the Queen of unlawful seduction. In order to protect his patron, Varney swears that Amy is his wife. Not altogether convinced, the Queen orders Varney to produce Amy in that capacity during the projected revels at Leicester's castle of Kenilworth. When Amy indignantly refuses to play this role, Varney has poisons administered, which will provoke a mild illness and thus excuse her absence. Amy, though, thwarts Varney's plan with the assistance of Tressilian's page Wayland Smith and makes her way to Kenilworth. Here, before she can make her husband aware of her presence, she comes face to face with the Queen and appeals for her aid against Varney. As she cannot bring herself to declare her marriage to Leicester against her husband's wishes, the Queen thinks her mad and consigns her, eventually, to Varney's care. Varney, who sees in Amy an obstacle to his own ambition, persuades his patron that she is having an affair with Tressilian, and the jealous Leicester orders him to put her to death. Varney leaves Kenilworth with Amy in order to carry out the murder at Cumnor Hall. A messenger sent to countermand the order, when Leicester has second thoughts, is brutally killed by Varney. Back at Kenilworth, Tressilian, who is ignorant of Amy's fate, makes a personal appeal to Leicester. Incensed, Leicester challenges him to a duel and is on the point of killing him, when the arrival of a delayed letter from Amy convinces him that Varney's accusations are false. Leicester confesses his marriage to Elizabeth who dispatches Tressilian to Cumnor Place to rescue Amy. He arrives at the moment that Varney has engineered her death through a fall. Varney is arrested and poisons himself in his prison cell; the heart-broken Tressilian enlists on the Virginia expedition and dies

---

[2] Lockart 1837, vol. 5, 28.
[3] The action of the novel is set in 1575, when Leicester entertained Elizabeth at Kenilworth. Alexander 1993, 476 (= 1999, 400) notes however: 'Scott violates chronology freely, and often obviously, to bring historical characters and events within range of this date.'

an early death; Leicester regains his privileged position at court after a brief period of disgrace.⁴

According to Lockhart's account quoted above, Scott derived the original idea of writing *Kenilworth* from 'Cumnor Hall', the favourite ballad of his childhood. The ballad was inspired by 'the story of the unhappy countess of Leicester, who was murdered there in Queen Elizabeth's time' and told of Amy's complaint to Leicester for having abandoned her at Cumnor Hall and of her subsequent death. It was first printed in 1784, in vol. 4 of Thomas Evans' *Old Ballads, Historical and Narrative, and Some of Modern Date* and was the work of the Scottish poet William Julius Mickle.⁵ Scott's main prose source for this particular story was Elias Ashmole's *Antiquities of Berkshire* (1719), to which the readers are also referred by Evans' prologue to 'Cumnor Hall'. Mickle and Ashmole are both cited in the first edition of *Kenilworth*, and stanzas of 'Cumnor Hall' are quoted four times.⁶ According to Ashmole, it was Leicester who ordered the murder of Amy Robsart and executed it with the aid of Richard Varney, the villain of Scott's novel:

> *Robert Dudley*, Earl of *Leicester*, a very goodly Personage, and singularly well Featur'd, being a great Favourite to Queen *Elizabeth*, it was thought, and commonly reported, that had he been a Bachelor, or Widower, the Queen would have made him her Husband; to this End, to free himself of all Obstacles, he commands, or perhaps, with fair flattering Entreaties, desires his Wife to repose herself here, at his Servant, *Anthony Foster*'s House, who then lived in the aforesaid Manor House; and also prescribed to Sir *Richard Varney*, (a prompter to this Design) at his coming hither, that he should first attempt to poison her, and if that did not take effect, then by any other Way whatsoever to dispatch her. [...].⁷

Scott's own view on what was reported by Ashmole is expressed in the Introduction to the Magnum Opus edition of *Kenilworth*:

---

4 Derived, with minor changes, from http://www.walterscott.lib.ed.ac.uk/works/novels/kenilw.html (Walter Scott Digital Archive, accessed 8 July 2016).
5 Evans 1784, 130–5.
6 Stanzas of Mickle's ballad are quoted as epigraphs of vol 1, chapter VI; vol. 2, chapter X; and vol. 3, chapter XVI. Following the conclusion of vol. 3, Scott mentions both Ashmole and Mickle and quotes the latter: 'The outlines of this melancholy tale may be found, at length, in Ashmole's *Antiquities of Berkshire*, and it is alluded to in many other works which treat of Leicester's history. The ingenious translator of 'Camoens', William Julius Mickle, has made the Countess' tragedy the subject of a beautiful elegy, called *Cumnor-Hall*, which concludes with these lines [last two stanzas quoted].' (Scott 1821: vol. 3, 347–8).
7 Ashmole 1719, vol. 1, 149–50.

> It is possible that slander, which very seldom favours the memories of persons in exalted stations, may have blackened the character of Leicester with darker shades than really belonged to it. But the almost general voice of the times attached the most foul suspicions to the death of the unfortunate Countess, more especially as it took place so very opportunely for the indulgence of her lover's ambition. If we can trust Ashmole's *Antiquities of Berkshire*, there was but too much ground for the traditions which charge Leicester with the murder of his wife. In the following extract of the passage, the reader will find the authority I had for the story of the romance...[8]

Though Robert and Amy had been publicly married in 1549 during the reign of Edward VI,[9] Scott made their marriage a well-kept secret. As the novel begins, Amy lives in seclusion and is a virtual prisoner at Cumnor Hall, so that Leicester may maintain his position at court. I will argue below that the setting at Cumnor Hall is modelled after Apuleius' tale of *Cupid of Psyche* and that this intertextual relation has wider implications for the novel as a whole.

I will start with a few words on Scott's acquaintance with Apuleius' *Metamorphoses*. Scott was familiar with major Latin authors. Latin quotations abound in *Kenilworth* as well as in his other novels.[10] For Scott as reader of Apuleius we have several testimonies. I begin with what Lockhart says about one of his notebooks:

> The note-book from which I have been copying is chiefly filled with extracts from Apuleius and Anthony-a-Wood [an antiquary]—most of them bearing, in some way, on the subject of popular superstitions. It is a pity that many leaves have been torn out; for if unmutilated, the record would probably have enabled one to guess whether he had already planned his 'Essay on Fairies'.[11]

---

8 Scott 1831, 5. In the following pages of the 'Introduction' Scott quotes the whole account of Amy's murder from Ashmole 1719: vol. 1, 149–54. Ashmole drew on the *Secret Memoirs of Robert Dudley*, also known as *Leicester's Commonwealth* (Parsons 1641, 35–7; Anonymous 1706, 44–7). See further the 'Historical Note' in Alexander 1993, 473–8 (= 1999, 397–402). According to Alexander 'The exact circumstances of Amy's death will probably never be known, but much modern historical opinion regards the accusations against Leicester as largely unfounded.'
9 Alexander 1993, 476 (= 1999, 400).
10 On Scott's education in general see Sutherland 1995, 26–44. Important information on his classical education is provided by Scott himself in his *Memoir(s)* (Lockhart 1937, vol. 1, 17–46; Hewitt 1981, 1–44); for further information see D'Andrea 2016, 46–59, with earlier literature. Her thesis offers a perceptive analysis of Scott's engagement with the classical past in a selection of the Scottish novels.
11 Lockhart 1837, vol. 1, 156. The entry for May 22, 1797 begins as follows: 'Apuleius, lib ii'.

The subject of witchcraft had fascinated Scott since childhood.¹² In the *Letters on Demonology and Witchcraft, Addressed to J.G. Lockhart, Esq.*, which was composed and published in 1830, he makes a direct reference to Lucian and Apuleius:

> The poets of the heathens, with authors of fiction, such as Lucian and Apuleius, ascribe all these powers to the witches of the pagan world, combining them with the art of poisoning and of making magical philtres, to seduce the affections of the young and beautiful;¹³

In a note added in 1827 to the 2ⁿᵈ edition of *Paul's Letters to His Kinsfolk* (1816), Scott notes the following:

> The apparition of the half-moon reminds us of Hecate, of the mysteries of Isis in Apuleius, and of a passage in Lucian's 'Lears,' [perhaps *Philopseudes sive incredulus* 14.1?] where the moon is forced down by magical invocation.¹⁴

The earliest and most rewarding testimony occurs in Scott's preface to the traditional ballad entitled 'Willie's Ladye' and contained in Scott's collection *Minstrelsy of the Scottish Border* (1802). Here Scott quotes a whole passage from Apuleius' *Metamorphoses* in the original Latin. It is the passage where the vindictive witch Meroe condemns a woman to perpetual pregnancy:

> Those who wish to know how an incantation, or charm, of the distressing nature here described, was performed in classic days, may consult the story of Galanthis's Metamorphosis, in OVID, or the following passage in APULEIUS: '*Eadem (Saga scilicet quaedam), Amatoris uxorem, quod in sibi dicacule probrum dixerat, jam in sarcinam praegnationis, obsepto utero, et repigrato foetu, perpetua praegnatione damnavit. Et ut cuncti numerant, octo annorum onere, misella illa, velut elephantum paritura, distenditur.*'—APUL. METAM. LIB I.[9.5–10]¹⁵

---

12 Lovecraft 2013, 44–5.
13 Scott 1830, 99.
14 Scott 1827, 492.
15 Scott 1802, vol. 2, 27–8. 'She (namely a witch) also condemned a lover's wife, who had wittily insulted her and was carrying the baggage of pregnancy at the time, to perpetual pregnancy by sealing her womb and delaying the birth; according to everyone's count, the poor woman now has been burdened for eight years and is swollen as if she were going to produce an elephant.' (transl. Hanson, adapted). The explanation *Saga scilicet quaedam* is obviously by Scott. The pronoun *sui* has dropped out after *amatoris* and *in eam* has been replaced by *in sibi*: the former may be a typographical error but the latter is probably Scott's error. Not all MSS give *iam* before *octo* and some early editions (like Price 1650 in Scott's possession) do not print it.

Finally, occasional references to Apuleius are also found in Scott's novels, as in the following passage from *The Fortunes of Nigel:* '[...] But here comes Maxwell, bending under his burthen, like the Golden Ass of Apuleius.'[16]

The catalogue of Sir Walter Scott's library at Abbotsford contains the following Apuleius books: an edition of *Apulegio volgare*, Matteo Maria Boiardo's famous translation of the *Metamorphoses* (1537); a French translation of the tale of *Cupid and Psyche* (*L'amour de Cupido et de Psiché*, 1586[17]); an annotated edition of the *Metamorphoses* by Ioannis Pricaeus (John Price, 1650); and an annotated edition of Apuleius' other works by Julianus Floridus (Julien Fleury, 1688). John Price's edition of the *Metamorphoses* was acquired after the publication of *Kenilworth* as part of the large donation to Scott by Constable in 1824.[18]

In *Kenilworth*, allusions to Apuleius' tale of *Cupid and Psyche* are most prominent in the first chapters of the novel where the scene is set. In the conversation that takes place at the inn in chapter II of vol. 1 we hear of a mysterious lady living in Cumnor Hall who never sees the light of day and is as beautiful as an angel:

> 'Nay,' said the mercer, 'it is not altogether pride in Tony[19] neither—there is a fair lady in the case, and Tony will scarce let the light of day look on her.' [...] 'Why, I wot not,' answered the host, 'except that men say she is as beautiful as an angel, and no one knows whence she comes, and every one wishes to know why she is kept so closely mewed up. For my part, I never saw her—you have, I think, Master Goldthred?'[20]

The readers will not of course be alerted at once by this account to the narrative of Psyche's divine beauty and her seclusion in the supernatural palace to await Cupid's nocturnal visits, until they later hear of a pictorial representation of *Cupid and Psyche* and learn of Amy's secret relationship to Leicester and his se-

---

16 Scott 1822, vol. 1, 130.
17 Translation generally attributed to Jean Maugin, but also to Claude Chappuys, Antoine Héroet, and Mellin de Saint Gelais.
18 Garside 2008, 253. Cf. Scott's letter to Constable dated 5 January, 1824: 'My dear Sir,-Yesterday I had the great pleasure in placing in my provisional library the most splendid present as I in sincerity believe which ever an author received from a bookseller, in the shape of the inimitable Variorums. Who knows what new ideas the Classics may suggest for I am determined to shake off the rust which years has contracted and to read at least some of the most capital of the ancients before I die. Believe me my dear and old friend I set a more especial value on this work as coming from you and as being a pledge that the long and confidential intercourse betwixt us has been agreeable and advantageous to both.'
19 Anthony Foster, steward of Cumnor Hall.
20 Scott 1821, vol. 1, 9–10. The text of *Kenilworth* is quoted from the 3-volume first edition. I have also consulted Scott 1831, Alexander 1993 and 1999.

cret visits to Cumnor Hall. In other words, the initial hints require a second reading in order to acquire significance. The conversation at the inn prepares for the visit to the mansion of two individuals with secret plans on their minds like Psyche's sisters (5.11–20). These are the unscrupulous Michael Lambourne,[21] who is determined to have the mystery resolved and profit by it in any way he can, and Amy's ex-fiancé Edmund Tressilian who conceals his true identity and is determined 'to save Amy from her betrayer and from herself and restore her to her father' even against her will.[22] Upon arrival at the mansion Lambourne notes that the huge door is stronger than that of a county jail,[23] and later Tressilian will perceive the house as a prison and Amy as a prisoner,[24] just as in Apuleius Psyche feels 'as if confined in a luxurious prison' (5.5.5 *beati carceris custodia septa*);[25] and though Amy is naïve enough to reply to Tressilian that it is her choice to inhabit that house, the truth of the matter is that both Psyche and Amy are kept in seclusion against their will. One question that Tressilian asks Amy without receiving a satisfactory reply regards the nature of her relationship to Leicester: '[...] does he claim a husband's right to control thy motions?'[26] Apuleius' reader will remember that Cupid, though not yet married to Psyche, is labelled Psyche's 'husband' when he first sleeps with her and she becomes his 'wife' (5.4.3 *iamque aderat ignobilis maritus et torum inscenderat et uxorem sibi Psychen fecerat et ante lucis exortum propere discesserat*)[27] and their relationship is from this point onward described in terms which suggest a legal marriage.[28] Though Robert and Amy are legally married, an aura of ambiguity surrounds their relationship: Leicester keeps the marriage secret to safeguard his interests at court, Varney will later declare himself before Elizabeth to be Amy's husband in order to protect his master,[29] and Tressilian will find out the truth only in the penultimate chapter of the novel.

---

21 The nephew of the landlord of the 'Black Bear' inn.
22 Scott 1821, vol. 1, 79.
23 Scott 1821, vol. 1, 61.
24 Scott 1821, vol. 1, 81, 83.
25 The text and translation of Apuleius' tale of *Cupid and Psyche* are quoted from Kenney 1990; for the text and commentary I have also consulted Zimmerman *et al.* 2004.
26 Scott 1821, vol. 1, 84. Cf. Tressilian's confession to Elizabeth in Scott 1812, vol. 3, 298: 'Art dumb, sirrah?' she continued; 'thou know'st of this affair – dost thou not?' 'Not, gracious Madam, that this poor lady was Countess of Leicester.'
27 'Now there entered her unknown husband; he had mounted the bed, made her his wife, and departed in haste before sunrise.'
28 Zimmerman *et al.* 2004, ad loc.
29 Scott 1821, vol. 3, 175.

In chapter VI of vol. 1, which bears as epigraph the opening stanza of Mickle's ballad,[30] we are told that a few days previously workmen sent from London, on Leicester's orders and in expectation of his visit, had converted the four rooms on the western side of the manor 'from the dilapidated appearance of a dissolved monastic house, *into the semblance of a royal palace.*'[31] The association with the gorgeous palace to which Psyche is conveyed at the beginning of *Metamorphoses* 5 is enhanced by the circumstances under which the operation took place, with absolute secrecy and unnoticed workmen:

> A mystery was observed in all these arrangements; the workmen came thither and returned by night, and all measures were taken to prevent the prying curiosity of the villagers from observing or speculating upon the changes which were taking place in the mansion of their once indigent, but now wealthy neighbour, Anthony Foster.[32]

All this brings to mind the circumstances at Cupid's palace where Psyche is served by unseen, disembodied attendants (5.2–3).[33]

The rich decoration of the rooms comprises works of art with mythological subjects: in the banqueting-room there is a salt-cellar 'moulded into a representation of the giant Briareus' (120); the withdrawing-room 'was hung with the finest tapestry representing the fall of Phaeton' (120); and in the sleeping room

> The curtains were of blue velvet, lined with crimson silk, deeply festooned with gold, and embroidered with the loves of Cupid and Psyche.[34]

The image of the loves of Cupid and Psyche functions as an intertextual marker that produces a ripple effect, spreading waves of meaning through the surrounding text. And *vice versa* it is the surrounding text which invests with meaning an image that could have been a commonplace and trivialized decoration for a bedchamber. Amy's reaction to the sight of the restored mansion wing adds further intertextual significance to the embroidered loves of *Cupid and Psyche:* it is clearly modelled after Psyche's heightened amazement in Apuleius when she first gazes at the splendour and the wonders of the divine palace (5.2):

---

30 'The dews of summer night did fall,/The moon, sweet regent of the sky,/Silver'd the walls of Cumnor-hall,/And many an oak that grew thereby.'
31 The italics are mine.
32 Scott 1821, vol. 1, 117–8.
33 Cf. 5.3.4: 'She could see no one but merely heard the words that were uttered, and her waiting maids were nothing but voices to her.'
34 Scott 1821, vol. 1, 122.

Inuitata Psyche talium locorum oblectatione propius accessit et paulo fidentior intra limen sese facit, mox prolectante studio pulcherrimae uisionis rimatur singula et altrinsecus aedium horrea sublimi fabrica perfecta magnisque congesta gazis conspicit. nec est quicquam quod ibi non est. sed praeter ceteram tantarum diuitiarum admirationem hoc erat praecipue mirificum, quod nullo uinculo, nullo claustro, nullo custode totius orbis thensaurus ille muniebatur. haec ei summa cum uoluptate visenti offert sese uox quaedam corporis sui nuda et 'Quid,' inquit 'domina, tantis obstupescis opibus? tua sunt haec omnia. [...]'

Attracted by the delights of this place, Psyche approached and, becoming a little bolder, crossed the threshold; then allured by her joy in the beautiful spectacle she examined all the details. On the other side of the palace she discovered lofty storehouses crammed with rich treasure: there was nothing that was not there. But in addition to the wonder that such wealth could exist, what was most astonishing was that this vast treasure of the entire world was not secured by a single lock, bolt or guard. As she looked at all this with much pleasure there came to her a disembodied voice: 'Mistress, why are you amazed at this great wealth? All of it is yours. [...]'

Four things merit our special attention regarding intertextual relations with Apuleius' tale: (a) in circumstances analogous to the narrative of the *Metamorphoses* (5.2–4) Amy sees the redecorated apartments *for the first time* and on the occasion of Leicester's expected *secret visit*; (b) Amy views the redecorated apartments as 'an enchanted palace', a perfect reminiscence of Apuleius' palace; (c) like Psyche, Amy is portrayed as spell-bound by the fabulously rich interior decoration introduced for her benefit; and (d) Amy recognizes in the marvellous sight the work of love produced for her sake by her lover whom she metaphorically identifies with Cupid, features which conspicuously evoke the situation in Apuleius' tale. I quote the relevant sections with the most significant passages italicized:

> She had been, therefore, introduced upon that evening to a part of the mansion *which she had never yet seen*, so different from all the rest, that it appeared, in comparison, *like an enchanted palace*. And when she first examined and occupied these splendid rooms, it was with the wild and unrestrained joy of a rustic beauty, who finds herself suddenly invested with a splendour which her most extravagant wishes had never shaped for her[35], and at the same time with the keen feeling of an affectionate heart, which knows that *all the enchantment that surrounds her is the work of the great magician Love.* [...] The Countess Amy [...] had for a time flitted hastily from room to room, *admiring each new proof of her lover* and her bridegroom's taste, and feeling that *admiration enhanced* as she recollected that all she gazed upon was one continued *proof of his ardent and devoted affection.* [...] I

---

[35] Changed to 'had never imagined' in the Magnum Opus edition of *Kenilworth* (missing from the 'Emendation list' of Alexander 1993, 433–72).

shall thank him more *for the love that has created such an unimaginable paradise* [...] stopping suddenly from her *tripping race of enraptured delight* [...]36

In the *Cupid and Psyche* tale the evil sisters convince Psyche that the husband who sleeps in her bed every night is a ferocious serpent planning to devour her when the child in her womb is fully grown (5.12–20). Following their advice she prepares to sever his neck with a sharp razor when the light of the lamp she raises over the creature reveals to her that he is actually 'of all wild beasts the most soft and sweet of monsters, none other than Cupid, the fair god fairly lying asleep'.37 Scott adapted Cupid's assumed and true identity to the situation of the Earl's double life and double identity. Driven by vanity and curiosity—the latter being of course the most distinguishing feature of Psyche's character—Amy had requested that her lover should appear before her not as 'a private cavalier' but as 'a great Earl' covered with jewels and decorations. When Leicester eventually arrives and enters Cumnor Hall he is 'muffled in the folds of a long dark riding-cloak' (145). Amy wants it removed in order to find out if he has kept his promise and so next 'as the cloak dropped on the floor, [and] shewed him dressed as princes when they ride abroad.' Then the excited Amy

> examined and admired from head to foot the noble form and princely attire of him, who formed the proudest ornament of the court of England's Maiden Queen, renowned as it was for splendid courtiers, as well as for wise counsellors.38

Inspired by the myth of *Cupid and Psyche*, Scott turned the distinction between Leicester's private and formal dress into a feature emblematic of his double life. The former he wore when he first met Amy and every time he was with her thereafter, and the latter he wore at Court and anywhere in the presence of Elizabeth, his Queen and would-be wife. Amy's request to see him dressed with all his jewels and decorations *marks a turning point in the novel* just as the revelation of Cupid's identity does. After satisfying her curiosity with the rich dress and the numerous decorations which the Earl enumerates for her pleasure, Amy takes one step further: she requests that she may publicly enjoy the honour of being '[as] the avowed wife of England's noblest Earl' (154). The Earl explains that the declaration of his marriage would ruin him, but things can no longer remain under his absolute control. Later however he confesses to Varney: 'I am well nigh

---

36 Scott 1821, vol. 1, 124–6.
37 5.22.2 *uidet omnium ferarum mitissimam dulcissimamque bestiam, ipsum illum Cupidinem formonsum deum formonse cubantem.*
38 Scott 1821, vol. 1, 149.

resolved to tempt the sea no farther, but sit me in quiet down on the shore'. Varney taunts him with an ironic but telling literary allusion to Cupid's power ('And gather cockle-shells, with Dan Cupid to aid you,')[39] and manages to dissuade him from his plan by exciting his ambition.

When in chapter XV of vol. 3 (= chapter 40 of the single volume edition), the penultimate one of the novel, Queen Elizabeth learns through the Earl's confession about his marriage to Amy, she becomes furious. At some point Leicester partly puts the blame on her for having concealed the marriage. Elizabeth is struck by his effrontery and when addressing her counsellors makes the following sarcastic comment:

> What ho! my lords, come all and hear the news—my Lord of Leicester's stolen marriage has cost me a husband, and England a King. His lordship is patriarchal in his tastes—one wife at a time was insufficient, and he designed us the honour of his left hand. Now, is not this too insolent,—that I could not grace him with a few marks of court-favour, but he must presume to think my hand and crown at his disposal? You, however, think better of me; and I can pity this ambitious man, as I could a child, whose bubble of soap has burst between his hands.[40]

In the opening lines of the Introduction to the Magnum Opus edition quoted above Scott states that he attempted to describe Elizabeth as 'at once a highminded sovereign, and a female of passionate feelings'. The concealment of the Earl's marriage concerns and affects both sides of her character, the Queen and the woman. Directly relevant to the topic of my study is the intertextual aspect of these features. Elizabeth is the analogue of Venus in Apuleius' tale, the former representing the highest authority on earth and the latter a major divine authority. Psyche is mortal and Venus immortal, and yet the former usurps the divine honours owed to Venus and rivals her in beauty rousing the goddess' indignation and setting in motion a mechanism of revenge (4.28–9). In an analogous fashion, though Elizabeth is Queen of England and Amy the daughter of an impoverished knight, they are nonetheless rivals for the hand

---

[39] According to *OED* 'Dan' or 'daun' is an honorary title derived from Latin *dominus* and meaning 'Master, Sir'. Applied to Cupid it would be an allusion to Chaucer's *House of Fame* 1.137 (Alexander 1993, 492 = 1999, 418). In Book 1 of the *House of Fame* the narrator falls asleep and dreams that he wakes within a temple made of glass decorated with words and images from the *Aeneid*, where Chaucer summarizes much of Virgil's epic with special attention to the capture of Troy and more extensively to the Dido and Aeneas story. Dido's Juno temple at Carthage has been turned into a temple of Venus who is accompanied by 'daun Cupido, hir blynde sone'.

[40] Scott 1821, vol. 3, 305.

of the same nobleman, while the Earl's secret marriage to Amy represents an outrage to Elizabeth as both a Queen and a woman. Elizabeth shares with Apuleius' Venus her outbursts of jealous anger,[41] but to her courtiers and people she is depicted as impervious to the passion of love. When Walter Raleigh recites to her those verses from Shakespeare's *A Midsummer Night's Dream* (2.1.155–64) in which Cupid shoots in vain 'At a fair vestal throned by the west', the Queen murmurs to herself the last line: 'In maiden meditation, fancy free'.[42] Scholars have seen in Shakespeare's 'fair vestal' an allusion to the Virgin Queen and in Cupid an allusion to the Earl of Leicester.[43] Incidentally, among Shakespeare's plays this one enjoys the strongest claim to Apuleian influence in the transformation of Bottom's head into that of an ass.[44]

Persisting in her sarcastic mood towards Leicester in the same chapter of the novel the Queen announces her decision to 'solemnize' at Kenilworth Castle the Earl's marriage with Amy now made public. The mortified Leicester pleads with Elizabeth to take his head rather than keep heaping such taunts on him and implores her as follows: 'Urge not a falling man—tread not on a crushed worm.' The Queen's reply provides a telling conclusion to the theme of the Earl's double life:

> 'A worm, my lord?' said the Queen, in the same tone; 'nay, a snake is the nobler reptile, and the more exact similitude—the frozen snake you wot of, which was warmed in a certain bosom' —[45]

By identifying Leicester with a snake Elizabeth takes the readers back to vol. 1, chapter VII of Scott's novel and intertextually to the story of *Cupid and Psyche*. They will recall that he had changed his 'slough' in order to please Amy and came dressed not as 'a private cavalier' but as 'a great Earl'.[46] In the present situation Amy's excitement and admiration is reversed: in vol. 3, chapter XV the viewpoint is that of a Queen and would-be wife who feels doubly betrayed by the Earl's furtive conduct. The comparison in this respect of Leicester to an insidious snake which Elizabeth warmed in her bosom, where 'bosom' connotes also 'female breasts', will alert learned readers to the fact that in Apuleius' tale Cu-

---

[41] *Met.* 4.29.5–30. Fearful of her wrath, the Earl of Leicester uses the Virgilian quotation *furens quid foemina* (*Aeneid* 5.6; Scott 1821, vol. 2, 223).
[42] Scott 1821, vol. 2, 134–5.
[43] Halpin 1843, with Kennedy and Kennedy 1999, 137–141; on Queen Elizabeth and the 'fair Vestal' see Holland 1994, 163 and Foakes 2003, 76.
[44] On *A Midsummer's Night Dream* and Apuleius' *Metamorphoses* see Gillespie 2001, 22–23 with literature; Carver 2007, 433–45.
[45] Scott 1821, vol. 3, 306–7.
[46] Scott 1821, vol. 1, 147.

pid's identity as claimed by her sisters is that of a serpent sleeping with Psyche only in order to devour her at the right time (5.17–18).

I have argued that the opening chapters of Walter Scott's *Kenilworth* set at Cumnor Hall, where the Earl of Leicester keeps his wife Amy Robsart secluded, rework aspects of Apuleius' tale of *Cupid and Psyche*. I have discussed the mystery surrounding the place, the marriage concealed from everyone but persons of Leicester's absolute trust, the Earl's secret visits to the mansion, the arrival of two outsiders with undisclosed plans on their mind, the transformation of the west wing apartments into an 'enchanted palace', and Amy's amazed and ecstatic reaction to a fabulous sight that is entirely new to her. All of these features evoke well-known situations and characters in Apuleius' tale of *Cupid and Psyche*. My point of departure for the suggested intertextual reading of the first chapters of Scott's novel was the mythological subject embroidered on the curtains of the couple's sleeping chamber, the loves of Cupid and Psyche, which I have treated as a marker that illuminates the surrounding text. Amy's request that her husband may appear before her not as 'a private cavalier' but as 'a great Earl' reworks Cupid's assumed and real identity and simultaneously points to the main theme of the novel's plot and its implications, Leicester's double life. I have also suggested parallelisms in the roles played respectively by the goddess Venus and Queen Elizabeth, the former representing the dominant divine authority in Apuleius' tale and the latter the highest authority on earth in Sir Walter Scott's novel. In later years, the novel naturally becomes one of the most important genres for the reception of the novelistic story of Cupid and Psyche, as Pasetti, Schultze, Gaisser and Provencal show.

1 Bibliography

Anonymous (1706), *Secret memoirs of Robert Dudley. Earl of Leicester, Prime Minister and Favourite of Queen Elizabeth*, London.
Ashmole, E. (1719), *The Antiquities of Berkshire*, in three volumes, London.
Alexander, J.H. (ed.) (1993), *W. Scott. Kenilworth. A Romance*, Edinburgh.
Alexander, J.H. (ed.) (1999), *W. Scott. Kenilworth. A Romance*, Edinburgh.
Carver, R.H.F. (2007), *The Protean Ass. The* Metamorphoses *of Apuleius from Antiquity to the Renaissance*, Oxford.
D'Andrea, P. (2016), *Classical Reception in Sir Walter Scott's Scottish Novels. The Role of Greece and Rome in the Making of Historico-National Fiction* (Thesis submitted for the Degree of Doctor of Philosophy), Oxford.
Halpin, N.J. (1843), *Oberon's Vision in the Midsummer-night's Dream*, illustrated by a comparison with Lylie's *Endymion*. London.
Hewitt, D. (1981), *Scott on Himself. A Selection of Autobiographical Writings of Sir Walter Scott*, Edinburgh.

Evans, T. (1784), *Old Ballads, Historical and Narrative, with Some of Modern Date*; now first collected, and reprinted from rare Copies and MSS. With notes by Thomas Evans. vol. IV, London.
Garside, P.D. (2008), 'The Baron's Book. Scott's *Waverley* as a Bibliomaniacal Romance', *Romanticism* 14, 245–258.
Gillespie, S. (2001), *Shakespeare's Books. A Dictionary of Shakespeare's Sources*, London and New Brunswick, NJ.
Hanson, J.A. (ed. transl.) (1989), *Apuleius. Metamorphoses*, 2 vols., Cambridge, Mass.
Kennedy, J.M./ Kennedy, R.F. (eds.) (1999), *A Midsummer Night's Dream* (Shakespeare: The Critical Tradition), London and New Brunswick, NJ.
Kenney, E.J. (ed.) (1990), *Apuleius. Cupid and Psyche*, Cambridge.
Lockhart, J.G. (1837), *Memoirs of the Life of Sir Walter Scott, Bart.*, vols. 1–7, Edinburgh.
Lovecraft, H.P. (2013), *Supernatural Horror in Literature*, Abergele.
Parsons, R. (1641), *Leicester's Common-wealth, conceived, spoken and published with most earnest protestation of dutiful goodwill and affection towards the Realme*, London.
Price, J. (ed.) (1650), *L. Apuleii Metamorphoseos Libri XI cum Notis et Amplifico Indice Ioannis Pricaei*, Gouda.
Scott, Sir W. (1802), *Minstrelsy of the Scottish Border. Consisting of historical and romantic ballads, collected in the southern counties of Scotland; with a few of modern date, founded upon local tradition*, in two volumes, Kelso.
Scott, Sir W. (1822), *Kenilworth. A Romance*, 3 vols., Edinburgh.
Scott, Sir W. (1822), *The Fortunes of Nigel*, 3 vols., Edinburgh.
Scott, Sir W. (1827), *The Miscellaneous Prose Works of Sir Walter Scott, Bart.*, in six volumes, vol. 5, *Paul's Letters to his Kinsfolk*, &c., Edinburgh.
Scott, Sir W. (1830), *Letters on Demonology and Witchcraft. Addressed to J.G. Lockhart, Esq.*, London.
Scott, Sir W. (1831), *Kenilworth*, Illustrated by C. J. Staniland, London and Glasgow.
Sutherland, J. (1995), *The Life of Walter Scott. A Critical Biography*, Oxford and Cambridge, Mass.
Zimmerman, M. et al. (eds.) (2004), *Apuleius Madaurensis/Metamorphoses Books IV 28–35, V and VI 1–24, The Tale of Cupid and Psyche*, Groningen.

Zacharias Andreadakis
Kierkegaard as a reader of Apuleius' *Metamorphoses*

In what follows, I will suggest that existentialism's origins may be rooted in the playful and provocative agenda of Apuleius' literary masterpiece, the *Metamorphoses*. More specifically, I will propose that the transformations that Lucius, and his alias figure, Psyche,[1] undergo in the wake of their displayed anxiety may have proved to be a stimulus from which Kierkegaard was able to construct his densely complex theory of anxiety—and with it, one of the core building blocks of existentialism.

Penetrating the work of Kierkegaard is meant to be like a spiritual trial, 'painful and excruciating and, in addition, dialectically complicated almost to the point of madness'.[2] His writing style is opaquely unsystematic—wavering constantly between prose and poetry—and he chooses to write mainly under various pseudonyms, frustrating and ironising any attempt to directly identify himself with any of his works.[3] What is more, his vast and profound knowledge of the classical and modern philosophical *corpora*[4] together with his own prolific —perhaps even compulsive[5]—writing require significant linguistic, historical and philosophical training, as well as philological patience, in order to be fully appreciated. Nevertheless, the benefits of working with such a thinker are significant. On Kierkegaard's revolutionary thought hinges the foundation of the philosophical and cultural movement of existentialism—expressed though his conceptions of freedom, anxiety, transformation, and irony—that still exerts great influence on the social sciences,[6] philosophy (continental and analytic)[7] and literature.[8]

---

[1] For the thematic and reflexive connection of *C&P* with the entirety of the *Metamorphoses*, and for the suggestive relationship of Psyche as an alias figure for Lucius see Kenney 1990, 12–17; Tatum 1969, 508–14; Harrison 1998; Zimmerman et al. 2004, 9.
[2] 1858 JP IV 4370 IX A 333 (see Kierkegaard 2016); Thomte and Anderson 1980, 175.
[3] Westphal 1996.
[4] Nun et al. 2015.
[5] In addition to the twenty books Kierkegaard wrote, his journals and incidental notes cover approximately 8000 pages (see Payne 1978, 302–3).
[6] Stewart 2011b.
[7] Aho 2014.
[8] Bloom 1989.

Given these high stakes, this study will explore manifestations of Apuleian influences on Kierkegaard in three areas: his biography, which is much more relevant to his work than with most writers;[9] his personal notebooks, journals, and library collection catalogue; and the published works, with the main emphasis on his existentialist manifesto, the *Concept of Anxiety*.

1 Direct contact

Let us start with the biographical ground that establishes Kierkegaard's close and life-long connection with Classics in general, and particularly with Apuleius. Søren Aabye Kierkegaard lived in the kingdom of Denmark from 1813 to 1855. During that time, deep knowledge of the Classics and speaking ability in Latin was a *sine qua non* in the educated ranks of Denmark. Kierkegaard came from an elite family and was educated at a prestigious boys' school in Copenhagen (*Borgerdydskolen*).[10] In this supportive environment, he immersed himself deeply in the world of Classics and the study of ancient languages, a fact that has left an indelible mark on his thinking. His dissertation, defended in 1841 and entitled 'On the Concept of Irony with Constant Reference to Socrates' (*Om Begrebet Ironi med stadigt Hensyn til Socrates*), displays a remarkable command of the ancient Greek sources, while discussing no less than thirty direct quotations of Platonic passages. On the Latin side, Kierkegaard not only defended his dissertation in Latin, but was also employed as a teacher of Latin from 1837–1838 at his old high school.[11] Kierkegaard had such extensive philological training in Greek and Latin that not only did he prepare a journal with a transcription of and comments on 10000 verses of Homer and 330 pages of Greek prose,[12] but he also wrote his own extensive Latin translations of what he considered the most difficult New Testament books.[13]

Kierkegaard's relationship with Latin texts, and particularly with Apuleius, is irrefutable and persistent. A surviving testimony, some new scholarly finds from Kierkegaard's personal library, notebooks and journals and, most importantly, direct quotations within Kierkegaard's published works provide sufficient proof of Apuleius' influence on the Danish philosopher. The most indirect testimony derives from one of his classmates, Frederik Peter Welding (1811–1894),

---

9 Mcdonald 2014.
10 McDonald 2014, 2.
11 Rosenmeier 1978, 16.
12 Cappelørn et al. 2007, 435–7.
13 Cappelørn et al. 2007, 435–70.

who maintained that Kierkegaard 'at an early age produced work in Latin composition and in Danish which showed signs of such unusual maturity and meticulous preparation'.[14] Given the nature and language of Apuleius' novel, as well as its popularity as a *Gymnasium* textbook at the time,[15] one might expect that young Søren had access to just such a book of diverse style. After all, there is a strong precedent for such familiarity with the text, since there is a long tradition of humanists like Boccaccio, Chaucer, Beroaldo, and Adlington treating Apuleius' novel as a handy manual of style,[16] if not taking from it directly, as in the case of Boccaccio.

Besides his mastery of prose composition, however, we can find perhaps more convincing evidence in some relatively new scholarly discoveries from Kierkegaard's extensive library catalogue, along with his personal diaries and marginal notes, published only recently by the online *SKS* database.[17] This catalogue shows that Kierkegaard owned several editions and reworkings of the *Metamorphoses*, including Orelli's 1833 edition of the story of *Cupid and Psyche*,[18] Valpy's 1825 edition of Apuleius, Kehrein's 1834 free poetic rendering of *Cupid and Psyche* along with what appears to be an early version of Nutzhorn and C. Paludan-Müller's 1867 Danish translation of *Cupid and Psyche*, and, last but not least, Hildebrand's 1843 Apuleius edition.[19]

Kierkegaard did actually read these editions of Apuleius, repeatedly so. In his Journal NB 25: 38, composed sometime between March and June 1852,[20] we can read the following: *'Jeg læser just idag igjen Fortællingen hos Apuleius. Den*

---

14 Ake 2009, 4 n11; Kirmmse 1996, 7.
15 For *Cupid and Psyche* as an especially popular textbook, after Bonaventura Vulcanius' adaptation of it into Renaissance Latin, see Ake 1999; Ake 2009, 3.
16 Gaisser 2008.
17 The new and superior online Danish edition of Kierkegaard entitled *Søren Kierkegaards Skrifter* (henceforth *SKS*) is found at http://sks.dk/forside/indhold.asp. and allows us to read not only the catalogue of the *Metamorphoses* editions that Kierkegaard owned, but also his personal short comments and marginalia on the novel. A search for Apuleius in this database returns the following results (extending in two pages): http://sks.dk/zoom/search.aspx?zoom_query=apuleius&zoom_page=2&zoom_per_page=10&zoom_and=1&zoom_sort=1&zoom_xml=0. From the 16 results that the search returns on Apuleius (which are also in reference to *Cupid and Psyche*), 13 are passing namedropping or lexical references and only NB 25:38, NB 17:40 and SKS 18:154/JJ:39 earn extensive mention.
18 Orelli's edition of *C&P* is peculiar in its inclusion of an extensive and philologically interesting *'lectiones memorabiles'* (a mixture of readings, comments and divinations) instead of the standard *apparatus criticus* and the addition of the epitome of Fabius Planciades Fulgentius (*Mythologicon Lib.* III, C. 6).
19 See Notebook (henceforth *NB*) *Komm. til SKS* 20: 36, 18 (in SKS).
20 For the dating of Kierkegaard's notebooks see Hannay 1996; Cappelørn et. al. 2007, 1–5.

4de Prøve paa hvilken Venus sætter P. er at hente den Æske hos Proserpina' (I just read today, again, the story of Apuleius. On the fourth test, Venus sets P<syche> to pick up the box of Proserpina).[21] The note goes on to praise courage and a fearless attitude toward danger, virtues that should be combined with compassion. Two things are particularly striking in this note. The first one is its date: 1852. Kierkegaard was at that time 39 years old, only three years before he passed away. We can thus see that even in the last stage of his life, he is still concerned with Apuleius' story, to which he returns 'again' (*igjen*). The second important aspect of this note is its use of abbreviations, especially 4de Prøve (4th trial) and P. (for Psyche), which are not naturally justified, given the fact that this note is a piece of correspondence, and not for personal use.[22] It would appear, then, that both the recipient of this piece of information and Kierkegaard himself seem to share a very good grasp of the primary source, which might mean, in turn, that it is a common topic of discussion.

Apuleius had also appeared in Kierkegaard's journals a few years earlier, in 1850. This is what Kierkegaard says about the nature of belief in NB 17: 40:

> Psyche vilde ikke nøies med at troe; det var jo muligt, at den Usynlige, der besøgte hende, var et Uhyre—saa saae hun, og saae, hvad hun tabte. Saaledes ogsaa med Reflexions-Forholdet i Forhold til Gud. Det Tilbagelagte, det kan Du maaskee see er det Overordentlige, saa altsaa dette var Dig forundt: vil Du ikke nøies hermed, nøies med at leve baglænds, forud have Sikkerheden, for at være ganske sikker paa, at den Vei Du | gaaer ikke er en Afvei—det var jo muligt (som det var muligt at hiin Usynlige, der besøgte Psyche, var et Uhyre, der just for at skjule dette, kun vilde sees i Mørke: ikke sees men troes—): saa er Alt tabt, Du faaer saa alligevel ikke Visheden men kun Visheden om, at nu er Alt tabt.

> Psyche was not content to believe; it was indeed possible that the invisible one who visited her was a monster—then she saw, and understood what she was losing. Thus, such is the 'reflection-relationship' in relation to God. What has passed, you may see it is extraordinary, so this was vouchsafed to you: you will thus not be content, to be content to live backwards, before having security, to be quite sure that the way you proceed is not a detour—that was indeed possible (as it was possible that the invisible one, who visited Psyche, was a monster, that, just to hide this, only wanted to be seen in the darkness, not seen but believed): so everything is lost, yet you do not arrive at certainty, but only the certainty that now everything is lost.

---

21 Cappelørn et al. 1997–2013 *SKS* 24, 461, *Notebook* 25, 38 (1852). Translations are all mine, unless otherwise indicated.

22 There are no exact statistical data on the use of abbreviations in Kierkegaard's work. Cappelørn et al. 2016, xiv, say that Kierkegaard 'made liberal use of a great many abbreviations', but they do not account for the obvious, yet understudied, differences in writing style and abbreviation occurrence between his correspondence and personal notes.

Psyche is chosen here as the archetype for the study of faith. Kierkegaard uses Psyche's exemplary tale in order to indicate the two horns of the impossible dilemma that faith represents: if you believe, you have to forget certainty, but you also have to set aside your drive to reflect. If you do not believe, you acquire the limited certainty of reflectiveness, but you lose the levity of existence that faith provides. It is as if Kierkegaard is saying that at the moment Psyche lit the lamp, she really entered the darkness, reminding us of the tragic inversion of vision: you have better insight into the divine when you are in the dark.[23] Cupid asks from Psyche, as God asks from all of us, to be better left in the darkness, but in return Psyche acquires a restlessness, an anxiety to reflect and see for herself, in order to reach for a certainty, which is in any case unattainable.

The impression of Apuleius is evident also within Kierkegaard's two most highly regarded books. The first one is found in the *Seducer's Diary*, in the first volume of his famous work, *Either/Or*, where the protagonist Johannes uses a German translation of *Cupid and Psyche* as a weapon in his campaign to win the love of Cordelia:

> 'As [Cordelia's] glance falls on the table, she sees a book... It is a German translation of a well-known work by Apuleius, *Amor and Psyche*. It is not a poetic work, and it should not be that either, for it is always an affront to a young girl to offer her a book of real poetry, as if she at such a moment were not herself sufficiently poetic to imbibe the poetry that is immediately concealed in the factually given and that has not first gone through someone else's thought. Usually one does not think of this, and yet it is so. She wants to read that book, and with that the goal is reached. When she opens it to the place where it was last read, she will find a little sprig of myrtle, and she will also find that this means a little more than to be a bookmark.'[24]

This reference shows knowledge of Apuleius' concealed, erotic nature that is embedded in *C&P*'s story and its unique, ambiguous literary status ('it is not a poetic work'). It seems also to serve as a subtle comment on how Cordelia displays the same curiosity and restless anxiety as Psyche in her attempt to access what is forbidden and what she is not ready for (remember Cupid's paradoxical reminder to Psyche in 5.11.4: *non videbis si videris* ('you will not see it if you see it')), be that real poetry or real love. Whichever the agenda behind using Apuleius on this occasion, Kierkegaard uses this story as a bookmark (perhaps even a translated guide) indicating how to entice a restless soul.

The *C&P* story returns in *Fear and Trembling*, this time to bring up the issue of faith (similar to NB 17: 40, as we saw above) and to explain in particular how

---

[23] Goldhill 1986, 199–221.
[24] See Cappelørn et al. 1997–2013 *SKS* 2, 420.

silence preconditions faith: 'Despite the rigorousness with which ethics demands disclosure, it cannot be denied that secrecy and silence make a man great, simply because they are qualifications of inwardness. When Amor leaves Psyche, he says to her: you will bear a child that will become divine if you remain silent but will be human if you betray the secret.'[25] These words, harking back to Met. 5.11.6,[26] reveal a constant pattern in Kierkegaard's thought, namely that faith requires muting a strong inner voice. This is a deliberate appropriation of Apuleius' thought for a different, religious context, yet it reveals the constant presence of C&P as a useful resource for illustrative examples in philosophical and theological arguments.

Besides knowledge of Apuleius's C&P, I would like to add that Kierkegaard was no stranger to Imperial prose fiction in general. Even though he does not mention by name Pseudo-Lucian's epitome of the *Onos*, he does display familiarity with the Lucianic corpus and that of broader Imperial prose fiction, appreciating greatly the humour and irony of Lucian, as well as his linguistic and intellectual touch.[27] Kierkegaard also displays knowledge of Longus' *Daphnis and Chloe*.[28] We do however not find in his works the same return again and again to any of these texts as we do with Apuleius, even if just as an illustrative reference point.

---

[25] Cappelørn et al. 1997–2013 SKS 4, 177; *Fear and Trembling*, 88. A very similar turn of phrase about the divine child of Cupid and Psyche appears also in Kierkegaard's notes (Cappelørn et al. 1997–2013 SKS 18, 154, JJ: 39), where Kierkegaard says the following: 'When Amor left Psyche, he said to her: You will be a mother to a child who shall be a divine child if you are silent, a mere human if you betray the secret. Every human being who knows how to keep silent becomes a divine child, for in silence lies a concentration upon one's divine origin; he who speaks remains a human being. How many know how to be silent, how many understand what it means to be silent?'

[26] Apul. *Met.* 5.11.6: 'hic adhuc infantilis uterus gestat nobis infantem alium, si texeris nostra secreta silentio, divinum, si profanaveris, mortalem'.

[27] For the exact references to Lucian's work see Notes on the 9th and 10th January 1938, II A 690/691; Hannay 1996, 113.

[28] See Kierkegaard's note in *Fear and Trembling* in Cappelørn et. al. 1997–2013 SKS 4, 192, 2: 'En græsk Forfatter skjuler i sin simple Naivitet saa uendeligt Meget, naar han siger: πάντως γὰρ οὐδεὶς Ἔρωτα ἔφυγεν ἢ φεύξεται, μέχρι ἂν κάλλος ᾖ καὶ ὀφθαλμοὶ βλέπωσιν (cf. Longi *Pastoralia*)'.

2 Apuleius: Inspiration for Kierkegaard's existentialism?

As Kierkegaard's great ease with the Latin language and his close familiarity with Apuleius's *Cupid and Psyche* are a given, let us move now towards Kierkegaard's broader engagement with Apuleius' own ideas. More specifically, I will examine how the transformative process of Lucius and his *alter ego* Psyche might have served as inspiration for Kierkegaard's existential philosophy in its inception, seen mainly (but not exclusively) through the manifesto of existentialism, the *Concept of Anxiety*.[29]

Let us first turn to the *Metamorphoses*. Apuleius' narrative is chiefly driven by the exploration of one question, namely, can we really change, can we really undergo a genuine transformation (*metamorphosis*)? The process of transformation is very nuanced and difficult to parse, since it negotiates the epistemic and fictional boundaries of belief.[30] The reader is constantly invited to ask: in what way and how much did Apuleius push these limits? These questions are brought to the fore by both the novel's conclusion and the inset narrative of *Cupid and Psyche*.

The very last book, the Isis Book (11), arguably contains the crux of unpacking the entire meaning of the story.[31] Often characterised as the 'joy' book, where *felicitas*, *gaudium*, *beautitudo* and *laetitia* are constantly present,[32] it includes a careful imbrication of satire and seriousness (*spoudaiogeloion*)[33]—a tension that seems to undercut the conversion moment, calling into question the nature of belief and ultimately the sincerity of the transformation. Scholarship has been very split as to the purpose and seriousness of this last book and the conversion/transformation story,[34] especially in a narrative that is driven overall by parodic Milesian tales. What is more, Lucius' conversion is also coloured by some rather buffoonish and ambiguous elements: his shaven head has perhaps been the most iconic one, allowing us to see him under various guises: a

---

29 For the Concept of Anxiety as a manifesto of existentialism see Grøn 2008, 1–5.
30 As Winkler (1985, 256) put it, the *Metamorphoses* is a 'vehicle for belief and ridicule of belief.'
31 See Keulen et al. 2015: 2–3.
32 Keulen et al. 2015, 18nn. 61–2, 496: 'dense web of reference to joy and happiness in book 11'.
33 For *spoudaiogeloion* in Greek and Latin literature in general see Giangrande 1972. For Apuleius' use of it see Beaujeau 1975; Schlam 1992; Graverini 2012, 124–6.
34 See Harrison 2012 with much relevant bibliography; Keulen et al. 2015 for extensive commentary.

comic actor, a headstrong Isis believer, or a Socrates-like philosopher.[35] Therefore, transformation is a very ambiguous process at the novel's conclusion: it can be seen as both sincere and simultaneously as ironic, reflecting the inconclusiveness of religious transformation itself. Such a transformation—together with all its ambiguities—is thus an integral part of Apuleius' novel. It is tied directly to the literal transformation of Lucius himself: he goes from a man obsessed with witchcraft (and who becomes a donkey as a result) to a man who is *for the time being* dedicated to the religious cult of Isis.

A second point of departure for analyzing transformation is the inset story of *Cupid and Psyche*. Apuleius, faithful to the agenda of an Alexandrian *doctus*, has inserted an intricate inset tale of transformation almost at the centre of his work, in order to create its reduced, reflective counterpart, as well as a suggestive cipher for the main story.[36] Traits of *improspera curiositas*, deviant behaviour, submission to the ordeals of the divine (with the complementary overlapping deities Venus and Isis) and final salvation by some undeserved divine intervention are among a long list of similarities between the protagonists of both narratives.[37] Perhaps the greatest similarity between them is their respective transformations, along with the ambiguity that these present to the reader. Like Lucius, Psyche displays lapses of judgment, frivolity and, after her failure to listen to her husband, signs of an existential crisis, which leads to an ultimate transformation: from mortality to immortality. The reader, upon finishing this inset story, is left wondering about Psyche's course of actions and the inexplicable divine providence that ordains her seemingly undeserved transformation into a goddess.

A careful reader could not have missed the sheer difficulty or the discomfort with either transformation, especially one like Kierkegaard, for whom transformation was a central preoccupation. Throughout his life, he seemed nearly obsessed with knowing whether or not genuine religious transformation is possible at all. As we saw in the previous section, for instance, the transformation of Psyche provided a fictional parallel to the religious transformations discussed in the works of Kierkegaard, where the doubt surrounding such conversions is of prime importance. The (Christian) believer needs to come to grips with how belief is constructed at large and how possible is it for the individual to become 'a

---

[35] Graverini 2012, 82–8 best encapsulates the stakes of the shaven head debate; see also Winkler 1985, 225–7; Schmeling and Montiglio 2006, 39 for the shaved head as the figure for the novel itself; Harrison 2012.
[36] For a detailed analysis of the similarities between the two stories and the two protagonists see Kenney 1990, 12–17; *contra* Penwill 1975, arguing for *C&P* as a point of intentional contrast to Lucius' narrative.
[37] Kenney 1990, 12–17.

new person'[38] in order to fully acquire the gift of faith. Without transformation, Kierkegaard suggests, we cannot achieve faith and belief, conditions that are essential for approximating the divine. Similarly, the problem of transformation is most decisively tackled in his *Concluding Unscientific Postscript*, where this transformation is considered as an attainable *desideratum*. According to Kierkegaard, the transition 'by which something historical and the relation to it becomes decisive for an eternal happiness is the *metabasis eis allo genos* [transition to another form]'.[39] In these works, transformation is thus still possible and sincere: a source of liberation, happiness and reinstatement of belief.[40]

However, Kierkegaard in his *Concept of Anxiety* seems to offer another mode of thought regarding the possibility of successful transformation—and thus the ensuing happiness it purports to have for the believer. After a careful analysis of Classical concepts of κίνησις and the intellectual challenges of transition as a category of thought,[41] he maintains that genuine transformation is actually reversible and thus impossible, since that would imply an inconceivable slicing up of the category of time between past and present. For him, time cannot be separated into the eternal and the ephemeral, but it always requires a third category, 'a Parmenidean third man', to explain it. Under these circumstances, any presentism and conclusiveness in transformation is simply a parody.

> 'Time is, then, infinite succession; the life that is in time and is only of time has no present. In order to define the sensuous life, it is usually said that it is in the moment and only in the moment. By the moment, then, is understood that abstraction from the eternal that, if it is to be present, is a parody of it.' (Thomte and Anderson 1980: 86.)

This passage is of notorious difficulty. What Kierkegaard maintains here is in a sense Heraclitean: if you cannot ever enter the same river twice, if you cannot ever disrupt the flow of time (infinite succession), then you can never have that one—transformative and key—moment of conversion. In fact, even speaking about it is a direct parody of how belief is constructed in a sincere relationship with time. In this way, then, transformation—the dissociation of the internal and the external for the individual—becomes impossible.

Of course, these two positions require some further qualification. In either case, possibility of and movement towards transformation is not to be equated

---

38 Hong and Hong 1985, 18.
39 Swenson and Lowrie 1968, 90.
40 See Davis 1992, 148–50.
41 For analysis of Kierkegaard's thought on Plato's *Sophist* and *Parmenides* on movement see Wild 1940.

with inevitability. Quite the opposite: Kierkegaard was persistently critical of any straightforwardness in the construction of belief.[42] However, this faltering between possibility and impossibility of the project of transformation is confusing and ambiguous—in a way not unfamiliar if compared to what we also saw at the conclusion of Apuleius' novel and in the story of *Cupid and Psyche*.

This doubt about the true effectiveness of religious conversion is theorised and metaphorical for Kierkegaard. In Apuleius' novel, however, it is represented literally, in the transformation of Lucius into a donkey and back, and in the transformation of Psyche from a naïve and curious human into an immortal. Could Kierkegaard have been inspired by the two stories in his own thoughts about the unattainability of genuine religious transformation? It is important also to look at the process in each by which such a conversion occurs. As we will now see, it is the concept of a transformative, productive, yet perilous anxiety that seems to surround and stimulate the transformations in both writers.

3 Anxiety in Apuleius and Kierkegaard

At the heart of all these transformations of belief in Apuleius lies a crisis, as Shumate 1996 has exemplarily shown. In that moment of crisis, Shumate explains, the individual experiences a complex mental state, that of anxiety.[43] This idea of anxiety as a restless curiosity has been seen by scholars of modern philosophy not as starting with Apuleius but as an idea of specifically Kierkegaardian lineage.[44] Thinkers like Freud, Sartre and Heidegger refer directly to Kierkegaard when they discuss the notion,[45] which is one of the prime reasons for Kierkegaard's persistent and interdisciplinary prestige. However, the same sort of anxiety can be seen to follow Apuleius' protagonist from the start until the very end of the novel—an anxiety that I argue below may have served as an inspiration for Kierkegaard's famous version many centuries later.

The first key moment of anxiety in the *Metamorphoses* appears at the beginning of Book 2. This is how Lucius presents himself to the reader: *anxius alioquin et nimis cupidus cognoscendi quae rara miraque sunt* ('anxious in general and excessively passionate for learning the rare and the marvellous').[46] Lucius, upon

---

42 Hannay 2001, 180–206, with much relevant bibliography.
43 Shumate 1996, 1–14; Freeman and Freeman 2012, 1–18.
44 Caron 1992; Marino 1998; Cope 2004; Wulfing 2008; McDonald 2013.
45 Freud 1933; Wulfing 2008.
46 *Met*. 2.1. All citations of the Latin text of Apuleius' *Metamorphoses* are from Zimmerman 2012 and all translations are from Hanson 1989, with slight alterations. Leigh 2013, 147 describes Lu-

arrival in Thessaly and before his conversion into a donkey, has woken up seemingly unperturbed, ready to go about his business in the city of Hypata. However, from that morning on, his epistemic crisis hinted at in the start of the book is greatly accentuated, as we can see from his thoughts about the city upon his arrival: *nec fuit in illa ciuitate quod aspiciens id esse crederem quod esset, sed omnia prorsus ferali murmure in aliam effigiem translata* ('nothing I looked at in that city seemed to me to be what it was; but I believed that absolutely everything had been transformed into another shape by some deadly infernal whisper', *Met.* 2.1). This moment has caught the scholarly eye for its peculiarity. In spite of the fact that Lucius has no obvious reason to be anxious at that moment, he displays a strong propensity to be so, by way of being impatient and incurably curious about things.[47] And it is this very anxiety that pushes Lucius more and more into the world of the occult, in order to try to gain some control over it, eventually leading to his transformation into an ass.

This key moment of anxiety near the beginning of the novel is paralleled by one at its end in Book 11, this time after Lucius undergoes the second, and more explicitly religious, transformation. Lucius, relieved from his ill-starred curiosity, is finally tasting the fruit of his liberty and can reach a state of happiness: *ad religiosam istam beatitudinem inprouida produxit militia... nam cum coeperis deae seruire, tunc magis senties fructum tuae libertatis* ('[Fortune], has brought you in its random wickedness to this holy state of happiness... When you start serving the goddess, it is only then that you most greatly feel the fruit of your liberty', *Met.* 11.15). Yet this freedom from his previous self does not seem all that permanent, nor does in fact his transformation: Lucius displays some strik-

---

cius as habitually anxious, and Keulen 2009, 104 makes the persuasive point that Lucius' natural anxiety needs curbing, like a child's by his parents. But nobody so far to my knowledge has pointed out a similar use of '*anxius*' in ancient literature elsewhere.

47 Van Mal-Maeder 2001, 54 says on Lucius' anxiety '*anxius:* "tourmenté par l'impatience" plutôt qu'"anxieux". Le mot apparaît souvent lié à un état de curiosité extrême: cf. 9, 12 (211, 29 s.) *familiari curiositate attonitus et satis anxius*, avec GCA [sc. Hijmans et al.] 1995, 117 s. ad loc. et 364, 11, 23 (285, 8 s.) *quaeras forsitan satis anxie, studiose lector, quid deinde dictum, quid factum.* Cf. aussi à propos de l'initiation de Lucius aux mystères d'Isis 11, 20 (281, 23 s.) et 11, 21 (282, 19 ss.), avec Fredouille 1975, 98 et 101 *ad loc'*. Moreover, according to Fredouille 1975, 98, 101: '*Anxius:* non pas "anxieux", mais "impatient, nerveux, intrigué"; cf. II, I, 1: *anxius alioquin et nimis cupidus cognoscendi*; IX, 1: *curiositate attonitus et satis anxius*; *infra*, 2.1, 3. ... *Anxium:* état d'esprit de celui qui va franchir une étape importante de sa vie: impatience mêlée d'appréhension, curiosité mêlée de gravité'.

ingly similar behaviour even after his initiation, first at 11.20,⁴⁸ and then more significantly at 11:21:

> at ille, uir alioqui grauis et sobriae religionis obseruatione famosus, clementer ac comiter et ut solent parentes inmaturis liberorum desideriis modificari, meam differens instantiam, spei melioris solaciis *alioquin anxium mihi* permulcebat *animum*.
>
> But he, being a serious man famous for his observance of austere religious discipline, gently and kindly put off my insistence, as parents try to restrain the premature desires of their children, and he soothed *my generally anxious spirit* with the comfort of hope for better things. (Apuleius, *Met.* 11.21)

It would seem that Lucius can never seriously rid himself of his anxiety, even when he has been changed back into a human, embraced religion, and entered the religious life of an Isis priest.

It is not surprising perhaps that right between these two moments that bookend Lucius' transformation, we find Psyche in a rather similar predicament, to the extent that several psychologists have analysed her anxiety, e.g. from a Jungian perspective, as Benson shows in this volume. Pestered by an insuppressible innate curiosity, Psyche is constantly inclined to have things done her way, as a child. However, in times of rapid change and crisis of belief, as when she is informed that she will be a mother, Psyche responds not only with mere curiosity but also with a forceful anxiety (*crescentes dies et menses exeuntes anxia numerat*, *Met.* 5.12), an anticipation very similar to the forceful one of Lucius in 2.1.⁴⁹ Conversely, she refers to herself as an anxious suppliant (*supplicis anxiae*, 5.13) when faced with the possibility of missing her sisters' company, begging to be soothed from her anxiety and be made joyful again (*animam gaudio recrea*, 5.13). Very much like Lucius, Psyche's anxiety is stimulated by liminal turns of events, yet persists, both in her restless search for her husband (*quanto magis inquieta animi, tanto cupidior*, 6.1) and in her ultimately failed search to help herself and please her husband (*mentem capitur temeraria curiositate... placitura*, 6.20). Psyche, however naïve, is in a constant state of restless uneasiness with her surroundings.⁵⁰

---

48 *sic anxius et in prouentum prosperiorem attonitus templi matutinas apertiones opperiebar* ('I was anxious and excited about this fortunate outcome as I awaited the morning opening of the temple', *Met.* 11.20).

49 For different, more standard uses of anxiety in *C&P* see 5.20 (Psyche's sister); 6.2 (Venus).

50 Other examples of Psyche's innate curiosity can be found at *Met.* 5.6 (*sacrilega curiositate*); 5.23 (*satis et curiosa*); 5.28 (*verbosa et satis curiosa*); 6.20 (*temeraria curiositate*); 6.21 (*perieras, misella, simili curiositate*).

For Lucius and for Psyche, anxiety is innate and simultaneously transient: Apuleius lets us see that they have never got rid of it in spite of their religious and/or transformative experiences, which can curb curiosity (or seemingly at least, in the case of Lucius), but not anxiety, the force that pushed them to undergo a transformation of belief in the first place. If the novel of Apuleius is complete, as I believe it is,[51] then this lingering anxiety might undercut or at least problematise Lucius' transformation (and, respectively, Psyche's): how much have things actually changed?

As Winkler and Shumate have pointed out, the story of Lucius' conversion presents a tease, a possibility that denies closure, and which oscillates between frames of reference, being simultaneously an invocation and a serious critique of transformation.[52] Lucius does present us with all the clues necessary in order to understand the instability of his experience and make us consider whether all that much has changed since 2.1. Lucius has been very motivated to believe and follow his new cult. Yet the more he tries, the more doubt creeps in, as a way to make the reader problematise the straightforward relationship with the divine and the freedom to act as you please while at the same time fully participating in the religious experience.

As integral as the concept of anxiety is to understanding Lucius' and Psyche's respective transformations, it is even more significant as one of the most important components of Kierkegaard's existential philosophy, if not the most important. Its content is famously elusive, though, perhaps even to the point of despair. However, there are a few elements that separate Kierkegaard from others in his understanding of anxiety, including its rather ambiguous role in the idea of genuine transformation.

Kierkegaard is considered to be the first thinker to dissociate anxiety from fear and claim that its object is indeterminate.[53] Of course, anxiety *per se* was not a new notion: the Romantics, Kant, Schelling and Hegel all grappled with the concept, with varying conclusions, from it being some sort of 'holy hypochondria' to its constituting a means to display trials of spirit.[54] In Hannay's terms, Kierkegaardian anxiety is 'generalised apprehensiveness with no particular "in case" in view, one might call it a state of global uneasiness'.[55] For Kierkegaard, however, anxiety had also gone further than that, being much more the-

---

[51] Here I follow Tilg 2014, 133–148, presenting a compelling philological argument for the completeness of the novel as finished at the end of Book 11.
[52] Winkler 1985; Shumate 1996, 326–8.
[53] Marino 1998; Bruun 2001; Cope 2004; McDonald 2013.
[54] Hannay 2001, 212–3.
[55] Hannay 2001, 213.

orised and systematised. Anxiety was Kierkegaard's ultimate philosophical challenge,[56] and he expressed the systemic boundaries of anxiety in a variety of ways: a pleasing and profound feeling;[57] an alien power that grips and shows the limits of freedom;[58] and a dizziness from staring at the limits of the self.[59]

Even if extensively theorised, then, anxiety in Kierkegaard still remains elusive, perhaps because of its pervasiveness in the philosopher's thought. These seemingly contradictory strands come together in the way that Kierkegaard shows anxiety to be a limbo situation that one should enter at all costs and learn to embrace, no matter how tantalising this may seem, as a dialectic possibility; in fact, Kierkegaard does not hesitate to mark it positively, as 'sweet', in spite of the fact that he describes in detail the serious predicament that anxiety presents for human existence. For him, the transformation that would rid us of anxiety, if totally final, would annul the possibility of our choice and freedom.[60]

As we saw above, Apuleius describes in some detail Lucius' anxiety before and after his conversion as a process ridden with a similar insurmountable ambiguity about its potentiality that if final would lead to an end of potentiality. Lucius throughout his transformations is never totally rid of his anxiety and thus his free will: it leads him through more than one transformation—and perhaps, it would seem, to possibly even more after the story has ended. This text, to remember Winkler's main tenet, is excruciatingly open.[61]

At this point, one may wonder where the examination of these similarities leaves us regarding the broader picture, namely, Apuleius' influence on the intellectual project of existentialism that Kierkegaard began.[62] And why is the connection between the two important?

To answer this, I should provide some background on existentialism in general. In nearly all academic accounts, existentialism is a modern philosophical and cultural movement that started as late as the nineteenth century, and more specifically, with Søren Kierkegaard, even though it may have found its most consistent definition in the works of Jean-Paul Sartre.[63] The term existentialism itself has been the subject of harsh criticism, and has often been reduced

---

[56] 'Whoever has learned to be anxious in the right way has learned the ultimate' (*Concept of Anxiety*, 155).
[57] *Concept of Anxiety*: 42.
[58] See JP I 94; Pap. III A 233, 1842 *Concept of Anxiety*, 234.
[59] *Concept of Anxiety*, 43.
[60] Davis 1992; Hannay 2001; Cameron 2007.
[61] Winkler 1985, 13.
[62] Dreyfus 2007.
[63] McDonald 2014; Crowell 2015.

to a catch-all term, employed only for historical convenience.[64] To such reproaches has been also added a commonly held, polemical position by analytic philosophers, which classifies existentialism as a bygone cultural movement rather than an identifiable philosophical position.[65] In spite of these criticisms, however, which have been carefully addressed and criticised in several different works,[66] the study of existentialism allows for the identification of some coherent philosophical premises, standardly summarised in two main points: understanding human existence requires new categories of thought not found in the conceptual repertoire of either the ancient or early modern tradition; and human beings can be understood neither as substances with fixed properties, nor as subjects interacting with a world of objects. Hence, the individual needs to develop a new, authentic relationship with his or her surroundings. On the basis of this new, authentic relationship with one's self and environment, existentialist thought has dealt with and constantly returned to some major issues and themes that constantly puzzle and provoke: dread, boredom, alienation, nothingness, freedom, and anxiety.[67]

How certain can we be that Apuleius influenced this movement via Kierkegaard?[68] Even though Kierkegaard's knowledge of Apuleius' novel is clear fact,

---

[64] For an outline of existential criticism see Reynolds 2006, 13–22.
[65] For the animosity between analytic and existential philosophy see Cavell 1964; Crowell 2012a. This view has lost ground especially after the consolidation of quantum physics, which openly praises and advances existentialism's understanding of uncertainty as 'the only rule in life'. See Schrödinger 1944, 1–3, as well as Flitney and Abbott 2008, 231–42.
[66] See Schrift 1995; Cooper 1999.
[67] Crowell 2015.
[68] In recent years, a few scholars have touched upon the issue of a latent proto-existentialism in Apuleius' transformational narrative. The prime example is Shumate 1996, who provides an extensive argument for the parallel function of the *Metamorphoses* and an existentialist novel, Sartre's *La Nauseé* (1938), in their capacity as quest narratives. After his apparent transformation, Lucius has Isis as his metaphysical anchor, a reference point which his previous self sorely lacked. In Sartre's novel, on the other hand, music is for the protagonist, Roquentin, the saving grace, the ballast that saves him from his chaotic existence. The melody that comes from the composer and the singer of the recurring jazz song in the book has saved them (*en voilà deux qui sont sauvés*), and through that melody Roquentin discovers a way out of his normal cynicism, out to something he did not know he could experience anymore: a sort of joy (*une espèce de joie*, 177). Another connection that Shumate makes is with Kafka's *Metamorphoses*, in that both narrators seem to be victimized in front of a relentless sequence of toil and struggle with an absurd, blind fate. Recalling Auerbach, and following Smith, Shumate sees in Apuleius' *Metamorphoses* a 'dreamlike, even nightmarish reality, in which we find a new kind of protagonist, that is racked by self-doubt… and in which they struggle to find someone to be on their side.'

our case regarding influence is far from straightforward to prove. Whoever is familiar with the work of Kierkegaard knows well that the Danish philosopher necessarily resists such sweeping certainties: he has been praised, after all, as the greatest proponent of the death of the author—insisting on the alienating deployment of his pseudonyms until his untimely death.[69] Yet the similarities with Apuleius appear extremely suggestive, even if Kierkegaard cites only the story of *C&P*, and not the *Metamorphoses* in its entirety.

Perhaps Kierkegaard never read the *Metamorphoses* besides the *C&P* story. In spite of his owning several copies of the work and his striking 'again' in his personal notebooks, we cannot entirely rule out this possibility. However, given the explicit similarities between Lucius and Psyche, along with the lifelong engagement of Kierkegaard with the issue of religious conversion, this is unlikely. I would like to conclude by pointing to a potential explanation for this difficult reality, from an interdisciplinary perspective, in what in experimental psychology, but also in literary theory, is called cryptomnesia: experiencing a memory or a thought as if it were a new inspiration.

Authors, especially philosophers, often fail to give *verbatim* credit to their sources, and even if they do, they still cannot be held fully accountable for their own originality.[70] Sometimes, they read so deeply and widely that they can internalise sources to such an extent that the boundaries between thought patterns and idea patronage become blurry. Borges' story 'Pierre Menard, Author of Don Quixote' is one of the most iconic metafictive enactments of this phenomenon of cryptomnesia.[71] In this 'review' of this fictive author, Borges describes the labours of Menard, who makes an effort to go further than the mere translation of Don Quixote by actually trying to recreate it, line by line, in the original 16th century Spanish. Hence, Menard raises questions about the nature of accurate translation or, in this case, the hermeneutics of cryptomnesia. How much do we really own our ideas?

Could it be that Kierkegaard was enveloped in Apuleius' thought to the extent of cryptomnesia (in Kierkegaard's words, a cryptogamia, only accessible to

---

69 Stewart 2011a.
70 Hansson 2008.
71 Jung 1957; Brown and Murphy 1989; Brown and Halliday 1991; Macrae et al. 1999; Defeldre 2005. Similar phenomena of cryptomnesia appear in Nietzsche's *Thus Spoke Zarathustra*, as noted by Jung (see Jung 1957; Brown and Halliday 1991, 47) and in Eco's comments on the composition of the *Name of the Rose* in his *Interpretation and Overinterpretation* (Eco 1992, 88).

the careful reader)?[72] We cannot be entirely certain if Apuleius's presence is a latent thread in the thought of Kierkegaard. However, the prominence of the themes of transformation and its ensuing anxiety, along with their insistence on unpacking the difficulties of the human condition, should invite further research. The establishment of connections or genealogies of ideas between authors is not always straightforward. Who would have thought, for instance, that the father of analytic philosophy, Wittgenstein, would be actually following Kierkegaard as one of the main pivots of his thought?[73] This paper has attempted to showcase such an indirect line of influence and re-establish the urgent relevance of Apuleius' intellectual heritage for re-examining anxious identities in crisis through the lens of a powerful philosophical undertaking, Kierkegaard's existentialism.

I have made the case that the intellectual affinity between the two authors splices philosophical and fictional vocabularies. Specifically, I have argued that Apuleius' deep nose-dive into themes with existential resonance, and particularly with anxiety and its transformative power, invites us to re-examine not only his significance for modern philosophical tradition, but also the seriousness of his own authorial intentions.[74] Apuleius, in other words, is more than an entertaining story-teller: he is an philosophical ironist par excellence, who defies monolithic interpretations of the Platonic philosophical tradition. And this defiant way of writing casts a new light on the philosophical irony in the meaning of transformation which seems to have conclusively inspired Kierkegaard, and perhaps on any of our further attempts towards inducing meaning from Apuleius' corpus.

4 Bibliography

Abbott, D./Davies, P.C.W./Pati, A.K. (eds.) (2008), *Quantum Aspects of Life*, London.
Aho, K. (2014), *Existentialism. An Introduction*, Cambridge.
Ake, S. (1999), 'Hints of Apuleius in the *Sickness unto Death*', *Kierkegaardiana* 20, 51–70.
Ake, S. (2009), 'Apuleius. Direct and Possible Indirect Influences on the Thought of Kierkegaard', in: Stewart, 1–10.
Andreadakis, Z. (2015). Review of "Stefan Tilg, Apuleius' Metamorphoses: A Study in Fiction (Oxford 2014): *Ancient Narrative* 68 (1), 159–65.

---

[72] 'For these fruits are like cryptogamia in the plant world: they escape the attention of the masses and only a solitary researcher discovers them and rejoices in their finding', 35 I A 68; Hannay 1996, 27. For picking up clues as a way of reading Classical texts see Andreadakis 2016.
[73] Creegan 1989; Miles 2012.
[74] See Andreadakis 2016, 164–165, Graverini 2010, Fletcher 2014.

Andreadakis, Z. (2016), 'Reading for Clues. Detective Narratives in Heliodorus' *Aithiopika*', PhD Dissertation (University of Michigan: Ann Arbor).
Beaujeu, J. (1975), 'Sérieux et frivolité au IIe siècle de notre ère. Apulée', *Bulletin De L'Association Guillaume Budé* 4, 83–97.
Bloom, H. (1989), *Søren Kierkegaard*, New York.
Borges, J.L. (1998), *Collected Fictions*, transl. A. Hurley, New York.
Brown, A.S./Halliday, H.E. (1991), 'Cryptomnesia and source memory difficulties', *American Journal of Psychology* 104, 475–90.
Brown, A.S./Murphy, D.R. (1989), 'Cryptomnesia. Delineating inadvertent plagiarism', *Journal of Experimental Psychology: Learning, Memory, and Cognition* 15, 432–42.
Bruun, S. (2001), 'The Genesis of the Concept of Anxiety', *Kierkegaard Studies Yearbook* 2001, 1–14.
Cameron, E. (2007), 'The Ethical Paradox in Kierkegaard's *Concept of Anxiety*', *Colloquy* 13, 93–113.
Cappelørn, N.J./Garff, J./Knudsen, J./Kondrup, J./McKinnon, A./Mortensen, F.H. (1997–2013), *Søren Kierkegaards Skrifter*, vols. 1–28, vols. K1–28, Copenhagen.
Cappelørn, N.J./Hannay, A./Kangas, D./Kirmsee, B.H./Pattison, G./Rumble, V./Söderquist, K.B. (eds.) (2007), *Kierkegaard's Journals and Notebooks. Volume 1: Journals AA–DD*, Princeton.
Caron, J. (1992), *Angoisse et communication chez S. Kierkegaard*, Odense.
Cavell, S. (1964), 'Existentialism and Analytical Philosophy', *Daedalus* 93, 946–974.
Cooper, D. (1999), *Existentialism*. Oxford.
Cope, C. (2004), 'Freedom, Responsibility and the Concept of Anxiety', *International Philosphical Quarterly* 44, 549–66.
Creegan, C.L. (1989), *Wittgenstein and Kierkegaard. Religion, individuality, and philosophical method*, London.
Crowell, S. (2012a) 'Existentialism and its Legacy', in: Crowell 2012b, 3–26.
Crowell, S. (2016), 'Existentialism', https://plato.stanford.edu/archives/spr2016/entries/existentialism/ [accessed 31st July 2017].
Crowell, S. (ed.) (2012b), *The Cambridge Companion to Existentialism*, New York.
Davis, W.C. (1992), 'Kierkegaard on the Transformation of the Individual in Conversion', *Religious Studies* 28, 145–63.
Defeldre, A.C. (2005), 'Inadvertent Plagiarism in Everyday Life', *Applied Cognitive Psychology* 19, 1033–40.
Dreyfus, H.L. (2007), 'The Roots of Existentialism', in: Dreyfus/Wrathall, 135–61.
Dreyfus, H.L./Wrathall, M.A. (eds.) (2007), *A Companion to Phenomenology and Existentialism*, Hoboken.
Eco, U./Collini, S. (1992), *Interpretation and Overinterpretation*, Cambridge.
Emmanuel, S.M./McDonald, W./Stewart, J. (eds.) (2016), *Kierkegaard's Concepts. Tome I*, New York.
Fletcher, R. (2014). *Apuleius' Platonism: The Impersonation of Philosophy*, Cambridge.
Flitney, A./Abbott, D. (2008), 'A semi-quantum version of the game of life', in: Abbott/Davies/Pati, 231–42.
Fredouille, J.C. (1975), *Apulei Metamorphoseon Liber XI. Apulée, Métamorphoses Livre XI. Édition, introduction et commentaire par J.-Cl. F.*, Paris.
Freeman, D./Freeman, J. (2012), *Anxiety. A Very Short Introduction*, Oxford.

Freud, S. (1933), 'Anxiety and instinctual life' in *New Introductory Lectures on Psychoanalysis*, vol. 2, London, 81–111.
Gaisser, J.H. (2008), *The fortunes of Apuleius and the Golden Ass. A study in transmission and reception*, Princeton.
Garff, J. (2005), *Søren Kierkegaard. A biography*, Princeton.
Giangrande, L. (1972), *The Use of Spoudaiogeloion in Greek and Roman Literature*, The Hague.
Goldhill, S. (2008), *Reading Greek tragedy*, Cambridge.
Graverini, L. (2012), *Literature and Identity in the Golden Ass of Apuleius*, transl. by B.T. Lee. Columbus.
Graverini, L., (2010) 'Amore, "dolcezza", stupore: romanzo antico e filosofia', in: R. Uglione (ed.), *Atti del convegno nazionale di studi:"Lector intende, laetaberis"*. Il romanzo dei Greci e dei Romani; Torino, 27–28 aprile 2009, 57–88, Alessandria.
Grøn A. (2008), *The concept of Anxiety in Søren Kierkegaard*, transl. by. B.L. Jeanette and M. Knox. Mercer.
Hannay, A. (1996), *Kierkegaard. Papers and Journals. A Selection*, London.
Hannay, A. (2001), *Kierkegaard. A Biography*, Cambridge.
Hannay, A./Marino, G. (eds.) (1998), *The Cambridge Companion to Kierkegaard*, Cambridge.
Hanson, J. (2011), 'Holy Hypochondria. Narrative and Self-Awareness in *The Concept of Anxiety*', *Kierkegaard Studies Yearbook* 2011, 239–62.
Hanson, J.A. (1989), *Apuleius. Metamorphoses*, Cambridge.
Hansson, S.O., (2008), 'Philosophical Plagiarism', *Theoria* 74, 97–101.
Harrison, S.J. (1998), 'Some Epic Structures in Cupid and Psyche', in: Zimmerman et al. 2008, 51–68.
Harrison, S.J. (2012), 'Narrative Subversion and Religious Satire in *Metamorphoses* 11', in: Keulen/Egelhaaf-Gaiser, 73–85.
Hijmans, B.L. et al. eds (1995), *Apuleius Madaurensis Metamorphoses Book IX. Text, Introduction, and Commentary*, Groningen.
Hildebrand, G.F. (1842), *L. Apuleii opera omnia*, 2 vols. Leipzig.
Hong, H.V./Hong, E.H. (1985), *Kierkegaard. Philosophical fragments. Johannes Climacus*, Princeton.
Hong, H.V./Hong, E.H. (1992), *Fear and Trembling/Repetition*. Princeton. https://rjh.ub.rug.nl/AN/issue/view/3264
Jung, C.G. (1957), 'Cryptomnesia', in: R.F.C. Hull (transl.), *Collected works* (vol.1). London, 95–106.
Kehrein, J. (1843), *Amor und Psyche. Freie, metrische Bearbeitung nach dem Lateinischen des Apulejus*. Gießen.
Kenney, E.J. (1990), *Apuleius: Cupid and Psyche*. Cambridge.
Keulen, W.H. 2009, 'Different Drinking Habits. Satirical Strategies of Self-fashioning in Antonine ego-narrative', *Ancient Narrative* 8, 85–113.
Keulen, W.H./Nauta, R.R./ Panayotakis, S. (eds.) (2006), *Lectiones Scrupulosae: Essays on the Text and Interpretation of Apuleius' Metamorphoses in Honour of Maaike Zimmerman*. Havertown.
Keulen, W.H./Tilg, S./Nicolini, L./Graverini, L./Harrison, S.J./Panayotakis, S./van Mal-Maeder, D. (2015), *Apuleius Madaurensis Metamorphoses. Book XI. The Isis Book*, Leiden.

Keulen, W.H/Egelhaaf-Gaiser, U. (eds.) (2012), *Aspects of Apuleius' Golden Ass. Volume III. The Isis Book*, Leiden.
Kierkegaard, S./Cappelorn, N.J./Hannay, A./Kangas, D./Kirmmse, B.H./Pattison, G./Rumble, V./Söderquist, K.B. (2016), *Kierkegaard's Journals and Notebooks. Volume 2: Journals EE-KK*. Princeton.
Kirmmse, B.H. (1996), *Encounters with Kierkegaard. A Life as Seen by his Contemporaries*, Princeton.
Leigh, M. (2013), *From Polypragmon to Curiosus. Ancient Concepts of Curious and Meddlesome Behaviour*. Oxford.
Macrae, C.N./Bodenhasen, G.V./Calvini, G. (1999), 'Contexts of cryptomnesia. May the source be with you', *Social Cognition* 17, 273–97.
Marino, D. (1998), 'Anxiety in the Concept of Anxiety', in: Hannay/Marino, 308–28.
McDonald, W. (2013), 'Anxiety', in: Emmanuel et al. 2013, 59–64.
McDonald, W. (2016), 'Søren Kierkegaard', https://plato.stanford.edu/archives/fall2016/entries/kierkegaard/ [Accessed 31st July 2017].
Miles, T. (2012), 'Wittgenstein. Kierkegaard's Influence on the Origin of Analytic Philosophy', in: Stewart, 209–241.
Nietzsche, F. (1993), *Thus spake Zarathustra*. transl. by Wilhelm, T.C./Birx, H.J., Buffalo, N.Y.
Nun, K. (2010), 'Cumulative Plato Bibliography', in: Stewart/Nun 147–66.
Nun, K./Schreiber, G./Stewart, J. (2015), *The Auction Catalogue of Kierkegaard's Library*, Farnham.
Nun, K./Stewart. J. (eds.) (2014), *Kierkegaard's literary figures and motifs. Agamemnon to Guadalquivir*, Burlington, VT.
Nutzhorn, F./C. Paludan-Müller. (1867), *Apuleius's amor og psyche*, Copenhagen.
Orellius, J.C. (1833), *Apuleii fabula de psyche et cupidine*, Zurich.
Pattison, G. (2005), *The philosophy of Kierkegaard*, Montreal.
Payne, S.L. (1978), 'Book Review. Søren Kierkegaard's Journals and Papers', *The Philosophical Review* 87, 302–16.
Penwill, J.L. (1975). 'Slavish Pleasures and Profitless Curiosity. Fall and Redemption in Apuleius' *Metamorphoses*', *Ramus* 4, 49–82.
Poole, R. (1993), *Kierkegaard. The indirect communication*, Virginia.
Reynolds, J. (2006), *Understanding existentialism*, Chesham.
Rosenmeier, H. (1978/2009), *Kierkegaard. Letters and documents*, Princeton.
Schlam, C. 1992, *The Metamorphoses of Apuleius. On Making an Ass of Oneself*, Chapel Hill, N.C.
Schmeling, G. and Montiglio, S. (2006), 'Riding the Waves of Passion. An Exploration of an Image of Appetites in Apuleius' *Metamorphoses*', in: Keulen/Nauta/Panayotakis, 28–41.
Schrift, A. (1995), *Nietzsche's French Legacy.A Genealogy of Poststructuralism*, New York.
Schrödinger, E. (1967), *What is life? The physical aspect of the living cell. Mind and matter*, Cambridge.
Shumate, N. (1996), *Crisis and Conversion in Apuleius' Metamorphoses*, Ann Arbor.
SKS = *Søren Kierkegaards Skrifter* (2016) http://sks.dk/forside/indhold.asp [accessed 31st July 2017].
Stewart, J. (ed.) (2009), *Kierkegaard and the Roman World*, Farnham.
Stewart, J. (ed.) (2011a), *Kierkegaard and Existentialism*, Farnham.
Stewart, J. (ed.) (2011b), *Kierkegaard's Influence on the Social Sciences*, Farnham.

Stewart, J. (ed.) (2012), *Kierkegaard's influence on philosophy. Tome 1. German and Scandinavian philosophy*, Farnham.
Stewart, J.B./Nun, K. (eds.) (2010), *Kierkegaard and the Greek World. Plato and Socrates Vol. 1*, Farnham.
Swenson, D.F./Lowrie, W. (1968), *Kierkegaard. Concluding Unscientific Postscript*, Princeton.
Tatum, J. (1969), 'The Tales in Apuleius' *Metamorphoses*', *Transactions and Proceedings of the American Philological Association* 100, 487–527.
Tatum, J. (1972), 'Apuleius and Metamorphosis', *The American Journal of Philology* 93, 306–13.
Thomte, R./Anderson, A.B. (1980), *The Concept of Anxiety. A Simple Psychologically Orienting Deliberation on the Dogmatic Issue of Hereditary Sin*, Princeton.
Tilg, S. (2014), *Apuleius'* Metamorphoses. *A Study in Roman Fiction*, Oxford.
Valpy, A.I. (1825), *L. Apulei opera. Ex editione Oudendorpiana cum notis et interpretationibus in usum Delphini*, London.
van Mal-Maeder, D. (2001), *Apuleius Madaurensis* Metamorphoses. *Livre II, texte, introduction et commentaire*, Groningen.
Westphal, M. (1996), *Becoming a self. A reading of Kierkegaard's 'Concluding unscientific postscript'*, Indiana.
Wild, J. (1940), 'Kierkegaard and Classic Philosophy', *Philosophical Review* 49, 536–51.
Winkler, J.J. (1985), *Auctor & Actor. A Narratological Reading of Apuleius' Golden Ass*, Berkeley.
Wulfing, N. (2008), 'Anxiety in Existential Philosophy and the Question of the Paradox', *Existential Analysis* 19, 73–80.
Zimmerman, M. et al. (eds.) (2004), *Aspects of Apuleius' Golden Ass. Vol. II. Cupid and Psyche*, Groningen.
Zimmerman, M., ed. (2012), *Apulei Metamorphoseon libri XI*, Oxford.
Zimmerman, M., et al. (2004), *Apuleius Madaurensis Metamorphoses. Books IV 28–35, V and VI 1–24. The tale of Cupid and Psyche*, Groningen.

Luca Ruggeri
Robert Bridges' *Eros and Psyche* and its models

Robert Bridges (1844–1930) now best remembered as the friend and posthumous editor of Gerald Manley Hopkins, was Poet Laureate of the United Kingdom from 1913 until his death and was admired in his lifetime especially for his exquisitely crafted lyrical poems. His swan song, the long philosophical poem *The Testament of Beauty* (published in 1929), was enthusiastically received by many contemporary critics and sold over 70000 copies. Soon afterwards, however, with the change in literary tastes brought about by Modernism, he fell out of favour.[1] As a result, while a handful of his short poems (*On a Dead Child*, *London Snow*, *Eros*, *Low Barometer*, and a few others) may be read in present-day anthologies, the bulk of his literary output has been out of print for over forty years— over eighty in the case of the dramas excluded from the single-volume Oxford edition of the *Poetical Works*.[2]

In the earlier phase of his career, before the turn of the century, Bridges often experimented with classical subjects, writing tragedies and masques on Nero, Prometheus, Ulysses, and the young Achilles, a Menandrean comedy based on Terence's *Heauton timorumenos*, and a poetic version of the story of *Cupid and Psyche*.[3]

The earliest surviving reference to *Eros and Psyche* (henceforth *E&Ps*) is found in a letter from G. M. Hopkins to Bridges dated July 18, 1884:[4]

> I find that 2557 is divisible by nothing ~~but~~ till you reach 20, beyond which I have not tried: what then can the length of the stanza be? And what is the subject of the poem?

---

[1] See e.g. Sparrow 1955, vii-xvii. For a general introduction to Morris' *Earthly Paradise* see introduction 1.6.
[2] Bridges 1953, last reprinted in 1971. The most recent sizeable selection of Bridges' poems is Cecil 1987.
[3] First published by George Bell and Sons in 1885 (Bridges 1885, henceforth referred to as *E&Ps* 1885); the second, heavily revised edition appeared in 1894 (Bridges 1894, henceforth *E&Ps* 1894), and in 1898 the poem was included in the first volume of Bridges' *Poetical Works*: Bridges 1898, 71–216, with a *Note on Eros and Psyche* at 290–291: henceforth *E&Ps* 1898. Quotations are from this edition unless otherwise stated.
[4] Thornton and Phillips 2013, vol. 2, 677.

Bridges's side of the correspondence is lost, but it is clear that in his previous letter he had tried to arouse his friend's curiosity about a new poem of which he had completed a draft[5] by giving him two seemingly incompatible pieces of information: that it was stanzaic, and that the number of lines was 2557, a prime number. E&Ps in fact consists of 365 seven-line stanzas followed by a two-line *Envoy*. The external structure of the poem matches that of the Roman calendar: the stanzas are arranged into twelve short cantos, or 'measures', representing the months from March to February, the number of stanzas in each measure being that of the days in the corresponding month. In the second edition Bridges would further group the measures into four 'quarters', naming the former after the months and the latter after the seasons.[6] The *Envoy* is probably meant to represent, albeit approximately, the difference in length between the typical calendar year of 365 days and the longer tropical year. As we shall see, there are in the poem many such references to the workings of the physical world, some of which seem to have passed unnoticed.

The main differences between Bridges's version and the Latin original have been discussed extensively by critics[7] and by the poet himself, both in a letter to Coventry Patmore[8] and in the *Notes* appended to the first and third editions of E&Ps,[9] and do not need to be examined at length here. A list of Bridges' innovations might include: the setting of the earlier part of the story on the island of Crete; the numerous allusions to Greek, and especially Cretan, places and myths; the Hellenisation of proper names (apparent from the very title of the work) and the erasure of Apuleius' references to Roman customs and institutions; the interpolation of long passages of description (of landscapes, people, objects, etc.); the frequent use of epic conventions such as catalogues, dressing scenes, and extended similes of the Homeric type; the smoothing away of perceived inconsistencies and improprieties, and in particular 'a gentler characterization of Psyche, who deserves more care in handling the motives of her conduct than was perhaps felt in Apuleius' time and country' (Bridges 1898, 290).

---

5 In *E&Ps* 1885, p. 155 the poem (i.e., presumably, the completion of its first draft) is dated June 30, 1884.
6 See also below. The temporal articulation of the story matches for the most part the calendrical frame that encloses it: see, for instance, *Sept.* 12.1 'Summer is over', *Jan.* 13.1 "Twas winter', and the nine 'external' months that pass between Eros' announcement of Psyche's pregnancy (*Jun.* 19) and the birth of Hedonè/Voluptas (*Feb.* 28).
7 See especially Hofmann 1908, 94–111; Young 1914, 192–197; Guérard 1942, 20–23 and 37–41; Bush 1969, 433–436; Stanford 1978, 58–67; Turner 1960 for further bibliography see Stanford 1978, 314 n. 28.
8 Patmore 1948, 199–200.
9 Bridges 1885, 156–158; Bridges 1898, 290–291.

All these embellishments and corrections have very little, if any, impact on the plot, so that Bridges could claim that he had 'amended Apuleius without altering him.'[10] Yet, as this paper will show, Bridges is keen to update Apuleius for his modern readers, with deliberate allusions to contemporary events, science, and literature.

1 "Borrowed Plumes"

In discussing Bridges' departures from Apuleius, Stanford (1978, 64) wrote: 'Undoubtedly, Bridges found delight at this stage of his career in indulging in fanciful invention'. This statement needs to be qualified: many of his additions to the original are borrowings from earlier works, both literary and artistic. The poet himself warns the reader in the *Note* to the first edition (Bridges 1885, 157):

> A reader unacquainted with the classics is warned that many beauties of the poem are borrowed plumes; and in the absence of notes it may be well to refer generally to Father Homer, Pindar, Plato, Moschus, Callimachus, the Greek Anthology, Lucian, Lucretius, Virgil, Dante [...], Petrarch, Botticelli, Titian, Rafael, Spenser [...], Wyatt, the mighty Shakespeare and others.

A closer look at two of Stanford's examples will provide an illustration of Bridges' method. One is the last section of the first canto: having asked her son to help her punish Psyche, Aphrodite heads to the seashore; the nine stanzas *March* 23–31, broadly corresponding to *Met.* 4.31.4–7 (463 words v. 153 in Taylor's literal translation of Apuleius' passage[11]), can be analysed as follows:

Stanza 23: mainly from *Met.* 4.31.4, with the addition of some topographical details (vv. 4–7 'The southward stretching margin of a bay,/Whose sandy curve she pass'd, and taking stand/Upon its taper horn of furthest land,/Lookt left and right to rise and set of day.').

Stanzas 24–26:

> Fair was the sight; for now, though full an hour
> The sun had sunk, she saw the evening light
> In shifting colour to the zenith tower,
> And grow more gorgeous ever and more bright.

---

10 Patmore 1948, 200.
11 Taylor 1795, 5–6.

Bathed in the warm and comfortable glow,
The fair delighted queen forgot her woe,
And watch'd the unwonted pageant of the night.

Broad and low down, where late the sun had been
A wealth of orange-gold was thickly shed,
Fading above into a field of green,
Like apples ere they ripen into red;
Then to the height a variable hue
Of rose and pink and crimson freak'd with blue,
And olive-border'd clouds o'er lilac led.

High in the opposèd west the wondering moon
All silvery green in flying green was fleec't;
And round the blazing South the splendour soon
Caught all the heaven, and ran to North and East;
And Aphrodite knew the thing was wrought
By cunning of Poseidon, and she thought
She would go see with whom he kept his feast.

The description of the twilight sky in these stanzas, which have no counterpart in Apuleius, 'is a portrait of the phenomena which followed the great eruption of Krakatoa' (Bridges 1898, 290). The eruption took place on 26–27 August 1883, and later in the year spectacular sunsets and twilights of the kind described here were witnessed in many regions of the world—in the British Isles especially in November-December. Although there is no reason to doubt that Bridges watched one or more such sunsets from his house at Yattendon, it has long been suspected that his account here depends on one by Hopkins published in *Nature* on 3 January 1884.[12] In stanza 26, Aphrodite's realizing that Poseidon, the Earth-shaker (Greek γαιήοχος, ἐννοσίγαιος, or ἐνοσίχθων), is responsible for what she sees is an ingenious allusion to the volcanic origin of the phenomena.[13] In the *Metamorphoses* the scene of Venus' departure takes place in the daytime

---

12 *Nature* 1884, 222–223. See Altick 1960, 253–356, and Hopkins's letter to Bridges of 1 January 1885 (Thornton and Phillips 2013, vol. 2, 704–706): 'One word on Psyche and volcanic sunsets. The description of th the one over the Cretan Sea is so closely agrees with an account I wrote ^in Nature^, even to details which were local only, that it is very extraordinary: you did not see my letter, did you?'

13 The modern reader may be struck by the blitheness with which Bridges turns one of deadliest eruptions in recent history (more than 36000 people were killed) into a night party with fireworks. A similar lack of empathy for the victims of natural disasters emerges from a letter Bridges sent to his friend Lionel Muirhead shortly after the 1908 Messina and Reggio earthquake (Stanford 1983–1984, vol. 2, 560–561).

(4.31.7 *ille serico tegmine flagrantiae solis obstitit inimici*[14]), and no reason is given for her sudden desire to sail.

Stanzas 27–31: As in Apuleius, a cortège of sea-gods rushes to pick up Aphrodite, but Bridges expands and varies his main model in several ways, by allusions, as promised, to Greek and Latin epic as well as to Renaissance paintings:

Stanzas 27–28:

> Swift to her wish came swimming on the waves
> His lovely ocean nymphs, her guides to be,
> The Nereids all, who live among the caves
> And valleys of the deep, Cymodocè,
> Agavè, blue-eyed Hallia and Nesæa,
> Speio, and Thoë, Glaucè and Actæa,
> Iaira, Melitè and Amphinomè,
>
> Apseudès and Nemertès, Callianassa,
> Cymothoë, Thaleia, Limnorrhea,
> Clymenè, Ianeira and Ianassa,
> Doris and Panopè and Galatea,
> Dynamenè, Dexamenè and Maira,
> Ferusa, Doto, Proto, Callianeira,
> Amphithoë, Oreithuia and Amathea.

Cf. *Met.* 4.31.5: *et ipsum quod incipit uelle, set statim, quasi pridem praeceperit, non moratur marinum obsequium: adsunt Nerei filiae chorum canentes [...].* The catalogue of the Nereids comes from the *Iliad* (18.37–49) and was perhaps meant to invite comparison with Spenser's adaptation of Hesiod's longer catalogue of the same deities in the *Faerie Queene* (4.11.48–51; cf. Hes. *Th.* 243–264).[15] Bridges' list, and expecially stanza 28, which consists entirely of proper names, is a veritable 'show of metrical virtuosity' (Guérard 1938: 85), retaining all the compactness of the original. Even though the metre forced Bridges to change the order of the names, he took care not to break such pairings as Δωτώ τε Πρωτώ τε (43), Δυναμένη τε | Δεξαμένη τε (43–44), Νημερτής τε καὶ Ἀψευδής (46), and Ἰάνειρα τε καὶ Ἰάνασσα (47).[16]

---

[14] Quotations from Apuleius follow the text of Kenney 1990.
[15] Cf. Bush 1969, 464–465 and Groom 1955, 19.
[16] As noted by Palacio 1999: 93, Beroaldus' commentary might be relevant here: *Nerei Filiae: Nereides. Hesiodus, Homerus, Maro noster poetae omnes nominatim Nereidas innumeras percensent.*

Stanza 29:

> And after them sad Melicertes drave
> His chariot, that with swift unfellied wheel,
> By his two dolphins drawn along the wave,
> Flew as they plunged, yet did not dip nor reel,
> But like a plough that shears the heavy land
> Stood on the flood, and back on either hand
> O'erturn'd the briny furrow with its keel.

This echoes *Met.* 4.21.6 *et auriga paruulus delphini Palaemon. iam passim maria persultantes Tritonum catervae* (noting that the sea-deity Palaemon is the apotheosed prince Melicertes according to Ovid, *Met.* 4.542) The first part of this description (ll.1–3) appears to have been based on, and be alluding to, a modern work of art. Raphael was the first to equip the vehicle of a marine deity with wheels without felloes in his *Triumph of Galatea*[17] for Agostino Chigi's villa in Rome (later known as the Villa Farnesina) [Figure 14], and everything points to that painting as Bridges' model here: Galatea's chariot-shell is also drawn by two dolphins; the fresco, which has long been known as one of the greatest masterpieces of the Italian Renaissance, is in the same building as Raphael's *Loggia di Psiche*, one of the most celebrated depictions of the story of *Cupid and Psyche* in painting;[18] and Raphael is included in Bridges's own list of models. At ll. 5–7, the commonplace comparison between sailing and ploughing was probably suggested by Beroaldus' conjecture *persulcantes* for *persultantes* or by Taylor's translation of it ('the company of Tritons everywhere furrowing the sea'[19]).

Stanza 30–31:

> Behind came Tritons, that their conches blew,
> Greenbearded, tail'd like fish, all sleek and stark;
> And hippocampi tamed, a bristly crew,
> The browzers of old Proteus' weedy park,
> Whose chiefer Mermen brought a shell for boat,
> And balancing its hollow fan afloat,
> Push'd it to shore and bade the queen embark:
>
> And then the goddess stept upon the shell
> Which took her weight; and others threw a train

---

17 See Meiss 1974.
18 See Simard's chapter in this volume, above.
19 Taylor 1795, 6. For Taylor's knowledge of Apuleius see Carver in this volume.

Of soft silk o'er her, that unfurl'd to swell
In sails, at breath of flying Zephyrs twain;
And all her way with foam in laughter strewn,
With stir of music and of conches blown,
Was Aphrodite launch'd upon the main.

In this passage both the conch-blowing Tritons and their green beards come from Apuleius, the latter from his description of Portunus *caerulis barbis hispidus* (*Met.* 4.21.6); the hippocampi, not in Apuleius, are nevertheless so common in scenes of this kind that it makes little sense to try to trace them to any one source;[20] by contrast, other details, especially the two flying Zephyrs that blow to swell the silken cloth, clearly allude to another celebrated painting whose artist is also in Bridges' list, Sandro Botticelli's *Birth of Venus*.[21] This stanza illustrates Bridges' mastery in combining Apuleius with various other allusions into a remarkable display of his learnedness, in a way that Apuleius himself might have approved of.

Bridges' handling of the *Galatea* and the *Venus* in this passage explains why writers and artists are grouped together in his list of models: in each case, instead of offering a general, more or less detailed, description of the painting as a whole, he picked just one or two details and integrated them into the Apuleian scene. This procedure is distinct from the one by which works of art usually come into play in classical and classicising literature, namely ekphrasis, and closely resembles the method of literary allusion. This in not to say that ekphrasis of art objects is absent from *E&Ps:* we find a clear instance in the third canto. The walls of Psyche's bedroom in her enchanted palace are adorned with paintings depicting 'Love's victories over the Gods renown'd,'[22] and Bridges describes five of them (four in *E&Ps* 1885: a fifth was added at the top of the list in *E&Ps* 1894). Here are the last two (*May* 20.1–6):

Here Dionysos, springing from his car
At sight of Ariadne; here uplept
Adonis to the chase, breaking the bar
Of Aphrodite's arm for love who wept:

---

20 There is, howerer, a sea-horse on the left in the *Galatea*.
21 Cf. also Stanley 1945, 412, on stanza 31: 'There is more than a reminiscence of Botticelli here.' It is probable, indeed almost certain, that Bridges, an ardent admirer of Italian Renassaince art, had visited both the Uffizi and the Villa Farnesina during his sojourns in Italy (the former perhaps as late as 1882: see Phillips 1992, 104–6).
22 *May* 12.5.

Figure 14: Raphael, *Triumph of Galatea*, Rome, Villa Farnesina. Source: https://commons.wiki media.org/wiki/File:Galatea_Raphael.jpg. Released through Wikimedia commons by Attilios 2007. [accessed 25th October 2017]

> He spear in hand, with leashèd dogs at strain;
> A marvellous work.

A visitor to the National Gallery in London will immediately recognise two large paintings by Titian, *Bacchus and Ariadne* and *Venus and Adonis*, on show in Rooms 2 and 9 respectively.

The other example is taken from canto 2 (*April*). On the king's return from consulting the oracle, his councillors begin to speculate about the identity of Psyche's destined husband. Some say he is none else than the giant Talos. Bridges, who never misses a chance to interpolate elements of Cretan mythology into the story, spends two stanzas describing him (*Apr.* 12–13):

> Some said that she to Talos was devote,
> The metal giant, who with mile-long stride
> Cover'd the isle, walking around by rote
> Thrice every day at his appointed tide;
> Who shepherded the sea-goats on the coast,
> And, as he past, caught up and live would roast,
> Pressing them to his burning ribs and side:
>
> Whose head was made of fine gold-beaten work,
> Of silver pure his arms and gleaming chest.
> Thence of green-bloomèd bronze far as the fork,
> Of iron weather-rusted all the rest.
> One single vein he had, which passing down
> From head to foot was open in his crown,
> And closèd by a nail; such was this pest.

Some elements of this description come ultimately from Greek sources, probably through the mediation of one or more modern mythological compendia; cf., for instance, the entry on Talos in Smith's *Dictionary of Greek and Roman Biography and Mythology*:[23]

> TALOS (Τάλως) [...] 2. A man of brass, the work of Hephaestus. This wonderful being was given to Minos by Zeus or Hephaestus, and watched the island of Crete by walking around the island thrice every day. Whenever he saw strangers approaching, he made himself red-hot in fire, and then embraced the strangers when they landed. He had in his body only one vein, which ran from the head to the ankles and was closed at the top with a nail.

Others, namely the roasting of the sea-goats, appear to be Bridges' own invention, while the first four lines of the second stanza are an almost literal translation of Dante, *Inferno* 14.106–109[24] (itself a versification of *Daniel* 2.32–33[25]):

---

[23] Smith 1849, vol. 3, 973.
[24] See Palacio 1999, 229.

> La sua testa è di fin oro formata,
> e puro argento son le braccia e 'l petto,
> poi è di rame infino a la forcata;
>
> da indi in giuso è tutto ferro eletto,
> salvo che 'l destro piede è terra cotta;
> e sta 'n su quel, più che 'n su l'altro, eretto.
>
> 'His head is formed of fine gold, and pure silver are his arms and breast; then he is of brass as far as the fork; from then downward he is all refined iron, except that his right foot is baked clay; and on that one, more than on the other, he stands erect.' (Durling's translation[26])

Dante is describing the Old Man of Crete, whose tears, dripping from cracks in his body, form the rivers of Hell. The relationship between the old and the new context is a nice combination of similarity (of size and location) and contrast (the Old Man's immobility v. Talos' superhuman speed).[27]

Translations that, like those seen above, occupy two or more lines and are as close to their original as the metre and the new context allow, are not rare in the poem and certainly fit Bridges' description of his literary debts as 'borrowed plumes'.[28] One appears toward the end of the poem, in the catalogue of the Olympian gods summoned to assembly by Mercury: *February* 17.5 'Athena, mistress good of them that know' seems to allude to Dante's famous reference to Aristotle as 'the master of them that know (It. '[i]l maestro di color che sanno') in *Inferno* 4.131.[29] The other is *January* 13.6:

---

25 Three stanzas later (*Apr.* 17.5–7), what was originally a biblical allusion was turned into an almost literal quotation in the second edition: *E&Ps* 1885 'Up to the mountains! for I heard the voice/Of my deliverance on the winds, *Rejoice,/Rejoice, arise, my Psyche, and come away!*' becomes *E&Ps* 1894 'Up to the mountain! for I hear the voice/Of my belovèd on the winds, *Rejoice,/Arise, my love, my fair one, and come away!*" (author's italics): cf. *Song of Solomon* 2.10 'My beloved spake, and said unto me, Rise up, my love, my fair one, and come away.' The italics signal the embedding of direct speech within direct speech (cf. *Aug.* 23.5–7, *Jan.* 9.5–10.4, 19.4–5).
26 During and Martinez 1996, 223–5.
27 Robert Carver (personal communication) convincingly suggests that Bridges is also alluding to Spenser's *Faerie Queene*, bk. 5, where Talus, representing retributive justice, is described as 'an yron man' and 'made of yron mould' (5.1.12.2 and 6); the same point was made by Hoffman 1908, 105.
28 But there are subtler ways in which works other than the *Metamorphoses* are exploited in *E&Ps*. Two references to Dante's *Comedy* may serve as an example.
29 Also Mar. 11.5–7 < Lucr. 1.22–23 (see below); May 6.3–7 < Il. 1.601–8; Oct. 13 < Call. Dem. 10–16; Nov. 3.2–4.7 < Il. 18.394–405.

> 'Twas winter; and as shivering Psyche sat
> Waiting for morn, she question'd in her mind
> What place the goddess meant, arrived whereat
> She might descend to hell, or how should find
> The way which Gods to living men deny.
> 'No Orpheus, nay, nor Hercules am I,'
> Said she, 'to loosen where the great Gods bind.'

Psyche is in the same situation and state of mind as Dante the character at the beginning of *Inferno* 2: both have just agreed to set out on a journey to the underworld but feel unequal to the task. Like Psyche, Dante compares himself unfavourably with two great men of the past that made a similar journey, Aeneas and St. Paul. His comparison climaxes with the powerful line 'Io non Enea, io non Paulo sono' (32), which is probably the model of Bridges' 'No Orpheus, nay, nor Hercules am I.'[30]

On the basis of these intertextual connections, the reader might be tempted to think that Bridges was in some way trying to emulate the allusive texture of the *Metamorphoses* and in particular of the story of Cupid and Psyche. This hypothesis is supported by some passages in which Bridges appears to have included references to the same classical text alluded to by Apuleius in the corresponding section of the *fabella*. The most striking instance occurs in the presentation (in Apuleius, self-presentation) of Aphrodite/Venus at the beginning of the tale. In his version, Bridges substituted the unmistakable echoes of the proem of Lucretius' *De rerum natura* in the first sentence of Venus' speech (*Met.* 4.30 *En rerum naturae prisca parens, en elementorum origo initialis, en orbis totius alma Venus...*) with an even clearer reference to the same proem (March 11.5–7 "Seeing that without her generative might / Nothing can spring upon the shores of light, / Nor any bud of joy or love be born", a translation Lucr. 1.22–23 *nec sine te quicquam dias in luminis oras / exoritur neque fit laetum neque amabile quicquam*). Another interesting case is that of Nov. 11. Apuleius ends the scene of Venus' meeting with Mercury with the words *nec Mercurius omisit obsequium* (*Met.* 6.8), which echo the Homeric line: ὡς ἔφατ', οὐδ' ἀπίθησε διάκτορος Ἀργειφόντης. Bridges did not translate Apuleius' sentence exactly but interpolated in their place a dressing scene clearly modelled on the one that follows the hexameter in both its occurrences in the Homeric poems (*Il.* 24.339, *Od.* 5.43).

---

30 Cf. also Verg. *Aen* 6.119–23. Orpheus and Hercules are respectively the first and the last in Aeneas' list of four katabatic heroes. For *Jan.* 20.2 'woolly Charon' cf. the 'woolly cheeks' (It. 'lanose gote') of *Inf.* 3.97. Bridges certainly had Dante's passage in mind when he translated Virgil's description of Charon in *Ibant obscuri* (1909): 'all filthily unkempt/That woolly white cheekfleece' ~ *Aen.* 6.299–300 *cui plurima mento/canities inculta iacet.*

2 Claims of originality

The list of writers and artists in the *Note* of *E&Ps* 1885 serves also another purpose: it tells the reader *where not to look* for Bridges' models:

> …Wyatt, the mighty Shakespeare and others. The author has never read any English version of the story.

Thus, Bridges refuses to engage with the rich tradition of translations, adaptations and rewritings of Apuleius' story in English and implies that any similarities that may exist between those works and his are due to chance only, so his claim needs to be analysed. In the previous section we met a passage that may, but does not need to, have been influenced by Taylor's translation. Here, I will focus on three narrative poems: *The Legend of Cupid and Psyche* by Shackerley Marmion,[31] *Cupid and Psyche: a Mythological Tale from the Golden Ass of Apuleius* by Hudson Gurney,[32] and *The Story of Cupid and Psyche* by William Morris. Since Bridge's *Note* was included in the first edition of the poem and never reprinted afterwards,[33] any discussion of his claim must be based on the text of that edition. I will start with Marmion.

The Legend of Cupid and Psyche is a poem of 2320 lines written mainly in heroic couplets. Like Bridges, Marmion expanded considerably on Apuleius while preserving the original plot in its essentials. The closest verbal correspondence with *E&Ps* is perhaps the rendering of *Met.* 5.22.7 *ceterum corpus glabellum atque luculentum* in Marmion 1.3.287 'His body sleek, and smooth,' *E&Ps* 1885 5.21.5–6 has 'and smooth to touch/His body sleek.' Moreover, in both Marmion and Bridges, but not in Apuleius, Venus wants Psyche's love interest to be physically deformed: compare Marmion 1.1.17 'deformed of limb' with *E&Ps* 1885 1.22.2 'deformed in body.' While Apuleius does not specify the number of the weavers that Psyche meets in the underworld, Marmion (2.2.262), Morris (l. 2093), and

---

[31] First published in 1637 (1638), it had a second edition in 1666. A reprint of the 1637 text, with modernised orthography, appeared in 1820: see Watson 1974, col. 1314. I quote it from George Saintsbury's edition (Saintsbury 1906, 2–60), which has the advantage of numbering the lines. Marmion's poem was certainly familiar to Morris: see Boos 2002, vol. 1, 384, 399 n. 18, 418–9 n. 44 (where 'Marmion 177–198' should be 'Marmion 1.2.177–198').

[32] Published anonymously in 1799 (1800²; 1801³: [Gurney] 1801, from which I quote), reprinted in Davenport 1812, 257–83. Later included in *The Works of Apuleius*, London: H. G. Bohn, 1853 (repr. by George Bell and Sons, the future publisher of *E&Ps*, in 1878), 407–430.

[33] There is a reference to it in *E&Ps* 1898, 290, where however no mention is made of the claim in question: 'In the first edition there was a note acknowledging the frequent translations from the Greek, and other robberies.'

Bridges (*E&Ps* 1885 11.22.2, 27.4) all say that there are three of them; only Marmion explains his choice of that number, and he does so by identifying them with the Parcae.[34] The most significant point of contact between Bridges and Marmion is to be found in their narration of the fall of the first sister from the rock. This is Bridges (*E&Ps* 1885 6.27):

> But as a dead stone, from a height let fall,
> Silent and straight is gathered by the force
> Of earth's vast mass upon its weight so small,
> In speed increasing as it nears its source
> Of motion—by which law all things soe'er
> Are clutched and dragged and held—so fell she there,
> Like a dead stone, down, in her headlong course.

There is nothing resembling this in the text of Apuleius. About this stanza (or an earlier version of it), Hopkins wrote to Bridges:[35] 'In suggestion it is one of the most brilliant in the poem but in execution ~~of the most~~ very imperfect.' Later critics too mention the passage, not always approvingly, for its most conspicuous feature, the versified account of Newton's law of general gravitation, as if it were Bridges' own invention. It is, in a sense; but compare the corresponding lines in Marmion's poem (1.4.152):

> ...she did herself bequeath
> Unto a fearful precipice, and threw
> Her body headlong down, whose weight it drew
> Towards the centre; for, without support
> All heavy matter thither will resort.

It is very hard to believe that the two passages are not directly related. Bridges updated his model by substituting Newton's law for Aristotle's theory of natural place, according to which all heavy bodies move naturally toward the centre of the Earth. This reference to the law of gravitation has been called an anachronism by more than one critic.[36] Since, however, *E&Ps* is not a faithful translation of an ancient work, any allusion to a universal law in it could be anachronistic only if attributed to one of the human characters, which is not the case here. In fact, all references to discoveries of modern science in the poem are made by either the external narrator or, in two instances, the Olympian gods. One is the re-

---

34 Hoffmann 1908, 99.
35 1 January 1885: Thornton and Phillips 2013, vol. 2, 705.
36 Guérard 1942, 41; Stanford 1978, 61.

alisation on Aphrodite's part that the extraordinary sunset she is watching is the result of some subterranean convulsion (1.26.4–6, on which see above). The other conveniently leads us to the second poet, Hudson Gurney.

His version is by far the shortest of those considered here, running as it does to 812 lines (mostly quatrains of iambic tetrameters with rhyming scheme abab). The plot is basically that of Apuleius, but Gurney inserted philosophical and ethical remarks, short similes, and other interpolations, and at the same time abridged his source, suppressing whole passages of description and speeches. His narrative is at times so condensed as to be hard to follow without making reference to the original.

The following stanza (*E&Ps* 1885 9.5) is part of Bridges' description of the chariot of Aphrodite, made for her by Hephaestos:

> 'Twas then he wrought this work within the cave,
> Embossed with rich design, a moonèd car;
> And when returned to heaven to Cypris gave,
> In form imagined like her crescent star;
> Which circling nearest earth, maketh at night
> To wakeful mortal men shadow and light
> Alone of all the stars in heaven that are.

I quote Apuleius' description in full for comparison:

> *iubet construi currum, quem ei Vulcanus aurifex subtili fabrica studiose poliuerat et ante thalami rudimentum nuptiale munus obtulerat, limae tenuantis detrimento conspicuum et ipsius auri damno pretiosum.*
> limae : lunae edd. vett.
>
> She ordered to be prepared the car that Vulcan the goldsmith had lovingly perfected with cunning workmanship and given her as a betrothal present—a work of art notable by what his refining tools had pared away, valuable through the very loss of gold. (Met. 6.6.1, Kenney's translation)

The 'moonèd car' is not in our texts of Apuleius, but it is not Bridges' invention, either. Several early editions of the *Metamorphoses* have *lunae* instead of *limae* ('file'), and the whole phrase *lunae tenuantis detrimento* was explained by Beroaldus as meaning that the chariot was in the shape of a crescent. *Limae*, the reading of F (codex Laurentianus 68.2, the source of all other extant manuscripts of the *Metamorphoses*) makes much better sense in the context, and editors and commentators have preferred it since the eighteenth century at the latest. However, *lunae* survived a little longer in the English-speaking world through Thomas Taylor's translation (Taylor 1795, 66):

> She orders the chariot to be made ready, which Vulcan, having fabricated with subtle skill, arched like the horned moon and precious with a waste of gold, had presented her before the consummation of her marriage

A moon-shaped chariot would perfectly suit Diana or Selene, much less so Venus, as Bridges himself realised. But, instead of simply dropping the whole concept, he chose to play with it and turn it into something more meaningful. As the pronoun 'her' in line 4 of stanza 9.5 shows, the celestial body described in lines 4–7 is not the Moon but the planet Venus. 'Moonèd' (l. 2) and 'crescent' (l. 4) refer to the corniculate shape Venus assumes when it is below the Sun, a phenomenon already alluded to by Milton in *Paradise Lost*;[37] 'circling nearest earth' (l. 5), is in itself ambiguous, but here means 'its orbit about the Sun being the closest to Earth's of any planet'. As for ll. 5–7's reference to shadows, both the Moon and Venus are capable of casting shadows,[38] but only Venus is commonly called a star. Bridges must have felt at some point that the allusion was too obscure, for in the second edition he changed 'Cypris' in l. 3 to 'Venus', breaking the general rule he had set against Roman names. Bridges could have devised his stanza solely on the basis of the reading *lunae* in Apuleius or of Taylor's translation, but the Moon and Venus are associated in the corresponding passage of Gurney's poem (11.5):

> VENUS then calls her doves, and soon
>   With quick steps mounts her golden car,
> Arch'd inwards like the waning moon,
>   And brilliant as the morning star

Admittedly, the two stanzas have little in common apart from the mention of the planet, and if this were the only point of contact between the two poems it would be safer to view it as a curious coincidence.

There are, however, other passages in *E&Ps* to which Gurney's version seems to offer a more or less close parallel. Both poets interpolate a personification of

---

[37] 7.366 (see Fowler *ad loc.*).The phases of Venus were first observed by Galileo in 1610. The discovery that the planet goes through a complete set of phases, from full to gibbous to crescent, showed for the first time that the Ptolemaic model could not be correct (see Palmieri 2001). It is tempting to read the mention of the crescent of Venus here and that of the law of gravitation in 6.27 as implicit tributes to their discoverers. In a later poem (*Wintry Delights*, published in 1903) Bridges declared that the glory of Alexander the Great and Napoleon cannot compare 'With the immortal olive that circles bold Galileo's | Brows, the laurel'd halo of Newton's unwithering fame.' (ll. 128–129, Bridges 1953, 413).
[38] For a 19th century popular account of Venus' shadows see Ward 1859, 97.

Time, although their respective contexts and connotations are very different (*E&Ps* 1.2: 'old hard-featured Time,' a lover of literature, has preserved the ancient story of the king's three daughters; Gurney 6.1–3: cruel Time, holding a scythe and surrounded by attendant Cares, hastens the arrival of Psyche's wedding day). Both close the stanza they devote to expressing the ineffability of Psyche's beauty (the fifth of each poem) with words borrowed from an earlier English poet and, what is more striking, they clearly mark them as a quotation, albeit with different means: *E&Ps* 1885 1.5.5–7 'Ideals out of being and above,/Which music worships, but if love should love,/'Tis, as the poet saith, to love a star.' echoes Shakespeare, *All's Well that Ends Well*, act. 1 sc. 1 "Twere all one/That I should love a bright particular star/And think to wed it, he is so above me';[39] Gurney 2.3 'The youngest—but no tongue so warm/Though matchless eloquence be given,/May dare pourtray her finish'd form,/The 'prodigality of heaven!" echoes Gray, *Stanzas to Mr. Bentley*, ll. 17–20 'But not to one in this benighted age/Is that diviner inspiration given,/That burns in Shakespeare's or in Milton's page,/The pomp and prodigality of heaven'. Later in the story, in the dialogue between Venus and the seagull, *E&Ps* 1885 7.14.4 'Or Naiad? say, or is a Grace his flame?' is remarkably similar in wording to Gurney 16.3.2 'No Grace, no Goddess is his flame'. Lastly, this is how Bridges describes Aphrodite's handmaids Care and Sorrow (9.24.1–5):

> These, like twin sharks that in a fair ship's wake
> Swim constant, showing 'bove the water blue
> Their shearing fins, and hasty ravin make
> Of overthrow or offal, so these two
> On Aphrodite's passing follow hard;

This simile is reminiscent of the nautical metaphor that opens Gurney's account of the visits of the two sisters (10.1):

> Gaily we launch our little bark,
>   The sun-beams on the water play,
> While close behind the ravenous shark
>   Expecting waits his destin'd pray.

Although none of these parallels is in itself sufficient to prove dependence, taken together they make it likely that Bridges knew Gurney's poem.

The last version considered here is also the most relevant to our discussion. William Morris published *The Story of Cupid and Psyche* in 1868—just sixteen

---

[39] See Hoffman 1908, 110.

years before Bridges began to write *E&Ps*—as part of the lengthy epic *The Earthly Paradise*, the work that finally established him as one of the foremost poets of his day. The popular success of *The Earthly Paradise* meant that readers and reviewers would naturally compare Bridges' version to that of Morris, whether the former had been influenced by the latter or not. It is against this background that we have to place Bridges' claim that he had not read any English version of the story.[40]

In fact, a number of *E&Ps*' departures from its main model have their closest parallel in Morris. First and foremost, the external structure of Bridges' poem (on which see above) is almost certainly based on that of *The Earthly Paradise*[41] as a whole, which, apart for a prologue and an epilogue, consists of twelve sections, corresponding to and named after the months from March to February.[42] Regarding the relationship between the two versions of the story (as opposed to that between *E&Ps* and *The Earthly Paradise*), it is perhaps significant that both poets eliminate the character of Psyche's mother: Bridges never mentions her, whereas Morris has one of Psyche's sisters recall the happier time when she was alive (l. 1096, Boos 2002: vol. 1, p. 420).[43] Both describe Psyche' first awakening in the secret valley in much greater detail than Apuleius, focusing on her confused state of mind:

> iamque sufficienti recreata somno placido resurgit animo.
> Presently, refreshed by a good rest, she rose with her mind at ease.
> (*Met.* 5.1.1 , Kenney's translation)

Morris ll. 441–448 (Boos 2002, vol. 1, pp. 400–1):

> Therewith did Psyche open wide her eyes,
> And rising on her arm, with great surprise
> Gazed on the flowers wherein so deep she lay,
> And wondered why upon that dawn of day
> Out in the fields she had lift up her head
> Rather than in her balmy gold-hung bed.

---

[40] The statement was discussed by reviewers exclusively in relation to Morris: Webster 1886, *The Month* 1886; *The Saturday Review* 1895. Other reviews comparing the two versions: Morshead 1886, *The Saturday Review* 1886, Mackail 1886, *The Spectator* 1898, Quiller-Couch 1899.
[41] See Evans 1933, 232.
[42] The twelve sections contain a total of twenty-four tales exchanged between a group of Greek sages and one of Scandinavian wanderers. *The Story of Cupid and Psyche* is the classical tale for May.
[43] Hofmann (1908, 99). Psyche's mother is also absent in the dramatic versions of Heywood and Molière.

Then, suddenly remembering all her woes,
She sprang upon her feet...

E&Ps 1885 3.1–2:

After long sleep when Psyche first awoke,
A smile delayed the opening of her eyes,
Fed from the confort of her spirit, that spoke
Delighted invitation to arise.
But soon the encompassment of sights so strange
Rebuffed her mood, nor could she piece the change,
But lay awhile embarassed with surprise.

Anon here quickening thought took up its task,
And all came back as it had happed o'ernight;
The sad procession of the wedding mask,
The melancholy toiling up the height,
The solitary rocks where she was left;
And thence in dark and airy waftage reft,
How on the flowers she had been disburdened light.

Finally, in both versions a bird helps Cupid find Psyche after her last trial. In Morris the Phoenix sees the girl asleep near the mouth of the cave and informs her lover, who immediately comes to her rescue (ll. 2350–2359, Boos 2002: vol. 1, p. 455); in *E&Ps* Eros flies to the Taenarian peninsula in search of Psyche, encounters 'that snowy bird/Of Crete, that late made mischief with his queen,' asks him whether he has seen Psyche, and then follows him to the spot where she lies (12.1–4).[44] There is, I believe, little doubt that Morris is Bridges' model here.

3 Conclusion

In this paper I have tried to highlight, through a close analysis of selected passages, the highly intertextual nature of Bridges's poem, which goes well beyond its obvious relationship with the *Metamorphoses*. The poet himself acknowleged his many 'robberies', even providing an (avowedly incomplete) list of classical authors to assist his readers in identifying them. At the same time, he sought to present his relationship with Apuleius as unmediated, and did so by denying that he had read—and thence that he had been influenced by—any English ver-

---

44 Hoffman 1908, 100.

sion of the tale. In order to challenge this claim, I have concentrated on the narrative poems of Marmion, Gurney and Morris; a further step would be to extend the comparison to other works such as Thomas Heywood's masque *Love's Mistress*, Mary Tighe's *Psyche*, and Richard Crowley's *Venus and Psyche*, but the parallels I have collected suffice to show that Bridges, for all his attempts at positioning himself outside the rich tradition of English retellings of the Apuleian story, is himself in dialogue, and sometimes in competition, with it.[45] Furthermore, Bridges' allusive adaptation of the story with many references to previous literature is in many ways similar to Apuleius' own working methods in his novel, and Bridges allows us to look at Apuleian intertextuality with fresh eyes.

4 Bibliography

Altick, R. D. (1960), 'Four Victorian Poets and an Exploding Island', *Victorian Studies* 3/3, 249–60.
Boos, F. S. (ed.) (2002), *The Earthly Paradise by William Morris*, 2 vols., New York and London.
Bridges, R. (1884), *Poems*, Oxford.
Bridges, R. (1885), *Eros & Psyche. A Poem in Twelve Measures*, London.
Bridges, R. (1894), *Eros & Psyche*. London.
Bridges, R. (1898), *Poetical Works*, vol. 1, London.
Bridges R. (ed.) (1909), *Select Poems of R. W. Dixon*, London.
Bridges, R. (1953), *Poetical Works. With the Testament of Beauty but Excluding the Eight Dramas*, Oxford.
Bush, D. (1969), *Mythology and the Romantic Tradition in English Poetry*, Cambridge, MA.
Cecil, D. (1987), *A Choice of Bridges' Verse*, London.
Davenport, R.A. (ed.) (1812.), *The Poetical Register and Repository of Fugitive Poetry for 1808–1809*, London.
de Palacio, J. (1999), *Les métamorphoses de Psyché. Essai sur la décadance d'un myth*, Biarritz.
Durling, R. M., R. L. Martinez (1996), *The Divine Comedy of Dante Alighieri*, vol. 1: *Inferno*, New York and Oxford.
Evans, B. I. (1933), *English Poetry in the Later Nineteenth Century*, London.
Groom, B. (1955), *The Diction of Poetry from Spenser to Bridges*, Toronto.
Guérard, A. J. (1938), *A Study of the Poetry of Robert Bridges*, diss. Stanford University.
Guérard, A. J. (1942), Jr., *Robert Bridges: A Study of Traditionalism in Poetry*, Cambridge, MA.
[Gurney, H.] (1801), *Cupid and Psyche: a Mythological Tale from the Golden Ass of Apuleius*, London.

---

[45] I am most grateful to Laura Banella, Emilio Capettini, Stephen Harrison, Regine May, Rino Modonutti, Glenn Most, and Giovanni Santucci for their criticisms and suggestions.

Hoffmann, A. (1908), *Das Psyche-Märchen des Apuleius in der englischen Literatur*, diss. Kaiser-Wilhelm-Universität zu Strassburg.
Kenney, E. J. (1990), *Apuleius. Cupid & Psyche*, Cambridge.
Mackail, J. W. (1886), review of Bridges 1885, *The Oxford Magazine*, 24 February, 85–6.
McCracken, U. E./ Randall, L. M. C. / Randall, R. H. jr, (eds.) (1974), *Gatherings in Honor of Dorothy E. Miner*, Baltimore.
Meiss, M. (1974), 'Raphael's Mechanized Seashell. Notes on a Myth, Technology and Iconographic Tradition', in: McCracken/Randall/Randall, 317–322.
Morshead, E. D. A. (1886), review of Bridges 1885, *The Academy*, 2 January: 2–3.
Nature (1884), 'The Remarkable Sunsets', 3 January: 222–5.
Palmieri, P. (2001), 'Galileo and the Discovery of the Phases of Venus', *Journal for the History of Astronomy* 32: 109–129.
Patmore, D. (1948), 'Coventry Patmore and Robert Bridges. Some Letters', *The Fortnightly*, n.s. 169, 196–204.
Phillips, C. (1992), *Robert Bridges: A Biography*. Oxford.
Quiller-Couch, A. T. (1899), review of Bridges 1898, 18 March, 317–8.
Saintsbury, G. (1906), *Minor Poets of the Caroline Period*, vol. 2, Oxford.
Smith, W. (ed.) (1844–1849), *Dictionary of Greek and Roman Biography and Mythology*, 3 vols., London.
Sparrow, J. (ed.) (1955), *Robert Bridges: Poetry and Prose*. Oxford.
Stanford, D. E. (1978), *In The Classic Mode: The Achievement of Robert Bridges*, Newark, NJ.
Stanford, D. E. (ed.) (1983–1984), *The Selected Letters of Robert Bridges, with the Correspondence of Robert Bridges and Lionel Muirhead*, 2 vols. Newark, NJ.
Stanley, C. (1945), 'Return to an Old Book', *University of Toronto Quarterly* 14/4, 409–413.
Taylor, T. (1795), *The Fable of Cupid and Psyche, translated from the Latin of Apuleius*. London. *The Month* (1886), review of Bridges 1885: 57, 294–295.
The Saturday Review (1886), review of Bridges 1885, 16 January, 91.
The Saturday Review (1895), review of Bridges 1894, 12 January, 41–2.
The Spectator (1898), review of Bridges 1898, 12 November, 688–9.
Thompson, E. (1944), *Robert Bridges: 1844–1930*. Oxford.
Thomson, J. (1880), *The City of Dreadful Night and other Poems*. London.
Thornton, R. K. R/ Phillips, C. (eds). (2013), *The Collected Works of Gerard Manley Hopkins*, vols. 1 and 2: *Correspondence*, Oxford.
Turner, P. (1960), 'Pater and Apuleius', *Victorian Studies* 3/3, 290–296.
Ward, M. (1859), *Telescope Teachings*, London.
Watson, G. (1974), *The New Cambridge Bibliography of English Literature*, vol. 1, 600–1660, Cambridge.
Webster, A. (1886), review of Bridges 1885, *The Athenaeum*, 3 April, 450–1.
Young, F. E. B. (1914), *Robert Bridges. A Critical Study*, London.

III *Fin de Siècle* and Psychology

Lucia Pasetti
From Psyche to psyche.
The interiorisation of Apuleius' *fabella* in D'Annunzio, Pascoli, and Savinio

1 Introduction. Gabriele D'Annunzio

The period between the late nineteenth and the early twentieth century is a high point in the European reception of Apuleius' *fabella:* late romantic spiritualism retraces the path of symbolic interpretation, travelled many times in the long story of our text, including by its ancient readers.[1] The point of greatest interest is undoubtedly the character of Psyche: in keeping with the perspective of decadent culture, this female figure is spiritualized as well as eroticized.[2]

In Italian post-Romantic culture, the prominence given to Psyche—documented by the essay of Ugo de Maria, *La favola di Amore e Psiche nella letteratura e nell'arte italiana* (1899)[3]—provides the background for the experience of Gabriele D'Annunzio (1863–1938), whose *Psiche giacente* is the starting point of our survey. Published on its own in 1892,[4] the poem was inserted a year later in the collection *Poema paradisiaco*, a milestone of Italian Decadentism, in which the memory of contemporary poets (from Baudelaire to Swinburne) mingles with a Pre-Raphaelite atmosphere. D'Annunzio's 'reclining Psyche' is not directly based on Apuleius,[5] but on a painting by Edward Burne-Jones: therefore, the myth is filtered through Pre-Raphaelite art, which exerted a great influence on D'Annunzio's poetry in the 1880s.[6] Giuliana Pieri has called the poem a

---

[1] Cf. Graverini 2007, 145–7.
[2] Brief overviews on late 20th century European reception in Haight 1927, 130–4; 155–60; Hummel 2008, 74–7; Auraix-Jonchière-Volpilhac-Auger 2000, esp. 326–91; a more detailed analysis in de Palacio 1999 and Sozzi 2000 and 2007, 115–38, 171–187.
[3] De Maria 1899: 5 takes for granted the symbolic interpretation, quoting also modern writers such as Leopardi, Zanella and Prati (34–41 and 224–7).
[4] Andreoli-Lorenzini 1982, 1168 *ad loc.*
[5] D'Annunzio does not count Apuleius among his favourite *auctores*, even if he is seemingly aware of the privileged position held by the *Metamorphoses* in Victorian England (see above, n. 2, particularly de Palacio 1999, 83–102): in *Il Piacere*, an improbable Marquis of Mount Edgcumbe bores his young friend 'talking of a rare edition of Apuleius' (Andreoli-Lorenzini 1988, 295 and 1225, n. 254). He clearly refers to the 1469 *editio princeps* of Andrea De Buxis.
[6] On D'Annunzio and Pre-Raphaelite art see the syntheses of Pieri 2009, 177–8. and 2009a.

case of 'double ekphrasis',[7] since Burne-Jones' painting, for its part, illustrates a scene from William Morris' *Earthly Paradise*; for his work's influence on contemporaries see the introduction and Ruggeri in this volume.

The episode is not present in the Apuleian tale: Cupid finds Psyche asleep in a garden, falls in love and kisses her without waking her.[8] Of course, D'Annunzio knew Morris;[9] still, the epigraph ('Da Burne-Jones') introducing the poem states its main dependence on a visual hypotext, in all likelihood not a drawing (as previously thought), but the watercolour owned by the Pre-Raphaelite painter and model Mrs. Marie Spartali Stillman[10] and now at the British Museum (Figure 15: 'Cupid finding Psyche', watercolour and bodycolour, signed and dated 1866, British Museum, London. Provenance: S. Elliot Lewis, in J. Gere, Pre-Raphaelite Drawings at the British Museum, 1994, cat. n. 58, p. 86).

In D'Annunzio's seven stanzas, each comprising seven hendecasyllables, Cupid contemplates a sleeping Psyche, lying on the edge of a marble basin. Here, water gushes from the marble mouth of a fountain (tracing an arch, just like in the British Museum's watercolour and unlike other versions created by Burne-Jones).[11] In the background, there is an enchanted garden, full of life and sensuality. The loving encounter is yet to come, but there is an allusion in the poem's last words already to the 'fatal lamp' (l. 39).

> Voi, rose, offritevi a la man che appresta
> il letto, empite quella man funesta
> che accenderà la lampada fatale!

> You, roses, offer yourself to the hand that ready the bed, fill that fatal hand that will set alight the fatal lamp!!

Certainly Burne-Jones, Morris and D'Annunzio share 'the decadent fascination for the sleeping woman, ultimately connected to the final embodiment of feminine passivity, the dead woman'.[12] Because of its interest in the cliché of female victimisation, decadentism glosses over the resourcefulness of Psyche and her determination to regain her beloved, thus fitting her into the sleeping-beauty ste-

---

7 Pieri-Everson 2012, 15.
8 Cf. Morris 1888 [1868–1870]: I.231, ll. 347–50: 'withal at last amidst a fair green close/hedged round about with woodbine and red rose,/within the flicker of a white-thorn shade/in gentle sleep he found the maiden laid', with de Palacio 1999, 86.
9 Cf. Marabini Moevs 1976, 17 n. 22.
10 Cf. Giuliana Pieri (2009a, 22–26 and Pieri-Everson 2012, 16–17).
11 A comparison of the different versions in Pieri 2009a, 23–4.
12 Pieri 2009, 190.

Figure 15: Edward Burne Jones 'Cupid finding Psyche', watercolour and bodycolour, signed and dated 1866, British Museum, London. Reprinted with permission of the Trustees of the British Museum.

reotype.[13] This figure in fact occurs several times in D'Annunzio's works,[14] representing (as we shall see) the most obvious *trait-d'union* between him and Pascoli.[15]

Over and above the clichés, the most interesting feature of the poem is the link established here between the Apuleian myth and the inner world of humanity. According to Leonello Sozzi's sensitive reading, the poem represents phenomena that take place in the most intimate secrecy. This idea is suggested by the image of the cradle[16] ('cuna', l. 15) on which the young woman is lying. Love establishes a deep and silent communication between Psyche and surrounding nature: thus, the breathing of the maiden is in rhythm with the cosmos and, while dreams well up from her heart, everything in the garden becomes animated. This process is illustrated through pervasive personifications: the water rises to kiss her (l. 12), the wind sighs languidly (l. 26), the roses reach forward to Psyche's tresses (ll. 29–30). In short, the garden of Psyche is a true 'Garden of the Soul',[17] an inner space inhabited by dreams, emotions, desires, a metaphor clearly belonging to late-romantic spiritualism.

2 Giovanni Pascoli

The effectiveness of the poem by D'Annunzio makes it easier to understand why, twelve years later, it is precisely Apuleius' Psyche that is chosen by the more discreet and subtle Giovanni Pascoli (1855–1912) in order to develop his complex reflection on the human soul. He includes in his *Poemi conviviali*—a passionate dialogue with the ancient tradition—the *Poemi di Psyche* (1904), a diptych focused, like others of the same collection, on the topic of the soul: its nature and its destiny after death.[18] While the first poem, *Psyche*, is a rewriting of Apuleius' *fabella*, the second one, *La civetta* (*The owl*), reworks the story of Socrates' death in the wake of Plato's *Phaedo*.

---

13 About victimization of women in decadent imagery, see the classic study by Praz 1948³, 97–172 and Dijkstra 1986, esp. 51–63 (the 'fetish of sleep'); on the 'sleeping beauty' in Burne-Jones' art, see Tatar 2014, 149–52.
14 Pieri 2009, 190 and n. 61.
15 D'Annunzio's Psyche, however, lapses into the opposite but complementary sterotype of the *femme fatale*, evoked by the 'fatal lamp' of the last verse.
16 Sozzi 2007, 181.
17 Sozzi 2007, 171–87.
18 The diptych belongs to the later phase of the collection (1903–1904), especially focused on the soul-theme: Bàrberi Squarotti 2009, 266.

Unlike D'Annunzio, Pascoli enters directly into dialogue with Apuleius' text.[19] However, like D'Annunzio, in his other works, he does not seem to care much for the Latin novel, either as a Latin scholar or as a poet.[20] Although the subject of Psyche played an important role in modern poetry,[21] the main reason for Pascoli's rewriting of Apuleius remains the possibility of an allegorical reading through Plato. The Platonic interpretation, consistent with the history of Apuleian reception, was also a well-established trend in *fin de siècle* culture. At the time of Pascoli—which is also the time of Erwin Rohde and his essay on the Greek conception of the Soul, *Psyche*[22]—Platonism is reinterpreted in the light of romantic spiritualism. The memory of Plato is then linked to the exaltation of the soul, which is immortal and independent from the body.

As for the poems on Psyche, the Platonic interpretation is explicitly provided by the the second poem of the pair, based, as already mentioned, on Socrates' death. An especially relevant hypotext is *Phaedo* 77e—a pervasive presence in Pascoli's corpus and Apuleius' own Platonism[23]—where Socrates reproaches his friends for their fear of death:

> You seem afraid, like children, that as the soul goes out from the body, the wind may literally blow it apart and disperse it, especially when someone happens not to die in calm weather but in a high wind.[24]

One of them, Cebes, replies:

> Try to reassure us, Socrates, as we were afraid ourselves, but maybe there's a child inside us, who has fears of that sort. Try to persuade him, then, to stop being afraid of death, as if it were a bogeyman.

---

19 Pascoli gives precise translations of some Apuleian expressions: for instance 'ignude voci' (l. 14) is a rendering of *nuda... corporis sui vox* (Apul. *Met.* 5.2.3), recognized by the commentators (e.g. Nava 2008, 255 *ad loc.*); other Apuleian syntagms concerning the movements of the ants assisting Psyche in her first task are translated in ll. 85–90 (Nava 2008, 260–1).
20 I was unable to find further references to Apuleius, except the ones mentioned below, n. 35.
21 Bàrberi Squarotti 2009: 267 and above, n. 3.
22 Pascoli probably knew Rohde's *Psyche* (Paratore 1965, 482 and Leonelli 1980, 211), even if the book is not found in his personal library.
23 Cf. Leonelli 1980, 221: not only did Pascoli recall this passage in his famous critical work, *Il fanciullino* (Garboli 2002, 935), but he also included a translation of it in his private papers (G. 76–6–1–12) and elsewhere in his writings (Valerio 1980, 62–3 n. 5). The same passage is also quoted in Rohde's *Psyche* (1970 [1894]: II.595, n. 2). For *Phaedo* in the 2nd century AD see Trapp 1990.
24 Transl. by Gallop 1993.

This passage is clearly echoed in lines 63 ff. of *La civetta*[25] ('in each one, in his heart,/was a child who was afraid of the dark'),[26] where Socrates' friends are waiting in fear for the fatal moment. The same passage is likely to provide a hypotext also for the frame narrative of the poem,[27] which opens with a group of *real* children playing just outside the jail of Socrates. For fun, they are keeping an owl tied to a thread. Soon, however, they have to interrupt their play, concerned for the fate of the prisoner ('an old kind Silenus', l. 150). As the philosopher dies from hemlock, the boys feel lost, when suddenly the owl frees herself and flies away: this final image clearly symbolizes the flight of the immortal soul, previously described by Pascoli's Socrates in his last words to his friends.[28]

The topic of death and destiny of the soul is also at the core of the second poem of the diptych, where Apuleius' tale is rewritten as a story of the soul: with a striking narrative ellipsis, the poem begins when Psyche, now abandoned by her Love (*Amore* in Pascoli), lives imprisoned in a house inhabited by mysterious voices. The alteration in the order of Apuleius' story is consistent with the character of Pascoli's Psyche: she does not embody the beautiful princess hated by the envious Venus, but the *Psyche misella*, the fragile and unhappy creature persecuted and humiliated by the goddess. Such psychological features help the identification of this character with the suffering and lonely soul, longing to be freed from the prison of the body.

In this respect, Plato's role as mediator is clear from the very beginning (ll. 1–9):

> O Psyche, tenue più del tenue fumo
> ch'esce alla casa, che se più non esce,
> la gente dice che la casa è vuota; ...
> sei prigioniera nella bella casa   6
> d'argilla, o Psyche, e vi sfaccendi dentro
> pur lieve sì che non se n'ode un suono;
> ma pur vi sei, nella ben fatta casa,
> ché se n'alza il celeste alito al cielo.

> O Psyche, more slight than the slight smoke
> that comes from the house: if it no longer
> comes out they say the house is empty; ...

---

[25] Cf. Leonelli 1980, 221; Belponer 2010, 260 n. 30; Garboli 2002, 1176; Nava 2008, 174; Bàrberi Squarotti 2009, 291.
[26] All the English translations of *Poemi conviviali* are from Lunardi-Nugent 1979.
[27] Interpreters generally mention Herodas, *Mimiambics* 3 and Theocritus, *Idylls* 16.
[28] See ll. 76–79 'And if the soul forever free departs/into the immortal night, there.../... will the soul then die?'; on the symbolic interpretation, see Nava 2008, 281, *ad loc*.

> you are a prisoner 6
> in your splendid house of clay, O Psyche,
> working there, so light not a sound is heard;
> but still you are there, in your well-made house,
> for, from there, your clear breath goes to the sky.

Here Psyche is described as a prisoner in *her* 'well-made' house (l. 9): several commentators on the poem have quickly recognised the Platonic metaphor of the body as the prison of the Soul.[29] It is not easy to find a correspondence for this house in the tale of Apuleius. The secret voices naturally recall the Palace of Love; still, in the first stanza, Psyche is herself a slave and, moreover, she is already separated from Love. Therefore, the mysterious house might also be the palace of Venus. This ambiguity is just the first example of a method applied throughout the poem: the symbolic meaning is put in the foreground, while the signifying element constantly remains undefined. So, in the next sequence, when Psyche, in order to regain Love, is forced to perform her tasks, the antagonist Venus and the many assistants that, according to the myth, help her, are replaced by mysterious voices that act out their conflict in Psyche's consciousness (ll. 50 – 58):[30]

> ... e le voci odi, che fanno
> all'improvviso a te cader dal ciglio
> la stilla che non ti volea cadere.
> Però che sono e sùbite e severe
> le più; ma più di tutte una che sempre
> contende e grida, ad ogni tuo sospiro 55
> verso l'alata libertà: 'non devi!'.
> Quella non t'ama, credi tu; ma un'altra
> è, sì, che t'ama, e favella a parte
> e ti consola, e teco piange e parla

> ... and you hear the voices
> which suddenly make you shed the tear
> that had tried not to fall from your eyelash.
> For most of the voices are unexpected
> and harsh; but one more than all, always
> scolds and cries each time that you sigh 55
> for winged freedom: 'You must not!'
> That one loves you not, you think; but there is
> another, yes, who loves you and speaks

---

29 Leonelli 1980: 211 mentions *Phaedo* 62b and 81; *Crat.* 399d-e, 400a-c.; *Gorg.* 493a.
30 On the psychological and symbolic interpretations of this conflict: Leonelli 1980, 211; Salibra 1999, 162 and Nava 2008, 258, in the wake of Froldi 1960, 162–163.

to you aside, consoles you, weeps with you,
speaks...

Such internalisation affects not only the characters, but also the plot: the period spent by Psyche with her mysterious husband and the fatal episode of the lamp are summarised in a brief flashback (ll. 32–41), where the past is filtered by the emotions of Psyche; the sort of emotions that Pascoli often expresses in his poetry: fear before the first experience of sex[31] and frustration over a lost happiness that is barely glimpsed and immediately vanishes (ll. 40–1):[32]

E lo sapesti solo allor che sparve,
l'Amore alato.

Only when it had fled did you find
winged Love.

Another noticeable consequence of this symbolic rewriting is the enhancement of Pan into Psyche's principal assistant who, at the beginning, comforts her with the memory of her past love and, in the end, saves the maiden, enclosing her in his embrace. He, along with Psyche and Love, is the only character who is not depersonalised and who maintains his (symbolic) name. A fleeting presence in Apuleius' text, Pan (of course meaning 'everything' in Greek) becomes pervasive in Pascoli, even replacing Love in the final rescue of the maiden.[33]

A third interesting consequence of Pascoli's symbolistic approach is the selective rewriting of Psyche's tasks, which decrease from the 'heroic' number of four[34] to three, the magic number of folklore. The reduction, which is not without consequences for the characterisation of Psyche as a passive and distressed creature, further emphasises the symbolic dimension of the poem. The task supressed is the second one, in which Psyche faces the ferocious sheep. Around 1895 the poet had thought to develop this episode in a Latin poem—entitled *Arundo viridis* —for the collection *Catullocalvos*, but the project was never rea-

---

31 Cf. Nava 2008, 257 and Bàrberi Squarotti 2009, 270.
32 Useful parallels in Garboli 2002, 1164; Nava 2008, 257; Bàrberi Squarotti 2009, 277.
33 In Decadent reception the psychagogic role of Cupid is often taken by other figures, such as Jesus and Satan: also Pan often occurs as a substitute for Cupid: see de Palacio 2000, 44–52; also below, pp. 180–1.
34 The interpreters of the tale explain this 'strange' number as a reference to the twelve labours of Hercules (12 is a multiple of 4), thus stressing the heroic identity of Psyche: see Harrison 1998, 61–62 and Zimmerman et al. 2004, 437.

lised.³⁵ In *Psyche* he concentrates, rather, on the first task—the sorting of the seeds—which lends itself to allegorical interpretation,³⁶ but also allows Pascoli to display his technical expertise in naming each type of seed. Consistent with the symbolic perspective is also the preservation of the last two tasks, in the course of which Psyche comes into contact with the Underworld; obviously the focus is on the topic of death, which pervades the whole poem (as well as Pascoli's poetry as a whole). An example of this topic is the recurrent metaphor of sleep (as death), already existing in Apuleius, but focused upon here.³⁷

The journey to the Underworld is arguably the centrepiece of the poem, the one in which Pascoli significantly deviates from the Apuleian hypotext. The failure of Psyche, who does not complete the journey and falls into the void ('nel queto vortice del nulla', l. 158) definitively confirms her passivity: finally overwhelmed by sleep-death, she is like D'Annunzio's sleeping beauty.

And, if the journey of Psyche is in all respects the journey of a soul, it is difficult to see in this lost and distressed figure³⁸ the immortal soul, capable of triumphing over death, that emerges from Platonism as interpreted along the lines of romantic spiritualism. It turns out that a Platonic reading, while very effective for the first part of the poem, is inconsistent with the Underworld section and the problematic end, where Psyche disappears within the embrace of Pan and is never seen again.

Still, some interpreters of Pascoli have tried to defend such a spiritualistic reading, typical of post-Romantic culture,³⁹ by comparing *Psyche* to Pascoli's essays on Dante, which undoubtedly offer interesting parallels to the Underworld section of the poem.⁴⁰ While Psyche's fall into the void is explained allegorically as a consequence of her fear (a lack of hope that prevents her from contemplation), the role of Pan is more difficult to explain, interpreted as an animal im-

---

35 '*Arundo viridis*. Apul. VI' numbers among the titles listed in G. 73–1–1–11 (Apostolico 2008, 183 and n. 176).
36 Sorting scattered seeds signifies to be discerning: cf. Salibra 1999, 163; Garboli 2002, 1164; Nava 2008, 259.
37 Cf. Apul. *Met*. 6.21.1 *infernus somnus ac vere Stygius... invadit eam*: cf. Bàrberi Squarotti 2009, 268–9.
38 Perugi 1980, 971 and Salibra 1999, 152 mention other female personifications of the soul in trouble in Pascoli's poetry; often recalled is Myrrine, in *L'etera* (*Poemi Conviviali*): cf. Salibra 1999, 175.
39 On the influence of this tradition (including neo-Orphism) on Pascoli, see Perugi 1996, 315, in the wake of Riffaterre 1970.
40 Perugi 1980, 971–81 and Salibra 1999, 147–78.

pulse coming from the unconscious to stop Psyche's journey.[41] Falling into Pan's arms, then, is essentially a diversion, which should be overcome and followed by the final ascent.[42] There is no ascent, however, in the final stanza, where Psyche disintegrates into the natural world (186–8):

> O Psyche! o Psyche! dove sei? Ma forse
> nelle cannucce. Ma chi sa? tra il gregge.
> O nel vento che passa o nella selva
> che cresce.
>
> O Psyche! o Psyche! where are you? Perhaps
> in the slender reeds. Who knows? 'Mid the flocks.
> Or in the passing wind, or in the woods
> that grow.

Inconsistent with the imagery of the soul's ascent, Pan is clearly imported from a large symbolic cluster typical of *fin de siècle* culture. In *Psyche*, Pan is a wild creature, symbolizing pre-civilised nature; he is eternal ('Pan l'etterno', l. 190), thus representing the *anima mundi*, an absolute in which Psyche gets lost, beyond the experiences of Love and Death. But Pan is also associated with music, the universal poetry, from which the individual soul of the poet (Psyche herself) draws its song.[43] All these symbols, which seem to reveal the influence of Schopenhauer and Nietzsche, perhaps through D'Annunzio,[44] certainly play a major role not only in *Psyche*, but in Pascoli's macrotext.

However, this final deviation from the Apuleian-Platonic hypotext can be better explained in the light of a peculiar conception of the soul that Pascoli himself was developing in the first years of the twentieth century.[45] This theory (named 'Psicogenesi' by the poet himself) was based on the evolutionary model outlined by the scientist Ernst Haeckel in his *Anthropogenie*, a text found in the personal library of Pascoli. The core of Haeckel's thought is epitomised by Pascoli in his private papers: 'Si rinnova in ogni uomo la storia dell'uma-

---

[41] Perugi 1980, 972 recalls Pascoli's interpretation of the lion that stands in Dante's way, hindering his journey (*Inf.* 1:45); according to Salibra 1999, 154–5, Pan is 'la Bestia che freme nelle profondità dell'inconscio'.

[42] This is the opinion of Perugi 1980, 972 (with references to Pascoli's essays on Dante).

[43] This does not imply that Psyche is merged with Syrinx or with other mythical figures: her identification with the soul is made, with all possible means, clear and unambiguous for the reader.

[44] Nava 2008, 255 *ad* l. 18 and Bàrberi Squarotti 2009, 267.

[45] See Valerio 1980, 11; Traina 1984, 10–11; Apostolico 2008, 10.

nità'.⁴⁶ Since, according to Haeckel, ontogenesis and phylogenesis overlap, every human being experiences, in the stages of his own life, the different stages of human evolution. By a regressive movement, the soul of the poet goes back in time and brings back to life the voices of the past.

Significant, in this regard, are some personal notes of Pascoli, dating to July 1904:

> Il poema della psyche umana. Io sento confuso in me il sentimento dell'evoluzione umana, da cellula a uomo—tutti i gradi di orrore e di bontà –,[sic] e da uomo primitivo a italiano del dì d'oggi (traverso la storia delle migrazioni e separazioni Ariane, alla vita celtica, romana, medioevale, ecc.), coi sogni dell'avvenire.⁴⁷

> The poem of the human psyche. I feel mixed inside me the sense of human evolution, from cell to man—all the degrees of horror and goodness –,[sic] and from primitive man to the Italian man of the present day (through the history of Arian migrations and divisions, up to Celtic, Roman, medieval life, etc.), with dreams of the future.

In connection with his project of a 'poem of the human psyche',⁴⁸ Pascoli describes a kind of metempsychosis—according to Alfonso Traina⁴⁹—that makes him able to re-live past lives. This peculiar 'sense of human evolution' also explains the need, deeply felt by him, to compose poetry in dead languages: by using Latin and Greek he is able to get in touch with the previous ages of the human soul.

But the same regressive movement allows the poet to return to the origins of mankind, reaching the very beginning of life. As highlighted by Aida Apostolico,⁵⁰ around 1905 Pascoli discovered the connection between his own soul theory and the concept of 'subliminal I' elaborated by the English classicist and psychologist Frederic Myers, according to whom, human consciousness (the conscious 'I') experiences a stream of ancestral memories and feelings. Taking some notes on Myers' essay, Pascoli even conceives the image of a 'Sister of Psyche', who is 'subliminal', lives beyond the threshold of consciousness, and sometimes emerges either temporarily or permanently.⁵¹ Hence arises the possibility of

---

46 'The history of humanity is relived in every man' (G. 76–6–1–11).
47 Cf. G. 72–4–1–22: the notes were posthumously published by Pascoli's sister in Pascoli 1924, 41.
48 A frame project (or a macrotext), including different poems, both in Italian and Latin, all related to the theory of 'Psicogenesi': cf. Citti 2014, 411–2.
49 Traina 2001², 11.
50 Apostolico 2008, 10–13.
51 G. 74–1–3–2, with Apostolico 2008, 13; Pascoli paraphrases Myers 1905, 22–3.

crossing the threshold and retrieving ancestral feelings, belonging to the simplest forms of life—to go back, as it were, 'from man to cell'. It is a regression experienced also by Psyche, who, in the last verses, is transformed into flocks, wind, and woods.[52]

The finale of *Psyche*, then, leaves Apuleius behind to incorporate Pascoli's 'poem of the human Psyche'.

3 Alberto Savinio

The third episode of reception belongs to a cultural atmosphere that is not much later in time, but totally different in spirit from the age of D'Annunzio and Pascoli: these poets (especially D'Annunzio)[53] are a target for the irony of Alberto Savinio (a pseudonym for Andrea De Chirico, 1891–1952), whose rewritings of *Cupid and Psyche* document the kind of reception, irreverent and caustic, that is typical of the twentieth-century avant-garde.

Savinio uses the myth for two long stories (or novellas), written almost twenty years apart: *Angelica o la notte di maggio* (*Angelica or the Night in May*, 1927) and *La nostra anima* (*Our Soul*, 1944); like Pascoli and unlike D'Annunzio, he establishes a direct relationship with Apuleius' *fabella*—which he admires[54]—but deconstructs it radically.

A good understanding of how Savinio treats myth is provided by Guido Guglielmi, according to whom, 'il mito può sopravvivere solo nel contesto della sua distruzione'.[55] Such a destruction begins with the setting of the myth, which in both of Savinio's stories is bleakly contemporary, and becomes more radical in the characterisation of Psyche, who, especially in *La nostra anima*, asserts a new identity that makes her different from the charming Psyche of Apuleius, and even more so from her pathetic *fin de siècle* incarnations.

The first text, *Angelica*, was written in 1925 and published in 1927[56] when Savinio, a painter as well as a writer and musician, came into contact with surrealist art, giving his own original interpretation. In 1926 Savinio had his first ex-

---

[52] A parallel metempsychosis ends *La civetta*, where the soul of Socrates transmigrates into the owl: cf. Bàrberi Squarotti 2009, 271, who, however, interprets such a transformation as an ascent to Hyperuranius (in the wake of Froldi 1960, 169–70).
[53] On Savinio's polemic against D'Annunzio in the 1920s, cf. Italia 2004, 209–210, 226.
[54] See the article *Metamorphoseon*, collected in Savinio 1993, 95–9. On this period, De Simone 2001, 214–5.
[55] Guglielmi 1986, 183: 'myth is able to survive only in the context of its own destruction'.
[56] Tinterri 1995, 936–7.

hibition, in Paris under the aegis of Jean Cocteau, whose place in the reception history of *Cupid and Psyche* is discussed in this volume by James.[57] *Angelica* can be defined as a surrealist novel, whose loose narrative structure is impacted by the search for new and disruptive forms of expression typical of the avant-garde.[58] Moreover, in *Angelica*, as in Cocteau's *Orphée*, mundane contemporary society is intermingled with mysterious presences from the world of myth.

The story looks like a parody of a *feuilletton* or hackneyed story from cheap fiction: the baron and financier Aaron Rothspeer suddenly falls in love with the poor and charming Angelica Mitzopulos, playing the role of Psyche in an ambiguous pantomime inspired by Apuleius' episode. The background is a trashy Greece (where Savinio had spent his childhood), marked by the contrast between the poor working classes, which includes the family of Angelica, and the unbridled luxury of the cosmopolitan *élite*, to which Rothspeer belongs. The setting moves constantly between run-down villas and luxury yachts.

Rothspeer—who embodies the cynical bourgeoisie despised by the avant-garde—recognizes in Angelica the beautiful Psyche of Apuleius. He immediately asks confirmation from his secretary, who is always immersed in reading Haeckel:

> Vero che dal tempo degl'Iddii replica più fedele della divina Psiche non era comparsa tra i mortali?[59]
>
> Isn't it true that, since the time of the gods, a more faithful copy of the divine Psyche had never appeared among mortals?

An analogy can be seen with the opening of the *fabella*, where Psyche, exalted for her 'divine' beauty, appears to mortals as a 'copy' of Venus.[60] Rothspeer, however, does not respect Psyche's superior nature: he overwhelms the girl by taking advantage of his social and economic superiority. The subsequent marriage, however, turns out to be a disaster, because Angelica, catatonic and perpetually absent, leaves her husband unsatisfied and sexually frustrated: in a sense, Angelica-Psyche returns to her status as sleeping beauty, although, unlike the 'lying Psyche' of D'Annunzio, she is not available to love.

---

57 Not coincidentally, perhaps, the fatal encounter between 'Psyche' and Rothspeer takes place in a cabaret called 'Orfeo' (the theatrical version of Cocteau's *Orphée* dates to 1926).
58 Guglielmi 1986, 185 speaks of 'istantanee che scorrono velocemente e in apparente disordine su uno schermo'; Savinio himself applied to his novel the adjective 'cinematografico' (Tinterri 1995, 934–5).
59 Savinio [1927] 1995, 358.
60 Apul. *Met.* 4.28–32, esp. 4.32.1 *mirantur... divinam speciem*, 'They admire her divine beauty'.

Finally, on a night in May, the baron discovers that his wife is cheating on him with a winged creature (Love). He shoots the 'angel', but this fatal act triggers a worldwide catastrophe (an outbreak of suicides and murders), which will end only when Psyche can once again meet Love. The situation is explained in a dialogue at the end of the novel between 'Io' (a projection of the author) and a secondary character:[61]

> *Io:* Diamo il tempo all'infelice Psiche di terminare il suo pellegrinaggio. E quando avrà ritrovato il suo sposo, che quello scemo di Rothspeer ha sbadatamente ferito in quella notte di maggio...
> *Berger:* Mais quoi! c'était elle, Psyche?
> *Io:* Questo non lascia dubbio. Allora tutto rientrerà nell'ordine nella tranquillità.
>
> *I:* Let's give the unhappy Psyche the time to end her pilgrimage. And when she has found her bridegroom, whom that idiot Rothspeer carelessly injured on that night in May...
> *Berger:* What?! That was Psyche?
> *I:* There is no doubt about it. Then everything will return to order again, to peace.

Angelica, ironically defined by Savinio himself as 'una leggera parafrasi della favola di Psiche',[62] swings between nostalgic evocation and ironic deconstruction of myth.[63] In this irreverent reading, Psyche becomes an allegory of the positive values exalted by the avant-garde:[64] as an embodiment of dream, myth and beauty, she escapes the economic logic of her rich husband and lives in a dimension that is apparently distant, but turns out to be essential for the survival of humanity. No wonder, then, that in the drawings created by Savinio for his French translation of the novel[65] (Figure 16), the figure of Angelica-Psyche has a 'metaphysical flavour'.[66]

Written 20 years after *Angelica*,[67] *La nostra anima* achieves a more radical destruction of myth. Even so, the relationship with Apuleius is even more explicit than in the previous rewriting: in this second novel the reader does not only

---

61 Savinio [1927] 1995, 437.
62 See the handwritten notes quoted in Tinterri 1995, 933–5.
63 Interesting considerations about the way Savinio reworks the Apuleian topics of curiosity and divine epiphany in: Zudini 2008, 146–150. Remarkable is also the ironic rewriting of some famous episodes of the *fabella*, such as the funeral wedding: in Savinio [1927] 1995, 384–7 the bridegroom faints and is taken for dead.
64 Cf. Cirillo 1997, 314–7.
65 In 1950 the novel was also translated into French, with the title *Psyché:* cf. Tinterri 1995, 937.
66 Cf. Zudini 2008, 151: 'une qualité meta-physique', with an implicit reference to the painting of Savinio's brother: Giorgio de Chirico; on this drawing, see also Fagiolo dell'Arco 1989, 59 and Vivarelli 1996, 362.
67 Cf. Tinterri-Italia 1999, 945–957.

Figure 16: Savinio, 'Angelica'; from: Alberto Savinio, *Hermaphrodito e altri romanzi, a cura di Alessandro Tinterri*. Introduzione di Alfredo Giuliani, Milano, Adelphi, 1995. Enhanced and reprinted under Fair Use Policy.

encounter Latin quotations,[68] as well as quite precise translations from the ancient tale,[69] but also hears from Psyche herself an ironic palinode of her famous story.

Similar to the *Metamorphoses*, *La nostra anima* has, in fact, a narrative frame: the primary narrator, Nivasio Dolcemare, one of the many alter egos of Savinio, says he has visited an uncanny museum of statues made of flesh, together with two friends: his lover, a romantic woman by the Shakespearean name of Perdita—an ironic borrowing from D'Annunzio[70]—and the enthusiastic doctor Sayas. Inside the museum, a veritable *locus horridus*, they see 'our soul', that is Psyche, who is in the hybrid form of a pelican-girl, as can be seen from the lithograph created by Savinio himself for the first edition of his novel (Figure 17). The iconographic motif of the bird-girl recurs in the art of Savinio (especially in the 1930s), in connection with the themes of family, infancy and myth (all of them interconnected): Savinio's human-animal hybrid figures are affectionate and self-mocking representations of his autobiographical mythology.[71]

Psyche, who lives surrounded by filth, like an animal in a zoo, is irritated by the attitude of her visitors, who seem to ignore her animality and, conditioned by an idealised memory of the myth, insist on being told the fascinating story of Psyche's encounter with Love. But when Psyche begins to tell *her* story, it immediately appears to be different from the charming tale of Apuleius, from which she quickly distances herself:

> Non è vero che fossimo figlie di un re e di una regina, come scrive il nostro biografo: *erant in quadam civitate rex et regina.*[72]
>
> It is not true that we were daughters of a king and a queen, as written by our biographer: *erant in quadam civitate rex et regina.*

In particular, the account of the discovery of Love by the light of the lamp completely disillusions the visitors, who are fascinated by the memory of the lovely *fabella*. First, the mysterious husband is seen in the light of a vulgar electrical switch, and not of the famous lamp, a detail that, according to Psyche, was arbitrarily inserted by Apuleius. She openly accuses the ancient novelist of being

---

[68] Savinio [1944] 1999, 525 (Apul. *Met.* 5.6.6); 528 (*Met.* 4.28.1); 546 (*Met.* 5.4.4); 550 (*Met.* 5.24.5).
[69] Savinio [1944] 1999, 546–7, from Apul. *Met.* 5.22.5–7 (the vision of Cupid): translations seem to be adapted from Bontempelli 1928, I, 247.
[70] See Italia 1997, 76–97.
[71] On the image of Psyche, see Vivarelli 1990, 316; Zudini 2008, 143; De Simone 2011, 215–6; about hybrid figures in Savinio's painting: Cammarella 1990, 75; Presilla 2011, 58; Cardano 2011, 59.
[72] Savinio [1944] 1999, 528.

Figure 17: Savinio, 'Psyche', lithograph created by Savinio for the novel 'Our soul'; from: Alberto Savinio, La nostra anima/Il signor Munster, Milano, Adelphi, 1981. Enhanced and reprinted under Fair Use Policy.

influenced by D'Annunzio's aestheticism. Next, the wonderful god described in the *Metamorphoses* turns out to be just a vulgar, monstrous phallus (represented by Savinio in a second lithograph). Again, Psyche does not hesitate to criticize Apuleius:

> Apuleio era uno sciocco che praticava un ottimismo di maniera, e credeva che per rendere le storie più gradite ai lettori, bisogna adornarle di lieto fine.[73]
>
> Apuleius was a fool, who practiced an affected optimism, and believed that, to make his stories most pleasant for his readers, it is appropriate to adorn them with a happy ending.

In fact, there is no happy ending for the Psyche of Savinio, who, stripped of her illusions of love, retains a perpetual distaste for her monstrous husband.

Moreover, direct references to the hypotext take the form of a corrosive commentary, constituting a total deconstruction of the myth. This new attitude comes from a new idea of the soul developed by Savinio during the 1940s, when he discovered Freud's theories and became a strong proponent and disseminator of Freudian psychoanalysis. In an article of this period (1948) Savinio proclaimed his conversion: 'allora usavo la parola 'anima', ora uso la parola 'psiche'.[74] While the Angelica-Psyche of the first novel was still the soul of the late-romantic theories—a spirit living apart, separated from the body—this second Psyche is precisely the psyche of psychoanalysts, inseparable from the body, and indeed strongly influenced by corporeality, even in its more violent and unpleasant manifestations.

Like Pascoli, then, Savinio, too, uses the myth of Psyche to express a strong sense of interiority. His bird-girl lives surrounded by the filth of her own body. She has tattooed on her skin inscrutable phrases representing the logic of the unconscious: she is, undoubtedly, an allegory of the Freudian psyche. Such disruptive innovation, however, upsets her visitors, still fond of the late-romantic soul.

4 Conclusion

To conclude, the *fin de siècle* reception of the *Cupid and Psyche* story in Italy is deeply influenced by the poetics of Aestheticism (D'Annunzio) and post-Romantic Spiritualism, which affect different areas of European culture, and mingles with Pascoli's Symbolism. A few decades later, Savinio's two rewritings (especially the second one) mark the end of this tradition. Savinio provides a caricature version of the myth, whose target is not Apuleius' *fabella*, but the way in which it had been treated by D'Annunzio's Aestheticism and by post-Romantic

---

73 Savinio [1944] 1999, 550.
74 'Then I used the word 'soul', now I use the word 'psyche''; cf. Savinio, [1943–1952] 2004, 733 (*Anima e psiche*).

Spiritualism; in other words, he satirises the glorious image of a soul that is immortal and separated from the body. By introducing a new conception of interiority (based on Freud's theories), Savinio causes the collapse of the post-Romantic interpretations of the myth, thus marking a turning point in the reception of the tale of *Cupid and Psyche*.

5 Bibliography

Andreoli A./Lorenzini N. (eds.) (1982), *Gabriele D'Annunzio. Versi d'amore e di gloria*, Milano.
Apostolico A. (2008), *'Uno strano lavorio di ricordi'. Autografi pascoliani*, Salerno.
Auraix Jonchière, P./Volpilhac-Auger, C. (eds.) (2000), *Isis, Narcisse, Psyché, entre Lumières et Romantisme. Mythe et écritures, écritures du mythe*, Clermont-Ferrand.
Bàrberi Squarotti, G. (2009), *Poesie di Giovanni Pascoli*, Torino, 4 vols.
Belponer, M. (2010), *Giovanni Pascoli, Poemi conviviali*, Milano.
Bontempelli, M. (1928), *Apuleio, Le trasformazioni*, Milano.
Cammarella, L. (1990), 'Savinio, l' 'eterno femminino' e la donna come idea', in: Savinio, 75–87.
Savinio, A. (1990), *Savinio, gli anni di Parigi: dipinti 1927–1932*, Milano.
Cardano, N. (2011), 'Miti dipinti', in: Trione, 59.
Cirillo, S. (1997), *Alberto Savinio. Le molte facce di un artista di genio*, Milano.
Citti, F. (2014), 'Un frammento "primitivo" delle "Eee" pascoliane e il poemetto "Leucothoe"', *Lexis* 32, 411–421.
De Maria, U. (1899), *La favola di Amore e Psiche nella letteratura e nell'arte italiana. Con appendice di cose inedite*, Bologna.
de Palacio, J. (1999), *Les métamorphoses de Psyché. Essai sur la décadence d'un mythe*, Paris.
De Simone, A.L. (2001), 'Cronologia critica di Alberto Savinio', in: Trione 2001, 211–7.
Dijkstra, B. (1986), *Idols of Perversity. Fantasies of Feminine Evil in Fin-de-siècle Culture*, Oxford.
Fagiolo dell'Arco, M. (1989), *Alberto Savinio*, Milano.
Froldi, R. (1960), *I poemi conviviali di Giovanni Pascoli*, Pisa.
Gallop, D. (1993), *Plato, Phaedo, Translated with an Introduction and Notes*, Oxford.
Garboli, C. (2002), *Giovanni Pascoli. Poesie e prose scelte, introd. e comm.*, Milano, 2 vols.
Gere, J. (1994), *Pre-Raphaelite Drawings at the British Museum*, London.
Graverini, L. (2007), *Le Metamorfosi di Apuleio. Letteratura e identità*, Pisa.
Gugliemi, G. (1986), *La prosa italiana del Novecento. Umorismo, metafisica, grottesco*, Torino.
Grigorian, N./Baldwin, T./Rigaud Drauton, M. (eds.) (2012), *Text and Image in Modern European Culture*, West Lafayette, Indiana.
Harrison, S.J. (1998), 'Some Epic Structures in *Cupid and Psyche*', in: Zimmerman et al. 1998, 51–68.
Haight, E. (1927), *Apuleius and his Influence*, New York.
Hummel, P. (2008), *D'Éros a Psyché. Tradition antique et moderne d'une mythe*, Paris.
Italia, P. (2004), *Il pellegrino appassionato. Savinio scrittore 1915–1925*, Palermo.
Leonelli, G. (1980), *Pascoli. Poemi conviviali*, Milano.

Lunardi, E./Nugent, R. (1979), *Giovanni Pascoli. Convivial poems. Part 1, Text and Translation*, Painesville, Ohio.
Marabini Moevs, M.T. (1976), *Gabriele D'Annunzio e le estetiche della fine del secolo*, L'Aquila.
Morris, W. (1868–70), *The Earthly Paradise*, Boston, 2 vols.
Myers, F. (1905), *La personnalité humaine, sa survivance, ses manifestations supranormales*, Paris (London 1903).
Nava, G. (2008), *Giovanni Pascoli. Poemi conviviali*, Torino.
Panayotakis, C./Panayotakis, S. (2015), 'The Human Characters in the Tale of Cupid and Psyche (*Metamorphoses* 4.28–6.24)', in: Harrison, 125–46.
Harrison, S.J. (ed.) (2015), *Characterisation in Apuleius' Metamorphoses*, Newcastle upon Tyne.
Paratore E. (1965), *Antico e nuovo*, Caltanissetta-Roma.
Pascoli, G. (1924), *Nell'anno mille. Sue notizie e schemi di altri drammi*, Bologna.
Perugi, M. (1996), 'Dantismo pascoliano e orfismo europeo', in: De Robertis/Gavazzeni, 315–27.
De Robertis, D./Gavazzeni, F. (eds.) (1996), *Operosa parva. Per Gianni Antonini*, Verona.
Pieri, G. (2009), 'The Effect of the Pre-Raphaelites on the Cultural Consciousness of D'Annunzio', in: Langford, 175–92.
Langford, R. (ed.) (2009), *Textual Intersections. Literature, History and Arts in Nineteenth-Century Europe*, Amsterdam-New York.
Pieri, G. (2009), 'D'Annunzio e Edward Burne-Jones. Il mito di Psiche tra preraffaelismo e decadenza', *Italianistica* 38, 21–9.
Pieri, G./Everson J. (2012), 'The Myth of Psyche in the Work of D'Annunzio and Burne-Jones', in: Grigorian/Baldwin/Rigaud Drauton, 15–31.
Praz, M. (1948), *La carne, la morte, il diavolo nella letteratura romantica*, Firenze.
Presilla, N. (2011), 'Miti dipinti', in: Trione, 58.
Riffaterre, H. B. (1970), *L'orphisme dans la poésie romantique, thèmes et style surnaturalistes*, Paris.
Rohde, E. (1970), *Psiche. Culto delle anime e fede nell'immortalità presso i Greci*, Bari, 2 vols. (*Psyche. Seelenkult und Unsterblichkeit der Griechen*, Freiburg in Breisgau, 1890–1894).
Russell, D. A. (ed.) (1990), *Antonine Literature*, Oxford.
Salibra, E. (1999), *Pascoli e Psyche*, Roma.
Savinio, A. (1993), *Torre di guardia. A cura di L. Sciascia, con un saggio di S. Battaglia*, Palermo.
Savinio, A. (1927), 'Angelica o la notte di maggio', in: Tinterri 1995, 353–437.
Savinio, A. (1944), 'La nostra anima', in: Tinterri/Italia 1999, 503–51.
Savinio, A. (2004), *Scritti dispersi (1943–1952)*. A cura di P. Italia, con un saggio di Alessandro Tinterri, Milano.
Sozzi, L. (2000), '*Amour et Psyché* entre romantiques et décadents', in: Auraix-Jonchière/Volpilhac-Auger, 377–391.
Sozzi, L. (2007), *Amore e Psiche. Un mito dall'allegoria alla parodia*, Bologna.
Tatar, M. (2014), 'Show and Tell. Sleeping Beauty as Verbal Icon and Seductive Story', *Marvels & Tales* 28, 142–58.
Tinterri, A. (ed.) (1995), *Alberto Savinio. Hermaphrodito e altri romanzi*, Milano.

Tinterri, A./Italia, P. (eds). (1999), *Alberto Savinio. Casa 'la Vita' e altri racconti*, Milano.
Trapp, M. (1990), 'Plato's *Phaedrus* in second-century Greek literature', in: Russell, 141–73.
Valerio, N. (1980), *Letteratura e scienza nell'età del positivismo. Pascoli-Capuana*, Bari.
Traina, A. (2001), *Giovanni Pascoli. Poemi Cristiani*, Milano.
Trione, V. (ed.) (2011), *Alberto Savinio. La Commedia dell'Arte*, Milano.
Vivarelli, P. (1990), 'Catalogo delle opere', in Savinio, *gli anni di Parigi: dipinti 1927–1932*, Milano 1990, 127–337.
Vivarelli, P. (1996), *Alberto Savinio. Catalogo generale*, Milano.
Zimmerman, M. et al., ed. (1998), *Aspects of Apuleius' Golden Ass. Vol. 2. Cupid and Psyche*, Groningen.
Zimmerman, M./Panayotakis, S./Hunink, V.C. et al. (eds.) (2004), *Apuleius Madaurensis, Metamorphoses, Books IV 28–35, V-VI 1–24. The Tale of Cupid and Psyche, Texte, Introduction et Commentary*, Groningen.
Zudini, C. (2008), 'Psiche et Amore dans l'oeuvre littéraire et figurative d'Alberto Savinio', *Travaux et Documents* 41, 130–51.

† Christoph Leidl
# Between Symbolism and Popular Culture. *Cupid and Psyche* in *Fin de siècle* Book Illustration

1 Introduction

Producing luxury editions of books was—given the improved methods for reproduction of images in print through the development of modern printing techniques like lithography (1798), steel engraving (1820), collotype (1856/1870), photogravure (1878)—not something new in the last third of the nineteenth century. The intended class of customers were the growing middle class, which combined aspirations towards higher education (and a material proof of being part of the educated class) with the appropriate funds. The number of books increased and illustrated magazines appeared on the market featuring engraved images, and offering both entertainment (serialized novels) and information of all sorts: in Germany, since 1853 *Die Gartenlaube, Illustrierte Familienzeitschrift* (The Garden Arbour, Illustrated Family Journal) was pioneering. In this context, the graphic arts served very practical purposes (mainly reproducing older works of art), where 'realistic' detail was more in demand than artistic innovation. On the other hand, new editions of 'classical' literary works (in Germany, Goethe and the Romantics) as well as modern texts were now furnished with artistic illustration of a higher quality in order to compete with the increasingly visual aspect of literary consumption. And one step further still, demands for the artistic shaping of the book—as a work of art and beauty, which would stand in contrast to the industrialized environment—were formulated, as for example in England by the proponents of the Arts and Crafts movement such as William Morris and his friends (as in the 1891 foundation of Morris's Kelmscott Press). This movement reverberated also on the continent, and in one way or another, the illustrated texts treated here may be compared to Morris's ideals, even though he and Edward Burne-Jones never managed to complete the illustrated edition of *The Earthly Paradise* which would have contained an elaborate series of woodcut illustrations of Morris' retelling of Apuleius' story of *Cupid and Psyche*.[1] This story

---

[1] An attempt to present the book as it had been designed is Morris, ed. Dufty 1974, cf. also Uerscheln 1998, 19–26. 37–8. For the influence of Burne-Jones on the Italian reception of Apuleius see Pasetti in this volume.

is a good test case for gauging the possibilities of keeping a text alive through adaptation and illustration, in close connection with both the development of the material culture of book-illustration (*Buchkunst*, book-art, became a very contested term towards the end of the nineteenth century) on the one hand and the interplay of the old and frequently reinterpreted story with modern sensibilities on the other.

Max Klinger's illustrated edition of Reinhold Jachmann's translation (1880) will take centre stage in this investigation; two other books, Robert Hamerling's retelling of the story with Paul Thumann's illustrations (1882) and Walter Tiemann's designs for the German translation of Eduard Norden (1902),[2] will serve to throw the tendencies of late nineteenth-century book illustration into relief. By way of introduction, a first impression of the overall character of the books and illustrators may be gained by a look at the covers. The gilt-edged luxury edition of Hamerling's 'poem in six cantos' *Amor und Psyche* ran to at least nine reprints (originally published in quarto, but later also in smaller formats, and in editions without illustrations) and had a red leather cover lavishly embossed in classicizing style with gold ornaments (palmettes and a double frame with meander and palmette motifs) and matching end-papers (gold meander and vegetative ornaments in brown, beige, red and turquoise), designed by G. Weidenbach and produced by renowned printing-houses in Munich, Vienna and Leipzig.

By contrast, the *Jugendstil* (Art Nouveau) cover of Norden/Tiemann is much more restricted in its artistic elements. It has a tripod drawn in gold on the left side (an allusion to Apollo's oracle) with fumes rising from it and forming a typical floral *Jugendstil* decoration around the left and top border of the brown cover. In general, all decorations in this book show extreme care for every detail (typical of the *Buchkunst*-movement of the early 20th century)[3] executed by the great typographer and illustrator Walter Tiemann.[4]

Finally, Klinger's *Amor und Psyche*, which can be found in a white (as in Heidelberg University Library) or dark blue cover (the book was produced to order by the publisher—which incidentally makes it difficult to assess the number of copies printed—so it seems that customers could chose some details of the decoration). This shows within a classicizing meander frame not unlike the Norden/Thiemann volume a lavish display of a mixture (characteristic of the period of

---

[2] Bibliographical details for the three books in the bibliography below.
[3] In the beautifully reprinted edition of 2016 with an afterword by Stephen Harrison the cover is different.
[4] Tiemann himself stresses the importance of Ruskin and Morris as forerunners for the development in Germany, Tiemann 1951, 184–5.

late historicism and early *Jugendstil*) of vegetative forms (a large palm tree with cyprus grass over the full height of the quarto page, crossed only by the text of the title in the upper third of the page), classical architectural forms (pillars with tendrils and candelabra), two Egyptian sphinxes on pedestals to the sides of the tree and Renaissance grotesque ornaments in the frames. All this is combined by the 23-year-old artist to produce the most elaborate artist's book of the time (and the first book to be designed in all artistic details—except the letter types—by one artist, at least in Germany).

2 Robert Hamerling—Paul Thumann

Robert Hamerling's *Amor und Psyche* is a literary adaptation. The classically educated Austrian poet, now almost completely vanished from literary consciousness, enjoyed enormous success in the middle and second half of the 19th century (in the Austrian city of Graz there is a monument to him) with his lyric poetry, historical verse epics and novels, where he celebrated life and beauty in contrast to a world dominated by technology, but was only able to express his ideas in a derivative, stilted language.[5] The illustrator's Paul Thumann's historic standing is much better than the author's; as an academic painter and a professor at art academies in Leipzig and Berlin (he also taught Max Klinger), he gained fame as one of the leading illustrators in mid-nineteenth century Germany for works by Goethe, Adelbert von Chamisso, Heinrich Heine or Alfred Tennyson (*Enoch Arden*) and as contributor to the *Gartenlaube*. He had travelled throughout Europe, including England; his wife was an English noblewoman, he was the father-in-law of Algernon Swinburne's brother, and knew painters like Frederic Leighton (who only became a Lord in the last weeks of his life) and Lawrence Alma-Tadema, whom Klinger, too, may have met in Berlin in 1878.[6]

Thumann's illustrations, executed with great skill and in perfectly balanced forms, are very much in harmony with the classicizing style of Hamerling's version of the story in six cantos (*Gesänge*).[7] He follows Apuleius' text (which Hamerling would have known quite well), but gives it a very 'classicising', idealized atmosphere. The tone is set by a decisive change to the motivation of the plot,

---

[5] Cf. Rieder 1966.
[6] Cf. Wolff-Beckh 1904; Vollmer, Thieme, Becker 1939, 113. A later Apuleius-inspired painting by Thumann, "Psyche at Nature's Mirror", 1893, became the logo for White Rock Mineral Water (still in use today) and is for example referred to by Paul Auster in his novel "4 3 2 1" (2017, beginning of ch. 2.1.) as an early inspiration for sexual fantasies of the novel's adolescent protagonist.
[7] Klimm 1974, 53–6 is rather inaccurate on Hamerling's reshaping of the story.

which gives Psyche's experiences a new meaning: it is Psyche's fear of being married, her obsessive chastity, which drives away numerous suitors and results in her punishment brought about through the oracle. Hamerling dwells particularly on descriptive passages (the idyllic life of Psyche on Cupid's island occupies a whole canto) which fitted his poetic persona better than dramatic narrative; he picks up vignettes from Apuleius and expands them rhetorically, almost following the 'theme and variation' principle well known to classical philologists from their reading of epic (earlier nineteenth or eighteenth century authors like Christoph Martin Wieland may also have played a role). So the poem begins in spring with Venus on Cyprus (symbolized with a decorated initial). But Hamerling also introduces new elements: one is the motif of the wings of Psyche, which are completely absent in Apuleius (though familiar from the iconographical tradition since antiquity[8]): as the new Venus, when she shows herself, although unwillingly, to the public (the full-page illustration is a good example of the smooth and elegant classical style of Thumann)—she is wingless (figure 18). Her wings start growing as she lives on Cupid's island (also unApuleian), as she discovers with great astonishment in the mirror of the water (illustrated in smaller format in the text), they are singed (without her noticing!) when she approaches Cupid with the lamp (but are not recognizable in the illustration which follows the classical tradition of this emblematic scene); finally she regains them when she is introduced into Olympus (in the final tableau she flies at Cupid's side).

All of this is a clear indication of the intended interpretation of the story as Psyche's way to the acceptance of her role as wife through perfect unity with her husband: there is much talk of love, kisses, embraces, but as Psyche is—as every reader must have noticed by now—pure innocence embodied, everything is very chaste and pure (even when she is in fear, text and illustration stress her decency): her pregnancy is suppressed (textually and visually), as is her second attempt at suicide, although at least in the descent to Hades there is some mild horror. Although it is not told as a full-fledged allegory, the message is a strongly idealised version of the role of sexual experience for a pubescent young girl, following what in Germany, too, has been tagged as 'Victorian morality'. In the illustrations this is well brought out in Venus' reproachful attitude matching the submissively crouching Psyche's repentance; here Thumann—unlike most other illustrators—takes great care to stress the physical resemblance of Venus and Psyche. Not that sexuality is completely under control, though; from time to

---

8 He may be inspired by wall-paintings designed by Moritz von Schwind in 1838/40, who (re-) introduces Psyche's ancient iconography with wings for the scene of her reception on Olympus, Holm 2006, 116–8 with note 41.

Figure 18: Paul Thumann, 'Psyche displays herself to the public'. Source: Robert Hamerling, Thumann, Paul 1882] Robert Hamerling, *Amor und Psyche. Eine Dichtung in sechs Gesängen. Illustriert von Paul Thumann*, Leipzig. Copyright: Christoph Leidl

time the illustrations put the viewer in the position of the voyeur, we get a peep at Psyche in all her lonely activities on the island, and she always tries to hide what has to be hidden, although she is alone. Particularly striking is her meeting with Pan, where she anxiously holds up her clothes to her breast and a lecherous note can be detected in Pan's otherwise friendly and joyful gaze. Even innocent narrative details reveal hidden mental pressures, as when a butterfly finds its way into the now lonely Cupid's room and crawls around his weapons, and Cupid feels an urge to perhaps crush the butterfly (he does not follow that urge; the illustration shows him watching the butterfly and pondering). So just as visually the wings of creatures like eagles or Cupid in Thumann's illustrations are never outside the picture frame,[9] so ideally all is under control. The final presentation of the couple as kissing and embracing (the last illustration) sums it up very well: we are in the classic academic tradition, which draws on ancient images of Cupid and Psyche kissing, in order to celebrate adolescent innocence and an idealistic concept of transcendent love. We may contrast this especially with the more eroticised eighteenth century portraits discussed by Simard in this volume with their focus on Psyche's humanity and fleshiness.

3 Klinger's concept of *Griffelkunst*, antiquity and the modern[10] artist

Now let us turn from teacher to pupil. Only two years before Thumann's 1882 illustrations, Max Klinger had designed for the publisher Stroefer one of the first *livres de peintre*, his *Amor und Psyche*. Klinger's concept of art and the artist was all-encompassing, aiming at a *Gesamtkunstwerk* (total work of art) in the visual arts to emulate Richard Wagner's achievement in the theatrical arts. Klinger's relationship with music was vital to his view of art; he frequently uses titles for types of pieces of music for his works, like *Intermezzo*, gives his cycles opus-numbers (the separately published set of his *Amor und Psyche* illustrations was Opus V, and he dedicated it to Johannes Brahms[11]), and later produced the cycle *Brahmsphantasie* as well as the famous designs for monuments for

---

9 Cf. Gross 1996, 70 f.
10 Brandes 1904, 71 finds Klinger's 'nervosity', the sign of the modern, late 19th century artist, exemplified in his treatment of Cupid.
11 On the separately published set (15 full-page plates, 8 plates combining the vignettes) cf. Singer 1909, 1978, 28.

Beethoven and Richard Wagner.[12] He wanted to invest the medium of graphic arts as opposed to painting with autonomous status (he called it *Griffelkunst*— art of the stylus/pencil), which stressed the subjectivity of the artist: the *Griffelkunst* presents the artist's world, his views, his impressions, his personal comments on the world, and nothing else.[13] So he can freely use but also change or transform what tradition offers him. He let his truly Wagnerian ego loose in a series of etchings entitled *Savings of Ovidian Victims* (retelling and changing stories from the *Metamorphoses* like Pyramus and Thisbe, Narcissus and Echo, Apollo and Daphne):[14] in the last picture, 'Satyre', he confronts in person Ovid the poet with his laurel wreath staging a duel in an open field where Klinger is armed with his giant spear-like engraving stylus and Ovid with his calamus or reed-pen (in the background an open grave and Charon await the loser).[15]

4 The book—form of presentation

Accordingly, it is not surprising to find Klinger's self-portrait as the right male caryatid on the frame of 'Psyche's wanderings'. This plate also introduces us to the role landscapes play in Klinger's imagination: here it is (typical for an inhabitant of the regions north of the Alps, and generations of Northern European artists before him) a typically Italian (not Greek) feeling that pervades most landscapes we see (including volcanoes etc.). But landscapes also echo the mental states of the figures depicted, as we will see. This illustration (figure 19) shows, too, the principle according to which all illustrations, both the 15 plates and the pages with text and the 31 vignettes, are designed: they have a central picture (and text) and a frame with individual design (consisting of architectural elements, vegetative and emblematic motifs and additional figurative vignettes (we shall come back to the relationship of these constituents). The frames for the text were woodcuts made from designs by Klinger, some with varying, though not arbitrarily chosen motifs, either connected with the sea in the form of fishes and sea monsters (often when Venus comes into play, or inner states of mind are depicted as in Apuleius), or with the world of ancient ritual and

---

12 Gleisberg 1988, 124 compares Klinger's relationship to Apuleius' text to that of a composer to his 'libretto'.
13 Cf. Klinger 1985, 30–5.
14 First published in 1879 as 'Sauvetages De Sacrifices d'Ovide, Dédiés A La Mémoire De Robert Schumann', Singer 1909, 1978, 11–9.
15 Gleisberg 1992, 17 sees in this confrontation spanning the millenia (like in science fiction) the same intellectual stance as in Klinger's later 'Christ in Olympus' cf. below.

Figure 19: Max Klinger, 'Psyche's wanderings'. Source: Klinger, Max 1880, 1988, *Amor und Psyche. Ein Märchen des Apuleius. Aus dem Lateinischen von Reinhold Jachmann*. Illustrirt in 46 Original-Radirungen und ornamentirt von Max Klinger. München 1880. Copyright: Christoph Leidl

(also non-Greek or Roman) gods (lions, bucrania, theatrical masks; a Dionysiac context), interspersed with exotic plants and butterflies (playing on Psyche's name), with inset vignettes in the top and bottom fields created through architecture. The combination of these elements, most of which were repeated several times, results in an impression of overwhelming variety for the reader as almost no frame is identical with another—though some are, as for example three frames show, all concerned with Venus: Venus in the sea and the scenes where when she is informed by the *gavia* (gull) and reproaches Cupid (notable here is the repetition of the seated Indian Goddess between sphinxes and worshippers in the bottom field). Thus, Venus' out-of-work priestesses sit above an image of Venus with her mirror, below ornaments formed by Cupid's bow and quiver—decorated with Venus' dove between plants with butterflies.

5 Cupid

Although the work was commissioned and remained the only text for which Klinger designed illustrations (it took him seven months of work day and night while living in Munich in spring and summer 1880, and he later claimed only to have done it for the money), the themes (love, death, dreams and imaginations, confrontation of ancient models and the modern world) and the characters interested Klinger all his life, especially Amor/Cupid, whom he had imagined in 1879 in a drawing as practising his bowmanship on the shooting range on naked girls tied to poles. It is not necessary to point out the underlying sexual fantasies here—but it shows Klinger as indeed the sensitive artist expressing what he feels but also senses in his environment. No wonder, again, that a much younger, childlike Cupid is shown getting his shooting lessons (at a different target, a shield held up in the bottom right-hand corner) from Chiron and satyrs as the first plate in *Amor und Psyche*—an episode wholly absent from Apuleius.[16] Let us follow Cupid growing up in his images: soon, when Venus first shows Psyche to him from the roof of a temple, he is not a child or a boy, but a young man, whose power is not only demonstrated by his muscular body, but also by his wings, which hardly fit into the frame of the picture (unlike Thumann's wings, as one might remember), and which in this picture fill a quarter of the frame, as his standing mother points out Psyche to her seated son (a motive famous from Raphael's paintings in the Villa Farnesina in Rome). Cavicchioli has

---

[16] For the identification of the scenes in plates or vignettes cf. the description in the bibliography.

aptly pointed out how the gesture is worthy of the great era of monumental silent movies,[17] but one should also note the contrasting postures of Venus, the middle-aged woman, her face in shadow, her back slightly arched, pointing in disgust to the earthly creatures, and of Cupid, leaning forward and intently gazing; their different attitudes to Psyche are immediately evident (not so in Apuleius' text) and Venus becomes a symbol of femininity. Also not expressly in Apuleius, but suggested to the careful reader, is Cupid's interference with the oracle; Klinger shows him actually fawning to Apollo in one of the vignettes. In a great night scene, he swoops down to a terrace of the palace, his elegant wings shine in the moonlight when he visits Psyche, his quiver dangles between his legs (a subtle hint at what he is going to do); the nocturnal landscape and the (only seemingly naturalistic, in fact very symbolically loaded) frame of this plate with an arabesque below, the kissing putti with roses on palms in the middle and the stars above all evoke the 'night of love' as a state of nature and a narrative element.

So far we have Cupid in his role familiar from Apuleius, but if we look at some of the pictures (vignettes) in the top part of the frames, another story begins to form in the viewer's mind. At irregular intervals, one very early, but most of them in the last third of the book, we see Cupid engaged in a number of activities (cf. figure 20). First, little Cupid is playing with a young lion, flanked by flamingoes, a peaceful sea setting (A); then he and a winged maiden with torches —this can only be Psyche—are driving away a group of horses (B); third, the two of them hunt a wild boar (C); fourth, Cupid alone pursues a stag (D); fifth, Cupid and Psyche sit on a bull swimming in the sea, with Neptune and Amphitrite watching (E); sixth, Cupid steals a girdle from Amazons (one of them is wounded) (F); seventh, Cupid and Psyche shoot birds (G). By now it should be clear, we are dealing with the Nemean lion, the horses of Diomedes, the Erymanthian boar, the Cerynthian hind, the Cretan bull, the girdle of Hippolyta and the Stymphalian birds. There follow the cleaning of Augeas' stables (H), the Lenaean Hydra (I) and Cerberus (J). The vignettes represent Labours of Hercules, performed by Cupid, sometimes with Psyche's help. The last two vignettes are non-canonical tasks of Hercules, but very evocative in connection with the story at hand: we find Cupid wrestling with Death to save Alcestis from the underworld (as he will save Psyche) (K) and Cupid and Psyche celebrating with a deadly wounded warrior to the right (most probably Laomedon, killed by Heracles at the first sack of Troy (L).[18] Finally there is a vignette representing the

---

17 Cavicchioli 2002, 244.
18 The warrior is strongly reminiscent of the fallen warrior in the east pediment of the temple of Aphaia in Aigina, exhibited in the Glyptothek in Munich (where Klinger worked at the illustrations) and usually identified with Laomedon.

Figure 20: Max Klinger, 'composite image of Cupid as Hercules'. Source: Klinger, Max 1880, 1988, *Amor und Psyche. Ein Märchen des Apuleius. Aus dem Lateinischen von Reinhold Jachmann*. Illustrirt in 46 Original-Radirungen und ornamentirt von Max Klinger. München 1880. Copyright: Christoph Leidl

liberation of Prometheus and Psyche(?) providing water for the eagle of Zeus (who had helped Psyche), thus making Psyche do Ganymede's job. This is in

Figure 20: Max Klinger, 'composite image of Cupid as Hercules'. Source: Klinger, Max 1880, 1988, *Amor und Psyche. Ein Märchen des Apuleius. Aus dem Lateinischen von Reinhold Jachmann*. Illustrirt in 46 Original-Radirungen und ornamentirt von Max Klinger. München 1880. Copyright: Christoph Leidl

fact on the last page of the book (figure 21) with the great finale of the birth of Voluptas.

Now this is not all without a basis in Apuleius, whose presentation of the labours of Psyche must have reminded every reader since antiquity of Hercules' deeds (only they were only four),[19] while Ganymede had been mentioned by

---

[19] Cf. on Hercules in Apuleius Harrison 2013. For Psyche as a female pendant to Hercules in 19th century reception cf. Holm 2006, e.g. 9. 233.

Figure 20: Max Klinger, 'composite image of Cupid as Hercules'. Source: Klinger, Max 1880, 1988, *Amor und Psyche. Ein Märchen des Apuleius. Aus dem Lateinischen von Reinhold Jachmann*. Illustrirt in 46 Original-Radirungen und ornamentirt von Max Klinger. München 1880. Copyright: Christoph Leidl

Apuleius as serving Jupiter at the wedding feast. But the way Klinger follows this motif, twists it (replacing Hercules with Cupid or Cupid/Psyche) and inserts it as a sort of commentary in the framing of the main story, has been convincingly described as mythological *bricolage* or improvisation from multiple sources (to borrow a term from structuralist theory).[20] If this is connected with the first plate (the young Cupid's education) we get a parallel story to that of Psyche: it is Cupid's coming of age, too, which runs parallel to Psyche's development. On the other hand, it may point to possible future achievements of Cupid and Psyche once they are united. The frames fulfil a double function as *parergon* or parallel product (this term is taken over from Jacques Derrida[21]) to the main text and illustration: they can and cannot be removed in so far as they invite the viewer/

---

20 Cf. Drude 2005.
21 See Derrida and Owens 1979.

Figure 21: Max Klinger, 'birth of Voluptas'. Source: Klinger, Max 1880, 1988, *Amor und Psyche. Ein Märchen des Apuleius. Aus dem Lateinischen von Reinhold Jachmann.* Illustrirt in 46 Original-Radirungen und ornamentirt von Max Klinger. München 1880. Copyright: Christoph Leidl

reader constantly to switch attention from centre to periphery and backwards, sometimes reinforcing the content of the narrative with the appropriate symbols, sometimes playing with illusion and ironically commenting on it.

This ironical illusionism, Klinger's playing with the viewer's expectations and his undermining attempts to construct an illusionistic unity from the image, is also evident in the use of architecture in illustration. For example, in the plate where Psyche is talking to her sisters on a terrace belonging to the palace, the observer first thinks he is watching from a different room in the palace, until he notices that the last Ionic column in a group is not really where it should be, and another group of Corinthian columns suggests an altogether different ground level of the building so that the observer is left suspended in mid-air or rather nowhere. Or, the plate with the very spectacular scene of Psyche fetching the water of Styx is designed as an image set into a huge gap in a Pompeian-style wall, letting us see the vast rocky landscape where the eagle gets the Styx's water for a tiny figure of Psyche; but the observer again starts to doubt whether this is really a wall with an opening or just a wall with a painting of the scene. No wonder Klinger was much admired by surrealists like Dali and Giorgio de Chirico (who hailed Klinger in his obituary as the modern artist *par excellence*,[22] and whose brother Alberto Savinio was fascinated by *Cupid and Psyche* throughout his life, as Pasetti in this volume shows).

6 Psyche

But what about Psyche? Certainly, she is depicted in the almost canonical image of her moment of revelation (figure 22) of the luminous body of Cupid framed by roses, the eternal symbol of love (even here it is not so clear whether we see a real bush—no roots—or an ornament), but at the bottom of the frame an androgynous face emerges from between the roses, lit by a tripod, and pulls the roses aside with the hands seen at the bottom corners. Faces like this have always been read as symbols of dreams and the unconscious: what is going on for Psyche—does she have a vision, or does she recognize the beastly creature before her? This scene is *de rigueur* for illustrators, but Klinger gives Psyche also some of the most unconventional and unclassical of his imaginative designs. Let us look back to earlier moments of the story: Psyche on the cliff (figure 23) is not a pure and innocent girl, there is no sentimentality, but we witness a young woman who does not know what to expect (though she is not trembling

---

[22] 'Klinger è stato l'artista moderno per eccellenza', De Chirico 2008b, 333.

Figure 22: Max Klinger, 'Psyche and the lamp'. Source: Klinger, Max 1880, 1988, *Amor und Psyche. Ein Märchen des Apuleius. Aus dem Lateinischen von Reinhold Jachmann*. Illustrirt in 46 Original-Radirungen und ornamentirt von Max Klinger. München 1880. Copyright: Christoph Leidl

like in Apuleius but quite composed, in an echo of well known contemporary images of Sappho on the rocks[23]). Her outside appearance is almost statuesque (Klinger would later turn towards sculpture), and the landscape and sea seem frozen, but some clouds over the sea signal unrest, even inner turmoil, in Psyche, the dark shadow is foreboding a dark future. Standing on top of the cliff does however not mean that she is on her way to some transcendental realm, but she remains firmly grounded on the rock, ready to face what is awaiting her. And that may be death: we get the motif of the 'bride of death'—a stark contrast to Venus—effacing the female power to give life, but the symbolic killing of Psyche lets her live to become a woman.[24]

In the plate 'Psyche abandoned' we get the only nude (view from the back) of Psyche (she is very often presented by other artists as only skimpily dressed) and we cannot but acknowledge that Psyche is facing the open sea and an open future, even though her gesture (arms spread out) signals distress. Her loneliness is impressively depicted in another 'modern style' pair of vignettes: in 'Psyche resting', that is, before she hands herself in to Venus, she is the only vertical element in a horizontal abandoned landscape with corn fields, with deep clouds and only a small strip of bright sky on the horizon. On the other hand, one is reminded of the atmosphere of paintings of the great Romantic painter Caspar David Friedrich. Klinger is constantly using, assembling material from the history of art in a technique of montage. The posture is repeated two pages later, when Psyche sits in the palace of Venus next to the heap of seeds she has to sort. The repetition of the figure could be interpreted as Klinger realising a *Pathosformel* as Aby Warburg would later call it—a visual formula of gestures universally conveying certain affective states—for melancholic brooding (Psyche is very similar to Dürer's Melencolia). Even on the plate with Psyche going to the underworld, Psyche is on her way to assert her own life: she has no eyes for Sisyphus on the hill in the background, or the persons she was told to ignore. Above, the bats in the frame (again meaningfully employed) signal the night, the poppy plants sleep, the snake at the bottom the powers of the underworld: at times Psyche suffers, but she seems determined to accept the challenge – that is the impression many scenes with Psyche make upon the reader. We have then a synthesis of psychology and mythology (as Thomas Mann commented on Richard Wagner) which gives a portrait of a woman completely at variance with what Thumann had drawn—or what Morris and Burne-Jones have drawn, for that.

---

23 E.g. Charles Mengin's 1877 Sappho, now in the Manchester Art Gallery.
24 On this motif cf. Kassimi 2006.

Figure 23: Max Klinger, 'Psyche on the cliff'. Source: Klinger, Max 1880, 1988, *Amor und Psyche. Ein Märchen des Apuleius. Aus dem Lateinischen von Reinhold Jachmann*. Illustrirt in 46 Original-Radirungen und ornamentirt von Max Klinger. München 1880. Copyright: Christoph Leidl

Speculatively (following Marsha Morton[25]) one might go a step further and point to the attempts at comparative mythology by authors like Creuzer, Schopenhauer and Bachofen, or the ideas of classical scholars like Ludwig Friedländer (1871), who interpreted the story as a *Märchen* (fairy tale), from whom lines of contact run into the 20th century to the Jungians Franz Riklin (discussed by Benson in this volume) and Erich Neumann: here we find the story in a symbolic interpretation (e.g. as initiation of the young woman as *rite de passage*) which is supported by comparative studies, for example involving Indian mythology. This might explain the many exotic features in Klinger:[26] the Indian deity on the Venus-pages, the symbols of Dionysos (bucrania, grapes, theatre masks, the many satyrs; his animal shapes: lions, bulls, snakes, bears), the sphinxes (in connection with Venus pointing to Isis?), and even the further oriental details (*japonisme*) may add up to a comparative vision of the myth. And did not Neumann suggest that it is really Psyche who rescues both herself and Cupid through the acceptance of suffering?[27] I would only stress that with the ironic mirroring of Hercules in Cupid and Psyche's development, we have in fact two initiations—the 'serious' one of Psyche and the 'ironic' version of it in Cupid/Psyche/Hercules, with their coming together leading to the happy ending.

But one final caveat: despite all psychological nuancing, it is not Klinger's intent to formulate a conceptually closed reading, but rather to demonstrate the artist's power over the story and the associations he chooses to bring to the story (about dreams, the female self, art); in a way, he is not very dissimilar to Apuleius in his treatment of his literary material. The vanishing point of all the images is the artist's imagination.[28]

---

25 Morton 2014.
26 Like, presumably, many superficial viewers, Leitmeier 1959, 186 found particularly the (mythical) animals in Klinger's decoration irritating and alien to the story while praising the plates as very fitting illustrations.
27 See Neumann 1971.
28 A postscript to the final note: The best one can say about Jachmann's translation is that it does not get into Klinger's way when his imagination soars high above the ground, but gives a solid basis which will help the reader/viewer to find connections between the illustrative ideas and Apuleius' text, even though he will hardly succeed in integrating it into an imaginative whole (that vanishing point is located in the artist's vision as we have seen).

7 Tiemann—*Jugendstil*

All of this is not obvious to the first time observer of Klinger's book. And so it is understandable that critics asked: 'What have all these lions and snakes and fishes to do with Cupid and Psyche?' and preferred the book designed by Walter Tiemann, published more than 20 years after Klinger.[29] Tiemann was really a 'man of the book', the leading typographer in the first half of the twentieth century in Leipzig, dedicating his life to illustration and typography (designing many fonts), especially for the Insel publishing house. His *Amor und Psyche* was an early work from the time when he had his brief *Jugendstil* period. He was fully aware of the achievements of English printing (overseeing German editions of the Kelmscott Press) and very much concerned about *Buchkunst*. This becomes immediately clear when we look at the (recently reprinted) book. From cover to the choice of coloured print (light brown for illustrations and green for the frames and text) to the interrelation of text and illustrations (besides seven plates, the other illustrations always form pairs of two on facing pages, set within the text), everything is carefully set out. He has nothing of the profusion of ideas on a single page of Klinger, but he gives a pronounced individual sensitiveness to the text. This text was translated by one of the greatest Latinists of his time, Eduard Norden, not a great admirer of Apuleius' style, who stated in the afterword that basically Apuleius had ruined his fine Greek source text with his sophistic Latin. Still, he translated the text, giving it a contemporary touch, which unfortunately—to my impression at least—does not fit very well with the style of the illustrations. Consequently, non-classicist art critics extolled Tiemann, but criticized the translation (Rode's eighteenth century version, still in print in Germany today, was judged much more favourably) for this modernizing style and regarded the afterword as utterly superfluous.[30] As the double title pages show, the ornamental line dominates—but the familiar roses for scenes of happy love in the frame persist[31] (Tiemann has only one more variant, for unhappy situations: a frame with thistles, used consequently as the story develops). As a kind of motto on the title page he gives the scene of Cupid discovering the sleeping Psyche, which will be mirrored formally through similar ges-

---

[29] The critical voice is Leitmeier's 1959, 186; on Tiemann's—not wholly successful—attempt to distance himself from Klinger cf. Hübscher 1989, 91.
[30] Leitmeier 1959, 198–200 regards the translation almost a 'travesty' of Apuleius.
[31] The reference to Lucius' quest for roses in the *Metamorphoses* is obvious, cf. Leitmeier 1959, 198.

tures and composition of the scene later in the book by the standard 'Psyche with the lamp'.

Already these two pictures characterize Tiemann's approach: Psyche and Cupid are on the same level, experiencing distress and joy together (though there is hardly much laughter in Tiemann), a young couple working at their relationship. We have few clearly antique trappings (a little column here and there, but all very much in the background); the figures are nude or half-nude, but there are few overt sexual allusions. It is all very natural and clean, with nothing of the darker, sarcastic, ironic view of love of Klinger. A comparison for example of Tiemann's Psyche seated on the lawn in Cupid's garden and gazing without much emotional expression with Klinger's Psyche on the cliff (cf. above) brings this out very well. There is a link as both are facing the observer and convey a feeling of uncertainty and expectation, but the pose is very different: Tiemann's sitting Psyche is in harmony with the garden, much more 'grounded', in contact with nature. When on another plate Cupid and Psyche debate about the visit of the sisters, it is not Cupid's commands that are stressed by his gestures and expression, but his gentle entreaties. And just as Psyche has her uncertainties, so Cupid is shown scowling when left alone. The plates are exclusively dedicated to the main characters (Cupid and Psyche), with only two plates with other figures (Psyche and Venus, Cupid and Jupiter). The 'action' passages are in the in-text illustrations, for example the journey to the underworld, but even here the heads of the characters dominate (as in Proserpina to the left). When the theme of water—so dear to *Jugendstil* artists—comes up, as in Venus' journey on the sea, Tiemann lets the lines flow and produces a fine effect by combining the two panels into one picture. The influence of painters like Arnold Böcklin— also much admired and followed by Klinger (especially in the presentation of sea-dwelling creatures) –comes into play, too. To sum up, the psychological view of the story (the wedding at the end is not presented) is shifted from an interest in the socialization of young women (both in Thumann and in Klinger) to the realm of the purely private life of a young couple, who have to live through a crisis (with two figures, Venus and Jupiter, as reflecting the position of the older generation), but overcome it in a dedication to a natural, harmonious life. The real story is the psychological development in the minds of two young persons.

8 Conclusion

The views of the Story of Cupid and Psyche in these three (or four, including Morris/Burne-Jones) books, artists, may be summarized as follows:
a) Psyche is the embodiment of chastity or sexual self-denial and the object of desire, who finds her place in a prestabilised social-sexual order by bodily incorporating society's idealised version of love, physically regaining her wings (Hamerling/Thumann).[32]
b) A variant of this concept is the consequent transcendental-allegorical interpretation given by Morris/Burne-Jones, which however diverges in its artistic realisation by a conscious recourse to older stages of reception (Renaissance woodcuts in the style of the illustrations to the *Hypnerotomachia Poliphili* from the circle around Mantegna) which are placed in contrast to contemporary art (and value-systems).
c) Psyche is the bride of death in an existential crisis within a world with uncanny backgrounds, borders, frames, facing the challenge but at the same time ironically transposed into a comic version of another myth (Klinger).
d) Psyche and Cupid are a young couple, on the same emotional level and with equal personal status, with little traces of subordination of one to the other, self-reflexive and trying to cope with an inner crisis that equally affects both, all in a private world, close to nature and not without idyllic elements (Tiemann/Norden).

Present and future will no doubt find their own variations of the theme. Klinger's own later incorporation of the myth into his monumental (2.51 x 4.65 m) painting *Christus im Olymp* (c. 1883–1890; a variation of the subject of Christ in Limbo) may—as appendix—serve to illustrate further possibilities.[33] From the left Christ, followed in solemn procession by personifications of Christian virtues clad in long robes and carrying his cross, enters Olympus, peopled by the ancient gods (frequently nude and posing in a typical antique way) and stops before Zeus seated on his throne with Ganymede. The central scene between Christ

---

32 Precisely its firm grounding in bourgeois moral, literary and artistic taste makes the Hamerling/Thumann book into welcome material for a destruction of this social myth through the fragmentation and rearrangement of Thumann's images in Max Ernst's Cycle *La femme 100 têtes* (in turn indebted to Klinger's next work *Paraphrase of the Finding of a Glove*), Hertel 1992, 111–2. Hertel 1987 explores the anticipation of surreal elements in Klinger's art around 1880, cf. e.g. on Psyche and the lamp: 117.
33 Cf. Dückers 1976, 113–7; Gross 1992.

and Zeus is taken up by a nude Psyche crouching on the ground and turning away from Cupid and towards Christ whilst Cupid (with Zeus' lightning-bolts in his hand) turns the other way. The strong eroticism in the scene (especially in Psyche as both the suffering woman and the human soul)[34] helps to underline that the apparent 'official' interpretation of the subject (the humanistic idea of a marriage of Christianity and Antiquity) is not the entire story: Klinger and his time are beyond the ideological and cultural dominance which these models once may have possessed. Rather, the design of the painting underlines the obsession of the late nineteenth century with the complex nature of the human soul, in the presentation of female suffering even hinting at the theme of violence and eroticism, recurrent in Klinger and in art in general well into the twenty-first century.

9 Bibliography with detailed description of the cycles of illustrations

9.1 The illustrated books:

Paul Thumann (1834–1908) Robert Hamerling (1830–1889)

[Robert Hamerling, Thumann, Paul 1882] Robert Hamerling, Amor und Psyche. Eine Dichtung in sechs Gesängen. Illustriert von Paul Thumann, Leipzig (Titze).
9 full-page **plates** (my titles: 1: Psyche worshipped as new Venus; 2: Psyche carried by Zephyrus, 3: Psyche with the lamp; 4: Psyche and Pan; 5: Psyche before Venus; 6: Psyche and Charon; 7: Cupid's Kiss awakens Psyche; 8: Cupid and Jupiter kissing; 9: Psyche on Olympus)
26 illustrations in the text: 9 half-page square, 4 figures unframed, 13 tondo-shaped (round)

Max Klinger (1857–1920)

[Klinger, Max 1880, 1988] Amor und Psyche. Ein Märchen des Apuleius. Aus dem Lateinischen von Reinhold Jachmann. Illustrirt in 46 Original-Radirungen und ornamentirt von Max Klinger. E.-F. Opus 5. Buchdruck von Gebrüder Kröner in Stuttgart. Papir aus der Gust. Schaeuffelenschen Fabrik zu Heilbronn. Holzschnitte von Kaeseberg & Oertel, R. Klepsch u. a. Kupferdruck von Fr. Felsing in München, München, Theo. Stroefer's Kunstverlag [1880].

---

[34] The poem 'Jesus und Psyche—Phantasie bei Klinger' from 1912 by the contemporary poet Richard Dehmel (1912, 2008) brings this out quite explicitly, cf. Spiekermann 2008.

Reprint (only with plates and vignettes, but only plain text without frames and ornamentation) Berlin 1988, with Nachwort by Dieter Gleisberg.

15 Plates (Klinger's titles, translated): 1: Cupid's Youth; 2: Venus shows Psyche to Cupid; 3: Psyche on a rock; 4: Cupid arriving; 5: Psyche and her sisters; 6: Psyche with the lamp; 7: Psyche abandoned; 8: Psyche wandering; 9: Jupiter and Venus; 10: Psyche and Venus; 11: Psyche and Jupiter's eagle; 12: Psyche in Tartarus; 13: Cupid finds Psyche; 14: Cupid with Jupiter 15: Wedding of Cupid and Psyche

31 Vignettes (Klinger's titles, translated): 1: Psyche worshipped by the people; 2: Venus' priestesses; 3: Venus in the sea; 4: Cupid and Apollo; 5: Oracle; 6: Parents mourning; 7: Psyche's wedding procession; 8: Psyche bathing; 9: Cupid (leaving) and Psyche; 10: The sisters, calling Psyche; 11: A sister and her husband; 12: Zephyrus carrying the sisters; 13: The sisters sailing home; 14: Zephyrus, carrying Psyche away; 15: Pan, comforting Psyche; 16: Psyche visiting one of her sisters; 17: The sister precipitating herself from the rock; 18: Venus learns about Cupid's liaison; 19: Venus in Cupid's room; 20: Venus encountering Juno and Ceres 21: Psyche and Ceres; 22: Psyche and Juno; 23: Psyche resting; 24: Venus and Mercury; 25: Psyche in the house of Venus; 26: Psyche and Arundo; 27: Psyche on her way to Tartarus; 28: Psyche on the Acheron; 29: Psyche received on Olympus; 30: Venus and Psyche; 31: Birth of Voluptas.

Walter Tiemann (1876–1951)

[Tiemann, Walter 1902, 2016] *Amor und Psyche. Märchen von Apuleius. Übertragen von Eduard Norden. Mit Buchschmuck von Walter Tiemann*, Leipzig (Seemann) 1902. Reprint Darmstadt 2016 with Nachwort by S.J. Harrison (tr. K. Brodersen), 65–126.

7 full-page wood-cuts, (including double title page) (my titles) 1: Cupid watching Psyche asleep (opposite title); 2: Psyche alone in Cupid's garden; 3: Cupid kneeling at Psyche's feet; 4: Psyche with the lamp; 5: Cupid distressed in his room; 6: Psyche before Venus 7: Cupid and Jupiter

18 double square illustrations in the text, (in 9 pairs on facing pages) (1–2: Venus in the sea; 3–4: Cupid kissing Psyche—parents mourning; 5–6: Sisters calling Psyche—Psyche answering; 7–8: Jealous sisters—concert for Psyche; 9–10: Psyche and Pan—Psyche unconscious on river bank, with young satyrs; 11–12: Ceres—Psyche weeping; 13–14: Venus with birds on her way to Olympus; 15–16: Psyche and the box—Venus commanding (last task); 17–18: Psyche in Charon's boat—Cerberus and Proserpina

9.2 Bibliography

Binder, G./Merkelbach, R. (eds.) (1968), *Amor und Psyche*, Darmstadt.
Brandes, G. (1901), 'Max Klinger', in: G. Brandes (ed.), *Moderne Geister. Literarische Bildnisse aus dem Neunzehnten Jahrhundert*, Frankfurt, 4th ed., 57–72.
[Burne-Jones, E./Morris, W.] (1998), *Amor und Psyche. Eine Holzstichfolge für das Buchprojekt 'The Earthly Paradise', dem Buch das niemals war (1866–1872)*, (exhib. catalogue) Clemens-Sels-Museum Neuss, Neuss.

Carmignani, M./Graverini, L./Lee, B.T. (eds.) (2013), *Collected Studies on the Roman Novel– Ensayos sobre la novela romana*, Córdoba.
Cavicchioli, S. (2002), *The Tale of Cupid and Psyche. An Illustrated History*, New York.
Debes, D. (ed.) (1989), *Traditionen Leipziger Buchkunst*, Leipzig.
De Chirico, G. (2008a), *Scritti 1. Romanzi e Scritti critici e teorici 1911–1945*, a cura di A. Cortellessa, Milano.
De Chirico, G. (2008b), 'Max Klinger', in: De Chirico 2008a, 321–333 (first publ. in *Il Convegno* I 10, 1920, 32–44)
Dehmel, R. (1912, 2008), 'Jesus und Psyche. Phantasie bei Klinger', in: Langer, 229–33.
Derrida, J./Owens, C. (1979), 'The Parergon', *October 9*, 3–41.
Drude, C. (2005), *Historismus als Montage. Kombinationsverfahren im graphischen Werk Max Klingers*, Mainz.
Dückers, A. (1976), *Max Klinger*, Berlin.
Dufty, A.R. (ed.) (1974), *The Story of Cupid and Psyche, with illustrations designed by Edward Burne-Jones, mostly engraved on the wood by William Morris; the Introduction by A.R. Dufty*, London, Cambridge.
Friedländer, L. (1871), 'Das Märchen von Amor und Psyche' in Binder and Merkelbach 1968: 16–43.
Gross, F. (1992), 'Vom Alltagsgetriebe fern: Der Große Einzelne in Klinger's "Kreuzigung Christi" und "Christus im Olymp"', in: Klinger 1992, 72–83.
Gross, F. (1996), 'Klingers graphische Modernität', in: Klinger 1996, 68–77.
Gleisberg, D. (1992), '"Ich muß mir stets ein kleines Monument errichten". Max Klinger in seinen Selbstdarstellungen', in: Klinger 1992, 13–25.
Gleisberg, D. (1988), 'Nachwort', in: Klinger (reprint 1988), 117–26.
Harrison, S.J. (2013), 'Heroic Traces. Theseus and Hercules in Apuleius' *Metamorphoses*', in: Carmignani/ Graverini/ Benjamin Todd, 141–56.
Hertel, C. (1987), *Studien zu Max Klingers graphischem Zyklus: Paraphrase über den Fund des Handschuhs (1878–1881)*, Diss. Tübingen, Frankfurt/M.
Hertel, C. (1992), 'Irony, Dream, and Kitsch. Max Klinger's Paraphrase of the Finding of a Glove and German Modernism', *The Art Bulletin* 74, 91–114.
Holm, C. (2006), *Amor und Psyche. Die Erfindung eines Mythos in Kunst, Wissenschaft und Alltagskultur (1765–1840)*, München, Berlin.
Hübscher, A. (1989), 'Walter Tiemann 1876–1951', in: Debes, 67–113.
Kassimi, S. (2006), 'Das Motiv der Totenbraut. Apuleius' Märchen von Amor und Psyche' in Illustrationen von Max Klinger und William Morris', in: Klinger 2006, 11–21.
Klimm, P. (1974), *Zwischen Epigonentum und Realismus. Studien zum Gesamtwerk Robert Hamerlings* (Diss. Wien 1974), Vienna.
Klinger, M. (1987), *Malerei und Zeichnung. Tagebuchaufzeichnungen und Briefe*, ed. A. Hübscher, Leipzig 1987.
[Klinger, M.] (1992), *Max Klinger 1857–1920* (exhib. catalogue). Städtische Galerie im Städelschen Kunstinstitut Frankfurt am Main 12. Februar bis 7. Juni 1992, Leipzig.
[Klinger, M.] (1996), *Max Klinger. Zeichnungen. Zustandsdrucke. Zyklen*, (exhib. catalogue). Museum Villa Stuck, München.
[Klinger, M.] (2006), *Zwischen Tag und Traum. Max Klinger. Graphische Zyklen* (exhib. catalogue), Neuss.
Langer, P. (ed.) (2008) *Max Klinger. Wege zur Neubewertung*, Leipzig.

Leitmeier, H. (1959), 'Die Bedeutung des Jugendstiles für das deutsche Buch und Walter Tiemanns Anteil daran', *Gutenberg-Jahrbuch* 34, 184–210.

Morton, M. (2014), *Max Klinger and Wilhelmine Culture. On the Threshold of German Modernism*, Farnham.

[NDB] (1966), Historische Kommission bei der Bayerischen Akademie der Wissenschaften, (ed.) (1966), *Neue Deutsche Biographie*, vol. 7, Berlin.

Neumann, E. (1971), *Amor and Psyche. The Psychic Development of the Feminine. A Commentary on the Tale by Apuleius*, Princeton.

Rieder, H. (1966), 'Hamerling, Robert', in: *NDB* 1966, 585–6.

Singer, H.W. (1909, repr. 1978), *Max Klingers Radierungen, Stiche und Steindrucke. Wissenschaftliches Verzeichnis*, Berlin (repr. New York).

Spiekermann, B. (2008), *Weltanschauungskunst. Richard Dehmels lyrische Bearbeitung von Klingers Christus im Olymp*, in: Langer, 212–28.

Tiemann, W. (1951), 'Der Jugendstil im deutschen Buch', *Gutenberg-Jahrbuch* 26, 182–91.

Uerscheln, G. (1998), 'Amor und Psyche im 'Irdischen Paradies' von William Morris and Edward Burne-Jones' in Burne-Jones, Morris 1998, 19–39.

Vollmer, H./Thieme, U./Becker, F. (eds.) (1939), *Allgemeines Lexikon der Bildenden Künstler von der Antike bis zur Gegenwart*, vol. 33, Leipzig, 113.

Wolff-Beckh, B. (1904), 'Paul Thumann', *Kunstchronik* N.F. 15, 568–70.

Geoffrey C. Benson
Psyche the psychotic. *Cupid and Psyche* in Dr. Franz Riklin's *Wishfulfilment and Symbolism in Fairy Tales*

1 Introduction. *Cupid and Psyche* and psychology

Since the early twentieth century, Apuleius' tale of *Cupid and Psyche*[1] has been the subject of many psychological interpretations from either the Freudian or the Jungian perspective.[2] In fact, as Gollnick notes, 'next to the Oedipus story there is hardly another [story] which has received more attention from depth psychologists.'[3] Freud himself, however, made only a few brief comments on the story, arguing that Psyche represents death in 'The Theme of the Three Caskets' (1913), an essay about trios of sisters in mythology and literature. Freud's cursory analysis is surprising in light of the central opposition between desire (Eros) and death (Thanatos) in his thought and the fact that his collection of ancient art included at least six statues of the god Eros.[4] Yet, the limited scope of Freud's interpretation created an opportunity for his colleagues and successors to analyze the story in their own creative ways.[5] Freudians generally treat the story as Psyche's dream and suggest that it deals with sexual anxieties of adolescent girls, although their interpretations differ on many points of detail. Jungians, on the other hand, argue that *Cupid and Psyche* symbolizes psychological development—in particular that of girls—although a few Jungians see Psyche as the feminine side or *anima* archetype of either Lucius' or Apuleius' unconscious.

Nevertheless, in spite of the popularity and diversity of the psychological interpretations of *Cupid and Psyche*, they have been neglected in Apuleian studies. While Walsh analyzed Neumann's Jungian interpretation in his groundbreaking book, subsequent monographs say little about Neumann and the other psycho-

---

1 The text of the *Metamorphoses* is Zimmerman 2012, and the translations are mine.
2 For discussion of the major Freudian and Jungian interpretations of *Cupid and Psyche*, with bibliography, see Gollnick 1992. The only important psychoanalytic interpretation Gollnick omits is Lacan 2015, 225–6 who argues the story is a Freudian allegory.
3 Gollnick 1992, 1.
4 For Freud's art collection and discussion of three of the Eros terracottas in it, see Gamwell and Wells 1989, 100–3.
5 The remarks in the rest of this paragraph build on Gollnick 1992, 58 and 106.

analytic interpreters.⁶ This is also the case in the commentaries on *Cupid and Psyche* that rightly prioritize philological research over psychoanalytic and folkloric approaches, which are not the expertise of the different commentators. Kenney, for instance, brings up Bettelheim (1976) on a few occasions—but only to reject his Freudian reading in favour of a Platonic one.⁷ The Groningen Commentators explicitly state that their commentary on *Metamorphoses* 4.28–6.24 does not discuss Freudian and Jungian interpretations or the reception of the tale in literature.⁸ In recent years, psychological approaches have received more attention in ancient novel studies, as we shall see. Nonetheless, the dominant view of the Freudian and Jungian readings is that they are 'tiresome and reductive.'⁹ Classicists have good reasons for maintaining this view, as I show later, but at the dawn of this era of 'Deep Classics' it is important to consider all the different strata that have built up 'over' *Cupid and Psyche*, especially the strata that have been ignored.¹⁰ What do we gain by paying closer attention to the Freudian and Jungian interpretations of Apuleius' tale? How might psychoanalysis and psychology help us to understand Apuleius' story better?

In order to address these questions, this essay focuses on the first psychoanalytic interpretation of *Cupid and Psyche* by Dr Franz Riklin (1878–1938), a Swiss clinical psychiatrist who collaborated with Jung on *Studies in Word Association* (1918).¹¹ Riklin's fascinating but largely forgotten retelling and interpretation of Apuleius' tale appears in *Wishfulfilment and Symbolism in Fairy Tales* (*Wunscherfüllung und Symbolik im Märchen*, 1908), translated into English in 1915. Riklin wrote this short book while he was still a Freudian,¹² as is evident from the first page where Riklin claims 'the psychology of fairytales stands in close relationship to the world of dreams, of hysteria, as we have learned to

---

6 Neumann 1956 is discussed in Walsh 1970, 219–20; Tatum 1979, 58; James 1987, 142, 174; and Schlam 1992, 96.
7 Kenney 1990, 18 n. 77, 126, and 182–3.
8 Zimmerman et al 2004, 3 and 3 n. 8. Grimal 1963: 32 refers in his annotated bibliography to Neumann 1956 but does not discuss psychoanalytic readings in detail; there is a single reference to Freud in Moreschini 1994, 216.
9 Lateiner 2005. For a review of psychoanalytic approaches the ancient novels, see Fusillo 2003, 293–300.
10 For the phrase 'Deep Classics,' see Butler 2016b, who also assesses Freud's analogy of the human psyche to the city of Rome in *Civilization and its Discontents* (1930).
11 For a brief account of Riklin's relationship with Jung, see Van den Berk 2012, 66.
12 Riklin stuck with Jung after Jung's break with Freud, see Jung 1989, 167–8.

know through Freud, and of mental disease.'[13] Riklin suggests that *Cupid and Psyche* symbolizes a psychotic's wishfulfilment fantasies, and this essay examines the fascinating way in which he presents this argument, and also assesses its legacy. In most circles, Riklin's interpretation has been rejected and ignored, but there are elements in Apuleius' narrative that suggest madness is a central concern. My aim is to show that Riklin might be a starting point for future psychological interpretations of the tale, and I suggest what such a reading might look like at the conclusion of this essay.

2 Franz Riklin's *Cupid and Psyche*. A fairytale with a case history in the footnotes

At the very end of the final chapter of his book, 'Chapter VII: Some Special Sexual Fairy-Tale Motives,' Riklin discusses fairytales where a heroine is persecuted for her beauty and prevented from marrying a prince. It is in this context that Riklin retells *Cupid and Psyche*, meaning that this story is the climax of his book. Riklin opens his account by acknowledging Apuleius as the author of the story, admiring the beauty of his language, and referring to *Cupid and Psyche* as a fairytale.[14] Riklin's positive assessment of Apuleius' style is not in line with trends in German scholarship of the time—in particular, Norden's critique of Apuleian Latinity in his *Die Antike Kunstprosa* (1898).[15] However, the idea that *Cupid and Psyche* is a fairytale (*Märchen*) is one that Riklin inherited from the Brothers Grimm and that was later developed in essays by Friedländer (1871) and Liebrecht (1879) that note parallels between *Cupid and Psyche* and tales from as far afield as New Zealand.[16] Riklin, as we shall see, has the same comparative impulse, which also has roots in Creuzer's discussion of *Cupid and Psy-*

---

13 Riklin 1915, 1; White's translation of Riklin 1908 has been altered on occasions where it strays too far from the original German. I thank Alexis Briley for her assistance with the revision of White.
14 Riklin 1915, 79; Riklin 1908, 92.
15 For Norden's attack on Apuleius' style, see Harrison 2013b, 22–3.
16 For the Brothers Grimm's response to *Cupid and Psyche* in *Über das Wesen der Märchen*, *Kinder- und Hausmärchen* (1819), see Friedländer 1871, 20–21; Schlam 1992, 85, and Morton 2014, 238. The view that Apuleius drew on motifs from an ancient, oral storytelling tradition has been disputed ever since Fehling 1977 argued that the notion of peasant-produced, orally transmitted folktales is a romantic fiction and that fairytales can trace their origin back to Apuleius; see also Reeve 2008, 295–297. Plantade 2014, however, revives the theory that *Cupid and Psyche* descends from an oral source.

che (1810–1812; 2nd ed. 1819). Riklin, however, does not have the same agenda as Creuzer, who was attempting to reconcile Greek religion with Christianity; Creuzer maintained that *Cupid and Psyche* came from Persia, and that it is an allegory with connections to Pythagoreanism and the Mystery cults.[17] Riklin is not explicit about another important influence; he in fact builds on Bachofen's analysis of *Cupid and Psyche* (1859), but Riklin's reading is much less positive, as we shall see.[18] Bachofen was known for his theories about prehistoric matriarchy and cultural evolution, and he argued that *Cupid and Psyche* describes the maturation of Psyche's consciousness—namely, the transition from the Tellurian state of sensuality, materialism, and illicit love (hetaerism) to the Lunar stage of matrimony. Subsequent psychological interpretations of the tale, particularly Jungian ones, generally depart from Bachofen.[19]

After these introductory remarks, Riklin starts retelling *Cupid and Psyche*, without any reference to the situation in which the story is told in the *Metamorphoses* or to its role in the novel (I cite his summary, followed by his footnotes as cued in the text):

> A king and a queen had three daughters of great beauty. The youngest, however, was of incomparable beauty.[7] She was admired like the beautiful Venus, the Goddess of love.[8] Psyche finds, however, only admirers but no husband and her sorrowing father receives the following answer from the oracle:
>
> Place the maiden high on the rocky crag of the mountain, adorned in the sorrowful garb of marital woe. Do not hope for a son-in-law of mortal birth; instead, he will arise terribly from the dragon's tribe. Then flying through the air he pursues them all and brings them all doom with fire and sword, Jupiter trembles before him, all the gods fear him, the sea shudders before him: even the Stygian night.[9]

Instead of to her wedding, Psyche was conducted, in obedience to the oracle, up the mountain in her bridal attire.

In characteristic manner she herself (like other fairy-tale princesses in similar sagas) is less troubled than those about her and urges herself to the fulfill-

---

17 Creuzer 1822, 709–14.
18 Schopenhauer's explication of *Cupid and Psyche* (1851), on the other hand, had little impact on Riklin. According to Schopenhauer 2015, 372–3, Psyche is punished for giving conscious thought to a process that should be unconscious and physiological—the act of procreation. Schopenhauer admits this is a 'very subtle and highly unusual allegorical interpretation' (p. 372), and the only point of comparison between his reading and Riklin's is that they both emphasize the darker aspects of the tale.
19 Bachofen 1967, 44–7. For Bachofen's influence on subsequent psychological interpretations of *Cupid and Psyche*, see Neumann 1956, 147–8 and 154–5 and Morton 2014, 231–2.

ment of the oracle's command. (One is tempted to say: She just knows that nothing evil will befall her!).

> From the top of the mountain, the anxious, trembling Psyche was seized by the soft zephyrs and wafted to a valley and placed on a bed of flowers.[10]
>
> Notes
>
> [7] As usual in fairytales, the number three has the purpose of making the heroine duly prominent, even as the fairytale often—and sometimes awkwardly—introduces a foil to the hero, a contrasting character who spoils everything and comes to a bad end.
>
> [8] Here Venus, the later mother-in-law, has the rôle of persecutor, similar to the witch, the giant, or the stepmother in other tales.
>
> [9] This verse reminds one of fairytales in which the insatiable dragon demands the virgin sacrifice. The subsequent funeral procession (= wedding procession) to the mountain also supports such a comparison and speaks for the correct interpretation of the dragon figure in the fairytale.
>
> [10] Here Psyche enters the sphere of enchantment. This instant corresponds to the appearance of the magic mist in the Icelandic fairy tales, the going astray in the forest in the German, etc. At the same time, Zephyr also corresponds to what often appears in fairytales as the magic cloak or similarly magical means of flying through the air. It is unfortunate that we today with our imperfect balloons are not so far advanced.

Here begins the production of a wish structure which improves upon the preceding and rather unpleasant position of Psyche. Why does it resemble so strikingly a dream and the wish phantasies of the psychotic?[20]

Riklin compresses events that Apuleius describes over the course of several pages in Book 4 (*Met.* 4.28–35) and hits the high points in the plotting—Psyche's background and beauty; the oracle; her exposure on the mountain; the transport into the hidden valley—but his account does not include several key formal features of the story such as the direct speeches of Venus (4.30.1–3; 4.31.1–3) and Psyche (4.34.3–6), and the vivid ekphrastic description of Venus' descent into the sea (4.31.4–7). Direct speeches and ekphrasis make *Cupid and Psyche* a *bella fabella* (6.25.1);[21] direct speech, moreover, accounts for nearly half of the lines of the tale and, as van Mal-Maeder and Zimmerman note, one of the central themes of the tale is 'the persuasive power and magic of the spoken word.'[22] Riklin's epitomisation of the tale, therefore, lacks the elements that make Apuleius' narrative sparkle.

---

20 Riklin 1915, 79; Riklin 1908, 92–3.
21 Cf. Zimmerman et al. 2004, 9.
22 Van Mal-Maeder and Zimmerman 1998, 84 and 95–102.

However, the footnotes are the most striking feature of Riklin's *Cupid and Psyche*. Riklin retells many fairytales in his book—for example, in Chapter III, he tells an Icelandic story and then two Russian fairytales over the course of nine pages—but no other story has as many footnotes as his version of *Cupid and Psyche*.[23] This sudden burst of footnotes is puzzling. One possible reason for them is that they allow Riklin to tell the tale without interruption but also let him draw attention to his psychological interpretation. Riklin's retelling, of course, is an interpretation, and I shall evaluate the overall direction of his interpretation after we make our way through the whole narrative. The footnotes may well be designed to obscure this fact, but they also let Riklin remind readers of earlier references to *Cupid and Psyche* in his book.

Whatever the case may be, the content of these footnotes is interesting and sometimes even bizarre. In notes 7, 8, and 9, Riklin develops his idea that *Cupid and Psyche* is a fairytale by pointing to motifs in the story that he believes are paralleled in other fairytales—the number three; Venus as step-mother/persecutor; virgin sacrifice. Note 10, however, is different. This note opens with the same sort of comparative material that is found in notes 7–9 (magic mist in Icelandic fairytales; the forest in German tales; magic cloaks that facilitate flight) and that Riklin uses to support his view that *Cupid and Psyche* is a fairytale. However, the decisive claim in the footnote comes after an unexpected lamentation about the deficiencies of modern-day air travel and a line break that signals the note will now move in a new direction—to the theory that the story symbolizes a psychotic's wishfulfilment fantasies. In Riklin's view, the sudden change in Psyche's fortunes—she was just about to wed a monster, when Zephyr intervenes and transports her to a magical valley—is the first 'wish structure' in the tale. For Riklin, wishfulfilment is the central motif in the tale. Further, as the final sentence in the note indicates, Riklin believes the plot of the story unfolds in the same way as 'the thought processes of some of his psychotic patients when they try to escape from difficult situations through dreams and fantasy,' as Gollnick puts it.[24] The psychotic in *Cupid and Psyche*, according to Riklin, is 'anxious' Psyche, who may have been influential on Kierkegaard's concept of 'anxiety', as Andreadakis argues in this volume. Riklin expands this idea in more detail in the footnotes that follow, but he never explains how he developed this theory.

Riklin continues to punctuate his narrative with footnotes when he retells the events that Apuleius handles in Book 5 of the *Metamorphoses*:

---

[23] Riklin 1908, 21–9; 1915, 15–23.
[24] Gollnick 1992, 36.

On awaking she found herself in a fairy grove and sees before her a house built by godly skill (a magic castle) from the richest and most splendid material. As she surveys all within, she heard servants' voices[11] which invited her to a most pleasing repose and to a most excellent table.[12] Also, afterwards, the most beautiful music was sung. In the evening she lay down to rest; startled by a soft sound, she trembled, fearing something undefined. Soon an unknown man appears, who weds Psyche, and hastens away again before daybreak.[13] He warns her later of her sisters who visit her and wish to tear from her the secret of her marriage to a god.[14] Unfortunately without success. The envious sisters who were carried by the same Zephyr into the magical realm, persuaded her, until at last she finally looked at her divine spouse by the aid of a lamp and awakened him by incautiously spilling oil upon him.

They suggest to her, that her husband was perhaps, as the oracle proclaimed, a hideous dragon, who would yet devour her. Amor, however, makes his escape.[15] Psyche revenged herself on her sisters by telling them that Amor was her lover, and declared that he had run away from her because of the exposure of his secret, but that he was now going to woo one of the sisters. They hastened to the mountain, threw themselves, without the help of the zephyrs, into the air, and were most miserably dashed to pieces.

Psyche wandered, full of misery, through all countries seeking Amor, while Venus, who had learned of Amor's adventure, pursued her rival with renewed anger in order to punish her.

Notes

[11] As expressed in psychoses.

[12] A 'little table, set yourself' [Brothers Grimm, *Kinder- und Hausmärchen* 36]

[13] It has already been mentioned that certain psychotics experience a quite identical nocturnal embrace of an invisible spouse.

[14] This mystic union with the god as a higher being occurs as a psychic, sexual wish structure again and again. Christian mysticism has produced wonderful cases of this sort. The painting of Correggio, 'The Mystic Marriage of St. Catherine,' in the Louvre, has represented such an event with ravishing loveliness. A comical counterpart suggests itself to me in a similar hallucinatory experience of a patient, whose beloved God appeared in checkered trousers! These trousers led us to a young man who, in the wish structure of the patient, had become a sort of God.

[15] We have already met this motive in different fairy tales.[25]

Riklin once again compresses a great amount of detail: he eliminates speeches and ekphrases, omitting the wonderful focalized description of Cupid's palace that opens Book 5 of Apuleius' novel (5.1.2–5.2.3) and Psyche's vision of her sleeping husband (5.22.2–7). However, the most significant alteration in this section of Riklin's retelling and also in what follows is the absence of repetition and the suspense it creates. In Apuleius' narrative, Cupid repeatedly warns Psyche

---

25 Riklin 1915, 80; 1908, 93–4.

about her sisters and instructs her not to investigate his identity and appearance (5.5.2–3; 5.6.2–3; 5.11.3–6; 5.12.4–6).[26] These sisters visit Psyche several times and badger Psyche with the same question—Who is your husband?—before returning home loaded with gifts (5.7–8; 5.14–15; 5.17). The sisters, moreover, exchange similar speeches in which they complain about Psyche's fortune and their own old and feeble husbands (5.9–10). After Psyche loses Cupid (5.24) the narrative becomes even more repetitive. Psyche, employing the same kind of poisonous rhetoric that the sisters used to trick her, gets one of her sisters to plunge to her death, and her second sister is killed in the same exact way moments later in the text (5.27). Psyche subsequently visits Ceres' temple and prays to this goddess for help, only to be turned down (6.1–2); she then comes across Juno's temple, and her prayers again fall on deaf ears (6.3–4). After all this, Venus forces Psyche to perform four tasks. The only repetitive elements from Apuleius' narrative that Riklin retains are the tasks. Riklin's *Cupid and Psyche*, as a result, is a simpler story, and I will discuss the larger ramifications of this shortly. At the same time as Riklin streamlines the tale, he subtly draws connections between *Cupid and Psyche* and other fairytales. For example, Riklin refers to Amor's palace as a 'magic castle,' whereas Kenney and the Groningen commentators connect Cupid's home with descriptions of the palaces of heroes and gods in Homer and the epic tradition, and Brodersen links it to Roman villas.[27]

Riklin's view that Psyche is psychotic and that the plot of the tale revolves around her fantasies and hallucinations becomes very clear in the footnotes that accompany this section of the narrative. In note 11, Riklin suggests the disembodied voices Psyche encounters (*Met.* 5.2) are similar to the auditory hallucinations of psychotics. Then in note 13, Riklin connects Psyche's nightly encounters with her unseen husband to the experience of psychotics who feel but cannot see their lovers. Riklin argued this point in greater detail in Chapter 5 by describing the experience of one of his own patients:

> As in the tale of Amor and Psyche, the heroine in the fairytale of the brown dog feels the embraces of a man she sleeps with but cannot see.
>
> One is thereby reminded in the liveliest manner of fully analogous hallucinatory perceptions which our patients frequently relate.
>
> One such patient experienced this connubial embrace clearly every night at two o'clock and had to answer it. That this automatism always appeared when the clock struck two, as a

---

[26] Cupid's warnings, however, become 'more precise and more dramatic,' see Zimmerman et al. 2004, 138. For analysis of the repetitions in the story, see Benson 2019, 132–134.
[27] Kenney 1990, 137; Zimmerman et al. 2004, 115–6; Brodersen 1998.

symbol for the existence of the two lovers, depends on a comic association similar to the one that connects the lark (Löweneckerchen) and the lion (Löwe).²⁸

Finally, in note 14, Riklin compares Psyche's marriage to a god to the mystical experiences of St. Catherine. However, he implies in the second half of the note that mystical religious experience is equivalent to psychotic hallucination by relating how one of his patients would picture God dressed up in checked trousers. Riklin consistently views mystical religious experience as a pathology, so I suspect he would support the satirical reading of Apuleius' novel.²⁹

Riklin retells the rest of *Cupid and Psyche*—specifically the events Apuleius describes in Book 6 of the *Metamorphoses*—in the same way he deals with the beginning and middle of the tale:

> Finally Psyche voluntarily gave herself up to the wrathful goddess, was naturally badly treated and was required to fulfil three difficult tasks.[16] First, like Cinderella, she must separate different kinds of seeds from a pile. Helpful ants quickly executed the task. Venus believed that Amor had helped her and charged her to bring her a lock of the golden fleece. Psyche, who frequently wished to end her life, was instructed by the nymph Arundo how she could solve this problem. Third she must bring water from a spring, guarded by dragons, which supplied the Stygian swamps and the waters of Cocytus. Jupiter's eagle helped her this time.
>
> Finally, Venus asks for a box full of the beauty of Proserpine. In despair, Psyche is about to throw herself from a tower, when the tower speaks to her in an encouraging and counseling voice,[17] telling her in what manner she can carry out this most difficult task and safely enter the underworld. Opening the box—out of curiosity and a desire to take for herself a bit of this otherworldly beauty—she nearly forfeited her life, overcome as she was with the feeling of sleep emanating from inside. The recovered Amor, escaping from the bondage of his mother, comes to her assistance and turns back the sleep into the box, and Psyche delivers the present of Proserpine. Amor—instead of, as in other tales, vanquishing the persecutrix as the hero—now goes to Zeus in order, as his favorite, to procure deliverance from the difficulties.
>
> Zeus charges him with having, in various ways, wounded and stained his heart through earthly passion and with having damaged his reputation and authority through an ugly and morally objectionable love affair, when he induced him to change into serpents and flames, into a bull and a swan.[18] However, he promises to help him; the mortal Psyche receives the nectar of immortality[19] and is united forever with the godly Amor.
>
> Notes
>
> [16] Difficulties, which interfere with the attainment of the goal. See earlier.

---

28 Riklin 1915, 45; Riklin 1908, 54–5.
29 Such as Harrison 2000, 210–259.

[17] Similarity with a teleological hallucination.

[18] What a beautiful collection of masculine sex symbols! Apuleius seems to have known it!

[19] Compare the fruit of the tree of life.[30]

Riklin again streamlines the narrative by eliminating speeches, descriptions, and characters with small roles such as Pan, Ceres, and Juno. Moreover, he draws further connections between *Cupid and Psyche* and other fairytales, comparing Psyche to Cinderella, for example. Lastly, he continues to suggest in his footnotes that the tale is about a psychotic's wishfulfilment. The proportion of the narrative dedicated to the tasks is surprising, and the transformation of the talking green reed (6.12.1) into a nymph named Arundo is also a new feature. The emphasis on the tasks may anticipate the Jungian approach to the tale in which the tasks are front and centre. However, as Riklin implies in note 16, the tasks are important to him because he had connected them with the behaviour of psychotics at the end of Chapter 5. They therefore help to support his view that the story is about psychotic wishfulfilment:

> The many tasks to be fulfilled correspond to those which must often be carried out in dreams and the wish-deliria of the mentally disturbed. To many psychotics, for example, the confinement in an asylum itself and the work accomplished therein appear as one of the tasks, which they must fulfil, in order to attain the object of their desires.[31]

Riklin continues his psychological interpretation in the next footnote, asserting that Psyche's conversation with the talking tower is similar to a 'teleological hallucination'—that is a hallucination in which the psychotic is told what he or she should do. However, what is most surprising about the end of Riklin's *Cupid and Psyche* is that Voluptas, the child of Cupid and Psyche (*Met.* 6.24), is not mentioned. As Gollnick notes, all the Freudian interpretations of the tale ignore Voluptas, and this is somewhat puzzling because 'Voluptas as delight or pleasure might seem to fit in with a generally sexual interpretation of the story as a woman's fantasies, dreams or anxieties.'[32] Yet, as Gollnick goes on to observe, 'sexual fulfillment is not the primary object of these fantasies, since the Freudians, for the most part, read this myth as an expression of repressed sexual impulses, projections and reaction formations.'[33]

---

30 Riklin 1915, 81; 1908, 94–5.
31 Riklin 1915, 50; 1908, 60.
32 Gollnick 1992, 125 and 27 n. 79.
33 Gollnick 1992, 125.

Riklin simplifies Apuleius' complex tale of *Cupid and Psyche* so that it resembles more closely the fairytales he discusses in the rest of his book; at the same time, the footnotes turn it into something that resembles a case history of one of his psychotic patients. The irony of this epitomisation is that Riklin erases the very features of Apuleius' story that are arguably best suited for psychoanalytic interpretation—namely, the situation of narration and the repetitive elements in the narrative. However, before I explain why Riklin may actually be on to a key feature of *Cupid and Psyche*, I want to evaluate the response to Riklin's argument.

3 The reception of Riklin in psychology and classics

Riklin's *Cupid and Psyche* has been neglected in the subsequent work on the tale by Freudians and Jungians, and it has had little influence on Classical scholarship. Among Freudians and Jungians, Riklin is recognized as a pioneer, but his interpretation is not taken seriously—perhaps because he sees *Cupid and Psyche* as a fairytale, not a myth. For example, von Franz regards Riklin as an important early psychoanalytic interpreter of fairytales but saves praise for later Freudians such as Bettelheim.[34] The most extensive discussion of Riklin's interpretation that I know of is by Gollnick. Gollnick criticizes Riklin for studying the tale outside of its larger context in Apuleius' novel and also for reducing 'religious experience to pathological wishfulfilment,' which makes it impossible for Riklin 'to appreciate the mystical potential of the Eros and Psyche myth.'[35] Gollnick is skeptical that Psyche is psychotic but suggests Riklin may have developed this idea 'by reading the frame narrative of Lucius being changed into an ass as an example of psychotic delusion,'[36] an interpretation that a classicist has countenanced.[37] C.S. Lewis, on the other hand, rejects the view that Psyche is psychotic and that the tale is made up of a series of wishfulfilment hallucinations in *Till We Have Faces. A Myth Retold* (1956), his novelistic adaptation of *Cupid and Psyche*.[38] Psyche's sister, Orual, entertains the idea that Psyche is 'mad' and hallu-

---

[34] Von Franz 1996, vii.
[35] Gollnick 1992, 38–9.
[36] Gollnick 1992, 38.
[37] Laird 1993, 170.
[38] Lewis was familiar with Freud and Jung, commentating on them in an essay titled 'Psycho-Analysis and Literary Criticism' (Lewis 1969, 286–300), but I am unaware of any evidence that Lewis read Riklin. For Lewis' novel see the chapter by Drews in this volume.

cinating, after Psyche shows her the palace, which is invisible in Lewis' version of the story.[39] Orual, however, has a vision of the palace that makes her realize madness is not an adequate explanation for Psyche's experiences or her own perceptions.[40]

Riklin's ideas have fared even more poorly in Classics because his work has been forgotten. As far as I know, the only classicist to refer to Riklin is Relihan, who includes Gollnick's table of Freudian and Jungian interpretations at the end of his translation of *Cupid and Psyche*.[41] Classicists have ignored Riklin and the other Freudians and Jungians because they 'have tended to remove the story from its literary context, and this procedure has encouraged a proliferation of meanings which seem to have little to do with the original setting of the tale in the *Metamorphoses*.'[42] Neumann, one of the major Jungian interpreters, justifies this separatist approach by asserting that Apuleius did not create the tale and that it actually originates from Minoan Crete,[43] a view that classicists do not support.[44] Moreover, Riklin's incorporation of material from his psychiatric practice, along with neglect of key details in the plot of the tale, make his interpretation susceptible to criticism from the angle that psychoanalytic literary criticism turns texts into vehicles for various psychological theories.

4 Rehabilitating Riklin. Madness and repetition in *Cupid and Psyche*

Despite this dismal reaction to Riklin, there has been a revival of interest in psychological approaches to *Cupid and Psyche* and the *Metamorphoses* as a whole. The socio-biological interpretation of *Cupid and Psyche* by Burkert and Bierl— that *Cupid and Psyche* is not about mystery initiation, as Merkelbach had it, but revolves around the rites of passage to adulthood, especially marriage—appears to have an unstated affiliation with Freudian and Jungian readings.[45] This work should encourage scholars to take a fresh look at the psychological interpretations of *Cupid and Psyche*. Freudian and Jungian readings, in Apuleian

---

[39] Lewis 1956, 117 and 122.
[40] Lewis 1956, 133–4.
[41] Relihan 2009, 86–7; Gollnick 1992, 114–5.
[42] Gollnick 1992, 17; von Franz 1970 and Ulanov 1971 are the only Jungian interpreters to keep the rest of the *Metamorphoses* in mind.
[43] Neumann 1956, 153 and 158–159. For the Minoan origin theory, see Gere 2009, 132–9.
[44] Schlam 1992, 89.
[45] Burkert 1996; Bierl 2013; Merkelbach 1962.

scholarship, are treated as something less than an interpretation and also different from responses to *Cupid and Psyche* in literature and the visual arts. Riklin's *Cupid and Psyche* and the other psychoanalytic interpretations, however, at the very least, should join the ranks of literary receptions of Apuleius' tale.

Furthermore, I think Riklin put his finger on an important dark current in *Cupid and Psyche*. While Apuleius' *Cupid and Psyche* might not consist of a series of wishfulfilment hallucinations, madness is an important element in the tale. Psyche is not in her right mind, particularly after she learns the true identity of her husband. Upon seeing Cupid for the first time, she is said to be *impos animi* or 'out of one's mind, demented, not responsible for one's actions' (*Met.* 5.22.3).[46] Psyche is so demented, in fact, that she attempts suicide: 'She sank faint and trembling to her knees. She tried to hide the weapon—in her own heart' (*defecta tremensque desedit in imos poplites et ferrum quaerit abscondere, sed in suo pectore, Met.* 5.22.4). This sentence is fairly awkward, thanks to a correcting adversative (*sed*) which makes *abscondere* a zeugma—to hide and to thrust.[47] This zeugma captures nicely Psyche's panicked confusion.

Finally, *Cupid and Psyche* is a prime candidate for the kind of psychoanalytic literary analysis that Peter Brooks champions in *Reading for the Plot* (1984) and *Psychoanalysis and Storytelling* (1994). Brooks argues in the latter that psychoanalytic criticism is at its most effective when it does not focus on the writer and the characters but on the form and rhetoric of a narrative.[48] The features of *Cupid and Psyche* that are most significant from this perspective are the repetitive narrative structures in the middle of the story and the scene of storytelling in the frame narrative—the very elements Riklin eliminates in his epitomisation. Brooks is particularly interested in the interplay between features that propel a narrative forward and those that keep characters or readers from reaching a goal —such as repetitive plot elements in the middle of *Cupid and Psyche*—developing a theory of narrative and desire that draws on Freud's pleasure principle. Brooks is also interested in transference (the dynamics between analyst and analysand during psychoanalysis) and accordingly focuses on stories embedded in other stories, the relationship between storytellers and their audiences, and the way in which narratives can 'cure' audiences.[49] Stories, as Brooks puts it, 'ultimately

---

[46] *OLD* s.v. *impos* b; Zimmerman et al. 2004, 270 and Kenney 1990, 148 stress the word play any time *animus/anima* is used in the text in association with Psyche.
[47] Cf. Zimmerman et al. 2004, 275.
[48] Brooks 1994, 23 and 43–44. Another potential model is Whitmarsh 2011, who employs psychoanalytic narrative theory to help describe the narrative dynamics of the Greek novels.
[49] Brooks 1994, 78.

seek to change the minds and lives of those they touch.'[50] But what is puzzling about the narrating situation in *Cupid and Psyche* is that we do not exactly learn how the primary recipient, Charite, responds to the tale.

The point of these concluding, suggestive comments is to demonstrate that it is worth thinking about Riklin's fascinating, but largely forgotten retelling and interpretation of *Cupid and Psyche*. I believe Riklin could be a good starting point for future interpretations of Apuleius' beautiful tale that draw attention to its darker tones.

5 Bibliography

Bachofen, J. (1859), *Versuch über die Gräbersymbolik der Alten*, Basel.
Bachofen, J. (1967), *Myth, Religion, and Mother Right: Selected Writings of J.J. Bachofen*, R. Manheim, transl., London.
Bettelheim, B. (1976), *The Uses of Enchantment: The Meaning and Importance of Fairy Tales*, New York.
Bierl, A. (2013), 'From Mystery to Initiation: A Mytho-Ritual Poetics of Love and Sex in the Ancient Novel—even in Apuleius' *Golden Ass?*', in: Futre Pinheiro/Bierl/Beck, 82–99.
Binder, G./Merkelbach, R. (eds.) (1968), *Amor und Psyche*, Darmstadt.
Brodersen, S. (1998), 'Cupid's Palace—A Roman Villa (Apul. Met. 5,1)', in: Zimmerman et al. (1998), 113–125.
Brooks, P. (1984), *Reading for the Plot: Design and Intention in Narrative*, New York.
Brooks, P. (1994), *Psychoanalysis and Storytelling*, Oxford and Cambridge, MA.
Burkert, W. (1996), *Creation of the Sacred: Tracks of Biology in Early Religions*, Cambridge, MA.
Butler, S. (ed.) (2016a), *Deep Classics: Rethinking the Classical Tradition*, London.
Butler, S. (2016b), 'On the origin of "Deep Classics"', in: Butler 2016a: 1–19.
Creuzer, F. (1822), *Symbolik und Mythologie der alten Völker, besonders der Griechen*, Leipzig and Darmstadt.
Fehling, D. (1977), *Amor und Psyche: Die Schöpfung des Apuleius und ihre Einwirkung auf das Märchen, eine Kritik der romantischen Märchentheorie*, Wiesbaden.
Freud, S. (1913), 'The Theme of Three Caskets', in: Strachey, 289–302.
Friedländer, L. (1871), 'Das Märchen von Amor und Psyche' in Binder and Merkelbach 1968: 16–43.
Fusillo, M. (2003), 'Modern Critical Theories and the Ancient Novel', in: G. Schmeling (ed.), 277–305.
Futre Pinheiro, M.P./Bierl, A./Beck, R. (eds.) (2013), *Intende, Lector—Echoes of Myth, Religion and Ritual in the Ancient Novel*, Berlin and Boston.
Gamwell, L./Wells, R. (eds.) (1989), *Freud and Art: His Personal Collection of Antiquities*, Binghamton, New York.
Gere, C. (2009), *Knossos and the Prophets of Modernism*, Chicago.

---

50 Brooks 1994, 67.

Gill, C./Wiseman, T.P. (eds.) (1993), *Lies and Fiction in the Ancient World*, Exeter.
Gollnick, J. (1992), *Love and the Soul: Psychological Interpretations of the Eros and Psyche Myth*, Waterloo, Canada.
Grimal, P. (ed.) (1963), *Metamorphoseis (IV, 28-VI, 24): Le conte d'Amour et de Psyché*, Paris.
Harrison, S.J. (2000), *Apuleius: A Latin Sophist*, Oxford.
Harrison, S.J. (2013a), *Framing the Ass: Literary Texture of Apuleius' Metamorphoses*, Oxford.
Harrison, S.J. (2013b), 'Constructing Apuleius: The Emergence of a Literary Artists', in: Harrison 2013a, 13–37.
Hooper, W. (ed.) (1966), *C.S. Lewis: Selected Essays*, Cambridge.
James, P. (1987) *Unity in Diversity: A Study of Apuleius' Metamorphoses with Particular Reference to the Narrator's Art of Transformation and the Metamorphosis Motif in the Tale of Cupid and Psyche*, Hildesheim-Zurich-New York.
Jung, C.J. (1989), *Memories, Dreams, Reflections*, transl. R. Winston/C. Winston, New York.
Kenney, E.J. (ed.) (1990), *Apuleius: Cupid and Psyche*, Cambridge.
Lacan, J. (2015), *Seminar VIII: Transference*, Bruce Fink, transl., Cambridge and Malden, MA.
Laird, A. (1993), 'Fiction, Bewitchment and Story Worlds: The Implications of Claims to Truth in Apuleius', in: Gill/Wiseman, 147–174.
Lateiner, D. (2005), 'Review of Zimmerman, M. et al., eds (2004), *Apuleius Madaurensis. Metamorphoses. Books IV. 28–35, V and VI. 1–24. The Tale of Cupid and Psyche. Text, Introduction and Commentary*, Groningen. Groningen Commentaries on Apuleius', *BMCR* 2005.08.24.
Lee, B.T./Finkelpearl, E./Graverini, L. (eds.) (2014), *Apuleius and Africa*, New York and London.
Lewis, C.S. (1956), *Till We Have Faces: A Myth Retold*, San Diego and New York.
Lewis, C.S. (1966), 'Psycho-Analysis and Literary Criticism', in: Hooper, 286–300.
Liebrecht, F. (1879), 'Amor und Psyche', in: Binder/ Merkelbach, 44–55.
Merkelbach, R. (1962), *Roman und Mysterium in der Antike*, Munich.
Moreschini, C. (ed.) (1994), *Il mito di Amore e Psiche in Apuleio: saggio, testo di Apuleio, traduzione e comment*, Naples.
Morton, M. (2014), *Max Klinger and Wilhelmine Culture: On the Threshold of German Modernism*, Farnham, Surrey.
Neumann, E. (1956), *Amor and Psyche: The Psychic Development of the Feminine: A Commentary on the Tale by Apuleius*, transl., R. Manheim, Bollingen Series LIV, Princeton.
Norden, E. (1898), *Die Antike Kunstprosa*, Leipzig.
Plantade, E./Plantade, N. (2014), '*Libyca Psyche:* Apuleius' Narrative and Berber Folktales', in: Lee/Finkelpearl/Graverini, 174–202.
Reeve, M. (2008), 'The Re-Emergence of Ancient Novels in Western Europe', in: Whitmarsh 2008, 282–98.
Relihan, J. (ed.) (2009), *The Tale of Cupid and Psyche*, Indianapolis.
Riklin, F. (1908), *Wunscherfüllung und Symbolik im Märchen*, Leipzig and Vienna.
Riklin, F. (1915), *Wishfulfilment and Symbolism in Fairy Tales*, transl., W. White, New York.
Schlam, C. (1992), *The Metamorphoses of Apuleius: On Making an Ass of Oneself*, Chapel Hill.
Schmeling, G. (ed.) (2003), *The Novel and the Ancient World*. (Revised Edition), Boston and Leiden.

Schopenhauer, A. (2015), *Parerga and Paralipomena. Short Philosophical Essays*, vol. 2, transl., A. del Caro and C. Janaway, Cambridge.
Strachey, J. (ed.) (1953–1974), *The Standard Edition of the Complete Psychological Works of Sigmund Freud, Volume XII (1911–1913): The Case of Schreber, Papers on Technique and Other Works*, London.
Tatum, J. (1979), *Apuleius and the Golden Ass*, Ithaca.
Ulanov, A. (1971), *The Feminine in Jungian Psychology and in Christian Theology*, Evanston.
Van den Berk, T. (2012), *Jung on Art: The Autonomy of the Creative Drive*, New York.
Van Mal-Maeder, D./Zimmerman, M. (1998), 'The Many Voices in *Cupid and Psyche*', in: Zimmerman et al. 1998, 83–102.
Von Franz, M.-L. (1970, Revised 1992), *The Golden Ass of Apuleius: The Liberation of the Feminine in Man*, Boston and London.
Von Franz, M.-L. (1996), *The Interpretation of Fairy Tales: Revised Edition*, Boston and London.
Walsh, P.G. (1970), *The Roman Novel*, Cambridge (reprinted with addenda 1995, Bristol).
Whitmarsh, T. (2011), *Narrative and Identity in the Ancient Greek Novel*, Cambridge.
Whitmarsh, T. (ed.) (2008), *The Cambridge Companion to the Greek and Roman Novel*, Cambridge.
Zimmerman, M. (2012), *Apulei Metamorphoseon Libri XI*, Oxford.
Zimmerman, M. et al. (eds. 1998), *Aspects of Apuleius' Golden Ass. Vol. II: Cupid and Psyche*, Groningen.
Zimmerman, M./Panayotakis, S./Hunink, V.C./ Keulen, W. H./Harrison, S. J. /McCreight, T. D./ Wesseling, B./van Mal-Maeder, D. (eds.) (2004), *Apuleius Madaurensis Metamorphoses, Books IV 28–35, V, VI 1–24, The Tale of Cupid and Psyche*, Groningen.

Clemence Schultze
Psyche and Cupid in the Novels of Charlotte M. Yonge and Sylvia Townsend Warner

1 Introduction

The reworking of mythical material can lead to unexpected associations, such as that between Apuleius of Madaurus, sophist and alleged magician, and the Misses Yonge and Warner, each of whom chose to address the Psyche and Cupid story, adapting the myth to her own ends. Both set the tale in a relatively recent period of English history; both worked out ingenious equivalences of name and situation. And in both cases the original source went unrecognised by readers— so that each author was later obliged to explain her book's basis in myth. But in other respects there is little similarity between the two writers.

Charlotte Mary Yonge (1823–1901), chiefly famed for her bestselling romantic novel *The Heir of Redclyffe* (1853), passed her life in her native village near the English cathedral city of Winchester. Here the Tractarian poet and theologian the Reverend John Keble was her mentor during her girlhood.[1] Educated at home, she had a good command of languages, classics and history.[2] Her time, marked out by duties to God, the High Anglican Church and her family, was spent in writing and study, in journalism (as editor of a magazine for young women), and in home, parish and mission responsibilities. She never married; if the law had permitted women to vote, Yonge would certainly have been a Tory.

Some circumstances of Sylvia Townsend Warner's life (1893–1978) superficially resemble Yonge's: upper middle class English background (her father was a master at Harrow School) and home education. She too later lived permanently in a country village and was an essayist and journalist as well as a successful novelist. But in other ways the two greatly differ. From her late teens Warner had a 17-year secret liaison with a male musicological colleague. Then in her 30s she began a lesbian relationship with poet Valentine Ackland, which endured life-long despite Valentine's infidelities and her problems with

---

1 Dennis 1992, 7–51.
2 Schultze 2007; Walton 2010, 181–7.

drink and depression. Ackland was a Roman Catholic convert; Warner was wryly non-religious; both were firmly committed to the radical Left.³

Love and Life. An Old Story in Eighteenth Century Costume is a work of Yonge's later years (1880); *The True Heart* comes early in Warner's career (1929), following her bestselling contemporary feminist tale *Lolly Willowes* (1926). Both are historical novels, set respectively in 1739 and 1873. Yonge draws on eighteenth-century memoirs and fiction written in or about the era (especially Scott) for period detail, utilising Gothic and sensation novel tropes. Warner's book was born out of an intense engagement with the Essex sea-marshes, a liminal landscape, by turns prosaic and uncanny. Maybe it is partly owing to these fully imagined settings that early readers failed to identify the Apuleian model, despite the ample clues in plot and nomenclature offered by the authors.⁴ In a preface added to the 1882 (second) edition Yonge outlines 'the old fable on which it was founded', and explains that, like other re-handlings, her treatment is to be read typologically, as an allegory of the Christian life (Yonge 1882, ix-xi). In the Virago Press re-issue of *The True Heart* Warner relates how her retelling began as an exercise in writing; and how reviewers missed her ingenuity in disguising the characters: 'Only my mother recognised the basis of the story' (Warner 1978, [vi]).⁵

The narrative of Psyche's passage from innocence through ordeals to fulfilment can be regarded as a kind of *Bildungsroman*, and also recalls Gothic literature, with its imperilled but ultimately empowered heroines.⁶ The present paper aims to illustrate how the two authors exploit the myth's manifold applicability. It concentrates on Yonge's allegory of a Christian soul's progress, where the author draws extensively upon Gothic motifs, only to undercut them in the interests of her overall typological purpose. Warner's tale, which will be more briefly examined, possesses what might be termed a 'pastoral-Gothic' quality as background to a young woman's growth towards autonomy.

In examining the authors' use of the *Bildungsroman* it is helpful to utilise Prewitt Brown's division of this genre into two categories: novels of accountability, and novels of empowerment:

---

3 Harman 1989.
4 *Love and Life*'s final words (426) are 'Cupid and Psyche'; *The True Heart* ends (297) with the birth of 'Joy'.
5 In a 1954 letter Warner describes the writing exercise in musical terms: 'I wanted to do some serious technical study—to develop my wrist for narrative. So I thought I would write a canto fermo, as one does in learning counterpoint. *The True Heart* is on a canto fermo.' Maxwell and Steinman 2001, 51–2.
6 Williams 1995, 157–72.

In the purest examples of the former... the main character's recognition of his or her culpability is the single dramatic event informing all others: the point to which all else either leads up or from which it follows as a consequence. In [the latter category] the main character tries and fails until he or she succeeds in staking his claim to a place in the world.[7]

Love and Life belongs to the first group: its Gothic and sensation novel elements are employed to show the process whereby the abandoned and repentant heroine is re-integrated into the social and (more importantly for Yonge) the spiritual community. *The True Heart*, by contrast, ends with retreat to a rustic idyll, a fairy-tale place of safety.

2 *Love and Life*

The sub-title Yonge gave her novel, *An Old Story in Eighteenth Century Costume*, draws attention to the 'dressing-up' of the fable of *Cupid and Psyche*. The protagonist is Aurelia Delavie (Psyche), her Christian name (also denoting a type of butterfly) plays with the Greek term denoting 'soul', 'breath', and 'butterfly', while her surname evokes 'life'. Sir Amyas Belamour (Cupid, 'beautiful love') meets and falls in love with her. To get Aurelia out of the way, his mother Lady Belamour (Venus) compels Aurelia's father to send her as governess to Lady Belamour's young children (the Graces) by her second marriage to Mr Wayland (named after the mythological Wayland the Smith, to represent Vulcan). Initially frightened by Bowstead House, abode of reclusive dark-dwelling Mr Amyas Belamour (Sir Amyas's uncle) and his black servant, Aurelia gradually learns to give him the Christian sympathy that helps lift his remorseful depression. Sir Amyas discovers Aurelia's whereabouts and, with his uncle's consent, meets her in the darkened rooms and woos her (uncle always being present). Lady Belamour is furious, and to protect Aurelia, uncle and nephew arrange a secret marriage. Aurelia believes she is marrying elderly Mr Belamour but in fact her still-unseen husband is young Sir Amyas; after the marriage, her life at Bowstead continues exactly as before. One of Aurelia's sisters (well-meaning, not wicked) persuades her that out of self-respect she cannot accept the ban on seeing her husband, and gives her a light-making device. When Aurelia uses it, the shock causes Sir Amyas to fall concussed. Just as Aurelia discovers who her real husband is, Lady Belamour arrives, threatening her with prosecution. Aurelia flees and Lady Belamour consigns Mr Belamour to a private asylum. Aurelia, finding no help from any neighbour (Ceres, Diana etc.), visits a church where she

---

7 Prewitt Brown 2013, 668.

repents of running away, choosing instead to throw herself on Lady Belamour's mercy. She is imprisoned in a grim mansion to make her sign a disclaimer of her marriage. Lady Belamour sets her tasks: one is to search out a recipe for cosmetics to be taken to Cora Darke, a perfumer (Kore/Proserpina). This aptly-named underworld figure is also a procuress, tasked with drugging Aurelia and dispatching her abroad. Meanwhile, father and husband rescue Mr Belamour from the asylum and search for Aurelia, reaching her just as she is put, still unconscious, on Captain Karen's (Charon's) ship that is to bear her off to a forced marriage in the Indies. Lady Belamour's husband Mr Wayland returns from abroad to see justice done for his wife's wicked plotting. The next morning Aurelia awakens to the presence and knowledge of her husband.[8]

3 'Gothic' and sensation novel tropes

This summary of the story makes clear both the Apuleian parallels and the narrative elements deriving from Gothic and from sensation novels. Its Gothic devices include: (i) architecture; (ii) darkness; (iii) sexual threat; (iv) experiences of near-death and apparent death.

In its *architecture*, Bowstead presents as 'a tall house, perfectly dark, with strange fantastic gables and chimneys... as still as death.' (*LL* 79). Later, however, Aurelia is totally isolated in Delavie House: 'the emptiness of Bowstead was nothing to this, and [Aurelia] smiled to herself at having thought herself a prisoner there' (*LL* 347). Architecture also functions in the Gothic as more than the physical building: as a container of the past, where lurk both specific mystery/mysteries and history/histories; these include the threat of being lost, and of losing oneself.[9] The history/mystery at Bowstead is revealed in the person and past of reclusive Mr Amyas Belamour, who is truly the one lost to light and life until recovered by Aurelia. At Delavie House, by contrast, Aurelia could actually lose herself if she succumbed to the temptation of disowning her marriage—as it were, rejecting her own past. The more sinister atmosphere of the latter house expresses the far greater danger to the heroine's identity.

Darkness is a key motif of a novel where light and life are equated on a real and on a spiritual level. The 'melancholic' Mr Amyas Belamour, having killed his

---

8 Yonge, brought up on Walter Scott's novels, also knew the multi-faceted Wayland Smith in *Kenilworth:* servant, physician, and fixer. 'Wayland' is thus a doubly appropriate name for the *deus ex machina* here. On *Kenilworth*, see Michael Paschalis's paper in this volume.
9 DeLamotte 1990, 14–6.

fiancée Mary's brother in a duel, has chosen from remorse to dwell in 'utter darkness and seclusion' (*LL* 24). Aurelia visits him out of compassion, and gradually brings him back to light and life, reminding him of the possibility of salvation through repentance.[10]

The motif of the *sexually threatened heroine*, a staple of romance, was adopted in the eighteenth century into realist novels by writers such as Samuel Richardson, whose Clarissa and Pamela resist seduction and rape until death or a triumphant vindication (even though Clarissa is raped when drugged). Gothic writers such as Sophia Lee and Ann Radcliffe extend the range of potential threats, depicting heroines whose virtue, socio-economic status and sanity are variously endangered.[11] Considerations of propriety made the sexual aspect a difficult area for Yonge; she addresses it via a quasi-Radcliffeian story of imprisonment and abduction. Aurelia travels from home to Bowstead (removal from first state of innocence), to Delavie House (imprisonment with ordeals), to Cora Darke's workshop, where she is drugged (threat of a forced marriage, implying rape).

Near-death or apparent death is experienced by three of the characters. Mr Belamour, self-sentenced in his darkened room, enacts a living death. His nephew Sir Amyas is accidentally struck unconscious when Aurelia ignites the phosphoric cotton given her by her sister. 'Death-like' at the time, he later reports feeling 'bound down' (Yonge 1882, 246–7; 276), an experience shared by many victims in Gothic novels, either literally bound, or paralysed by fear. Here the association with his mother's presence evokes the compelling power which she (Venus) exercises over the other characters. Sometimes this manifests itself as charm, at other times as a kind of force, inspiring awe and obedience (e. g. 330, 404). And finally, Aurelia, in the drug-induced sleep facilitating her abduction on the ship, lies 'like [a] chrysalis' (375, 400), without 'power to move' (402).

Plots abounding with such Gothic motifs are unusual in Yonge's repertoire. The protagonists in her contemporary-set novels are tested through moral situations requiring patience, endurance and forbearance in ordinary daily existence. Aurelia too undergoes the like, but the historical setting gives scope for much more dramatic ordeals, imposed by Lady Belamour's machinations. Yet what Yonge is demonstrably doing here is to employ these trappings of the Gothic, but then largely to undercut them. The atmosphere of Bowstead belies its architecture; those who are dark (the black servant) or dwell in the dark (Mr Bela-

---

10 On this key concept in Yonge's novels see Colón 2012, 54–61.
11 Wallace 2013, ch. 1 and 2. Clery 2002 discusses the relationship between romance, realism and the Gothic.

mour) prove to be friendly or pitiable rather than threatening. The suggestions of sexual threat are understated. Sir Amyas' phase of unconsciousness is admittedly quite alarming in evoking total powerlessness; by contrast, Aurelia's drugged sleep is quasi-natural, for it is the 'chrysalis' phase from which the Aurelia butterfly (from antiquity onwards linked to Psyche as an emblem of the soul)[12] will emerge. In short, *Love and Life*'s Gothic aspects in setting and incident are played with but then played down, while significant elements which allude to the 'sensation novel' genre are embedded within it.

The sensation novel which flourished from the 1860s onwards was typically plot-driven, featuring crimes, secrets, madness and extreme passions in the heart of the respectable home: bigamy, illegitimacy, impersonation and incarceration abound. Doubleness (mistaken or pretended identity) has been claimed as the 'generic principle' of the sensation novel[13] and Victorian authors saw the eighteenth century as the characteristic locus of doubleness.[14] This element features in *Love and Life*, the plot of which depends on the doubling of the hero and his homonymous uncle. Linked with it is confusion and derangement of faculties (an experience common to both Gothic and sensation novel characters). Guilt has brought Mr Belamour to morbid reclusiveness that is close to insanity; and Aurelia is almost overthrown by the deliberate mystification surrounding her wooer's identity.

The role of Cupid is in fact shared between no fewer than three characters. With these triune Cupids Yonge may be alluding to the tradition that this god, one of the oldest on Olympus, nevertheless looks like a boy.[15] The young son of Lady Belamour and her second husband is Archer Wayland: this minor character represents Cupid as mischievous child. The significant doubling, however, is that of the homonyms, Mr and Sir Amyas Belamour. On this depends the plot's central element, the secret wedding in a darkened room. But before a wedding there must be a wooing. Here Yonge exploits the doubleness theme in order to reveal the awakening of love between Aurelia and Sir Amyas. In the Apuleian version that love is a consummated sexual relationship. In typological terms, it stands as the Type of the Soul's relation to Christ as the Beloved; it is the strength and power of that love which enables the Soul to withstand the ordeals it encounters before the final eternal union. But it would be unthinkable for Yonge to allow a sexual union to take place: even after the secret wedding ceremony, the only physical intimacy she permits is a single kiss. It appears that, ir-

---

12 Icard-Gianolio in *LIMC* 7.1, 582–5 and 7.2, pl. 60.
13 Hughes 1980, 20.
14 Williams 2004, 60–1.
15 I thank Regine May for this point.

respective of eighteenth-century marriage legislation, Yonge does not regard a secret marriage as a valid Church sacrament. Indeed, Yonge's Victorian sense of propriety will not even countenance any unchaperoned encounter between Aurelia and Sir Amyas. She is faced, therefore, with the problem of making Aurelia fall in love without actually seeing her husband-to-be. How, then, is she to be wooed?

The role of 'Cupid as lover' is accordingly divided between the two Amyases. Young Sir Amyas falls in love at first sight at a country dance. Fidelity to the fable requires that Aurelia, on the other hand, must not actually *see* the beloved, so Yonge makes her too shy to look higher than her partner's feet. Thereafter Mr Amyas Belamour functions as a proxy wooer, for Yonge can permit her heroine to be alone in a dark room with a man some thirty years older than herself. Since he is early established as refined and considerate, as well as reclusive, Aurelia's honour and chastity are secure. The age disparity is balanced by the light (first metaphorical, later literal) which Aurelia (whose name may be a pun on Aurora/Dawn) brings into his life. In physical terms, all each knows of the other is by voice and an occasional touch of the hand. But in order to reinforce the story's parallel with what Yonge terms the 'fairy myths' of Beauty and the Beast and the Black Bull of Norroway (Yonge 1882: ix), there is necessarily a repellent aspect to the hermit. This has Gothic overtones: when giving Aurelia a ring, Mr Belamour lightly kisses her fingers—but, at a period when clean shaving was customary, the feel of his hermit's beard 'conveyed a sense of squalor and neglect almost amounting to horror' (153).

Yonge, needing to make credible a degree of attraction between heroine and husband-to-be, emphasises the beauty and charm of youthful Sir Amyas. But in comparison with his uncle's developed personality he is an immature Prince Charming, whose chief trait is devotion to Aurelia. Well may Aurelia's father ask her, after her rescue, for which of the two Amyases she really feels love (Yonge 1882, 403; 406–7): a valid doubt, given that the two young people have scarcely spoken to each other. Aurelia, however, emphatically asserts her love for the younger Amyas. Yonge has prepared the ground for this by delicate but clear intimations of the increasing physical attraction between the two on the occasions when Sir Amyas, concealed in his uncle's darkened room, addresses Aurelia. She is bewildered by varying voices from different directions; and unsettled yet excited by the passionate words and warm handclasps so at odds with Mr Belamour's usual demeanour (199).

Aurelia, in saying 'yes' to the right Amyas in the belief that he is the other one, is thus implicated in the doubleness plot, her confusion as to her own (future) identity expressed through the stirring of her senses and her fainting. There is recognition not only that men (males) operate in two modes but also that these evoke reactions in women, whether of alarm or response. As the meetings go on, and the suitor varies between staid and ardent, Aurelia finds that his 'endearments... thrilled her with such strange emotions' (Yonge 1882, 207). After the secret marriage has taken place, Aurelia is embraced by her husband (213) with one kiss, so that then a further sensation novel trope comes into play: the wedded bride who is not a wife.

4 Typology, myth and Tractarian 'reserve'

The 1882 preface to *Love and Life* shows Yonge knew other typological renderings of this myth, and she specifically mentions Calderón's two *autos sacramentales*, sacred dramas that employed it to teach the lesson of Faith, not Sight (viii-ix). Her magazine *The Monthly Packet* published a retelling which described Psyche as 'a type of the soul thirsting after perfection, yet subject to the weaknesses ... [of] a mortal nature'.[16] Significantly, that article took its epigraph from Isaac Williams: 'They spoke of things more glorious than they knew.' (*The Cathedral*, 'The North Transept', stanza XXII.) This was a quotation favoured by Tractarians who discerned in the 'pagan' writers of classical antiquity the foreshadowing of Christian belief.[17] Just as Old Testament persons related as Types to the Christian Antitype, so too could classical figures function typologically. And, importantly, the natural world itself did the same. John Keble's *Tract* 89 'On the Mysticism attributed to the Fathers of the Church' (1841) laid out a system of typological thinking applied to nature (itself the providential work of God).[18] Lecturing as Professor of Poetry at Oxford in the 1830s, he developed a theory of poetry which held

> that the associative coherence which characterizes the work of a great poet must make their poetry expressive of, or stand in a typological relationship to, the 'idea' of the providential economy of Christianity even in cases such as Virgil or Aeschylus where this could not be a conscious intention.[19]

This conception, which also entails a hermeneutical practice of close reading, applies to other literary forms—including the novel. Charlotte Yonge, acquainted with Keble from 1836 and greatly influenced by his thinking, discussed with him

---

[16] 'Yarach' 1854, 370–1.
[17] Williams 1849 applies the theory of Types to the university teaching of classical literature.
[18] Shaw 1987, 189–98.
[19] Budge 2007, 114; cf. 46–50.

her books in progress. Not surprisingly, therefore, 'typological realism' pervades her own approach to novel-writing, 'informing minute details of plot and characterization'.[20] This operates irrespective of setting, applying, as Budge demonstrates apropos *The Heir of Redclyffe*, to her contemporary-set works, just as much as to those novels which actually draw their plots from myth.[21]

Closely connected with this typological mode of viewing the world is the important Tractarian doctrine of Reserve.[22] Far from being (as misperceived or deliberately caricatured by some opponents) a deliberate and sinister concealment of 'Romish' doctrines, it was in fact a temper of restraint or 'economy' (J.H. Newman's term) in addressing sacred subjects. This entails far more than respect for place and person, or self-control in expression and demeanour: it requires a sustained attitude of self-disciplined obedience in the great and small matters of daily life, work, and intellectual activity so as to lead to a gradual increase in understanding. '[S]alvation depends upon habits of holy living and reverence towards God' not on 'broadcast[ing] religious instruction'.[23] Reserve was as vital to Tractarian aesthetics as to their theology and liturgy. Allegory and typology were embraced as being appropriate to the treatment of doctrine and belief: this applied equally to poetry, to novels, and to children's tales. The minutest details of natural phenomena or everyday life point, by analogy, to spiritual truths, that are to be grasped ever more fully. A novel such as *Love and Life* is accordingly typological not only in its overall structure—the mapping of a soul's progress onto a classical myth—but in many tiny individual points of plot, theme and incident.

5 Natural typology. Light

An instance of Yonge's method is shown by the constant equation of light with truth—both factual and scientific truth, and also religious truth. A Newtonian clergyman-scientist supplies the phosphorised cotton that provides Aurelia with the light to see her husband. In Yonge's view, science, rightly understood, did not controvert religious faith but supported it.[24] So it is appropriately through this man's agency that Sir Amyas' identity is revealed.

---

20 Budge 2007, 126.
21 Schultze 1999, 2014.
22 Pereiro 2008, 115–121.
23 Colón 2010, 224.
24 Chen 2010, 368–73.

Mr Belamour is introduced as living in the darkness of despair; hence light represents his gradual acceptance that salvation is possible. Texts recited by Aurelia, especially those placed on his fiancée's grave ('Love is as strong as Death', *Song of Solomon* 8.6–7, and 'Sorrow not as others that have no Hope', 1 *Thess.* 13), serve to recall Christian redemption (Yonge 1882, 114, 119). Soon afterwards he is able to go out by night to visit the grave, remaining until dawn (120). This marks the dawning of spiritual light; thereafter he gradually returns to the enjoyment of society and normal life.

Darkness also typifies the spiritual trials which Aurelia undergoes before achieving reunion with her Love. When imprisoned, she is nightly plagued by rats, representing the dread of total abandonment. Daylight disperses the rats; patience and self-imposed occupation enable her to endure the forsakenness; she recites her sacred texts from memory (Yonge 1882, 341–349). This is the phase in which, typologically speaking, the Soul has come to feel love for the Bridegroom, Christ, but has achieved only partial knowledge, owing to distraction and dissipation of effort. Trust and faith must still be learnt during the ordeal of separation. Only after death will there be full union of the Soul with Christ.

Here too Yonge employs markers of light and darkness. The perfumer/procuress, Mrs Darke, is the pitiless goddess of death in unrepented sin. The drug she administers produces a death-like sleep, in which Aurelia remains for some time before gradually coming back to life in the glow of sunset (Yonge 1882, 399–404). At dusk she is restored to her family, but it is only after confessing at dawn (405) her mistrust and disobedience that she finally (for the first time ever) properly beholds her Love, Sir Amyas: he is 'dazzling' in the full light of day (407).[25]

Despair and loss of faith are phenomena which Yonge recognises in her contemporary novels. She would deem it more than impertinent to scrutinise their effects directly or to depict characters in the act of self-examination or prayer. So it is all very un-Evangelical, very unlike the dramatic tracts of confession, conversion and death-bed repentance which formed an important strand in English religious literature from the eighteenth century onwards. Accordingly, Mr Belamour does not analyse his own spiritual progress; instead, he is shown as gradually regaining faith through hearing God's word via Aurelia's recitation of psalms and texts, until he literally sees the light of day at Mary's grave. In this portion, roles are reversed: Aurelia is the medium whereby the Church's message

---

[25] Similarly in *The Heir of Redclyffe*. a glorious sunset leads Guy towards the duty of forgiveness. Budge 2007, 141–4 brings out the difference between typology and symbolism here.

is brought to the sinner, and Mr Belamour is the Everyman figure, the awakening Soul. This makes it clear that Yonge's narrative, on the realist level apparently highly gendered, is in fact, when regarded typologically, not gendered at all: Aurelia and Mr Belamour are on a par as regards faithlessness and near-despair. The young girl and the man who killed another in a duel are in need of exactly the same message of love and hope. Thus, later, at a morning service where she again sees the first text from the grave, Aurelia recognises how she has failed in obedience to her husband and in trust in God's protection; accordingly, she gives herself up to Lady Belamour (Yonge 1882, 261–265). The use of scripture and/or a church service to mark such a turning point is a characteristic instance of Reserve in Yonge's novels.

So Yonge is shaping a very particular kind of *Bildungsroman*, one portraying the formation of a Christian soul by means of obedience and endurance through temptations and tribulations, and culminating in its union with the divine. As Mr Belamour reflects at the close: 'A soul trained by love and suffering, as in the old legend' (Yonge 1882, 409).

6 *The True Heart*

Sylvia Townsend Warner's novel of 1926 can be treated more briefly. The protagonist is Sukey Bond, a 16-year-old orphan whose chief characteristic is naïve obedience: her surname expresses the constraints imposed on her by society and her own personality. She is sent as a servant to some Essex farmers, the Nomans, silent incurious people who represent the unseen denizens of Cupid's palace. The job has been arranged for her by the Venus character, the aptly named Mrs Seaborn, wife to the Reverend Smith Seaborn and a supporter of the orphanage. Mrs Seaborn, ashamed of her simple 'idiot' son, Eric (Eros), has chosen to keep his existence a secret by housing him with the Nomans. He is kind but fey, loving, and incapable of inflicting pain. He and Sukey fall in love and wish to marry. Prudence, a former servant in the house, (characterised by a knowing worldliness that equates her to Psyche's sisters), asserts herself by forcing Sukey to kill a cockerel. Sukey fails to get Eric's help, resents his lack of understanding, and finally kills the bird herself. This causes Eric to fall in a fit, and a furious Mrs Seaborn descends and removes him. Sukey pleads in vain to Mrs Seaborn and is spurned by her servants Rew and Grieve (Sollicitudo and Tristities), but meets Pan as a helpful tramp, Ceres as publican Mrs Disbrowe, and ox-eyed Juno as Mrs Oxey, brothel-keeper. She finds work on another farm. Here Prudence visits her, and recounts how Mrs Seaborn is aggrieved to the point of madness by social slights caused by the unexplained arrival of a son hitherto unknown to her neighbours. Sukey conceives the notion that a Bible from Queen Victoria will assuage Mrs Seaborn's anguish, and sets off to London. Encountering helpers who take her to the mourning Queen, she receives the Bible. Sukey and Eric are reunited as Mrs Seaborn, maddened by disgrace, spurns the Bible. Her relative Mr Warburton (Jupiter) intervenes, sending Mrs Seaborn for a rest-cure and establishing Sukey and Eric as bee-keepers. The book ends as their daughter, Joy, is born.

7 A feminist fairy-tale?

Warner makes Sukey's story a feminist *Bildungsroman*, expressing female empowerment via growth in (i) self-assertion; (ii) self-knowledge; and (iii) discernment in handling others.

Self-assertion develops in a character whose 'one salient gift was a knack for obedience—a knack that amounted almost to a genius' (Warner 1978, 6). Warner describes her employment with characteristic irony:

> Her wages were to be ten pounds a year, and nothing more was required of her than honesty, industry, cleanliness, sobriety, obedience, punctuality, modesty, Church of England principles, good health and a general knowledge of housework ... (4).

But later Sukey sticks to her decision to leave the Nomans' farm: 'She felt herself slipping back into the dominion of the old tender conscience, the old docility, but she held on to her resolution and was silent.' (88).

Sukey's quest also demonstrates her new assertiveness, for it is not an ordeal imposed by Venus but an undertaking determined by herself. One motive is her concern for Mrs Seaborn's pain but more important is her resolve to recover Eric: 'free, bartered for a Bible, ransomed by her slyness' (Warner 1978, 204). Warner's version diverges from the Apuleian tradition, downplaying Venus' agency in order to emphasise the heroine as autonomous and active, in contrast to the passive and vulnerable Eric.

Self-knowledge grows in Sukey concomitantly with understanding of others and of love itself. This climaxes in the cockerel-killing scene when Eric seems to her beautiful and beloved as never before (Warner 1978, 67) and yet he fails the test. What she wishes to say is given, in a lengthy imagined speech, ending: 'Show yourself be real to me, let me trust you, come alive and take this love that I cannot give you properly unless you open yourself to it and take it in!' (69). What she actually does is to ask him—indeed, attempt physically to force him—to kill the cockerel. His complete inability to do so and his empathy with the bird evokes remorse in her for even trying to compel him. Though herself pitying the bird, she nevertheless dispatches it. As Eric collapses, seemingly dying, 'his face convulsed, his breath snoring and sobbing' (72), Sukey is devastated but enlightened. Just at the moment when her malicious quasi-sister Prudence shows her that the world sees only 'an idiot in a fit' and herself as an ignorant fool (73), Sukey recognises that her own love for Eric transcends his total failure to help her.

Discernment is a quality the guileless Sukey initially lacks, making her vulnerable to manipulation. But she learns how to engage with others so that they will act in her interests, sometimes employing judicious silence, sometimes by speech. Questioned by Queen Victoria about Mrs Seaborn's son, she replies: 'Your Majesty… I am afraid he is not a comfort to her, just now.' (Warner 1978, 265). This induces the Queen—worried (the reader infers) about the reprobate Prince of Wales—to respond positively to Sukey's request for a Bible.

The setting for Sukey's growth in autonomy is the agricultural Essex marshland, reclaimed from the sea; its mists and tides create a dreamlike and unreal quality. The Nomans, though quite kindly, are silent and bearlike in their movements, as befits the non-human inhabitants of a magical realm. In this pastoral-Gothic isolation, Eric, ungraspable and playful, is the most physically real being that Sukey encounters. Love emboldens Sukey to go on her London quest where, protected by her innocence, she finds a variety of improbable helpers.[26] The end result of Sukey's *Bildung*, however, is essentially a retreat.[27] Sukey and Warburton (Jupiter), considering what Eric's well-being demands, agree on 'a country life… a settled life… Bees would do excellently well.' (Warner 1978, 287; 291). In a certain sense this fits the myth admirably; but, adopting Prewitt Brown's categorisation of *Bildungsromane* (mentioned above), Sukey's growth towards empowerment has ceased, and the plot's fairy-tale elements come to the fore. The heroine has learnt to assert herself and gained her love-object—an unheroic lover, whose vulnerability requires protection.

8 Conclusion

Two more different authors can scarcely be imagined; two diverse novels result from exploration of the same myth. Yonge's may be judged more successful in

---

26 David Garnett objected that here 'you invite the reader to feel superior to your heroine.' (Garnett 1994, 45).
27 Beer 1999, 76 holds that the novel 'struggles awkwardly with innocence and ends with the acceptance of a yoked life'.

achieving her specific aims, in that every element of the myth coheres with the allegory. Warner, on the other hand, appears in the end constrained by the need to retain the structure of the Apuleian story, resulting in a mismatch between the thrust of the ongoing narrative and its conclusion.

In several respects, Warner's work seems to provide an ironic response to issues addressed by Yonge's retelling: was Warner aware of the earlier novel? It is not inconceivable. Nineteenth century children's books featured in Warner's wide childhood reading,[28] and Yonge's were still popular and widely available, many of them in print, others obtainable from libraries. It is impossible to read the description of the requirements imposed on Sukey—honesty, industry, Church of England principles, and so on (quoted above)—without recalling Miss Yonge's support, in life and in her contemporary-set fiction, for the Girls' Friendly Society, an organisation aimed at providing social and educational contacts for girls and young women of good character working in domestic service. It is hard to avoid the notion that in depicting Mrs Seaborn/Venus as a vicar's wife Warner is having a little joke at the expense of the numerous worthy women (and the few lazy or snobbish ones) who fulfil this role in Yonge's novels. It seems unlikely that Yonge would have been happy with a cross-class match between an orphanage girl (however industrious) and a clergyman's son, quite apart from the supposed health considerations.[29] And churchgoing and church beliefs play only a very minor role in Sukey's life, and are handled with a sparkling irreverence that Yonge would doubtless have deplored.[30] Finally, one of Yonge's most admired authors was Sir Walter Scott, himself a reader of Apuleius, as Paschalis shows in this volume, and *The Heart of Midlothian* was one of his best-regarded novels.[31] In dispatching her heroine on her unprotected quest to London and Queen Victoria, does not Warner have in mind Jeanie Deans and her mission to beg for mercy for her sister Effie from Queen Caroline, consort of George II? It is during the reign of that very king that *Love and Life* is set. None of this is provable, of course, but it seems not unlikely that from the vantage point of 1929, even as she addressed the same classical myth, the younger author of advanced opinions and modern life-style looked back upon the worldview of her predecessor, and bade farewell to all that Victorianism stood for.

---

28 Maria Edgeworth, for one: Warner and Maxwell 1982, 12.
29 Warner addresses contemporary eugenic concerns in this risky love between unprivileged Sukey and 'idiot' Eric: Wachman 2000.
30 e.g. the preachers described in: Warner 1978, 23–4.
31 Yonge 1864, ch. 15.

9 Bibliography

'Yarach' (1854), 'Mythological legends—Eros and Psyche', *Monthly Packet* 7/41, 342–71.
Beer, G. (1999), 'Sylvia Townsend Warner: "the centrifugal kick"', in: Joannou, 76–86.
Budge, G. (2007), *Charlotte M. Yonge: religion, feminism and realism in the Victorian novel*, Bern.
Chen, M. (2010), '"To face apparent discrepancies with revelation": examining the fossil record in Charlotte Yonge's *The Trial*', *Women's Writing* 17/2, 361–79.
Clery, E. J. (2002), 'The genesis of "Gothic" fiction', in: Hogle, 21–39.
Colón, S. E. (2010), 'Realism and reserve: Charlotte Yonge and Tractarian aesthetics', *Women's Writing* 17/2, 221–35.
Colón, S. E. (2012) *Victorian parables*, London.
Courtney, J./Schultze, C. (eds.) (2007), *Characters and scenes: studies in Charlotte M. Yonge*, Abingdon.
DeLamotte, E. C. (1990), *Perils of the night. A feminist study of nineteenth-century gothic*, New York.
Dennis, B. (1992), *Charlotte Yonge (1823–1901), novelist of the Oxford Movement: a literature of Victorian culture and society*, Lampeter.
Gardner, H./Murnaghan, S. (eds.) (2014), *Odyssean identities in modern cultures: the journey home*, Columbus, OH.
Garnett, R. (ed.) (1994), *Sylvia and David. The Townsend Warner/Garnett letters*. London.
Harman, C. (1989), *Sylvia Townsend Warner: a biography*, London.
Hogle, J. (ed.) (2002), *The Cambridge companion to Gothic fiction*, Cambridge.
Hughes, W. (1980). *The maniac in the cellar: sensation novels of the 1860s*, Princeton.
Joannou, M. (ed.) (1999), *Women writers of the 1930s. Gender, politics and history*, Edinburgh.
Maxwell, W./Steinman, M. (eds.) (2001), *The element of lavishness: letters of Sylvia Townsend Warner and William Maxwell, 1938–1978*, Washington, D.C.
O'Gorman, F./Turner, K. (eds.) (2004). *The Victorians and the eighteenth century: reassessing the tradition*, Aldershot.
Pereiro, J. (2008), *Ethos and the Oxford Movement: at the heart of Tractarianism*, Oxford.
Prewitt Brown, J. (2013), 'The moral scope of the English *Bildungsroman*', in: Rodensky, 663–78.
Rodensky, L. (ed.) (2013), *The Oxford handbook of the Victorian novel*, Oxford.
Schultze, C. (1999), 'Manliness and the myth of Hercules in Charlotte M. Yonge's *My Young Alcides*', *International Journal of the Classical Tradition* 5, 383–414.
Schultze, C. (2007), 'Charlotte Yonge and the classics', in: Courtney/Schultze, 159–88.
Schultze, C. (2014), 'Absent fathers and faithful wives: Penelope-figures in the novels of Charlotte Yonge', in: Gardner and Murnaghan, 64–85.
Shaw, W. D. (1987), *The lucid veil: poetic truth in the Victorian age*, Madison, WI.
Wachman, G. (2000), 'The true story of England's greatness: degeneracy, primitivism, eugenics', *Journal of the Sylvia Townsend Warner Society* 2000, 34–42.
Wallace, D. (2013), *Female gothic histories: gender, history and the gothic*, Cardiff.
Walton, S. (2010), *Imagining soldiers and fathers in the mid-Victorian era. Charlotte Yonge's models of manliness*, Farnham.
Warner, S.T. (1978), *The True Heart*, (second edition), London. (First edition 1929).

Warner, S.T. /Maxwell, W. (ed.) (1982), *Letters*. London.
Williams, A. (1995), *Art Of Darkness: A Poetics Of Gothic*, Chicago.
Williams, C. D. (2004), '"The dreams of thy youth": Bucks, belles and half-way men in Victorian fiction', in: O'Gorman/Turner, 57–75.
Williams, I. (1849), *The Christian Scholar*, Oxford.
Yonge, C. M. (1853), *The Heir of Redclyffe*. London.
Yonge, C. M. (1864), *The Trial*. London.
Yonge, C. M. (1882), *Love and Life: an old story in eighteenth century costume* (second edition), London. (First edition 1880).

IV Twentieth Century and Modernism

Julia Haig Gaisser
Eudora Welty's *The Robber Bridegroom*. *Cupid and Psyche* on the Natchez Trace

Eudora Welty (1909–2001) was one of the most highly regarded American writers of the twentieth century. She spent most of her long life in her birthplace, Jackson, Mississippi; but her influence and interests extended far beyond the American South.[1] Although Welty is best known for her short stories, she also wrote memorable essays about books and writing, reviews of authors as different as William Faulkner and Virginia Woolf, a novel, and a memoir, *One Writer's Beginnings*.[2] This short memoir is a superb introduction to Welty's life and work, and especially to her unique literary voice, which is colloquial and expressive, humane, attuned to darkness and injustice, but often extremely funny. My subject in this paper is an early work, published in 1942: her only novella, *The Robber Bridegroom*.

The Robber Bridegroom has as its principal themes identity and the inexorable changes wrought by the passage of time.[3] These themes are developed in a narrative that is a complex amalgam of characters, stories, and genres from three disparate sources: the Grimms' fairy tales, Apuleius, and Mississippi legend. Its most obvious component is the Grimms' eponymous tale, 'The Robber Bridegroom' ('Der Räuberbräutigam'), embellished with touches of other tales, including 'Cinderella' and 'Snow White'. Apuleius' story of *Cupid and Psyche* is embedded in the old fairy tale, and together the Robber Bridegroom and Psyche are transported to the real world of Mississippi legend, the Natchez Trace, a beautiful and dangerous wilderness inhabited by settlers, bandits, and Indians in the eighteenth and early nineteenth centuries.[4] The story of *Cupid and Psyche* is the least conspicuous element of the three. It is so inconspicuous, in fact, that critics usually ignore or pass over it.[5] Welty herself, as we shall see, barely men-

---

1 See Marrs 2005, with earlier bibliography.
2 Welty 1984.
3 Important discussions include French 1979; Randisi 1982, 1–28; Kreyling 1986.
4 But Welty put it the other way: 'I transposed these horrors [of life along the Natchez Trace]— along with the felicities that also prevailed—into the element that I thought suited both just as well, or better—the fairy tale'. Welty 1978, 309.
5 The few critics who mention it tend to speak only in general terms, treating it as a myth rather than a specific literary model (e.g. Chamlee 1991; Kreyling 1999, 38; Randisi 1982, 3–5). Weston (1994, 173–83), following Neumann 1956, discusses 'Welty's use of the myth of Psyche in the light of female psychic development'.

tioned it. In what follows, however, I will suggest that it is a major intertext in the work and that it plays an essential role in its shape and conception. I will begin with Welty's three sources and their use in the narrative and then turn to their relation to her overarching themes of identity and time and change.

First, the Grimms. In their tale a beautiful young girl is betrothed by her father to a suitor whom she instinctively dislikes. The man insists that she visit him in his house deep in the forest, and she reluctantly proceeds through the dark woods to his dark and silent cottage. As she enters, a bird in a cage hanging on the wall calls out to her:

> Turn back, turn back, young maiden dear,
> 'Tis a murderer's house you enter here.[6]

In the cellar she finds an old woman who warns her that her betrothed and his gang are murderers and cannibals who kill young girls, chop them up, and eat them for dinner. The old woman hides her behind a barrel—and just in time, too, for in come the drunken robbers, dragging another girl with them. They poison her, chop her up, and season the pieces with salt. One cuts off her finger to get her golden ring, but the finger flies up and into the lap of the lurking heroine. Fortunately for her, the murderers are too drunk to retrieve it, and after they fall into a stupor, the girl and the old woman escape. Later, the girl tells the whole tale at her wedding feast, producing the finger as evidence, and her bridegroom and his henchmen are arrested and executed.

From the Grimms Welty borrowed her title along with several other elements: the beautiful girl and her two-faced suitor, the forest, the dangerous house, the talking bird, the robbers, and the hideous murder. She transformed them all, changing the fairy tale into a work of fiction. It is still fantastic, but it follows the dictum in Welty's article, 'Place in Fiction': that 'fantasy itself must touch ground with at least one toe'.[7] For her that grounding is above all specificity of place and time, and this specificity gives rise to the characters that belong to them.

This brings us to our second source, Mississippi legend and the Natchez Trace. Welty's setting is the looming forest in which most of the action takes place. The forest is a standard fixture of fairy tales, a place apart from the safe hamlet of ordinary life —dangerous to enter, hard to escape, and filled with human and animal predators. Consider *Hansel and Gretel* or *Little Red Rid-*

---

6 Welty 1978b, 307.
7 Welty 1978c, 126. She continues: 'and ghost stories must have one foot, so to speak, in the grave'.

ing Hood—or, for that matter—the Grimms' *Robber Bridegroom*. Welty's forest has the same qualities, but differs in one profound and essential respect. Fairy tale forests are imaginary; they have no name and are not to be found on a map. But Welty's forest is real. It is the wilderness that once surrounded the Natchez Trace, a primeval track starting at the Mississippi River and running north-east for over four hundred miles—from present-day Natchez, Mississippi to Nashville, Tennessee. The track was formed thousands of years ago by animals migrating along the ridge lines above the river. Much later came various tribes of Native Americans, building settlements and enlarging and deepening the trail, which, like the city at its base, gets its name from the Natchez people. A millennium later, European settlers followed, living on uneasy terms both with each other and with the Indians. In 1729 the Natchez massacred a French garrison and were massacred in turn, and by the end of the century only a few remained.[8]

The Robber Bridegroom is set in a small corner of this wilderness, the area around the town of Rodney's Landing at the first bend of the river some thirty miles upstream from Natchez. It was a place Eudora Welty knew well. In the 1930s she had a position for a time with the WPA (Works Progress Administration), a jobs program of the U.S. government during the Depression. Her position as a 'junior publicity agent' required her to travel the state of Mississippi from one end to the other, and she took her camera with her.[9] She developed a special interest in the area around Rodney—by that time almost a ghost town and on its way back to forest.[10] She came back often, and her photographs convey the spirit of the place.[11]

Welty set her story at the end of the eighteenth century—'just before 1798', as she told the Mississippi Historical Society in a talk about her novella.[12] This specificity of time, like that of place, is another departure from fairy tale, which is always set in a remote and indefinite past: 'long ago' or 'once upon a time'. As Welty puts it elsewhere:

> there are only four words... that a novel rules out: 'Once upon a time'. They make a story a fairy tale by the simple sweep of the remove—by abolishing the present and the place where we are instead of conveying them to us.[13]

---

8 For the Natchez see Milne 2015, 1–44; Brown 1989, 8–28.
9 Welty 1984, 91–3.
10 Writing in 1944, Welty said, 'Today Rodney's Landing wears the coat of vegetation that has caught up with the whole land for the third time, or the fourth, or the hundredth'. Welty 1978a, 295.
11 Welty 2003.
12 Welty 1978b, 302.
13 Welty 1978c, 117.

The words abolish not only the present, however, but also any moment in the real past. Welty's date, by contrast, is very specific: the story takes place on the eve of the final political transition of the Natchez area, which had been controlled first by the Indians and then in succession by European absentee landlords: France, England, and Spain. In 1795 Spain ceded it to the United States, and in 1798 the town of Natchez was made capital of the Mississippi Territory.[14] The political transition marked the beginning of the end of the wilderness and the slow approach of what Huckleberry Finn would derisively call 'civilization'. Before 1798, however, the area was still wild—a place for fantasy, we could say, with at least a toe—but not a whole foot— touching the ground.

Settlers travelled the Trace or came down the river in flatboats, and some built cabins, cleared a little land and stayed. A few became wealthy enough to sell their tobacco down river in New Orleans. Welty's story opens with one such man, arriving back from a successful trip:

> It was the close of day when a boat touched Rodney's Landing on the Mississippi River and Clement Musgrove, an innocent planter, with a bag of gold and many presents, disembarked. He had made the voyage from New Orleans in safety, his tobacco had been sold for a fair price to the King's men.[15]

Please note the phrases: 'innocent planter' and 'in safety'. Innocence and safety in this wilderness were in short supply. Musgrove's first wife and infant son had been killed by Indians before the story begins. They had been set upon as they landed their boat for the night—by Indians waiting on the shore, 'on all fours, disguised in their bearskins'.[16] Indians also attacked in the forest and along the Trace; and bandits—either singly or in gangs—infested both forest and river. Bandits, like the Indians, are prominent in Welty's story—not only the Robber Bridegroom of the title and his band, but also two figures of the historical record: Mike Fink, a larger than life keelboat man, and Little Harp, a vicious killer.[17]

Mike Fink was famous on the frontier for brawling, tall tales and occasional brutality.[18] He swaggers into the story in the first chapter. Clement Musgrove,

---

14 Sass 1989.
15 Welty 1970, 1.
16 Welty 1970, 22.
17 The lives of both men extended into the nineteenth century, well past the dramatic date of Welty's story.
18 For a succinct account, see Davis 1995, 49. See also Baldwin 1941, 110–14 and 218 n. 27.

back from New Orleans and just arrived at Rodney's Landing, comes to an inn and finds that he must share his room and bed with two other travellers. The first to arrive is Mike Fink:

> a brawny man six and a half feet high, with a blue coat, red shirt, and turkey feather stuck in his cap, and he held a raven on his finger which never blinked an eye, and could say,
> 'Turn back, my bonny,
> Turn away home'.[19]

The third traveller is a little smaller than Mike Fink but almost as imposing, a yellow-haired man 'dressed up like a New Orleans dandy'.[20] This is Jamie Lockhart, the Robber Bridegroom in his character as a respectable man. After Fink and Jamie drink and fight and trade insults for a while, Fink hints that he knows Jamie's other identity:

> 'I will bet... that your name is Jamie Lockhart, Jamie Lockhart the-'... .But the yellow-haired stranger smiled... and said... 'Say *who* I am forever, but dare to say *what* I am, and that will be the last breath of any man'.[21]

Eventually everyone goes to sleep. But in the middle of the night Jamie gets Clement up and puts two large bundles of sugar cane in their places in the bed. Soon Mike Fink wakes up. Deceived by Jamie's substitution, he attacks the bundles with a board and beats them to a pulp. With his companions dispatched, as he thinks, he seizes their bags of gold and goes back to sleep. In the morning when he finds Clement and Jamie standing in front of him, he believes that they are ghosts and jumps out the window in terror, leaving the gold and the raven behind.

Little Harp was a much more depraved and vicious character. He and his brother, called Big Harpe (Welty has dropped the *e* from their name), were not so much robbers as men who killed for the fun of it.[22] At the end of the eighteenth century they murdered dozens of men, women, and children along the rivers from Kentucky to Mississippi. Big Harpe was killed in 1799 by the husband of

---

19 Welty 1970, 5–6. The feather in Fink's hat is historical, a sign of his prowess: 'The boatman who wore in his cap the red feather of victory and boasted that he had never been whipped was bound to fight everyone who challenged him'. Baldwin 1941, 100.
20 Welty 1970, 6.
21 Welty 1970, 12–13.
22 For the Harpes, Micajah (Big Harpe) and Wiley (Little Harpe), see Coates 1930, 21–70; Baldwin 1941, 122–31.

one of his victims, who beheaded him and stuck his head in a tree.²³ Little Harpe lived until 1804, when he was caught and hanged near Natchez—his head fixed to a pole on the Natchez Trace.²⁴ Welty takes a few liberties with this grisly history and its chronology, but she does not pretty it up. Big Harp is already dead when the story begins, and his brother carries his head around locked in a trunk. As Welty later noted: 'He can always turn it in and claim the reward on it—it's like money in the savings bank'.²⁵ Little Harp commits the horrible murder corresponding to the one in the Grimms' story and is later killed by Jamie Lockhart, now in his character as robber. The head of Big Harp—finally freed from its trunk—becomes a valuable commodity and is used to claim the reward on Jamie's own head.

Welty's third source is Apuleius' story of *Cupid and Psyche*. Her Cupid, of course, is Jamie Lockhart, both robber and 'New Orleans dandy'. The part of Psyche is played by Clement Musgrove's beautiful young daughter, Rosamond, and Psyche's jealous sisters are embodied in Clement's second wife Salome (the name is important), who had escaped with him from the Indians before the story begins. Rosamond, like Psyche, is driven to discover her lover's identity, and does so when he is asleep. Welty acknowledged the parallel:

> Bandits, adventurers, lovers and gods have the disguise in common. But girls always fall for taking it off. Psyche, in the fable, held a candle over Cupid's sleeping face—a god who only came in the dark—then let a drop of hot wax fall, and up he jumped, away he flew.²⁶

But the girl's discovery of her lover is by no means Welty's only borrowing. I have already noted that Rosamond's stepmother plays the part of Psyche's sisters, but the extent of the Apuleian intertext is not apparent until the very heart of the story, where elements from *Cupid and Psyche* weave in and out of a narrative as strange as anything in Apuleius.

On the day after Clement comes home with his gold and many presents, Rosamond's wicked stepmother sends her out to gather herbs on the other side of the forest. She does this every day, in hopes that something awful will happen to her. This time, just in case, she sends her familiar, a poor neighbor boy called Goat, to try to make sure that it does. I should note that Goat (the name is significant) emerges as a major character, although to start with he mostly just reports to Salome, as on this occasion. But although generally ineffective, he has

---

23 Coates 1930, 64–7; Baldwin 1941, 124.
24 Coates 1930, 163–4; Baldwin 1941, 131. See also Welty 1978b, 311–12.
25 Welty 1978b, 310.
26 Welty 1978b, 308.

one notable habit that will turn out to be essential. He invariably opens things—gates, boxes, cages, doors—and releases anything inside. With Goat following her, then, Rosamond goes tripping through the forest and meets the robber Jamie Lockhart, 'out for a devilment of some kind, with his face all stained in berry juice for a disguise'.[27] Since he is a robber, Jamie takes all her clothes—a good haul, since she is wearing the beautiful silk dress her father had brought from New Orleans. He rides off, leaving her naked in the woods. When Rosamond tells her parents what happened, Clement is determined to bring the unknown bandit to justice, and thinks that his new friend Jamie Lockhart is just the man to do it.

The next day, Salome sends her off again, and she wanders into the forest—this time not to be robbed, but to be carried off by her bandit. He seizes her up on his great horse, and they ride off like the wind.

> Up the ridge they went, and a stream of mist made a circle around them... . Rosamond's hair lay out behind her, and Jamie's hair was flying too... . Rosamond's cloak filled with wind, and then in the one still moment in the middle of a leap, it broke from her shoulder like a big bird, and dropped away below.[28]

Rosamond's abduction is a much wilder affair than Psyche's gentle wafting by Zephyr down from her rock, but no reader of Apuleius can miss the way that the description of her wind-filled cloak evokes Psyche's billowing garment at the same point in the story.[29] Psyche is terrified, Rosamond thrilled, but each is just about to be joined with her unknown lover. Psyche's union will be delayed for a few chapters, but Rosamond's is immediate. At the end of their ride, Jamie 'stopped and laid her on the ground... and robbed her of that which he had left her the day before'.[30]

Rosamond goes home, and is at once put to work again by Salome, cleaning and cooking in preparation for the night's dinner guest, who of course is Jamie Lockhart. Clement wants him to hunt down the bandit who took Rosamond's clothes and plans to reward him with her hand. When Clement and Jamie arrive, Rosamond, treated like Cinderella all day, is a terrible sight—'with ashes all in her hair and soot on either cheek and her poor tongue all but hanging out,

---

[27] Welty 1970, 51.
[28] Welty 1970, 63–4.
[29] Compare Apuleius 1990, 4.35.4. The wind-filled garment is a *topos* in classical abductions, as Kenney notes *ad. loc.*
[30] Welty 1970, 65.

and her dress burned to a fringe all around from the coals'.[31] The two lovers do not recognize each other: 'this time he was too clean and she was too dirty'.[32] When Clement tells about the stolen clothes and makes his proposition, Jamie is appalled, for he never associates Clement's daughter, obviously dirty and ugly and behaving almost like an imbecile, with his girl in the woods. He just assumes that the news of his theft has gone through the bandit community, inspiring a copycat crime.

The next day Rosamond sets out to find the house of her bandit, going deeper and deeper into the forest. It is a glorious summer day, and the woods are full of flowers and birdsong.

> At last she crossed a dark ravine and came to a place where two long rows of black cedars were, and at the end sat a house with the door standing open. It was a little house not as pretty as her own, made of cedar logs all neatly put together.[33]

As she goes up the lane, she hears a voice saying:

> 'Turn back, my bonny,
> Turn away home',

and sees a raven in a cage at the window. The raven says the same thing again when she enters the empty house, but "'I'll do nothing of the kind', said Rosamond, who had had enough commands from her stepmother".[34] The house is in just the mess one would expect from a gang of robbers, so she washes the dishes and puts everything in order. Just as she is putting the kettle on, she hears the robbers coming home and hides behind a big barrel in the corner. The bandits come in, Jamie Lockhart at their head, his face all covered with berry juice. Dismayed at the unwonted tidiness of their cottage, the robbers turn it upside down to see if anything is missing, and discover Rosamund behind the barrel.

After some discussion they vote not to kill her, but have her stay on to cook and clean. It is understood that she belongs to Jamie, their chief. What happens next is an amalgam of the Grimms and Apuleius, for Rosamond is like both Snow White keeping house for the dwarves and Psyche in her love idyll with Cupid. She cooks and cleans all day, but spends the night with Jamie, who always

---

[31] Welty 1970, 68.
[32] Ibid.
[33] Welty 1970, 78.
[34] Welty 1970, 79.

rides off before dawn. Like Psyche before her, she does not know her lover's name; and like Psyche, she longs to see his face.

> She begged him every night to wash off the stains from his face...but he would never do it. He told her that this was for the best of reasons, and she had to be content with that.[35]

She understands that her lover has two lives: his raiding and robbing, and the hours he spends with her. But he also has another life she does not know about. He is not just the berry-stained bandit in the woods, but a respectable man, well known in town. The barrier between these two identities is thin— only the berry juice, and it cannot be kept up. One day as Jamie has just started to put on his berry juice after a trip to town, he hears screams coming from a nearby cave and discovers Little Harp inside, complete with his trunk, along with a girl that he is going to kill.[36] After stopping him, Jamie hears what he recognizes as the voice of doom.

> 'Aha, but I know who you are...', said Little Harp... . 'Your name is Jamie Lockhart and you are the bandit in the woods, for you have your two faces on together, and I see you both'.[37]

Jamie starts to kill him, but finds that he cannot do it, even though he knows it is a terrible mistake.

Meanwhile, Rosamond has gone back home to see her parents. She bears rich gifts and is visibly pregnant, and the scene familiar from Apuleius ensues as Salome questions her closely about what she calls Rosamond's robber bridegroom.[38] No doubt he had sent her away, she claims; but Rosamond, who could almost be quoting Apuleius, says that she had been missing her father and had begged and pleaded until her lover gave her permission to come. She cheerfully admits that she does not know his name and has never seen him 'by the light of day without his robber's disguise'.[39] But Salome keeps at it:

> 'I fear, my dear, that you feel in your bosom a passion for a low and scandalous being, a beast who would like to let you wait on him and serve him, but will not do you the common

---

35 Welty 1970, 84.
36 It is appropriate that Little Harp first appears in a cave, for the real Harpe brothers once operated out of a cave known as Cave-in-Rock on the Ohio River that they shared for a time with other notorious bandits. See Coates 1930, 47–53.
37 Welty 1970, 112.
38 Welty 1970, 116.
39 Welty 1970, 119.

courtesy of letting you see his face. It can only be for the reason that he is some kind of monster.'[40]

When Rosamond finally breaks down, Salome gives her the recipe for removing berry stains and advises her to take a tomahawk with her 'in case her husband should turn out to be too horrible to look at'.[41] Rosamond takes the recipe but not the tomahawk and goes back to the woods.

But by now Little Harp has moved in with the robbers. This time Rosamond's trip through the forest is like that of her predecessor in the Grimms'version — dark and fearful, with a cold wind rustling dry leaves. The raven utters his warning, but she goes in. All the bandits are there except hers, and a strange man is now in charge—Little Harp, still with his trunk. She hides behind the barrel to watch. They are all drunk, and when Little Harp keeps demanding the girl that used to belong to their chief, they drag in an Indian girl to appease him and drug her. Little Harp cuts off her wedding finger (it offends him, he says), and it flies into Rosamond's lap. He rapes and murders the Indian girl. Just then Jamie Lockhart bursts in, and little Harp brags:

> 'I have killed your bride, and that is the first payment... And the next thing, I will speak out your name and cast evil upon it'.[42]

Again Jamie starts to kill him, but refrains. He orders the other robbers to throw him into the ravine, discovers that the murdered girl is not his bride, and falls into bed. Rosamond creeps in beside him, and we are back in the story of *Cupid and Psyche*. As she sees him 'dreaming there with his face stained dark with berry juice', she is driven as never before to know 'his name and true appearance'.[43] So she follows Salome's recipe and washes off the berry stains, holding up a candle to see by.

Jamie Lockhart opened his eyes and looked at her. The candle gave one long beam of light, which traveled between their two faces.

> 'You are Jamie Lockhart!' she said.
> 'And you are Clement Musgrove's silly daughter!' said he.
> Then he rose out of his bed.
> 'Good-by',' he said. 'For you did not trust me, and did not love me, for you wanted only to know who I am. Now I cannot stay in the house with you'.

---

40 Welty 1970, 123.
41 Welty 1970, 125.
42 Welty 1970, 132–3.
43 Welty 1970, 134.

> And going straight to the window, he climbed out through it and in another moment was gone.
> Then Rosamond tried to follow and climbed out after him, but she fell in the dust.[44]

We have been here before: with the girl revealing her unknown lover, the light that shows his face, his angry departure, and the girl's failed attempt to follow him that ends with her collapsed on the ground. But this is not Apuleius' *Cupid and Psyche*. The recognition is double, and neither one is delighted. We could say that Rosamond is merely surprised: '"You are Jamie Lockhart!" she said'. But Jamie is surely disgusted: '"You are Clement Musgrove's silly daughter!" said he'. His reproaches, unlike Cupid's, cannot be made from a position of superiority. He is no god, but only a bandit, and all he can say is that she did not love him enough not to try to discover his identity. This is weak, and Rosamond clearly thinks so, too, for she may be Clement Musgrove's silly daughter, but she is no docile and humble Psyche. In the next chapter she angrily laments:

> 'My husband was a robber and not a bridegroom.... . He brought me his love under a mask, and kept all the truth hidden from me, and never called anything by its true name, even his name or mine, and what I would have given him he liked better to steal. And if I had no faith, he had little honor, to deprive a woman of giving her love freely'.[45]

But that is later, after another important event that clearly evokes *Cupid and Psyche*, although Welty—typically—takes it in a different direction. The morning after Jamie's departure Rosamond regains consciousness, still lying where she had fallen, and she sees a head looking out from her bedroom window. It is Goat, and now we see the reason for his name. His counterpart, Pan, at the same point in the story, tried to calm the desolate Psyche, and gave her some advice:

> '...put away your grief. Instead pray to Cupid, the greatest of the gods, and worship him and earn his favor with flattering deference...'[46]

Goat does not advise Welty's Psyche, although he does try to cheer her up; in any case, she is in no mood to hear about prayers and deference. Instead, he has news: that Jamie Lockhart is the bandit of the woods, that murder was done in his house, that the first man who brings in his head will get a hundred pieces of gold, and that everyone will be looking for him. As Goat is leaving, a voice

---

[44] Welty 1970, 134–5.
[45] Welty 1970, 146.
[46] Apuleius 1989, 5.25.6.

emanates from the trunk left behind when Little Harp had been thrown out the night before.

> 'Let me out!'... . 'What did you say?' asked Goat. .. 'Let me out', said the voice... So Goat lifted up the lid. And there sat the head of Big Harp, Little Harp's brother, all wrapped up in the blue mud, and just as it came down off the pole in Rodney.
>
> 'Will you look what was doing the talking!' cried Goat, and pulled the head out by the hair, holding it up at arm's length so it turned round like a bird cage on a string, and admiring it from all directions.[47]

Rosamond faints, and Goat goes skipping down the hill with the head, crying, 'Jamie Lockhart is the bandit of the woods! And the bandit of the woods is Jamie Lockhart!'

Now things move quickly. The murder of the Indian maiden, unlike that of her counterpart in Grimm, is not unavenged. The Indians capture all the characters except Goat, burn down the robbers' house, and torture Salome, forcing her to dance like her biblical counterpart until she falls dead when she blasphemes their chief god, the Sun.[48] The most important event, however, is the final confrontation of Jamie and Little Harp. Goat, who likes to open things, first frees Rosamund, who steals away, and then the two men. He has already turned in Big Harp's head for the reward for Jamie's, he tells them: it 'is resting on a new-cut pole in Rodney square under the name of Jamie Lockhart, the bandit of the woods'.[49] Jamie protests: 'But I am Jamie Lockhart, the bandit of the woods!'[50] Little Harp snatches the reward and contradicts him: 'You, sir, my good stranger, are *not* Jamie Lockhart, the bandit of the woods'.[51] What happens next echoes the exchange with Mike Fink at the beginning, fight and all—except for two points. This time Jamie does not deny but claims his double identity:

> 'I am Jamie Lockhart, the bandit of the woods!' cried Jamie. 'Not a man in the world can say I am not who I am and what I am, and live!'[52]

---

[47] Welty 1970, 139–40.
[48] The Natchez, who called themselves People of Sun, worshipped the sun as their principal deity; they called their chief The Great Sun. See Milne 2015: 15; Brown 1989. Salome's dancing death replicates that of Snow White's stepmother.
[49] Welty 1970, 155.
[50] Welty 1970, 156.
[51] Ibid.
[52] Welty 1970, 156–7.

And this time he kills his opponent. In doing so, perhaps he is destroying his evil alter ego. I think myself that he is killing his own *potential* evil self—which is not quite the same thing.

Jamie gives the reward to Goat ('the bandit's life is done with', he says), and goes looking for Rosamund.[53] Finding just a few small bones in the embers of his house, he thinks she is dead and heads to New Orleans to take ship. Rosamund finds him with his foot already on the gangplank:

> ... he... came down and brought her home, not failing to take her by the priest's and marrying her on the way. And indeed it was in time's nick.[54]

Like Psyche, Rosamond is transported to Olympus, or at least to New Orleans, its frontier equivalent, and married just in time by her lover. A few months later Clement finds her the mother of twins, dressed like a queen, and living in a beautiful mansion on Lake Pontchartrain with her Cupid, now a rich and respectable man, who, as she says—in a final Apuleian touch, 'used to scorn her for her curiosity'.[55]

In *The Robber Bridegroom* Welty has blended her diverse ingredients into a confection far greater than the sum of its parts—a narrative that is fantastic and amusing, but also fundamentally serious because of its recurrent themes of identity and time and change. She emphasized the importance of identity to the Mississippi Historical Society.

> Crucial, or comical, scenes of mistaken identity take place more or less regularly as the story unwinds. There's a doubleness in respect to identity that runs in a strong thread through all the wild happenings—indeed, this thread is their connection, and everything that happens hangs upon it.[56]

Identity is the engine driving Welty's plot. It comes up in connection with almost all the characters, but especially with her two protagonists. With Rosamond it takes the form not of disguise but of mistaken identity and surrogates. Jamie does not know who she is until their mutual recognition scene. Both the girl Harp was going to kill in the cave and the Indian maiden are surrogates for her, and so is Salome, who tries to replace her at the end, claiming that her daughter is dead and that she is now the fairest.[57] The case of the Indian girl

---

53 Welty 1970, 166.
54 Welty 1970, 181.
55 Welty 1970, 184.
56 Welty 1978b, 310.
57 Welty 1970, 159–60.

is particularly chilling, especially when Little Harp cuts off her wedding finger, the symbol, he thinks, that identifies her as Jamie's bride. Jamie, on the other hand, is leading a double life; in his case identity is a matter not of *who* he is but *what* he is. The Grimms' robber bridegroom is his obvious ancestor, but in terms of plot Apuleius' Cupid is more important. The unmasking of the Grimms' character is both the point and the end of the tale. Cupid's discovery by Psyche, by contrast, is not the end, but the turning point of the story, which is above all the story of Psyche: her trials, her reunion with Cupid, and her final apotheosis. Welty uses the discovery for a different purpose: to propel the plot to its resolution, and to move Jamie and Rosamond—and all the other characters—to confront, question, and decide who and what Jamie Lockhart really is. To put it another way, Welty's story is less about the apotheosis of her Psyche than the identity of her Cupid.

The theme of time and change, important in itself, also bears on that of identity. I said earlier that the story was set at a moment marking 'the beginning of the end of the wilderness'.[58] But in fact change had been coming on the wilderness for a long time, and would continue far into the future—into Welty's own day and far beyond. This is a fact that only the innocent planter Clement Musgrove, the work's only thoughtful and perceptive character, understands. Near the end of the story he learns that Jamie Lockhart, whom he has known as a respectable man, is also the bandit of the woods. He walks into the forest to reflect, and sits down in the pinegrove, concerned, as Welty says, 'with the identity of a man'.[59] He muses—not on Jamie—but on the primeval track through the wilderness created long ago in an unending succession of the seasons by 'the buffalo on his sinking trail... and the deer following behind to the salty places'.[60]

> 'Across this [forest] floor, slowly and softly and forever moving into profile, is always a beast, one of a procession, weighted low with his burning coat, looking from the yellow eye set in his head'.[61]

In his mind's eye Clement sees travellers and settlers, planters and slaves, bandits and flatboat men, and always the Indians—all moving down the forest track into oblivion. Later, as a captive in the Indian camp, he thinks:

---

58 On the end of the wilderness see French 1979 and Kreyling 1986.
59 Welty 1970, 141.
60 Welty 1970, 142.
61 Welty 1970, 141.

'The savages have only come the sooner to their end; we will come to ours too… The planter will go after the hunter, and the merchant after the planter, all having their day'.[62]

But the land itself also changes, through both human and natural agency. Clement himself, goaded by his ambitious wife Salome, constantly fells more trees to make room to plant more indigo and tobacco.[63] Over time, fifty years or so after the events in the novel, the Mississippi River itself would change course, and Rodney's Landing would be left behind and become simply Rodney; by Welty's time the town was officially described as 'extinct'.[64] The former settlers will move from forest to town to city, where Jamie, former bandit, is now a rich merchant:

> All his wild ways had been shed like a skin… . the outward transfer from bandit to merchant had been almost too easy to count it as a change at all, and he was enjoying all the same success he had ever had.[65]

Jamie the merchant, unlike Clement the planter, is a creature of the new age, and we see him at the end, able to shed one identity and take on another, all without changing his essential self.

Welty's *Cupid and Psyche* is a far cry from Apuleius', just as her *Robber Bridegroom* is a far cry from the Grimms'. She has fused them, adding countless touches all her own, and transformed them—not quite out of recognition—by moving them out of the timeless, placeless world of fairy tale into the Mississippi frontier, a real world already vanishing into legend.

1 Bibliography

Apuleius (1989), *Metamorphoses*, ed. and transl., J. A. Hanson. Cambridge, Mass.
Apuleius (1990), *Cupid and Psyche*, ed. and transl., E. J. Kenney, Cambridge.
Baldwin, L. D. (1941), *The Keelboat Age on Western Waters*, Pittsburgh.
Benson, G. (2019), *Apuleius' Invisible Ass: Encounters with the Unseen in the Metamorphoses*, Cambridge.
Brown, I. W. (1989), 'Natchez Indians and the Remains of a Proud Past', in: Polk, 8–28.
Chamlee, K. (1991), 'Grimm and Apuleius. Myth-Blending in Eudora Welty's *The Robber Bridegroom*', *Notes on Mississippi Writers* 23, 37–45.

---

[62] Welty 1970, 161.
[63] Welty 1970, 28, 99.
[64] 'In 1938 the town of Rodney…was designated "extinct" by Mississippi's official *Guide to the Magnolia State*'. Devlin 1979, 170.
[65] Welty 1970, 183–5. And see French 1979, 186: 'No *inner* change has been required by the transformation'.

Coates, R. M. (1930), *The Outlaw Years. The History of the Land Pirates of the Natchez Trace*, New York.
Davis, W. C. (1995), *A Way through the Wilderness. The Natchez Trace and the Civilization of the Southern Frontier*, New York.
Devlin, A. J. (1979), 'Eudora Welty's Mississippi', in: Prenshaw, 157–78.
French, W. (1979), '"All Things are Double": Eudora Welty as a Civilized Writer', in: Prenshaw, 179–88.
Kreyling, M. (1986), '*The Robber Bridegroom and the Pastoral Dream*' in H. Bloom, ed., *Eudora Welty. Modern Critical Views*, New York: 135–48. (Reprinted from Kreyling, *Eudora Welty's Achievement of Order*, Baton Rouge, 1980.)
Kreyling, M. (1999), *Understanding Eudora Welty*, Columbia, South Carolina.
Marrs, S. (2005), *Eudora Welty. A Biography*, Orlando.
Milne, G. E. (2015), *Natchez Country. Indians, Colonists, and the Landscapes of Race in French Louisiana*, Athens, Georgia and London.
Neumann, Erich (1956), *Amor and Psyche: the psychic development of the feminine*, New York.
Polk, N. (ed.) (1989), *Natchez before 1830*, Jackson and London.
Prenshaw, P. W. (ed.) (1979), *Eudora Welty. Critical Essays*, Jackson.
Randisi, J. L. (1982), *A Tissue of Lies. Eudora Welty and the Southern Romance*. Lanham, New York and London.
Sass, J. (1989), 'Chronology of Natchez', in: Polk, 3–7.
Welty, E. (1970), *The Robber Bridegroom*, San Diego, New York, London. (First published in 1942.)
Welty, E. (1978a), *The Eye of the Story. Selected Essays and Reviews*, New York.
Welty, E. (1978b), 'Fairy Tale of the Natchez Trace. A Talk Delivered to the Mississippi Historical Society in 1975', in: Welty 1978a, 300–14.
Welty, E. (1978c), 'Place in Fiction', in: Welty 1978a, 116–33. (Reprinted from *The Archive* (Duke University) 67 (April, 1955).
Welty, E. (1978d), 'Some Notes on River Country', in: Welty 1978a: 286–99. (Originally published in *Harper's Bazaar*, 1944.)
Welty, E. (1984), *One Writer's Beginnings*, Cambridge, MA.
Welty, E. (2003), *Some Notes on River Country*, illustrated with twenty-eight of her photographs, ed., H. Cole, Jackson.
Weston, R. D. (1994), *Gothic Traditions and Narrative Techniques in the Fiction of Eudora Welty*, Baton Rouge and London.

Friedemann Drews
Cupid & Psyche and C.S. Lewis' Till We Have Faces.
A Christian-Platonic metamorphosis

1 Introduction. Apuleius—only a 'source' for C.S. Lewis?

In his 'note', printed at the very end of the Harcourt Edition of *Till We Have Faces* (*TWHF*), C.S. Lewis summarizes his 'source', Apuleius' famous tale of *Cupid and Psyche* (*CP*). Lewis adds some remarks on his adaptation:

> The central alteration in my own version consists in making Psyche's palace invisible to normal, mortal eyes—if 'making' is not the wrong word for something which forced itself upon me, almost at my first reading of the story, as the way the thing must have been. [...] I felt quite free to go behind Apuleius [...]. Nothing was further from my aim than to recapture the peculiar quality of the *Metamorphoses*—that strange compound of picaresque novel, horror comic, mystagogue's tract, pornography, and stylistic experiment. Apuleius was of course a man of genius: but in relation to my work he is a 'source', not an 'influence' nor a 'model' (Lewis, *TWHF*, 313).

Although I do not see any reasons to doubt Lewis' self-assessment, in what follows I would like to challenge Lewis' own view on his reworking of Apuleius—at least in part. For, even if it is fairly obvious that Lewis would have never thought of writing such a 'strange compound' as he labels Apuleius' *Metamorphoses* (*Met.*)—in *TWHF* we get neither pornography nor comic tales etc.—there might be some features that *TWHF* and the *Met. as a whole* do have in common. And if this assumption is right, it would be rather surprising if these similarities were coincidental: should Lewis have downplayed or perhaps simply overlooked them?

Maybe the conclusions we draw concerning the relation between Lewis and Apuleius also depend on our interpretation of the *Met.*—or, maybe Lewis simply did not want his own novel to be associated too much with such a 'strange compound'.

In the following pages, I shall first briefly rehearse the plot of *TWHF* and show how Apuleius' original version of *CP* causes insanity in Orual, the principal character in Lewis' novel; second, I would like to argue that the whole of the *Met.* in a certain sense *is* present in *TWHF*; and third, I will explore what role Stoic and Platonic philosophy play in *both* novels, with a view to the end of *TWHF* and its Christian dimension.

2 The Plot of *TWHF* and the challenge of Apuleius' *CP* for Orual in *TWHF*

The first major plot difference between *CP* and *TWHF* consists in the fact that in Lewis' novel the principal character is not Psyche, but one of her two sisters, Orual, who at the same time is the first person narrator and the intradiegetic or fictitious 'author' of 'her' book, in which she intends to 'accuse the gods, especially the god who lives on the Grey Mountain' (*TWHF* 3) as she tells us, her readers, from the outset: the issue of theodicy is present throughout Lewis' novel. Orual is driven by what Lewis in his book *The Four Loves* describes as 'Need-Love',[1] an obsessive and possessive love for her sister Psyche.[2] Accordingly, Orual cannot at all endure that her sister Psyche is going to be sacrificed for the well-being of their state Glome and in order to appease the goddess Ungit, who grew angry at the people of Glome for worshipping Psyche as a goddess. This matches of course the veneration of Psyche in the place of Venus in Apuleius' *CP*[3]. The reason why it is Psyche who is chosen as a sacrifice is, as the priest of Ungit tells us, that 'in the Great Offering, the victim must be perfect' (49). This clearly is a tenet of Lewis' Christian theology as expounded in his book *Mere Christianity:*[4] at this stage already we can see that Lewis metamorphosizes his 'source' into Christian shape.

After having been supposedly sacrificed to the monster by her parents, Psyche arrives in a marvellous world similar to the one in *CP*. However, Orual, visiting her sister there, can neither see the best china nor taste the wine (for her it is only water, 119[5]) nor can she see the palace: when it starts raining, Orual thinks

---

[1] 'And the Need-Love, like Need-Pleasure, will not last longer than the need' (Lewis 1977, 19).
[2] Cf. Hunt 2016, 126, 142; Jacobs 2005, 239–240; Myers 1994, 192; Donaldson 1988, 19, 70; Adey 1998, 154.
[3] *Met.* 4.28.3.
[4] 'Only a bad person needs to repent: only a good person can repent perfectly' (Lewis 2001, 57). Cf. Hunt 2016, 121: 'Like Christ, Psyche has taken upon herself evil that she has eradicated, and yet is persecuted, cursed.'
[5] See Adey 1998, 159 for the 'eucharistic symbol of what Psyche perceives spiritually as wine and Orual materially as springwater'. For more allusions to the Eucharist in *TWHF* see Hunt 2016, 121–3.

her sister is getting wet while Psyche points to the roof of the palace.[6] Only once, at night time, while kneeling, does Orual catch a glimpse of the palace, but in the next moment 'as I rose (for all this time I was still kneeling [...]), almost before I stood on my feet, the whole thing was vanished' (133). Consequently, she regards this vision as an illusion. In contrast to Apuleius, but according to the account Orual gives in her book, she is the only sister who visits Psyche: Redival, her other sister, is not present, so that Orual is left alone to decide whether or not what she saw was real.[7] In vain does Orual try to persuade Psyche to return to their former world where they used to live together.

Meanwhile, Orual has succeeded her father in Glome: as queen she writes her book in order to accuse the gods because of the injustice that has happened; all the time she is complaining that 'there is no judge between gods and men, and the god of the mountain will not answer me' (3). The first part of the novel finishes after 250 pages, the second one follows with only 60 pages. Now Orual states that she should rewrite everything from the start, for 'the past which I wrote down was not the past that I thought I had (all these years) been remembering' (253). Gradually, the reader learns that, in many visions, Orual has not only seen the truth about herself, her obsessive love and selfishness, but also the truth about Psyche, the goddess Ungit, and the true God.[8]

With hindsight, the new viewpoint Orual takes on her past life seems to be prepared for at the end of part one—at least if we focus on the key question: what was the real past? Orual finally decides to leave Glome and to do some travelling. In Essur she meets the priest of Istra. Istra is also the real name of her sister, whose nickname 'Psyche' is only the Greek translation of Istra, as the reader learns at the beginning of the novel (20). When the priest starts talking of Istra, Orual is not 'startled' since the name is 'not so uncommon in Glome'. The priest reveals that Istra is 'a very young goddess. She has only just begun to be a goddess' (241). And then he tells Orual 'the sacred story. Once upon a time in a certain land there lived a king and a queen who had three daughters, and the youngest was the most beautiful princess in the whole world...' (241–2). This is, of course, almost a verbatim translation of Lewis' 'source': *Erant in quadam civitate rex et regina. Hi tres numero filias forma conspicuas habuere* (*Met.* 4.28.1).

---

[6] *TWHF* 125–6.
[7] 'If both sisters went, they could agree that there was nothing to see, that Psyche's palace was simply her illusion' (Myers 2004, 148; similarly Myers 1994, 192).
[8] Cf. Myers 2004, 147.

What happens here is that Orual (and we as readers) suddenly seems to hear the original version of *CP* from Apuleius' *Metamorphoses*. On the metaliterary level this might appear as a clever inclusion and mirroring of the 'source', but that is not the only reason why the story is included. Orual reports:

> And to me it was as if the old man's voice, and the temple, and I myself and my journey, were all things in such a story; for he was telling the very history of our Istra, of Psyche herself—how Talapal (that's the Essurian Ungit) was jealous of her beauty and made her to be offered to a brute on a mountain,[9] and how Talapal's son Ialim, the most beautiful of the gods, loved her and took her away to his secret palace. He even knew that Ialim had there visited her only in darkness and had forbidden her to see his face. But he had a childish reason for that: 'You see, Stranger [sc. Orual], he had to be very secret because of his mother Talapal. She would have been very angry with him if she had known he had married the woman she most hated in the world.' [...] Then, suddenly [...], I asked him; 'Where did you learn all this?' He stared at me as if he didn't well understand such a question. 'It's a sacred story,' he said (242).

So far there is nothing unsettling for Orual in the priest's words. But now the twist of the priest's story—that is, the distressing effect this version has on Orual—becomes more and more tangible: 'But now all the dreamlike feeling in me suddenly vanished. I was wide awake and I felt the blood rush into my face. He was telling it wrong—hideously and stupidly wrong. First of all, he made it that both Psyche's sisters had visited her in the secret palace of the god' (243). (This mirrors, of course, Apuleius' version,[10] but marks a stark contrast with Orual's own experience.) '"And so," he said, "when her two sisters had seen the beautiful palace and been feasted and given gifts, they—"— "They saw the palace?"' (243).

For Orual this is a dumbfounding and threatening detail: Not only does it question the 'fact' that she alone went to see Psyche in the other world; it simply makes her former doubts whether the palace existed at all unjustified and untrue. (The issue of so-called 'fake facts' the postmodern world is facing nowadays is at stake here.[11]) Immediately, new doubts and irritations arise in her:

---

9 Cf. Schakel 1984, 62–63: 'The story told to Orual by the Priest of Essur becomes a middle level between Apuleius's telling and Lewis's re-telling [...] By interrupting the Priest, Orual prevented him from completing his sentence with the word *sacrifices*' (63).
10 *Met.* 5.14 f.
11 Myers 1994, 209–10 interprets this differently: '[...] Orual learns that her history has become a myth [...]. Just as the slight error in the priest's story does not destroy it as evidence [...].' As far as I can see, Lewis does not present the priest's version with a 'slight error', rather Orual's former experience is challenged here—the past she remembers was not the real past (see below). This would be in line with Myers' own interpretation: 'In the second part of the story, he [sc. Lewis]

It was as if the gods themselves had first laughed, and then spat, in my face. So this was the shape the story had taken. You may say, the shape the gods had given it. For it must be they who had put it into the old fool's mind or into the mind of some other dreamer from whom he'd learned it (243). [...] And now to tell my story as if I had had the very sight they had denied me... is it not as if you told a cripple's story and never said he was lame [...]? And I saw all in a moment how the false story would grow and spread and be told all over the earth; and I wondered how many of the other sacred stories are just such twisted falsities as this. [...] That moment I resolved to write this book (244).

Now, you who read, judge between the gods and me. They gave me nothing in the world to love but Psyche and then took her from me. But that was not enough. [...]; they have now sent out a lying story in which I was given no riddle to guess, but knew and saw that she was the god's bride, and of my own will destroyed her, and that for jealousy. As if I were another Redival. I say the gods deal very unrightly with us. For they will neither (which would be best of all) go away and leave us to live our own short days to ourselves, nor will they show themselves openly and tell us what they would have us do. For that too would be endurable. [...] I say, therefore, that there is no creature (toad, scorpion, or serpent) so noxious to man as the gods. Let them answer my charge if they can. It may well be that, instead of answering, they'll strike me mad or leprous or turn me into a beast, bird, or tree. But will not all the world then know (and the gods will know it knows) that this is because they have no answer? (248–250)

Let us leave Orual's speech for a moment—at the end, we shall come back to it and to the question what the past is like in *TWHF*.

3 Comparing the structure of Apuleius' *Met.* and Lewis' *TWHF*

The similarities and differences between *TWHF* and *CP* have, of course, not gone unnoticed in scholarship.[12] As I try to argue that there are similarities between *TWHF* and the *whole* of Apuleius' *Metamorphoses*, I want to draw our attention to the following three observations: 1. In *TWHF*, Orual is both the protagonist and the first-person narrator, as is Lucius in the principal storyline of the *Metamorphoses*. 2. In the same way as the eleven books of Apuleius' *Met.* can be divided into a dual structure of ten books plus one,[13] *TWHF* is divided into a bigger first and a much shorter second part. 3. The latter is set apart from the first because Orual now starts to reconsider her own past and story. This can be compared to

---

portrays the dissemination of the Psyche myth as an event brought about by God' (ibd., 211)—'errors' would undermine it.
12 See e.g. Myers 2004, 148–150; Donaldson 1988, 10–12.
13 Cf. Heller 1983.

the eleventh book of Apuleius' *Metamorphoses:* Lucius, having just regained his human form, is reconsidering his former life in front of an image of the goddess Isis ('but keenly intent on the statue of the goddess I recalled my former tribulations'[14]). Both novels implicitly ask their readers to follow the protagonists' example.

4 Stoic and Platonic philosophy in Apuleius' *Met.* and C.S. Lewis' *TWHF*

Another similarity between both novels, hitherto unnoticed, surfaces when we look at the role philosophy plays in the *Met.* and in *TWHF* or, put more precisely, at the way Stoic philosophy is gradually superseded by Platonic philosophy. Since this is not only a structural parallel between both novels, and since it especially involves the question of how Apuleius is interpreted, I will briefly tackle these issues in more detail, starting with the *Met.* and summarizing some lines of interpretation I have elaborated on elsewhere.[15] 1. Whereas in his philosophical works Apuleius is eager to show that there is *no* all-determining fate in the Stoic sense, pervading the whole universe in every detail,[16] Lucius—at the start of the novel—declares his belief in precisely such a kind of fate.[17] 2. Whereas in book 2 Lucius welcomes the opportunity to 'plunge' (*praecipitare*) into the abyss of magic adventures[18] (not paying any attention to his aunt Byrrhena's warnings) and whereas in book 5 Psyche, 'out of her mind, plunged (*praecipitavit*) into the abyss of calamities' (forgetting about Cupid's warnings and her own promises) and later tries to commit suicide by 'plunging' (*praecipitem se dedit*) into the river,[19] the author Apuleius expounds in his *De Platone* that a truly free vo-

---

[14] *intentus <in> deae specimen pristinos casus meos recordabar* (*Met.* 11.17.5; transl. Keulen et al. 2015, 322).
[15] See Drews (2009, 2012, 2015, 2017).
[16] *quare nec omnia ad fati sortem arbitratur esse referenda.[...] nec sane omnia referenda esse ad vim fati putat, sed esse aliquid in nobis et in fortuna esse non nihil* (*De Platone* 1.101.16–102.17). The text follows the edition by Moreschini 1991.
[17] 'Ego vero', inquam, 'nihil impossibile arbitror, sed utcumque fata decreverint, ita cuncta mortalibus provenire [...]' (*Met.* 1.20.3).
[18] *Met.* 2.6.2.
[19] *Extra terminum mentis suae posita prorsus omnium mariti monitionum suarumque promissionem memoriam effudit, et in profundum calamitatis sese praecipitavit [...]* (*Met.* 5.18.4–5); [...] *per proximi fluminis marginem praecipitem se dedit* (*Met.* 5.25.1); [...] *saltu se maximo praecipitem dedit* (*Met.* 5.27.2).

lition intends a certain good: bad and harmful things were willed only because somebody mistakes them for good ones and thus unwittingly 'plunges' (*praecipitatur*) into difficult circumstances.[20] 3. Soon after, Lucius becomes an ass. He is now the animal the goddess Isis regards as detestable;[21] it is only when he finally prays to the 'queen of heaven' (whose name is yet unknown to him), that he, by the help of Isis, regains his human nature and is instructed by her priest what the difference between the true providence of the goddess and blind fortune consists in.[22] Here some Platonic lines of thought lurk under the surface, as becomes obvious if one compares the novel to Apuleius' philosophical works.[23] However, before he turns to Isis in book 11, Lucius-the-ass (like the two sisters in *CP*[24]) repeatedly accuses blind fate or fortune respectively,[25] without considering the possibility that he might—at least to some degree—be himself responsible for his 'asinine life'. Only at the very end of book 10 does he suddenly remember his inner faculty of free will;[26] immediately thereafter he turns in prayer to the queen of heaven.

The conclusion to be drawn from this brief outline is that in the first ten books of his novel, the author Apuleius makes his figure Lucius and other char-

---

20 *sed virtutem liberam et in nobis sitam et nobis voluntate appetendam; peccata vero esse non minus libera et in nobis sita, non tamen ea suscipi voluntate. [...] Sed si eiusmodi mala pergit ac sibi usuram eorum utilem credit, deceptus errore et imagine boni sollicitatus quidem, <in->sciens vero ad mala praecipitatur* (De Platone 2.122. 9–20).
21 [...] *pessimae mihique iam dudum detestabilis beluae istius corio te exue* (Met. 11.6.2).
22 '*Eat [sc. Fortuna] nunc et summo furore saeviat et crudelitati suae materiem quaerat aliam; [...]. In tutelam iam receptus es Fortunae, sed videntis, quae suae lucis splendore ceteros etiam deos illuminat*' (Met. 11.15.2–3).
23 Cf. Drews 2012.
24 '*En orba et saeva et iniqua Fortuna!*' (Met. 5.9.2); '*Videsne quantum tibi periculum <minatur>? Velitatur Fortuna eminus, ac nisi longe firmiter praecaves, mox comminus congreditur*' (Met. 5.11.3).
25 *talibus fatis implicitus* (Met. 4.3.1); *sors deterrima* (Met. 4.5.1). Cf. *caecam et exoculatam esse Fortunam* (Met. 7.2.4); *Fortunae scaevitate* (Met. 7.3.5); *Sed illa Fortuna mea saevissima [...] rursum in me caecos detorsit oculos* (Met. 8.24.1); *Sed nimirum nihil Fortuna rennuente licet homini nato dexterum provenire nec consilio prudenti vel remedio sagaci divinae providentiae fatalis dispositio subverti vel reformari potest* (Met. 9.1.5); *Sed haec bene atque optime plenaque cum sanctimonia disposita feralem Fortunae nutum latere non potuerunt, cuius instinctu domum iuvenis protinus se direxit saeva Rivalitas* (Met. 10.24.1).
26 [...] *meis cogitationibus liberum tribuebatur arbitrium [...]* (Met. 10.35.2). Cf. Drews 2009, 519–24.

acters in the novel think precisely the opposite of what he as a philosopher deems rational. Therefore, the *Met. as a whole* cannot be a *Mysterienroman*.[27]

In Lewis' *TWHF* we get something similar: from the outset, with much more profundity and seriousness than Lucius in the *Met.*, Orual puts the question of theodicy: 'I will accuse the gods' (3). In their sympathy for Plato, both Lewis[28] and Apuleius share a certain common ground as regards philosophy, even though Christianity is much more important to Lewis—and disapproved of by Apuleius.[29] However, like in the first ten books of the *Met.* (as regards belief in determinism, the accusation of blind fortune/fate), it is Stoic philosophy that prevails in the first and bigger part of *TWHF*, embodied by the figure of the Fox, the teacher of Orual and her two sisters.[30]

When the Fox advises his pupils: '"We must learn, child, not to fear anything that nature brings"' (14), or: '"All is to be borne"' (141), then these words sound like Seneca's: 'Therefore everything is to be borne bravely [...]; ourselves about to perish, we receive what is about to perish.',[31] or like Marcus Aurelius: 'If something is troubling you, then you forgot that everything happens according to universal nature.'[32] When the Fox is talking of Stoic *ataraxia* ('The body is shaking. I needn't let it shake the god within me', 18), this is again reminiscent of Marcus Aurelius: 'If you keep the god within you pure and steadfast [...], you'll lead a happy life.'[33]

It is important for the issue of theodicy that, according to Stoic teaching, evil things subsist only in one's misguided opinion. 'Everything is as good or bad as our opinion makes it' (7), the Fox says.[34] Marcus Aurelius agrees: 'The evil you

---

27 This interpretation was, of course, proposed by Merkelbach, who had to admit certain discrepancies ('Unstimmigkeiten', Merkelbach 2001, 423–435) involved in this hermeneutical enterprise. For a brief criticism of Merkelbach cf. Drews 2009, 454, n. 126.
28 'For Lewis, Plato was the philosopher of first importance. As Digory says in *The Last Battle*, 'It's all in Plato, all in Plato' (*LB* 170)' (Myers 2004, 212; cf. Adey 1998, 272.
29 Cf.: '[...] this is rightly interpreted as Isis' deliverance of Lucius from the beast of Typhon, but in Africa it could also bear the additional interpretation of deliverance from Christian superstition' (Walsh 2006:,187).
30 Cf. Hunt 2016, 119; Duriez 2015, 151 and Myers 2004, 210, 216–8: 'The Fox tried to free her [sc. Orual] from Glomish superstition with his rational Stoicism' (ibd., 140).
31 *Ideo fortiter omne patiendum est [...]; accipimus peritura perituri* (*De prov.* 3). All translations are my own if not stated otherwise.
32 Ὅταν δυσφορῇς ἐπί τινι, ἐπελάθου τοῦ, ὅτι πάντα κατὰ τὴν τῶν ὅλων φύσιν γίνεται (Aur. 12.26).
33 Ἐὰν [...] τὸν ἑαυτοῦ δαίμονα καθαρὸν ἑστῶτα τηρῇς [...], εὐζωήσεις (Aur. 3.12).
34 Cf. Orual: 'All those wilder misgivings, all the fluttering to and fro between two opinions, was (for that time) quite over. I saw in a flash that I must choose one opinion or the other; and in the same flash I knew which I had chosen' (126). For the Stoic view that every part of reality (suffer-

experience does not subsist in another one's guiding thought, nor in any turn or change that affects your body. Where then? Where you have the mastery of shaping your opinion about evil things. This [sc. the *hêgemonikon*], therefore, should not have such an opinion, and everything is well.'[35]

> Because the Fox is a Stoic, his worldview excludes the supernatural and the hard-to-explain. He believes that everything happens in accordance with the laws of Nature and that Nature is a seamless web. When Orual points out the objective improvement in Glome's situation since the sacrifice of Psyche [...] the Fox replies that the apparent cause-effect relationship is mere chance. But then Orual reminds him, 'How often, Grandfather, you have told me there's no such thing as chance.' He blames the apparent contradiction on language, 'an old trick of the tongue', and reaffirms his belief that all events have been determined from the beginning ([sc. *TWHF*] 84–85) (Myers 1994, 204–5).

In *TWHF*, the Fox and the philosophy he stands for gradually lose their power of persuasion.[36] Facing death as the so-called 'perfect victim', Psyche expresses her doubts: "'I have come to feel more and more that the Fox hasn't the whole truth'" (70).[37] In the same way Orual says: "'Of course the Fox is wrong. He knows nothing about her [sc. the goddess Ungit]. [...] He thought there were no gods, or else (the fool!) that they were better than men'" (71). After Psyche has been sacrificed, it becomes obvious that the Fox is not able to live up to his own philosophical standards:[38]

> Then his love got the better of his philosophy [...] (85); Next day he said, 'You saw yesterday, Daughter [sc. Orual], how little progress I have made. I began to philosophise too late. You are younger and can go further. To love, and to lose what we love, are equally things appointed for our nature' (86).

---

ing, pleasure, death etc.) has to be stripped of its 'clothes' in order to arrive at the sophisticated conclusion that 'everything is only opinion' see Marcus Aurelius (ὅτι πάντα ὑπόληψις 12.8).
35 Ἐν ἀλλοτρίῳ ἡγεμονικῷ κακὸν σὸν οὐχ ὑφίσταται· οὐδὲ μὴν ἔν τινι τροπῇ καὶ ἑτεροιώσει τοῦ περιέχοντος. ποῦ οὖν; ὅπου τὸ περὶ κακῶν ὑπολαμβάνον σοί ἐστι. τοῦτο οὖν μὴ ὑπολαμβανέτω, καὶ πάντα εὖ ἔχει. (Aur. 4.39).
36 For this reason, I find it hard to assume that Lewis wants the Fox to be seen as 'a forerunner of Jesus' (Myers 2004, 218) as well as that '[a]s a Stoic, the Fox's perspective is closer to Lewis's Christian view' (ibd., 22).
37 On this point, I cannot see how Myers arrives at her interpretation of Psyche: 'The Fox believes that gods like Ungit do not exist. He insists that either there are no gods at all or they rise above the petty jealousies that human myths ascribe to them. Psyche finds light in his teaching' (Myers 2004, 45).
38 Cf. Myers 2004, 217.

As regards Orual's accusation of the gods, Stoic philosophy remains predominant even though her doubts increase, especially in the shorter second part of the novel. Here Orual is surprised when Arnom, priest of Ungit, answers her question of who Ungit is by stating: "'she signifies the earth, which is the womb and mother of all living things'" (270). This appears to be a typical kind of Stoic allegory: a deity is simply replaced by a physical phenomenon.[39] Accordingly, Lewis makes Orual, the narrator, immediately emphasize: 'This was the new way of talking about the gods which Arnom, and others, had learned from the Fox' (270–1). Orual doubts the sense of such a 'theology':[40] "'If that's all they [sc. the holy stories] mean, why do they wrap it up in so strange a fashion?'" (271) In other words: Why do we need mythological pictures if a simple look at nature suffices?

In the course of the visions Orual experiences at the end of the novel and the realism of which she can no longer deny,[41] she dissociates herself from Stoic philosophy. No longer does she believe in the deification of the physical world nor in an all-encompassing determinism which precludes the possibility to distinguish between the things that gods and those that men are responsible for.

Like Lucius in Apuleius,[42] Orual now considers the possibility that it is she herself who might to a certain extent be responsible for what she suffered from in her past life:[43] it might not be her outward ugliness (because of which she veiled her face) that is the problem of her life, but her obsessive love for people like Psyche and Bardia (her loyal friend and adviser) and her selfishness.[44] Now she recalls ways to perceive reality that seem to be true alternatives to the Fox's teachings:

> I knew there were certain initiations, far away at Eleusis in the Greeklands, whereby a man was said to die and live again before the soul left the body. But how could I go there? Then I

---

[39] See Bernard 1990.

[40] Myers 2004, 148 sees a Christian underpinning here: 'He [sc. Lewis] is also demonstrating that the Christian Modernists' effort to strip the faith of the supernatural by sophisticated allegorization, like Arnom's explanation of Ungit (*TWHF* 270–1) is, in the final analysis, not very convincing.'

[41] 'This vision, anyway, allowed no denial. Without question it was true' (276); 'What followed was certainly a vision and no dream' (285).

[42] '[...] *redde me meo Lucio. ac si quod offensum numen inexorabili me saevitia premit, mori saltem liceat, si non licet vivere*' (*Met.* 11.2.4). Cf. Egelhaaf-Gaiser 2000, 78.

[43] Tellingly, Orual is also afraid of being transformed into an animal: 'Often, remembering that it is sometimes the gods' way to turn us into beasts, I put my hand up under my veil to see if I could feel cat's fur [...]' (175).

[44] Cf.: 'To say that I was Ungit meant that I was as ugly in soul as she; greedy, blood-gorged' (281–2).

remembered that conversation which his friends had with Socrates before he drank the hemlock, and how he said that true wisdom is the skill and practice of death. And I thought Socrates understood such matters better than the Fox (281).

With this allusion to Plato's *Phaedo*,[45] C.S. Lewis makes Orual reveal that, in her eyes, the Fox as the proponent of Stoicism has finally been overtaken by Socrates and Plato, whose name, as Myers (2004: 210) observes, 'is never mentioned in book 1 of *TWHF*'. Similarly, in the *final* book of the *Met.*, Apuleius put (at least some bits of) his Platonic theory of providence, fortune, and free will into the sermon of the priest of Isis, so that Lucius' former belief in blind fortune and fate is superseded by Isiac-Platonic teaching, as it were. Lucius' former education he had been so proud of at the beginning of the *Met.* was of no avail to him[46] nor were the Fox's lessons to Orual.

When, in one of her visions, Orual steps forward and wants to read out her long accusation to the assembly of the gods, she discovers that the book has become small and somehow different from what she had been writing for so long (289). She finally realizes that 'the complaint was the answer. To have heard myself making it was to be answered' (294).[47] In a panoramic view, she is now seeing the ghosts of all her deceased ancestors as well as of the Fox. The Fox cannot hold back any longer and confesses:

> 'Oh, Minos, or Rhadamanthus, or Persephone, or by whatever name you are called,[48] I am to blame for most of this, and I should bear the punishment. I taught her, as men teach a parrot, to say, 'Lies of poets,'[49] and 'Ungit's a false image.' I made her think that ended the question. I never said, Too true an image of the demon within. And then the other face of Ungit (she has a thousand) ... something live anyway. And the real gods more alive. Neither they nor Ungit mere thoughts or words. [...] Of course, I didn't know; but I never told her I didn't know. I don't know now. [...] Send me away, Minos, even to Tartarus, if Tartarus can cure glibness. I made her think that a prattle of maxims would do, all thin and clear as water. [...] So I fed her on words' (295).

---

45 Cf. Myers 2004, 211. 'In book 2, there is evidence that Orual had read the *Phaedo*' (ibd., 212).—Cf. the description of the library in Glome, which includes 'some of the conversations of Socrates' (*TWHF* 232).
46 *Nec tibi natales ac ne dignitas quidem vel ipsa, qua flores, usquam doctrina profuit [...]* (*Met.* 11.15.1).
47 'This insight represents a major step forward in Orual's freeing herself spiritually from the paralyzing effect of self-centeredness' (Hunt 2016, 139).
48 Cf. Lucius' prayer to the *regina caeli: [...] quoquo nomine, quoquo ritu, quaqua facie te fas est invocare [...]* (*Met.* 11.2.3).
49 Cf. *TWHF* 8, 28, 303.

In the last vision, the Fox and Orual together see Psyche, who—as in Apuleius' *CP*—

> must go down into the deadlands to get beauty in a casket from the Queen of the Deadlands, from death herself; and bring it back to give it to Ungit so that Ungit will become beautiful.[50] But this is the law for her journey. If, for any fear or favour or love or pity, she speaks to anyone on the way, then she will never come back to the sunlit lands again[51] (301).

The Fox and Orual see that they themselves have been false friends for Psyche: "'She had no more dangerous enemies than us'", the Fox says (304).[52] Stoic theology as the Fox had taught the sisters now becomes a kind of direct temptation for Psyche as, within the vision, the former[53] Fox tells her:

> 'O Psyche, Psyche,' said the Fox in the picture (say, in the other world; it was no painted thing), 'what folly is this? What are you doing, wandering through a tunnel beneath the earth? What? You think it is the way to the Deadlands? You think the gods have sent you there? All lies of priests and poets, child. [...] There are no deadlands such as you dream of, and no such gods. Has all my teaching taught you no more than this? The god within you[54] is the god you should obey: reason, calmness, self-discipline. Fie, child, do you want to be a barbarian all your days? I would have given you a clear, Greek, full-grown soul. But there's still time. Come to me and I'll lead you out of all this darkness [...]' (302–3).

---

50 Cf. *Met.* 6.16.4.
51 Cf. *Met.* 6.18–19.
52 Cf.: 'For it began to be like those vile dreams I had had in my ravings when the cruel gods put into my mind the horrible, mad fancy that it was Psyche who was my enemy' (200). From Orual's new perspective of the second part of *TWHF*, it seems as if this 'fancy' was not sent by 'cruel gods'; rather, Orual received a kind of revelation about her obsessive love (s. above section 2), which she did not understand.
53 'The Fox was with me [sc. Orual] still; but he who rose up in the cold light to meet Psyche by the wayside was also the Fox—but older, greyer, paler than the Fox who was with me' (302). Tellingly, the old Fox, when alive, seems paler than the deceased, i.e. 'otherworldly' Fox, seeing the vision together with Orual. (Within the 'real world' of part one, the Fox died and was buried by Orual, *TWHF* 236).
54 See above: 'I needn't let it shake the god within me' (18).

5 Christianity in *TWHF*[55] and the (anti-Aristotelian) transformation of the past

In stark contrast to Apuleius, Psyche in Lewis' novel has meanwhile become a Christ-like figure:[56] She is the innocent sacrifice,[57] literally 'takes her cross upon her'[58] in spite of all adversities and bites herself 'in the lip till the blood came and wept bitterly' (304). From this Christian perspective, it also seems fitting that Orual (a few pages before, in a different vision), when awaiting the sentence of the gods, at first is frightened by the thought that the gods might *not* be just at all; but then, the transformed Fox (as witness of the vision together with Orual) soothes her, saying: '"Be sure that, whatever else you get, you will not get justice."—"Are the gods not just?"—"Oh no, child. What would become of us if they were?"' (297)

In line with Lewis' Christianity, justice in terms of the New Testament is however one of the highest goods; though at the same time no one would be able to face the divine gaze if God was merely just (and not more than just).[59] Only a mediator who is perfectly just is able to produce and obtain justice—and Psyche does this kind of job in *TWHF* when she goes 'a long journey to fetch the beauty that will make Ungit beautiful' (306).[60] And in the end, this Ungit is Psyche's sis-

---

55 For the reading of *TWHF* as Lewis' critique of modern Christian theology and as 'an oblique criticism of "the quest for the historical Jesus"' cf. Myers 1994, xiii: The Fox 'is like the biblical critics who would demythologize the Gospel by removing the dramatic, poetic miracles in order to concentrate on the principles of virtue but then find themselves loving the stories' (ibd., 203).
56 Cf. Hunt 2016, 120–1. '[...] yet Lewis intended her [sc. Psyche] to signify not Christ but the naturally Christian soul' (Adey 1998, 155). 'Psyche is in a sense the Church, the Bride of Christ, but also every believer insofar as every believer is a member of the Church' (Jacobs 2005, 262). See Hunt 2016, 141; Donaldson 1988, 19–20 and Duriez 2015, 152 for the Christian 'doctrine of exchange' and atonement in *TWHF*.—Psyche: '"How can I be the ransom for all Glome unless I die?"' (72); The Fox: '"She bore much for you then. You have borne something for her since"' (304). The last passage might be compared with the New Testament, *Col* 1.24.
57 Cf. Psyche's words: '"I know that I am betraying the best of lovers and that perhaps, before sunrise, all my happiness may be destroyed forever. This is the price you have put upon your life. Well, I must pay it [...] Go. You have saved your life; go and live it as you can."—I [sc. Orual] found I was becoming afraid of her' (166–7).
58 Cf. the New Testament, *Mt* 16.24.
59 Cf.: 'Therefore no one will be declared righteous in his sight by observing the law; rather through the law we become conscious of sin' (*Rom* 3.20); 'Who then can be saved?' (*Mt* 19.25b). (Translations from the *New International Version*, [10]1998).
60 Cf. *Met*. 6.16.4.

ter Orual:[61] from the goddess[62] Psyche, who is 'the old Psyche still; a thousand times more her very self than she had been before the Offering' (306), from Psyche Orual now is receiving her true self. As Lewis puts it in his book *Mere Christianity* (225): '[...] our real selves are all waiting for us in Him [sc. Christ]'. There might also be a parallel with Apuleius' novel: In a way Lucius 'becomes' Apuleius in the end and receives his new self.[63]

All this comes to the fore only by looking back on the past from a completely different point of view as happens in Orual's visions in the shorter second part of *TWHF*. However, it also happens—although, of course, in a non-Christian context—at the end of Apuleius' novel: having just regained his human form, Lucius is reconsidering his former life in front of an image of the goddess Isis: 'but keenly intent on the statue of the goddess I recalled my former tribulations' (*Met.* 11.17.5). Similarly, in Lewis' novel Orual discovers: 'The past which I wrote down was not the past that I thought I had (all these years) been remembering' (253).[64] And here we get back to the end of part one of *TWHF*: Orual was struck with insanity when she heard, as it were, the Apuleian version of Psyche's story the priest of Essur told her.

That the past should itself have changed comes, of course, as a paradox: how on earth could the past—i.e. the things that once happened—not be the past? C.S. Lewis tries to give a hint how to solve this riddle by turning a quotation[65] from the Greek tragedian Agathon,[66] as transmitted by Aristotle, into its opposite meaning. In his *Nicomachean Ethics* (6.2) Aristotle says: 'What happened is not possible not to have happened', and then quotes Agathon: '"For,

---

[61] '"But Maia, dear Maia, you must stand up. I have not given you the casket. You know I went a long journey to fetch the beauty that will make Ungit beautiful"' (305–6).
[62] '"Oh Psyche, oh goddess", I said' (305); 'Goddess? I had never seen a real woman before' (306). This might even be reminiscent of the Christian theology expressed in the Chalcedonian dogma: The human nature and the divine nature, unmingled and without separation, are one in Christ.
[63] Cf. Drews 2009, 437–43.
[64] Cf.: '[...] the whole of *TWHF* [,] is a "narrative of transformation"' (Donaldson 1988, xvii, 24); for the second part as a reinterpretation of part one of *TWHF* see ibd., 77–8 (albeit without a reference to the *recordabar* in Apuleius). Donaldson's (re-) reading of *TWHF* remains entirely on a metaphorical level: 'such an approach counters the psychological/reductionist interpretations which lose Orual altogether' (ibd., 80). However, also the opposite can be argued: A strictly metaphorical interpretation might lose sight of the metamorphosis, the reality of which (maybe analogous to a Christian resurrection) appears to be crucial for the novel's ending. Perhaps this question of interpretation asks for a balanced solution, somewhere 'in the golden mean'.
[65] Orual hints at this verse earlier on in the novel: 'A Greek verse says that even the gods cannot change the past. But is this true?' (173).
[66] Cf. Plato, *Symp.* 172a7.

this alone even God is deprived of, to turn whatever has been done into something that never happened.'"⁶⁷

Thinking of Lewis' Christian-Platonic metamorphosis of Apuleius' *Cupid and Psyche* in general and of Orual suffering from the unanswered question of theodicy in particular, the words spoken by the Fox in order to comfort her seem to be right in place: "'[...] Only this I know. This age of ours will one day be the distant past. And the Divine Nature can change the past. Nothing is yet in his true form'" (305).

6 Bibliography

Adey, L. (1998), *C.S. Lewis. Writer, dreamer & mentor*. Grand Rapids, Michigan.
Bernard, W. (1990), *Spätantike Dichtungstheorien. Untersuchungen zu Proklos, Herakleitos und Plutarch*. Stuttgart.
Bywater, I. (ed.) (1984 [1894]), *Aristotelis Ethica Nicomachea*, Oxford.
Dalfen, J. (ed.) (1987), *Marcus Aurelius. Ad se ipsum libri XII*, Leipzig.
De Luise, F./Moore., C./Stavru, A., eds. (2017), *Socrates and The Socratic Dialogue*, Leiden/Boston 'A man of outstanding perfection.' Apuleius' admiration for Socrates, für: Socrates and the Socratic Dialogue. ed. F. de Luise/C. Moore/A. Stavru (forthcoming).
Donaldson, M.E. (1988), *Holy places are dark places: C.S. Lewis and Paul Ricoeur on narrative transformation*. Lanham, Md.
Drews, F. (2009), *Menschliche Willensfreiheit und göttliche Vorsehung bei Augustinus, Proklos, Apuleius und John Milton*. (2 vols.) Frankfurt.
Drews, F. (2012), *Asinus Philosophans. Allegory's Fate and Isis' Providence in the Metamorphoses*, in: Keulen/Egelhaaf-Gaiser, 107–131.
Drews, F. (2015), 'A Platonic Reading of the Isis Book', in: Keulen et al, 517–528.
Drews, F. (2017), 'A man of outstanding perfection'. Apuleius' admiration for Socrates in de Luise et al., 760-71.
Duriez, C. (2015), *Bedeviled. Lewis, Tolkien and the Shadow of Evil*. Westmont.
Egelhaaf-Gaiser, U. (2000), *Kulträume im römischen Alltag. Das Isisbuch des Apuleius und der Ort der Religion im kaiserzeitlichen Rom*. Stuttgart.
Heller, S. (1983), *Apuleius, Platonic Dualism, and Eleven*, AJPh 104, 321–339.
Hunt, M. (2016), *The Divine Face in Four Writers. Shakespeare, Dostoyevsky, Hesse, and C.S. Lewis*. New York.
Jacobs, A. (2005), *The Narnian. The life and imagination of C.S. Lewis*. New York.
Keulen, W. and U. Egelhaaf-Gaiser, eds. (2012), *Aspects of Apuleius' Golden Ass III*. Leiden, Boston.
Keulen, W./Tilg, S./Nicolini, L./Graverini L./Harrison S.H./Panayotakis, S./van Mal-Maeder D. (2015), *Apuleius Madaurensis. Metamorphoses Book XI*, Leiden. (Groningen Commentaries on Apuleius).

---

67 τὸ δὲ γεγονὸς οὐκ ἐνδέχεται μὴ γενέσθαι· διὸ ὀρθῶς Ἀγάθων · μόνου γὰρ αὐτοῦ καὶ θεὸς στερίσκεται./ἀγένητα ποιεῖν ἄσσ' ἂν ᾖ πεπραγμένα. (Aristotle, *EN* 1139b8–11).

Lewis, C.S (1977 [1960]), *The Four Loves*, London.
Lewis, C.S (1984 [1956]), *Till We Have Faces*, New York.
Lewis, C.S (2000 [1952]), *Mere Christianity*, New York.
Merkelbach, R. (^{2}2001), *Isis regina—Zeus Sarapis. Die griechisch-ägyptische Religion nach den Quellen dargestellt*. Munich.
Moreschini, C. (ed.) (1991), *Apuleius. De philosophia libri*, Stuttgart, Leipzig.
Myers, D.T. (1994), *C.S. Lewis in Context*. Kent, Ohio.
Myers, D.T. (2004), *Bareface. A Guide to C. S. Lewis's Last Novel*. Columbia.
Schakel, P. (1984), *Reason and Imagination in C. S. Lewis. A Study of* Till We Have Faces. Grand Rapids, Michigan.
Walsh, P.G. (2006), *The Roman Novel*. Cambridge. [1970].
Zimmerman, M. (ed.) (2012), *Apulei Metamorphoseon libri XI*, Oxford.

Vernon L. Provencal
Faulkner's reception(s) of Apuleius' *Cupid and Psyche* in *The Reivers*[1]

I believe that man will not merely endure: he will prevail. He is immortal ... because he has a soul, a spirit capable of compassion and sacrifice and endurance.
William Faulkner, Nobel Prize Banquet Speech, 1950[2]

1 Faulkner and *The Reivers*

Many works by the Nobel Prize-winning American novelist, William Faulkner (1897–1962), including *The Reivers* (1962), are set in the fictional Mississippian county of Yoknapatawpha. Published a month before his accidental death with the subtitle, *A Reminiscence*,[3] *The Reivers* recollects characters and storylines from Faulkner's earliest to most recent work, preserving an unintended final comment on his entire corpus and its preoccupation with race, class, religion, gender and sexuality, especially as experienced through the modernization of the American South in the traumatic aftermath of the Civil War.[4]

In his Nobel speech, Faulkner identified 'the problems of the human heart in conflict with itself' as that 'which alone can make good writing because only that is worth writing about'.[5] *The Reivers* concerns the conflict of 'Virtue' and 'Nonvirtue' in the heart of an eleven-year old boy, Lucius Priest[6], who, in 1905, aided his family's adult white employee, Boon Hogganbeck, in the theft of an automobile from family patriarch, Grandfather Boss Lucius Priest, which they then

---

[1] My thanks to Stephen J. Harrison and Regine May for editorial suggestions incorporated into this paper.
[2] Hoffmann and Vickery 1960, 348.
[3] Unless otherwise noted, textual citations for *The Reivers* (*TR*) reference chapter (following its use of lower case Roman numerals) and pagination in the first edition, prepared under Faulkner's guidance, published by Random House (1962), followed by pagination in the scholarly corrected edition, prepared by Blotner and Polk, published by The Library of America (1999).
[4] Themes addressed in Moreland 2007.
[5] Hoffmann and Vickery 1960, 348.
[6] First personified *TR* iii.51 and repeatedly addressed from iii through xii, e.g. v.93–4/800, xii.259/933). As narrator, Lucius recognizes their subjection to an 'Over-goddess' (*TR* iii.51/766), a reception of Apuleian Isis and Fortune.

drove from their rural hometown of Jefferson, Mississippi, to the tenderloin (rough) district of Memphis, Tennessee.

Unexpectedly accompanied by the family's adult black employee, Ned McCaslin, the three reivers (robbers)[7] arrive the next day at Miss Reba's brothel.[8] Accommodating Boon's desire to room with Miss Corrie (as her regular paying customer), Miss Reba rooms Lucius with Miss Corrie's perverse fifteen-year old nephew, Otis, visiting from Arkansas.[9] Upon first sight, Lucius falls in love with Miss Corrie, whose real name he learns to be Everbe Corinthia. Wounded in a knife-fight with Otis in defence of her honour, Lucius' chivalry so moves Everbe that she vows—much to Boon's dismay—to reform, and she immediately quits the profession into which she had first been placed as a twelve-year old orphan by a certain 'Aunt' Fittie. Meanwhile, Ned goes off to trade the stolen automobile for a stolen racehorse, returning that evening with a plan that includes winning back the automobile by setting up a horserace in Parsham, a rural community one hour by train from Memphis. In Parsham, where Lucius stays with the black family of Ned's relative, Uncle Parsham, they fall prey to the lust and greed of a corrupt deputy, Butch Lovemaiden. Sent for by Miss Reba, the district constable, Mr. Poleymus, arrives to strip Butch of his gun and badge, but not before Everbe enrages Boon by submitting to Butch's ransom demand for 'a piece of her flesh', which she does to enable the horserace to proceed as Ned had planned, so that Lucius might win his way back home to Jefferson, which Lucius does by winning the final heat of the horserace. By this time, Grandfather Boss Priest has arrived in Parsham to bring Boon back to Jefferson with his recovered automobile and to take Lucius back home to his father, where he will graciously intercede on Lucius' behalf and instruct him in the wisdom to be gained from his fall into 'Non-virtue'. Lucius' narrative ends with the birth of his namesake, Lucius Priest Hogganbeck, which draws our attention to *The Reivers*' reception of *Cupid and Psyche*, which ends with the birth of Voluptas.

There is no explicit reference to *The Golden Ass* in *The Reivers*. Although scholars have averred a strong connection (Wagner 1975, 252; Samjay 1989, 254), external evidence does not wholly confirm it. An unsigned copy of the 1943 Black & Gold edition of Apuleius resides in Faulkner's library at his former home Rowan Oak in Oxford, Mississippi; the pages are cut but there are no an-

---

[7] Faulkner defined 'reiver' as 'an old [Scottish] Highland name for a robber'. Elnimeiri (1987) 1, s.v. 'Title'.
[8] Different aspects of Apuleian Lucius are received in all three 'reivers'.
[9] Jones 2007, 56–7 reflects on Otis' dramatic function as a figure of 'evil', albeit misrepresenting him as Everbe's son. *TR* v.102/806 explicitly identifies Otis as Everbe's 'nephew'.

notations or other signs of usage.[10] No explicit reference to Apuleius or *The Golden Ass* is catalogued in Serafin 1983,[11] but Faulkner's familiarity with *The Golden Ass* is evinced by the occurrence of 'Risibility' in *The Hamlet* (1940),[12] unmistakably a reception of the Roman deity Risus, Laughter, known only from *The Golden Ass* (2.31, 3.11; cf. Lewis & Short 1966), and 'in all likelihood an Apuleian invention' (May 2006, 188).[13]

Faulkner's alleged use of *The Golden Ass* to compose *The Reivers* conforms to his adoption of the 'mythical method' of using a classical model to render order from the chaos of contemporary experience from T.S. Eliot and James Joyce.[14] Lifelong friend and mentor, Phil Stone, who 'regaled Faulkner with classics in their original tongue', lent him copies of *Ulysses*, Eliot's poetry, and issues of *The Dial* (Stone 1961; McHaney 2007, 324). Faulkner undoubtedly read Eliot's seminal 1923 review of *Ulysses* in *The Dial*, which first identified the 'mythical method', and may have also read his 1928 review there of a new edition of Adlington's translation of *The Golden Ass* (Apuleius 1927).

In a classical reception study, however, proof of an author's acquaintance with a classical text is not a prerequisite. We do not regard the relationship between the classical and contemporary primarily through the lens of an author who employs a classical model to create a contemporary work. Instead, we view it primarily through the lens of the reader—the ultimate receiver—who employs a classical model to interpret a contemporary work.[15] So, while our ability to read *The Reivers* as a reception of *The Golden Ass* presumes its use in the act of creation, this is not prerequisite to our reception in the act of reading.

---

10 Apuleius 1943, perhaps not the 1927 edition Blotner 1964, 79 lists.
11 In 1956, Faulkner admitted that 'I taught myself a little of Latin, reading poetry'. Jellife 1956, in Serafin 1983, 132.
12 The same year Faulkner conceived *The Reivers*; cf. 'Letter to Robert K. Haas, dated 3 May 1940', Faulkner 1977, 123.
13 Just as Lucius learns that he was the victim of a practical joke in celebration of Risus (3.10), *The Hamlet*'s Jack Houston believes 'he had been victim of a useless and elaborate practical joke at the hands of the prime maniacal Risibility' (3. 3. 905). The Apuleian provenance of 'Risibility' is strengthened by the 'Milesian' context of Houston's cow becoming the beloved of the 'idiot' Ike Snopes.
14 Wagner 1975, McHaney 2007, Weinstein 2007. Serafin 1983, 16, 'Notably structured upon classical models are *The Marble Faun* (1924), *Mosquitoes* (1927), *As I Lay Dying* (1930), *Sanctuary* (1931), "Black Music" (1934), and *Absalom, Absalom!* (1936).'
15 Martindale 1993, 3, 'meaning is at the point of reception'.

2 Reception(s) of Apuleius' *Cupid and Psyche*

Faulkner's reception of Apuleius' *Cupid and Psyche* in *The Reivers* is twofold: (1) a *burlesque* reception in which the divinely beautiful Cupid and Psyche are received as the notably unhandsome, forty-year old Boon Hogganbeck, and a plain-looking prostitute about half Boon's age, known to Boon by her working name, 'Miss Corrie'; (2) a *chivalrous* reception in which eleven-year old genteel Lucius Priest plays Cupid to Miss Corrie's Psyche, but as a *lady*.[16] Although 'named for Grandmaw' (*TR vii*.155/851), Everbe Corinthia takes the name of a beautiful young woman of common birth who meets a tragic end in Faulkner's short story, *The Leg* (1934).[17] In *The Reivers*, 'Everbe' can be associated with the immortality bestowed upon Psyche and possessed by Isis; 'Corinthia' can be associated with Corinth, Lucius' hometown, as well as the insatiable Corinthian noblewoman with whom he has sex as an ass (10.19–22).

In the burlesque reception, Cupid/Boon's relationship to Psyche/Corrie is lustful, servile and self-serving; in the chivalrous reception, Cupid/Lucius' relationship to Psyche/Everbe is romantic, idealist, and self-sacrificing. The Apuleian-Platonic theme of the division and relation of the sensible and ideal is at the heart of the relationship between the burlesque and chivalrous receptions:[18] as antagonist Cupids yoked together by their relation to Corrie/Everbe, Lucius and Boon resemble the noble and ignoble steeds yoked to the chariot of the soul (*psyche*) in Plato's *Phaedrus* (246b),[19] with Boon overriding Lucius as Cupid in the burlesque reception, and Lucius overriding Boon as Cupid in the chivalrous reception. Eventually, the servile lust of Boon is overtaken and reformed by Lucius' romantic idealism, even as Lucius is educated by Boon in the experience of what Lucius refers to as 'Non-virtue' (lying, stealing, gambling and prostitution) that serves as a rite of passage from childhood to adulthood.[20]

---

[16] 'Lucius saves Corrie from a life of prostitution through his chivalric treatment of her,' Jones 2007, 57.
[17] In Faulkner 1950a.
[18] See notably Apuleius, *Apologia* 12, on the Platonic Vulgar and Celestial Venuses. For brief introductions to Platonic influence on *Cupid and Psyche*, see Hooker 1955; Kenney 1998, 9–10; Walsh 1999, xli-xlii; bibliography in Schlam and Finkelpearl 2000, 109–12; Tilg 2014; C. and S. Panayotakis 2015. Harrison 1999b acknowledges its presence but 2000, 224–5, 252–9 and 2013,165–66 (guided by Winkler 1985) insists on its 'sophistic' status.
[19] Compare Lucius' horse Candidus, see Griffiths 1978, 159–61.
[20] Hönnighausen 2007, 248.

The Reivers concludes with the rivalry of these competing receptions resolved in Everbe's marriage to Boon and the naming of their son after Lucius.

In the larger context of *The Golden Ass*, the mythic relationship of Cupid and Psyche is mirrored by and serves to interpret Lucius' sensual relationship to the slave girl Photis on the one hand, and on the other, his spiritual relationship with the goddess Isis. Likewise, in *The Reivers*, Boon's burlesque relationship with Miss Corrie as a prostitute resembles Lucius' relationship to Photis, while Lucius Priest's chivalrous relationship with Everbe Corinthia as a lady resembles Lucius' relationship with Isis.[21] It is also possible to regard Boon and Lucius as receiving contrary aspects of Cupid in his relationship with Psyche: Boon's illegal and lustful relationship with Miss Corrie as a prostitute corresponds roughly to Cupid's disobedient and impassioned relationship with Psyche whom his mother has sentenced to ignominy (5.5–25); Lucius' salutary relationship with Everbe Corinthia corresponds to Cupid's renewed relationship with Psyche in which he saves her from his mother's enmity (6.21–24).[22]

3 Burlesque reception of *Cupid and Psyche* in *The Reivers*

In addition to the reception of Cupid and Psyche as the ugly Boon and plain Miss Corrie (both orphaned in early childhood and thereafter employed in servile positions on the lowest rungs of the social ladder),[23] Venus is received as Miss Reba, 'a young woman …with a hard handsome face and hair that was too red' (*TR* v.98–99/804), a younger version of the brothel owner of Faulkner's most lurid novel, *Sanctuary* (1931). Miss Reba is 'callipygian' by association as owner and operator of the brothel: her 'girls' are described as 'nymphs' descending from 'callipygian grottoes' to greet customers (*TR* vi.133/832), 'callipygian'

---

21 On Cupid's relationship with Psyche as a mirror of Lucius' relationships with Photis and Isis: Sandy 1974; Schlam 1978; Walsh (1994: xli), n.32 quoting Kenney 1990, 148 (5.6.9); Harrison 2000, 249, n.174; Carver 2013, 256 ff.; May 2015, 69–79.
22 On the initial passionate relationship between an irascible Cupid and passionate Psyche, see Zimmerman et al. 2004, 286–88 on 5.23.121,6–8; on the renewed relationship between a salvific Cupid and imperiled Psyche, see Zimmerman et al. 2004, 524–5 on 6.21.144,8–12. Of especial note is the correspondence between the end of the passionate relationship and the beginning of the salutary relationship: 'Cupid's final flight to rescue Psyche reverses the earlier flight by which he abandoned her', Zimmerman et al. 2004, 525.
23 Boon as orphan, *TR* ii.21–22/739–40, and servile employee, *TR* ii.23–24/743; Everbe as orphan, *TR* vii.155–6/851–2.

('with beautiful buttocks') being a well-known epithet of Venus.[24] The magisterial Jupiter is received as the corrupt deputy, Butch Lovemaiden, repeatedly described as 'jovial'. It is Butch who affixes the derogatory epithets, 'Sugar Boy' and 'Sweet Thing', to Boon and Miss Corrie.

The signature passage in Faulkner's burlesque reception of *The Reivers* is Butch's reply to the proposal that he leave Boon and Everbe alone:

> 'Ha ha ha,' Butch said, without mirth, without anything. 'How's that for a idea? Huh, Sugar Boy? You and Sweet Thing bobbasheely on back to the hotel now [...].' He moved easily along the fence to where Boon stood, watching Boon ... 'I cant let Sugar Boy leave without me. I got to stay right with him, or he might get everybody in trouble. They got a law now, about taking good-looking gals across state lines for what they call immortal purposes. Sugar Boy's a stranger here; he dont know exactly where that state line's at, and his foot might slip across it while his mind's on something else–something that aint a foot. At least we dont call it a foot around here. Huh, Sugar Boy?' He slapped Boon on the back, still grinning, watching Boon–one of those slaps which *jovial* men give one another, but harder, a little too hard but not quite too hard.'[25] (*TR viii*.177/868; emphasis added)

The derogatory epithets 'Sugar Boy' and 'Sweet Thing' are apt signifiers for the burlesque reception of Cupid and Psyche as Boon and Everbe, just as 'jovial' and 'Lovemaiden' are apt descriptors to signify the burlesque reception of Jupiter as Butch. Repeated twice in subsequent passages (*TR ix*.189, 192/877, 879), 'jovial' characterizes Butch's despotic abuse of his power and authority as an officer of the law in service to his base passions of lust and greed. Equally burlesque is the reception of Jupiter's chastisement and binding of Cupid as the source of lawless immorality among gods and mortals in Butch *Lovemaiden*'s chastisement and binding of Boon: 'I got to stay right with him, or he might get everybody in trouble' (*TR viii*.177/868).[26]

A notable aspect of the burlesque reception is that the Apuleian relationships of Cupid, Psyche, Venus and Jupiter are inverted: where devout Cupid attends to a fallible Psyche, it is long-suffering Everbe who rescues Boon from

---

24 In the original August 1961 typescript (*TR* 157) Faulkner corrected 'kallipygian' to 'callipygian'. *LSJ*⁹ cites καλλίπυγος as an 'epithet for Aphrodite', after Athenaeus (*Deipnosophists* 12.554c/12.80), who reports a Syracusan temple to *Venus Kallipygos*. Also, as Elnimeiri 1987, 74 notes, 'Callipygian is the name of a famous statue of Venus, the Callipygian Venus' (*Museo Nazionale Archeologico di Napoli*).

25 The original 1961 and corrected 1999 editions of *The Reivers* preserve Faulkner's idiosyncratic punctuation; see Blotner and Polk 1999, 1001.

26 Among revisions made in January 1962, Butch's last name was changed from Lovelass to Lovemaiden; either name alludes to Jupiter's affairs with mortal women that degrades his *maiestas* and offends Juno.

his impetuosity; where irate Venus persecutes Psyche, the tough but warm-hearted Miss Reba does her utmost to protect Everbe; finally, and most notably, where the magisterial Jupiter intervenes to elevate Psyche to immortality so as to contain Cupid within the holy and lawful bonds of marriage, a debauched 'jovial' Butch Lovemaiden intervenes solely to abuse his office for the purpose of degrading a reformed Everbe by tearing her apart from Boon and forcing her back into prostitution to satisfy his own lust.

Key to the burlesque reception of *Cupid and Psyche* is Butch's ominous warning to Boon: 'They got a law now, about taking good-looking gals across state lines for what they call *immortal* purposes' (*TR viii*.177/868; emphasis added).[27] In the original typescript of August 1961, Faulkner had written '*immoral* purposes'; in the annotated typescript of October 1961, 'immoral" has been changed to 'immortal'.[28] In this final form, the text reads as though Butch the deputy meant to say what Faulkner originally wrote for him to say: '*immoral* purposes', but 'butchers' his line and misspeaks *immortal* for *immoral*. Whatever its provenance (deliberate revision, happy accident, or both), Butch's misspeaking *immortal* for *immoral* alerts the reader to his mythic role as the 'jovial' Jupiter in Faulkner's burlesque reception of *Cupid and Psyche*.

In Apuleius, Jupiter uses his power to make Psyche *immortal*, and uses the law to bind lawless Cupid to his beloved; in Faulkner, Butch abuses his power with the intent to keep Everbe *immoral* and the law to keep Boon apart from her in custody. But there seems to be a deeper meaning in Butch's misspeaking *immortal* for *immoral*—a deeper sense in which we should take him at his unintended word, that he is somehow imposing a law that prohibits 'Sugar Boy' Cupid from transporting 'Sweet Thing' Psyche across the boundary separating mortals and immortals. In his perverse enforcement of a law aimed at imposing a federal limit on state prostitution (with its implicit parallel to the Roman *lex Julia* cited by the Apuleian Jupiter, *Met*. 6.22), the border that Butch is really preventing Everbe from crossing is that which stands between her servitude as any man's 'whore' and her hope for freedom in becoming one man's 'wife'. From the Christian perspective soon brought to bear on Everbe's predicament by the intercession of the district constable, Mr Poleymus ('he's a Baptist first, and then he's

---

27 Butch anachronistically cites The *White-Slave Traffic/Mann Act* of 1910, which made it a felony to knowingly enable a woman or girl to cross state lines 'for the purpose of prostitution or debauchery, or any other immoral practice' (Langum 1994, 262).

28 That 'immortal' replaces 'immoral' in the first (1962) and corrected (1999) editions indicates that the revision was deliberate rather than negligent; cf. Elnimeiri 1987, 94, '117.20 "immortal": Butch's malapropism for 'immoral'. Cf. 'the divinity of simple unadulterated uninhibited immortal lust', *The Town* (1957) 1.1.13.

the Law', *TR* ix.210/894),[29] the line between mortality and immortality *is* the line between morality and immorality: the damnation of mortal sin through Adam and the hope of eternal salvation through Christ. As with Psyche, the law that would set Everbe free of bondage socially and spiritually is the lawful bond of holy matrimony.[30]

Despite her vow to reform, Everbe remains in the base employ of Miss Reba (kindhearted, but still a brothel owner), and it has not yet occurred to Boon to ask for her hand in marriage. In his relationship with Everbe as Miss Corrie, Boon remains on a par with his rival Butch: both degrade Everbe to the slave-status Psyche suffers under *ira Veneris*. The lustful, servile, self-serving character of Boon's burlesque relationship with Everbe Corinthia as the prostitute Miss Corrie is put most clearly by Boon himself in terms of his own status as the servile employee of Lucius' family:

> 'God damn it, she's a whore, cant she understand that? She's in the paid business of belonging to me exclusive the minute she sets her foot where I'm at like I'm in the paid business of belonging to Boss and Mr Maury exclusive the minute I set my foot where they're at. But now she's done quit. For private reasons. She cant no more. She aint got no more private rights to quit without my say-so too than I got to quit without Boss's and Mr Maury's say-so too—' (*TR* ix.197/884)

By their mutual disregard for Everbe's person (her *psyche*) in their claims upon her as a prostitute, Boon and Butch approximate the *immoral* Jove whose divine *maiestas* is debased by his desire for mortal women (Ov. *Met*. 2.846–7), for which the Apuleian Jupiter chastises Cupid even as he demands that he procure a surrogate for Psyche (*Met*. 6.22). The ugliness of character shared by Boon and Butch vis-à-vis Everbe Corinthia is matched by their physical appearance, Butch being 'a man almost as big as Boon and almost as ugly' (*TR* viii.172/864). In one respect, however, the redeemable Boon clearly differs from the irredeemable Butch: whereas the jovial Butch lords it over Boon and Everbe in his fraudulent exercise of the Law, Boon shares with Everbe a common servility of those subject to the Law.

---

29 'Faulkner was famously equivocal concerning the influence of religion on his work, explaining that "the Christian legend" was an inescapable part of "his background" and also averring that he believed in humanity's religious aspirations' (Duck 2007, 269).

30 Jupiter's decree to Psyche, *immortalis esto* (6.23), 'reflects the Roman formula of manumission … Psyche's passage from mortal to immortal can fittingly be seen as a form of manumission, especially as Venus has treated her as a runaway slave (*fugitiua*, 5,31 and 6,8)'. Zimmerman et al 2004, 545.

Outraged by Butch's despotic abuse of power (especially as exercised upon Everbe), Lucius dearly wishes upon him the wrath that a disgraced Ovidian Jove would face in an outraged Juno (Ov. *Met.* 2.846–7), mother of the ambidextrous god, Vulcan:[31]

> I hoped that maybe he [Butch] had a wife in it [his home] … an ambidextrous harridan who could cope with him by at least recording into his face each one of his countermarital victories. Because probably half the pleasure he got out of fornication was having it known who the victim was. But I wronged him. He was a bachelor. (*TR* ix.194–95/882)

Lucius' confession of error that he wronged Butch in wishing upon him Jove's 'ambidextrous harridan' might suggest that Butch's jovial abuse of his office may have misled us to mistake him for Jove, and that we ought to replace him with the incoming constable, Mr. Poleymus, who after all, is, like Jove and unlike Butch, married. Yet, Mr. Poleymus' sacrificial devotion to his invalid wife bears little resemblance to the dysfunctional relationship of Jove and Juno (*TR* xii.257/932). The true import of Lucius' error is not that the bachelor Butch has been mistaken for Juno's harangued husband, but that jovial Butch is no more the Law he pretends to be than, from a Christian standpoint, the pagan god Jupiter is truly the deity who presides over human affairs. For it is soon revealed that Butch Lovemaiden is an unlawful pretender to the throne of justice in Parsham. We learn this as a result of the arrival of the district authority, the constable Mr. Poleymus, sent for by Miss Reba to intervene (chiefly on Everbe's behalf) against Butch's machinations (*TR* xi.242/920). Although the constable's intercession comes too late to save Everbe from paying the ransom Butch demands for their freedom, when Mr Poleymus does intervene it is by way of stripping his despotic usurper of his false claim to power and authority (*TR* xii.257/932).

Despite his Greco-Roman sounding name, the heroic provenance of Mr. Poleymus is not Classical, but Christian.[32] The most memorable line going right to the heart of *The Reivers*, moreover, is delivered by Ned in his dispute with the constable's discomfort (perhaps more professional than personal) with allowing Lucius to stay with Ned's relative, Uncle Parsham (Possum), 'a white boy staying with a family of niggers':

> 'There's somewhere the Law stops and just people starts,' Ned said ….
> 'You're right,' he said. He said to me: 'That's where you want to stay? with old Possum?'

---

31 The Hephaestean epithet 'Ambidexter' (like Callipygian Venus) is here taken to be common knowledge; it appears to originate in a tradition of translating ἀγχίμολος in *Odyssey* 8.300, Hesiod *Th.* 571, 579, and *Op.* 70 as 'strong in both arms' rather than 'lame in both legs'.
32 Cf. Skaggs 2007, 173, '*polymerus* means "having many parts"'.

'Yes sir,' I said.
'All right,' he said. (*TR* xi.243–44/921, emphasis added)

The constable justifies Miss Reba's faith in his Christian ability to recognize and enforce the *limit* of the law, which sets him over and above Butch Lovemaiden, and his ancient predecessors, the Pharaoh of Egypt, who persecuted the Hebrews, and the Caesars of Rome, who persecuted the Christians:

> 'When he can be a Baptist and the Law both at the same time, he will. But any time the law comes conflicting up where nobody invited it, the law knows what it can do and where to do it. They tell how that old Pharaoh was pretty good at kinging, and another old one back in the Bible times named Caesar, that did the best he knew how. They should have visited down here and watched a Arkansas or Missippi or Tennessee constable once.' (*TR* ix.210/894–95)

Caesar and Pharaoh enjoyed absolute power as the avatars of divine law—a lawful reign that knew no limit to the exercise of their power as the law of the land. In his despotic abuse of power as a lawman to satisfy his lust for Everbe Corinthia, Butch Lovemaiden transgresses the unwritten line 'where the Law stops and people starts'. That he does so in the role of a debased Jove invites us to read Faulkner's burlesque reception of *Cupid and Psyche* as a critique of Apuleius from a modern humanist standpoint which Faulkner here identifies with Christianity vis-à-vis Rome and antiquity generally, where the salutary power of divine grace intervenes to save humanity from paying the penalty of damnation for its transgression against divine law.

The dominance of the burlesque reception of *Cupid and Psyche* in *The Reivers* under the aegis of Butch Lovemaiden wanes in (the penultimate) chapter *xii* once the unlawful deputy is stripped of his badge and gun by the lawful constable Mr Poleymus. With the serendipitous arrival of Grandfather Boss Priest in chapter *xiii* to replace Butch as Jupiter, the chivalrous reception of *Cupid and Psyche* finally gains the upper hand, with both receptions reaching their conclusion back in the Jefferson homestead of the Priest clan as a reception of the conclusion of *Cupid and Psyche* on Mount Olympus. Under the aegis of Boss Priest, Boon is moved to emulate Lucius and marry Everbe Corinthia:

> 'You mean you're going to marry her?' Grandfather said. But it was not Grandfather: it was me [i.e. Lucius] that Boon pounced, almost jumped at.
> 'God damn it,' he said, 'if you can go bare-handed against a knife defending her, why the hell cant I marry her? Aint I as good as you are, even if I aint eleven years old?' (*TR* xiii.299/966)

By way of the patronage of Boss Priest as Jupiter (and a final push by Miss Reba as Venus), the burlesque reception concludes with the marriage of Boon as a reformed Cupid to Everbe as an ascendant Psyche, followed by the birth of their son. As Lucius' namesake, the newborn Lucius Priest Hogganbeck fully reconciles the (reformed) burlesque reception of *Cupid and Psyche* with its chivalrous reception in the relationship of Lucius and Everbe:

> Then the day came at last. Everbe sent for me and I walked across town to the little backstreet almost doll-size house that Boon was buying by paying Grandfather fifty cents every Saturday. She had a nurse and she should have been in bed. But she was sitting up, waiting for me, in a wrapper; she even walked across to the cradle and stood hand on my shoulder while we looked at it.
> 'Well?' she said. 'What do you think?'
> I didn't think anything. It was just another baby, already as ugly as Boon even if it would have to wait twenty years to be as big. I said so. 'What are you going to call it?'
> 'Not it,' she said. 'Him. Cant you guess?'
> 'What?' I said.
> 'His name is Lucius Priest Hogganbeck,' she said. (*TR* xiii.304–5/971)

4 Chivalrous reception of *Cupid and Psyche* in *The Reivers*

The chivalrous reception of *Cupid and Psyche* germinates the moment Lucius and Everbe set eyes upon each other.[33] Seeing her first as the homely counterpart of Boon in the burlesque reception of Psyche, Lucius is moved by Everbe's gaze to respond in his heart to her inner beauty.[34]

> ... a big girl. I dont mean fat: just big, like Boon was big, but still a girl, young too, with dark hair and blue eyes and at first I thought her face was plain. *But she came into the room already looking at me, and I knew it didn't matter what her face was.* (*TR* v.102/806, emphasis added)[35]

---

33 'Perhaps it is because of his innocence and idealism that Lucius conceives of the world in chivalric terms. From the moment he first meets Miss Corrie in Reba's brothel he makes it his task to protect her good name, and in this respect he has a great deal in common with another of Faulkner's crusaders—Gavin Stevens', Levins 1976, 178.
34 Everbe's and Lucius' first glances at one another parallel those of Psyche (5.22) and Cupid (5.24).
35 Cf. Elnimeiri 1987, 63, 'Lucius' impression of Corrie becomes a fixed idea ... [that] expresses Lucius' idealization of Corrie and his sense of her as beyond the vulgar experience of which she is a part.'

What immediately impresses both Miss Reba and Everbe Corinthia about Lucius is not his childhood but his chivalry, the 'refinement' he learned from his family forbears, displayed by his courteous gesture of 'drugging' his foot upon meeting them, a courtesy which graciously confers upon the brothel owner and prostitute the status of 'lady', which society denies to their servile profession.

The chivalrous relationship between Lucius and Everbe develops by way of usurping the burlesque relationship of Boon and Miss Corrie, as first happens when Boon, piqued by his jealousy of Miss Corrie's relationship with a rival customer, attempts to take possession of her physically:

> 'Come here,' Boon said. Miss Corrie stopped. 'Come here, I said,' Boon said. She approached then, just outside Boon's reach; I noticed she wasn't looking at Boon at all: she was looking at me. Which was perhaps why Boon, still sitting, was able to reach suddenly and catch her arm before she could evade him, drawing her toward him, she struggling belatedly, as a girl that big would have to, still watching me. (*TR vi*.131–32/831)

The horrific shame Everbe experiences when Boon then grabs hold of her buttocks is such as to measure Boon's burlesque act by the chivalry of Lucius' gaze:

> But again too late, his hand dropping and already gripping one cheek of her bottom, in sight of us all, she straining back and looking at me again with something dark and beseeching in her eyes—shame, grief, I don't know what—while the blood rushed slowly into her big girl's face that was not really plain at all except at first. But only a moment; she was still going to be a lady. She even struggled like a lady. But she was simply too big, too strong for even anyone as big and strong as Boon to hold with just one hand, with no more grip than that; she was free. (*TR vi*.132/832)

Miss Reba's response to the situation paves the way for Miss Corrie's redemption as Mrs. Hogganbeck, saying to Boon:

> 'If you're going to run fevers over her purity, why the hell don't you set her up in a place of her own where she can keep pure and still eat?' (*TR vi*.132/832)

The critical episode in the chivalrous relationship of Lucius and Everbe which brings it to fruition is his heroic defence of her honor in the knife fight with Otis, from whom he learns her real name, Everbe Corinthia (*TR vii*.155/851), the real name of the private person—the true self, or *psyche* of Miss Corrie—yet unknown to Boon. The fight transforms Lucius' relationship with Boon and Everbe, and marks the point from which his chivalrous relationship with Everbe begins to gain ascendancy and influence over her burlesque relationship with Boon, established in a subsequent diptych of Boon and Lucius followed by Lucius and Everbe.

First, Boon good-naturedly acknowledges the superiority of Lucius' character to his own, in a manner which also emphasizes their inseparability:

> 'Eleven years old,' he said, 'and already knife-cut in a whorehouse brawl.' He looked at me. 'I wish I had knowed you thirty years ago. With you to learn me when I was eleven years old, maybe this time I'd a had some sense too. Good night.' (*TR vii*.159/854)

Second, Everbe comes and promises her virtue to Lucius, in a manner that stands proxy for a marriage vow, providing an intertextual parallel to Psyche's marriage to Cupid:

> 'You fought because of me. I've had people—drunks—fighting over me, but you're the first one ever fought for me. I aint used to it, you see. That's why I don't know what to do about it. Except one thing. I can do that. I want to make you a promise. Back there in Arkansas it was my fault. But it wont be my fault any more.' (*TR vii*.159–60/854)

In return, Everbe demands Lucius avow his acceptance: 'But you'll have to say you'll take it. You'll have to say it out loud.' 'Yes,' I said, 'I'll take it' (*TR vii*. 160/854). Hereafter, Boon's burlesque relationship to Miss Corrie the prostitute is subject to, reformed by, and ultimately identified with Lucius' chivalrous relationship to Everbe Corinthia as a lady, which finds fulfillment in the birth and naming of Lucius Priest Hogganbeck.

With Everbe's climactic presentation of the newborn Lucius Priest Hogganbeck to his namesake, Lucius Priest, the chivalrous reception of *Cupid and Psyche* concludes *The Reivers* in Lucius' hometown of Jefferson, Mississippi, as a reception of the Apuleian conclusion on Mount Olympus. Here, Lucius' mother, Alison Priest, replaces Miss Reba to receive Apuleius' transformed Venus, now restored to her (Virgilian) *maiestas* as divine *mater*.[36] Psyche's escape from servitude to *ira Veneris* in her elevation to membership in the immortal family of Olympus is received in Everbe Corinthia's escape from prostitution in her rebirth as a respectable member of human society through her marriage to Boon, which she owes to the chivalrous influence of Lucius. Jupiter's pre-marital interview with Cupid is received first as Boss Priest's interview with Boon, in which Boon professes his desire to marry Everbe (*TR xiii*.298–99/966), followed by Lucius' interview with Grandfather Boss Priest which invests Lucius with the patri-

---

[36] Kenney's (1990, 18) vengeful Venus Vulgaris (Virgilian Juno) and maternal Venus Caelestis (Lucretian Venus/Isis) corresponds to Faulkner's Miss Reba as Vulgar Venus and Lucius's mother, Alison Priest, as Celestial Venus, save that Miss Reba's vengeful wrath against Butch Lovemaiden arises from a maternal concern for Everbe like that of Virgilian Venus for Aeneas, unlike the self-regard of Virgilian Juno.

archal genteel code of *noblesse oblige,* which governs relations between races and sexes (*TR xiii*.301–03/968–69).

5 Reciprocal readings of reception

Reception confers universality on the historical particularity of contemporary receiver and classical received alike. The 'figures and fortunes' (*Met.* 1.1) of ancient Rome and modern America are superimposed on one another. Cupid and Psyche are modernized; in their modern guise, they are universalized. Boon, Lucius and Everbe gain new identities and purpose as avatars of classical antiquity in the present-day, their quotidian existence exalted to exemplary status. A comprehensive examination of the two-way effect of reception on receiver and received alike is beyond our present scope; we conclude by focusing on certain aspects of it.

By their reception in *The Reivers,* the mythical divine beauty of Apuleian Cupid and Psyche is re-imagined in the earthly and mundane existence of a pair of servile orphans and a genteel boy in the American South at the beginning of the 20th century. The result of the burlesque reception is that we can imagine Cupid in modern guise as an unhandsome buffoon, Psyche as a plain-looking prostitute, even as we recognize Boon as a modern-day Cupid and Everbe as a modern-day Psyche. Boon and Everbe become more meaningful in reading them as *our* Cupid and Psyche, and this renders the Apuleian Cupid and Psyche more meaningful in reading them as *our* Boon and Everbe. Miss Reba as a kind-hearted Venus reminds us that the goddess of love was also the patron deity of prostitution in the classical world.[37] Like Everbe Corinthia, Psyche is stripped of her place in human society and placed into a life of servitude. Butch Lovemaiden as a corrupt Jupiter reminds us and gives us insight into the significance of the division between mortal and immortal in classical antiquity, as well as slavish dependence of the *populus Romanus* upon the whim of their god-like emperors.

In the chivalrous reception of Lucius and Everbe, we can understand Psyche as a plain-looking prostitute rescued by the idealistic love of a young Cupid who sees her for the *person* she truly is. The love Everbe inspires vaguely in Boon and acutely in Lucius is a love that responds to the inner beauty of the soul illuminated by nobility of character—by what Lucius calls 'Virtue'. Such is the love which the beauty of Psyche ultimately inspires in the heart and soul of Cupid. The marriage of Boon and Psyche inspired by Lucius' chivalry helps us to understand the *human* aspect of the divine marriage of Cupid and Psyche, as a union

---

[37] Cf. Pomeroy 1995, 6–7; McGinn 1998; Neils 2000, 216.

which offers a resolution to 'the human heart in conflict with itself' where 'Virtue' finally prevails over 'Non-virtue'. The paternal beneficence of Grandfather Boss Priest that enables this victory mirrors that of Jupiter as *paterfamilias* of the Olympic pantheon (and of Augustus as *Pater Patriae*). Jupiter as Grandfather Boss Lucius Priest places divine *imperium* in a human context where power and authority is exercised to enable the downtrodden to acquire *libertas* and *dignitas* as the rightful possession of 'a spirit capable of compassion and sacrifice and endurance'.[38]

The manner in which *The Reivers* doubles up the story of *Cupid and Psyche* into two interwoven narrative strands, one comic, one idealistic, reflects again on Apuleius' own metamorphic version with its own doubling: Psyche is a version of Lucius, and both play out the salvation narrative we see in *The Reivers*. In sum, the reception of *Cupid and Psyche* in Faulkner's novel elevates both tales to universal paradigms by which to interpret the classical and contemporary through one another.

6 Bibliography

Andrews, E. A./Freund, W./Lewis, Charlton T./Short, C. (1879; 1966), *A Latin Dictionary*, Oxford.
Apuleius (1927), *The Golden Ass of Apuleius, Being the Metamorphoses of Lucius Apuleius. An English Translation by W. Adlington, 1566. Revised 1915–1927 with an Essay by Charles Whibley*, New York, 3rd edn., 1930.
Apuleius (1943), *The Golden Ass of Apuleius, Being the Metamorphoses of Lucius Apuleius. Translated by W. Adlington, 1566. Revised 1915–1927 with an essay by Charles Whibley*, New York, Black & Gold edition.
Brodsky, L.D./Hamblin, R. (1982), *Faulkner. A Comprehensive Guide to the Brodsky Collection, Volume 1: The Biobibliography*, Jackson.
Carver, R.H.F. (2013), 'Between Photis and Isis: fiction, reality, and the ideal in *The Golden Ass* of Apuleius', in: Paschalis and Panayotakis, 243–74.
Cohen, B. (ed.) (2000), *Not the Classical Ideal. Athens and the Construction of the Other in Greek Art*, Leiden.
Eliot, T.S. (1923), '*Ulysses*, order and myth', *The Dial* 75.5, 480–83.
Eliot, T.S. (1928), 'The Golden Ass of Apuleius', *The Dial* 85.3, 254–57.
Elnimeiri, A.M. (1987), *William Faulkner's The Reivers. A Reminiscence. Annotations to the Novel*, Diss. Ann Arbor.
Faulkner, W. (1950a), *Collected Stories of William Faulkner*, New York.
Faulkner, W. (1950b), 'The Stockholm Address', in: Hoffman/Vickery, 347–348.

---

38 Hoffmann and Vickery 1960, 348.

Faulkner, W. (1961a), *The Reivers. A Reminiscence,* Original Typescript Dated 21 August 1961, Faulkner Archives, Alderman Library, University of Virginia.
Faulkner, W. (1961b), *The Reivers. A Reminiscence,* Annotated Typescript, Dated October 1961, Faulkner Archives, Alderman Library, University of Virginia.
Faulkner, W. (1961c), *The Reivers. A Reminiscence* [partial copy of 1961b], Faulkner Archives, Alderman Library, University of Virginia.
Faulkner, W. (1962), *The Reivers. A Reminiscence,* [Random House] New York.
Faulkner, W. (1977), *Selected Letters of William Faulkner,* ed. J.L. Blotner, New York.
Faulkner, W. (1985), *Novels 1930–1935: As I Lay Dying, Sanctuary, Light in August, Pylon,* eds. J. Blotner and N. Polk, New York.
Faulkner, W. (1990), *Novels 1936–1940: Absalom, Absalom!, The Unvanquished, If I Forget Thee Jerusalem [The Wild Palms],The Hamlet,* eds. J. Blotner and N. Polk, New York.
Faulkner, W. (1992), *The Reivers. A Reminiscence,* Vintage International edition, New York.
Faulkner, W. (1999), *Novels 1957–1962: The Town, The Mansion, The Reivers,* eds. J. Blotner and N. Polk, New York.
Faulkner, W. (2006), *Novels 1926–1929: Soldiers' Pay, Mosquitos, Flags in the Dust, The Sound and the Fury,* eds. J. Blotner and N. Polk, New York.
Griffiths, J. Gwyn (1978), 'Isis in the *Metamorphoses* of Apuleius', in: Hijmans Jr./van der Paardt, 141–66.
Hanson, J.A. (1989), *Apuleius.* Metamorphoses, 2 vols., Cambridge Mass.
Harrison, S.J. (ed.) (1999a), *Oxford Readings in The Roman Novel,* Oxford.
Harrison, S.J. (1999b), 'Introduction' in Harrison 1999a.
Harrison, S.J. (2000), *Apuleius: A Latin Sophist,* Oxford.
Harrison, S.J. (ed.) (2015), *Characterisation in Apuleius' Metamorphoses. Nine Studies,* Newcastle upon Tyne.
Hijmans Jr., B. L./van der Paardt, R. T. (eds.) (1978), *Aspects of Apuleius' Golden Ass,* Groningen.
Hoffman, F.J./Vickery, O.W. (eds.) (1960), *William Faulkner. Three Decades of Criticism,* New York and London.
Hönnighausen, L. (2007), 'Violence in Faulkner's major novels', in: Moreland, 236–51.
Hooker, W. (1955), 'Apuleius's *Cupid and Psyche* as a Platonic Myth', *The Bucknell Review* 5, 24–38.
Jones, A.G. (2007), 'A loving gentleman and the corncob man. Faulkner, gender, sexuality, and *The Reivers*', in: Moreland 46–64.
Kenney E. J. (1990), *Apuleius. Cupid and Psyche,* Cambridge.
Kenney E. J. (1998), *Apuleius. The Golden Ass. Translated with an Introduction and Notes,* London.
Kenney, E. J. (2008), 'Introduction and Notes', in: Ovid transl. Melville.
Langum, D.J. (1994), *Crossing Over the Line. Legislating Morality and the Mann Act,* Chicago.
Levins, L.G. (1976), *Faulkner's Heroic Design. The Yoknapatawpha Novels,* Athens, GA.
Martindale, C. (1993), *Redeeming the Text. Latin Poetry and the Hermeneutics of Reception,* Cambridge.
May, R. (2006), *Apuleius and Drama. The Ass on Stage,* Oxford.
May, R. (2015), 'Photis (*Metamorphoses* Books 1–3)', in: Harrison 2015, 59–74.
McGinn, T.A.J. (1998), *Prostitution, Sexuality, and the Law in Ancient Rome,* Oxford.
McHaney, T.L. (2007), 'Faulkner's genre experiments', in: Moreland, 321–41.

Moreland, R.C. (ed.) (2007), *A Companion to William Faulkner*, Malden, MA.
Neils, J. (2000), 'Others within the Other: An Intimate look at heterai and maenads', in: Cohen, 203–26.
Ovid (2008), *Metamorphoses*. transl. A.D. Melville. With an Introduction and Notes by E. J. Kenney, Oxford.
Panayotakis, C./Panayotakis, S. (2015), 'The human characters in the Tale of Cupid and Psyche (*Metamorphoses* 4.28–6.24)', in: Harrison 2015, 125–45.
Paschalis, M./Panayotakis, S. (eds.) (2013), *The Construction of the Real and the Ideal in the Ancient Novel*, Groningen. (Ancient Narrative Supplementum 17).
Pomeroy, S. (1995), *Goddesses, Whores, Wives, and Slaves. Women in Classical Antiquity*, New York.
Sandy, G.N. (1974), '*Serviles voluptates* in Apuleius' *Metamorphoses*', Phoenix 28, 234–44.
Schlam, C. (1978), 'Sex and sanctity. The relationship of male and female in the *Metamorphoses*', in: Hijmans/van der Paardt, 95–105.
Schlam, C./Finkelpearl, E. (2000), 'A review of scholarship on Apuleius' *Metamorphoses* 1970–1998', *Lustrum* 42, Göttingen.
Serafin, J.M. (1983), *Faulkner's Uses of the Classics*, Ann Arbor.
Skaggs, M.M. (2007) *Axes. Willa Cather and William Faulkner*, Lincoln.
Stone, P. (1961), 'Letter from Phil Stone to Richard P. Adams, October 4, 1961', listed as '1503i', in: Brodsky/Hamblin, 296–7.
Tilg, S. (2014), *Apuleius'* Metamorphoses, Oxford.
Wagner, L.W. (1975), *Hemingway and Faulkner: Inventors/Masters*, Meteuchen, N.J.
Walsh, P.G. (1999), *Apuleius: The Golden Ass. Translated with an Introduction and Notes*, Oxford.
Weinstein, P. (2007), '"Make it new": Faulkner and modernism', in: Moreland, 342–58.
Winkler, J.J. (1985), *Auctor & Actor. A Narratological Reading of Apuleius'* Golden Ass, Berkeley.
Zimmerman, M./Panayotakis, S./Hunink, V./Keulen, W.H./Harrison, S.J./McCreight, T.D./Wesseling, B./ van Mal-Maeder, D. (eds.) (2004), *Apuleius Madaurensis. Metamorphoses. Books IV. 28–35, V and VI. 1–24. The Tale of Cupid and Psyche. Text, Introduction and Commentary*, Groningen. Groningen Commentaries on Apuleius.

Holly Ranger
'I have tried to be blind in love'. Psyche and the quest for feminine poetic autonomy in Sylvia Plath's *House of Eros*

In a photograph taken in the spring of 1960, Sylvia Plath stands at home in London with her infant daughter Frieda in front of what Plath describes in a letter as a 'lovely engraving of Isis from one of Ted's astrological books'; the engraving is titled 'Isis: Magnae Deorum Matris: as described by Apuleius'.[1] In Hughes' poem 'Isis'—published in his letter-poems to Plath, *Birthday Letters*—this engraving steps off the wall to take possession of Plath's body as she gives birth to Frieda, 'The great goddess in person... waxing full'.[2] Hughes is a careful reader of Plath; but he seems here to have interpreted the Isiac imagery that permeates Plath's work—of moons, and roses, for example—biographically, that is, as representations of Plath-the-woman, rather than as signals of her literary classical engagement. Hughes' poem provides a useful example of how, when Plath's classicism is noted, it is often only to mythologize Plath herself, overlooking her sophisticated employment of ancient texts.[3] This essay takes Plath's Isiac symbols as a signal of a sustained engagement with Apuleius, particularly with his tale of *Cupid and Psyche*. I argue that Plath explores the dimensions of the Latin text in a critical dialogue which develops from an early poetic response to Psyche-as-woman, to the refiguration of Psyche's tale to allegorize a feminine quest for embodied knowledge and artistic autonomy.

In part one of the essay, I explore Plath's early engagement with Apuleius' tale in her poems and short stories; in part two, I detail the episode's appearance in Plath's series of Yorkshire Moors poems. I argue that Plath's bathetic presentation of the House of Eros in her moor poems is filtered through its dilapidated appearance in Charlotte Brontë's *Jane Eyre* (1847). Against a critical tradition that

---

[1] Plath 1976, 357 (photograph), 365. The engraving provides the cover to Athanasius Kircher's *Oedipus Aegyptiacus* (1652–4); cf. *Met.* 11.3–4.
[2] Hughes 1998, 111–12. Hughes' own use of Apuleius centres on the statue of Diana and Actaeon described at Met. 2.4 and Actaeon's presence in the text as a cipher for Lucius' lustful curiosity; Ingleheart 2009, 206 suggests that it is the character of Lucius who informs Hughes' additions to Ovid's Latin in his translation of the Actaeon episode in *Tales from Ovid*, and Hughes' presentation of the young hunter's lustful, but guiltless 'surges of curiosity' (Hughes 1997, 107). For Hughes' classicism more broadly, see the essays collected in Rees 2009.
[3] For Plath-as-Isis see Sagar 2006 and Rollyson 2013.

https://doi.org/10.1515/9783110641585-021

reads Plath's Yorkshire poems as a rewriting of Emily Brontë's *Wuthering Heights* (1847), I suggest instead that Plath draws on the literary authority of Charlotte Brontë's earlier Psyche-narrative to self-consciously position herself within a tradition of women readers and rewriters of Apuleius, using the tale to foreground a difference between masculine and feminine poetic vision. In part three, I discuss in detail Plath's verse-play *Three Women,* in which Psyche is presented with three alternative endings to her story. It is through this final iteration of Psyche's tale that Plath harnesses Apuleius to forge an identity as both a woman and a woman poet.

1 Early poems and short fiction

Plath studied Plato's allegorical myths of Eros and the Soul as found in *Phaedrus* (246a-254e) and *Symposium* (180d2–181b8, 189c2-d6) for the philosophy paper whilst at Newnham College, Cambridge in 1955–1956, and she owned both dialogues in the Harvard Loeb editions.[4] She likely first read Apuleius' artful recombination of Platonic myth and folk-tale in his *Cupid and Psyche* in the 1940s in her school Latin class—US contemporaries of Plath, Rachel DuPlessis and Alicia Ostriker, both recall reading Apuleius at school and both have written their own Psyche sequences—although, to Plath, Apuleius' story is always read through a Platonic lens.[5]

Apuleius' tale first appears in the narratives of two poems written in Plath's teenage years, 'To a Jilted Lover' and 'On Looking into the Eyes of a Demon Lover'. Plath responds primarily to the narrative of the story, and her speakers take on the roles of young women, Psyche-characters, who offend—and lose—

---

[4] Plath's autographed and annotated copies of *Euthyphro, Apology, Crito, Phaedo, Phaedrus* (1953, Loeb Classical Library, transl. H.N. Fowler) and *Lysis, Symposium, Gorgias* (1953, Loeb, transl. W. R. M. Lamb) are held in the Smith College Archives. Plath's tutor at Newnham, Dorothea Krook-Gilead, recalls Plath's intellectual engagement with Plato in her philosophy supervisions in Krook 1976.

[5] DuPlessis 1979 and Ostriker 1982, 1983b; both write their Psyche sequences explicitly in response to Neumann's psychoanalytic reading of Apuleius' tale (1956). Additional likely intertexts for Plath's response to Apuleius include H.D.'s 'Psyche: *"Love drove her to hell"'* and the tale's appearance in Woolf's *Mrs Dalloway* (1925); Plath was familiar with Graves' *The White Goddess* (1948), which quotes Adlington's translation of Apuleius, and she may have been aware of Graves' own translation *The Golden Ass* (1950). As Plath was familiar with the Loeb Classical Library (n. 4, above), she may also have seen S. Gaselee's revised 1915 Loeb edition of Adlington's translation. On Plato in the second century, see Trapp 1990; for Platonist readings of *Cupid and Psyche* see Hooker 1955, Penwill 1975, Kenney 1990b, Dowden 1998, and O'Brien 1998.

a lover. In 'To a Jilted Lover', the Psyche-figure laments her infliction of a burning wound upon a supernatural lover:

> Cold on my narrow cot I lie
> and in sorrow look
> through my window-square of black:
> figured in the midnight sky,
> a mosaic of stars
> diagrams the falling years,
> while from the moon, my lover's eye
> chills me to death
> with radiance of his frozen faith.
>
> Once I wounded him with so
> small a thorn
> I never thought his flesh would burn
> or that the heat within would grow
> until he stood
> incandescent as a god;
> now there is nowhere I can go
> to hide from him:
> moon and sun reflect his flame.[6]

Plath's Psyche lies awake waiting for the 'angry dawn', alone in the House of Eros: 'blazing in my golden hell'. Plath stresses Psyche's guilt, rather than her helpless distress, for her Psyche is not the partner who has been abandoned. Unfolding through the stanzas from the ambivalent 'cold' that sharply opens the poem, a self-reflexive monologue castigates the emotional chill displayed in jilting a lover—an injury the speaker perceived at the time to be 'so | small a thorn'. Plath reimagines and elaborates Apuleius' tale by transposing minor details; here, Cupid's arrow upon which Psyche pricks her finger becomes the thorn which wounds her lover—a symbol which may draw upon Apuleius' description of Psyche's 'rose-red blood' as much as it draws upon the fairy tale tradition through which Psyche has been transmitted, a tradition whose thorny roses and spindles symbolise menarche and sexual initiation.[7] In another inversion of Apuleius' *Cupid and Psyche*, Plath's Psyche feels that it is the memory of Cupid that she cannot escape, rather than the vengeful Venus: 'there is nowhere... to hide'. Plath's characters swap identifications throughout the poem as Cupid metamorphoses into Venus, and Psyche shifts into the role of Lucius

---

[6] Plath 1982, 309–10.
[7] *sanguinis rosei*, *Met.* 5.23.2; on symbolism in the fairy tale tradition e.g. the spindles and thorns in Psyche-variant 'Briar Rose' ('Sleeping Beauty'), see Vaz da Silva 2014.

as Plath draws from the *Metamorphoses* more widely for the poem's Isiac imagery. The 'moon' appears in both the first two stanzas—echoed in the rhyme of 'noon' in the final third stanza—and Psyche's sleepless, guilt-wracked night in 'To a Jilted Lover' is shaded by Lucius' night beneath the stars before his Isiac epiphany.[8]

In her second early response to Apuleius, 'On Looking into the Eyes of a Demon Lover', the poem's imagery of moons, magic mirrors, and reflections continues Plath's blend of Isiac symbolism with fairy tale tropes:

> Here are two pupils
> whose moons of black
> transform to cripples
> all who look:
> each lovely lady
> who peers inside
> takes on the body
> of a toad.
> Within these mirrors
> the world inverts:
> the fond admirer's
> burning darts
> turn back to injure
> the thrusting hand
> and inflame to danger
> the scarlet wound.
> I sought my image
> in the scorching glass,
> for what fire could damage
> a witch's face?
> So I stared in that furnace
> where beauties char
> but found radiant Venus
> reflected there.[9]

If 'To a Jilted Lover' staged the aftermath of the break between Cupid and Psyche, 'On Looking into the Eyes of a Demon Lover' captures Psyche earlier in dramatic time, at the moment of revelation. On the verge of uncovering the face of her monstrous husband, her 'thrusting hand'—bearing the lamp that inflicts a 'scarlet wound'—is pricked upon Cupid's 'burning darts'; their mutual love 'inflames' each wound. Again, subjectivities shift across the poem with its referen-

---

[8] In this early poem, however, the moon takes on a hostile, male role.
[9] Plath 1982, 325.

ces to metamorphosis ('transforming'), as Plath's speaker takes on in turn the roles of Psyche, the witch Meroe, who transforms rivals into frogs, and the goddess Venus (we recall in Apuleius that Psyche is hailed as Venus-on earth; here she sees herself as Venus in her mirror: 'the world inverts').[10]

While Plath's early poems focused on the point of crisis in the relationship, 'The Other Two', a poem written shortly after Plath's own wedding, reimagines Cupid and Psyche's marriage: the reader meets the contemporary double—and ghostly original—of Apuleius' lovers.[11] The poem ostensibly describes the villa in Benidorm in which Plath and Hughes spent the first weeks of their honeymoon, but Plath turns to Apuleius once more, borrowing from his description of Cupid's palace (ll. 1–14):

> All summer we moved in a villa brimful of echoes,
> Cool as the pearled interior of a conch.
> Bells, hooves, of the high-stepping black goats woke us.
> Around our bed the baronial furniture
> Foundered through levels of light seagreen and strange.
> Not one leaf wrinkled in the clearing air.
> We dreamed how we were perfect, and we were.
>
> Against bare, whitewashed walls, the furniture
> Anchored itself, griffin-legged and darkly grained.
>
> Two of us in a place meant for ten more—
> Our footsteps multiplied in the shadowy chambers,
> Our voices fathomed a profounder sound:
> The walnut banquet table, the twelve chairs
> Mirrored the intricate gestures of two others.

Like Apuleius' Psyche wandering alone through the dazzling palace lighted by the glint of its gold walls—gazing upwards at the animals carved onto the walls, and spoken to by voices without bodies who lay a banquet before her—Plath's Psyche moves through this villa of floating furniture, 'brimful of echoes'

---

10 Meroe *cauponem... aemulum deformavit in ranam* ('Semblably she changed one of her neighbours... into a Frog, in that he was one of her occupation, and therefore she bare him a grudge'), *Met.* 1.9.3; Psyche is worshipped *ut ipsam... deam Venerem... terras Venerem aliam... pullulasse* ('[as] if she were Lady Venus indeed... [as if] the earth... had budded and yeelded forth a new Venus'), 4.28.4. Psyche's reflection here also alludes to and inverts the animate mirror in Psyche-variant 'Snow White', into which the stepmother stares but sees only the girl reflected. On Psyche in the fairy tale tradition, see Warner 1995; Anderson 2000, 61–71; on *Cupid and Psyche* as folktale, see Thompson 1946, 97–101, 281–2.
11 Plath 1982, 68–9.

and disembodied 'voices', 'bells', and 'profound sounds'.[12] As in the earlier poems, the 'moon-blanched' (l. 22) night suggests the background presence of the goddess Isis; and in a reprisal of the mirror imagery of 'On Looking into the Eyes of a Demon Lover', Plath's newlyweds attend an uncanny banquet 'above love's ruinage' (l. 34) at which a ghostly couple appear reflected in mirrored cabinets and lacquered wooden table-tops.

By the close of the poem, the line between reflection and reality has blurred and the real and ghostly lovers become confused: 'Ourselves the haunters, and they, flesh and blood... we were | The heaven those two dreamed of, in despair'. The poem emphasizes the perfection and completeness of the contemporary couple, and uses the mirrored lovers to darkly foreshadow the strife ahead in Psyche's tale; the ghostly lovers are trapped in a 'purgatory'. Although Psyche here is accompanied on her journey to the Underworld by Cupid, the mythic couple's 'arguments' and 'stricken voices' contrast with the happy marriage and birth of *Voluptas* that concludes *Cupid and Psyche*, and is suggestive rather of a mutual hell. Plath's ghostly couple comments ironically on promised marital 'bliss', a theme that is explored further in Plath's later Psyche-poems.[13]

Plath is not uncritically mythologizing her life, nor suggesting that the two couples are equivalent. Unlike the clear image in the mirror of the early

---

12 Cf. the *sonus* that signals Cupid's approach, *Met*. 2.4.2. Plath's description of the villa borrows particularly from the description at *Met*. 5.1.–5.3: there 'was a princely Edifice, wrought and builded not by the art or hand of man, but by the mighty power of God: and you would judge at the first entry therein, that it were some pleasant and worthy [*luculentem*, 'full of light, splendid'] mansion for the powers of heaven. For the embowings above were of Citron and Ivory, propped and undermined with pillars of gold, the walls covered and seeled with silver, divers sorts of beasts were graven and carved, that seemed to encounter with such as entered in. All things were so curiously and finely wrought, that it seemed either to be the worke of some Demy god, or God himselfe. The pavement was all of pretious stones, divided and cut from one another, whereon was carved divers kindes of pictures... Every part and angle of the house was so well adorned, that by reason of the pretious stones and inestimable treasure there, it glittered and shone in such sort, that the chambers, porches, and doores gave light as it had beene the Sunne... And when with great pleasure [Psyche] had viewed all these things, she heard a voyce without any body, that sayd, "... we whose voyces you heare bee your servants, and ready to minister unto you according to your desire..." ... [at once] shee saw the table garnished with meats, and a chaire to sit downe. When Psyches was set downe, all sorts of divine meates and wines were brought in, not by any body, but as it were by a winde, for she saw no person before her, but only heard voyces on every side' (transl. Adlington). The 'echoes', 'conch', and 'goats' in Plath's opening three lines anticipate the appearance of Pan and Echo in Apuleius' story.
13 Plath may have read *Cupid and Psyche* ironically, arguably as Apuleius wrote it, positioned in the middle of a work filled with infidelity and adultery.

poems, the reflections here are merely ghosts glimpsed in shining walnut-wood and immaterial dreams; and unlike her relatively direct rewriting of the myth as a teen, Plath has begun to critically examine the story, asking whether her contemporary couple mirror Cupid and Psyche perfectly or imperfectly. This seems to be a recognition by Plath of the difference and distance between the classical and the present, for despite the heaviness of the pull of mythic romance (the mirrored lovers are 'Heavy as statuary... They poise and grieve as in some old tragedy'; ll. 15; 21), her 'intricate gestures' are 'swallowed in a great darkness' (ll. 14; 25), an image evocative of both the self-conscious sense of belatedness in Plath's act of reception, and the thick palimpsest of the classical tradition whose layers obscure and refract the Apuleian tale. Plath begins to experiment with *Cupid and Psyche* in 'The Other Two', using the tale to meditate on her act of reception at the same time as she rewrites Apuleius.

In a series of journal entries and fictional sketches written a few months later, Plath further considers not only the possibility of looking at old stories in new ways, but that reception may be a gendered process.[14] Plath wrote this series of variations on the Psyche narrative while she was staying with Hughes' family at their home in Yorkshire and adventuring on the trail of the Brontë sisters. In the first sketch, a young woman runs out from a house 'clustered with ghosts' on to the Yorkshire moors following a quarrel with her lover; Plath describes it as the 'story of a lost woman' who must show a 'match-flare of courage in the dark'.[15] Plath's aim was to foreground the theme of vision by telling the story from four points of view, 'each with [a] different vision of day, changing', and the themes were to be 'aloneness... aloneness & difference... —eternal paradox of identity'. If this first sketch told of Psyche's flight from the House of Eros, a second tells of her quest to reunite with Cupid. Titled 'House of Wind', the character Elly sets off on a Jane Eyre-like quest—although here to find 'career or

---

14 Around the same time (Spring/Summer 1957), Plath details working on a second novel—a sequel to her as-yet-unpublished *The Bell Jar*—the plot of which follows the *Cupid and Psyche* narrative closely: the novel recounts 'the voyage of a girl through destruction, hatred and despair to seek and find the meaning of the redemptive power of love' (Plath 2000, 275). Provisionally titled *Falcon Yard* (the place in Cambridge where she first met future husband Hughes), the novel's theme was to be 'love, a falcon, striking once and for all' (Plath 2000, 284). The manuscript of this novel seems unfortunately to have been mostly destroyed, although a few pages remain in archives under the working title *Venus in the Seventh*, an astrological designation of the planet Venus in the seventh astrological 'house'—the 'house of partnership', or 'house of marriage' (but also a word-association play on the 'house of love/eros'); in astrology, in which Hughes encouraged Plath to take an interest, Venus is valent as 'Magna Deorum Mater', or Isis.
15 Plath 2000, 302–3.

man'. She must overcome 'jealousy' and 'selfishness' to find 'faith in her fiancé'.[16] In this story sketch, Psyche's envious sisters become aspects of Elly's personality that must be conquered, and Plath plays with using a Psyche narrative to portray the quest of a 1950s woman who feels caught between art and domesticity. In this story, Psyche chooses her fiancé.

In a third variation, 'Four Corners of a Windy House', Plath considers the framing narrative of a 'trip to & from Wuthering Heights told by four characters—each seeing a different facet of absolute reality—which is nearest truth?'.[17] As in the poem 'The Other Two', Plath uses two doubled or mirrored couples, but does so here to foreground a male character's voice. Whereas in Plath's first sketches the story was narrated by Psyche herself, foregrounding the woman's perspective on the myth, here Plath looks at Psyche through the eyes of a Gravesian male poet. Plath draws upon the Platonic reading of *Cupid and Psyche*—in which there are two forms each of Eros and Psyche, and a distinction is drawn between the respectively base and higher pleasures of body and soul—to allegorize the male poet's struggle between 'his muse, versus his woman—flesh & spirit'.[18] Plath links Psyche here to male artistic vision, and the woman of the myth is split or doubled to create the seemingly irreconcilable 'real' woman and Muse.

These journal notes offer an insight into Plath's working process and reveal her experimentation with different (re)reading and (re)writing strategies to approach Apuleius' text—narratively, thematically, or allegorically. The link that Plath makes between Apuleius and Yorkshire at first seems curious, and perhaps secondary to the emphasis on allusions to the Brontës; but Plath further develops the association in a series of five poems written during and about her stay in Yorkshire that draw heavily on Psyche's tale: 'The Snowman on the Moor', 'Hardcastle Crags', 'The Great Carbuncle', 'Two Views of Withens', and 'Wuthering Heights'. In his own series of moor poems that recall this trip, Hughes explicitly forges the biographical connection between the doomed author of *Wuthering Heights* and Plath herself, taking the novel as his reference point and blurring the lines between Emily-Cathy-Sylvia.[19] I would like to suggest that the titles of Plath's poems—with their too-obvious allusions to *Wuthering Heights*—are a misdirection, and that an understanding of Plath's intertextual models freshly illuminates her Yorkshire poems.

---

16 Plath 2000, 303.
17 Plath 2000, 303.
18 Plato, *Symp.* 180d$_2$-181b$_8$; Kenney 1990a, b.
19 See esp. 'Emily Brontë', Hughes 2005, 485.

2 Yorkshire poems

The reputation of Emily Brontë's novel *Wuthering Heights* as a classic romance narrative may have led Plath by word association or plot similarities to think of a gnomic 'house of love' when she visited Yorkshire. Plath certainly was rereading *Wuthering Heights* whilst staying there, but she noted in a letter that Cathy and Heathcliff's love is destructive and often fuelled by jealousy and hatred.[20] Plath's choice of title, 'Wuthering Heights', coupled with the poem's atmosphere of oppression, ironizes both the common romanticizing elision of the devastating sexual and racial politics that drive the plot of *Wuthering Heights*, and an uncritical reading of Cupid and Psyche's 'house of love'—the social institution of marriage which necessarily (in the 1950s) is at the expense of the woman's intellectual freedom. Yet the Brontë sisters had read translations of Apuleius—alongside essays on the philosophical allegory of the *Cupid and Psyche* tale—published in the 1830s-40s in the journals *Blackwoods* and *Fraser's*.[21] The influence of *Metamorphoses* is reflected in the structural framework of *Wuthering Heights*, which borrows the form of Apuleius' super-narrative and inset *fabula anilis*: Brontë's Lucius, Mr Lockwood, records in his diary the 'tale' of Cathy and Heathcliff as narrated to him by the old housekeeper, Nelly Dean.[22] It seems to me, however, that Plath's reassessment of *Cupid and Psyche* takes its main cue rather from the tale's striking appearance in *Jane Eyre*, whose narrative structure is clearly influenced by the story of Psyche.

In the central section of the novel, the eponymous and innocent Jane is sent to work as a governess at a grand house—like 'some Bluebeard's castle'—with opulent furnishings, moulded ceilings, and wooden panels carved with bestial scenes.[23] Like Psyche, Jane enters Rochester's house before she has met him; and like Plath's description of the Benidorm villa, Jane's tour of Rochester's ornately-decorated mansion borrows heavily from Apuleius' House of Eros.[24] As Jane's tour of the house comes to a close, a 'sound... struck my ear' (cf. *sonus aures eius accedit*, *Met.* 5.4.2), a disembodied and 'curious laugh... a clamorous peal that seemed to wake an echo in every chamber'.[25] The first time Jane meets

---

[20] Plath 1976, 270.
[21] Imlay 1989, 105–10.
[22] Brontë 2000, 65.
[23] Brontë 1999, 92.
[24] Brontë 1999, 90–2, esp. the ornately carved oak bed, 'portraying effigies of strange flowers, and stranger birds, and strangest human beings,—all which would have looked strange, indeed, by the pallid gleam of moonlight'.
[25] Brontë 1999, 92–3.

Rochester whilst out walking one evening, the 'metallic clatter' of his approach on horseback causes her to take fright at the thought that the beast approaching her is the Gytrash, a shapeshifting spectre that takes on animal forms, a possible hint at Apuleius' theme of animal metamorphosis.[26] Although the appearance of '[t]he man, the human being, broke the spell at once', Rochester remains aloof and mysterious—a man rumoured to have a 'violent' temperament—and a man whom Jane only meets in the house at night.[27] On the day of their wedding, Jane discovers Rochester's secret (his wife, Bertha Mason, the 'madwoman in the attic' and author of the disembodied laugh) and flees onto the moors; like Psyche's, Jane's flight is interspersed with repeated fainting and near-death experiences, and she is aided by friendly helpers.[28] Finally, Jane is reunited with Rochester, now blinded and living in a woodsman's cottage of 'moderate size, and no architectural pretensions'—his former mansion a blackened ruin following a fire.[29] While in Apuleius Psyche must earn her husband's love to be raised to immortality, in Brontë, it is Rochester who must earn Jane's goodness and be humbled by the experience.

In two Yorkshire poems, 'The Snowman on the Moor' and 'Hardcastle Crags', Plath draws upon Brontë's narrative reversal of Apuleius in which it is Psyche-Jane who abandons Cupid-Rochester. Both poems narrate a woman's flight from a lover's quarrel onto the moors alone, reprising the theme from Plath's short stories now understood to be indebted to *Jane Eyre*'s version of Psyche.[30] Plath echoes Brontë's imagery and vocabulary in her descriptions of the moor, dilapidated mansion, and the wind, which 'Pours by like destiny, bending | Everything in one direction' (cf., for example, the storm on the eve of Jane's aborted

---

26 Brontë 1999, 97.
27 Brontë 1999, 97; 92.
28 In the novel, Jane also plays the role of Cupid herself, as she awakes at night to find Bertha in her room (Brontë 1999, 249–520). Although it is Bertha's face which Jane sees lit by candlelight, Bertha holds the secret to Rochester's identity and history.
29 Brontë 1999, 380. The fire in *Jane Eyre* is started by Bertha, in the role of Psyche again as she steals into Rochester's bedroom at night; recalling the demise of Psyche's sisters, Bertha dies when she leaps from the roof of the flaming mansion.
30 Picking up imagery from Brontë and Apuleius, both poems are crowded with echoes, and set under the moonlight; 'echo' appears three times in 'Hardcastle Crags', linked to its occurrences in 'The Other Two' and *Three Women*. In 'The Great Carbuncle', the House of Eros informs the uncanny atmosphere of a journey over a moor-top, 'air-streaming and green-lit', aiming 'Toward that great jewel… hidden, yet | Simultaneously seen… | Knowable only by light || Other than noon, than moon, stars'; the speaker is 'suspended' by enchantment 'among the floating | Tables and chairs', Plath 1982, 72–3 (cf. *inhumanae mensae*, *Met*. 5.8.1).

wedding, which 'poured' 'one way', 'bending' the trees').³¹ The characterizations of Plath's speakers also borrow from the bold Jane Eyre in their wilful natures and first-person narration (Jane addresses her reader directly).

In a further nod to Brontë, Plath's setting of the tale of *Cupid and Psyche* is no longer idyllic as in 'The Other Two' ('We dreamed how we were perfect, and we were'), but gothic: 'The whole landscape | Loomed absolute as the antique world was | Once... || Enough to snuff the quick | Of her small heat out'.³² In an inversion of the flowery meadow into which Psyche is conveyed softly down, Plath describes the valleys in 'Wuthering Heights' as 'narrow and black as purses' full of 'small change'; a biting contrast both between the romantic Brontë-myth and the contemporary tourist-trap, and between the myth of romance and the quotidian reality of domesticity and purse-strings (Plath describes the romanticized Yorkshire life as one in reality spent 'pottering' around kitchens).³³ The House of Eros is no longer palatial but—as in *Jane Eyre*—a burned-out and abandoned, yet animate, whispering house of echoes and repeated 'odd syllables', the 'Black stone, black stone' an echo of 'love's ruinage' first seen at the Spanish villa.

Like the distorted reflections of the earlier poems, this dystopic setting may suggest an image of the woman writer wandering Psyche-like through a fragmented literary landscape in search of female classical models. Plath's use in her various Psyche poems of the fairy tale and gothic traditions may be a means of aligning herself more explicitly with feminine oral and literary cultures and to wryly literalize and positively reclaim the self-described *fabula anilis* of Apuleius' inset story.³⁴ Cupid's burned-down palace becomes a literary detail

---

31 Brontë 1999, 343–4; Stoneman 1996, 235. The goddess Isis appears again: 'As I looked up... the moon appeared momentarily... her disk was blood-red', Brontë 1999, 343–4.
32 Plath 1982, 68; 62.
33 Plath 1982, 167–168; Plath 2000, 588–9.
34 At a time when women's writing was widely dismissed—the first three editions of *Jane Eyre* were published under the pseudonym Currer Bell—Charlotte Brontë draws upon the cultural power of the classical tradition to authorise her tale of a modern Psyche; but there is a self-conscious dry irony in Brontë's choice of a text that explicitly dismisses itself as women's speech. In a published biographical note, Brontë writes that the three sisters' choice of the gender 'ambiguous' pseudonyms Currer (Charlotte), Ellis (Emily), and Acton (Anne) was 'dictated by a sort of conscientious scruple at assuming Christian names positively masculine, while we did not like to declare ourselves women, because—without at that time suspecting that our mode of writing and thinking was not what is called "feminine"—we had a vague impression that authoresses are liable to be looked on with prejudice; we had noticed how critics sometimes use for their chastisement the weapon of personality, and for their reward, a flattery, which is not true praise' (Bell [Brontë, C.] 1850a, ix). On 'old wife's tales' and the role of the female storyteller of *Cupid*

passed down between generations of women writers via the gothic tradition. To me, this detail of the burned-down palace also suggests a witty postscript to the moment of crisis in Apuleius; that is, Brontë, and in turn Plath, take Psyche's burning of Cupid to its narrative conclusion with a common-sense domestic touch—carelessly carried flames risk burning the house down.[35]

A complementary poem, 'Two Views of Withens', describes a journey to visit the alleged setting for *Wuthering Heights*, the now-ruined farmhouse Top Withens.[36] Again, despite the overt link to *Wuthering Heights*, the poem is covertly informed by the description of the House of Eros in *Jane Eyre*. Plath plays with Romantic tropes throughout the poem, and explores the nature of poetic vision as a gendered experience by staging an experiment: two poets looking at the House of Eros:

> I found bare moor,
> A colorless weather,
> And the House of Eros
> Low-lintelled, no palace;
> You, luckier,
> Report white pillars, a blue sky,
> The ghosts, kindly.[37]

Plath counterpoints two imagined ekphraseis; while the male poet describes the dazzling beauty of the palace, the poem's speaker describes it with a knowingly bathetic, yet disappointed realism, comically deflating classicizing male poetic vision with an unromantic assessment of a dilapidated cottage.[38] In Hughes' ver-

---

and Psyche, see Warner 1995; Zimmerman and van Mal-Maeder (1998) discuss the female perspective in Apuleius' text; Finkelpearl (1998) suggests that 'old wife's tale' is not derogatory, but is meant to emphasize the tale as oral, epic (masculine) tradition which heroizes Psyche; Graverini 2006 argues for Apuleius' self-ironic use of the term, and warns us against reading Apuleius too literally.
35 Compare the burned-down robber's house in Welty's *The Robber Bridegroom* (1942), with Gaisser's paper in this volume.
36 Plath 1982, 71–2; for Plath's 1956 pen and ink drawing of Top Withens, 'Wuthering Heights Today', see Hughes 2013, 5.
37 Plath 1982, 72.
38 Nor does the woman poet have a Zephyr to magically transport her to Cupid's palace in 'Two Views', but she must trek there 'over hill | And hill, and through peaty water' (Plath 1982, 72); here, Plath turns her ironic poetic eye on herself, as there is more than a touch of comedy in this image of the American facing the reality of the 'great' British outdoors. The poem also presents two readings of *Wuthering Heights*, one romantic, one realistic. In the 1850 preface written for Emily Brontës' *Wuthering Heights*—the edition in which the true gender of the author is revealed (n. 34, above)—Charlotte Brontë invokes the myth of Psyche in relation to poetic inspiration: 'the

sion of this visit, a poem also titled 'Wuthering Heights', he casts himself as the clear-visioned Yorkshireman and Plath as the romanticizing American abroad. Yet Plath's presentation of an alternative viewpoint questions the authority of male poetic vision and declares that this reading of the House of Eros will be a woman's.[39]

In her pitching of masculine against feminine poetic vision and interpretation, Plath uses the tale of Psyche—filtered via *Jane Eyre*—to foreground issues of reading and reception, turning the lovers' quarrel over literal vision into one of poetic vision. Plath's Yorkshire poems announce Plath's intention to tell Apuleius' story in a new way, and document her attendant rejection of male poetic vision by consciously situating herself in a tradition of women readers and rewriters of Apuleius' text. At the close of 'Wuthering Heights'—written four years after 'Two Views'—Plath seizes control of Apuleius' tale, directing it to her own purposes and reclaiming poetic narrative authority with a strong personal voice: the 'tilted and disparate', 'unstable horizons' of the myth 'dissolve and dissolve | Like a series of promises, as I step forward... me, me.' A few months later, Plath presents her most innovative reworking of Apuleius' tale yet, her verse-play *Three Women: A Monologue for Three Voices*.[40]

3 *Three Women*

While the earlier poems and short stories featured both lovers, in *Three Women*, Plath focuses on the pregnant Psyche. She also explicitly draws on *Metamorpho-*

---

writer who possesses the creative gift owns something of which he is not always master—something that at times strangely wills and works for itself. He may lay down rules and devise principles, and to rules and principles it [creativity] will perhaps for years lie in subjection; and then, haply without any warning of revolt, there comes a time when it will no longer consent to "harrow the vallies, or be bound with a band in the furrow"—when it "laughs at the multitude of the city, and regards not the crying of the driver"—when, refusing absolutely to make ropes out of sea-sand any longer, it sets to work on statue-hewing, and you have a Pluto or a Jove, a Tisiphone or a Psyche, a Mermaid or a Madonna, as Fate or Inspiration direct" (Bell [Brontë, C.] 1850b, xxiii–xxiv).

39 Hughes 1998, 59–61. Hughes' poems 'Two Trees at Top Withens', 'Top Withens', and 'Two Photographs of Top Withens' all directly respond to—and borrow imagery and vocabulary from—Plath's 'Two Views of Withens'; Hughes' 'Haworth Parsonage' describes their visit to the Brontës' home. On masculine and feminine modes of reading/writing *Cupid and Psyche*, cf. *Jane Eyre*: Rochester quotes poetry to woo Jane, while Jane answers in prose: 'a fitting vehicle for the plain truth', Imlay 1989, 40.
40 Plath 1982, 176–87.

ses more widely here than in the earlier Psyche poems, which focused on the inset tale, as the previously background role of the attendant moon now comes to the fore. Plath reworks the moonlit apparition of Isis and the initiation of Lucius that forms the end of Apuleius' super-narrative to represent three women's journeys through pregnancy, and to stage three alternative endings to Psyche's story.[41] With a nod to the modernists, Plath sets the action of the play over one night and updates the setting of the myth to a maternity ward of a hospital—a wholly new interpretation of the 'house of love'. The play comprises three monologues—separate, yet sharing imagery and vocabulary—representing three Psyches (or perhaps Psyche and her two sisters): First Voice bears a son; Second Voice, a secretary, miscarries; and Third Voice, a student, bears a daughter who is placed for adoption.[42] Here, Plath's women face the trials of pregnancy rather than the tasks set for Psyche, and unlike the fleeing woman of the moor poems, the three Psyches of the play are static; instead, their journeys are of self-knowledge, and the landscape they must traverse is physiological and psychological. The three temples of the goddesses are replaced in *Three Women* by the home, the office, and the university, while Plath nimbly replaces the points of crisis in Apuleius—Psyche's repeated fits of swooning—with the blackouts of anaesthesia and labour pain.

The explicitly aural premise for *Three Women*—comprising three women narrating their stories, and written as a radio-play for a BBC audience—echoes the Apuleian frame narrative of the old woman and Charite.[43] Plath's subject-matter and use of the Psyche-tale to meditate on pregnancy and women's bodies suggests that her imagined audience is also female. Although the old woman in Apuleius offers a cautionary tale—Plath's tale is more informative—the intention in both ancient and modern texts is to pass on feminine knowledge. Although Apuleius is sympathetic to Psyche's perspective, Plath's shift from third to first person narration enables her to stress Psyche's voice and interiority in a way that counteracts the emphasis on physical beauty in the Latin. Plath also removes Cupid from the myth, rejecting the latent narrative of feminine acculturation that has been accentuated by the fairy-tale tradition, and transforming Psyche's quest from a punishment and a search for the masculine (her male lover) into a celebration of feminine curiosity—a gendered quest for self-knowledge

---

[41] For an Isiac reading of *Cupid and Psyche* see Merkelbach 1958; Walsh 1970, 52–3, 202, 207 discusses Psyche-as-Io/Isis; Walsh 1994 reconciles the Isiac reading with the Platonic allegory.
[42] Plath acknowledged a debt of inspiration to Ingmar Bergman's *Brink of Life* (1958), likewise set in a maternity ward and recording the conversation between three expectant women.
[43] First broadcast 19 August 1962.

about herself, her body, and her sexuality.⁴⁴ Psyche's quest is not a monolithic or universalising account of motherhood, however, nor is it predicated upon the experience of motherhood; that the three voices are separate demonstrates a recognition by Plath that motherhood can divide as well as unite women. Plath's Psyche is not reconciled with Cupid, but with her own body and her own desires and choices. In *Three Women*, Plath finally rejects the romance narrative to stress instead the love and equality of the mother-infant relationship ('I will him... to love me as I love him'); moreover—as threatened in Apuleius—Plath's Psyche is willing to sacrifice the divinity of her child in order to achieve this love: 'He is human after all... There is no guile or warp in him'.⁴⁵

In the play, Psyche's quest is refigured as an initiation ritual; just as Lucius wakes on a moonlit beach, the moon which gazes 'luminous as a nurse' through the windows of the maternity ward is mentioned explicitly five times in the opening dialogues of the three women.⁴⁶ The moon is a favourite image of Plath's (occurring 104 times across her poetry), but is often read by critics negatively as representing sterility and barrenness. An understanding of the Apuleian allusion that links the moon and the fertility goddess Isis (*Met.* 11.3; in conjunction with a host of other Isiac imagery in the play—waxing and waning, tides and tidal movements, roses, Egypt, Africa, and hieroglyphs), reveals Plath's positive and gendered use of the moon and metamorphic Isiac imagery to describe the ill or menstruating body, and the transformations of pregnancy. Further suggestions of the initiation ritual can be found in First Voice's description of herself as 'sacrificial' (recall Psyche's sacrificial exposure on the rocks), and ready for the 'great event', although Plath is careful to emphasize a woman's choice and to reject a simple bourgeois celebration of motherhood: Third Voice is not censured for giving away her daughter, saying repeatedly, 'I wasn't ready'.⁴⁷ In stressing

---

44 Cf. the distinction Lucius makes at the beginning of the novel between information-gathering and curiosity (if ironic), '[I] am not so *curious* as *desirous to know* all', *Met.* 1.2.6. Psyche's naivety is also a fault (Cupid upbraids her at 5.11.5, 5.1.45, and 5.24.3, *simplicissima*); Plath seizes the potential for subversion here, highlighting the danger of denying women knowledge about their bodies and desires.
45 Plath 1982, 186, 181.
46 Plath 1982, 176.
47 Plath 1982, 179, 176, 178. In *Metamorphoses*, the priest restrains Lucius until he is ready to be initiated, 'as parents commonly bridle the [*inmaturis*, 'untimely, immature'] desires of their children', 11.21.3. Plath redirects and literalizes the simile: here, the initiate is the woman who takes control both of her body and the decision regarding the timeliness and readiness to become a parent. As the priest comments, the great mystery is not one to be undertaken thoughtlessly (*temerarium*, 11.21.6).

Psyche's autonomy Plath resituates the active, questing woman at the centre of Apuleius' text that has been obscured by the fairy-tale tradition.

First Voice is the Psyche who has followed Cupid's commands ('I see nothing'), and she gives birth to the son promised to Psyche before she disobeys.[48] Her happy altruism is not presented without irony, however, but this ambivalence likewise refuses to trivialise motherhood by idealising it; First Voice describes her labour pains in honest detail: 'I am the centre of an atrocity'.[49] Third Voice, who gives her daughter away, is a composite of mythic characters perhaps more familiar from Ovid—Procne, Io, Echo, Narcissus, Danaë and Leda—but who appear in Apuleius in Jupiter's reminiscences of his transformation into 'snakes, fire, beasts, birds, and oxen' for past 'adulteries'.[50] Here, Third Voice describes the moment of conception:

> I remember the minute I knew for sure.
> The willows were chilling,
> The face in the pool was beautiful, but not mine—
> It had a consequential look, like everything else,
> And all I could see was dangers: doves and words,
> Stars and showers of gold—conceptions, conceptions!
> I remember a white, cold wing
> And the great swan, with its terrible look,
> Coming at me, like a castle, from the top of the river.
> There is a snake in swans.
> He glided by...
> ... The white clouds rearing[51]

Carver in this volume makes a case for Yeats' poem on Leda and the swan being inspired by Apuleius. Plath's specific use of these stories introduces the masculine threat that pervades *Three Women* and hints at the latent narrative of mar-

---

48 Plath 1982, 180; *infantem... divinum* ('divine male child'), *Met.* 5.11.6, cf. *filia* ('daughter'), 6.24.4; Jane Eyre's first-born is a son, and Rochester's 'happiness' at the birth restores his sight (Brontë 1999, 400).
49 Plath 1982, 180.
50 *Met.* 6.22; Narcissus at *Met.* 4.34 and 5.26.
51 Plath 1982, 177–8. The snake in feathers also evokes the rumoured serpentine nature of the winged Cupid. Third Voice is Procne ('what is this bird that cries | With such sorrow in its voice?'); Second Voice is Niobe (hard as stone, in perpetual grieving), Tiresias ('neither man nor woman, | Neither a woman, happy to be like a man, nor a man'), and Philomela via Lavinia of *Titus Andronicus* ('learn to speak with fingers, not a tongue. | The body is resourceful'). Plath may add Io here as a cipher for Isis.

riage as rape, epitomized by the figure of Proserpina and emphasized by the woman's violent experience of the Christian *rapture* of 'doves and words'.[52]

Plath emphasizes Apuleius' theme of vision and sight in Lucius' story through her dense employment of the imagery of vision, faces, and reflections, to comment on her evolving reception practice. In a development from the distorted reflections of her earlier Psyche poems, the face Plath's speaker finds reflected back now is not her own as she breaks free from the 'pull' of Apuleius' text to make it wholly her own. For despite the disturbing presentation of conception-as-rape, Plath counterbalances this imagery with a celebration of embodied subjectivity—Plath's women are no longer passive victims or passive receptacles for the masculine element, but active drivers of their pregnancies. The voice who loses her child will try again on her own terms, as—perhaps—will the voice who 'wasn't ready'. The *raptus* of conception is replaced at the close of the play by the transcendental pleasures of a woman's body and the rapture First Voice experiences when contemplating her new-born—a constructive loving look that neutralizes both the 'terrible look' of Jupiter's swan and the destructive consequences of Psyche's female gaze in Apuleius.

Second Voice, however, sees only the terrifying face of a patriarchal society when she searches for the faces of her lover and unborn child:[53]

> Is this my lover then?
> ...
> I have tried not to think too hard. I have tried to be natural.
> I have tried to be blind in love, like other women,
> Blind in my bed, with my dear blind sweet one,
> Not looking, through the thick dark, for the face of another.
> I did not look. But still the face was there,
> The face of the unborn one that loved its perfections,
> The face of the dead one that only be so perfect
> In its easy peace, could only keep holy so.
> And then there were other faces. The faces of nations,
> Governments, parliaments, societies,
> The faceless faces of important men.[54]

Plath's Second Voice is closest to Apuleius' Psyche, who hopes to discover her unseen lover's face in that of her child; yet despite her adherence to the rules of Love's game ('I did not look'), in a world defined—or written—by men Psyche

---

[52] Symbols of the Holy Spirit and the Son, with echoes of the immaculate conception, that cast Psyche as a Mary.
[53] Cf. '[your] face I shall learne at length by the childe in my belly', *Met.* 5.13.3.
[54] Plath 1982, 178–9.

miscarries her child; the jealousy of her male office colleagues renders her 'flat because they are'.[55] Masculinity is associated throughout the play with destruction, war, industry, and invasive medical practices, and is threatened by feminine fertility, education, and growth. The Psyche who loses her child in *Three Women* is the one most embroiled in masculine society, a secretary who orders 'parts, || Parts, bits, cogs' for 'destructions, | Bulldozers, guillotines, white chambers of shrieks'.[56] On first reading, this dichotomy seems to reflect the mutually exclusive choice between career and motherhood presented to women in the 1950s and 1960s. I do not think that Plath is arguing that masculine and feminine worlds are incompatible, however, only that women cannot unite work and domesticity in a masculine world, following masculine rules. That the Psyche who miscarries her child is the one who is punished for her attempt to have a career is a savage critique on Plath's part of the behavioural codes for and expectations of contemporary women.

Although there is a tension between women and masculine spheres, Third Voice returns to university; perhaps Plath suggests that constructive forms of education and art are more compatible with motherhood, and that feminine creativity can produce both intellectual and physical offspring. Plath's verse-play itself demonstrates that a synthesis is possible—that is, writing poems about motherhood—offering a particularly feminine alternative or solution to the Platonic allegory, refuting the implicit denigration of both women and the body by multiplying and flaunting the physicality of the pregnant Psyche.[57] Plath's Psyche-tale thus both explicitly celebrates women's bodies and functions allegorically, metapoetically reflecting on its act of reception at the same time as Plath literalizes male poetic tropes of poetry as giving birth, using infants as ciphers for poems—here, for works of classical reception. In this reading, Psyche is transformed by Plath into the woman artist, and the three voices represent three methods of approaching Apuleius—three different quests for feminine artistic autonomy and fulfilment. This reading is strengthened by the final image of the

---

55 Plath 1982, 179; in Apuleius, Psyche's sisters warn her that her monstrous husband is rumoured to eat pregnant women, and is fattening her up for that purpose alone: 'hee will not pamper thee long with delicate meats, but when the time of delivery shall approach, he will devoure both thee and thy child', *Met.* 5.18.1.
56 Plath 1982, 177.
57 Plath uses the word 'soul' repeatedly throughout *Three Women* filtered through a Platonic lens; the rows of babies in incubation cots are 'innocent souls... beginning to remember'. Haskins 2014, providing a useful survey of gendered readings of *Metamorphoses*, notes that reading Psyche allegorically negates her femaleness. Plath may, however, have read a feminine allegory for the trimesters of pregnancy in Psyche's trials of seeds, containers, and water; her three voices embody each stage—a feminine allegory that does not negate Psyche-as-woman.

poem, in which the Psyche who has lost her child sits at home stitching a piece of lace, here used metonymically for writing; although she has not received the promised patriarchal reward of a child, the next act of feminine creative composition is already under way. Psyche will get to re-take her trial.[58]

4 Conclusion

Plath repeatedly demonstrates an intimate knowledge of the original Latin text of *Cupid and Psyche* through close verbal, thematic, and structural echoes. Her repetition, re-viewing, and re-writing of the tale mimics Psyche's gaze as she looks and then looks again at the story, narrating it first literally, and then allegorically. In her early poems, Plath refigured the Apuleian theme of sight as one about artistic vision and competition; in later poems, she refigures the quest. Plath's evolving engagement enacts different modes of reading and writing—from retelling the story thematically or narratively, to critically examining the story, to rewriting both the story and the allegory, at the same time as she critically re-examines her own reception practices. While Apuleius' Psyche is characterized by her helplessness and need, Plath's Psyches are characterized by their artistic activity, as Plath restores the active nature of Psyche's quest that has frequently been elided in receptions of Apuleius' tale which heighten Psyche's passivity and 'feminine' naivety. Yet in a contrast to the rather domestic nature of Psyche's original tasks (sorting beans, gathering wool—albeit from flesh-eating sheep—and sourcing an exotic beauty cream), the quest faced by her Psyches is to narrate their lives and creative processes. In this way, Plath harnesses Apuleius' tale to comment on feminine modes of reading, speaking, and writing, and the intellectual pleasure taken by a woman in artistic creativity and poetic fulfilment—to consider a woman's artistic production as well as reproduction.

Plath's blend of the domestic and the classical makes her engagement with Apuleius both uniquely personal and deeply literary. In *Three Women* Plath not only creates a synthesis between the worlds of art and domesticity, but also between classical myth, Platonic allegory, and the denigrated feminine literary traditions of fairy tale and gothic romance. Plath's achievement is to reclaim to subversive ends a latent narrative of female acculturation that has traditionally been used to police women's bodies and behaviours, to celebrate instead women's

---

58 On sewing and weaving as feminist poetics, see e.g. Joplin 1984, Marcus 1984, and Ford 1997; see Homans 1988 on the appeal of classical female weavers such as Penelope and Arachne to contemporary women writers.

bodies and feminine knowledge-seeking as positive and creative forces. In the quest for artistic, not romantic fulfilment, Plath uses Psyche to represent an identity as both a woman and a woman poet. Plath's rewriting of a Latin text to foreground women's creativity and embodied experiences represents a radical feminine reclaiming of the classical tradition; writing before women began to take a political approach to theorizing their lives, Plath, using Apuleius, takes a poetic one.

5 Bibliography

Adlington, W. (1566), *The Golden Asse of Lucius Apuleius*, first printed 1566; reprinted from an edition of 1639, London.
Anderson, G. (2000), *Fairytale in the Ancient World*, London.
Bell, C. [Brontë, C.] (ed.) (1850), Wuthering Heights *and* Agnes Grey *by Ellis and Acton Bell, A New Edition Revised, with a Biographical Notice of the Authors, A Selection from Their Literary Remains, And a Preface*, London.
Bell, C. [Brontë, C.] (1850a), 'Biographical Notice of Ellis and Acton Bell', in: Bell 1950, vii-xvi.
Bell, C. [Brontë, C.] (1850b), 'Editor's Preface to the New Edition of *Wuthering Heights*', in: Bell 1850, xvii-xxiv.
Brontë, C. (1999), *Jane Eyre*, Ware.
Brontë, E. (2000), *Wuthering Heights*, Ware.
Dowden, K. (1998), '*Cupid and Psyche.* a question of the vision of Apuleius', in: Zimmerman et al. 1998, 1–22.
DuPlessis, R. (1979), 'Psyche, or Wholeness', *The Massachusetts Review* 20(1), 77–96.
Finkelpearl, E. (1998), *Metamorphosis of Language in Apuleius: A Study of Allusion in the Novel*, Ann Arbor.
Ford, K. J. (1997), *Gender and the Poetics of Excess: Moments of Brocade*, Jackson.
Graverini, L. (2006), 'An Old Wife's Tale', in: Keulen et al. 2006, 86–100.
Haskins, S. (2014), 'A Gendered Reading for the character of Psyche in Apuleius' *Metamorphoses*', *Mnemosyne* 67(2), 247–69.
Homans, M. (1988), 'The Woman in the Cave: Recent Feminist Fictions and the Classical Underworld', *Contemporary Literature* 29, 369–402.
Hooker, W. (1955), 'Apuleius' "Cupid and Psyche" as a Platonic myth', *The Bucknell Review* 5(3), 24–38.
Hughes, T. (1997) *Tales from Ovid*. London.
Hughes, T. (1998), *Birthday Letters*, London.
Hughes, T. (2005), *Collected Poems*, ed. P. Keegan, London.
Ingleheart, J. (2009) 'The transformations of the Actaeon myth: Ovid, *Metamorphoses* 3 and Ted Hughes's *Tales from Ovid*', in: Rees 2009, 199–215.
Hughes, F. (ed.) (2013), *Sylvia Plath: Drawings*, London.
Imlay, E. (1989), *Charlotte Brontë and the Mysteries of Love: Myth and Allegory in Jane Eyre*, New York.
Joplin, P. K. (1984), 'The voice of the shuttle is ours', *Stanford Literary Review* 1, 25–53.
Kenney, E. J. (1990a), 'Psyche and her mysterious husband', in: Russell 1990, 175–98.

Kenney, E. J. (ed.) (1990b), *Apuleius: Cupid and Psyche*, Cambridge.
Keulen, W. H. et al., (eds.) (2006), *Lectiones Scrupulosae: Essays in Honour of Maaike Zimmerman*, Groningen.
Krook, D. (1976), 'Recollections of Sylvia Plath', *Critical Quarterly* 18(4), 5–14.
Marcus, J. (1984), 'Still Practice, A/Wrested Alphabet: Towards a Feminist Aesthetic', *Tulsa Studies in Women's Literature* 3(1/2), 79–97.
Merkelbach, R. (1958), 'Eros und Psyche', *Philologus-Zeitschrift für antike Literatur und ihre Rezeption* 102, 103–16.
O'Brien, M. (1998), 'For every tatter in its mortal dress. Love, Soul, and her sisters', in: Zimmerman et al. 1998, 22–34.
Ostriker, A. (1982), 'Message From the Sleeper at Hell's Mouth', *Poetry* 139(4), 189–94.
Ostriker, A. (1983a), *Writing Like a Woman*, Ann Arbor.
Ostriker, A. (1983b), 'I Make My Psyche from My Need', in: Ostriker 1983a, 132–45.
Penwill, J. L. (1975), 'Slavish pleasures and thoughtless curiosity: fall and redemption in Apuleius' *Metamorphoses*', *Ramus* 4, 49–82.
Plath, S. (1976), *Letters Home: Correspondence 1950–1963*, ed. A. Plath, London.
Plath, S. (1982), *Collected Poems*, ed. T. Hughes, London.
Plath, S. (2000), *The Journals of Sylvia Plath*, ed. K. Kukil, London.
Rees, R. (ed.) (2009), *Ted Hughes and the Classics*. Oxford.
Rollyson, C. (2013), *American Isis: The Life and Art of Sylvia Plath*, New York.
Russell, D. A. (ed.) (1990), *Antonine Literature*, Oxford.
Sagar, K. (2006), *The Laughter of Foxes: A Study of Ted Hughes*, 2nd edn., Liverpool.
Stoneman, P. (1996), *Brontë Transformations: The Cultural Dissemination of Jane Eyre and Wuthering Heights*, New York.
Tatar, M. (ed.) (2014), *The Cambridge Companion to Fairy Tales*, Cambridge.
Thompson, S. (1946), *The Folktale*, Berkeley.
Trapp, M. (1990), 'Plato's *Phaedrus* in second-century Greek literature', in: Russell 1990, 141–73.
van Mal-Maeder, D. and Zimmerman, M. (1998), 'The Many Voices in "Cupid and Psyche"', in: Zimmerman et al., 83–102.
Vaz da Silva, F. (2014), 'Fairy-tale symbolism', in: Tatar 2014, 97–116.
Walsh, P. G. (1970), *The Roman Novel*, Cambridge.
Walsh, P. G. (ed.) (1994), *Apuleius: The Golden Ass*, Oxford.
Warner, M. (1995), *From the Beast to the Blonde: On fairy tales and their tellers*, London.
Zimmerman, M. et al., (eds.) (1998), *Aspects of Apuleius' Golden Ass. Volume II: Cupid and Psyche*, Groningen.

V New Audiences

Lisa Maurice
Cupid and Psyche for children

Although the narrative of *Cupid and Psyche* contains many elements that feature in traditional fairy tales throughout the Western world, there are also aspects of the myth that may not seem particularly suitable for the young. Nevertheless, the story has long been beloved of authors of juvenile literature, and throughout the twentieth and twenty-first centuries the story has appeared in multiple versions for children, all of which must deal with the issue of how exactly to adapt or 'censor' the story for youth.[1] In this paper I provide a chronological overview of the various retellings of the myth, examining how it has been adapted and utilized in children's literature over the past 150 years.

1 Popularising *Cupid and Psyche*. Thomas Bulfinch's *The Age of Fable*

Although not originally written for children, Bulfinch's retelling of Apuleius' tale has been so influential on later juvenile versions that it only makes sense to start with this version. An obituary of Bulfinch described him as:

> the author of several books of decided usefulness, which he prepared with great painstaking and taste. ... The Age of Fable, ... in which, expurgated of all that would be offensive, he presented in a succinct and lucid manner a large amount of information needed by readers, and especially by young readers, in regard to the beliefs, superstitions and traditions of the past.[2]

Bulfinch's work, according to his own introduction to *The Age of Fable*, was aimed at a general, non-specialised audience, and its aim was:

> To teach readers who are not yet familiar with the writers of Greece and Rome, ... enough of the stories which form what is called their mythology, to make those allusions intelligible which one meets every day, even in the authors of our own time.[3]

---
1 On the issue of censorship see McClure 1983, 22–5; Foerstel 2006; Booth 2011, 26–30; Hutcheon 2006, 118.
2 The *Boston Daily Evening Transcript*, May 27, 1867.
3 Bulfinch 1855, 3

https://doi.org/10.1515/9783110641585-022

This was necessary since 'the literature of our time, as of all the centuries of Christendom, is full of allusions to the gods and goddesses of the Greeks and Romans'. First published in 1855, this book has remained in print until the present day, and, principally because of its 'expurgation' of the 'offensive', has been a major source text for the later adaptations of *Cupid and Psyche* for children. In particular, Bulfinch's expansion of Cupid's role has been influential. Where Apuleius' tale moves from Venus' commands and departure to the sea to the oracle, Bulfinch's version adds the following paragraph:

> Cupid prepared to obey the commands of his mother. There are two fountains in Venus's garden, one of sweet waters, the other of bitter. Cupid filled two amber vases, one from each fountain, and suspending them from the top of his quiver, hastened to the chamber of Psyche, whom he found asleep. He shed a few drops from the bitter fountain over her lips, though the sight of her almost moved him to pity; then touched her side with the point of his arrow. At the touch she awoke, and opened eyes upon Cupid (himself invisible) which so startled him that in his confusion he wounded himself with his own arrow. Heedless of his wound his whole thought now was to repair the mischief he had done, and he poured the balmy drops of joy over all her silken ringlets.

These details, which add a romantic love to Cupid himself and may be a sign of the pervasive influence of Mary Tighe's *Psyche*, which features two fountains of sorrow and joy (discussed in this volume by O'Brien), have overtly or subtly been incorporated into later retellings so extensively that they are sometimes even quoted as being by Apuleius himself, as in a recent academic article which includes the remarkable citation:

> Apuleius, T (1855), 'The golden ass – books 4–6', *The Age of Fable; or, Stories of Gods and Heroes* in T Bulfinch, (Online), retrieved from < http://www.pitt.edu/~dash/cupid.html> in 19 March 2012.[4]

Another recent (2008) M.A. thesis also uses Bulfinch as the source text, but in this case justifies the choice, since not only is it more accessible and available, but, as a Victorian version, it has been adapted for its audience and therefore demonstrates 'recontextualized versions of the story within specific cultural frameworks'.[5] This recontextualization is not discussed further, and one is left with the impression that the Bulfinch version is felt to be the natural and 'correct' choice of text in some manner, in a way that Apuleius' version is not.

---

[4] Marlina 2015, 44.
[5] Zabolotney 2008, 10n1.

Bulfinch's adaptation then, with its alterations in order to conform to Victorian sensibilities, was enormously influential, not only in content and tone, but also in its attitude towards 'translation', and its attempt to suit the ancient text to another society. This was in itself of course a feature of Victorian attitudes, and similar approaches can be seen in succeeding versions that appeared subsequent to Bulfinch, in the first half of the twentieth century, to which we will now turn.

2 The early twentieth century

The retellings from the early decades of the twentieth century reflect, unsurprisingly, quite different *mores*, and a noticeably different style from later versions. In this period, the question of how children should be brought up and educated was becoming a subject of great interest and attention.[6] Ideas about childhood were the concern of those involved in fields as wide as literary fiction, modernism and primitivism, social and political reforms concerning the rights, education and welfare of children, educational psychology and psychoanalysis.[7] In particular, it was a golden age for children's literature,[8] which became a vehicle for educating the young, prominently featuring themes such as imperial ideology and ideas about concepts of civilization and savagery. Gender politics, typically acculturated female and male behaviour patterns, are scripted into the story.

Although it is often claimed that this golden age moved away from didacticism,[9] the collections that include the tale of *Cupid and Psyche* demonstrate that juvenile literature was very much regarded as an educational and moral tool. The story appears, for example, in Carolyn Sherwin Bailey's *Favorite Stories for the Children's Hour*, published in 1906, in which the stories were shortened, and, according to the preface, include,

> only such salient facts retained as will result in clear mental concepts and make the stories easily told without undue taxing of the child's attention... A *large place* has been given to the *fanciful tale*, which has a direct educational value in the training of the *imagination*... The book is offered to kindergarteners, teachers and mothers who realise the large part the story plays in the development of the child, mentally and morally.[10]

---

6 Prior 2013, 79–98.
7 Gavin and Humphries 2009,1–20; Watson and Thomas 2017, 124.
8 See e.g. Carpenter 2012; Gubar 2010.
9 See e.g. Grenby 2008, 82; Heyman 2003, 16–7.
10 Carolyn Sherwin Bailey 1906, 11 (emphasis added).

Thus in this version, which runs to only two pages, the relationship between Cupid and Psyche is a love match between two children, in which naughty Psyche hides from poor Cupid. Venus then punishes her by making her sort grains before being allowed to see Cupid again, whereupon they live happily ever after. 'Naughty' Psyche's childish behaviour and youth are stressed, and the pastoral setting is emphasised. These elements reflect the Edwardian obsession with the pre-pubescent child,[11] as well as another common theme, that of the idealized Arcadia.[12]

Andrew Lang's *The Red Romance Book* (1905) also sets out an educational and moral agenda:

> In this book you will read of men who, like Don Quixote, were often mistaken but never mean, and of women, such as Una and Bradamante, who kept patient and true, in spite of fierce trials and temptations.[13]

In its version of *Cupid and Psyche*, there is no sexual act, and the marriage instead is consummated rather strangely, as follows:

> So the hours flew by, and the sun was sinking, when suddenly a veil of golden tissue was placed on her head, and at the same time a voice that she had not heard spoke thus: 'Dip your hands in this sacred water'; and Psyche obeyed, and, as her fingers sank into the basin she felt a light touch, as if other fingers were there also. 'Break this cake and eat half,' said the voice again; and Psyche did so, and she saw that the rest of the cake vanished bit by bit, as if someone else were eating it also. 'Now you are my wife, Psyche,' whispered the voice softly.[14]

Psyche's suffering in this version is the punishment for her own untrustworthiness and deceit—she feigns happiness, fooling her husband—and indeed her fate is referred to as a deserved penalty by Cupid himself.

Similarly, Frances Jenkins Olcott's *Good Stories for Great Holidays* (1914) highlights in her table of contents, 'the *ethical*, historical, and other subject-matter of interest to the teacher', while she explains that the selection 'touches all sides of wholesome boy and girl nature', again emphasizing the moral didacticism that is the purpose even of a book devoted to holidays. Margaret Evans Price also included the story in her beautifully illustrated *A Child's Book of Myths and Enchantment Tales* (1924). The introduction to this book once again

---

11 Gavin and Humphries 2009, 1–3.
12 Paul 2015, 53; Marciniak 2015, 56–7.
13 Lang 1905, preface.
14 Ibid. 254.

emphasizes the importance of classical myth, reflective of the fact that the centrality of classical studies was at that stage unchallenged, and that they were a tool through which children could, and should, be educated to be better people.

3 The post-war period (after 1945)

Between the two world wars, and throughout the second world war, there appear to have been no new versions of *Cupid and Psyche* for children; perhaps at such a time romantic tales seemed too far-fetched to be appealing, while the reduced importance of classics in education,[15] and a factor as prosaic as paper rationing, also played their part.[16] In the immediate post-war period, the drop in popularity of the tale continues, for it features in only one collection I have found, namely, Olivia Coolidge's *Greek Myths* (1949). This book is an anthology centring on the Greek gods,[17] and its aim is the intellectual imparting of material rather than moral education. This is a fairly close retelling of the myth, although Psyche's pregnancy, whipping and torture at Venus' command are discarded, along with the death of the sisters, the meeting with Pan, and her visits to the temples of Juno and Ceres. These changes are in order to simplify and to tone down elements of the story perhaps regarded as unacceptable for younger readers. There is however none of the moral censure or educational nature of the earlier juvenile versions.

By the time the story reappears in juvenile literature, love has taken centre stage in the retellings.[18] Almost twenty years after Coolidge's book, another collection featured the tale of *Cupid and Psyche*, Bernard Evslin's, *Heroes, Gods and Monsters of the Greek Myths*.[19] Like most of Evslin's adaptations, this is a very free version of Apuleius, and one in which almost no blame is cast upon Psyche, who does not even ask for her sisters to visit, who is victimized through no fault of her own by Venus, and who is motivated not by curiosity but by passionate love.

---

15 See Stray 1998.
16 See Hunt 2004, 330.
17 It should be noted, of course, that scholars tend to agree is that this is not really a Greek myth, but the invention of Apuleius, a Latin author.
18 There is a vast body of work on the role of love and romance in children's fiction, in light of changing gender roles in the twentieth century. For a few representative examples see Lieberman 1972; Stone 1975; Zipes 1986; Segal 2008.
19 Evslin 1967.

In 1976, a longer standalone version of the story appeared by Edna Barth, *Cupid and Psyche. A Love Story*. This is a 63-page, rather bland retelling, illustrated by Ati Forberg, who, according to the book, had 'long been interested in Greek and Roman mythology and has traveled extensively in Greece and Italy'.[20] Rather strangely in a version of a Roman myth, these illustrations are influenced by Minoan art, since it was from Cretan culture that 'many of the Greek myths arose';[21] they are described by one Goodreads reviewer, whose views are fairly representative, as 'the best part of this book', although they are also characterised as being very seventies in style.[22] This reference to Greek myth is repeated by the author as well, as she explains her motivation in writing this book in an author's note, describing her 'old fondness for this romantic and lovely story'.[23]

In this note, Barth refers to the story as a fable by Apuleius, yet it seems that Bulfinch is at least as important a source for Barth, who includes details that appear in the latter but not the former, particularly increasing the role of Cupid on his first encounter with Psyche, and mentioning, again the two fountains, Cupid's quiver, the vials of water and other such elements. Despite this clear romanticizing of the tale, however, a deeper allegorical meaning is also explained in the author's note:

> The soul (Psyche), originating in heaven where all is love (Cupid) is condemned for a time to wander the earth, undergoing hardship and misery. If the soul proves worthy, it will in the end return to heaven and be reunited with love, as Psyche is reunited in the story with Cupid.[24]

Nevertheless, this aspect does not actually figure in the retelling itself in any way, and in fact the target audience is hard to gauge. The text is long and too complex for a young child's picture book, but at the same time seems too simple for an older child. Some elements are again left out—Psyche's pregnancy and the subsequent birth of a daughter, the second visit of the sisters, her own trip to their homes and their subsequent deaths, the beating and torture of Psyche, the third task—in order to make the tale more palatable for children.

---

20 Barth 1976, inside flap of the dustjacket.
21 Ibid.
22 http://www.goodreads.com/book/show/2020217.Cupid_and_Psyche [accessed 4th May 2017].
23 Barth 1976, 64.
24 Ibid. 62.

This book also has a somewhat didactic side, and in fact has a rather unusual message, for it seems that Psyche's great sin here is in fact curiosity.[25] One startling paragraph runs:

> True, she was inclined to be somewhat too curious. From time to time she would begin to muse over where she might be in a year or even five or ten years hence. And now and again she was heard to remark, 'I do wonder what my future husband will look like.' Of course this was none of her concern at all. This was something for her father, the King, to decide.[26]

Such a description in fact produced an outraged response from one Goodreads reviewer, who comments regarding this message:

> This seems too patriarchal even for a Victorian adaption, and this one is from the 70s! Psyche is also criticized for what seemed to me to be a perfectly natural discontent at living completely alone with no human contact except an invisible husband who comes to sex her up in the night. No conversation is mentioned between the two, and the first meeting occurs while she is sleeping and wakes to find him in her bed making out with her! Overall, I really felt like the author was affirming the importance of beauty and obedience, rather than trust, humility, and courage as in other versions I have read.[27]

Despite these objections, in this version the fault is actually on both sides; Psyche is too curious, but Cupid does not trust her, is frightened of his mother, and is in fact imprisoned by her as punishment. The marriage at the end of the story is a way of taming Cupid, the mischievous child, who 'has lived the life of a carefree child long enough' and indeed realizes this himself, but it is also a rite of passage and adulthood for both husband and wife, at the end of which, as Jupiter declares, the two share both true love and true trust, enabling them to wed. This marriage of Cupid and Psyche is a stabilizing influence in the world, where monogamous harmony will take the place of heedless love affairs, a portrayal that must owe something to the turbulent changes in society, particularly with regard to feminism and familial gender roles, of the late sixties and early seventies.

Two other standalone versions of the story were produced in the nineteen eighties, I. M. Richardson's *The Adventures of Eros and Psyche* (1983), and Margaret Hodges' *The Arrow and the Lamp* (1989). Both of these books are beautifully illustrated, Richardson's by Robert Baxter, and Hodges' by Donna Diamond, and both are aimed at younger children, although Hodges' in particular is over-

---

25 In Apuleius' text, Psyche also exhibits habitual curiosity.
26 Bath 1976, 7.
27 http://www.goodreads.com/book/show/2020217.Cupid_and_Psyche [accessed 4th May 2017].

laid with philosophy, as she utilizes the Neoplatonic tradition, whereby Psyche grows butterfly wings at the end of the tale. Antoinette Brazouski and Mary J. Klatt suggest that influences such as Dungeons and Dragons, and the Harryhausen *Clash of the Titans* with its fascination with monsters, were reasons for the retellings of this 'beauty and the beast' style monster tale, and its fantastical depictions at this period.[28] Mary Pope Osborne's *Favorite Greek Myths* (1989) demonstrates a similar approach, with the introduction referring to the world of Greek myth as 'a strange and beautiful world where human forms turn into seagulls, lions, bears and stars... where the impossible seems common, where the moon, the sun and the wind are all gods', and Greek civilisation as 'very young' and 'very close to nature'. Thus the ancient world has become a place of magic and fantasy, giving it new relevance in the modern world, since, despite the technological advances, 'our feelings are still much the same as theirs'.[29]

4 The late twentieth to twenty-first centuries

From the 1990s until the present day, the popularity of the tale continues. All of the more modern versions of the tale adapt elements of the story in different ways, and have slightly different nuances, dependent partly on authorial preferences and partly on the intended audience. Nevertheless, all attempt, to different degrees, to sanitise the story in some way, and to moderate the sex and violence of the Latin text. As Lily Glasner points out, in all of these adaptations,

> the sexually suggestive kiss Aphrodite gives her son upon asking him to avenge her ... is excluded; so too Mercury's pronouncement that whoever brings the runaway Psyche to Venus will win from the very mouth of the goddess erotic kisses ...; and Jupiter's request that Cupid pay him back by providing him with a lovely human girl...[30]

Similarly, such versions usually avoid mention of Psyche's suicide attempts, while some authors remove any vindictiveness on her part towards the sisters, either by omitting their role altogether or by placing the blame squarely on their own curiosity.

---

[28] Brazouski and Klatt 1994, 13.
[29] Osborne 1989, ix-x.
[30] Glasner 2017, 206.

5 The compilations

The story of *Cupid and Psyche* has appeared in different compilations by four different authors over the past two decades. Of these, three are relatively bland retellings of the tale. The first, Kathy Elgin's *Stories From Around the World. Roman Myths* (2008), part of a series entitled *Myths from Many Lands* and sold as school reference books, features the myth in a very condensed version, in which 'mischievous' Cupid is sent to make Psyche fall in love with an ugly man, but falls in love himself. As a result of Psyche's disobedience, Cupid runs away, causing her to search the world over, overcoming 'all kinds of problems' created by 'jealous Venus'. Eventually Cupid takes pity on her and forgives her, and at his request Jupiter makes Psyche immortal, allowing her to join the gods in heaven. Although the book is ostensibly aimed at 8 to 12-year-olds, and contains an introduction explaining some elements of Roman attitudes towards the gods, it has more of a picture-book format, and the language and style are extremely simplified, reducing the story to a bare love story told in the most minimal terms, and the pair themselves to the status of naughty children.

Philip Freeman's *Heroes of Olympus* (2012, adapted by Laurie Calkhoven) is a rather more detailed and faithful retelling of Apuleius' myth, leaving few elements out, and culminating in the birth of a daughter, rather more tamely named 'Happiness'. Diane Namm's *Classic Starts. Roman Myths* (2014), on the other hand, although relatively short, is a more unusual version, in that there is no happy ending, and the emphasis is on the importance of trust in a loving relationship. In this version, Psyche, on discovering her husband's identity, loses him not temporarily but permanently, and the story ends with Cupid disappearing after he wakes up and discovers the truth, declaring as he goes that 'Love cannot live where there is no trust'.

The most interesting of these adaptations is the earliest of them, that by Geraldine McCaughrean (1997), which has been published in a range of different collections,[31] and makes some interesting alterations to the story. In this version, Psyche is a virtuous girl, as opposed to Venus who 'was all passion, all instinct, all rash impulse and emotion'. We are told that in contrast, 'There is a cool, deep stillness in a thoughtful woman, which attracts like a deep lake on a hot day. Perhaps that is why mortal Psyche's quiet, pensive beauty was so appealing' and why 'some' say that she was even more beautiful than the goddess of love. Nowhere is it suggested that she is worshipped, however, or that she seeks anything except modesty and peace.

---

[31] McCaughrean 1997, 20–5; 1999, 289–94; 2011, 173–81.

She is also a victim, innocent of all blame, and, despite the emphasis on modesty and peace, a somewhat feisty figure. Psyche's parents and sisters do not feature until a later point in the story; as Psyche is doomed by Venus to a fearful death, it is Cupid who is instructed by Venus to tie Psyche to the rock in order that she will be devoured by the sea monster, Typhon. Disgusted by this, he nevertheless obeys while Psyche struggles and pleads with him. In this struggle, Cupid scratches himself with one of his arrows, but, strangely, no love is mentioned. After she is rescued and spirited by Zephyrus to the palace (in this case a 'seashell palace' where 'the sound of the sea whispered everlastingly through whorled walls of shining shell'), she meets the invisible Cupid who loves her and wants her for his wife'. He does not force himself upon her, however, and this is a match of two virtuous souls, freely entered into. The independent-minded Psyche considers his proposal of marriage, thinking for a moment, and then declaring that, 'If in a while I find you are as kind and gentle as you seem, I shall be your wife and never wish for the sun to shine on us both'.

This wise and virtuous soul is not even really blamed for her curiosity, which leads to the loss of her beloved. She is, we are told 'a thinker, a ponderer and puzzler over riddles', who is tormented by curiosity. In this case, it is actually Cupid who seems more at fault, for her response upon seeing him is '*You!*', implying that she recognises him as the one who had chained her to the rock to await Typhon, and that Cupid had remained invisible in order to conceal this from her. Nor is she aware, even after seeing him, that her husband is the god, Cupid, or that Venus has any antipathy towards her. In place of the four tasks imposed by Venus, Psyche must become the goddess' slave for seven years during which time she suffers such torments that 'every day the gods liked Venus a little less and admired Psyche a little more'. Through her suffering and willing servitude, Psyche earns Cupid's deep love and the subsequent apotheosis as Cupid claims her for his wife. This is not the end of this version of the story, however, for the monster Typhon, still wanting his prey, turns on Venus and Cupid, who turn themselves into 'starry fishes' in the 'dark pools of space'. Happily however, for some unexplained reason, Psyche is also there, 'gentle and silent as a sea anemone caressing the liquid night'. Although a far more independent and lively creature than in many retellings, this idealised version of gentle, serene womanhood, such a contrast to Venus' brash ways, is the enduring picture of McCaughrean's retelling. As such, it seems to encapsulate somewhat confused feelings with regard to female behaviour and roles, a product of its time, characterised by third wave feminism, as much as the earlier versions had been products of theirs.[32]

6 Longer retellings

Five more standalone narrations of the tale have also been published in the last twenty years.[33] Two of these are from the 1990s, Doris Orgel's *The Princess and the God* (1996), Craft and Craft's *Cupid and Psyche* (1997) while one more recent version, Sarah Coghill's *The Story of Cupid and Psyche*, is from 2011. The story also features as the backdrop to one of Randi Reisfeld's *Sabrina, the Teenage Witch* books, *All You Need is a Love Spell* (1998), while a longer modern adaptation, Jendela Tryst's *Origin of Love* trilogy, was published between 2014 and 2017.[34]

In all but one of these retellings, a clear change can be seen from earlier periods, obviously a result of the rise of feminism in Western society, in that the character of Psyche is developed more fully and becomes a far more interesting character. The exception is the version by Sarah Coghill, an ebook from 2011, perhaps the most attractive feature of which is the use of the Bouguereau painting, *Psyche*, as a front cover, albeit without acknowledgement or attribution. Billed as 'a short story' this is a six-page, rather stilted, retelling of the story, closely modelled on Bulfinch, but the story is told with little charm or detail, and considerably simplified. The Amazon review of the story, 'this was the bare bones story for Cupid and Psyche, it worked for me and my research. Quick and fast read' seems a fitting description of the piece.[35]

The other longer adaptations are of a far superior quality, and all present Psyche as a fully developed character, and an often confident and independent female. In the first of the four, Doris Orgel beautifully narrates the tale of *Cupid and Psyche* as a charming coming-of-age story, told mainly in the first person by a 16-year-old Psyche. *Publisher's Weekly* describes this book as 'a work sure to ensnare girls who have outgrown picture books but still prize the sort of love stories told in fairy tales', and explains that,

---

32 On third wave feminism, see Gillis, Howie and Munford 2007, xv-xxxi.
33 There are also two comic book versions, (*Stolen Hearts: The Love of Eros and Psyche* by Ryan Foley and artist Sankha Banerjee (2009), and *Psyche & Eros: The Lady and the Monster*, by Marie P. Croall and artist Ron Randall (2010)) which space does not allow me to address here.
34 Published as Tryst 2014, 2015, 2017.
35 https://www.amazon.com/Story-Cupid-Psyche-Sarah-Coghill-ebook/dp/B005QE9YSY/ref=asap_bc?ie=UTF8 [accessed 30th April 2017].

> While adhering to the classical story, Orgel embroiders patterns from other beloved tales... At the same time she maintains Psyche as a fully and thrillingly human figure among the mighty Olympians, giving readers a character to identify with completely. The target audience will like the love scenes especially—they're passionate and innocent at the same time.[36]

This Psyche is a flesh and blood character, and the love between her and her husband, whom she names 'Amor' is deep and genuine. Nor is there any idle curiosity leading to this heroine's downfall. Guided by a mixture of the misleading and terrifying prophecy that her husband is a dragon, reinforced by her sisters' scaremongering, and unfortunate coincidence—the discovery of the mangled body of a dead lizard—she acts to discover the truth as much for fear for her unborn child as for her own safety. This is emphasized by the words of the gods in council near the end of the book, in which Diana blames Apollo for the whole sorry business. In answer, Apollo stresses the truth of the prophecy while Diana charges Cupid with responsibility for events, suggesting that the prophecies were 'a smoke screen for the benefit of shameful little Cupid while he indulged his fancy for the human princess and had his little fling'. At this point Cupid himself appears, declaring that he has changed, and is now to be called Amor, the name his bride, the princess Psyche, gave to him.[37]

Not only is Psyche the innocent victim here, it is Cupid who is portrayed, at least to some extent, as the villain, who has, however, been rehabilitated by Psyche herself. Psyche has striven 'nobly and bravely for love', and her only weakness, the opening of Persephone's box, is caused by her catching sight of her own reflection and believing that Cupid's love is lost to her forever. Juno's reply that this is a very human response produces a paean of praise for humanity: 'It is to her very humanity that I owe the godhead you now recognize. By her own example, Psyche has led me to my truest self'. Jupiter then asks Minerva whether 'by commingling human with divine' he will diminish their godhood, to which his daughter answers that on the contrary, he will 'exalt what is valiant and good in humans'.[38] This version of the tale therefore glorifies humanity at the expense of the divine, extolling the worth of mortals,[39] and rehabilitating the virtuous but anguished Psyche, a noble yet flesh-and-blood teenager, who regards her beauty as a curse rather than a blessing.

---

36 http://www.publishersweekly.com/978-0-531-09516-4 [accessed 30th April 2017].
37 Orgel 1996, 104–5.
38 Ibid. 106–7.
39 A similar trend can be seen in recent movies dealing with divinities, from *Immortals* (2011) to *Noah* (2014).

In M. Charlotte Craft and K.Y Craft's visually beautiful adaptation, *Cupid and Psyche* (1996), it is the lonely Psyche herself who journeys to Delphi and receives the oracle, making her a far more active participant in the plot. Along with this sense of independent agency, this version also eliminates all sexual references. This Cupid is described as Psyche's 'companion' or 'host', and he even has his own bedroom. This is not a marriage, and therefore there is no sexual act or mention of pregnancy at this stage. Rather, marriage takes place only at the end of the book followed 'in due time' by the birth of a daughter, named 'Joy.'[40]

The other book-length treatments of the story feature very interesting twists on the old tale. Randi Reisfeld's *All You Need is a Love Spell* tells the story of how Cupid, Venus and Mars come to earth to capture Sabrina whom they think is Psyche. Cupid (here Quentin Pid i.e. Q. Pid, while Venus and Mars are Veronica and Martin) falls in love with Sabrina and defies his parents. In this story, Cupid is a weak character, manipulated by his parents, while Psyche does not even appear at all, since Sabrina is a witch rather than the character from Apuleius' myth. Sabrina is, however, a powerful female figure, and the story is an interesting and refreshingly fun spin on the ancient story.

Perhaps the most fascinating juvenile version of Apuleius' story, however, is the most recent one, Jendela Tryst's trilogy entitled *The Origins of Love*, which narrates the tale in three volumes, the first of which, *Struck. Eros and Psyche— A Myth* was published in 2014, the second (*Scorched*) in 2016, and the third (*Rupture*) in 2017. With each book running to close to 200 pages, this retelling, aimed at the young adult market, is a thoroughly twenty-first century approach to the story, in which Cupid and Psyche are star-crossed lovers, but with a contemporary twist, namely that the books feature a powerful, determined and strong heroine. Cupid, on the other hand, is a weaker figure who comes, over the course of the books, to learn and take responsibility for his actions. All the gods in this version are not only anthropomorphized as one would expect, but fascinatingly real and fleshed out, while retaining their otherworldliness and godliness, and their lack of humanity is actually contrasted negatively with that of mortals.

This Psyche is not a princess but a farmer's daughter. Her beauty is unconventional and the physical descriptions of her that speak of her skin that is 'not quite bronze and not quite gold', and long hair that is dark brown, with natural red and blond streaks in it, perhaps owe more to Tryst's Indian heritage than to Hollywood ideals of beauty. Her Psyche is also a thoroughly modern woman, despite living in bronze-age Greece (the Trojan War is taking place at the time of the events of the story)—she is 'strong-willed', 'spirited' and 'intelligent', and this is

---

40 See Glasner 2017, 206–7.

a match of true love, and of justice and freedom from oppression, as part of a much wider universal story. The book is also far more graphic in its sexuality. It is truly a rendering for the twenty-first century, and yet, paradoxically, in some ways it seems closest to the feeling of the original in its sophistication and creation of a fully developed world.

7 Conclusion

To conclude, it is apparent that Cupid and Psyche, despite its apparent unsuitability for a juvenile audience, has been, and continues to be, retold for children. In the early years of both the twentieth and twenty-first centuries in particular, it has proved to be a popular story, in the former case being interpreted didactically, and in the latter reflecting altered ideas regarding the role and status of women. Sometimes retold simply, due to a belief that classical tales need to be taught and understood, and on other occasions reinterpreted in order to promote ideas regarding moral values, the richness of Apuleius' story continues to inspire both those writing for a juvenile audience, and the young readers to whom the works are directed.

8 Bibliography

Bailey, C.S. (1906), *Favorite Stories for the Children's Hour*, Springfield. Reprinted (2014).
Barth, E. (1976), *Cupid and Psyche. A Love Story*, New York.
Booth, D. (2011), 'Censorship', in: Nel/Paul, 26–30.
Brazouski, A./Klatt, M.J. (1994), *Children's Books on Ancient Greek and Roman Mythology. An Annotated Bibliography*, Westport, CT.
Bulfinch, T. (1855), *The Age of Fable: Stories of Gods and Heroes*, Boston.
Bulfinch, T. (1867), *Bulfinch's Mythology: Legends of Charlemagne or Romance of the Middle Ages, The Age of Chivalry or Legends of King Arthur and The Age of Fable or Stories of Gods and Heroes*, New York.
Carpenter, H. (2012), *Secret gardens. A study of the golden age of children's literature*, London.
Coghill, S. (2011), *The Story of Cupid and Psyche* (kindle ebook).
Coolidge, O. (1949), *Greek Myths*, Boston.
Craft, C.M./Craft, K.Y. (1996), *Cupid and Psyche*, New York.
Elgin, K. (2008), *Stories from Around the World. Roman Myths*, London.
Evslin, B. (1966), *Heroes, Gods and Monsters of the Greek Myths*, New York.
Evslin, B. (1976), *The Dolphin Rider. And Other Greek Myths*, New York.
Foerstel, H.N. (2012), *Banned in the U.S.A. A Reference Guide to Book Censorship in Schools and Public Libraries*, Westport, CT.
Freeman, P. (2012), *Heroes of Olympus*, New York.

Gavin, A.E./Humphries, A.F. (2009), *Childhood in Edwardian Fiction: Worlds Enough and Time*, Basingstoke.
Gillis, S./Howie, G./Munford, R. (2007), *Third Wave Feminism. A Critical Exploration*, New York.
Glasner, L. (2017), 'Cupid and Psyche. A Love Story (?) in Comics and Children's Literature', in: Maurice 2017, 198–217.
Grenby, M.O. (2008), *Children's Literature*, Edinburgh.
Gubar, M. (2017), *Artful Dodgers. Reconceiving the Golden Age of Children's Literature*, Oxford.
Heyman, M. (2003), 'The Decline and Rise of Literary Nonsense in the Twentieth Century', in: McGillis, 13–22.
Hodges, M. (1989), *The Arrow and the Lamp*, Boston.
Hunt, P. (2004), *International Companion Encyclopedia of Children's Literature*, Oxford and New York.
Hutcheon, L. (2006), *A Theory of Adaptation*, New York.
Lang, A. (1905), *The Red Romance Book*, London
Lieberman, M.R. (1972), '"Some Day My Prince Will Come". Female Acculturation through the Fairy Tale', *College English* 34: 383–95.
Marciniak, K. (2015), '(De)constructing Arcadia. Polish Struggles with History and Differing Colours of Childhood in the Mirror of Classical Mythology', in: Maurice 2015, 56–82.
Marlina, L. (2015), 'The Discussion on Female Heroes in Respect of Gender Socialisation of Girls. Retelling Myths of Psyche, Artemis and Katniss', *Linguistics and Literature Studies* 3, 41–5.
Maurice, L. (2015), *The Reception of Ancient Greece and Rome in Children's Literature. Eagles and Heroes*, Leiden.
Maurice, L. (2017), *Rewriting the Ancient World. Greece and Rome in Modern Popular Fiction*, Leiden.
McCaughrean, G. (1997), *The Bronze Cauldron. Myths and Legends of The World*, New York.
McCaughrean, G. (1999), *Silver Myths and Legends of The World*, London.
McCaughrean, G. (2011), *King Arthur and a World of Other Stories*, London.
McClure, A. (2014), 'Censorship', *Children's Literature Association Quarterly* 8, 22–25.
McGillis, R. (2003), *Children's Literature and the Fin de Siècle*, Westport CT.
Namm, D. (2014), *Classic Starts Roman Myths*, New York.
Nel, P./Paul, L. (2011), *Keywords for Children's Literature*, New York.
Olcott, F.J. (1914), *Good Stories for Great Holidays*, Boston.
Orgel, D. (1996), *The Princess and the God*, New York.
Osborne, M.P. (1989) *Favorite Greek Myths*, New York.
Paul, J. (2015), '"Time is only a mode of thought, you know" Ancient History, Imagination and Empire in E. Nesbit's Literature for Children', in: Maurice 2015, 30–55.
Price Evans, M. (1924), *A Child's Book of Myths and Enchantment Tales*, New York.
Prior, C. (2013), *Edwardian England and the Idea of Racial Decline. An Empire's Future*, Basingstoke.
Reisfeld, R. (1998), *All You Need is a Love Spell*, New York.
Richardson, I.M. (1983), *The Adventures of Eros and Psyche*, Mahwah.
Segal, F. (2008), 'Who Said Romance Was Dead?' *The Guardian*, January 27, https://www.theguardian.com/books/2008/jan/27/fiction.features1 [accessed 1st May 2017].

Stone, K. (1975), 'Things Walt Disney Never Told Us', *The Journal of American Folklore* 88, 42–50.

Stray, C. (1998), *Classics Transformed. Schools, Universities, and Society in England, 1830–1960*, Oxford.

Tryst, J. (2014), *Struck: Eros and Psyche—A Myth*, New York.

Tryst, J. (2015), *Scorched*, New York.

Tryst, J. (2017), *Rupture*, New York.

Watson, J./Thomas, J.G. (2017), *Faulkner and History*, Jackson.

Zabolotney, B.R. (2008), *Transforming Beauty and the Beast. Literary and Typographic Adaptations of an Ancient Tale*, Simon Fraser University. (unpublished thesis).

Zipes, J. (1986), *Don't Bet on the Prince. Contemporary Feminist Fairy Tales in North America and England*, Aldershot.

Hendrik Müller
Cupid and Psyche on stage in the 21st century

Soon after its reception and translation into the modern languages,[1] Apuleius' *Metamorphoses* was adapted for the stage, as the author himself made constant use of dramaturgical and theatrical elements in the novel.[2] Yet for centuries these theatrical adaptations were limited to the inset tale of *Cupid and Psyche*,[3] as Lucius' encounters in asinine form were obviously not considered to be a suitable topic for theatre audiences of former times.

As shown elsewhere,[4] this attitude has changed due to the radical shift of moral values in Western civilization in the last decades, so that some of the existing twentieth and twenty-first century theatre productions of the *Metamorphoses* especially make use of the open sexual and comic connotations of Apuleius' novel.[5] Even so, until today the inset tale of *Cupid and Psyche* remains the most popular source for various kinds of theatrical adaptations of Apuleius' work.

This paper aims to present an overview of some of these very recent theatrical productions from the twenty-first century that deal explicitly with the *Cupid and Psyche* story. The adjective 'theatrical' in this case does not only cover theatre plays proper, but, according to the taste of modern audiences, also other stage productions like musical, comedy and ballet adaptations that are based on the *Cupid and Psyche* myth. A complete discussion therefore also has to include modern cinematic and musical theatre releases of the story. My paper will also touch upon a handful of early and especially late twentieth century versions, without which the more recent adaptations would possibly not have been realized.

---

[1] The reception of the novel during the Renaissance has recently been described in detail by Gaisser 2008 and Carver 2007.
[2] Frangoulidis 2001, May 2006.
[3] Cf. the survey of the separate reception of the tale in the introduction to Moreschini 1994. Müller-Reineke 2009 has collected various theatrical adaptations of *Cupid and Psyche* since the Renaissance until recent times.
[4] Cf. Müller-Reineke 2009.
[5] The Catalan group 'La fura Dels Baus' (Sewer Rats) included a video sequence of the mating of a naked woman with an ass, clearly inspired by Lucius' sexual encounters in Apul. *Met.* 10 in their production 'XXX' at the Kampnagel Summer Festival in Hamburg in 2004, cf. Müller-Reineke 2009, 12–3.

It is worth mentioning that Apuleius' tale of *Cupid and Psyche* tale has inspired other European versions of the story, for example the 'Beauty-and-Beast'-story, which is itself based on internationally prevalent folk motifs and which has triggered a reception of its own.[6] The 'Beauty and Beast'-version has produced a wide reception in the popular culture of the 20th century, e.g. Jean Cocteau's movie version (1946), Disney's 1991 animated film, a successful Broadway musical running between 1994 and 2007, and most recently the 2017 film version directed by William Condon which is a remake of Disney's earlier animated version. This paper will however deliberately concentrate on those modern theatrical adaptations that follow the original version of *Cupid and Psyche* much more closely both in relation to cast and story line, since James in this volume focuses on film adaptations.[7]

1 Theatre

In a review of recent theatrical versions of *Cupid and Psyche*, it is worth mentioning that most of the productions are naturally adapted to the prevalent public taste of the 21st century. On the one hand, this affects the genre of the productions itself, so that many of the plays are either musical or comedy versions (we even find a rock opera); on the other hand, in some of these productions additional characters were added to the original ancient cast so that some of the ancient stock characters are changed into their twenty-first society equivalents.

Undoubtedly there seemed to be quite a renaissance of the *Cupid and Psyche* story in theatrical terms at the beginning of the new millennium, as we find a handful of American productions and a recent German one, the details of which are easily accessible via the Internet.

New York based playwright Joseph Fisher adapted the tale in his 2002 version as a comedy: His play 'Cupid & Psyche' is more than two hours in length and includes a cast of eight actors, i.e. apart from Cupid, Psyche and Aphrodite, the latter's servant Runt, Psyche's father the king and her two sisters named Maleen and Kris, and the god Apollo,[8] who perform the complicated romance with a contemporary spin, as the production reminds the audience of a celebrity reality show in which the gods communicate via mobile phones. The play set in irregular verse was first produced at the Stark Raving Theatre in Portland, Oregon,

---

6 Cf. Müller-Reineke 2009, 7.
7 Cf. Accardo 2002, 68–87.
8 Cf. Fisher 2002.

where the author Joe Fisher at that time was playwright in residence.[9] The play covers barely half of the original myth, as a jealous Aphrodite devises a plan to marry off Psyche, a 'beautiful, highly-adored mortal'[10] to whom the goddess loses all her followers, to the most ugly, pestilent creature she can find: her servant with the speaking name Runt. She sends Cupid to shoot Psyche with one of his golden arrows in the hope that the first person Psyche sees will be Runt. Cupid falls in love with Psyche at first sight, and cannot bring himself to make the shot. For the first time in Cupid's life, he is faced with the concept of falling instantly in love with someone and does not know how to proceed. In desperation, Cupid consults his uncle Apollo for advice. Apollo, however, is seeking personal revenge for Cupid's misdeed long ago, when he was struck by Cupid's arrow, which resulted in his falling in love with a nymph who would rather face death than be pursued by a god.[11] Because of this, Apollo, who carries a memento of the nymph throughout the play,[12] devises a plan that will ultimately destroy the young couple. Following Apollo's advice, Cupid marries Psyche, but is forbidden by his uncle from showing his face to his bride. Advising Cupid this way, the latter takes revenge for the disastrous outcome of his entanglement with the nymph Daphne. Psyche appears to feel as though she has been kidnapped rather than betrothed. Aphrodite soon finds out what happened and tries to put a stop to the heartless game with a wager between the gods. Psyche who 'finds herself straddling the divide between mortals and Gods'[13] finally descends into the depths of Hades to achieve reconciliation with her mother-in-law.

Sometimes Fisher's version seems to be more of an intellectual discourse about the nature of love and beauty, including lengthy monologues for which the author was attacked by the critics.[14] Yet, all in all the play was a success

---

9 A biography of the artist can be found at https://www.playscripts.com/playwrights/bios/290.
10 Schlichting 2012.
11 An allusion to the well-known myth of Apollo and Daphne in Ov. *Met.* 1.452–567.
12 Although regarding the leaves of Apollo's wreath the play itself mentions a hyacinth instead of a laurel, it certainly references the Ovidian myth of Apollo and Daphne instead of the tale of Apollo and Hyacinthos in Ov. *Met.* 10.162–219. The element of competition between the god and the boy (*certamina*, Ov. *Met.* 10.177), however, could give a symbolic hint to the rivalry of Cupid and Apollo in Fisher's play.
13 Intended for Use 2012.
14 Cf. Cashman 2006, reviewing the production by the Themantics Group, a group of theatre professionals founded in 2002 and based in downtown New York, devoted to presenting seasonal work with a particular social or political theme, at Altered Stages 212 West 29th Street New York.

and had several reruns performed by professional, academic and amateur theatre groups all over the United States.[15]

A similar success story is the musical 'Cupid and Psyche' by Sean Hartley, currently Director of Music at the Kaufman Center in New York, and set to music by composer Jihwan Kim. It had its world premiere in 2000 at the 12th Annual Festival of New Musicals which is regularly organized by the American National Alliance for Musical Theatre (NAMT) in New York.[16] A number of subsequent regional productions followed, e. g, at the Oregon Cabaret Theater, Ashland (OR) in 2002, off-Broadway at the John Houseman Theater (NY) in 2003, at the Orlando Fringe Festival (FL) in 2008, and the New Jersey Repertory (NJ) in 2008 and 2009. The musical script also tries both to retell the story for a modern audience and to keep to the original myth:[17] the characters behave like contemporary humans, so that typical stock characters of our society are blended into the ancient myth: Venus, for example, acts like an over-protective mother who forbids her son Cupid to fall in love.[18] For that reason she has a dreaded Cyclops 'waiting in the wings for any mortal foolish enough'[19] to mess with her son. Venus plans to remove Psyche as a threat and asks her son to make her fall in love with that awful creature, but Cupid immediately falls in love with Psyche (additionally his arrow strikes the Cyclops who from that moment on follows him, lovesick). Hartley has kept quite closely to the ancient myth: 'His most significant deviations ... include giving the overprotective mother Venus a greater role in the couple's breakup and reunion and adding Mercury to the mix as Cupid's hard-partying best friend'.[20] All characters of the four-person cast are spitting images of up-to-date stereotypes. To quote a 2008 *New York Times* review: 'Psyche's a genuine babe, her belly-button diamond offset by the studious glasses she wears while reading Aristotle.'[21]

Hartley, who is a regular collaborator with The Walt Disney Company, managed to create a verse libretto which can be understood by children as well as adults. In the best tradition of American musical theatre, the production,

---

15 E. g. Oregon Shakespeare Festival, Ashland, OR in 2002, 2006 at Altered Stages Theater, New York; 2007 at The Ohio State University-Lima, OH; in 2010 at the Lonesome Valley Playhouse, Prescott Valley, AZ; 2012 at the Chetco Playhouse, Brookings, OR; 2013 at Hutchinson High School, KS.
16 https://namt.org/festivals/2000/#overview.
17 According to the review of New York based critic Pierce from September 2003.
18 Cf. Murray 2003, reviewing the off-Broadway production at John Houseman Studio Theatre.
19 Siegel 2008.
20 Pierce 2003.
21 According to Siegel 2008 and her review of a production by the New Jersey Repertory Company at 179 Broadway, Long Branch, New Jersey.

while making you laugh, also manages to tug at the heartstrings by underscoring lessons to be learned and underlining the allegorical character of the story.

A recent German adaptation of the *Cupid and Psyche* story is the play 'Amor & Psyche. Ein Spiel mit Masken für einen Mann und eine Frau' by Claudia Hann[22] and Udo Mierke, which tells the story of *Cupid and Psyche* as a masque play. The production had its premiere in 2001 at the Cassiopeia Theater in Cologne (which is owned and run by Hann and Mierke). Hann played the female part opposite her colleague Waldemar Hooge.[23] The masks are not actually worn by the two actors but carried by them in front of their bodies, so that they become autonomous objects, and the audience gets the impression that at times four actors are on the stage. The production interprets Psyche's tale as an act of inner maturing, as Psyche gradually moves away from the influence of her family.[24] This accentuation also gives the story a contemporary twist aimed at attracting an audience of adolescents aged 16 years and older.

Another adaptation of the *Cupid and Psyche* story is of a completely different nature. On 2nd September 2014, the premiere of composer-librettist Cindy Shapiro's 'Psyche. A Modern Rock Opera' took place at Greenway Court Theater in Los Angeles.[25] It tells the *Cupid and Psyche* story as a stylish musical hybrid of post-modernism and rock. Psyche was conceived by Shapiro during an artist-in-residence period at 'Cité Internationale des Arts' in Paris in the autumn of 2011.[26] The opera production followed the strapline: 'Dreams are private myths. Myths are public dreams', and featured an impressively painted set. The *LA Times*, although essentially criticizing the production for its mediocrity, labelled the show a 'modern-day retelling of the Psyche myth' that features 'a mind-bogglingly intricate staging that includes spectacular design elements, a wonderful cast, terrific choreography and the kind of dream musical direction that would grace a Broadway show.'[27]

American playwright and novelist Emily C.A. Snyder's 'Cupid & Psyche. A New Play in Blank Verse' is a five-act play in iambic pentameters which had its 'Bad Quarto' performance in Boston in 2009, presented by Emerson College

---

22 Information about the artist under: http://www.claudia-hann.de/theatertext/thextertext_amorpsyche.htm
23 Pictures can be seen under http://www.cassiopeia-buehne.de/pressebild/amor/.
24 Cf. Linden 2001.
25 The production has its own website under http://www.psycherockopera.com/.
26 More information about Cindy Shapiro can be found at her personal website http://www.cindyshapiro.net/.
27 Cf. Foley 2014.

Performing Arts Department,[28] and celebrated its world premiere at TBG Theatre in Midtown, New York City during the Valentine weekend of 2014. It was performed by the 'Turn to Flesh Production' company which Snyder founded together with fellow student Michelle Kafel, to sold-out houses during its initial New York City run. It is a modern interpretation of the myth and especially focuses on the anthropomorphization of the allegorical figures of Love and Soul. It opens with the wedding reception of two mortals Dareia and Chrysos, where all the men are so fascinated by the bride's sister Psyche that Aphrodite is shocked that she has lost their attention—and decides to kill Psyche.[29] Cupid is set to the task, but becomes infatuated with Psyche's body and soul [sic]. Psyche, who generally disdains love, initially rejects the advances of her invisible admirer and only gives in when her family is terrorized, so that Psyche marries Cupid 'to rid the world of "Love"…and then must rediscover what Love really is'.[30]

Snyder has successfully transferred the timeless issue of love and rejection into modern times, and with the help of the 'eclectic cast of characters helped flesh out what those unfamiliar with the mythological texts would view as ancient relics, truly carrying them into the 21st century.'[31] This modernization of the ancient myth was mirrored by the costumes of the gods and mortals, which ranged from Victorian dress to contemporary blue jeans and bomber jackets.[32] Snyder's pentameter verses are likewise contrasted with contemporary guitar music.

A very recent amateur production of the *Cupid and Psyche* story had its world premiere in April 2016 at the Calhoun Cabaret of Yale University: Music major Solon Snider had asked his mother Terry Zyporin about an old script of hers that had been neglected for 30 years and which was eventually updated by the mother-son duo so that 'Cupidity. A Brand New Musical Comedy' was revived. Snider especially updated the story for the twenty-first century, adding references to Buzzfeed, blinding cell phone camera flashes and effervescent talk

---

28 Snyder received her Masters in Theatre Education from Emerson College in the same year. See May and Harrison's 'Introduction' for Snyder's participation at the Leeds conference.
29 As a reviewer at the Facebook page of the production company writes: 'The story is easy to follow while maintaining the poetic beauty of blank verse': cf. https://www.facebook.com/turntofleshproductions/posts/10151984485916448.
30 Marran and Ross 2014.
31 Taghap 2014.
32 Photographs of the costumes of the NY production are shown under http://www.emilyroseparman.com/cupid-and-psyche.

show hosts. He also wrote and composed all of the music and finally brought his mother's script to a Yale stage.

'Cupidity' tells the *Cupid and Psyche* story quite faithfully, except for a few modifications required by the modern setting and cast. Set in contemporary Beverly Hills, the show uses the magic of Hollywood instead of the magic of the gods to advance the narrative, by grafting the mythic tale onto a world of online dating, Hollywood internships, and talk show therapy.[33] The musical showcases a diverse cast of complex characters. Rather than the fairest maiden in the land, Psyche is 'Buzzfeed's #1 Natural Beauty'. The mythical oracle of Apollo does not exist in this world, but instead, Dr Apollo—a gregarious, larger-than-life talk show therapist (reminiscent of American talk show 'Dr Phil's' host Phil McGraw)—doles out advice and counsel on his hit talk show. Queen Venus is portrayed as an over-the-top, has-been diva followed around by her two assistants Doreena and Cleo. As one critic wrote, 'these modernizations are funny and contribute to the light-hearted feel of the story, though they are occasionally delivered in a heavy-handed, overly simplified way. The adaptation itself is coherent and full, parsing the myth in a way that's easy for the audience to experience.'[34]

2 Ballet

For centuries the story of *Cupid and Psyche*, or at least single episodes from it, has formed an apt subject for various ballet productions, most famously the *tragicomédie et ballet* by Moliere and Lully given for the first time by the Académie royale de musique at the Théâtre du Palais-Royal of Paris on 17th January in 1671, discussed by Harrison in this volume.[35]

In this grand tradition, the Paris Opera ballet under artist-in-residence at the American Ballet Theatre and former director of the Bolshoi Ballet, Alexei Ratmansky, opened the season 2011 with the Greek-myth pairing of Serge Lifar's 'Phèdre' from 1950[36] and Ratmansky's new 'Psyché'. The latter is a 50-minute ballet which is set to César Franck's homonymous choral symphony. The French

---

[33] Pictures, song snippets and a synopsis can be found under http://terraziporyn.com/?page_id=668.
[34] Cf. Veeramani 2016 in the *Yale Daily News*, following the premiere of the play at Calhoun Cabaret, Yale University, April 22–24, 2016.
[35] Cf. Call 2015, 221. See also Bötger 1979, 83f.; Sallmann 1997, 316.
[36] Lifar directed the Paris Opera Ballet from 1930 to 1947 and was quite a controversial figure in French post-war culture: He was ousted for collaborating with the Vichy regime and later reinstated.

composer César Franck wrote his 'symphonic poem' for chorus and orchestra in seven movements over the summer of 1886. In Franck's retelling, Psyche first dreams of Eros and then is carried by zephyrs to Eros' secret garden, where the orchestra enacts a rapturous love duet as the chorus warns her that she must never seek to see the face of her mysterious lover. The aftermath of her transgression is again narrated by the chorus, and is, like her final apotheosis, profoundly moving.

Following Franck's storyline, the choreography by Ratmansky likewise presents episodes inspired by *Cupid and Psyche* rather than the full story of the myth. The heroine is at first cast into a deep sleep by jealous Venus; Cupid nevertheless later falls in love with her, but Psyche is not allowed to see his face. In the end, of course, true love prevails, and the whole storyline is underlined by fascinating solo and ensemble dances. Ratmansky has enlisted the American painter and installation artist Karen Kilimnik to provide the stage with settings of 'ferocious unsuitability'[37]: the production has been described by critics as a magical, otherworldly ballet, fittingly aligned with the slightly discomfiting surrealism of Kilimnik's backdrops which raise curious eyebrows while at the same time appealing to children in all in their depictions of fantastical landscapes, oversized birds and pirouetting cherubim.[38] Others have labelled the background as a 'Looney Tunes design' that might reflect Ratmansky's mistrust in the perfect match.[39] While Cupid and Psyche were lastly dressed in unalluring bathing suits, their technique compensated the audience for the odd scenery as both soloists provided classical and energetic yet charming dance movements.

A couple of years earlier, towards the end of the twentieth century, a different ballet version was put on stage in another European capital: commissioned by the Royal Danish Ballet and under the choreography of Kim Brandstrup, 'Amor og Psyche' had its premiere at Det Kongelige Teater, Copenhagen in May 1997.[40] Yet, this version did not use the traditional musical background of César Franck or others, but was set to music by the contemporary Danish composer Kim Helweg (1956-). Brandstrup wanted to tell the myth 'in a modern version, but with antiquity close at hand';[41] this aim is visually supported by the scenery of a Mediterranean square from the 1950s packed with scooters and neon signs. Cupid appears as an attractive seducer, while Psyche displays an icy attitude, isolating and exiling her from the very beginning to her own uni-

---

37 Crisp 2011.
38 'It verges on kitsch, but retains a sense of the fantastical and the marvelous': Sulcas 2011, 6.
39 Cf. Crisp 2011.
40 Cf. http://kimbrandstrup.org/project/amor_og_psychen_kim_brandstrup_choreographer.
41 Cf. Clarke 1997.

verse. The scenic accompaniment of the story then suddenly jumps backwards to the classical pillared hall where Psyche meets Cupid during the night. The choreography of Brandstrup's first major full-length ballet was widely praised for its dramatic structure and 'cinematic drive',[42] underscored by composer Helweg's filmscore-like music which proves that the genre boundaries in late 20th and 21st century productions are fluid.

3 Film

It might come as a surprise that the tale of *Cupid and Psyche* has never been made into a successful Hollywood film.[43] We do have a very early silent movie from 1897 (running for 27 seconds), in which inventor Thomas Edison on a stage at San Francisco's Sutro Baths, in front of what looks like a large crowd, filmed the Leander sisters, a young woman portraying Psyche and a girl of about ten portraying Cupid, performing a simple dance as they are watched by a crowd of bathers.[44] There are two other French silent films that have picked up the *Cupid and Psyche* theme, 'La Fable de Psyché' by Gaston Velle (1908)[45] and 'Le Mariage de l'amour', directed by Maurice Le Forestier from 1913.[46]

But if one searches the International Movie Database for more recent versions, the results are quite disappointing. There exist only an animated short film 'Cupid & Psyche' (running for 25 min) from 1994 produced in the UK, and a horror porn version 'Amore & Psiche' (1996) by the Italian director Joe D'Amato (who is more famous for the well-known Emanuelle series) which a disappointed online reviewer has called a '… a pretty bland and boring hardcore feature from D'Amato, which features some rather unattractive sex scenes as well as a boring story thrown in. The movie is very slow paced and is yet another example of the director not being too interested in the subject.'[47]

But although the story never made it to the big screen as a whole, the motif *of Cupid and Psyche* has found its way into several cinematic productions: One might think of the American TV-movie 'Love-Struck' from 1997 by director Larry Peerce, which retells the ancient story with a twist: two years after her last failed relationship, Emily Vale has stopped believing in love. This brings her to the at-

---

42 Dithmer 1997.
43 See Elsom 1989, 141–50.
44 Cf. http://www.imdb.com/title/tt0217344/?ref_=fn_al_tt_2.
45 See Bouquet 1993, 150.
46 Cf. Yumibe 2012, x.
47 Elliott 2009.

tention of Venus, who sends her son Cupid down to Earth to pierce her with an arrow in the hope of changing her mind. Unfortunately, the handsome but hapless Cupid misses and the arrow strikes his own heart so that he falls hopelessly in love with Emily.[48]

A completely different perspective is taken by 'Spike' (2008), a Gothic horror-romance directed by Robert Beaucage, in which four friends find themselves lost in a forest and entangled in a twisted love story. As they are each picked off one by one by a bizarre beast it becomes clear that none of them will make it out of this forest alive, unless the one the monster so desires is left behind. Beaucage with his version clearly also follows the 'Beauty and Beast' tradition and commented himself that with his film he wanted to: 'tell a fantasy story exploring dark and dangerous possibilities of a condition we have all experienced in one way or another: romantic love. Why do we love? What causes us to love particular individuals? What is love? Can we control it, or does it control us?'[49]

Apart from these versions clearly aiming at an adult audience, it is not surprisingly the genre of animated film that offers the unique opportunity to produce versions of the *Cupid and Psyche* myth that are also suitable for children. The late 1990s Canadian-produced animated television series 'Mythic Warriors. Guardians of the Legend' was a fixture of CBS' Saturday-morning cartoon lineup. The show featured several retellings of popular Greek myths that were slightly altered so as to be more appropriate for younger audiences. The story of 'Psyche and Eros' is the subject of the first episode of the second season (1999) and is to a large degree reminiscent of the ancient plot:[50] Psyche, the most beautiful princess in Greece, is sought after by everyone. She could not walk through her hometown without being protected by bodyguards. Eros falls in love with Psyche for her kind and caring nature, not for her beauty. He decides to see if she will fall in love with him based on his personality by turning himself into an invisible host who will not reveal his identity. When Psyche's sister starts filling her mind with awful ideas about her invisible suitor, she decides to see covertly who he is, only to discover an angry Eros. Psyche must find a way to regain his love, even if it means losing her beauty. In the end, she sacrifices her beauty for the price of love and becomes a normal female with normal looks.[51]

---

48 Plot and cast under http://www.imdb.com/title/tt0119580/.
49 Beaucage 2008.
50 The series has its own Wiki including its cast of characters, stills etc. under http://mythicwarriors.wikia.com/wiki/Psyche_and_Eros.
51 For her wish cf. http://mythicwarriors.wikia.com/wiki/Psyche.

In the animated Disney film 'Hercules' from 1997 Cupid appears as a tall, teenage God with fuchsia-colored skin and angelic wings,[52] but in the non-canon animated follow-up series which 'notably contradicts several events in in the original film and is not considered canon'[53] he is portrayed as a short, overweight, pink-skinned man with tiny wings wearing a nappy and featuring a thin mustache and a gap in his teeth.[54] A possible explanation for this could be that he (like his family the Olympians), is known to shapeshift, and if that is the case, the animated version could be a transformation and the film version of him could be his true form. Unfortunately, Psyche only makes a short appearance sitting silently next to Cupid in the film[55] as an attractive vamp with green hair and blue skin wearing a tight green dress matching the colour of her hair.[56] The absence of Psyche in the series might be another reason why Cupid can be infantilized there.[57]

Psyche also plays a minor role in the production 'Hercules. The Legendary Journeys', an American television series filmed in New Zealand. It was produced from 1995 to 1999, and was based on the tales of the classical Greek culture hero Heracles. In the seventh episode of season 2 from 1996 with the title 'The Green-Eyed Monster' Heracles is accidentally shot by one of Cupid's arrows and he falls in love with Psyche, the beautiful woman Cupid loves. That makes Cupid turn very jealous, and because of a curse of Hera, he becomes a dangerous green-eyed monster.[58] As the monster, Cupid kidnaps Psyche and takes her to Hephaestus' cathedral. In the meantime, Hercules finds a way to escape the power of the arrow and Psyche comes to realize that Cupid is in love with her. Fearing their love would cause Cupid harm, Aphrodite turns Psyche into an old woman. But Cupid loves her anyway and Hercules convinces Aphrodite to give Psyche ambrosia to make her immortal, so the couple could live together happily. On Olympus, Psyche and Cupid marry and conceive a son, Bliss. When Bliss escapes their home, Psyche searches all of Olympus for him, before Cupid finds him in a Greek village.[59]

---

52 A picture can be found under https://de.pinterest.com/pin/291185932134658818/.
53 https.//disneychannel.fandom.com/wiki/Hercules:_The_Animated_Series
54 See under https://www.pinterest.com/pin/557179785121520426/.
55 Psyche's name is never explicitly mentioned, cf. http://disneyshercules.wikia.com/wiki/Psyche.
56 Cf. http://disneyshercules.wikia.com/wiki/Psyche.
57 I thank Regine May for her thoughtful suggestion.
58 Picking up Shakespeare's term for jealousy from 'Othello'.
59 Cf. the wiki under http://hercules-xena.wikia.com/wiki/Cupid.

Apart from these retellings of the original myth that makes a younger audience at least familiar with the characters and the basic outline of the original ancient version, twenty-first century digital culture has come up with completely new formats that anyone interested in the modern reception of the ancient world surely has to include more and more in her or his research.

'The further adventures of Cupid and Eros' is a web series with 9 episodes of several minutes each released in 2010 and 2011, and available exclusively on YouTube. It is about two love gods trying to set the world, and their own lives, right.[60] In this version by L.A.-based writer, director and producer Avi Glijansky, Cupid and Eros are not identical, but colleagues, each one the god of love in their respective pantheon. To quote the series' website: 'They still match up mortals and do their best to stem the tide of infidelity and divorce, but besides their common mission they are as different as night and day.'[61] Cupid is male and a sweet and charming character, Eros on the other hand is female and represents the other side of love: she is passionate, sexually insatiable and attracted by mortals and gods likewise. At the beginning Cupid is depressed, as his love, Psyche, has run away with a dermatologist and the god of love therefore visits a therapist regularly. Cupid and Eros might have their rival approaches, but in the end they have to work together and are irrevocably entangled. So the first season ends with a scene where Eros rests her head on Cupid's shoulder, when suddenly Psyche enters the scene and seems unpleasantly surprised.[62] The series features a number of ancient heroes and gods, partly related to the *Cupid and Psyche* myth, such as Apollo or Venus, partly completely unrelated to it, such as a winged Achilles as a flirty barman in episode 8. Likewise, the goddess Isis prominent in book 11 of Apuleius' *Metamorphoses* has a cameo appearance in episode 1, and reappears along with Pan and Loki [sic] as a judge of the singing competition 'Olympian Muse' in Episode 5, which is clearly inspired by shows like *American Idol*.

YouTube is also the source for a number of other amateur and semi-professional cinematic versions of the *Cupid and Psyche* story produced all over the world, among others a short film trailer from 2014 by director Noli Evan Catre

---

60 Cf. https://www.youtube.com/watch?v=_XKbWP4dc-M.
61 Http://www.cupidanderos.com/the-show/.
62 A second season of the self-financed web series had been planned, but the necessary goal of $ 10.000 for the first episodes has not nearly been reached via crowdfunding platform Indiegogo.com, cf. https://www.indiegogo.com/projects/the-further-adventures-of-cupid-and-eros-season-2#/.

from the Philippines,[63] or the outcome of a school project in which the story is played by different Barbie dolls.[64]

4 Music

Quite naturally when it comes to purely musical adaptations, the direct reception of the ancient myth is much more difficult to grasp, as we often simply do not know the exact source or idea of the composer's inspiration. There are two very well-known musical pieces by the title of 'Cupid and Psyche' from the late 19th and 20th Century. César Franck's symphonic poem has been mentioned above in section 2 as the accompaniment for a ballet version. Similarly, German composer Paul Hindemith had the idea of a whole ballet in mind, but in the end only finished the overture of 'Amor und Psyche' in 1943. The subtitle 'Farnesine' indicates that he was inspired by the frescoes of the story painted by Raphael and his workshop in 1518 in the Loggia of Cupid and Psyche in the Villa Farnesina in Rome (described and discussed by Simard in this volume).

This tradition of writing music based on *Cupid & Psyche* was picked up decades later by the German composer Eberhard Schoener, who wrote a short opera 'Palazzo del Amore' (1996), in which Amor and Psyche meet Romeo and Juliet and sing together about eternal love. In the course of the plot the lovers are threatened by modern cosmopolitan and multicultural society as well as by the gods. But love is triumphant in the end, for one pair of lovers in death, for the others in heaven. Alongside Argentinian mezzo-soprano Nidia Palacios as Juliet and Italian tenor Andrea Bocelli as Amor, the cast of the CD production of Schoener's opera included Italian rock icon Gianna Nannini as Romeo and the American singer Helen Schneider as Psyche, each couple pairing a classical singer with a rockier one.

Lesser known is the fact that German composer Eugen D'Albert included a song with the title 'Amor und Psyche' sung by the main character Myrtocle in his opera 'Die toten Augen' ('Dead Eyes') from 1914; Myrtocle is blind and believes that her husband Arcesius is beautiful, but in fact he is disfigured. A miracle lets Myrtocle regain her sight, and when she finds out the truth about her husband she blinds herself again after Arcesius has killed himself. So the libretto of the opera plays with a complete reversal of the *Cupid and Psyche* motif.

---

63 Cf. https://www.youtube.com/watch?v=fpKiPHGkKQ4&t=5s.
64 Cf. https://www.youtube.com/watch?v=d4F6f35MlPY&t=108s.

But the story of *Cupid and Psyche* has also formed the inspiration for various instrumental compositions of the 21st century. American composer Jack Curtis Dubowsky (1968-) in 2001 composed a Neo-baroque string quartet with the title 'Cupid & Psyche Dance No.1',[65] and most recently in 2016 Italian musician Fabio Zuffanti (1968-) collaborated for his 'Symphony n. 1—Cupid & Psyche' with keyboardist Luca Scherani. Zuffanti is well known for his 'Höstsonaten' with an ever-changing line-up:[66] classical symphonic elements, always present in every Höstsonaten album, are constantly mixed with the elements of rock music, jazz and folk music. The whole album is instrumental, but each of the ten songs is associated with an episode of *Cupid and Psyche*.[67] For this reason, Italian philosopher and writer Pee Gee Daniel wrote a libretto of the symphony based on the ancient version which has been translated into English for the CD inner sleeve by flautist Joanne Roan.[68]

Following public taste, the *Cupid and Psyche* story even found its way into vocal expressions of contemporary pop music. Most famous is the British synth-pop group Scritti Politti, whose album 'Cupid and Psyche 85' appeared in 1985 and is even today considered to be one of the most influential albums of its time. One might guess that the title recalled Antonio Canova's famous marble sculpture of 'Amore e Psiche', which was carved almost exactly two hundred years earlier in 1787, as in the inner sleeve photograph of the album singer Green Gartside and his colleagues, like in René Magritte's famous painting 'La reproduction interdite', turn their backs to the camera, but their faces appear clearly visible in the bathroom mirror. The polished stone of the hotel washroom underneath the mirror similarly reminds the viewer of the marble of Canova's statue[69] which shows the awakening of Psyche by Cupid with a kiss.[70]

Some years later, in 2001, Stephen Coates aka (The Real) Tuesday Weld published 'When Cupid Meets Psyche', a song-cycle about love and its inevitable demise that contains speaking titles like 'Am I in love?' or 'L'amour Et la morte', linking love constantly with death.[71]

---

65 Cf. Yumibe 2012, 126 and colour plate 25.
66 Cf. https://fabiozuffanti.bandcamp.com/album/symphony-1-cupid-psyche.
67 1. The Sacrifice/2. Zephyr/3.Love Scene/4. Unmasking/5. Venus (1st trial)/6. Entrapped (2nd trial)/7. Sheep and Water (3rd trial)/8. Underworld (4th trial)/9. The Awakening/10. The Ascension.
68 Cf. http://www.btf.it/symphony-n-1-cupid-psyche-clear-purple-vinyl.html.
69 Following Tomlinson 2015.
70 Magritte, like Canova, created one of the most renowned paintings of a kiss, but in his painting "Les Amants II" two individuals are locked in an embrace and are kissing one another through veils.
71 See Müller-Reineke 2009, 7 (and footnote 65).

A close resemblance to the *Cupid and Psyche* myth can also be found in a song by British singer and multi-instrumentalist Brendan Perry, who is best known for his work as the male half of the duo Dead Can Dance with Lisa Gerrard. In the still unreleased song 'Eros', which he has been performing live since 2011 and which can be found in various versions on YouTube,[72] he sings about an unrequited love, and with the lines 'We would come in disguise/To the Le Grand Bal masquerade/Where I would try To find my/Electric, green-eyed girl/ But it's just a game/To keep on playing/Like hide and seek with your feelings/.../And I must sing, sing my unrequited love song' picks up various aspects of the ancient myth, such as unrequited love, jealousy and disguise.

5 Conclusion

The story of *Cupid and Psyche* remains a successful inspiration for contemporary stage productions in the twenty-first century. All adaptations have in common that they continue to follow the ancient myth more or less closely and stress the timeless testimony of the narrative. Regardless of the form of the various technical and artistic implementations, this means that even for the fastidious audience of the twenty-first century the story clearly has an enduring fascination and has furthermore found its way into formats that are typical of and unique to our digital age. The focus on family relationships and the love story, where the gods become humans wielding worldly powers, reflects modern concerns. The sheer existence of a web series, or the numerous cinematic versions filmed by amateurs and especially students on YouTube are clear proof that the myth of *Cupid and Psyche* will continue to be retold and not forgotten in our times.

6 Bibliography

Accardo, P. (2002), *The Metamorphosis of Apuleius. Cupid and Psyche, Beauty and the Beast, King Kong*. Cranbury, NJ.
Bötger, F. (1979), *Die "Comedie-Ballet" von Moliere-Lully*, Hildesheim. Repr.
Bousquet, H. (1993), *Catalogue 'Pathé' des années 1896 à 1914 (1907–1909)*, Bures-sur-Yvette.
Call, M (2015), *The Would-be Author. Molière and the Comedy of Print*, West Lafayette.
Carver, R.F.H. (2007), *The Protean Ass. The Metamorphoses of Apuleius from Antiquity to the Renaissance*, Oxford.

---

72 Cf. https://www.youtube.com/watch?v=WItBtYMqgZU.

Cashman, C. (2006), Cupid and Psyche, http://www.nytheatre.com/Review/josephine-cashman-2006-4-13-cupid-and-psyche [Accessed 5th March 2017].
Clarke, M. (1997), 'Danish Delights', in: *Dancing Times* July 1997: 922–923.
Crisp, C. (2011), Psyché and Phèdre, Paris Opéra, https://www.ft.com/content/191b3660-e5e5-11e0-8e99-00144feabdc0 (accessed 16th April 2017).
Elliott, M. (2009), 'D'Amato Again', http://www.imdb.com/title/tt0329988/ [Accessed 6th March 2017].
Elsom, H. (1989), 'Apuleius and the Movies', in: Hofmann, 141–150.
Hofmann, H., (ed.) (1989), *Groningen Colloquia on the Novel*, II, Groningen.
Dithmer, M. (1997), Amor og Psyche, *Politiken* 26.05.1997
    http://kimbrandstrup.org/page/amor_og_psyche_review_kim_brandstrup_choreographer
Fisher, J. (2002), Cupid and Psyche, https://www.playscripts.com/play/413 [accessed 13th March 2017].
Foley, K. (2014), Rock opera 'Psyche' at Greenway Court aims high, falls short, http://www.latimes.com/entertainment/arts/la-et-cm-psyche-at-the-greenway-court-theatre-20140902-story.html [accessed 10th March 2017].
Frangoulidis, (2001). *Roles and Performances in Apuleius'* Metamorphoses. Beiträge zum antiken Drama und seiner Rezeption 16, Stuttgart.
Gaisser, J.H. (2008), *The Fortunes of Apuleius and* The Golden Ass. *A Study in Transmission and Reception.* Princeton.
[Intended for Use] (2012), Olympian Reviews: Cupid and Psyche, https://intendedforuse.wordpress.com/2012/02/09/olympian-reviews-cupid-and-psyche/ (accessed 15th April 2017).
Linden, T. (2001), 'Figurentheater Cassiopeia zeigt Lucius Apuleius 'Amor und Psyche'. Wenn einen die Liebe quält', *Kölnische Rundschau* 09.05.2001.
Marran, P & Ross, J.A. (2014), CUPID & PSYCHE to Open 2/13 at The TBG Theatre, http://www.broadwayworld.com/off-off-broadway/article/CUPID-PSYCHE-to-Open-1213-at-Barrow-Group-Theatre-20140120 (accessed 16th April 2017).
May, R. (2006*), Apuleius and Drama. The Ass on Stage.* Oxford.
Moreschini, C. (1994), *Il mito di Amore e Psiche in Apuleio*, Naples.
Müller-Reineke, H. (2009), 'Recent Theatrical and Musical Adaptations of Apuleius' Metamorphoses', *New Voices in Classical Reception Studies* 4: 1–26.
Murray, M. (2003), 'Off Broadway Reviews: Cupid and Psyche', http://www.talkinbroadway.com/page/ob/09_24_03.html [accessed 10th March 2017].
Pierce, B. (2003), Cupid and Psyche, http://www.theatermania.com/new-york-city-theater/reviews/09-2003/cupid-and-psyche_3922.html [accessed 11 March 2017].
Sallmann, K. (1997), *Handbuch der Lateinischen Literatur der Antike, Vol. 4: Die Literatur des Umbruchs: von der römischen zur christlichen Literatur 117 bis 284 n. Chr.*, München.
Schlichting, B. (2012), 'Cupid and Psyche: A modern tale of Greek desire on stage', http://www.currypilot.com/csp/mediapool/sites/CurryPilot/News/story.csp?cid=4303084&sid=919&fid=151 (accessed 15th April 2017).
Siegel, N. (2008), 'Buff Cupid, Meet Spunky Psyche', *The New York Times*, https://mobile.nytimes.com/2008/12/21/nyregion/new-jersey/21cupidnj.html [accessed 12 March 2017].
Sulcas, R. (2011), 'Myths and Legends Open Paris Ballet', http://www.nytimes.com/2011/09/29/arts/dance/paris-opera-ballets-phedre-and-psyche-review.html [accessed 12th March 2017].

Taghap, J. (2014), 'The Power of Love', https://www.offoffonline.com/offoffonline/12906?rq=emily%20snyder (accessed 12th April 2017).

Tomlinson, (2015), '30 Years On: Scritti Politti's Cupid and Psyche '85', http://www.walesartsreview.org/30-years-on-scritti-polittis-cupid-and-psyche/ [accessed 12th March 2017].

Veeramani, A. (2016), 'Mother-Son Duo Brings a Mother and Son to Stage', http://yaledailynews.com/blog/2016/04/22/mother-son-duo-brings-a-mother-and-son-to-stage/ [accessed 6th March 2017].

Yumibe, J. (2012), *Moving Color. Early Film, Mass Culture, Modernism,* New Brunswick.

Janice Siegel
Undertones of Apuleius' *Cupid and Psyche* in Guillermo del Toro's *Pan's Labyrinth*[1]

1 Introduction

Guillermo del Toro has spoken widely about the fantasy films and stories that influenced his 2006 blockbuster film *Pan's Labyrinth*, including L. Frank Baum's *The Wizard of Oz*, Hans Christian Andersen's *The Little Match Girl*, and Lewis Carroll's *Alice in Wonderland*. But it is Apuleius' Tale of *Cupid and Psyche*—not mentioned in any known interview with the filmmaker—that best tracks overall with this extraordinary film in terms of the structure of the narrative, progression of the conflict leading to resolution, characterization techniques, and themes. Indeed, a comparative analysis reveals the film's systematic reflection of almost every aspect of the ancient tale.

The main narrative of *Pan's Labyrinth* unfolds five years after the end of the Spanish Civil War on the grounds of a dilapidated rural mill-turned-military outpost of the Falangist (fascist) Captain Vidal, whose job is to eradicate a stubborn band of local resistance fighters. The film begins as Vidal's very pregnant wife Carmen and her daughter from a previous marriage, eleven-year old Ofelia, join him there. Carmen will die in childbirth only five days later. Meanwhile, a captured rebel confesses under torture that some member of Vidal's household staff has been abetting their cause. Vidal catches this housekeeper—a key character named Mercedes—attempting to escape with Ofelia and the newborn. They resist his tyrannical attempts to dominate them, but in their final confrontation, Ofelia is killed by Vidal while protecting her baby brother. The resistance fighters then strip the Captain of his son, his life, and his legacy.

On the face of it, *Pan's Labyrinth* does not seem to have much in common with Apuleius' story, but subtle invocations and inversions of the tale of Cupid and Psyche are clearly perceptible in the fantasy sub-plot that shadows the film's main storyline. In this other narrative layer, Ofelia finds her way into a

---

[1] The Latin text of Apuleius is Helm's as published in Zimmerman et al. 2004. The translation is Hanson's. Dialogue and set directions of del Toro's film are cited from the English translation of the screenplay (© Picturehouse 2006) published online here: http://www.dailyscript.com/scripts/PansLabyrinthEnglishScreenplay.pdf. Unless otherwise stated, all images are taken from the New Line Home Entertainment, Inc. DVD of 'Pan's Labyrinth' in accordance with laws governing fair use.

https://doi.org/10.1515/9783110641585-024

world filled with magical creatures, one of whom—the Faun—informs Ofelia that she is really the reincarnation of Princess Moanna, long lost daughter of the King and Queen of the Underworld. The Faun explains that she can return to that wondrous world through an open portal located deep inside the mystical labyrinth in the nearby woods if she can accomplish three tasks within three days' time. Although the English title's 'Pan' appears to be a coincidental mistranslation of the Spanish title *El laberinto del fauno*, this is fortuitous, since, as Pasetti in this volume demonstrates, the god Pan in Apuleius can carry significant symbolism that is also observable in this Faun who acts as Ofelia's psychopomp.

2 The two worlds

The heroines Psyche and Ofelia are both young virginal girls who are provided an escape from their normal existence into a fantastic world populated by wondrous yet dangerous characters. These other worlds are accessible only through mystical means: Zephyr, who gently transports Psyche from the cliff, and the fairy that leads Ofelia into the labyrinth. Rather than remaining distinct, the two worlds of each heroine overlap one another. Psyche's sisters visit her in her enchanted world, and later Psyche will visit them in theirs. Ofelia's two worlds are juxtaposed from the beginning of the film via simple alternation of scenes as well as through cross-cutting. del Toro explains that '[t]hese two worlds start to intertwine among themselves' until the final scene, when 'they will lead to a single outcome' (DVD Commentary). This merging of the two plot lines is signalled by the mixing of their distinct colour palettes as well as by the appearance in one world of objects and people associated with the other.

Each heroine's fantastical world comes complete with a guide (Cupid/Faun), supernatural aides (Psyche's talking animals and objects/Ofelia's three fairies), and magic (e.g., the death-spell cast over Psyche/a piece of chalk with which Ofelia can create doorways). Each heroine must endure the oppressive behaviour of a terrible tyrant (Venus/Vidal) and is commanded to complete a series of dangerous tasks, during the course of which she violates a rule of such mythic import that her very survival is threatened. But in the end, each heroine is given a second chance and achieves her desired brand of immortality.

3 Psyche and Ofelia: Two lost souls

In Apuleius' tale, when a drop of hot oil from Psyche's lamp awakens him, the winged Cupid flies away, Psyche dangling from his leg until 'at last, exhausted, she fell to the ground' (5.24.1).

Scholars have long considered the apparent similarities between the fall of Psyche, whose name, of course, literally means 'soul', and the scenario sketched by Plato in his *Phaedrus*, where Socrates explains the plight of a fallen soul:[2]

> ...the Law of Destiny is this: 'If any soul becomes a companion to a god and catches sight of any true thing, it will be unharmed until the next circuit; and if it is able to do this every time, it will always be safe. If, on the other hand, it does not see anything true because it could not keep up, and by some accident takes on a burden of forgetfulness and wrongdoing, then it is weighed down, sheds its wings, and falls to earth.' (Pl. *Phaedrus* 248c).[3]

But this description of a fallen soul resonates even more with the backstory of Ofelia's fantasy-*Doppelgänger* Moanna, thus providing us with our first palpable link to Psyche's tale. *Pan's Labyrinth* begins with a striking image: a mortally wounded Ofelia lying on the edge of a well set deep in an ancient labyrinth, a ribbon of blood flowing *backwards* into her nose (suggesting that death might not be the end for her after all). A voiceover describes a scenario that sounds remarkably similar to Plato's dramatization of the soul's journey:

> Long ago in the Underworld Realm... where there are no lies or pain, there lived a princess who dreamt of the human world. She dreamt of blue skies, the soft breeze and sunshine. One day, eluding her captors, the Princess escaped. Once outside, the brightness blinded her and erased her memory. She forgot who she was and where she came from. Her body suffered cold, sickness, and pain. Eventually she died. Her father, the King, always knew that the Princess would return, perhaps in another body, in another place, at another time (2–3).

When the immortal Princess Moanna left the Underworld, she suffered the very effects warned about earlier in the *Phaedrus:* '...A soul that sheds its wings wanders until it lights on something solid, where it settles and takes on an earthly body...' (Pl. *Phaedrus* 246c).[4] When Ofelia meets the Faun, he will tell her that

---

[2] For example, see C. Panayotakis 2001, 576; O'Brien 2002, 77–90; Zimmerman et al. 2004, 283 and 294; Panayotakis and Panayotakis 2015, 145.
[3] Tr. Nehamas, A. and Woodruff, P. in Cooper 1997, 526.
[4] Tr. Nehamas, A. and Woodruff, P. in Cooper 1997, 524.

she is the reincarnation of this lost princess and that his sole concern is 'to make sure that your essence is intact, that you have not become a mortal' (24).

Figure 24: Screengrab from Guillermo del Toro, Pan's Labyrinth 2006. 'Stick insect transforming into winged fairy'. Taken from the New Line Home Entertainment, Inc. DVD of 'Pan's Labyrinth' in accordance with laws governing fair use.

Figure 25: Detail, white-ground terracotta funerary lekythos showing winged representation of the deceased's soul. Attic Greek, ca. 440 B.C. Metropolitan Museum of Art 1989.281.72. http://www.vroma.org/images/mcmanus_images/paula_chabot/ker.jpg. Credit: Paula Chabot. Reprinted in accordance with laws governing fair use.

And, too, the fairy in *Pan's Labyrinth* (see figure 24) resembles the standard rendering in Greek funerary art of the just-released winged soul (*psyche*) escaping its mortal prison and setting course for the Underworld (see figure 25). In the same way, Ofelia's fairy will facilitate the journey of Princess Moanna's soul (also to the Underworld) once it is released from Ofelia's body. Both the tale of *Cupid and Psyche* and *Pan's Labyrinth* tell the story of a lost soul's journey to its eternal home.

4 The character of a heroine

Because the two heroines are in different stages of life, their plots follow different trajectories. Psyche is of marriageable age, and Apuleius' tale thus focuses on her conjugal interests. Her fantastical journey begins with her magical teleportation to her new home, the enchanted palace of her new, mysterious husband. Moreover, Psyche's natal bonds are severed, leaving her despairing parents to wither away in ignorance of her fate. She even orchestrates the deaths of her own scheming sisters.

On the other hand, Ofelia is a pre-pubescent child, and the relationships she holds dear are thus necessarily those with her immediate family.[5] Early in the film, she is also relocated (in an utterly ordinary way) to her new home, her new stepfather's military outpost (a far cry from the comfort and opulence of Cupid's palace). She treasures her mother and her brother, both before and after the latter's birth. While Apuleius lingers over descriptions of the newly wed Psyche luxuriating in bed with her husband, the child Ofelia is repeatedly shown snuggling in bed with her pregnant mother. Further, Ofelia's fantasy goal is not marriage but reunion with her 'real' father, the King of the Underworld, who, she will be delighted to discover, has been searching for her all along.

In comparable scenes, it even happens that illness/injury separates both couples, each member relegated to a different room in the same house. While Cupid recovers from his wound in a room earlier identified as 'his mother's own bedchamber' (5.28.1), Venus holds Psyche prisoner elsewhere in the house: 'Thus, sundered and separated under one roof, the lovers dragged out an anguished night' (6.11.3). After Carmen hemorrhages in the bed she had been sharing with her daughter, the doctor explains to Vidal that this arrangement is no longer suitable: 'Your wife needs absolute bedrest. She'll be sedated from now on. The girl should sleep somewhere else.' (48) Ofelia is then relocated to the attic.

Each heroine's character is revealed through the traditional narrative elements of thought, diction, and deed, as well as dramatically through her alliances and conflicts with other characters. In the opening lines of her tale, Psyche is described as weeping and 'sick in body, wounded in heart' (4.32.4) simply because her inordinate beauty makes her lonely. She repeatedly presents herself with some combination of frightened, pale, trembling, weeping, and lamenting: while waiting to be sacrificed, before losing her virginity, in three different scenes as she attempts to persuade Cupid to allow her to visit with her sisters, in response to her sisters' claims that her husband is a monster, after Cupid abandons her for her treachery, and when she comes upon Pan. When her tears and prayers fail to convince Ceres and Juno to help her, she gives in to her grief.

---

5 An alternative interpretation of the film argues the significance of Ofelia's transition into womanhood (for example, see Salzman-Mitchell and Alvarez 2017). Such studies do have the virtue of exploring del Toro's rich 'gynecological/obstetrician motifs' (del Toro, DVD Commentary), but suffer for missing the significance of Ofelia's eternal status as pre-pubescent tween. del Toro is on record about how Ofelia's fantasy 'is about the girl's dreaming about going back into the womb of the mother' (Vaz and Nunziata 2016: 96), a very different thing than becoming a woman herself.

It is hardly Psyche's fault that she is ultimately unequal to the four tasks assigned by her tormentor. But described as 'weak in both body and spirit' (5.22.1), Psyche easily falls victim to despair. She is 'dismayed by the enormity' (6.10.4) of one task and 'completely overwhelmed by the magnitude of her inescapable danger' (6.14.6) regarding another. In response to challenges she sits 'silently dumbfounded' (in 6.10.4) and 'transformed into stone' (in 6.14.6). More often than not, she settles on suicide as her only way forward: after realizing that the monster in her bed was really a god, and on three separate occasions while completing her tasks. But some magical agency always intervenes: the knife refuses to stab her, and the reed, the eagle, and the tower solve her logistical problems. Psyche is happiest when following orders: 'Once she had been carefully instructed she never faltered or had reason to regret obeying' (6.13.1). She is repeatedly described with variations of the Latin word *simplex*, meaning 'honest, guileless,' but also suggesting gullibility or being easily manipulated.[6]

Ofelia, too, reveals her true character through her actions. But Ofelia literally and figuratively blazes her own trail through a very difficult landscape. While Psyche remains desperate for the gods' blessings and embrace, Ofelia is never obsequious to, or even compliant with, Vidal. She resists all attempts to control her. Despite her mother's entreaties, she refuses to accept Vidal as family ('he's not my father,' 10) and impishly delights in irritating him. She is repeatedly chastised and punished for breaking rules big and small. But when her mother and Mercedes can no longer protect her and she faces very real danger from the enraged Captain Vidal, the understandably terrified Ofelia shows remarkable self-assurance and courage for an eleven-year-old.

Like Psyche, Ofelia is given dangerous, fantastical tasks to accomplish: retrieve a key from the stomach of a monstrous Toad, use that key to open a cabinet that turns out to contain a golden dagger, and, as she will only find out later, use that dagger to draw the blood of an innocent. But unlike Psyche, Ofelia routinely shows bravery in dangerous situations. She is saved numerous times by her quick thinking. Ofelia even learns from her own mistakes, something Psyche seems incapable of doing.[7]

Poor Psyche never has any real hope of success as she is simply the victim of a vengeful bully much too powerful to thwart. Venus' tasks start out as demeaning busywork but devolve into traps the vengeful goddess hopes will destroy her. In contrast, Ofelia's tasks offer lessons about the benefits and risks of disobedience. But because Ofelia's fantasy world is thematically tied to her grim reality,

---

6 See 5.14.4, 5.15.10, 5.18.4, 5.19.5, 5.24.3, and 6.15.3.
7 Concerning this trait of Psyche, see Panayotakis and Panayotakis 2015, 141.

her tasks are more than just fairytale-style obstacles. They are moral dilemmas writ large.[8] And although both task-masters set time limits, only Ofelia's urgency to complete her tasks 'before the moon is full' (24) has meaning: her immortal soul depends on it. Venus puts time constraints on Psyche (in 6.10.3, 6.11.6, 6.13.5, and 6.16.5) that are just cruelly arbitrary.

5 *Katabasis* and the Pale Man

Venus' revenge culminates in her final assignment: Psyche must descend to the Underworld on a fool's errand. Ofelia's required visit to the Pale Man's lair offers a remarkable parallel. Each episode is a sort of *katabasis*, or descent to the Underworld typical of mythic heroes. But rather than returning with information (à la Odysseus or Aeneas), both Psyche and Ofelia are tasked with retrieving an object: Proserpina's beauty for Psyche, and the dagger for Ofelia. Both characters embark on a quintessentially mythic journey, but it is Ofelia, not Psyche, who best displays the heroic qualities of her mythic predecessors: adventurousness, intrepidity, determination, and the kind of over-confidence that trips up even mythic heroes.[9] In contrast, Apuleius' Psyche at best recalls the less impressive female protagonists of the Greek novels and New Comedy.[10]

Before they go, Ofelia and Psyche are both given explicit instructions as well as a specific interdiction. Psyche is warned by the talking tower not to give away even one barley-cake and 'to be especially careful not to open or look into the jar' (6.19.7).

The Faun provides a comparable warning to Ofelia: 'You are going to a very dangerous place. The thing that slumbers there, it is not human. You will see a sumptuous feast, but don't eat or drink anything. Absolutely nothing. Your life

---

[8] For example, the Faun explains that only by killing the Toad 'will the fig tree flourish again' (34). Because Ofelia's journey into the magical forest is intercut with scenes of Falangist soldiers rooting out resistance fighters in the same wood, the tree-killing Toad clearly stands for the blight of fascism. And indeed, the very last shot of the film will show that fig tree flowering once again.
[9] In her role as descender to the Underworld, Psyche falls far short of the mythic models of Aeneas, Orpheus, and Hercules, although she is often compared with them. See e.g. Harrison 2013, 153.
[10] For elements of Apuleius' tale lifted from New Comedy see May 2006, 208–46, Zimmerman et al. 2004, 542, and Panayotakis and Panayotakis 2015, 144. For Greek romance, see Zimmerman et al. 2004, esp. 412, 427, 543 and 544. For suicide as a typical recourse of heroines of Greek novels, see Zimmerman et al. 2004, 146; and for its frequency and common methods in New Comedy, see Zimmerman et al. 2004, 229.

depends on it' (51–2). (This, of course, is the very misstep that led to Proserpina's incarceration in the Underworld).

Both heroines ignore their instructions. Crucially, however, their motives are different. Psyche's curiosity (always a dangerous quality) is driven by the character flaw of vanity: 'I am a fool to be a porter of divine beauty and not take out a tiny drop of it for myself' (6.20.5). Ofelia's appetite is more forgivable: the child is simply hungry because she had been sent to her room without dinner.[11]

Yet the equally dire consequences of their disobedience are mythically equivalent. Ofelia barely escapes with her life after she eats from the Pale Man's table, which causes the monster to awaken and devour two of the fairies horribly, Cyclops-like. When she later faces the wrath of the Faun, Ofelia will try to minimize this 'accident,' as she calls it: 'It was only two grapes. I thought no one would notice' (70). This perfectly resonates with the tower's warning to Psyche: 'Do not suppose that this paltry loss of a barley-cake is of no consequence: if you lose either cake you will never see the daylight again' (6.19.2). Had Psyche lost a barley cake, she would be forever imprisoned in the Underworld. But the rule she does break—peeking into the jar—causes 'a deathlike and truly Stygian sleep' to come over her, making her 'no better than a sleeping corpse' (6.21.1–2). The Faun explains that death is also the consequence for Ofelia's violation: 'You'll get old like [humans], you'll die like them' (70). Later we will see how each heroine escapes this ultimate punishment.

The Pale Man, a raw-eater of human beings, is not unlike the ubiquitous anthropophagic monsters of classical mythology who represent a generally mythic threat to humanity. This monster though, is also specifically a child-eater.[12] Notably, Psyche also faces a similar threat she at first fails to recognize. Cupid had warned her against listening to her sisters, whom he specifically identified as 'Lamiae' (5.11.5), the child-devouring monsters of myth. But they in turn convince Psyche that the child-devouring threat comes from her husband, who, they claim, is really the monster she was prophesied to wed: '…he will not long continue to fatten you with the charming indulgences of nourishment, but as soon as a full womb brings your pregnancy to completion and endowed you with more luscious fruit, he will eat you up' (5.18.1). It is her sisters' plea that she not allow

---

[11] Calling it the 'biggest editing faux pas in the movie,' del Toro bemoans their decision to cut Mercedes' 'crucial' line in which she explains why Ofelia is so hungry (Vaz and Nunziata 2016, 109). Yet at the time, Carmen is quite clear about Ofelia's punishment for disobedience: 'What you've done hurts me. When you get out of the tub, you'll go to bed without dinner' (43).
[12] See Vaz and Nunziata 2016, 95 for a special insert containing sketches of the twelve illustrated panels adorning the dining room's walls: six of the Pale Man killing children with a sword and six of him devouring them raw.

herself 'to be buried in the bowels of a ferocious beast' (5.18.2) that persuades Psyche to murder her husband.

But the Pale Man represents an even more specific kind of threat in *Pan's Labyrinth*. del Toro links the Pale Man to Captain Vidal by using a technique he calls 'visual rhyming,' whereby similar imagery connects the otherwise distinct narratives, a method similar to Apuleius' 'motif correspondences'.[13] The Pale Man's dining room is a fantasy mock-up of the very dining room where earlier Vidal had hosted the village's leaders at a sumptuous banquet while they plotted to reduce the already inadequate rations of the locals. del Toro himself lists the similarities: 'the long table with the food, the chimney in the bottom, at the back, and the faceless monster at the head of the table' (DVD Commentary). (see figure 26 and figure 27).

Figure 26: Screengrab from Guillermo del Toro, Pan's Labyrinth 2006. 'Captain Vidal at head of table'. Taken from the New Line Home Entertainment, Inc. DVD of 'Pan's Labyrinth' in accordance with laws governing fair use.

Figure 27: Screengrab from Guillermo del Toro, Pan's Labyrinth 2006. 'Pale Man at head of table'. Taken from the New Line Home Entertainment, Inc. DVD of 'Pan's Labyrinth' in accordance with laws governing fair use.

Yes, both the Pale Man and the Captain 'restrict the consumption of food, and tempt with their possession of it' (Salzman-Mitchell and Alvarez 2017: 207). But each is also portrayed as a devourer of those unlucky enough to find themselves within his reach. As a consumer of innocents, the Pale Man has much in common with the fascist Captain. del Toro has explained that for him 'the Pale Man represents all institutional evil feeding on the helpless' (Twitter.com@RealGDT, 3:05 AM, 2 Feb 2017), specifically 'fascism and the Church eating the children when they have a perversely abundant banquet in front of them' (Guillén 2006).

---

[13] Other images that appear in both narrative layers and serve to connect the two storylines include goat's horns, a key, a knife, the moon, and a root. 'Motiventsprechungen': Riefstahl 1938.

By presenting the horrid Pale Man as the true essence of the outwardly handsome Captain, del Toro reveals the insidious evil of fascism, how it 'has a whole concept of design, and a whole concept of uniforms and set design that made it attractive to the weak-willed' (Guillén 2006). Both characters are monsters who see the world from their own odd perspective and are driven by bloodlust.[14] The Pale Man is simply the Captain stripped of the illusion of civility. His blood-red banquet and the artwork that covers his walls lay bare the beast and tyrant that also lurk behind the Captain's veneer of charm, manners, and elegance.

6 The character of a tyrant

del Toro's Vidal has much in common—in both character and deed—with Apuleius' tyrannical Venus. Both are destructive personality types sharing the same narcissistic traits of preening vanity, hypersensitivity, an arrogant sense of entitlement, and lack of empathy for others. They are ruthless abusers of power who need to control all aspects of their world (in the DVD Commentary, del Toro describes Vidal with the word 'minutiose'). They rage explosively when their delicate egos are wounded. They use humiliation and torture to punish their enemies. And both unleash the full force of their significant powers against a mere girl who threatens them. One expects such behaviour from a god in a myth. In the real world, such a man is truly a monster.

Despite his commanding presence, Vidal is a small man who despises his own inadequacies and lashes out in his anger and shame. Throughout the film, he obsesses over his appearance. He repeatedly shines his boots, checks that his hair is in place and his uniform square, and admires his shirtless reflection in his shaving mirror. But he has an equal measure of self-loathing, illustrated when he viciously slashes his reflection's throat in that same mirror. del Toro identifies Vidal's obsession with his physical appearance as a way to gain 'the illusion of power' and hide his inner ugliness: 'Perfection is a conceit' (Guillén 2006). When a fellow soldier regales the dinner party with the story of how Vidal's war-hero father purposely smashed his watch 'so his son would know the exact hour and minute of his death...so he would know how a brave man dies' (43), Vidal denies that his father ever owned a watch. But it does exist, and we

---

14 The metaphorical identification of tyrants with man-eaters is also a popular classical trope, as early as Plato. See Hook 2005, esp. p. 24.

see him obsessively tinkering with it in private. Vidal yearns for the kind of reputation he lacks the character to earn for himself.

At least the reputation Venus fights to regain is rightfully hers. Venus' anger is initially caused by the news that a young beautiful girl named Psyche is being venerated by the pious prayers of the people 'as if she were the very goddess Venus herself' (4.28.3). Worse yet, Venus discovers that her rites are being abandoned because 'It was the girl that people worshipped' (4.29.4). Venus is threatened not only by Psyche's youth, beauty, and virginity (4.28.4), but also by her potential to become pregnant by her son (5.29.4). But while Venus is jealous of Psyche's ability to *provide* a baby to her son, Vidal will be threatened by Ofelia's threat to *deny* him his own.

In Apuleius' tale, the goddess of Love and Sex is repeatedly shown engaged in her legendary beauty regimen (5.28; 6.11.1). And like Vidal, she cannot help but constantly admire her own image: when her retinue gathers to convey her to Olympus, one of the many Tritons in her entourage 'carried a mirror before his mistress's eyes' (4.31). But it is this vanity that makes Venus vulnerable. When she discovers that Psyche is being worshipped in her stead, she suffers a narcissistic injury of mythic proportions.

Venus reacts to the assault on her godhood as any god would: by using pain and humiliation to punish a human for her *hubris*. When Venus learns that her divine honours were usurped by this mortal girl (4.29.4), she charges Cupid to avenge her not by killing Psyche but by stealing her dignity and happiness by making her fall in love with a lowly man (4.31.2–3).

But instead, Cupid fell in love with her 'enemy' (5.29.2). Venus' fury derives from her fear of having been humiliated and made irrelevant: 'But now that I have been made a laughing stock, what am I to do?' (5.30.3). In retaliation for the wound to her vanity, she threatens to give him over to Temperance to disempower as well as to drug him, and clip his hair and wings.

Venus then turns her full attention to getting her hands on Psyche, the author of her original betrayal. After learning that Venus had promised divine kisses to whomever would deliver her to the goddess, the utterly defeated Psyche, now with virtually the whole world against her, decides that she must now surrender herself to Venus. Upon arriving at Venus' home, Psyche is yelled at and struck by the goddess' handmaiden Habit. Then Venus verbally abuses the unresisting girl, repeatedly referring to her as her slave.[15] Then the goddess hands

---

[15] Psyche is referred to as her 'slave girl' by Venus (in conversation with Mercury, 6.7.3 and to Psyche's face, in 6.9.5 and 6.10.2), and by Habit (to Psyche's face, in 6.8.6). Venus is called Psyche's 'mistress' by the narrator of the tale (in 6.8.5) and by Habit (in 6.8.6).

Psyche over to her handmaidens Care and Sorrow, who 'scourged poor Psyche with whips and tortured her with every other sort of device' (6.9.3). Venus then ridicules Psyche some more, dismissing her pregnancy as illegitimate, and even threatening to 'not allow [her] to go through with the birth at all' (6.9.6). Then more physical punishment: 'Venus flew at her, ripped her dress into several pieces, tore her hair, and beat her head, hurting her sorely' (6.10.1). And then Psyche is locked in a room and given the first of her several impossible tasks.

In much the same way, when the Captain captures Mercedes trying to escape the compound with Ofelia and his baby son, Vidal deals first with his (step)child who abetted the crime. Just as Venus was 'furious and angry' (5.31.1) with Cupid, so too is Vidal with Ofelia. He roughly grabs her as he pushes her into the attic, slapping her twice across the face. Just like Venus, Vidal is stung by the humiliation of his betrayal: 'How long have you known about her? How long have you been laughing at me behind my back?' (83). And while Venus melodramatically threatens to replace Cupid 'with another son much better than you' (5.29.5), Vidal has already created a replacement for Ofelia in the person of his newborn son. Her life is not worth much, and she knows it. Then Vidal leaves the weeping orphan in a locked room just as Venus does to Psyche, but worse, he orders the guards to kill Ofelia if anyone tries to rescue her.

But while the goddess Venus was in a position to offer a rich reward for information leading to Psyche's capture, the despised fascist must resort to torturing (and humiliating) a captured rebel soldier in order to find his traitor:

> *[Vidal] goes over to a toolbox and takes out a hammer, some needle-nosed pliers, and a leather-working blade.*
> VIDAL: At first I won't be able to trust you. But when I use this one—
> *He lifts the hammer.*
> VIDAL: you'll own up to a few things...
> *Next he shows off the pliers.*
> VIDAL: When we get to this one, we'll have a closer relationship, almost like brothers. You'll see.
> *He picks up the blade.*
> VIDAL: And when we get to this one, I'll believe everything you tell me.
> *Vidal picks up the hammer.*
> VIDAL: Now, I'll make you a deal. If you can count to three without st-t-tuttering, you can go.
> *He approaches the shivering man, who looks around as if in search of an answer.*
> VIDAL: Don't look around, look at me. There's no one above me. Garcés, if I say this asshole can leave—
> GARCÉS: Then he can leave, Captain -
> VIDAL: So there. Count to three—
> *And Stutter tries—sweating—making a supreme effort.*
> STUTTER: One—

> VIDAL: Good.
> STUTTER: Two.
> VIDAL: One more and you will be free.
> *And he goes for it. But—*
> STUTTER: T— t-t-t-t
> *He looks up at Vidal, imploring.*
> VIDAL: Pity.
> *His arm is a blur as the hammer lands a terrible blow.*

Stutter's vague confession and clues left behind after a rebel supply raid reveal to Vidal that the traitor is a member of his household staff. Soon thereafter he captures Mercedes in mid-escape with Ofelia and his newborn son. Like Stutter before her, Mercedes is tied to a post in the storeroom. Just as Venus did with Cupid, Vidal alternates between reproaches and threats. But then in a surprising break with protocol he dismisses his aide Garcés. In response to his objection, Vidal scoffs, revealing his disdain for Mercedes: 'For God's sake, she's just a woman.' After Garcés departs, Mercedes speaks truth to power:

> MERCEDES: That's what you always thought. That's why I was able to get away with it. I was invisible to you.
> VIDAL: Damn. You found my weakness. Arrogance. How perceptive. But we're here to find your weak points (83).

Just as he did in preparation to torture Stutter, Vidal has already rolled up his sleeves and unbuttoned his shirt. But now, as he turns away from the camera, he also casually shrugs off his suspenders, a motion del Toro intends to be 'vaguely menacing about rape or intimacy' (DVD commentary).[16] As Vidal fondles each torture-tool, he begins to recite his script: 'It's very simple. You will talk. And I have to know that everything you say is the truth...' But Mercedes, who has cut through her bonds with the paring knife she keeps in a fold of her apron, suddenly breaks loose and stabs him—once in the back, then again in the chest as he veers round. Then she thrusts the knife inside his mouth:

> 'I'm not some old man! Not a wounded prisoner! Sonofabitch! Sonofabitch! Don't you dare touch the girl! You won't be the first pig I've gutted' (85).

And then Mercedes slices open Vidal's face from the inside out, horribly and purposely wounding him in his vanity. Rather than inflict a mortal wound, the

---

[16] Although it is absent from Psyche's tale, rape is a fundamental expression of tyranny in Latin literature, too.

newly empowered Mercedes chooses to disfigure Vidal in a way that del Toro himself identifies as a castration (DVD commentary). With one slash of her knife, Mercedes deflates this petty tyrant earlier dismissed by the no-nonsense kitchen staff as 'a fussy dandy' (27). And then she escapes. Vidal stitches his cut using the same mirror that once reflected a vision of power. His ravaged face now reveals a wound that has struck his core.

7 Choice and disobedience

In the meantime, Ofelia still sits alone and fearful in a guarded attic room awaiting her punishment. She has no reason to expect rescue from her guardian Faun because on the previous night he had rebuked her for failing to follow his directions during her *katabasis*, and abandoned her:

> 'You broke the rules!'
> 'You failed. You can never go back. The moon will be full in three days. Your spirit will stay forever among the humans. You'll live among them, you'll get old like them, you'll die like them… and your memory of us will fade. And we'll vanish along with it!' (70–1).

But now, in Ofelia's moment of greatest need, the Faun returns to guide her: 'I've decided to give you one last chance' (87). His only demand is that she obey his every command:

> FAUN: You promise to listen, to do everything I tell you? Without question?
> *Ofelia nods yes.*
> FAUN: Pick up your brother and bring him to the labyrinth—as fast as you can. (88)

The grateful Ofelia draws a new door in the wall with her magic chalk, enters the Captain's study, drugs his drink with her mother's sleeping draught, collects her baby brother from his cradle, and bravely rushes out of the house into the midst of a rebel attack, keeping only a few steps ahead of the drugged and stumbling captain.

Upon her arrival in the centre of the Labyrinth, the Faun demands that she hand over the baby. Despite her promise to obey unquestioningly, Ofelia asks, 'What's that in your hand?' The Faun is holding the golden dagger Ofelia had retrieved from the locked niche in the Pale Man's Room:

> FAUN: The portal will only open if we shed the blood of an innocent. A pin-prick, that's all. Just a drop of blood. It's the last task! Hurry!!

And then he reveals his own selfish need:

> FAUN: You promised to do it, so give me the boy. I want to leave this place, I can't wait any longer!
> *The Faun comes closer to the girl. His face radiates a wicked hunger. She steps back, horrified.*
> OFELIA: No, my brother stays with me.
> FAUN: You would give up your sacred rights for this brat?
> OFELIA: Yes, I would.
> FAUN: You would give up your throne for him? He who has caused you such misery, such humiliation?
> *Vidal comes into the rotunda. He sees Ofelia alone. He can't see the Faun. With enormous effort, Vidal lifts his gun.*
> OFELIA: I will.
> FAUN: As you wish—your Highness—
> *As he recedes into the darkness, Vidal shoots. The bullet hits Ofelia in the stomach. She falls gently to the ground, at the edge of the well, clutching her baby brother.* (93–94)

In the end, it turns out that Ofelia's task-master, the Faun, is a trickster-god figure whose real purpose is not to help her but to test her. Ofelia's strength of character allows her to disobey the Faun, despite the certain consequence of death and the threat of the loss of her immortality. This pivotal moment in Ofelia's life was presaged by the Latin inscription chiseled into the arched entrance to the labyrinth, which the camera lingered on as she passed beneath it to enter this mystical space for the last time:

> *In consiliis nostris fatum nostrum est*
> ('Our fate lies in our own counsels')

Ofelia does indeed choose her own fate by following her own counsel (*consilium*) despite tremendous pressure to do otherwise. But what about Psyche? Remarkably, *consilium* is also the Latin word Apuleius uses repeatedly (in 5.6.6, 5.10.6, 5.11.1, 5.21.3, and 5.26.3) to define the advice she followed, the bad advice given by her sisters to kill her husband.

And just as Ofelia must determine for herself how to respond to the Faun's charge, a pivotal scene in Apuleius' tale shows how Psyche also must determine for herself her own path after being counseled by a comparable figure, the god Pan. Immediately after she is abandoned by Cupid and before she delivers herself to Venus, fresh from a thwarted suicide attempt, Psyche happens upon the god himself lolling on a riverbank. Fully informed of her plight and sympathetic to her situation, Pan gives her advice:

'... do not try to kill yourself again by a fatal leap or any other sort of suicide. Stop your mourning and put away your grief. Instead pray to Cupid, the greatest of the gods, and worship him and earn his favor with flattering deference, since he is a pleasure-loving and soft-hearted youth.' (5.25.5)

Until this moment, Psyche has done exactly what others have told her to do. But now she concocts and executes the only idea in the entire tale she herself can lay claim to: deceiving both of her sisters into leaping to their deaths. By following this, her own counsel, Psyche punishes her tormentors, avenges the wrong done to her husband, and successfully courts Cupid's favour, for he had told her that he looked forward to the day he would 'be revenged on these advisors (*consiliatrices*) for their disastrous instructions' (5.24.5).

While Psyche sacrifices her sisters to win back her husband, Ofelia chooses to sacrifice herself to save her brother. She is 'the only character in the film who decides not to enact any violence, not to take any lives' (Guillén 2006). This heroism Ofelia shows in the face of tyranny mirrors an earlier act of disobedience in the main narrative. The Captain's doctor, a rebel sympathizer, knew he would die when he chose to put the torture victim Stutter out of his misery rather than prolong his life as he had been ordered to do. The doctor had to explain to an incredulous Vidal why he did it: 'To obey without thinking—just like that—well, that's something only people like you can do, Captain' (77). del Toro always stresses the importance of the theme of choice and disobedience in interviews about this film: 'You choose to be destructive or you choose to be all encompassing and love-giving' (Guillén 2006).[17]

As the camera lingers on the figure of the dying Ofelia—the same image with which the film began—the scarlet and golden colours of her fantasy world illuminate her. A voice rich with authority and kindness speaks: 'Arise my daughter.' And Ofelia, now transformed into Princess Moanna, unharmed and in regal dress, enters a vast, radiant hall and approaches the enthroned King and Queen of the Underworld, their (Ofelia's and Moanna's) real mother and father. A third pillar throne sits empty. Her father explains: 'It was your blood and not that of an innocent that made you worthy of the throne. It was the last task, the most important one' (96). And at that, the Faun appears, accompanied by all three fairies, unharmed after all. He compliments her with a bow: 'And you chose well, Your Highness.' Thunderous applause rings out from the surrounding galleries as the scene dissolves back to the labyrinth where Ofelia dies in Mer-

---

[17] For similar statements, see e.g. Kermode 2006, DVD commentary 2006, and Vaz and Nunziata 2016, esp. 125.

cedes' arms, in the light of the full moon (on moon imagery and Apuleius see Ranger in this volume).

But while Ofelia is driven to disobey the directions regarding her final task out of conscience, Psyche is driven only by vanity. Even so, Psyche too, is saved —by a recovered Cupid who wipes away the infernal Sleep of Death that came upon her when she peeked in Proserpina's jar. Cupid restores Psyche to life with a prick of his arrow and makes a successful appeal for clemency directly to Jupiter. Psyche is transported by Mercury to Mt. Olympus where she is given ambrosia to make her immortal. She is then joined in eternal marriage to Cupid in an elaborate wedding celebration attended by all the gods. Like Ofelia, Psyche, too, comes full circle from the beginning of her tale, when her whole town had come out to witness 'the wretched maiden's funereal wedding' (4.33.4) in fulfillment of the divine oracle.

8 Conclusion

In Apuleius' tale, Cupid, Psyche, and Venus are all able to be reconciled only because Jupiter, a power greater than the tyrannical Venus, intervenes. Venus' hysterical tantrums all track comically, and she is limited in the damage she can do because Psyche enjoys divine protections. The wounded goddess Venus nevertheless gets her righteous vengeance for the injury to her godhood. And the principals achieve an eternal, loving union, the fruit of which is that splendid gift to mankind, Pleasure.

Pan's Labyrinth's Captain Vidal is a sociopath who acts like a god, but one with unlimited power to harm. His victims cannot appeal to a higher authority, for none exists. But while the resistance fighters cannot stop Vidal from killing Ofelia, they can—and do—get satisfaction from denying him the immortality he seeks. As he emerges from the labyrinth and hands over his newborn son to the rebels, Vidal smashes his now-working pocket watch in an attempt to garner the kind of renown once earned by his truly heroic father: 'Tell him about his father, about the time his father died' (95). But right before a bullet tears through his skull, Mercedes lets him know that only oblivion waits for him: 'No. He won't even know your name.'

In the end, both Psyche and Ofelia/Moanna leave the 'real' world behind as they are transported to their forever home (on Olympus or in the Underworld), where they thrive in conjugal union (Psyche) or natal reunion (Ofelia/Moanna) with their divine family. Psyche is apotheosized. Ofelia's alter-ego, the film's concluding voiceover recounts, 'reigned with justice and a kind heart for many centuries' and 'was loved by all her subjects' (97).

The many resonances of Apuleius' text in *Pan's Labyrinth* convince us that in comparison with Psyche, the child Ofelia comes off as smarter, braver, more principled, and the only one worthy of being called a mythic heroine. Despite her unrelentingly dark circumstances, Ofelia never displays any of Psyche's wavering uncertainty, suicidal despair, or lazy inclination to have others solve her problems. Ofelia is a stalwart opponent of evil, uncowed by the tyrant's threats, resourceful beyond measure, true to her family, and guided by her own inner moral compass to help rather than harm others. Ofelia is able to save her soul by learning lessons that Psyche never does. Nor does she need to, for unlike Ofelia, Psyche is not a character whose destiny is determined by the choices she makes.

9 Bibliography

Cooper, J. M./ Hutchinson, D. S. (eds). (1997), *Plato: Complete Works*, Indianapolis.
del Toro, G. (2006), *Pan's Labyrinth* screenplay, translated (Picturehouse). http://www.dailyscript.com/scripts/PansLabyrinthEnglishScreenplay.pdf [accessed July 2017].
del Toro, G. (2007), Director's Commentary and DVD Extras on *Pans' Labyrinth* DVD.
Guillén, M. (17 December 2006), 'Pan's Labyrinth—Interview with Guillermo del Toro,' https://screenanarchy.com/2006/12/pans-labyrinthinterview-with-guillermo-del-toro.html [accessed July 2017].
Hanson, J.A. (ed.) (1989), *Apuleius: Metamorphoses*, Cambridge, Mass.
Harrison, S. J. (ed.) (2015), *Characterisation in Apuleius'* Metamorphoses. Cambridge.
Harrison, S.J. (2013), *Framing the Ass: Literary Texture in Apuleius'* Metamorphoses, Oxford.
Hook, B. S. (2005), 'Oedipus and Thyestes Among the Philosophers', *CP* 100, 17–40.
Kermode, M. (25 November 2006), 'Interview with Guillermo del Toro' https://www.youtube.com/watch?v-iqdEKahV-gs [accessed July 2017].
May, R. (2006), *Apuleius and Drama: The Ass on Stage*, Oxford.
O'Brien, M. (2002), *Apuleius' Debt to Plato in the Metamorphoses*, Lewiston, N.Y.
Panayotakis, C./Panayotakis, S. (2015), 'The Human Characters in the Tale of Cupid and Psyche (*Metamorphoses* 4.28–6.24)', in: Harrison 2015, 125–45.
Panayotakis, C. (2001), 'Vision and Light in Apuleius' Tale of Psyche and Her Mysterious Husband', *CQ* 51/2, 576–83.
Riefstahl, H. (1938), *Der Roman des Apuleius: Beitrag zur Romantheorie*, Frankfurt.
Salzman-Mitchell, P. and Alvarez J. (eds.) (2017), *Classical Myth and Film in the New Millenium*, Oxford.
Vaz, M. C. and Nunziata, N. (2016), *Guillermo del Toro's Pan's Labyrinth: Inside the Creation of a Modern Fairy Tale.* Harper Design.
Zimmerman, M./Panayotakis, S./Hunink, V./Keulen, W.H./Harrison, S.J./McGreight, T.D./Wesseling, B./van Mal-Maeder, D. (2004), *Apuleius Madaurensis Metamorphoses, Books IV.28-VI.24. The Tale of Cupid and Psyche,* Groningen.

Paula James
Beauty and the Beast as a myth and metaphor in the contemporary world. Looking forward with Apuleius' fable of Cupid and Psyche

1 Introduction

Cupid and Psyche is a fable full of conundrums and, over the years, I have written about a number of paradoxes and tensions that emanate from the god of love appearing in his own myth.[1] The naming of the supernaturally beautiful but mortal princess as Psyche (Soul) reinforces the metamorphic nature of the narrative, as conceptual phenomena become characters with back stories and bodily extension. In this story, at the heart of Apuleius' novel, Cupid takes time out from propelling the action in stories about other gods and helpless mortals in the throes of passion with tragic and comic consequences. He becomes a willing victim of his own force and appears to settle down at the end of the story. Or we could say that Cupid's self-harming (he confesses to shooting himself with an arrow in order to fall in love with Psyche at *Met.* 5.24) gives him autonomy.

In *Cupid and Psyche*, Apuleius proves himself a worthy heir of Ovid in putting his indelible mark upon what could be characterised as a mythologized version of artistic representations of Love and Soul. He also gives philosophy its own fable, making a new story out of sacrifice rituals, and incorporating a few narrative elements familiar to us from subsequent folktales, for instance taboos and also testing tasks for the heroine. The fairy-story genre as popularized in and beyond Europe in later centuries includes scenes and narrative arcs from *Cupid and Psyche*. The sojourn of Psyche in the palace of a non-human and her relationship with an unusual suitor captured the imagination of post-classical writers and artists.

Cupid and Psyche, transformed into the Beast and Beauty, are a host and guest with, it seems, endless possibilities for visualisation, but also life lessons. Movie-makers have recognised the pulling power of physical and psychological mismatches in love and its potential for intensifying romance and eroticism. Star-crossed lovers are perennially popular, but the bestial meeting the beautiful

---
[1] James 1987, 140–79; 1998, 42–6.

possesses a particular piquancy for cinema audiences. The unity of the supernatural (vampiric) male and the 'special' female proved a winning formula in the four *Twilight* movies (from the books by Stephenie Meyer) which attracted mass teenage audiences with its interminable relationship between insipid Edward and the significantly named Bella.

2 From the complex to the simple?

Apuleius' novel has inspired allegorical, sententious and satirical treatments and critiques with *Cupid and Psyche* recognised as the structural and thematic fulcrum of the mainframe ass story.[2] It might seem counter intuitive to reduce the reception of *Cupid and Psyche* to a simple fairy story, but its afterlife as *Beauty and the Beast* benefits from the 'adaptation studies' approach so that we search for what is added to the source text rather than what has been lost from it.[3]

It would appear that Apuleius' fable introduced motifs that resonate with contemporary concerns and popular perceptions about love, identity, porous bodies, and strange couplings. It can even provide a commentary on modern life and virtual reality, although this approach may require a stretch of credulity comparable to the donkey-hero Lucius' willingness to suspend disbelief:

> 'Ego vero' inquam 'nihil impossibile arbitror, sed utcumque fata decreverint, ita cuncta mortalibus provenire.'

> 'Well,' I said, 'I consider nothing to be impossible. However the fates decide, that is the way everything turns out for mortal men.' (Apuleius, *Met.* 1.20)[4]

Cupid and Psyche as *bella fabella* is not submerged by this woody way of reception; on the contrary, there are additional layers of narrative sophistication and visual aesthetics to behold in the adaptations of *Beauty and the Beast* that can reconnect it to the rich literary texture of Apuleius, while simultaneously remind readers of the Latin novel that the fable of Love and the Soul is always an old wives' creation.

---

[2] On Apuleius' source see the introduction and Tilg 2014, *passim* who revisits the relationship between the Greek fantasy, *Metamorphoses* and *The Golden Ass*. However, no-one has been bold enough to suggest that the fable of *Cupid and Psyche* was one of the inserted stories in the Greek original.
[3] Bakogianni 2017, 470.
[4] All translations are taken from the 1989 Loeb edition by J. Arthur Hanson.

Taking refuge in generalities, we could say that within the old woman's fantasy lurk age-old preoccupations about relationships between human, animal, the divine and the hidden nature of such dangerous liaisons. The theme of miscegenation in Apuleius' fable adds spice to the scenario of star-crossed lovers that dominates the Greek romances. *Beauty and the Beast* stories have taken up the restoration and redemption of the male but it is Psyche who needs transformation and elevation in the Latin novel, while the donkey-hero Lucius plays the part of the beast in the mainframe narrative.

In both cases the 'happy-ever-after' of Psyche and Lucius can be deconstructed as an ending that operates on a satirical rather than a spiritual plane.

3 Monsters, maidens and mutual manipulation

The miscegenation or strange coupling theme is not confined to the central diversion of the *Cupid and Psyche* narrative in Apuleius' prose narrative. The re-layer of the fable to the reader, namely Lucius, is himself a beast by this point in the story. After his unfortunate transformation his human identity remains inside the skin of a donkey. Our hero is not the intended audience of the *Cupid and Psyche* story but, as an enslaved donkey, he overhears the *bella fabella* (aptly named by the ass as a 'beautiful little story' at 6.25) told by the drunken housekeeper in the brigands' hideout in the mountains. As an animal Lucius enjoys a close encounter with Charite, the lovely captive in the cave to whom the story is told, and whom he helps to make an escape bid. Later in his adventures (*Met.* 10.20–22) he is seduced by a good-looking, high-born woman eager to pay for sex with the well-endowed ass.

Lucius' erotic encounters in his donkey form have a distinct *Beauty and the Beast* timbre. The way in which the maiden (or in this case, *matrona*) manipulates and transforms the 'monster' by appealing to his human empathy, passion and fallibility has proved an enduring *topos* for creative artists and writers. [5] Movie treatments of mismatched couples that give a beautiful female a restorative and redemptive role in her relationship with a supernaturally strong and

---

[5] Lucius in bestial form becomes a lover of a beautiful woman. This found a place in the union of the hairy and the fairy (Bottom the Weaver, turned into an ass, and Titania, queen of the fairies) in the Shakespearean canon, and is seated at the numinous centre of a play, *A Midsummer Night's Dream*, which is full of resonances from Ovid as well as Apuleius. The bard certainly borrowed not just myths and mythical vignettes from these ancient authors, but recognised that both presented the reader with a canvas of connected themes and motifs. See Carver 2007, on the Renaissance reception.

dangerous male can also highlight this aspect of Psyche's influence over Cupid. Fairy and fantasy stories end with the beast restrained of his own free will. Screen versions relish the revelation that the monster is a man of beauty; once released from the spell the heroine of the movies is as entranced as Psyche when she sees the love god in his supernatural splendour.

In Apuleius, the fable suggests that the love god is tied down in the arms of his wife, Psyche, and so reformed. Taming and civilizing the beast has become an important part of the narrative's *Nachleben*. This strand, the manipulation of the magical partner, as well as the matter of ill-matched couples, and this might mean in status, appearance or personality, is present throughout Apuleius' prose fiction on a figurative as well as an actual plane.[6] In the fable, Cupid agrees to a disastrous course of action, namely opening up his house to Psyche's mischief-making sisters who are cunning, insanely jealous, and without any redeeming features. Their story of the snake spouse seems to confirm the text of the oracle at 4.33, which predicted her sacrifice to something monstrous.

On taking a lamp and a razor to their bed, Psyche discovers that her mysterious husband is Cupid, a winged god with a supernaturally alluring appearance. Seeing the beast as he really is and recognising her love for him is a persistent resolution to the narrative arc of *Beauty and the Beast* in its fairy-story form. The depiction of the beast as a monster to be slaughtered was graphically resurrected by Disney in the 1991 movie. The reluctance of the heroine's husband or host to pander to her feelings for family is another correspondence between the classical text and later versions, as Beauty's temporary departure risks abandoning the spellbound suitor to grief and death. Apuleius' imaginative play upon the relationship between human and less than or more than human creatures has proved an inspiration for the popular romance, but, like so many fairy stories, it has darker elements which take the audience out of its comfort zone.

In mass consumption, Cupid and Psyche may have morphed into the Beast and Beauty, raising the motif of miscegenation between maiden and monster, but this allows us to revisit the original from the perspective of romance and horror that continues to enthral readers and audiences alike. [7] The civilising power of female love possesses a persistent cachet. In 2016, Joss Whedon, director of the *Avengers* franchise, (after a notable career as creator of *Buffy the Vampire Slayer* and other critically acclaimed television series) highlighted the taming

---

6 I remain indebted to a conference presentation by Lisa Hughes at the Classical Association 2008. For a full acknowledgement see James 2014, 325–7.
7 James 2014 covers some of the horror story features of the fable foregrounded in its later incarnations (322–5) and engages with Accardo's chapter 'The Beast goes to the Movies.' (Accardo 2002, 88–101).

of the Hulk (Bruce Banner) by super strong Natasha Romanova (Black Widow, who in the Marvel comics tradition is fighting against a long training to be ruthless and inhuman).[8] In a slightly disturbing, if stimulating, keynote presentation at the June 2016 Euroslayage conference (the annual celebration of the works of Joss Whedon) held in Kingston University, Surrey, Lewis Call argued that empowered women (always beautiful or 'hot' in the words of Whedon) give certain men a safe space in which to be subdued and submissive. The monstrous men in question willingly partake in infantilization (succumbing to stroking and lullabies, amongst other therapeutic techniques).

Female domination is, in this context, loving, healthy, and effective for calming ultra-masculine men who are conflicted by their exceptional physical powers. In such fantasy scenarios where the woman takes the risk of confronting the beast, she can, in turn, be cared for, comforted and saved by her uncanny lover (the humanized hero) once she has established her strength and authority over him. Elements of this relationship might sound familiar to readers of Apuleius, and it puts an additional spin upon Psyche's ambiguous feelings for her spouse: *in eodem corpore odit bestiam, diligit maritum.* 'in the same body she loathed the beast but loved her husband.' (*Met*.5.21).

A suitably lyrical and aesthetic approach to what could be seen as a myth of miscegenation was presented at the University of Washington in May, 2016. In the fascinating exhibition, *Just One Look*, at the Seattle Conference, *Feminism and Classical Myth*, in which artists visualised the form, content and meaning of myths, Mari Eckstein Gower's Psyche becomes the butterfly, the winged woman, and has to undergo phases of transformation before she is made immortal. Gower states (p.27) that 'this is not the hero's saga; this is the maiden's tale.' Psyche does not believe that as a young girl she deserves a better fate than mating with a monster. And she says 'who was I a new wife to look upon the true face of my husband?' (*ibid.*) The work is suffused with symbolic all-seeing eyes (a concept we find in Cocteau's film, *La Belle et La Bête*, discussed below) which suggest that the gaze changes the narrative and that the gods watch over the world. According to the summary accompanying the Gower panels (figure 28), this all takes place because a flustered Cupid accidentally wounds himself with his own arrow, so the 'willing victim' motif is noted by Gower (p.26).

---

[8] Joss Whedon and team aired various narrative arcs on the theme of miscegenated couples in his now canonical TV series *Buffy the Vampire Slayer*. The central relationship between slayer and reformed vampire occupied the first three seasons. The tormented Angel, her vampire lover, returns from a Hell dimension (where the slayer was forced to send him) as a wild and snarling creature, and he urgently needs to be de-traumatised by Buffy's tender loving care.

Figure 28: Mari Eckstein Gower: 'Cupid and Psyche', exhibition: 'Just One Look'. Reprinted with permission of the artist and the University of Washington Libraries Special Collections.

If we apply what is suspect psychology with a dose of wishful thinking, even in the modern discourse of female empowerment and gender reversals, to Apuleius' fable, it could be said that Cupid has deliberately made himself vulnerable and human in the relationship with Psyche, firstly by self harming:

> 'Sed hoc feci leviter, scio, et praeclarus sagittarius ipse me telo meo percussi teque coniugem meam feci.'

> 'But that [i.e. flying to Psyche as her lover] was a frivolous thing to do, I know. Illustrious archer that I am, I shot myself with my own arrow and made you my wife.' (Apuleius, *Met*.5.24).

Cupid subsequently allows himself to be persuaded by Psyche's gentle and erotic endearments against his better judgement, to become the true mistress of his palace and invite her own guests in, this in spite of Psyche being the lesser being in the marriage. Apuleius is clearly drawing upon the language of female domination and male (faux) submission that Ovid perfected in his love poetry (Hindermann 2009, *passim*[9]).

Though her beauty is divine, Psyche is still the mortal consort of a cosmically powerful husband. The tipsy old woman who narrates the beguiling story (*lepida fabula*) is herself an unusual hostess who is actually casting distracting shadows on the cave about the nature of Love for a captive guest, Charite, the girl fated to be destroyed by Passion or *Amor* unconfined: the all-consuming desire that unsuccessful suitor Thrasyllus conceives for the lovely Charite destroys her husband and her happiness, a particularly poignant turn of events as this occurs

---

9 There are close verbal similarities between the persuasive techniques and flattering terms employed by the noblewoman in her seduction of the donkey and Psyche's blandishments to Cupid: *Met.* 10.22 and 5.6.

after her rescue from the robbers' cave and joyful nuptials to her suitor and saviour, Tlepolemus. The love god's flames of passion have turned Thrasyllus into a ruthless killer, so Cupid has clearly reverted to being the wayward boy after the fantasy finishes and Charite's interrupted tragedy continues. The *Cupid and Psyche* fable was always an elaborate fiction about a supernatural male being subdued by an exceptional girl, just as the *Avengers*' lovers play out a utopian scenario of dominance and submission.

4 The French connection

Jean Cocteau's ravishing cinematic production *La Belle et La Bête* was 70 years old in 2016 (the year of the *Cupid and Psyche* reception conference.) Disney's Oscar-nominated *Beauty and the Beast* was celebrating its 25th anniversary, and both this cartoon movie and the non-animated remake of 2017 take a modicum of inspiration from the influential 1946 art house film of the same name. Helen Elsom (1983, 149–150) was the first classical scholar to engage with the Cocteau movie as an Apuleian reception piece. This Latin legacy was most certainly unwitting on the part of the French director who, according to Elsom, believed *Beauty and the Beast* to be an English fable and cited as his text the version of the fairy story by Mme Leprince de Beaumont (1711–1780) who had spent time in England. Hers is a linear and less complicated narrative compared with Gabrielle-Suzanne de Villeneuve's *Beauty and the Beast* of 1740.

I am grateful to Stephen Harrison for pointing out that Cocteau was very likely to have encountered La Fontaine's work during his studies at the prestigious Parisian Lycée Condorcet, but the director nowhere acknowledges any such influence. Harrison 2016 demonstrates that La Fontaine's *Les Amours de Psyché et de Cupidon* of 1669 'marked the connection between the reception of *Cupid and Psyche* and the history of the modern European fairy fable.'[10] There are perhaps elements in the cinematographic choices Cocteau made that evoke Cupid's palace as imagined by La Fontaine. On the other hand, Cocteau was independently committed to 'make wonderful things happen and film them',[11] which is an unintentional echo of Apuleius' promise in the prologue:

---

[10] See Accardo (2002, 68–87) for summaries of the stories by Comtesse d'Aulnoy, Barbot de Villeneuve and Leprince de Beaumont, which he critiques from the perspective of inner psychic processes, the fear and ignorance of the virgin, and the humanization and socialization of the id by the superego.

[11] Elsom 1983, 149.

> *figuras fortunasque hominum in alias imagines conversas et in se rursum mutuo nexu refectas ut mireris.*
>
> so that you may be amazed at men's forms and fortunes transformed into other shapes and then restored again in an interwoven knot.
> (Met.1.1).

The movie, too, begins with a plea to its viewers to become artless and childlike. The young would see that the plucked rose signified tragedy and that a monster might feel shame in front of the maiden. Of course, Cupid hides his identity from Psyche, but for different motives. He is a sight to behold, but dangerously beautiful in the Apuleius fable. In *Cupid and Psyche* the bestial creature (a voracious serpent) masquerading as Psyche's husband is the invention of the spiteful sisters who also have an afterlife in *Beauty and the Beast*. Cocteau conflates them with Cinderella's vain and envious step-siblings, and reduces the number of her siblings from five to three, departing from his source, de Beaumont. He includes an equally feckless brother playing his part in Belle's bad decisions. It is this brother, Ludovic, and her suitor, Avenant, who, with the encouragement of the sisters, ride off to steal the beast's treasure.[12]

One of the most interesting correspondences between the Cocteau film and the fable is the depiction of Belle's *carcer beatus* or luxurious imprisonment. On her arrival at the palace she is struck with wonder, just as Psyche stands amazed at the wealth and workmanship of her new home.[13] Hospitality invariably brushes up against horror and the macabre, as the palace, like the beast, is under a magic spell. Lighting and music make the ambience of the palace disturbing. Bodiless hands and arms serve Belle and illuminate her way. Beauty, unlike Psyche, is not sexually possessed by her captor but she is imprisoned in a castle full of eyes, and we, as viewers or voyeurs, participate in the surveillance, while simultaneously identifying with the victim (figure 29).

In Apuleius, Psyche is not a willing guest but a sacrificial victim just as Beauty takes the place (rather Alcestis-like) of her father in what is a sumptuous monster's den. Psyche is wafted down to a palatial residence in a kind of *katabasis*,

---

[12] For the coincidental correspondence between Lucius' steed, Candidus, and the luminous white horse, Magnifique, see James 1998, 46, n.18. Cocteau went to great pains to choreograph Aramis, the circus pony cast in the role.

[13] I am indebted to Janice Siegel who commented at my presentation (Leeds Reception Conference) upon the possible presence of Zephyr, the West Wind, in the arrival scenes. The drapery of the Beast's palace billows gently around Belle who glides along the floor in an ethereal slow motion, as if she is being magically transported. Cocteau greatly admired Josette Day's (Belle) grace and naturalness in speech and demeanour. See his journal, 1947/1972, 18, 62.

Figure 29: Still from Jean Cocteau, *La Belle et La Bête*, 1946. 'Belle and the beast dine'. Taken from the BFI DVD of 'La Belle et La Bête' in accordance with laws governing fair use.

but in fact she is entering an earthly paradise (or having a taste of the Olympus which will become her eternal home by the end of the story). Purveyors of the fable as fairy story on screen love to linger, as does the narrator in Apuleius, over Psyche's entrance and her exploration of the magnificent and magical interior of her new home. The princess is fearful and overawed by the luxury and also the magical properties of the palace. The reader or viewer is made aware of the material riches of the rooms (apparently unguarded, as the robber housekeeper exclaims, providing the narrative focalization that is the equivalent of the point-of-view shot) while an entranced Psyche is waited on and watched over by unseen servants.[14] The divine residence is modelled upon a Roman villa (Brodersen 1998, 113–125), and Psyche's reactions also remind the reader of Lucius' wonderment at the lavish house of his aunt in Hypata (*Met.* 2.4 and 19).

Hospitality and the unusual behaviour of hosts and guests is part of the fabric of Apuleius' narrative, and Cocteau was not the only movie director to exploit its possibilities in the *Cupid and Psyche* storyline of his cinematic work.[15] The

---

[14] Zimmerman and van Mal Maeder (1998, 94–95) pinpoint this moment as a shift to Psyche's perspective upon events. They argue persuasively for a 'symphony of voices and subjective perceptions' throughout the fable.

[15] I shall argue that the much later Disney cartoon of *Beauty and the Beast* engages with the French film in spite of being a very different cinematic genre aimed at a mass audience. This

movie does incorporate a half-hearted taboo in that the Beast warns Belle not to look into his eyes and, like Cupid, he confines his visits to the evenings and the dimness of the lamps. In response to his self-knowing remarks about being a monster but having a gentle heart, Belle says that many men hide their monstrosity beneath pleasing exteriors. The beast is made up to be frightening, and he behaves at times like a wild animal, in hunting and slaughtering his prey, or slaking his thirst in a stagnant pond. The brutish side of him as beast limits his intellectual vigour, something that de Villeneuve and Leprince de Beaumont emphasize in their versions. However, in both Cocteau and later in Disney it is the village suitor who is heartless and destined to die.

When Belle's beau, Avenant, is killed (trying to burgle the beast's temple of treasure, he is shot by an arrow from the vivified statue of Diana), the dying beast revives in the warmth of Belle's declaration of love. As she embraces him, the heroine utters the line: 'I am the monster!' The feckless human hero becomes the beast (suggesting he was brutish at his core), but the beast turns into Ardent, identical to the heroine's would-be lover, Avenant (both are played by Jean Marais). He is suitably handsome (figure 30).

Figure 30: Still from Jean Cocteau, *La Belle et La Bête*, 1946. 'Belle and Ardent'. Taken from the BFI DVD of 'La Belle et La Bête' in accordance with laws governing fair use.

---

is partly because the uncanny nature of the household servants intrigues those in the business of visualisation and the moving image.

This is a quirky and bizarre resolution with Belle confessing she did love Avenant, and saying, coquettishly,[16] to her new-found prince that she likes being frightened with him. He carries her through the clouds to his kingdom and this reprises both the transporting of Psyche to Cupid's palace by Zephyr and her translation to Olympus by the god, to meet the family, as it were. Cocteau hints that Belle is just a little disappointed to lose the distinctive looking beast, an unconscious and very distant echo of the scorn heaped upon handsome Loukios in the Greek *Onos* finale (see the introduction for the relationship between the *Onos* and Apuleius' *Metamorphoses*): in the ancient epitome, the hero returns to the woman who loved him in his ass skin, but she points out that his sexual prowess has been much reduced from the abilities of the noble and well-hung donkey. Modern miscegenation myths from *Buffy the Vampire Slayer* to the *Twilight* franchise and Marvel Comics' *Avengers* movies echo the desire of the heroine to 'have a little monster in her man', a pithy observation from the vampire Spike, in regard to super-slayer Buffy's preference when it comes to sexual satisfaction.

It is a challenge to add to Elsom's skilful and succinct summary of the movie's place in Apuleian reception and the way in which it was also telling the story of Lucius, as a man turned into a beast by a bad fairy but restored to humanity by the love of a female. In 1998 I made some new observations upon the happy coincidences in the imagery and narrative arc between not just the *Cupid and Psyche* fable and *La Belle et La Bête,* but also motifs from Lucius' adventures that featured in the film. Elsom notes implicit metamorphoses throughout the screen fairy fable and the feminist slant that Cocteau intended to give the story. She also acknowledges that it is a 'baroque but finely wrought artefact full of charm,' that allows us, the viewers, to steep ourselves in a fantasy that also enjoys uniting the ethereal with the mundane. Cocteau is a true heir to Apuleius in that respect.[17]

---

16 See Elsom 1988, 150.
17 Sadly, there is not space to discuss Cocteau's fascinating *Belle et La Bête: Journal d'un Film* (1947) translated by Ronald Duncan in 1972. Amongst many nuggets in the diary are Cocteau's approach to the poetic and fantastic via the realistic, the precise and deliberately documentary style, his admiration for the Daedalian skills of his film set workers and lighting crew (creating the miraculous images of the palace and its treasures), and his pleasure in actor Jean Marais' portrayal of the beast. Cocteau describes how Marais met the director's intentions: 'he made of him a monster, which, instead of being awful, remains seductive, with that kind of monster's seductiveness in which one feels at once the man and the beast.'

5 Disneyfication and looking for Sourcery!

The 1991 Disney production of *Beauty and the Beast* was conceived in the style of a Broadway musical, and yet it is partly a pastiche and homage to Cocteau. Gaston, the muscle-bound suitor in the village is the real monster, 'primeval' as a modern bookworm Belle dubs him. He is 'a catch', a muscle man, but has none of the charm of Avenant in the 1946 film, although they are united by an irritating narcissism. However, Gaston does also die, falling from the precipice at the top of the castle, which is the fate engineered by Psyche for her evil sisters who attempted to destroy her happiness. Belle discovers the dying beast and, full of remorse, declares her love. This animated beauty is only indirectly responsible for the wounding of her unknown lover (Figure 31). Psyche bent over Cupid and accidentally spilled hot oil on the god, but Belle strikes a similar pose to resuscitate her beast.

Figure 31: Still from Disney 1991 *Beauty and the Beast.* Source: https://animationscreencaps.com/beauty-and-the-beast-1991/52/#box-1/180/beauty-and-the-beast-disneyscreencaps.com-9360.jpg?strip=all Released through Animationscreencaps [accessed 12th June 2019]

The movie gives a knowing wink to fairy fable genres and the history of animation, so it is consciously self-referential.[18] Belle loves to read romantic fairy

---

[18] Linda Wolverton, screenwriter, mentions seeing the Cocteau movie in college, but admits that Disney's animate objects (talking candlesticks and clocks) were principally introduced to be vehi-

stories (more meta-fiction) and is delighted when the beast bestows his library upon her. The Disney Belle is more resourceful and proactive than Cocteau's heroine. A modern miss, she helps the beast to remember his reading skills and, they start, appropriately, by revisiting Shakespeare's *Romeo and Juliet* who know they will be regarded by their warring families to be a disastrous mismatch. The movie demonstrates that the intellectual nurturing of the beast is, as ever, therapeutic and life changing.

Like Cocteau, Disney exploits the sinister and scary aspects of the beast's sumptuous abode. When the eccentric inventor father loses his way, he finds himself on a dark path to what could be Dracula's castle from a Hammer Horror movie. Towards the end of the fantasy, Beauty's would-be suitor in the village rounds up a posse of angry villagers to kill the beast, a notable example of the 'harrying of the monster' motif which is reminiscent of the cinematic *Frankenstein* of 1931, directed by James Whale. There are other odd Apuleian resonances, for instance the single wilting red rose that marks time running out for the enchanted prince to regain his human form. Lucius was transformed into an ass by accident and yet it is a consequence of his curiosity. Eating roses will restore him to his human form. All these correspondences have to come with the *caveat* that they could simply be cultural mnemonics and shared symbols uniting texts separated by centuries.

The prince has been punished for being inhospitable towards a superhuman creature, failing the divine encounter test, but, like Apuleius' hero, he has fallen foul of a witch. Belle's curiosity, when banned by the beast from the West Wing where the rose is encased under glass, is possibly an import from *Bluebeard* rather than an echo of Psyche's breaking of the taboo imposed by Cupid.[19] The palace boasts impressive Baroque architecture (Belle is given a tour in stately home style, a scene omitted from the 2017 Disney version), and the whole human household have been transformed into objects of utility and luxury.

They are comical and friendly, welcoming and hopeful that Belle will break the spell. There is an erotically disposed candlestick which, unlike the oil lamp in *Cupid and Psyche*, does not injure the beast but remains undyingly loyal to his master. The clock is another head servant, and veteran actor Angela Lansbury voices the singing teapot as the metamorphosed housekeeper, a role reprised

---

cles for singing Howard Ashman's songs. Wolverton (*The Guardian* 14/03/17, 'Reviews' p.20) set out to create a heroine who was about more than her looks, not passive but in keeping with the times (the 1990s). She also remembers that the final scenes were rushed and some of the later animation was 'not great', with frames borrowed from an earlier cartoon, *Sleeping Beauty*.

19 See the introduction 6 on links between *Bluebeard* and *Cupid and Psyche* in Perrault's fairy tales.

by Emma Thompson in the recent Disney production. The metamorphosed servants look on with pleasure and approval when Belle and the Beast are finally united.

6 Beauty and the Beast regenerated for the 21st century

The most recent of cinematic incarnations of *Beauty and the Beast* saw its general UK distribution on March 17th 2017. The history of her 'favourite fairytale' was explored in *The Guardian* (Sunday March 12th 2017, 19) by author Amanda Craig who brought the fable of *Cupid and Psyche* in Apuleius' *Golden Ass* (*Metamorphoses*) to the attention of the reader. As well as identifying the Latin fable as the source text for this enduring theme in global culture, which was refreshing for classical scholars, Craig selected a few key novels spanning the 18th to the 21st century, which, in her opinion, have creatively reworked the premise of maiden and monster, citing Marina Warner's study (1995) of the miscegenation motif and its various subtexts. Craig rates the Disney animated musical version the best version yet and she was eagerly anticipating the 'live' remake. Her willingness to be entranced by the 2017 big budget movie was based upon her approval of Disney's 1991 empowerment of the heroine Belle, and the Beast's back story with its redemption of a selfish prince who needs to learn about love and self-sacrifice.[20]

As in the original movie, all the staff are moving and speaking household objects, but the added piquancy is the emergence of real-life actors at the finale rather than animated drawings, as they are all re-transformed. In fact, the transition of the flat surface and drawn figures to flesh and blood characters on screen that the Disney industry has fashioned could be a metaphor for the move from representation to real in the history of the fable, with the proviso

---

[20] Craig suggests that 'the marriage of true minds' (Warner's phrase) is a determining factor in the plotlines of Richardson's *Pamela* and Austen's *Pride and Prejudice*. See Warner 1994, 273–97. She also mentions Trollope's *Ayala's Angel* and one of Angela Carter's subversive 'takes' on the fable, *The Tiger's Bride*, though I would say that *The Courtship of Mr Lion* is just as iconoclastic with its Belle becoming a narcissist before reforming and returning to the beast. Accardo (2002, 86–7) argues for the strong subtext of *Cupid and Psyche*, lightly filtered through *Beauty and the Beast*, in Brontë's *Jane Eyre* and du Maurier's *Rebecca*. A legion of correspondences between the fable and Hitchcock's screen adaptation of du Maurier's novel are creatively and intriguingly identified and explored by Padilla 2016, 151–209.

that the cinematic experience is still an illusion of corporeality.[21] The number 'Human Again' as sung by the enchanted servants at an earlier point in the film was edited out of the 1991 version and was not reinstated for the remake. However, the 2017 movie did not demur from the height of kitsch and, as crockery and furniture, they sing with gusto *Be Our Guest*, before an amused and bemused Belle, played by an elfin Emma Watson. I am indebted to Regine May for her observation that the 2017 heroine somewhat mischievously suggests that the prince might grow a beard when she sees that he is a handsome human. See also the ambivalence expressed in Charlotte Yonge's version, whose Aurelia-Psyche must chose between a young but vague and an older but grizzled suitor, discussed by Schultze in this volume. It seems that a succession of 'Belles' might miss the beast and yearn to retrieve their 'bit of rough'!

Whereas in Cocteau the music score is part of the ambience of the palace, Disney is truer to Apuleius in demonstrating that the captive girl is right royally entertained by the Beast's servants. At *Met.* 5.3, Psyche is entranced by an invisible lyre and a melodious choir. Disney's central production number *Be Our Guest* is discussed in Scott (2015), who notes that the song in the popular and Oscar-nominated original of 1991 demonstrates the ecstasy of consumerism in a world where the servants in the form of furniture and kitchen utensils revel in service with their quasi-erotic desire to be used: 'they act as avatars communing with the guest.'[22] His critique appears in a chapter entitled 'Anatomically Correct.' For Scott (and he may be marginalising the irony and the incongruity of this set piece), both the *Beauty and the Beast* story and its Disney vision and visualisation encapsulate what is on offer when strangers take up residence in holiday rentals. He sees the beast as a metaphor for generous hospitality; nevertheless, rules of reciprocity must be obeyed.

Scott targets the corporate firm Airbnb as the providers of the modern-day magical experience which operates on a superficial trust economy, and he believes that the company is consciously buying into *Beauty and the Beast* (Airbnb indeed!) as everyone's favourite fairy story. The internet corporation offers an opportunity for holiday-makers and home owners to save money or profit from the renting exchange.

---

[21] It is interesting that aficionados of quality cinema and cinematography judge the 2D version as superior to the 3D screening. 3D effects can impress with artefacts leaping out into the audience, but this only draws attention to the artificiality of our experience. A movie that by depth of composition and power of performances in a strong narrative absorbs its audience into the screen is invariably a far better triumph of illusion.

[22] Scott 2015, 34.

Airbnb claims that living in the homes of others is fantasy become reality, that 'every day, hosts around the world create magical experiences for thousands of guests' (quoted in Scott 2015, 34), but there is a downside to featuring the monstrous host and the imprisoned guest of the fable as symbolic figures and subtexts in their advertising. The beast of the fable has hidden powers (a magic mirror and other sorceries) which just might reveal that Airbnb's service to their hosts (via their tracking screen) is predicated upon their ability to follow the movements of the guests inside and outside their temporary abodes.[23] In the surveillance society, such transactions come with an insistence that all users (Scott 2015: 28) 'accumulate an online history of consistent, amiable personhood, so that we can be recognised wherever we crop up in digital space.'

The company offers an uncanny homeliness for its customers, a contradiction recognised by initial online discussions about the service as far back as 2011, which yielded evidence that a mutual paranoia about predator and prey was developing alongside an uneasiness about occupying an unknown house. On the 14th of April 2017 there were various news reports of Airbnb needing to introduce additional security checks on accounts and bookings, as bogus identities had been created and houses to let had been burgled. The American user was required in 2014 to have their government ID scanned into their profiles, but the company is still being duped by dummies (Scott 2015, 36). The cunning and skilful surfers of the net are fully capable of god-like elaborate fictions which hide their true selves. Thus the corporate dream has descended into the personal nightmare. It is worth recalling that Cupid, once he is master of his own abode, is protective of his privacy and wary of guests. However, he has been introduced in the fable as the 'thief of love' who runs through other folks' houses armed with flames and arrows, so he suffers like his victims, and not just in terms of the pains and pangs of passion (*Met.* 4.30).

Cupid, the eternal and ubiquitous force of passion, takes refuge in his own tailor-made fable and craves being in a fixed place, his domain, whatever the consequences for the world. Thus the god morphs from being Love to being a lover. Herein lies the tension of wanting to be connected and also private and remote. The flighty god settles down, but he can only do so 'off the radar', and he takes pains not to be discovered. He does not succeed, being forced by Psyche's betrayal to fly wounded back to his mother. In the meantime, the

---

23 The beast, after his outrage at the merchant's theft, namely plucking a single rose for his daughter, then offers him an exchange, his life for that of a replacement companion. The merchant departs and agrees to supply a substitute guest, just as, later in the narrative, Beauty promises to return, and just as Psyche vows that her sisters will not cause trouble as guests in the palace of Cupid.

gavia, the interfering and chattering sea-bird, lets Venus know what has been happening in her absence. A mythical prototype of Twitter ensures that there is nothing sacred or secret about the divine family's conduct and its consequences.

7 That's all folks. A conclusion

This essay has tentatively explored the potential of the central fable to become a metaphor for modern anxieties and desires, as Apuleius has invested it with a subtext or implied commentary on the representational becoming the real, of mortal aspirations to the divine, and of the descent (by design or accident) into the bestial. After all, the story sits within a prose romance originally (probably!) entitled *Metamorphoses*, and the prologue promises the reader wonderment at the transformations and re-transformations to come. In *Cupid and Psyche* the challenge of fluid identities, be they corporeal, elemental (or, transposed to the modern world, digital) possesses a particular piquancy. The blurring of boundaries between human and animal, puny mortals and powerful deities, the mundane and the supernatural, heightens the charm and the comedy of the old wives' fable.

In its guise as a fairy story, *Beauty and the Beast*, the fable can bring unexpected and new subtleties to the surface. Whether it can provide a philosophical template for the 21st century is open to question, but it might allow us to debate the complexity of Apuleius' invention in the language of new technology or virtual reality. In a world where we are not sure whether we are striving to get a happy ending, or to be godlike at the cost of acquiring thick digital skins, we need to discern the difference between dreams and reality. As Charite found to her cost, the pleasure produced by the fable of Cupid and Psyche (*Voluptas* is their child) is not immortal but fantastic and fleeting.

8 Bibliography

Accardo, A. (2002), *The Metamorphosis of Apuleius. Cupid and Psyche, Beauty and the Beast, King Kong*, Madison, Teaneck, London.
Bakogianni, A. (2017), 'The Ancient World is Part of Us: Classical Tragedy in Modern Film and Television', in: Pomeroy 2017, 467–90.
Brodersen, S. (1998), 'Cupid's Palace—A Roman Villa (Apul.*Met*.5,1)', in: Zimmerman *et al* 1998, 113–26.
Cocteau, J. (1947), translated Ronald Duncan 1974, *Beauty and the Beast. Diary of a Film*, New York.

Craig, A. (2017), *The Other Side of You*, Quick Reads. (untitled review of *Beauty and the Beast* in literature and film, in: *The Guardian*, Saturday March 11th 2017, 19).
Cueva, E.P./Byrne, S.N. (2014), *A Companion to the Ancient Novel*, Chichester.
Elsom, H. (1989), 'Apuleius and the Movies', in: Hofmann 1989, 141–52.
Gilson, R. (1988), *Jean Cocteau Cinéaste*, Paris.
Gower, M. Eckstein (2016) 'Cupid and Psyche' (artistic panel), in: Huntington/Moore/Dudley, 26–7.
Harrison, S.J. (2013), *Framing the Ass. Literary Texture in Apuleius'* Metamorphoses, Oxford.
Harrison, S.J. (2016), 'Nachwort: Amor und Psyche', in: Norden, 66–126.
Hindermann, J. (2009), *Der elegische Esel. Apuleius' Metamorphosen und Ovid's Ars Amatoria*, Frankfurt am Main.
Hofmann, H./Hijmans, B. edd. (1989), *Groningen Colloquia on the Novel*. Groningen.
Huntington, W./Moore, S.K./Dudley, L. (eds.) (2016), *Just One Look. An Exhibition of Contemporary Book Arts, Exploring the Theme of Women and Vision*, Seattle.
James, P. (1987), *Unity in Diversity*, Hildesheim.
James, P. (1998), 'The Unbearable Lightness of Being. Levis Amor in the *Metamorphoses* of Apuleius', in: Zimmerman *et al*, 35–50.
James, P. (2001), 'Kicking the Habit. The significance of *Consuetudo* in interpreting the fable of Cupid and Psyche', *Ramus* 30.2, 152–168.
James, P. (2014), 'Apuleius' *Metamorphoses*. A Hybrid Text?', in: Cueva/Byrne, 317–29.
Mal-Maeder, van D./ Zimmerman, M. (1998), 'The Many Voices in *Cupid and Psyche*' in Zimmerman *et al*., 83–102.
Norden, E. (2016), *Amor und Psyche*, Darmstadt.
Padilla, M.W. (2016), *Classical Myth in Four Films of Alfred Hitchcock*, New York.
Pomeroy. A.J. (ed.) (2017), *A Companion to Ancient Greece and Rome on Screen*. New York: John Wiley.
Scott, L. (2015), *The Four Dimensional Human. Ways of Being in the Digital World*, London.
Warner, M. (1995), *From the Beast to the Blonde. On Fairy Tales and their Tellers*, London.
Wolverton, L. (2017), 'How we made—Beauty and the Beast', *The Guardian* 14th March: 20.
Zimmerman, M. et al (eds.) (1998), *Aspects of Apuleius' Golden Ass Volume II. Cupid and Psyche*. Groningen.

List of Figures

Figure 1: William Morris, 'Zephyrus and Psyche'. Source: William Morris and Sir Sydney Carlyle Cockerell, *A note by William Morris on his aims in founding the Kelmscott Press. Together with a short description of the Press by S.C. Cockerell, & an annotated list of the books printed thereat.* Kelmscott Press 1898. Reproduced with the permission of Special Collections, Leeds University Library (Brotherton Collection).

Figure 2: Atelier Dufour, Wallpaper no. 3 = Psyche's bath in the palace. Copyright: Tapetenbilder aus dem Ovalen Saal des Großherzoglichen Palais in Bad Doberan. Edeltraud Altrichter, ITMZ Universität Rostock

Figure 3: Atelier Dufour, Wallpaper no 7 = Psyche encountering the fisherman. Copyright: Tapetenbilder aus dem Ovalen Saal des Großherzoglichen Palais in Bad Doberan. Edeltraud Altrichter, ITMZ Universität Rostock

Figure 4: Atelier Dufour, Wallpaper no. 8 = The delivery of the vase with Stygian water. Copyright: Tapetenbilder aus dem Ovalen Saal des Großherzoglichen Palais in Bad Doberan. Edeltraud Altrichter, ITMZ Universität Rostock

Figure 5: Charles-Joseph Natoire, 'Psyche Carried Away by Zephyrus', Salon de la Princesse, Hôtel de Soubise. Paris. Copyright: Jared A. Simard

Figure 6: Charles-Joseph Natoire, 'Psyche Contemplates Her Sleeping Husband', Salon de la Princesse, Hôtel de Soubise. Paris. Copyright: Jared A. Simard

Figure 7: Charles-Joseph Natoire, 'Psyche with the Shepherds', Salon de la Princesse, Hôtel de Soubise. Paris. Copyright: Jared A. Simard

Figure 8: Charles-Joseph Natoire, 'Psyche Faints From Fright Before Venus', Salon de la Princesse, Hôtel de Soubise. Paris. Copyright: Jared A. Simard

Figure 9: Charles-Joseph Natoire, 'Psyche Taken to Heaven by Cupid', Salon de la Princesse, Hôtel de Soubise. Paris. Copyright: Jared A. Simard

Figure 10: William Blake, 'Psyche repents' (1794/1796). Copyright Chetham's Library, Manchester

Figure 11: William Blake, *The Night of Enitharmon's Joy* (1795). Reprinted with permission of The Tate Gallery London

Figure 12: 'Master of the Die', Engraving 1 (1530s/1540s). Copyright Stephen Harrison

Figure 13: Spence, Joseph (1747), *Polymetis. Or, An Enquiry Concerning the Agreement Between the Works of the Roman Poets, And the Remains of the Antient Artists. Being an Attempt to Illustrate them Mutually from One Another. In Ten Books*, London, plate VI (between p. 82 and 83). Reproduced with the permission of Special Collections, Leeds University Library (Brotherton Collection Ltq SPE)

Figure 14: Raphael, *Triumph of Galatea*, Rome, Villa Farnesina. Source: https://commons.wikimedia.org/wiki/File:Galatea_Raphael.jpg Released through Wikimedia commons by Attilios 2007. [accessed 25th October 2017]

Figure 15: Edward Burne Jones, 'Cupid finding Psyche', watercolour and bodycolour, signed and dated 1866, British Museum, London. Reprinted with permission of the Trustees of the British Museum.

Figure 16: Alberto Savinio, 'Angelica'. Source: Alberto Savinio, *Hermaphrodito e altri romanzi, a cura di Alessandro Tinterri*. Introduzione di Alfredo Giuliani, Milano, Adelphi, 1995. Enhanced and reprinted under Fair Use Policy.
Figure 17: Alberto Savinio, 'Psyche', lithograph created by Savinio for the novel 'Our soul'. Source: Alberto Savinio, La nostra anima/Il signor Munster, Milano, Adelphi, 1981. Enhanced and reprinted under Fair Use Policy.
Figure 18: Paul Thumann, 'Psyche displays herself to the public'. Source: Robert Hamerling, Thumann, Paul 1882] Robert Hamerling, *Amor und Psyche. Eine Dichtung in sechs Gesängen. Illustriert von Paul Thumann*, Leipzig. Copyright: Christoph Leidl
Figure 19: Max Klinger, 'Psyche's wanderings'. Source: Klinger, Max 1880, 1988, *Amor und Psyche. Ein Märchen des Apuleius. Aus dem Lateinischen von Reinhold Jachmann*. Illustrirt in 46 Original-Radirungen und ornamentirt von Max Klinger. München 1880. Copyright: Christoph Leidl
Figure 20: Max Klinger, 'composite image of Cupid as Hercules'. Source: Klinger, Max 1880, 1988, *Amor und Psyche. Ein Märchen des Apuleius. Aus dem Lateinischen von Reinhold Jachmann*. Illustrirt in 46 Original-Radirungen und ornamentirt von Max Klinger. München 1880. Copyright: Christoph Leidl
Figure 21: Max Klinger, 'birth of Voluptas'. Source: Klinger, Max 1880, 1988, *Amor und Psyche. Ein Märchen des Apuleius. Aus dem Lateinischen von Reinhold Jachmann*. Illustrirt in 46 Original-Radirungen und ornamentirt von Max Klinger. München 1880. Copyright: Christoph Leidl
Figure 22: Max Klinger, 'Psyche and the lamp'. Source: Klinger, Max 1880, 1988, *Amor und Psyche. Ein Märchen des Apuleius. Aus dem Lateinischen von Reinhold Jachmann*. Illustrirt in 46 Original-Radirungen und ornamentirt von Max Klinger. München 1880. Copyright: Christoph Leidl
Figure 23: Max Klinger, 'Psyche on the cliff'. Source: Klinger, Max 1880, 1988, *Amor und Psyche. Ein Märchen des Apuleius. Aus dem Lateinischen von Reinhold Jachmann*. Illustrirt in 46 Original-Radirungen und ornamentirt von Max Klinger. München 1880. Copyright: Christoph Leidl
Figure 24: Screengrab from Guillermo del Toro, Pan's Labyrinth 2006. 'Stick insect transforming into winged fairy'. Taken from the New Line Home Entertainment, Inc. DVD of 'Pan's Labyrinth' in accordance with laws governing fair use.
Figure 25: Detail, white-ground terracotta funerary lekythos showing winged representation of the deceased's soul. Attic Greek, ca. 440 B.C. Metropolitan Museum of Art 1989.281.72. http://www.vroma.org/images/mcmanus_images/paula_chabot/ker.jpg. Credit: Paula Chabot. Reprinted in accordance with laws governing fair use.
Figure 26: Screengrab from Guillermo del Toro, *Pan's Labyrinth* 2006. 'Captain Vidal at head of table'. Taken from the New Line Home Entertainment, Inc. DVD of 'Pan's Labyrinth' in accordance with laws governing fair use.
Figure 27: Screengrab from Guillermo del Toro, *Pan's Labyrinth* 2006. 'Pale Man at head of table'. Taken from the New Line Home Entertainment, Inc. DVD of 'Pan's Labyrinth' in accordance with laws governing fair use.
Figure 28: Mari Eckstein Gower, 'Cupid and Psyche', exhibition: 'Just One Look'. Reprinted with permission of the artist and the University of Washington Libraries Special Collections.

Figure 29: Still from Jean Cocteau, *La Belle et La Bête*, 1946. 'Belle and the beast dine'. Taken from the BFI DVD of 'La Belle et La Bête' in accordance with laws governing fair use.
Figure 30: Still from Jean Cocteau, *La Belle et La Bête*, 1946. 'Belle and Ardent'. Taken from the BFI DVD of 'La Belle et La Bête' in accordance with laws governing fair use.
Figure 31: Still from Disney 1991 *Beauty and the Beast*. Source: https://animationscreencaps.com/beauty-and-the-beast-1991/52/#box-1/180/beauty-and-the-beast-disneyscreencaps.com-9360.jpg?strip=all Released through Animationscreencaps [accessed 12th June 2019].

Index

A
Accademia degli Incogniti 32
Ackland, Valentine 289 f.
Actaeon 159 f., 357
adaptation 8, 10, 12–20, 23 f., 37, 39, 44, 47, 51 f., 54 f., 58, 63 f., 120–122, 150, 160, 183, 207, 214, 221, 248 f., 283, 323, 382 f., 385, 388 f., 391, 393, 397 f., 401, 403, 409, 411, 434, 446
Adlington, William 11, 15, 19, 120 f., 135, 139, 147–149, 151, 153 f., 156, 158–163, 183, 341, 358, 362
Aeneid 53 f., 57 f., 102, 177 f.
Aeolus 34, 40, 43
Aeschylus 54, 296
aestheticism 154, 241 f.
Airbnb 447 f.
aisling 101, 104, 107–111, 113 f.
Albani, Alessandro 38, 44
Alcestis 256, 440
Alice in Wonderland 415
allegoresis 128, 130, 132
allegory 10, 13, 16, 23 f., 63, 66, 106 f., 121, 123, 130–132, 229, 233, 238, 242, 250, 268, 273, 276, 290, 297, 302, 332, 358, 365, 370, 374 f., 386, 401 f., 434
allusion 5, 9, 17–19, 36, 38, 69, 75, 106, 143, 148, 158 f., 163, 172, 177 f., 204–207, 209, 212, 215, 217, 226, 248, 267, 324, 333, 364, 371, 381 f., 399
Alma-Tadema, Lawrence 249
Amato, Joe D' 405
American South 307, 339, 352
Amore innamorato 31, 33 f., 38–40, 42–44
Andersen, Hans Christian 415
antiquarianism 103, 107
anxiety 37, 148, 181 f., 185, 187, 189–195, 197, 278
Apollo 6, 11, 49, 53, 55, 57, 67, 104, 151, 248, 253, 256, 270, 392, 398 f., 403, 408
apotheosis 1, 8, 85 f., 114, 149, 154, 156, 320, 390, 404

Ariadne 36, 38 f., 67, 94, 209, 211
Aristotle 123, 212, 215, 335–337, 400
Art Nouveau 248
Arts and Crafts 18, 247
Ashman, Howard 445
Ashmole, Elias 169 f.
ataraxia 330
Atelier Dufour 68, 71 f., 451
Augustan age 151, 153, 155, 163
Augustine of Hippo 17, 160
Avengers 436, 439, 443

B
Bachaumont, Louis Petit de 87 f.
Bachofen, Johann Jakob 265, 276
Bad Doberan 13, 61, 68, 71 f., 451
Bailey, Carolyn Sherwin 87, 383
ballad 107, 167–169, 171, 174
ballet 10, 14, 47–49, 51 f., 65, 124 f., 397, 403–405, 409
Banerjee, Sankha 391
Barlas, John Evelyn 122
Baroque 12, 14, 34, 42–44, 445
Barth, Edna 386
Baum, L. Frank 415
Baxter, Robert 387
Bayle, Pierre 119
Beaucage, Robert 406
Beauty and the Beast 14 f., 23, 295, 433–436, 439–441, 444, 446 f., 449, 453
Beloe, William 125, 131, 133
Beroaldo, Filippo 183
Bettelheim, Bruno 274, 283
Bible 121, 300 f., 335, 348
Bildungsroman 16, 290, 299–301
Black Bull of Norroway 295
Blake, William 125–128, 137, 451
Blondel, Merry-Josef 13, 61
Bluebeard 13, 365, 445
Boccaccio, Giovanni 11, 16, 19, 132, 183
Bocelli, Andrea 409
Böcklin, Arnold 267
Boffrand, Germain 92–94
Boiardo, Matteo Maria 11, 20, 172

Bonaventura Vulcanius 183
book illustration 20, 247 f.
Borges, Jorge Luis 196
Bosio, François Joseph 65
Botticelli, Sandro 205, 209
Boucher, François 85–89, 92, 94–96
Brahms, Johannes 252
Brandstrup, Kim 404 f.
Bridges, Robert Seymour 19, 203–209, 211–221
Brontë, Charlotte 22, 357 f., 363–369, 372, 446
Brontë, Emily 22, 358, , 363–369, 372, 446
Browning, Elizabeth Barrett 18
Buchkunst 248, 266
Buffy the Vampire Slayer 436 f., 443
Bulfinch, Thomas 102, 381–383, 386, 391
Bulwer-Lytton, Edward 17
burlesque 32, 342–346, 348–352
Burne-Jones, Edward 20, 225 f., 228, 247, 265, 268
butterfly 8, 96, 153 f., 158, 163, 252, 291, 294, 388, 437

C
Calderón de la Barca, Pedro 296
Calkhoven, Laurie 389
canon 24, 148, 407, 435
Canova, Antonio 65, 410
Carroll, Lewis 415
Catre, Noli Evan 408
Catullus 36, 38, 134, 147
Cavalli, Francesco 14, 31
Cerberus 73, 256, 270
Ceres 7, 19, 34, 130, 270, 280, 282, 291, 299, 385, 419
Chamisso, Adelbert von 249
Charite 16, 127 f., 286, 370, 435, 438 f., 449
Charles I 58, 120
Charles II 55, 58, 120
Charon 41, 49, 73, 213, 253, 270, 292
Château de la Chevrette 87 f.
Chaucer, Geoffrey 19, 177, 183
Chigi, Agostino 88–90, 208
childhood 203, 384

children literature 23, 381–394
Chirico, Giorgio de 236, 238, 261
chivalry 340, 342 f., 348–352
Christianity 20, 61, 63, 103, 123, 131, 141, 188, 232, 268 f., 276, 279, 290 f., 296, 298 f., 323 f., 330–332, 335–337, 345–348, 367, 373
Cinderella 13, 281 f., 307, 313, 440
Civil War 120, 339, 415
class 32, 102–104, 121, 237, 247, 289, 302, 339, 358
Classical tradition 1–2, 32, 35, 101, 195, 228, 249, 279, 303, 367, 376, 381
classicism 147, 357
Coates, Stephen 311 f., 315, 410
Cockney poets 147
Cocteau, Jean 237, 398, 437, 439–445, 447, 453
Coghill, Sarah 391
Coleridge, Samuel Taylor 141, 143
comedy 1, 9 f., 12–14, 22, 31, 33, 38 f., 41, 45, 52, 112, 124, 188, 203, 212, 268, 279, 281, 319, 323, 353, 368, 391, 397 f., 402, 421, 433, 437, 443, 445, 449
Condon, William 398
Coolidge, Olivia 385
Corneille, Pierre 47, 52, 73
Corneille, Thomas 14, 47, 52, 73
Craft, K.Y. 391, 393
Craft, M. Charlotte 391, 393
Crete 204, 206, 211 f., 220, 256, 284, 386
Creuzer, Georg Friedrich 265, 275 f.
Croall, Marie P. 391
Crowley, Richard 221
cryptomnesia 196
Cumberland, George 125, 127
Cumnor Hall 168–170, 172 f., 176, 179
Cupid 1–20, 22–24, 31, 33–35, 37–41, 43, 47–56, 58, 61, 63 f., 67, 69 f., 75, 79–82, 84–91, 94, 96, 101 f., 106–114, 119 f., 122–128, 130–135, 137, 139–143, 147–151, 153–155, 157–163, 167, 170, 172–179, 183, 185–188, 190, 203, 208, 213 f., 218–220, 226 f., 232, 236 f., 240, 242 f., 247, 250, 252, 255–259, 261, 265–270, 273–286, 289–291,

294f., 299, 307, 312, 314, 316f., 319–321, 323, 328, 337, 339f., 342–346, 348f., 351–353, 357–372, 375, 381–394, 397–411, 415–419, 422, 425–427, 429–431, 433–446, 448f., 451f.
curiosity   4, 7, 35, 37, 49, 70, 74, 112, 122, 131, 135, 138, 154, 174, 176, 185, 190–193, 204, 238, 281, 319, 357, 370f., 385, 387f., 390, 392, 422, 445

D

D'Albert, Eugen   409
Daniel, Pee Gee   211, 410
D'Annunzio, Gabriele   20, 225f., 228f., 233f., 236f., 240–242
Dante Alighieri   19, 205, 211–213, 232f.
d'Aulnoy, Marie-Catherine Le Jumel de Barneville   14, 439
Davenant, William   54
De Buxis, Andrea   225
Dead Can Dance   411
death   6f., 9, 12, 19, 24, 42, 49, 53, 56, 58, 63, 74, 81, 89, 91f., 101, 131, 153f., 158, 167–170, 196, 203, 228–230, 233f., 255f., 263, 268, 273, 280, 292f., 298, 318, 331, 333f., 339, 359, 366, 385f., 390, 399, 409f., 416–418, 422, 429–431, 436
decadentism   225f.
decorative program   79, 91, 96
Deep Classics   2, 274
del Toro, Guillermo   23, 415f., 418f., 422–424, 427f., 430, 452
Demoustier, Charles-Albert   64, 67–70, 73–75
desire   3, 24, 56, 91, 110, 112f., 130f., 137, 169, 192, 207, 228, 268, 273, 281f., 285, 340, 346, 351, 371, 406, 438, 443, 447, 449
determinism   330, 332
Diamond, Donna   387
Diana   40, 94, 159f., 217, 291, 357, 392, 442
Die Gartenlaube   247
Disney   15, 398, 400, 407, 436, 439, 441f., 444–447, 453

donkey   4f., 5, 7f., 11, 12, 24, 119, 121, 124, 127, 142, 158, 178, 188, 190f., 191, 283, 329, 342, 382, 397, 434f., 438, 443, 445
doubleness   294f., 317–320, 361, 368
dream vision   107f., 113, 149, 159
Du Maurier, Daphne   446
Dubowsky, Jack Curtis   410
Dudley, Robert, Earl of Leicester   167, 169f.
Duffett, Thomas   14
Dufour, Josef   61–65
d'Urfé, Honoré   52

E

Edison, Thomas   405
Edward   107, 120, 227, 434, 451
Edward VI   170
Edwardian   384
Egypt   348, 371
ekphrasis   159, 209, 226, 277
Elgin, Kathy   389
Eliot, T.S.   341
Elizabeth I   167
Emerson, Ralph Waldo   140f., 401f.
epic   9f., 12, 18, 53, 157, 177, 204, 207, 219, 249f., 280, 368
epitome   8, 183, 186, 277, 283, 285, 443
eroticism   23, 269, 433
Euripides   9, 36, 54
everyman   299
Evslin, Bernard   385
existentialism   181, 187, 194f., 197

F

fable   121, 125f., 130, 381f., 405
fairy tale   10, 13, 15, 23, 105, 131, 265, 273–280, 282f., 291, 300f., 307–309, 321, 359–361, 367, 370, 372, 375, 381, 391, 421, 445f.
fantasy   22, 278, 292, 308, 310, 319, 388, 406, 415–417, 419f., 423, 430, 434–437, 439, 443, 445, 448f.
fate   44, 369
Faulkner, William   22, 307, 339–346, 348f., 351, 353
Faun   341, 416f., 421f., 428–430
Federico II Gonzaga   90
female readership   16

feminism 23, 150, 256, 387, 391, 437
film 1, 3, 15, 23, 25, 398, 405–408, 415f., 419, 421, 424, 430f., 433, 435–437, 439–441, 443f., 447
fin de siècle 19, 229, 234, 236, 242, 247
Firenzuola, Agnolo 35, 120f.
Fisher, Joseph 398f.
fisherman 13, 63f., 70f., 87, 451
Flaxman, John 125
Floridus, Julianus 172
Foley, Ryan 391, 401
folklore 232
Fontenelle, Bernard Le Bovier de 47
Forberg, Ati 386
Fortuna 113, 136, 172, 191, 329, 339
Fragonard, Jean-Honoré 65
France 13, 31, 51, 54, 58, 63, 79, 86, 93, 96, 131, 310
Franck, César 403f., 409
free will 194, 329, 333, 436
freedom 2, 108, 181, 191, 193–195, 231, 345, 347, 365, 394
Freeman, Philip 190, 389
Freud, Siegmund 190, 242f., 273–275, 283, 285
Friedländer, Ludwig 265, 275
Friedrich, Caspar David 263
Fulgentius 8, 10f., 18, 122, 131f., 140, 183
Furies 36, 50, 55f., 124
Fusconi, Giovan Battista 14, 31–33, 38

G
Gardel, Pierre-Gabriel 124f.
genre 1, 3, 23, 31–33, 39, 47, 52f., 57f., 101, 121, 179, 290, 294, 307, 398, 405f., 433, 441, 444
George II 302
Gérard, François 61, 63, 65
Gesamtkunstwerk 252
Gildon, Charles 15, 121f., 135–140, 160
Glijansky, Avi 408
Goethe, Johann Wolfgang von 247, 249
Gothic 290–295, 301, 406
Gower, Mari Eckstein 437f., 452
Graces 73, 86, 94, 291
Grimm, Brothers 275, 279, 307–309, 312, 314, 316, 318, 320f.

Gurney, Hudson 16, 214, 216–218, 221

H
Hades 42, 131, 250, 399
hallucination 280–283, 285
Hamerling, Robert 248–251, 268f., 452
Hann, Claudia 401
Harryhausen, Ray 388
Hartley, Sean 400
hedonism 43
Heine, Heinrich 249
Helweg, Kim 404f.
Hely, James 103
Hercules 95, 213, 232, 256–259, 265, 407, 421, 452
Heywood, Thomas 12, 53f., 56, 120, 219, 221
Hildebrand, Gustav Friedrich 183
Hindemith, Paul 409
Hodges, Margaret 387
Hogg, Thomas Jefferson 119, 122, 141
Homer 9, 19, 65, 182, 205, 280
Hooge, Waldemar 401
Hopkins, Gerald Manley 2, 4, 203, 206, 215
Horace 23, 104, 147,
hospitality 90, 440f., 447
Hôtel de Soubise 13, 63, 79f., 82–88, 91–96, 451
Hughes, Ted 294, 357, 361, 363f., 368f., 436
Hunt, Leigh 107, 122, 151, 324, 330, 333, 335, 385
Hypnerotomachia Poliphili 268

I
idealism 21, 103, 153, 240, 249, 252, 268, 342, 348, 351–253, 372, 389
immortality 6–8, 11, 16, 44, 49–51, 57, 63, 94, 109–111, 113f., 130, 148, 153, 156f., 161–163, 177, 186, 188, 190, 216f., 229f., 233, 237, 243, 276, 281, 296, 323, 339, 342, 344–346, 351f., 366, 389, 392f., 399f., 402, 407f., 416–418, 421, 425, 427, 429, 431, 433f., 437f., 449
inconstancy 43–45
indeterminacy 192

inspiration 1, 11, 13, 17, 20, 22, 24, 31, 33, 35, 38, 41f., 45, 49, 61, 107f., 137, 141, 147–151, 156–159, 161–163, 169, 176, 187, 190, 196f., 218, 237, 249f., 352, 368–370, 372, 397f., 404, 408–411, 434, 436, 439
interior decoration 65, 79, 92, 175
intertextuality 4, 10, 19, 151, 170, 174f., 177, 179, 213, 220f., 351, 364
Iphigenia 52, 54, 57
Ireland 101–104, 107–110, 113f., 123
irony 182
Isis 5, 7, 16, 127f., 140, 158, 161, 163, 171, 187f., 191f., 195, 265, 328–330, 333, 336, 339, 342f., 351, 357, 360, 362f., 367, 370–372, 408

J
Jachmann, Reinhold 248, 254, 257–260, 262, 264f., 269, 452
James II 103
Jane Eyre 22, 357, 363, 365–369, 372, 446
Joyce, James 341
Jugendstil 248f., 266f.
Jung, Carl 196, 274, 283
Juno 7, 9, 34, 177, 270, 280, 282, 299, 344, 347, 351, 385, 392, 419
Jupiter 7, 40, 49, 51, 56, 75, 85, 89, 94f., 153, 211, 258f., 267–270, 276, 281, 300f., 344–349, 351–353, 372f., 387–389, 392, 431
Just One Look 437f., 452

K
Kafel, Michelle 402
katabasis 9, 41–43, 132, 421, 428, 440
Keats, John 17, 102, 104, 111, 141, 147–151, 153–163
Keble, John 289, 296
Kehrein, J. 183
Kenilworth 17, 167–170, 172, 175, 178f., 292
Kierkegaard, Søren 15, 181–190, 193–197, 278
Kilimnik, Karen 404
Kim, Jihwan 400
King Lear 56
kiss 153, 228, 268, 293, 296, 387, 409

Klinger, Max 248f., 252–270, 452
Krakatoa 206

L
La Belle et La Bête 437, 439, 441–443, 453
La Fontaine, Jean de 12–14, 20, 47, 51–53, 58, 61–70, 72–75, 79, 83, 87f., 96, 135, 439
La Live de Bellegarde, Louis-Denis de 87
La Motte, Antoine Houdar de 31
labours 87, 133, 196, 232, 256, 258
Lafitte, Louis 13, 61
lament 38, 40, 48f., 124, 317, 359
Lamiae 422
lamp 6, 50, 74, 82, 109, 112, 124, 149, 159, 176, 185, 211, 218, 226–228, 232, 240, 250, 262, 267f., 270, 276, 279, 281, 312, 316, 318, 359f., 366, 368, 372, 387, 417, 436, 439, 442, 445, 448, 451f.
Lang, Andrew 61, 384
Lansbury, Angela 445
lateness 24, 154
Le Forestier, Maurice 405
Leda 141f., 372
Lee, Sophia 293
Leighton, Frederic 249
Lemprière's Classical Dictionary 153
Leprince de Beaumont, Jeanne-Marie 439, 442
Lewis, C.S. 22, 226, 283f., 323–328, 330–333, 335–337, 341, 437
Lifar, Serge 403
Locke, Matthew 14, 54f.
Lockhart, John Gibson 22, 167, 169–171, 311–318, 320
Lockman, John 13, 135, 139
London 12, 14, 54, 58, 109, 119–122, 124f., 127f., 152, 174, 203, 211, 214, 226f., 300–302, 357, 451
Longus 186
Loredano, Giovan Francesco 31f.
Lorrain, Claude 92, 151
Louis XIV 47f., 51, 56, 58, 91f., 96
Louis XV 86
Loukios of Patrae 8

love 1, 3, 6–10, 12 f., 15–17, 22–24, 33–35, 38–43, 45, 48–51, 54–57, 79, 82, 84, 86, 89–91, 93–96, 101 f., 104–106, 109–114, 130, 135, 137, 142 f., 147–150, 154 f., 159, 162 f., 170 f., 174–176, 178 f., 185, 209, 212–214, 218, 220 f., 226, 228, 230–232, 234, 237 f., 240, 242, 250, 252, 255 f., 261, 266–268, 276, 279, 281, 290 f., 294–302, 312–317, 319, 324 f., 327, 331 f., 334, 340, 352, 357–360, 362 f., 365–367, 370 f., 373, 382, 384–387, 389–394, 399 f., 402, 404–411, 425, 430, 433–439, 441–444, 446, 448
Love and the Soul 10, 106, 434
Love in love 33–35
Lucian 8, 141, 171, 186, 205
Lucius 4 f., 7–9, 15, 17, 22, 24, 121, 127, 133, 140, 147, 158–163, 181, 187 f., 190–196, 266, 273, 283, 327–330, 332 f., 336, 339–343, 346–353, 357, 359 f., 365, 370 f., 373, 397, 434 f., 440 f., 443, 445
Lucretius 57, 205, 213
Lully, Jean-Baptiste 14, 47, 52, 65, 403

M

madness 181, 275, 284 f., 294, 299
Maginn, William 123 f.
maiden 9, 37, 40–43, 107, 162, 176, 178, 226, 228, 232, 256, 276, 308, 318 f., 403, 431, 435–437, 440, 446
Marcus Aurelius 18, 330 f.
Maria, Ugo de 1, 31, 58, 225, 302
Marino, Giovan Battista 33 f., 39, 42, 44, 190, 193
Marlborough Gem 125
Marmion, Shackerley 12, 120, 214 f., 221
marriage 10, 55–57, 64, 75, 79, 89, 91–96, 109, 123, 125, 137, 151, 159 f., 162, 168, 170, 173, 176–179, 217, 237, 269, 279, 281, 284, 291–293, 295 f., 343, 345 f., 349, 351 f., 361–363, 365, 373, 384, 387, 390, 393, 415, 419, 431, 438, 446
Martianus Capella 132, 140

Mary, Queen of Scots 17, 34, 64, 101, 104, 107, 114, 147, 167 f., 221, 293, 298, 373, 382, 388
masculinity 282, 358, 367, 369, 372–374, 437
Master of the Die 127, 129, 451
Mathias, T. J. 123
McCaughrean, Geraldine 389 f.
Medea 9, 36 f.
Mercury 44 f., 51, 89, 212 f., 270, 388, 400, 425, 431
Merriman, Brian 104, 114
Metamorphoses 1, 3 f., 7, 9, 12, 15 f., 18, 22–24, 47, 79, 104 f., 106, 109, 112, 114, 119–124, 126–128, 139–141, 147, 153, 158, 163, 170–172, 174 f., 178, 181, 183, 187, 190, 195 f., 206, 212 f., 214, 216, 220, 225, 240 f., 253, 266, 273 f., 276, 278, 281, 284, 323, 326–328, 340 f., 343, 358, 360, 365, 370 f., 374, 397, 408, 434, 443, 446, 449
metamorphosis 121, 126, 135, 158, 161, 171, 187, 323, 336 f., 361, 366
metaphor 36, 112, 147, 218, 228, 231, 233, 433, 446 f., 449
metempsychosis 235 f.
methodology 20, 24
Meyer, Stephenie 434
Meynier, Charles 65
Michiel, Pietro 31–33, 40
Mickle, William Julius 167, 169, 174
Midsummer Night's Dream 11, 178, 435
Mierke, Udo 401
Milton, John 141, 151, 217 f.
miscegenation 435–437, 443, 446
mise en abyme 7
Mississippi 307–311, 319, 321, 340, 351
modernism 22, 203, 332
Molière 14, 47, 50, 52, 54–57, 65, 87 f., 219
monster 6, 48, 57, 67, 69, 73, 105, 176, 184, 253, 278, 316, 324, 385, 388, 390 f., 406 f., 419 f., 422–424, 435–437, 440, 442–446
moon 126, 171, 174, 206, 217, 357, 359 f., 362, 366 f., 370 f., 388, 421, 423, 428, 431
Moore, Thomas 11 f., 104, 107

Morris, William 18 – 21, 214, 218 – 221, 226, 247 f., 265, 268, 451
Muse 114, 364
music 50, 125, 137, 341, 400, 402, 409
mysteries 123, 125, 129, 158, 161, 163, 171, 292
mysticism 16, 123, 133, 279, 296
myth 2 f., 22, 31, 33 f., 37 – 39, 41, 44, 63, 79 – 81, 84, 86 – 88, 90 f., 95 f., 103, 114, 127, 143, 148, 150, 154, 159, 176, 204, 225, 228, 231, 236 – 238, 240, 242 f., 265, 268, 282 f., 289 f., 295 – 297, 301 f., 307, 326 f., 331, 358, 363 f., 367 – 370, 375, 381, 384 – 386, 388 f., 393, 397, 399 – 404, 406, 408 f., 411, 422, 424, 433, 435, 437, 443
mythology 16, 52, 64, 127, 143, 150, 153, 155, 174, 179, 211, 214, 240, 259, 263, 265, 273, 291, 332, 381, 386, 402, 422

N

Namm, Diane 389
Nannini, Gianna 409
Napoleon I 62
narrator 17, 19, 21, 72, 104, 147 – 150, 157, 160, 177, 194, 215, 240, 324, 326, 332, 339, 425, 440
Natchez 307 – 310, 312, 318
Natoire, Charles-Joseph 79 – 89, 91 – 96, 451
nature 6, 9 f., 23, 34, 39, 41, 70, 72 f., 101, 127, 130, 133, 147 f., 150 f., 153, 161, 167, 171, 173, 183 – 185, 187, 196, 206, 220, 228, 234, 237, 249, 256, 267 – 269, 296, 329 – 332, 336 f., 367 f., 372, 375, 384 f., 388, 399, 401, 406, 433, 435, 438, 442
Neoplatonism 388
Neumann, Erich 265, 273 f., 276, 284, 307, 358
Newton, Isaac 215, 217
Nietzsche, Friedrich 196, 234
Night of Enitharmon's Joy 127 f., 451
nobility 79, 86, 92, 95 f., 352
Norden, Eduard 248, 266, 268, 270, 275
Noverre, Jean-Georges 124
Nutzhorn, Frederik 183

Nymph 50, 53, 68, 81 f.

O

Ó Rathaile, Aodhan 107
Ó Súilleabháin, Eoghan Rua 107
Odyssey 53, 347
O'Flaherty, Roderic 103
Olcott, Frances Jenkins 384
old wives' tale 365, 367
Olympus 7, 53, 80, 84 – 86, 89, 161, 212, 215, 250, 253, 268, 270, 294, 319, 348, 351, 389, 392, 407 f., 425, 431, 441, 443
Onos 8, 186, 443
Opera 124, 401, 403
oracle 6, 48, 50, 53, 55, 64, 67, 104 f., 156 f., 211, 248, 250, 256, 270, 276 f., 279, 382, 393, 403, 431, 436
Orellius, J.C. 182
Orgel, Doris 391 f.
originality 8, 24, 196, 214
Orpheus 42, 114, 125, 213, 421
Orphism 153, 233
Osborne, Mary Pope 388
Ovid 38, 41, 53, 114, 126, 171, 208, 253, 357, 372, 433, 435, 438
Owenson, Sidney 104
owl 127, 158 f., 228, 230, 236

P

paganism 11, 32, 123 f., 131, 135, 141 f., 156, 171, 296, 347
palace 6 f., 12 f., 47 – 51, 53, 55, 61, 64, 67 f., 70, 73, 75, 81 f., 84, 86, 88, 113, 127, 130, 139, 149, 156, 162, 172, 174 f., 179, 209, 231, 256, 261, 263, 279 f., 284, 299, 323 – 326, 361, 367 f., 390, 418 f., 433, 438 – 441, 443, 445, 447 f., 451
Palacios, Nidia 409
Palazzo del Te 63, 75, 90 f., 93
Paludan-Müller, C. 183
Pan 40, 55, 105, 142, 150, 232 – 234, 252, 270, 282, 299, 317, 362, 385, 408, 416, 419, 429
Pan's Labyrinth 23, 415, 417 f., 423, 431 f., 452
parergon 259

Paris 12f., 54, 58, 61f., 79f., 82–85, 92f., 124f., 131, 237, 401, 403, 451
parody 33, 38, 102, 104, 189, 237
Pascoli, Giovanni 19, 225, 228–230, 232–236, 242
Pater, Walter 18, 353
Pathosformel 263
patron 32, 86f., 91, 168, 195, 349
Peerce, Larry 405
Perrault, Charles 13f., 445
Perry, Brendan 411
philosophy 3f., 15, 22, 107, 123, 125, 131f., 141, 181, 187, 190, 193, 195, 197, 324, 328, 330–332, 358, 388, 433
Photis 128, 132f., 139, 158f., 343
Plath, Syvia 22, 143, 357–376
Plato 9, 15, 123, 125, 127, 131, 142f., 160, 189, 205, 228–230, 330, 333, 336, 342, 358, 364, 417, 424
Platonism 10, 15f., 18f., 22f., 119, 123, 125–127, 129, 136, 141, 153f., 160, 162, 182, 197, 229, 231, 233f., 274, 323f., 328f., 333, 337, 342, 358, 364, 370, 374f.
Plautus 9f., 41
plot 4, 9–12, 17, 19, 22, 24, 32f., 38, 41, 45, 51–56, 64f., 105, 149, 154, 167f., 179, 205, 214, 216, 232, 249, 278, 280, 284f., 290, 293–295, 297, 301, 319f., 323f., 363, 365, 393, 406, 409, 415f., 418
Plotinus 125, 129, 131f.
Poetry 103, 141, 296
Porson, Richard 123, 133
post-Romanticism 225, 233, 241, 243
Prasch, Johann Ludwig 17
Pre-Raphaelites 225f.
pregnancy 6, 9, 24, 52, 170, 203, 250, 314, 368–375, 384–386, 393, 414, 419, 422, 425f.
Pricaeus, Ioannis 172
Price, Margaret Evans 171, 384
primitivism 383
Procne 372
procuress 32, 40f., 292, 298
Prometheus 19, 203, 258
Propertius 41

Proserpina 7, 9, 37, 42f., 49f., 56f., 64, 84, 87, 127, 130, 184, 267, 270, 281, 292, 333, 373, 392, 421f., 431
prostitution 39f., 342–346, 350–352
proto-existentialism 15, 194
providence 135, 188, 295, 329, 333
Prud'hon, Pierre-Paul 61
Psyche 1–24, 31, 33–45, 47–58, 61, 63f., 66–75, 79–91, 93–96, 101–114, 119f., 122–128, 130–135, 137–143, 147–151, 153–163, 167, 170, 172–179, 181, 183–188, 190, 192f., 196, 203–206, 208f., 211–214, 218–221, 225–238, 240–243, 247–270, 273–286, 289–291, 294, 296, 299, 307, 312–317, 319–321, 323–328, 331f., 334–337, 339f., 342–346, 348f., 351–353, 357–376, 381–394, 397–411, 415–423, 425–427, 429–441, 443–449, 451f.
psychoanalysis 3, 15, 242, 273f., 283–285, 358, 383
psychology 2, 15, 18–20, 22–24, 105, 109–111, 192, 196, 230–234, 263, 265f., 273–286, 336, 370, 383, 433, 438

Q

Quarrel of the Ancients and Moderns 13
Quinault, Philippe 47, 52, 87f.

R

Radcliffe, Ann 293
Raleigh, Walter 178
Randall, Ron 391
Raphael 63–65, 75, 89–91, 127, 151, 208, 210, 255, 409, 451
Ratmansky, Alexei 403f.
reception 1–4, 9–13, 15, 17, 20, 22–25, 31, 47, 55, 58, 62f., 75, 79, 96, 112, 114, 140f., 147, 179, 225, 229, 232, 236f., 242f., 247, 250, 259, 268, 274, 283, 285, 339–345, 348f., 351–353, 363, 369, 373–375, 397f., 402, 408f., 434f., 439f., 443
reciprocity 352, 447
redemption 298, 350, 435, 446
Reisfeld, Randi 391, 393

Renaissance 1, 10–12, 18, 20, 23, 44, 103, 183, 207f., 249, 268, 397, 435
repetition 135, 150, 255, 263, 279f., 284, 375
representation 13, 91, 93f., 129, 132, 172, 174, 240, 357, 418, 433, 446, 452
reserve 296f., 299
Richardson, I.M. 387, 446
Richardson, Samuel 293, 387, 446
Riklin, Franz 22, 265, 273–286
rite of passage 265, 283, 341, 387
rivals 177, 361
River god 49f., 54f., 82, 136f.,
Roan, Joanne 410
Robber Bridegroom 15, 22, 307, 309–311, 319, 321, 368
Robison, John 132
rococo 79, 92–96
Rode, August von 15, 266
Rohan, François de 91f., 95
Rohan, Hercule Mériadec de 91f., 94f., 95
Rohde, Erwin 229
romance 12f., 52, 103, 121, 167, 293, 363, 365, 367, 371, 375, 384f., 398, 406, 421, 433, 435f., 449
Romano, Giulio 63–65, 75, 89–91
Romanticism 15, 141, 148, 162
Rome 5, 9, 11, 63, 86, 88, 91, 161, 208, 210, 255, 274, 348, 352, 381, 409, 451
Romeo and Juliet 409, 445
roses 75, 107, 111, 122, 127, 140, 161, 163f., 196, 226, 228, 256f., 357–359, 374, 440, 445, 448
Rostock 61, 68, 71f., 451

S
Salon 13, 61, 79–85, 451
Sartre, Jean-Paul 190, 194f.
Savinio, Alberto 22, 225, 236–243, 261, 452
Scherani, Luca 410
Schneider, Helen 409
Schoener, Eberhard 409
Schopenhauer, Arthur 234, 265, 276
Schwind, Moritz von 250
Scott, Walter 17, 55, 92f., 159, 167–174, 176–179, 290, 292, 302, 447f.
Scritti Politti 410
semi-opera 14, 54
Seneca 36, 330
sensation novel 290–292, 294, 296
Shadwell, Thomas 14, 47, 54–58
Shakespeare, William 3, 11, 16, 55, 178, 205, 214, 218, 400, 445
Shapiro, Cindy 401
Shelley, Mary 122, 136, 141, 143, 153
Shelley, Percy Bysshe 122, 136, 141, 143, 153
shepherd 83f., 87f., 141, 451
Sidney, Sir Philip 12
Siedler, Johann 11, 20
sisters 81, 270, 130, 136f., 235
snake 13f., 105, 134, 178, 262, 265f., 372, 436
Snider, Solon 402
Snow White 307, 314, 318, 361
Snyder, Emily C.A. 14, 401f.
Socrates 182, 188, 228–230, 236, 333, 417
Sophocles 9, 53
soul 1, 3, 8–11, 13, 16f., 19, 23, 34, 36, 44f., 96, 105f., 108–113, 124, 127, 129–133, 136f., 142f., 148, 153f., 158, 162f., 185, 228–231, 233–236, 240–243, 269, 290f., 294, 296–299, 332, 334f., 339, 342, 352, 358, 364, 374, 386, 390, 402, 417f., 421, 432f., 452
space 5, 20, 58, 64, 66, 90, 93, 95, 113, 120, 153, 228, 390f., 429, 437, 443, 448
Spartali Stillman, Marie 226
spéirbhean 104, 114
Spence, Joseph 151f., 154, 451
Spenser, Edmund 12, 104, 161, 205, 207, 212
spiritualism 225, 228f., 233, 242f.
star crossed lovers 393, 433, 435
Stoicism 18, 323, 328, 330–334
subjectivity 253, 360, 373, 441
suicide 7, 52, 55f., 82, 87, 238, 250, 285, 328, 388, 420f., 429f.
Synesius of Cyrene 132

T
taboo 6, 9, 11, 112–114, 159, 433, 442, 445

Talos 211 f.
taming 387, 436
tapestry 10, 85–88, 94, 174
Taylor, Thomas 15, 18, 119 f., 122–143, 153 f., 205, 208, 214, 216 f.
television 405, 437
Tennyson, Alfred 249
Terence 9, 52, 203
Thackeray, William Makepeace 18
The Reivers 22, 339–344, 347–349, 351–353
The Wizard of Oz 415
theatre 2, 7, 10, 14, 54, 58, 124, 265, 397 f., 400, 402 f.
Thompson, Emma 361, 446
Three Women 358, 366, 369–372, 374 f.
Thumann, Paul 248–252, 255, 265, 267–269, 452
Tiemann, Walter 248, 266–268, 270
Tighe, Mary Blachford 17, 34, 64, 101–114, 147–151, 154–157, 159, 161, 221, 382
Tiresias 372
Titian 205, 211
tractarianism 289, 296
tragedy 9 f., 12–14, 35–38, 45, 52 f., 73, 169, 185, 342, 363, 433, 439 f.
tragicomedy 14, 47
transcendentalism 130, 139 f., 161, 163, 252, 263, 268, 373
transformation 4, 7, 11, 121, 125, 158, 160, 178 f., 181, 187–195, 197, 236, 282, 321, 335 f., 371 f., 407, 435, 437, 449
Trémolière, Charles 92, 94 f.
Tryst, Jendela 391, 393
typology 296–298

U
Underworld 7, 9, 40, 42 f., 52 f., 56 f., 233, 362, 410, 416–419, 421 f., 430 f.
Ungit 324–326, 331–336

V
Valpy, Abraham John 183
Van Loo, Carle 95
Velle, Gaston 405
Venice 11, 14, 31 f.
Venus 6 f., 9, 33–35, 37 f., 40–42, 48–52, 55 f., 63 f., 72–74, 80, 84, 86 f., 89, 94 f., 105, 111–113, 133, 140, 153 f., 156, 177–179, 184, 188, 192, 205–207, 209, 211, 213 f., 216–218, 221, 230 f., 237, 250, 253, 255 f., 263, 265, 267, 270, 276–281, 291, 293, 299 f., 302, 324, 342–347, 349, 351 f., 359–361, 363, 382, 384 f., 388–390, 393, 398–400, 402–404, 406–408, 410, 416, 419–421, 424–427, 429, 431, 449, 451
Vergil 9, 23, 54, 57 f., 129, 147, 157, 177, 205, 213, 295, 351
Versailles 12 f., 47, 63, 92 f.
Victorian 18, 20, 225, 250, 294 f., 382 f., 387, 402
Villa Farnesina 63, 75, 88–91, 93 f., 151, 208–210, 255, 409, 451
Villeneuve, Gabrielle-Suzanne de 15, 439, 442
vision 22, 101, 104, 108, 110 f., 114, 126 f., 141, 154, 157, 185, 240, 261, 265, 279, 284, 325, 332–336, 358, 363 f., 368 f., 373, 375, 428, 447
Voluptas 7 f., 16, 66, 75, 102, 131 f., 135, 204, 258, 260, 270, 282, 290, 300, 324, 340, 362, 393, 431, 449, 452
Vulcan 40, 48, 50, 53–55, 216 f., 291, 347

W
Wagner, Richard 252 f., 263, 340 f.
wallpaper 13, 61–73, 75, 451
Walpole, Horace 123
Warburton, William, Bishop of Gloucester 121–123, 129 f., 300 f.
Warner, Sylvia Townsend 15, 22, 289 f., 299–302, 361, 368, 446
Wayland 168, 291 f., 294
web series 408, 411
wedding 6, 9, 13, 95, 105, 110, 125, 161 f., 218, 220, 238, 259, 267, 270, 276 f., 294, 308, 316, 320, 361, 366 f., 402, 431
Wedgwood, Josiah 125
Welty, Eudora 15, 22, 307–321, 368
Whale, James 445
Whedon, Joss 436 f.
Wieland, Christoph Martin 16, 250
Williams, Isaac 107, 290, 294, 296

Wishfulfilment 273f.
Woolf, Virginia 307, 358
Wordsworth, William 101, 109, 140f., 153
Wuthering Heights 358, 364f., 367–369

Y
Yeats, W.B. 106, 141–143, 372
Yoknapatawpha 339
Yonge, Charlotte Mary 22, 289–299, 301f., 447

Yorkshire 357f., 363–367, 369
YouTube 23, 408, 411

Z
Zephyr 6f., 20f., 48–50, 55, 64, 67, 79–82, 88, 149, 209, 270, 277–279, 313, 368, 390, 410, 416, 440, 443, 451
Zuffanti, Fabio 410
Zukofsky, Louis 134

www.ingramcontent.com/pod-product-compliance
Lightning Source LLC
Chambersburg PA
CBHW051552230426
43668CB00013B/1830